NEWCAST SUNDERLAND, DURHAM
STREET ATLAS

CONTENTS

Key to Map Pages	2-3	Index to Places	145
Map Pages at 6" to 1 mile	4-141	Postcode Map	146–147
Enlarged City Centre	142-143	Index to Streets	148 onwards
Road Map	144	Metro Map	Back Cover

REFERENCE

Motorway	**A1(M)**	County Boundary	+ · + · + ·
A Road	A193	District Boundary	· — · — · — ·
Under Construction		Posttown Boundary By arrangement with the Post Office	——
Proposed		Postcode Boundary Within Posttowns	– – – –
B Road	B1284	Ambulance Station	✚
Dual Carriageway		Car Park (Selected)	P
One Way Street Traffic flow on 'A' Roads is indicated by a heavy line on the drivers left.	→	Church or Chapel	†
Pedestrianized Road		Fire Station	■
Restricted Access		Hospital	H
Track		House Numbers Selected Roads only	2 ... 45
Railway	Level Crossing / Station	Information Centre	🛈
Metro Network Stations	M	Police Station	▲
Map Continuation 23	Large Scale City Centre 61	Post Office	★
Washington District Boundary	· · · · · ·	Toilet With Facilities for the Disabled	▽ ♿
Built Up Area	NORTH STREET		

SCALE

6 inches to 1 mile

0 — ¼ — ½ Mile
1:10,560

0 — 250 — 500 — 750 Metres

Geographers' A-Z Map Company Ltd.

Head Office:
Fairfield Road, Borough Green, Sevenoaks, Kent, TN15 8PP
Telephone 0732-781000

Showrooms:
44 Gray's Inn Road, London, WC1X 8LR
Telephone 071-242 9246

Edition 1 1994 © Copyright of the Publishers

G000292791

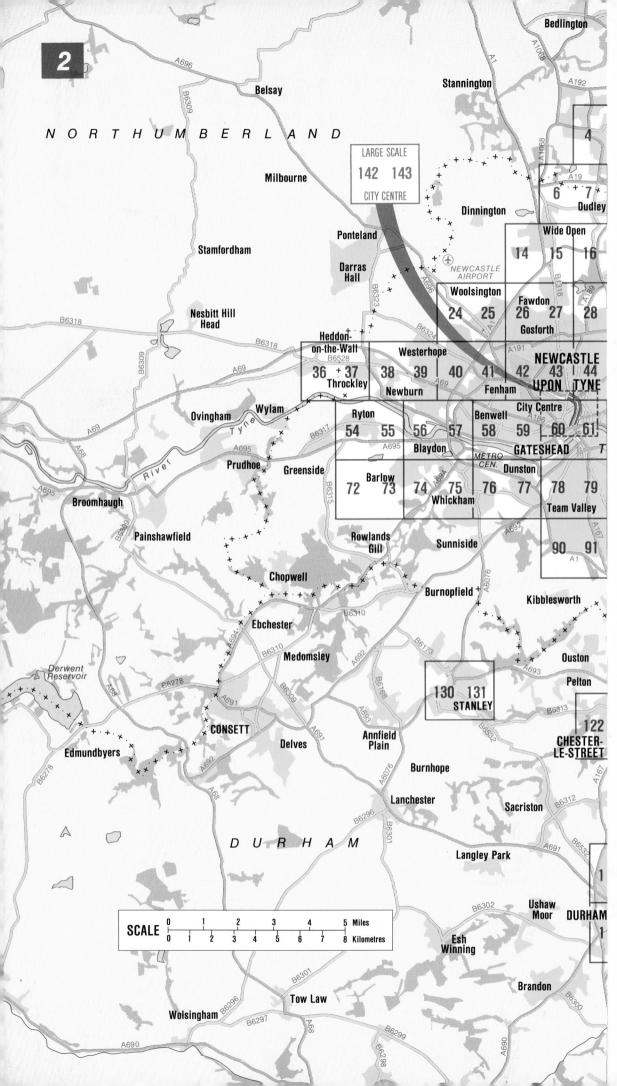

2

NORTHUMBERLAND

Belsay

Milbourne

Stamfordham

Nesbitt Hill Head

Stannington

Bedlington

LARGE SCALE
142 143
CITY CENTRE

Dinnington

Ponteland

Darras Hall

Heddon-on-the-Wall

Throckley

Ovingham   Wylam

River Tyne

Prudhoe   Greenside

Broomhaugh

Painshawfield

Chopwell

Ebchester

Medomsley

Derwent Reservoir

Edmundbyers

CONSETT   Delves

Wolsingham

Tow Law

DURHAM

Dudley

Wide Open

| 14 | 15 | 16 |

Woolsington

NEWCASTLE AIRPORT

Fawdon

| 24 | 25 | 26 | 27 | 28 |

Gosforth

Westerhope

| 36 | 37 | 38 | 39 | 40 | 41 | 42 | 43 | 44 |

Newburn   Fenham

NEWCASTLE UPON TYNE

City Centre

Ryton   Benwell

| 54 | 55 | 56 | 57 | 58 | 59 | 60 | 61 |

Blaydon

GATESHEAD

METRO CEN.   Dunston

Barlow

| 72 | 73 | 74 | 75 | 76 | 77 | 78 | 79 |

Whickham   Team Valley

Rowlands Gill   Sunniside

| 90 | 91 |

Burnopfield

Kibblesworth

Ouston

Pelton

| 130 | 131 |
STANLEY

122
CHESTER-LE-STREET

Annfield Plain

Burnhope

Lanchester

Sacriston

Langley Park

Ushaw Moor   DURHAM

Esh Winning

Brandon

SCALE

| 0 | 1 | 2 | 3 | 4 | 5 Miles |
| 0 | 1 | 2 | 3 | 4 | 5 | 6 | 7 | 8 Kilometres |

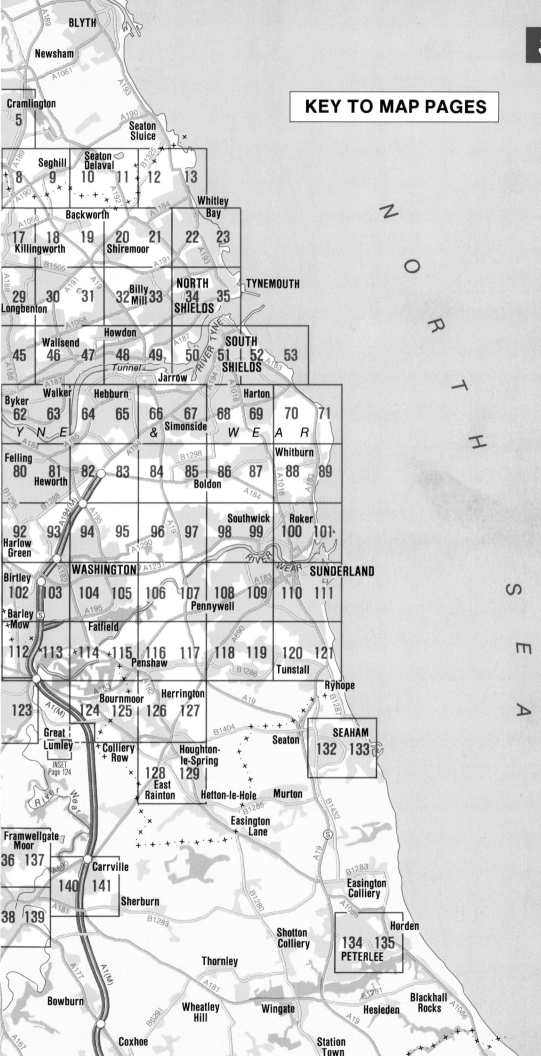

3

KEY TO MAP PAGES

NORTH SEA

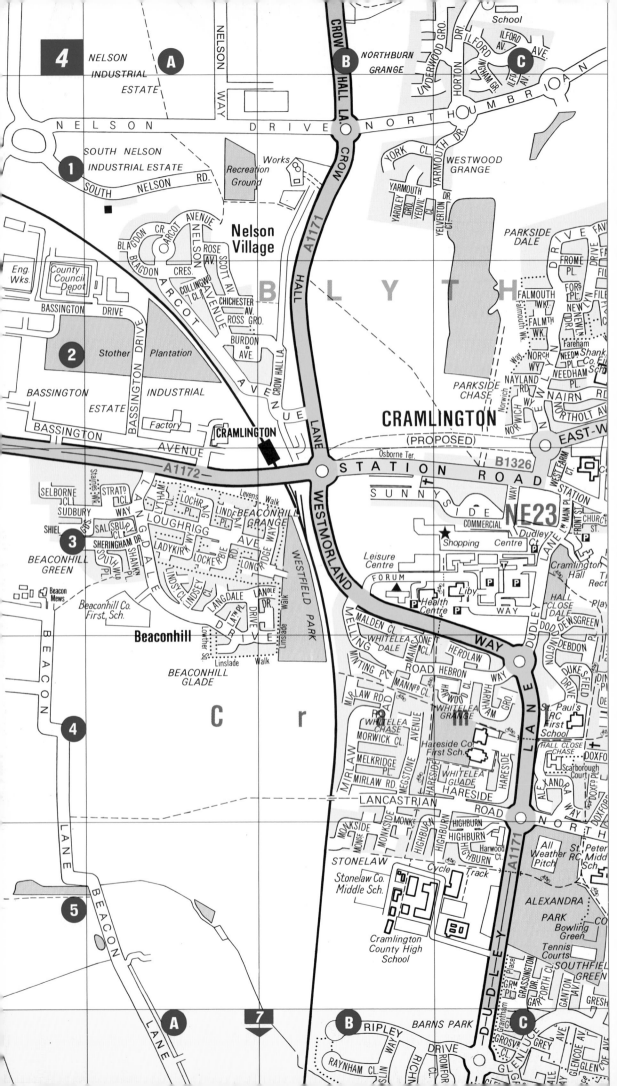

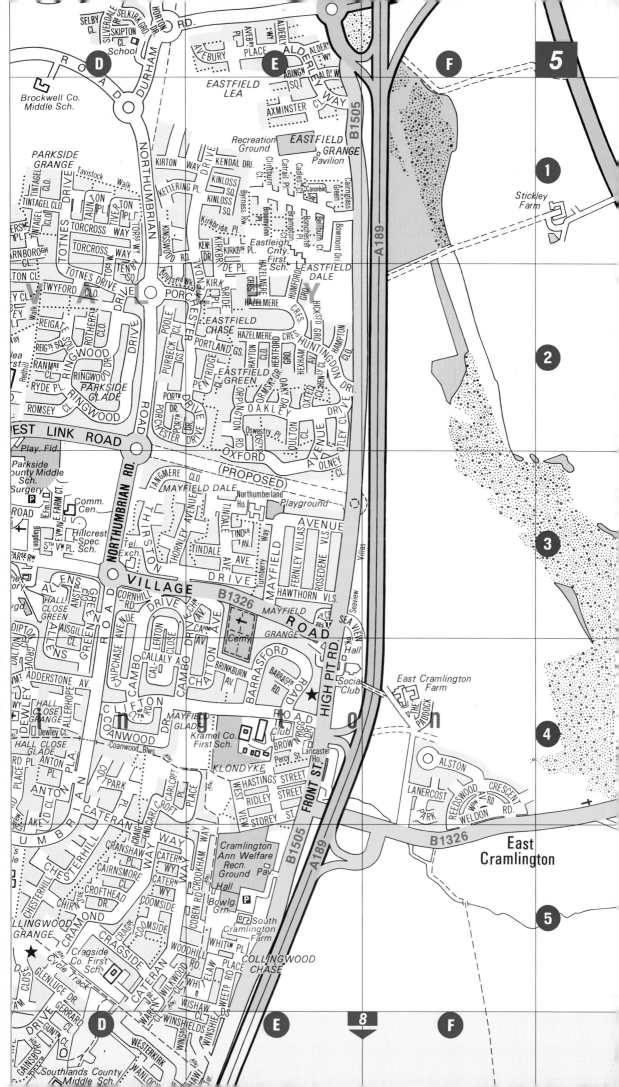

Plantation

Plessey South
Moor Farm

White Wood

ARCOT HALL
GOLF COURSE

6

New
Jubilee
Plantn.

Sir Jasper's
Plantation

A

B

C

1

BLYTH VALLEY
CASTLE MORPETH

A1068

FISHER LANE

ARCOT

B L Y T H

Sandy's Letch

Arcot Hall
(Club House)

2

A19

C r a m l

NORTHUMBERLAND
TYNE & WEAR

FRONT

Seaton Burn
Miners' Welfare
Park
Playgd.

Bowlg.
Grn.

Pav.
Tennis
Ct.

Football
Ground

3

B1318

HORNTREE AV.

Horntree Cotts.

STREET

N O R T H

T

Blezard
Business
Park

BRENKLEY WAY

SEATON BURN

Brenkley Ct.

Chapel Ct.

CHAPEL PL.

Blagdon

GARDEN CL.

★

Chapel
ville

NE13

DUDLEY

Seaton Burn High School

Weetslade
Cemetery

4

BRIDGE ST.

Mason
View

War
Mem.

BURNBRIDGE

Jubilee
Terr.

RUSSELL SQ.

BRIGSDE COTTS.

BRIGSIDE

PATIENCE

PINE ST.

CLAY ST.

ELM STR.

MEADOW

AV.

ROOKWD. DR.

NEARNE CL.

MEADOW DR.

B1321

Y

Green's
Houses
Farm

BURNBRIDGE

Depot

DRIVE

Rook
Wood

Seaton Burn
Dairy Farm

Hartley
Burn

Seaton Burn
First School

West
View

East
View

CHANTRY DRIVE

**Newcastle
-upon-
Tyne**

Seaton
Burn

Seaton Burn
House

5

NORTH TYNESIDE

NEWCASTLE

Nursery

RAYLEIGH
DR.

RAYLEIGH

126

147

B1318

McCRACKEN DR.

McCRACKEN AV.

GRAY AV.

Mitford

MORPETH AV.

WARKWORTH AV.

WOOLER

TAYLR. AV.

TAYLR. AV.

A

CRANWELL DRI.

EWESLEY
GDS.

BOULMER
GDS.

LESBURY
GDS.

HAVANT GDS.

SWINHOE GDS.

WALK

WOODHORN
DR.

HALTON DR.

15

ROTHBURY
GDS.

Gardens

TAYLOR AV.

View
View

B

Wideopen
Middle School

East
Wideopen

C

Aged
Miners
Homes

DRYSDALE CT.

Robert
Allen Ct.

Club

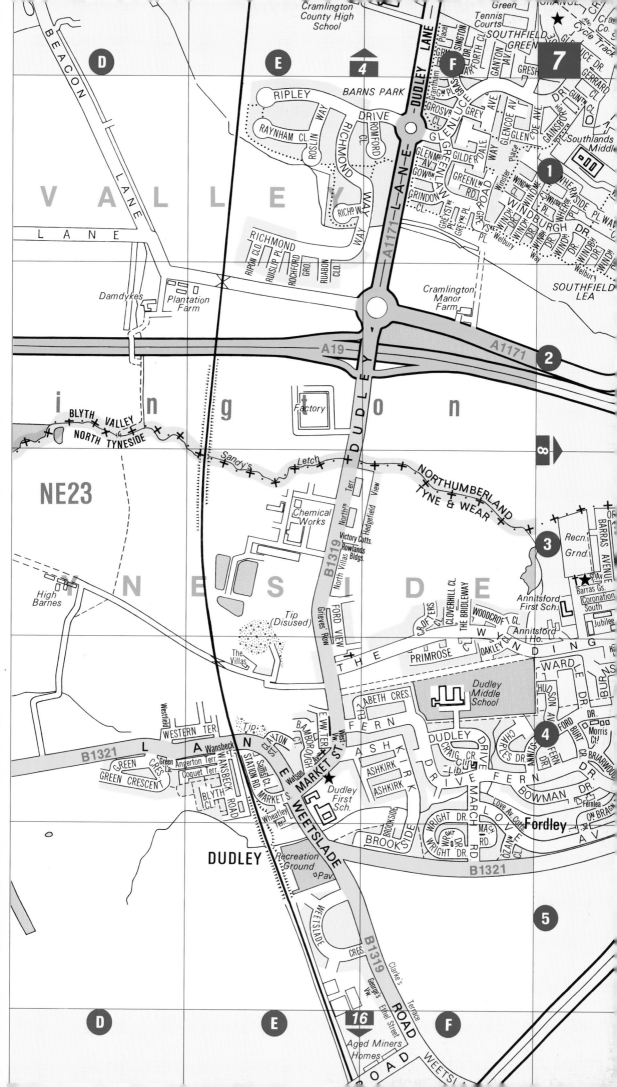

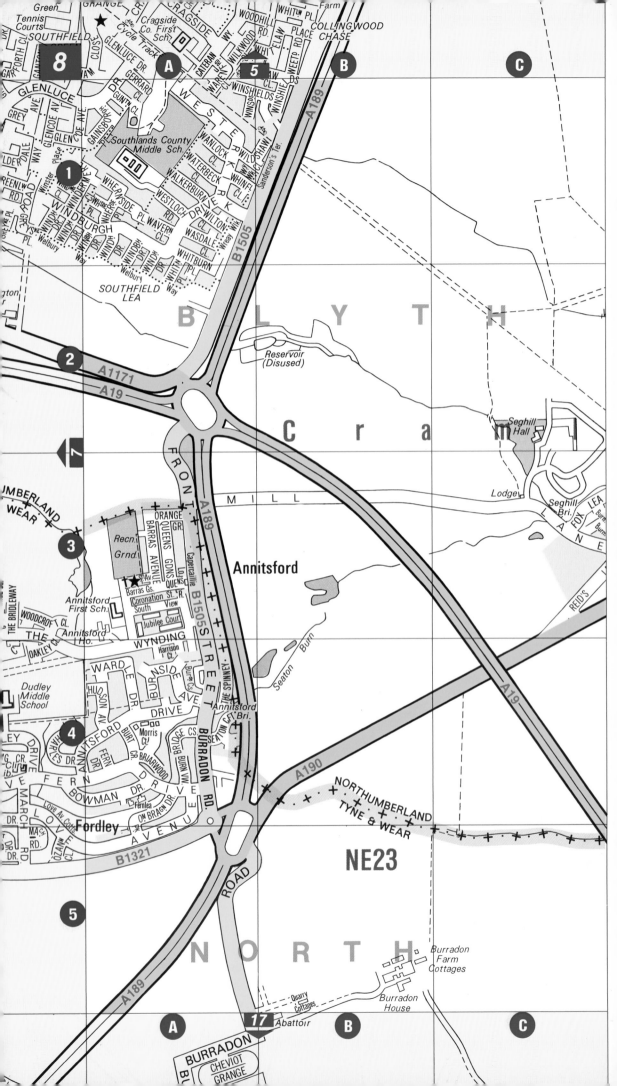

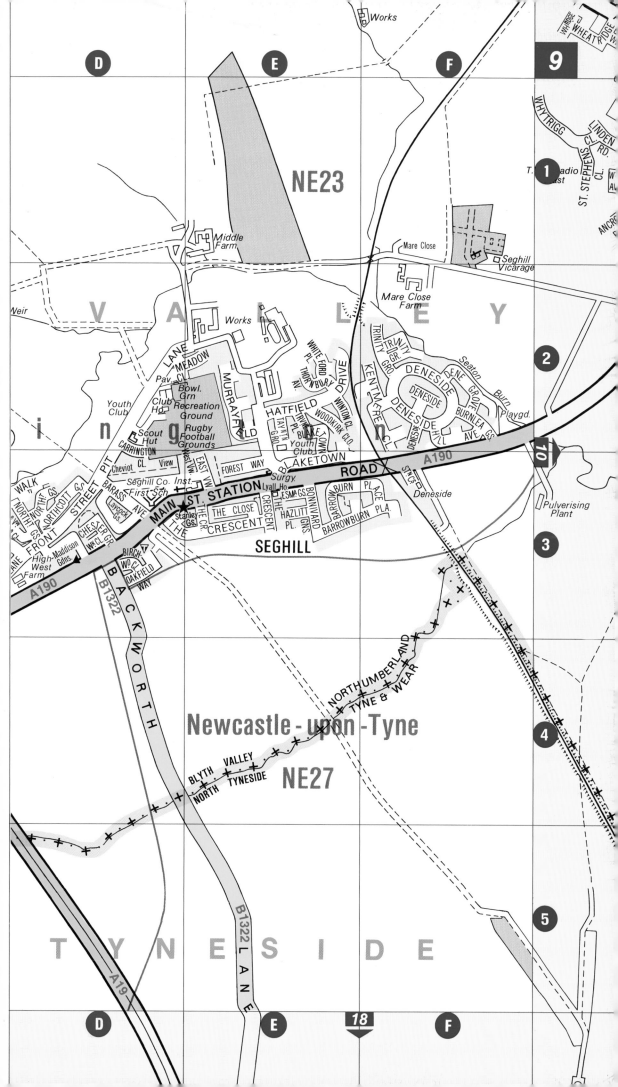

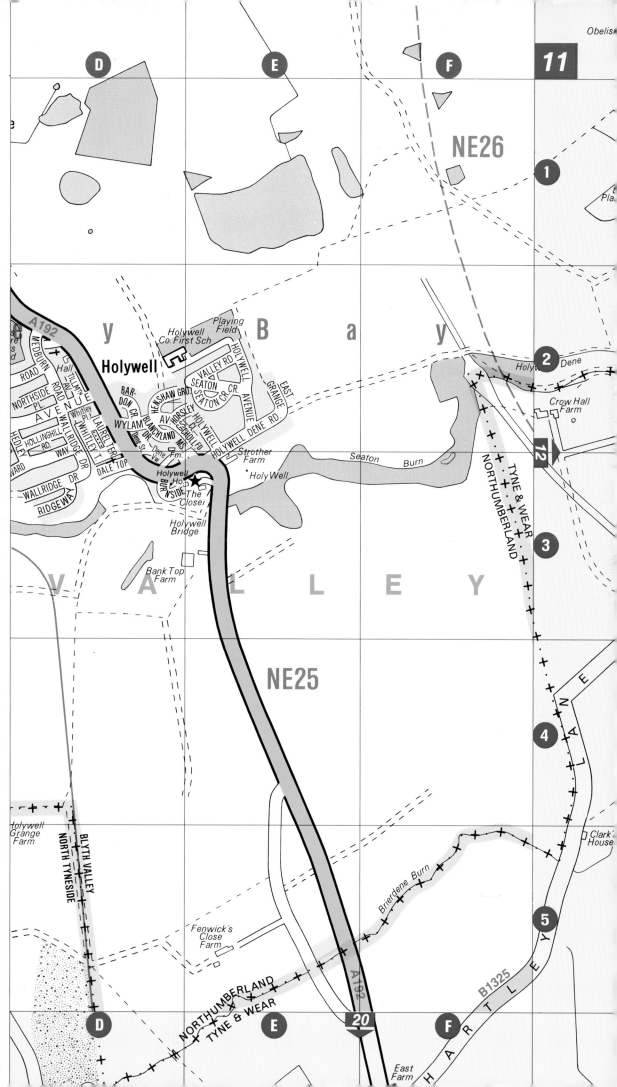

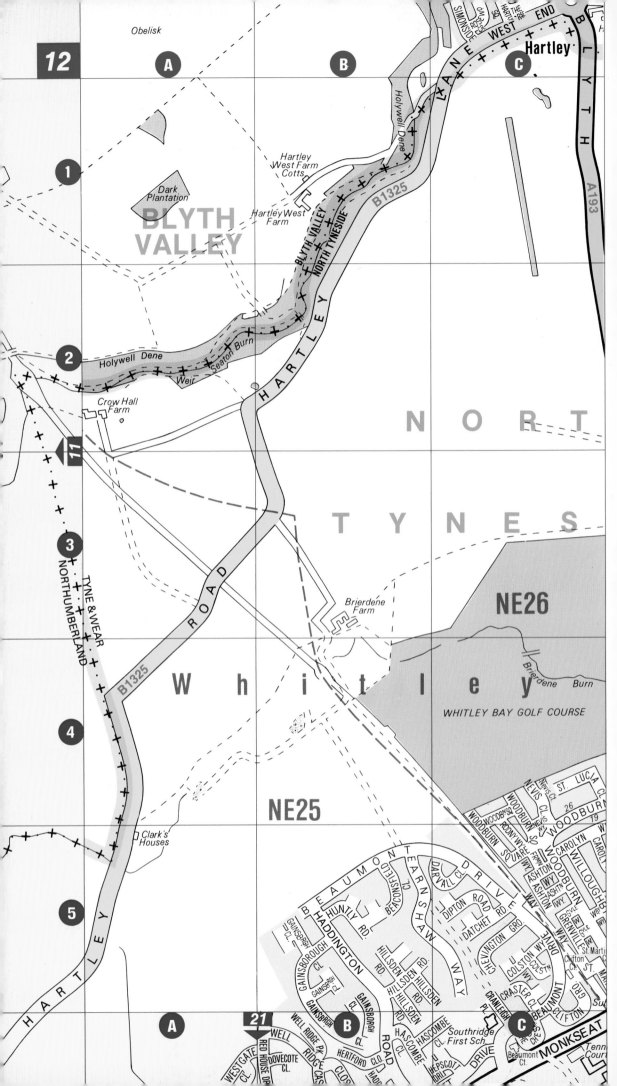

Obelisk

A　　　**B**　　　**C**

1

Dark Plantation

BLYTH VALLEY

Hartley West Farm Cotts

Hartley West Farm

LANE　**WEST END**

Hartley

B1325

BLYTH VALLEY NORTH TYNESIDE

Holywell Dene

A193

BLYTH

2

Holywell Dene

Weir

Seaton Burn

Crow Hall Farm

HARTLEY

11

N O R T

3

TYNE & WEAR

NORTHUMBERLAND

ROAD

T Y N E S

Brierdene Farm

NE26

Brierdene Burn

W h i t l e y

WHITLEY BAY GOLF COURSE

B1325

4

NE25

Clark's Houses

NEVIS CL

ST. LUCIA CL

WOODBURN SQ

WOODBURN SQUARE

NEVIS CLS

RODNEY WY

26

19

WOODBURN

CAROLYN W

CARO

ASHTON WY

WILLOUGHBY

WBN

5

HARTLEY

BEAUMONT

TEARNSHAW

DARVAL CL

DIPTON ROAD

DATCHET RD

DRIVE

WY

CAROLYN WY

GRENVILLE WY

CLIFTON ST.

St. Martin

BEAUMONT

GAINSBOROUGH CL

HADDINGTON

HUNTLY RD.

BEACONSFIELD

WAY

HILLSDEN RD

HILLSDEN RD

CHEVINGTON GRO

COLSTON WYE

COLSTN

CRASTER CL

CRANLEIGH PL.

BEAUMONT

CLIFTON

BEAUMONT Ct

GAINSBRGH CL

GAINSBRGH CL

HILLSDEN RD

HILLSDEN RD

HASCOMBE CL

Southridge First Sch

MONKSEAT

Tenn Court

A　　**21**　　**B**　　　**C**

WESTGATE CL

RED HOUSE DR

DOVECOTE CL.

WELL RIDGE PK.

WELL RIDGE CL.

HERTFORD CLO

GAINSBOROUGH CL

HASCOMBE CL.

HEPSCOTT DRI

HADDN CL

HASCOMBE ROAD

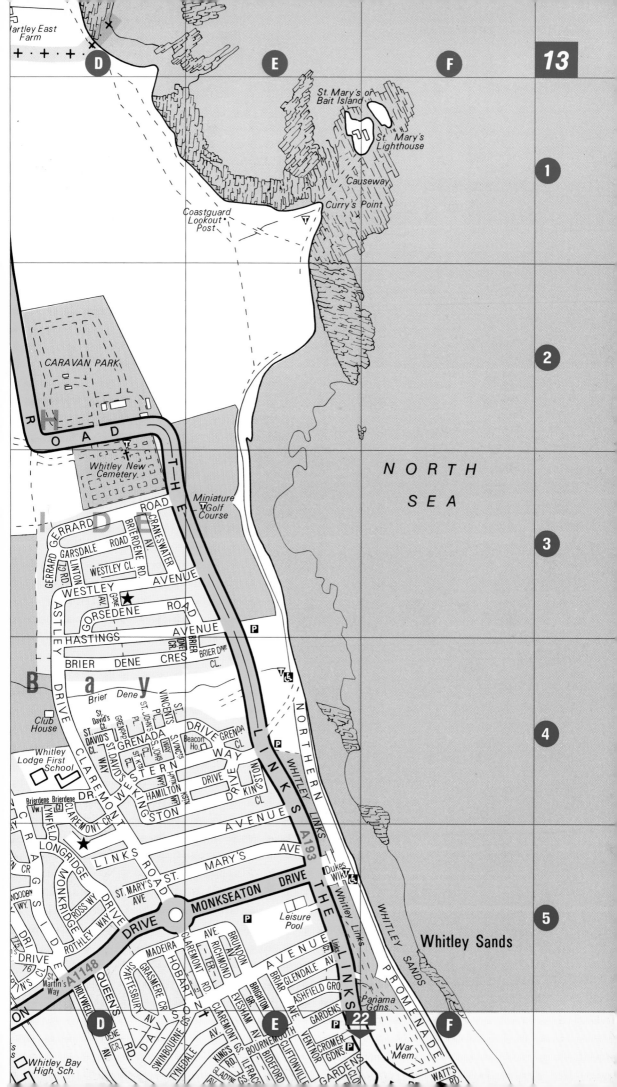

Hartley East Farm

D

E

F

St. Mary's or Bait Island

St. Mary's Lighthouse

1

Causeway

Curry's Point

Coastguard Lookout Post

CARAVAN PARK

2

ROAD

Whitley New Cemetery

THE

Miniature Golf Course

N O R T H

S E A

3

HIDE

GERRARD ROAD

CRANESWATER AV.

BRIERDENE RD.

GARSDALE ROAD

LINTON RD.

WESTLEY CL.

BRIERDENE

AVENUE

WESTLEY

AV.

GDNE.

GORSEDENE ROAD

ASTLEY

HASTINGS AVENUE

DENE CR.

BRIER DENE CR.

BRIER DENE CL.

BRIER DENE CRES.

P

Bay

DRIVE

Brier Dene

ST. VINCENTS PL.

ST. JOHN'S AV.

DRIVE WAY

GRENDA

WHITLEY LINKS

V

E

Club House

St. David's CL.

GRENADA

ST. JOHN'S CL.

ST. K'TH.

Beacon Ho.

DRIVE

NORTHERN LINKS

4

P

Whitley Lodge First School

ST. DAVID'S CL.

DAVID'S WAY

ESKING

ST. DAVID'S WAY

GRENADA

HAMILTON

HMLTN. WY.

ST. K'TH. WY.

DRIVE

KING'S CL.

KINGSTON

LINKS

DRIVE

Brierdene Brierdene Vw. Ct.

LYNFIELD

CLAREMONT CRNT.

DR.

AVENUE

A193

Dukes WIK.

V E

CRAIG'S CR.

CLAREMONT

★

LINKS ROAD

MARY'S

AVE.

WHITLEY LINKS

5

WOODB'N. WY.

CROSS WY.

MONKRIDGE

ROTHLEY WAY

LONGRIDGE DRIVE

ST. MARY'S AVE.

MARY'S ST.

THE LINKS

Whitley Sands

WHITLEY SANDS

DRIVE

DRIVE

MONKSEATON DRIVE

P

Leisure Pool

PROMENADE

S

DRI'S.

76

A1148

St. Martin's Way

HS.

QUEEN'S

HOLWELL

MADEIRA

GRASMERE CR.

SHAFTESBURY AV.

DAVISON AV.

CLAREMONT RD.

AVE.

BRUNDON TER.

RICHMOND RD.

BRIAR AVE.

GLENDALE AV.

ASHFIELD GRO.

BRIGHTON GR.

Panama Gdns.

D

E

F

22

War Mem.

Whitley Bay High Sch.

SWINBOURNE GS.

TYNEDALE

DENE CR. AV.

KING'S GS.

GLADTINE

BOURNEMOUTH GDNS.

ILFRACOMBE GDNS.

BIDEFORD GDNS.

VENTNOR GDNS.

CLIFTONVILLE GDNS.

CROMER GDNS.

GARDENS

WATT'S RD.

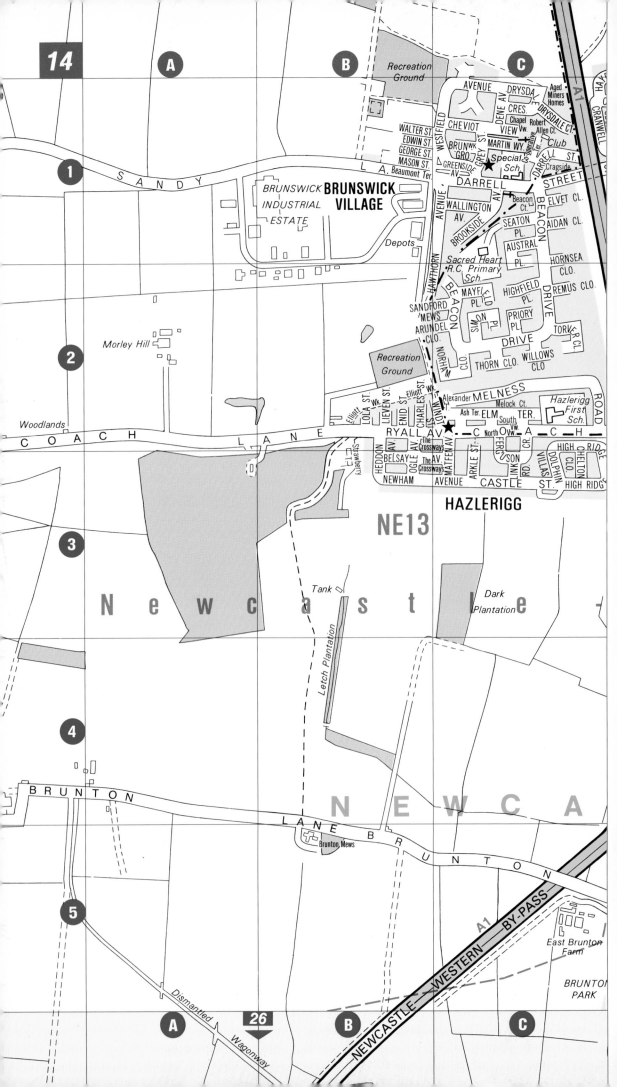

Ⓐ Ⓑ Ⓒ

Recreation Ground

AVENUE DRYSDALE
DENE AV.
Aged Miners Homes
DRYSDALE CRES.
CHEVIOT
Chapel VIEW
Robert Allen Ct.
DRYSDALE CT.
WESTFIELD
GREY ST.
BRUN WK. GRO.
MARTIN WY.
Co-operative Ter.
Club
DARRELL ST.

1 SANDY L. A. Beaumont Ter.

WALTER ST.
EDWIN ST.
GEORGE ST.
MASON ST.

BRUNSWICK INDUSTRIAL ESTATE

BRUNSWICK VILLAGE

Depots

GREENSIDE AV.
Special Sch.
Cragside
STREET

AVENUE
WALLINGTON AV.
BROOKSIDE AV.
Beacon Ct.
ELVET CL.
SEATON PL.
AIDAN CL.
BEACON
AUSTRAL PL.
HORNSEA CLO.

HAWTHORN
Sacred Heart R.C. Primary Sch.
BEACON
MAYFIELD PL.
HIGHFIELD PL.
REMUS CLO.
DRIVE

SANDFORD MEWS
SIMON Pl.
PRIORY PL.
TORVER CL.
ARUNDEL CLO.
DRIVE
THORN CLO.
WILLOWS CLO.
NORHAM CLO.

Morley Hill

2

Recreation Ground

Alexander MELNESS
Hazlerigg First Sch.
ROAD
Melock Ct.
Woodlands
Elliott Wk.
LOLA ST.
LIEVEN ST.
ENID ST.
ELLIOTT ST.
CHARLES ST.
LONIN Wk.
Ash Ter. ELM
South Vw.
TER.

COACH LANE
Elliott St.
RYALL AV.
The Crossways
North O Vw.
A C H
C A H

HEDDON AV.
BELSAY AV.
OGLE AV.
The AV.
The Crossways
MATFEN AV.
ARKLE ST.
FERGUSON INK RD.
CR.
HIGH RIDGE
CHELTON CLO.
DOLPHIN VILLAS
ST.

NEWHAM
AVENUE
CASTLE
HIGH RIDGE

HAZLERIGG

Strawberry

NE13

3

N e w c a s t l e

Tank
Dark Plantation

Letch Plantation

4

BRUNTON

LANE BRUNTON
N E W C A

Brunton, Mews
BRUNTON

5

A1
NEWCASTLE — WESTERN — BY-PASS

East Brunton Farm

BRUNTON PARK

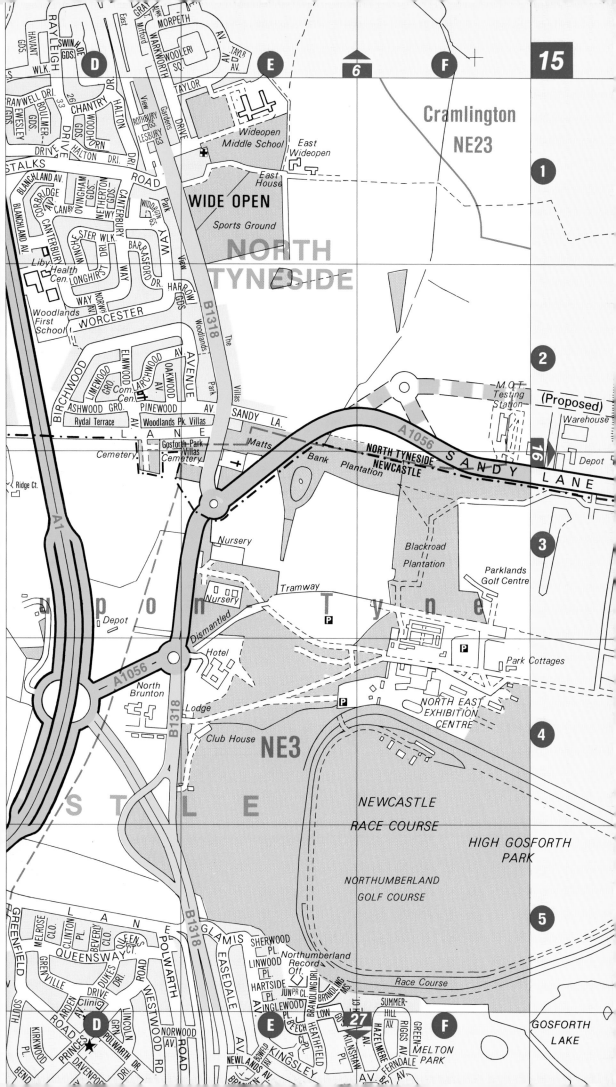

D

E

6

F

RAYLEIGH GDS.
SWIN HOE GDS.

HAVANT GDS.

WLK.

CRANWELL DRI.

BOULMER GDS.

EWESLEY GDS.

BLANCHLAND AV.

CORBRIDGE AV.

CANBY

BLANCHLAND AV.

CANTERBURY

STALKS

MORPETH

WARKWORTH

WOOLER

TAYLR AV.

VIEW

ROTHBURY GDS.

LESBURY GDS.

GARDENS

CHANTRY
GDS.
WOODHORN
GDS.
HALTON
DRI.

HALTON DRI.

ROAD

33

26

DRIVE

CANTERBURY WAY

Park

OVINGHAM GDS.

NETHERTON GDS.

WIDDRINGTN. GDS.

WINCHESTER WLK.

NEWBY

BARRASFORD DRI.

HARROW GDS.

Liby.

Health
Cen.

LONGHIRST

WAY

NORWICH WAY

WORCESTER

NORTH

TYNESIDE

Wideopen
Middle School

East
Wideopen

East
House

WIDE OPEN

Sports Ground

**Cramlington
NE23**

1

Woodlands
First
School

BIRCHWOOD

ASHWOOD GRO.

LIMEWOOD GRO.

Com.
Cen.

ELMWOOD GRO.

LARCHWOOD AV.

OAKWOOD AV.

PINEWOOD AV.

Rydal Terrace

Woodlands Pk. Villas

AVENUE

Woodlands

The

Villas

Park

SANDY LA.

SANDY

LANE

B1318

LANE

LANE

Cemetery

Gosforth Park
Villas Cemetery

Matts

Bank

Nursery

2

M.O.T.
Testing
Station

(Proposed)

A1056

16

Warehouse

Depot

Ridge Ct.

A1

NORTH TYNESIDE

NEWCASTLE

SANDY

LANE

Blackroad
Plantation

Plantation

3

Parklands
Golf Centre

u p o n   T y n e

Depot

Nursery

Tramway

Dismantled

Hotel

North
Brunton

A1056

B1318

Lodge

Club House

NE3

T

P

P

P

P

North EAST
EXHIBITION
CENTRE

Park Cottages

4

S T L E

**NEWCASTLE
RACE COURSE**

**HIGH GOSFORTH
PARK**

**NORTHUMBERLAND
GOLF COURSE**

5

GREENFIELD

QUEENSWAY

GRENVILLE

MELROSE
CLO.

LINTON
PL.

BEVERLEY
CLO.

QUEENS
CT.

DUKES
DRI.

LANE

ROAD

GRENVILLE

DRIVE

GREENFIELD

SOUTH

KIRKWOOD
PL.

BEND

POLWARTH

WESTWOOD RD.

NORWOOD
AV.

GLAMIS

EASEDALE AV.

B1318

SHERWOOD
PL.

LINWOOD
PL.

HARTSIDE
PL.

INGLEWOOD
PL.

Sherwood
PL.

Northumberland
Record
Off.

JUN PR CL.

BRANDLING
MS.

BEECH
GRO.

Race Course

27

SUMMER-
HILL

HAZELMERE AV.

RIGGS AV.

FERNDALE AV.

GREEN
MELTON
PARK

GOSFORTH
LAKE

D

E

F

Clinic

ARDEN
AV.

LINCOLN CT.

GRN.WARTH DRI.

PRINCES

DAVENPORT

POLWARTH DRI.

KINGSLEY AV.

NEWLANDS AV.

HEATHFIELD
PL.

KILNSHAW
AV.

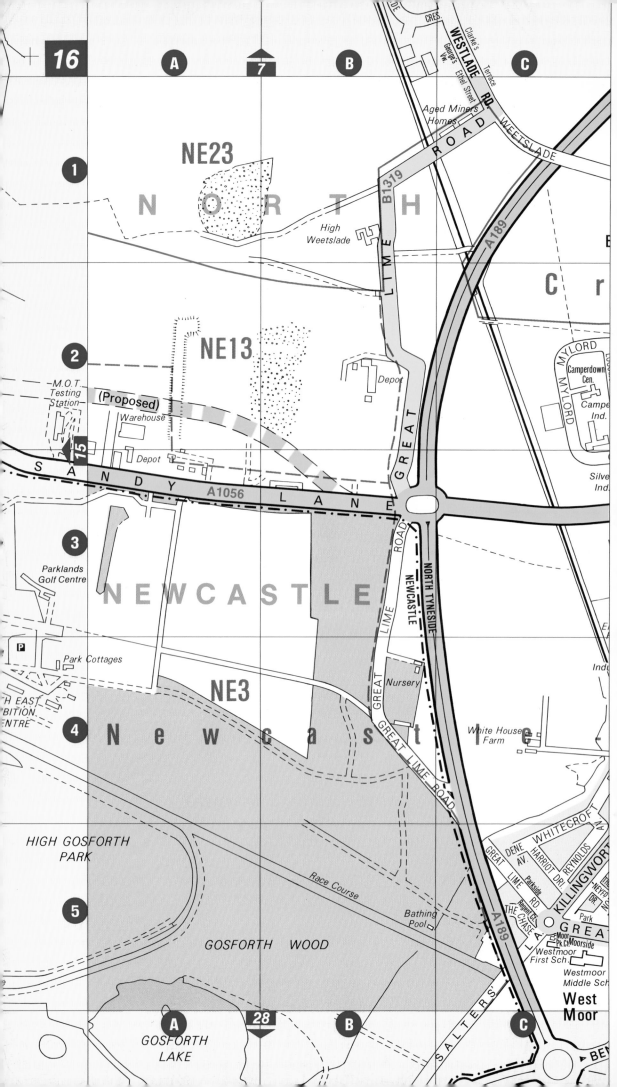

A   ⌂ 7   B   C

1

NE23

N O R T H

CRES.

WESTLADE

Clarke's Terrace

Ethel Street

George's Vw.

Aged Miners' Homes

ROAD

WEETSLADE

RD.

A189

B1319

High Weetslade

LIME

2

NE13

M.O.T. Testing Station

(Proposed)

Warehouse

Depot

Depot

GREAT

MYLORD

MYLORD

Camperdown Cen.

Campe Ind.

Silve Ind.

C r

E

15

S A N D Y   A1056   L A N E

3

Parklands Golf Centre

N E W C A S T L E

GREAT

LIME

ROAD

NORTH TYNESIDE

NEWCASTLE

Nursery

E

Indu

P

Park Cottages

H EAST BITION NTRE

NE3

4

N e w c a s t l e

GREAT

LIME

White House Farm

WHITECROFT

DENE AV.

HARRIOT DR.

REYNOLDS

KILLINGWORT

Parkside

HIGH GOSFORTH PARK

Race Course

5

GOSFORTH WOOD

Bathing Pool

A189

GREAT LIME RD.

THE CHASE

Regent Ct.

Moor Pk.Ct.

Moorside

Westmoor First Sch.

Park

GREA

Westmoor Middle Sch

West Moor

A   28   B   C

GOSFORTH LAKE

SALTERS

BEN

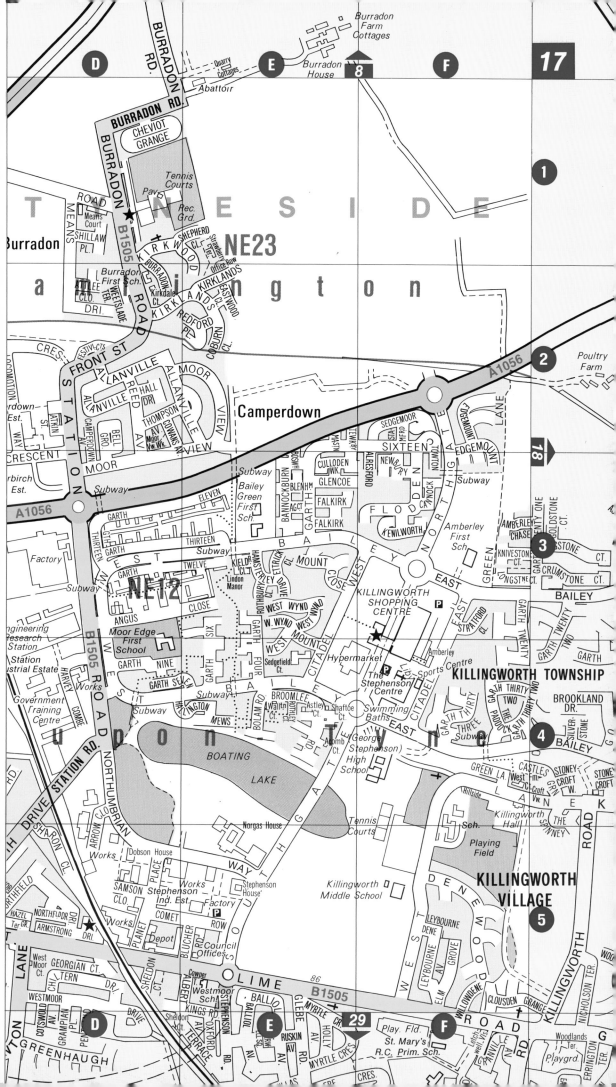

A **9** **B** **C**

Cramlington
NE23

1

A19

LANE

BACKWORTH

B1322

A1056

2

West Farm

BACKWORTH

LANE

Poultry
Farm

High Farm

N O R T H

LANE

CASTLE
SQUARE

EDGEMOUNT

17

Subway

Amberley
First Sch.

KILLINGWORTH LA.

B1317

KILLINGWORTH

NE27

GREEN

Amberley
Close

ALDERLEY CL.

FOXLEY CL.

ASHLEY CL.

Dismantled Mineral Railway

A19

3

ASHMEAD CL.

GARTH TWENTY ONE

GOLDSTONE CT.

MEGSTONE CT.

BERKELEY CL.

DRIVE

CRANHAM CL.

DARDEN CL.

SIMONSIDE

BLUEBURN DR.

GARLEIGH CL.

WAY

EAST

KNIGHTONGSTNE CT.

CRUMSTONE CT.

GARTH TWENTY TWO

GARTH TWENTY

GARTH

BARLEY

FOUR

GARTH TWENTY

TWENTY FIVE

HARWOOD DR.

N e w c a

EAST

STRATFORD CL.

arley
Centre

GARTH THIRTY THREE

GARTH THIRTY TWO

THE PADDOCK

BROOKLAND DR.

SILVER-STONE

GOODWOOD

GOODWOOD

ULLSWATER DR.

RYDAL CLOSE

THIRLMERE CL.

GARTH TWENTY SEVEN

GREENWOOD

East House
Farm

APPLE-WD.

DOWNS-WD.

HAZEL-WOOD

ROSE-WOOD

DR.

NORTH

- u p

KILLINGWORTH TOWNSHIP

NE12

Subway

EAST

GREEN LA.

West Fm
Ct.

CASTLES

STONEY-CROFT GRN.

CROFT
Vw.

STONEY-CROFT W.

STONEY-CROFT E.

CHERRYTREE CL.

OAKFIELD CL.

ORCHARD CL.

GREENWOOD

KILLINGWORTH

T y

WEST

Hillside

Killingworth
Hall

THE SPINNEY

LANE

KILLINGWORTH

ROAD

Sch.

Playing
Field

**KILLINGWORTH
VILLAGE**

5

B1317

STEPHENSON

TRAIL

Stores

Highfield
Well

KILLINGWORTH MOOR

GROVE

WILLOWDENE

GLENEWOOD

URNE

CLOUSDEN GRANGE

ROAD

NICHOLSON TER.

WOODLANDS GRANGE

WOODLANDS GRANGE

GREEN

THE PALMERS

A **30** Pav. Spor round **B** **C**

Woodlands
Ter.

FOREST HALL RD.

GRANVIL

VIEW

ANVIL

CROXDEN DR.

ERRINGTON TER.

FELTON DRIVE

GRT. LIME

CROSSLEY TER.

Palmersville
Meadowfield
Ter.

★ Bamford Ter.
Osborne

Palm
Ct.

LAUREL

LAUREL

Palmersv

AV.

AV.

RD.

LAUREL
END

Palmersville

**Benton
Square**

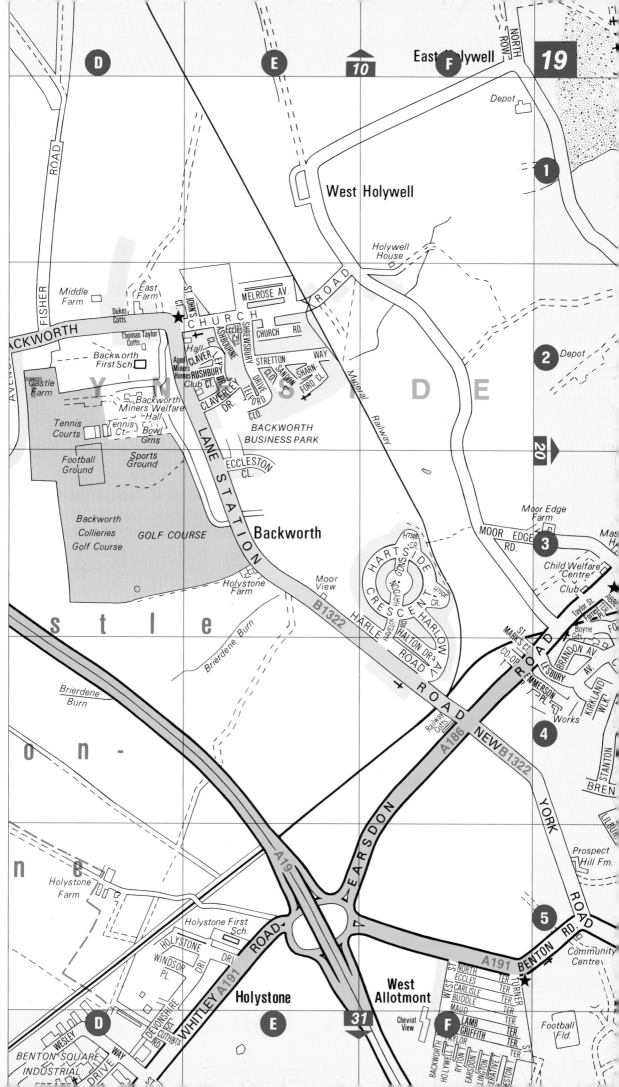

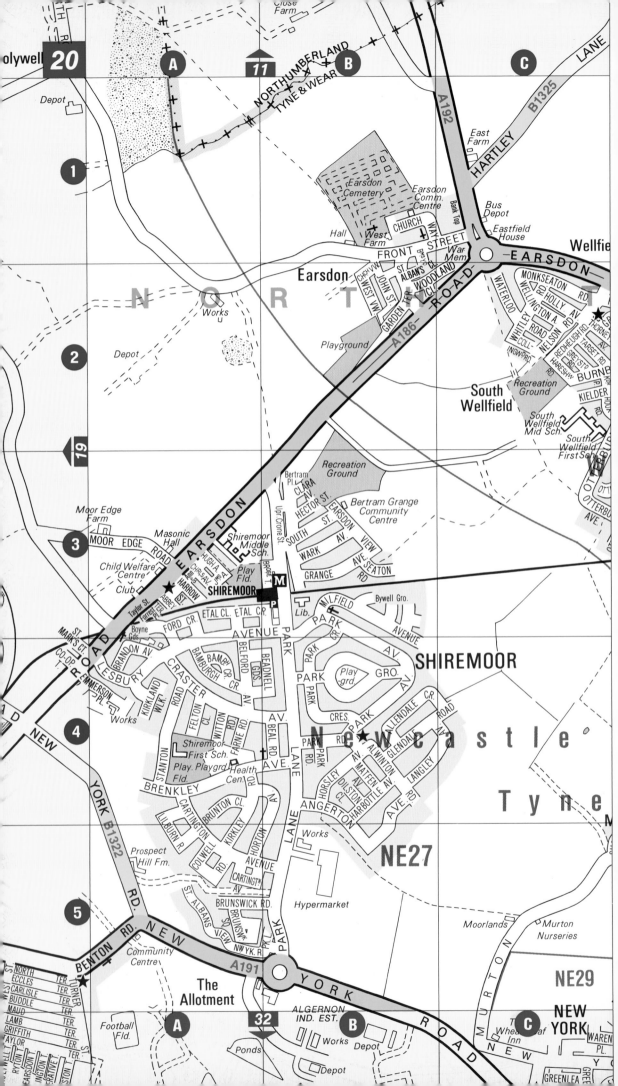

A · B · C

11 NORTHUMBERLAND

TYNE & WEAR

1

Depot

Close Farm

Earsdon Cemetery

Earsdon Comm. Centre

East Farm

Bus Depot

Eastfield House

Wellfi

Hall

West Farm

CHURCH

War Mem

EARSDON

Earsdon

FRONT STREET

ROAD

WAY TOP

Bank Top

A192

HARTLEY LANE

B1325

MONKSEATON RD

WELLINGTON A

WATERLOO

WHITLEY

HOLLY AV.

NELSON RD

WELLINGTON RD

REDHEUGH RD.

GREY ST.

HARESHW RD.

TARGET RD

THORNEY

BURNB

KIELDER

OTTERBU AVE.

BU

OTT

Playground

South Wellfield

Recreation Ground

South Wellfield Mid Sch.

South Wellfield First Sch

2

Depot

Works

A186

EARSDON

19

Moor Edge Farm

MOOR EDGE ROAD

Masonic Hall

Child Welfare Centre

Club

Shiremoor Middle Sch.

Play Fld.

HARROW

SHIREMOOR

Recreation Ground

Bertram Pl.

CLARA AV.

HECTOR ST.

SOUTH ST.

EARSDON ST.

WARK AV.

GRANGE

VIEW AV.

SEATON RD

Bertram Grange Community Centre

Upr Crone St.

3

Taylor St.

Forrest

HUGH A.

CHURSAV.

ABBEY

ST. MARK'S CT.

CO-OP T.

EMMERSON PL.

ALESBURY

FORD CR.

ETAL CL.

ETAL CR.

AVENUE

Boyne Gds.

BRANDON AV.

KIRKLAND WLK.

CRASTER ROAD

BAMBURGH CR.

BAMB

BELFORD GDS.

BRADNELL

PARK

M

P

Lib.

MILFIELD

Bywell Gro.

PARK AVENUE

PARK AV.

PARK GRO.

SHIREMOOR

Play grd.

PARK CRES.

PARK

ROAD

GLENDALE CR.

4

Works

SHIREMOOR

Shiremoor First Sch.

Play. Playgrd. Fld.

Health Cen.

FELTON

WITTON RD.

FARNE RD.

STANTON

BRENKLEY

LILBURN R.

BRUNTON CL.

CARTINGTON

COLWELL RD.

KIRKLAV

HORTON

CARTINGT. AV.

BEAL RD.

PARK LANE

AVE.

HORSLEY

ALWINTON

MATFEN AV.

DILSTON CL.

HARBOTTLE

ANGERTON

LANGLEY

AVE. RD.

Newcastle

Tyne

NE27

YORK B1322 RD.

NEW

Prospect Hill Fm.

ST. ALBANS

AVENUE

BRUNSWICK RD.

BRUNSK VIEW

NWYK. R.

NWK R.

SQ.

Hypermarket

Moorlands

Murton Nurseries

5

BENTON RD.

NEW

Community Centre

A191

PARK

YORK ROAD

MURTON

NE29

NORTH

ECCLES

CARLISLE

BUDDLE

MAUD

LAMB

GRIFFITH

TAYLOR

RYTON

NGTON

RATIVE

TER.

TER.

TER.

TER.

TER.

TER.

TURNER

ST.

The Allotment

Football Fld.

32

A191

ALGERNON IND. EST.

Works

Depot

Ponds

Depot

Wheat Sheaf Inn

GREENLEA

WAREN PL.

NEW YORK

A · B · C

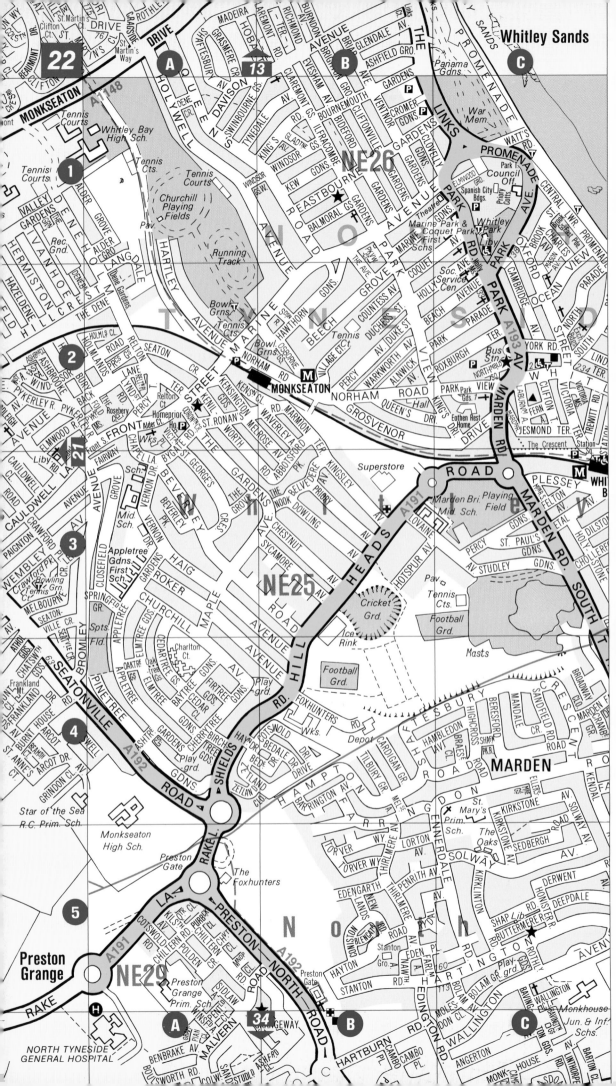

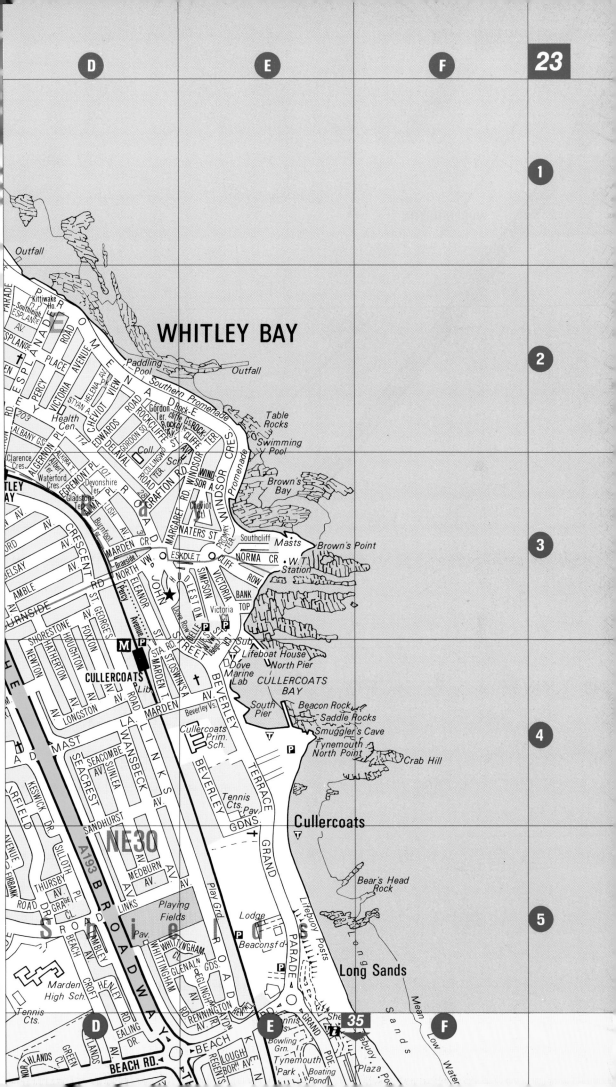

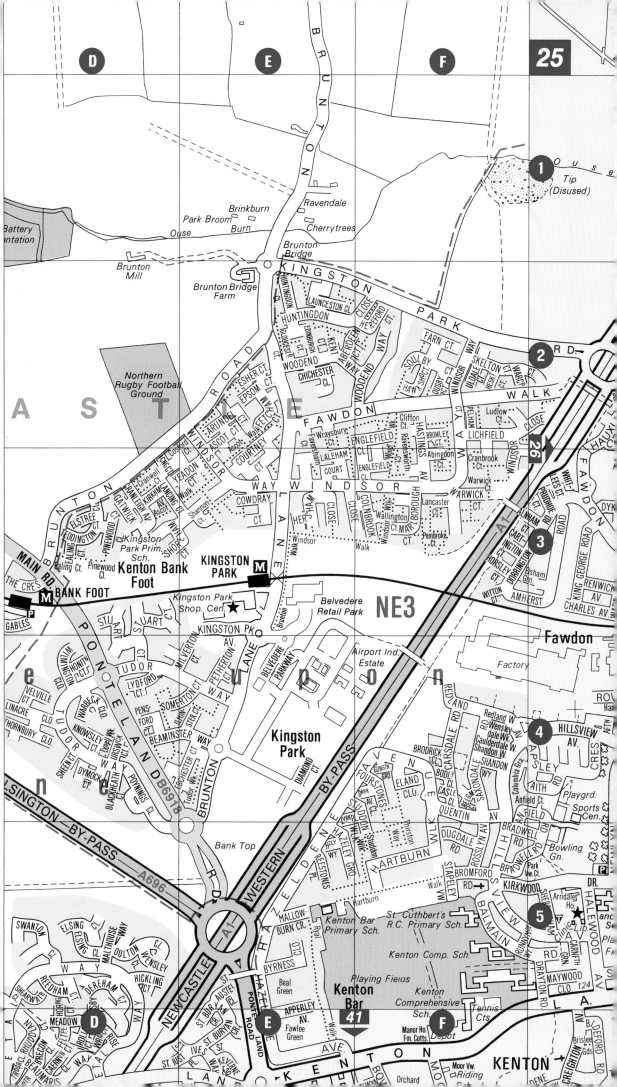

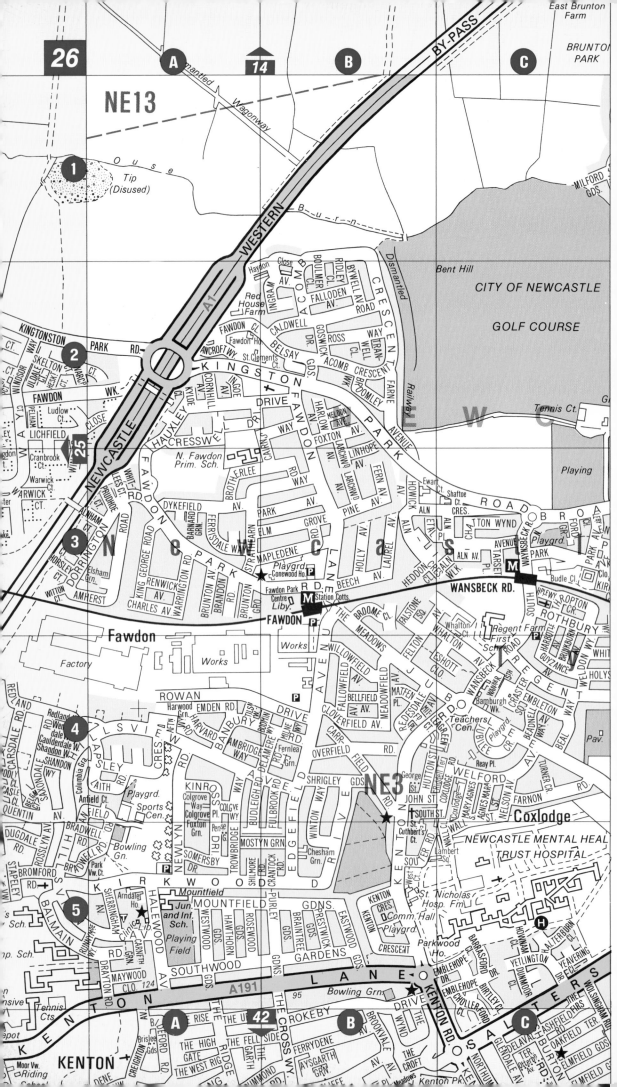

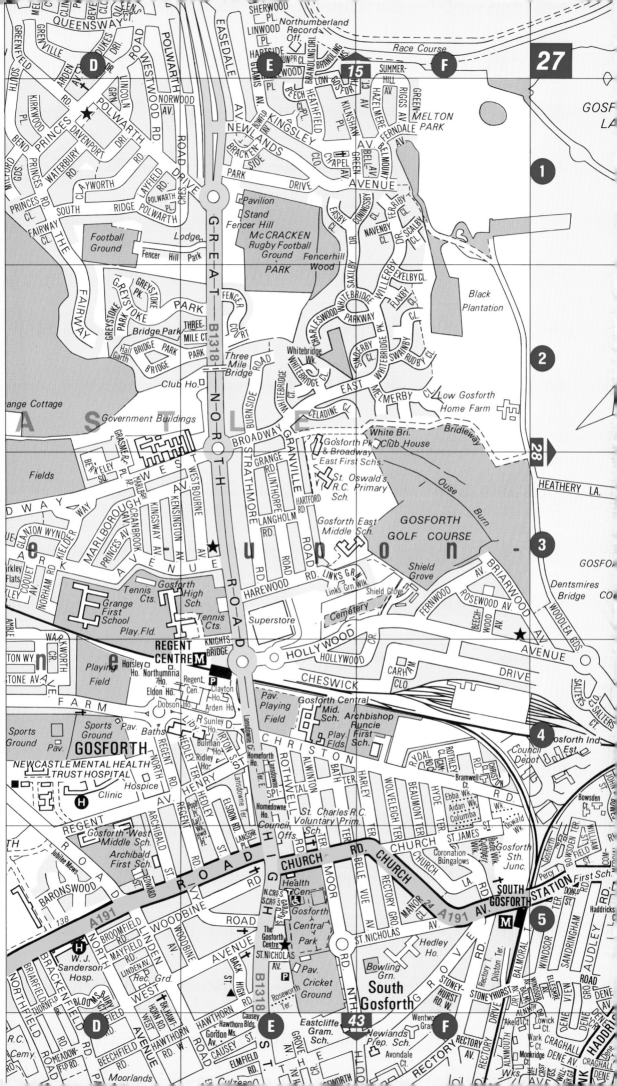

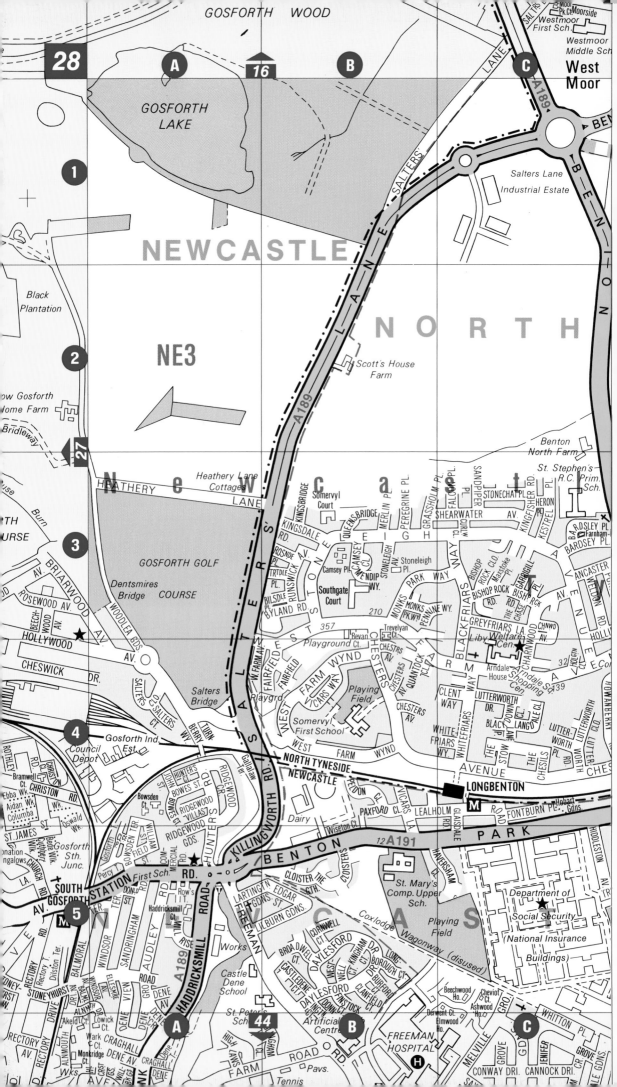

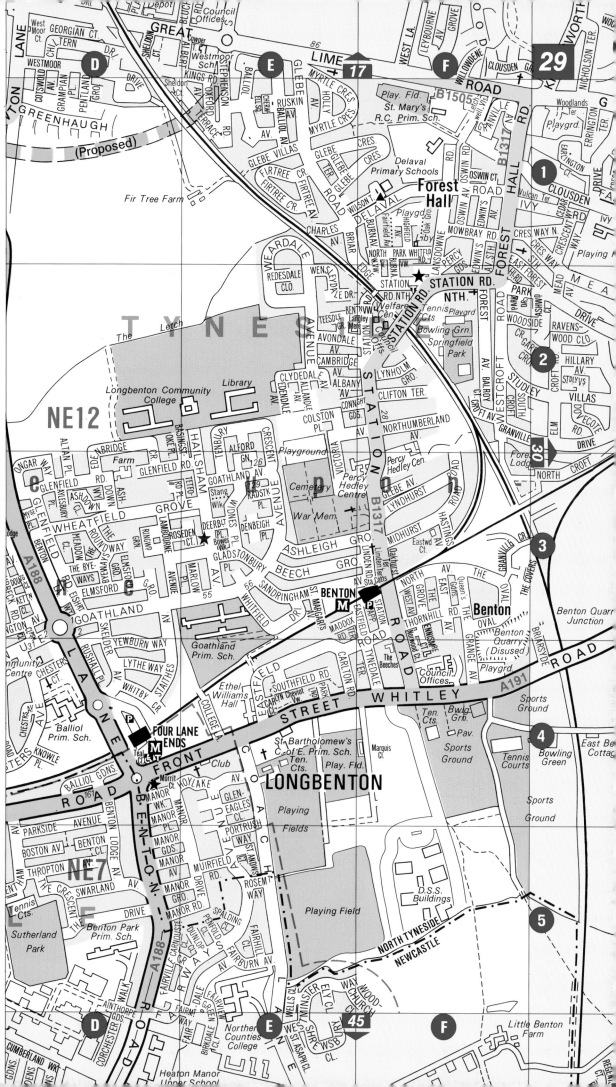

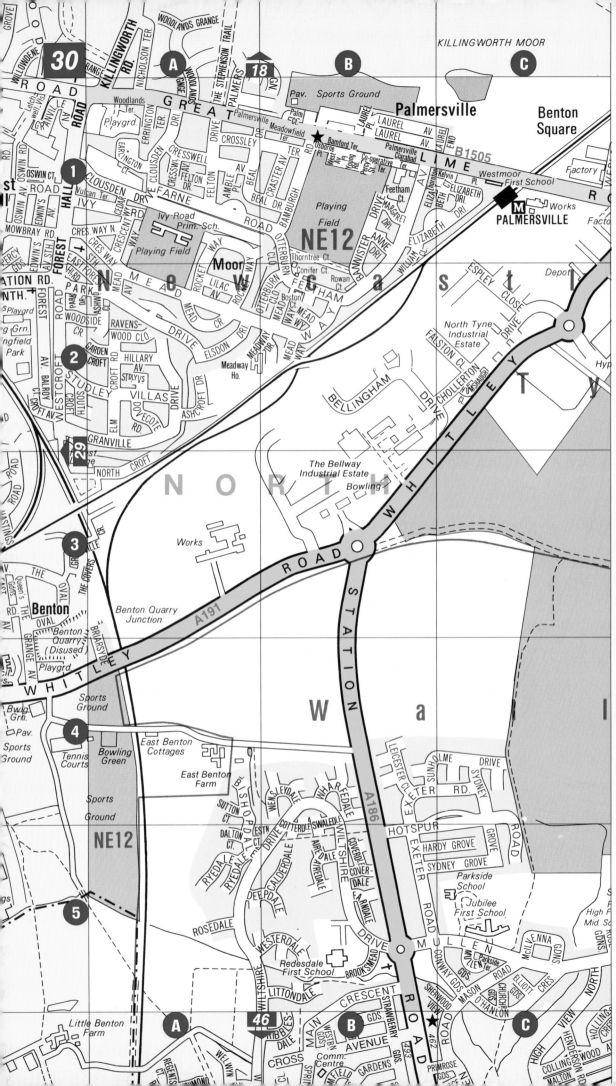

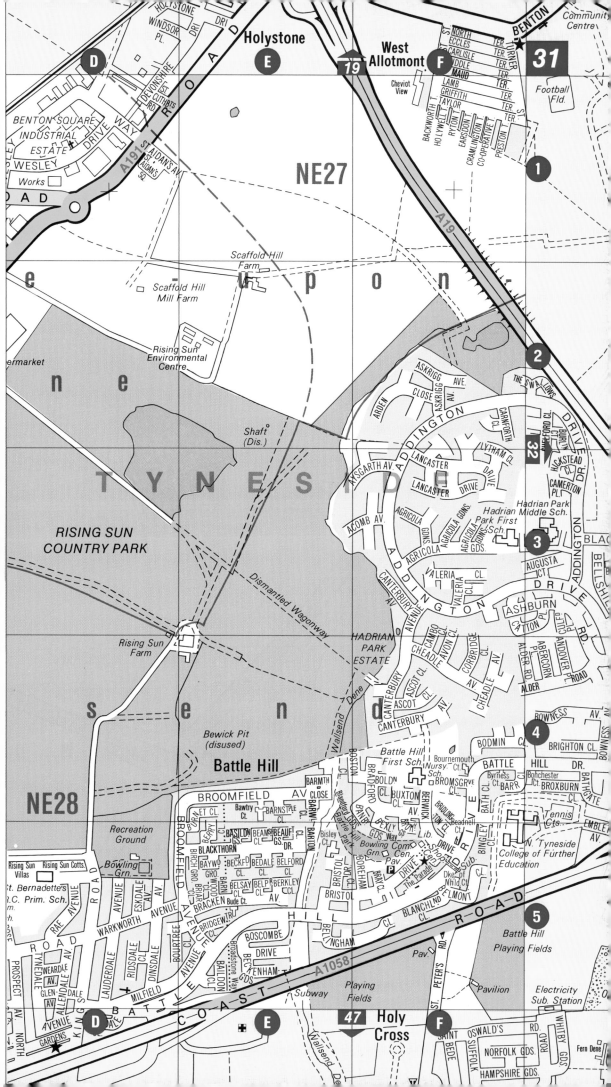

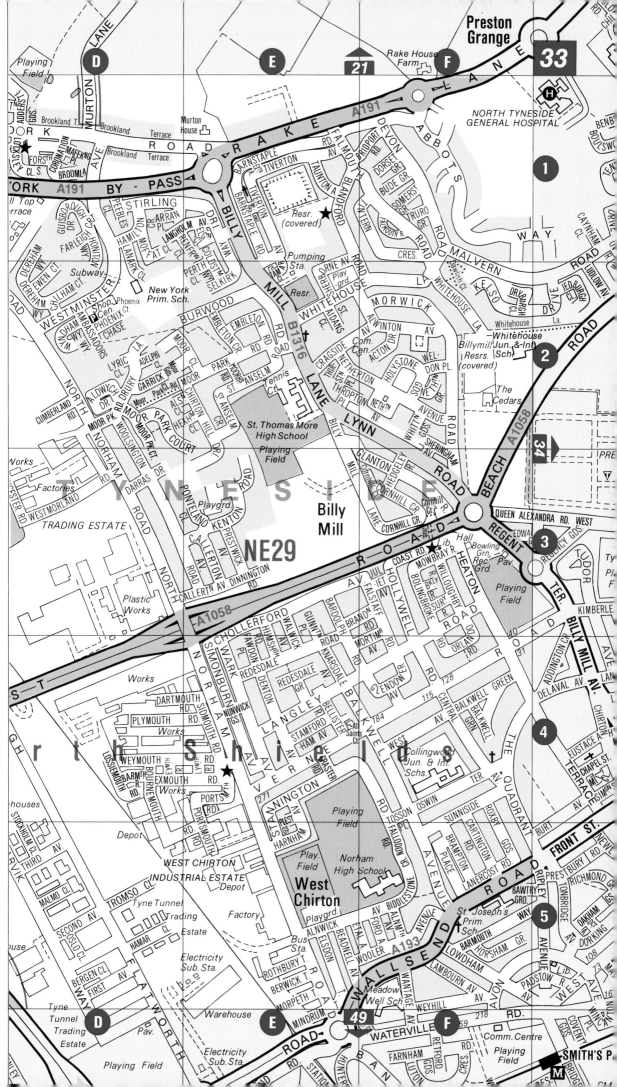

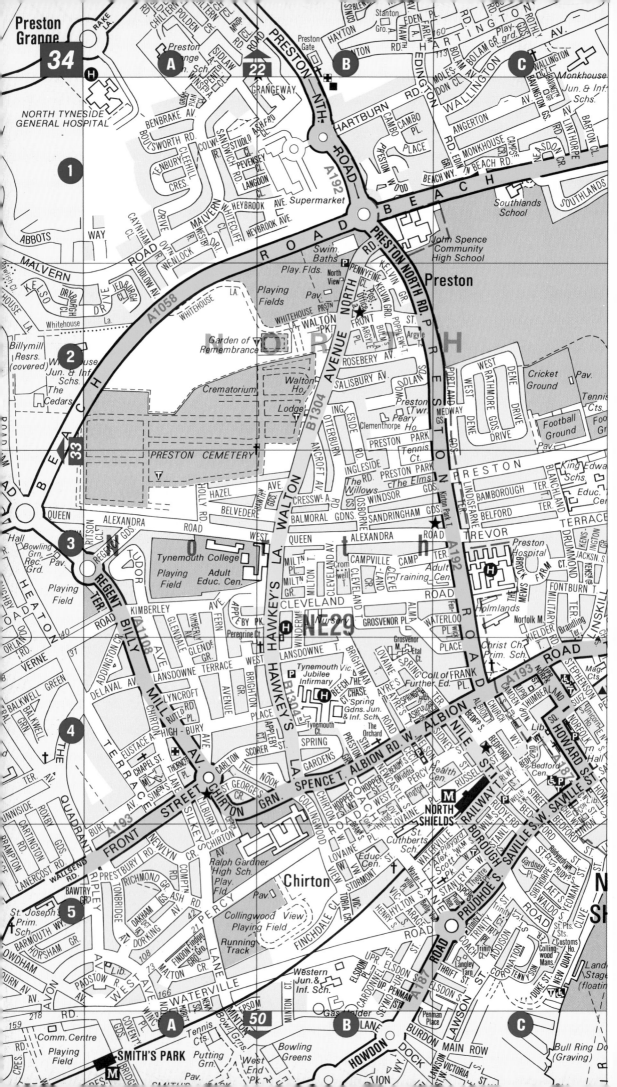

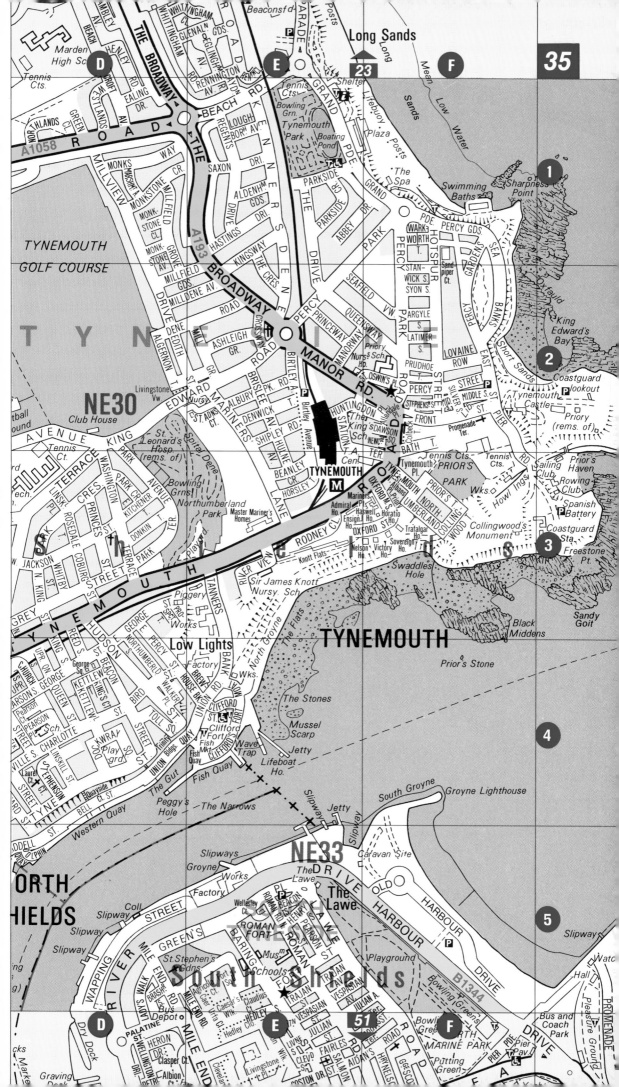

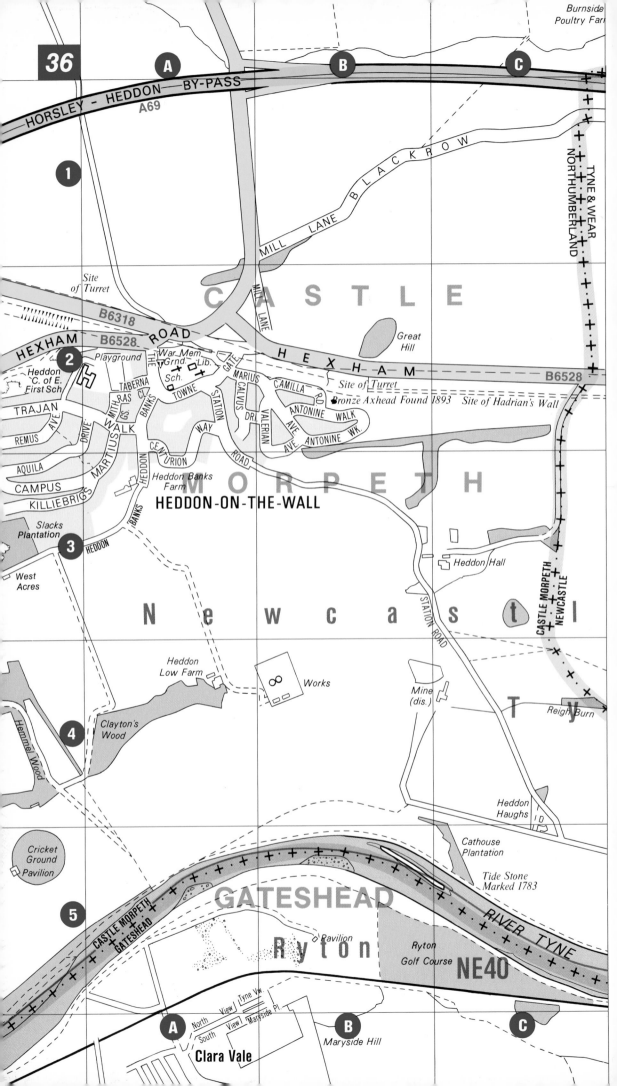

HORSLEY – HEDDON – BY-PASS
A69

A · B · C

1

Burnside
Poultry Far

MILL LANE BLACKROW

TYNE & WEAR
NORTHUMBERLAND

Site
of Turret

C A S T L E

B6318

HEXHAM · B6528 · ROAD

H E X H A M

B6528

Great
Hill

2

Playground

Heddon
C. of E.
First Sch

War Mem.
Grnd.
Sch.

Lib.

GATE

MARIUS

CAMILLA RD.

Site of Turret

Bronze Axhead Found 1893

Site of Hadrian's Wall

TABERNA

MITHRAS CL.

THE

TOWNE

STATION

CALVUS DRI.

VALERIAN AVE.

ANTONINE AVE.

ANTONINE WK.

WALK

TRAJAN AVE.

BANKS

WALK

MARTIUS

DRIVE

WAY

REMUS

CENTURION

ROAD

AQUILA

HEDDON

Heddon Banks
Farm

M O R P E T H

CAMPUS

KILLIEBRIGS

HEDDON-ON-THE-WALL

Heddon Hall

Slacks
Plantation

3

HEDDON

BANKS

West
Acres

N e w c a s t l

CASTLE MORPETH
NEWCASTLE

STATION ROAD

Heddon
Low Farm

Works

Mine
(dis.)

Reigh Burn

4

Clayton's
Wood

Hemmel Wood

T Y

Heddon
Haughs

Cathouse
Plantation

Cricket
Ground
Pavilion

Tide Stone
Marked 1783

5

CASTLE MORPETH
GATESHEAD

GATESHEAD

R y t o n

Pavilion

Ryton
Golf Course

RIVER TYNE

NE40

A

North View
South View

Tyne Vw.

Maryside Pl.

B

Maryside Hill

C

Clara Vale

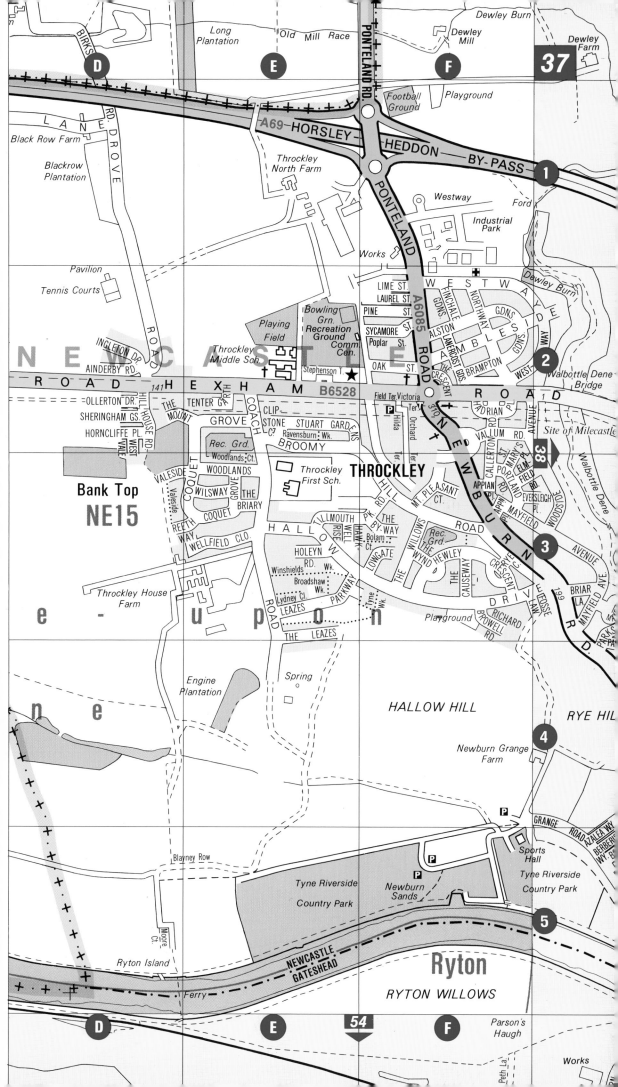

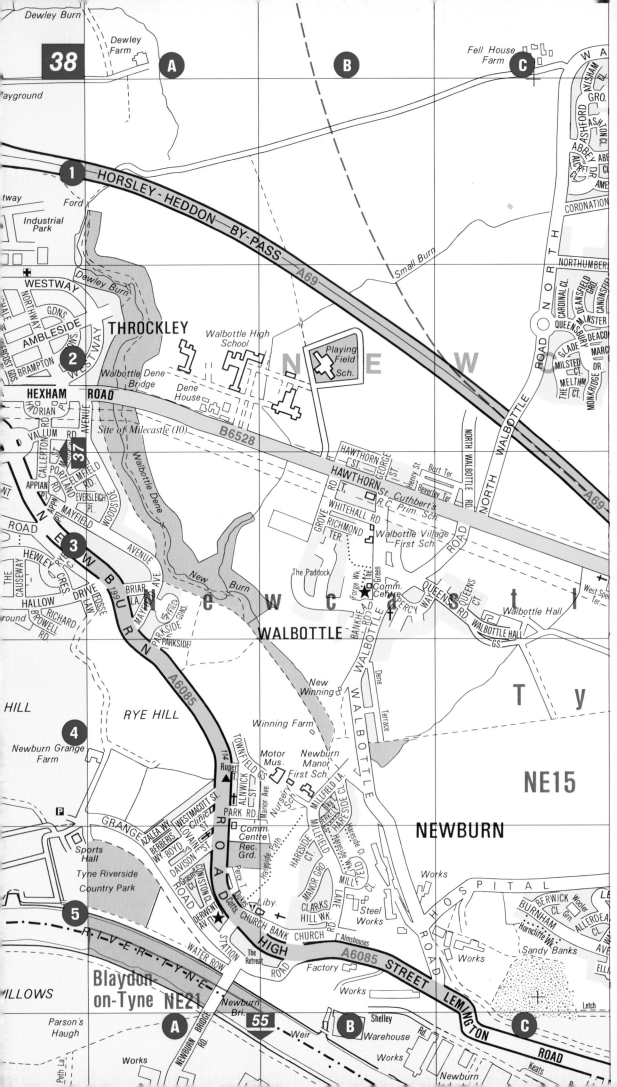

A   B   C

Dewley Burn

Dewley Farm

Playground

1 HORSLEY - HEDDON - BY-PASS   A69

Ford

Industrial Park

Fell House Farm

AYLSHAM GRO.
ASHFORD GRO.
ABBEY
ALLCROFT CL.
ABB
CL.
AME

CORONATION

Small Burn

NORTHUMBERL

WESTWAY
NORTHWAY
GDNS.
AMBLESIDE
BRAMPTON
2 WESTWAY

THROCKLEY

Walbottle Dene Bridge

Dene House

Walbottle High School

Playing Field Sch.

NE W

CARDINAL CL.
QUEENSBURY
DEANSHELD GRO.
CANONS
GLADE
THE
CT.
MINSTER
DEACON
MILSTED
MARCH
CT.
MELTHM
CT.
MONKRIDGE

HEXHAM   ROAD

HADRIAN
VALLUM   RD.
37

APPIAN
PORTLAND
ELMFIELD
RD.
MAYFIELD

CALLERTON   AVENUE
WESTWAY

Site of Milecastle (10)

B6528

Walbottle Dene

HAWTHORN   ST.
GEORGE   ST.
Henry St.
Burt Ter.
Beverley Ter.
St. Cuthbert's R.C. Prim. Sch.

NORTH WALBOTTLE   RD.

NORTH   WALBOTTLE   ROAD

A69

THE CT.

ROAD

EVERSLEIGH PL.

WHITEHALL RD.
RICHMOND TER.
GROVE
Walbottle Village First Sch.

3

THE CAUSEWAY
HEWLEY CRES.
FOSSE
RYE CL.
BRIAR LA.
MAYFIELD GDNS.

HALLOW
RICHARD
B POWELL RD.
DRWE
LAW
WOODSOME

NEWBURN   ROAD   B 199

New Burn

New Burn   AVENUE

The Paddock

PARKSIDE GDNS.
PARKSIDE

Forge Wk.
Comm. Centre
The
Green
QUEENS   WAY
PERCY
QUEENS   RD.
QUEENS CT.
WALBOTTLE HALL
GS.
Walbottle Hall
West Sper   Ter.

WALBOTTLE

BANKHEAD

WALBOTTLE   ROAD

New Winning

Dene

Terrace

HILL

RYE HILL

A6085

4 Newburn Grange Farm

Winning Farm

Motor Mus.

Newburn Manor First Sch.

NE15

NEWBURN

P

GRANGE
AZALEA WY.
BERBERIS WY.
BOYD
DAVISON
RUPERT
ALNWICK ST.
WESTMACOTT ST.
GLOVAINE ST.

TOWNFIELD GS.

PARK RD.
Clinic
Comm. Centre
Rec. Grd.
Nursery Sch.
Manor Ave.
MILLFIELD LA.
BERKLEY CT.
HARESIDE CL.
HARESIDE CT.
Hareside Cl.

HOSPITAL

ROAD
LEMINGTON   ROAD

BERWICK CL.
BURNHAM
Horncliffe Wk.
ALLERDEAN CL.
Wooler
LE
AVE.
ELL

Sports Hall

Tyne Riverside Country Park

GRAMERCY
GRASMERE CL.
CONISTON ST.
DERWENT AV.

5

R I V E R   T Y N E

WILLOWS

Parson's Haugh

Blaydon-on-Tyne NE21

WATER ROW

NEWBURN BRIDGE RD.

STATION   ROAD

The Retreat

Percy T.
Duke St.
Liby.
CLARKS HILL WK.
HILL

CHURCH BANK
HIGH   STREET   A6085
CHURCH
Almshouses
Factory

MANOR GRO.
MILLFIELD GRO.
HARESIDE CL.
MILL LANE
Steel Works
Works

Sandy Banks

Letch

55

Newburn Bri.

Weir

Shelley Rd.
Warehouse

Keats

Newburn

Peth La.

Works

Works

A   55   B   C

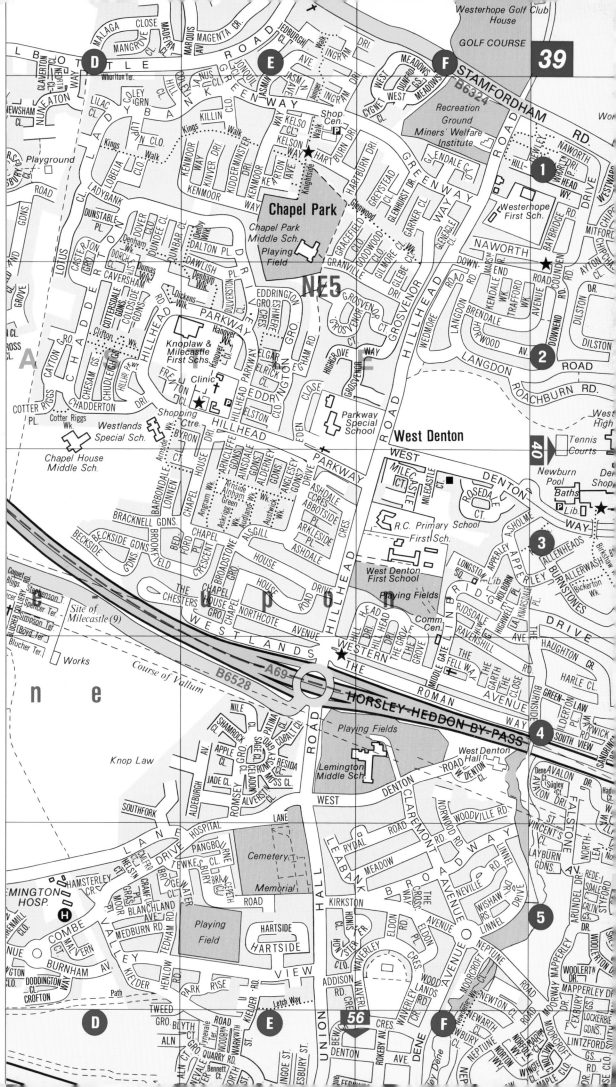

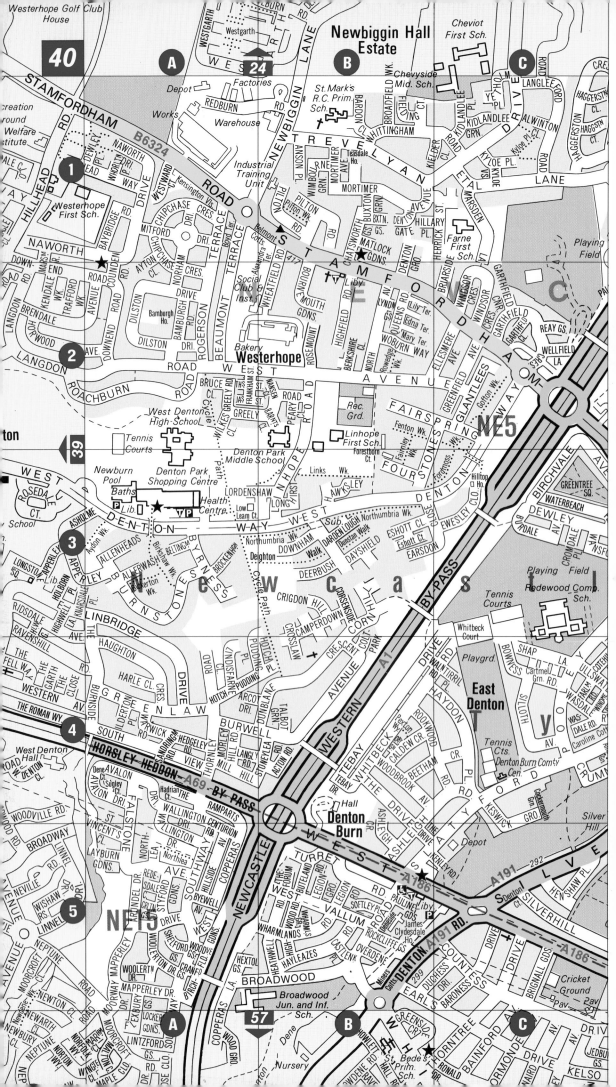

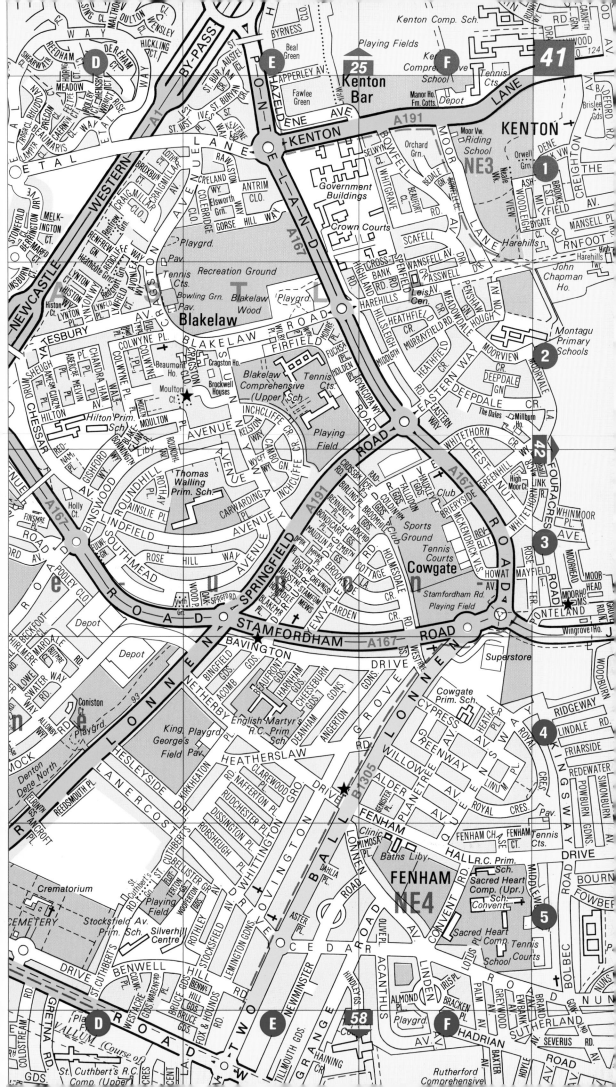

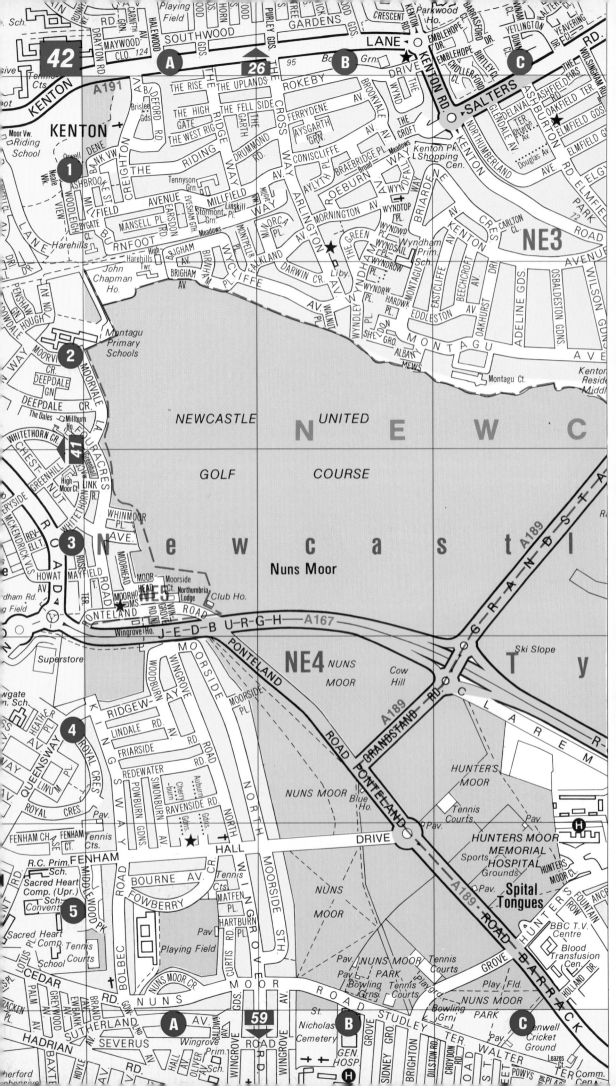

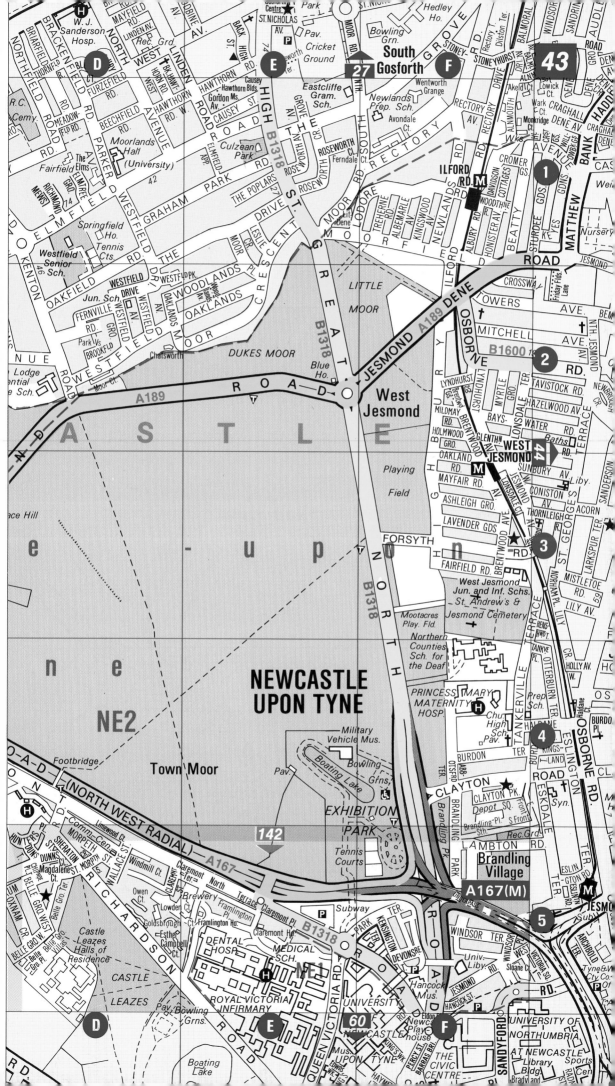

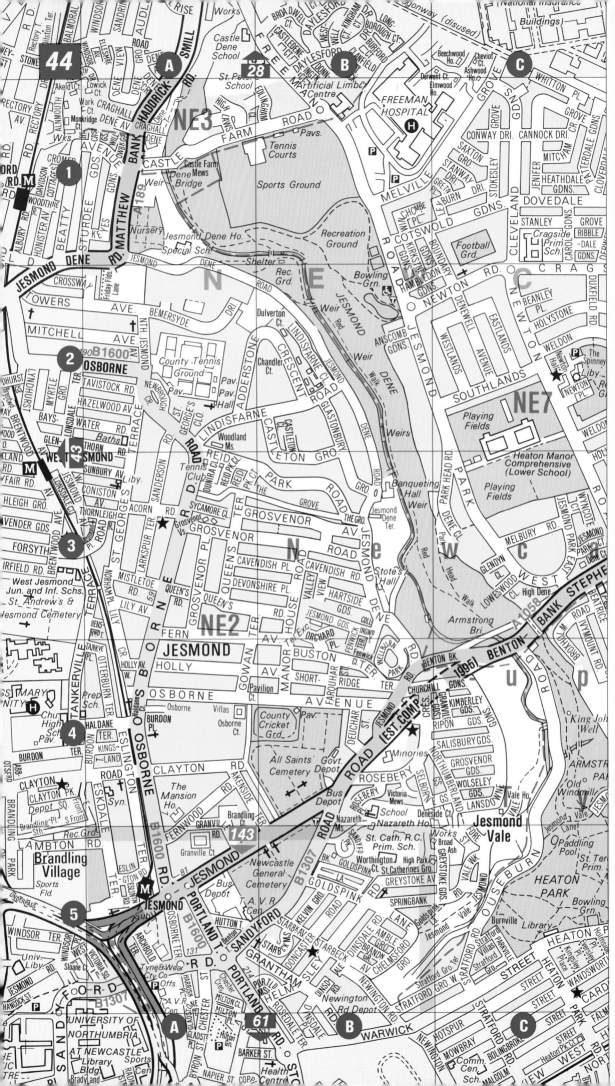

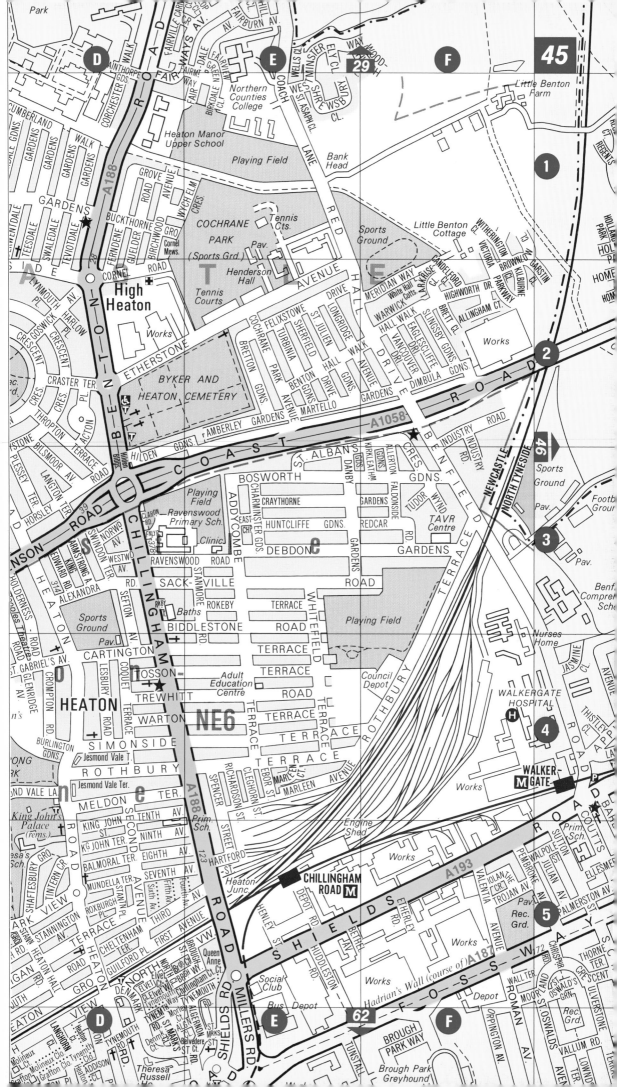

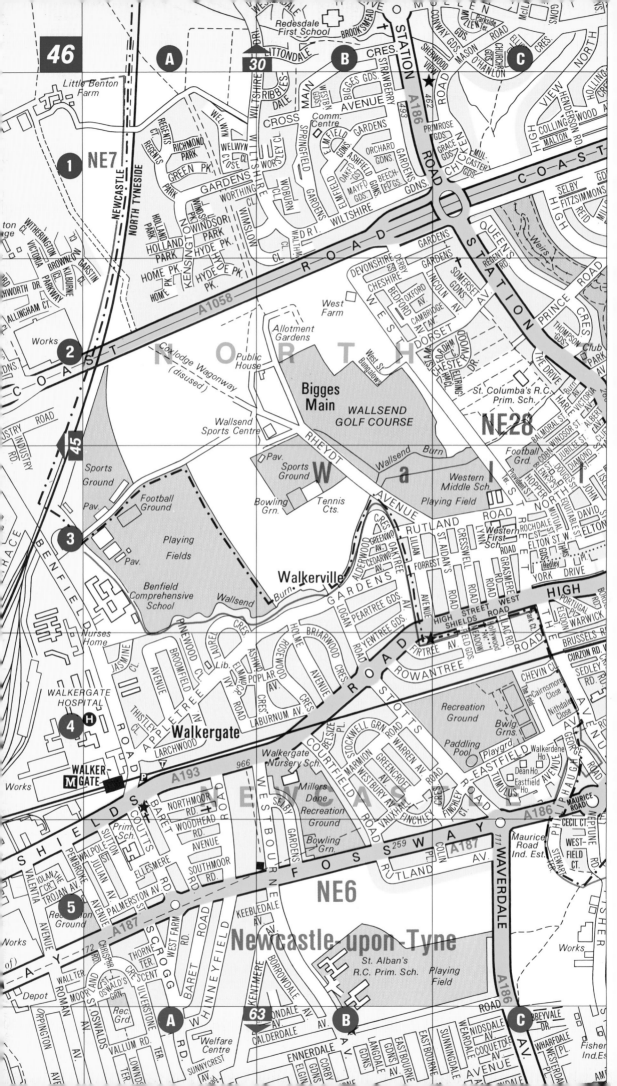

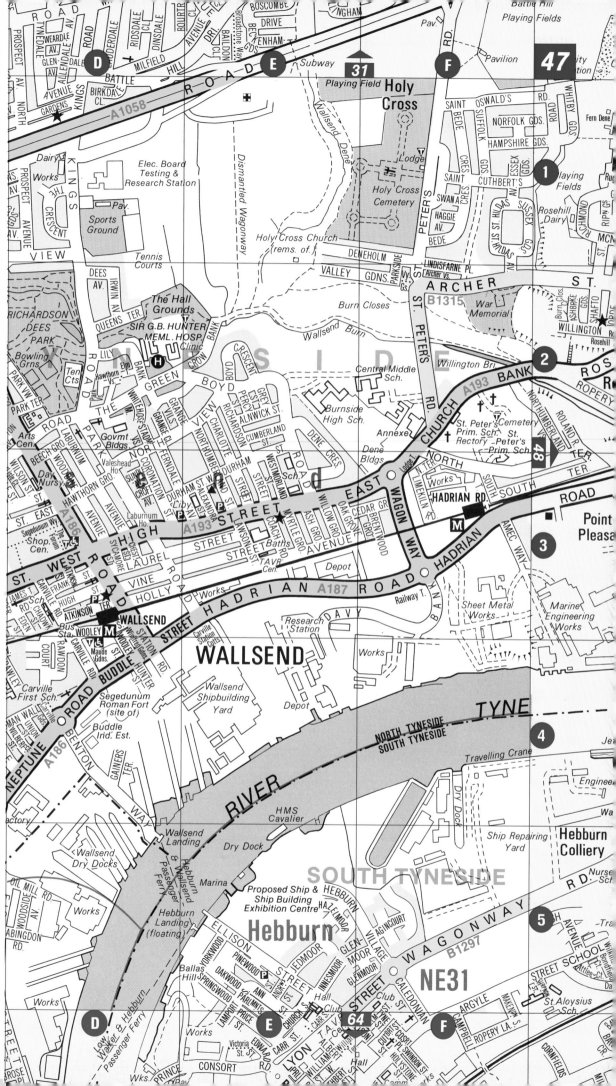

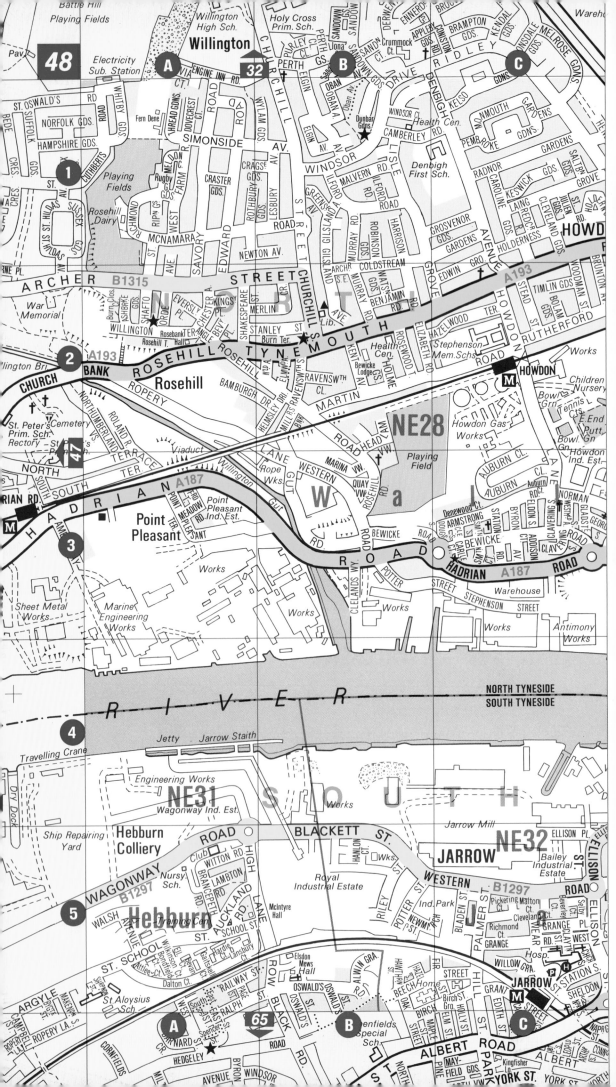

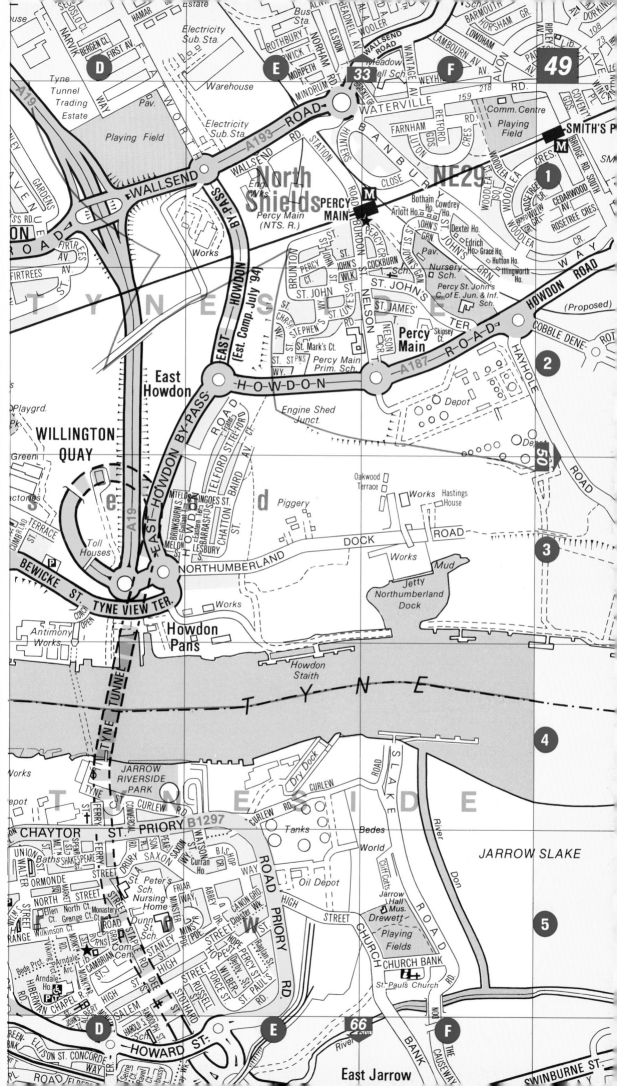

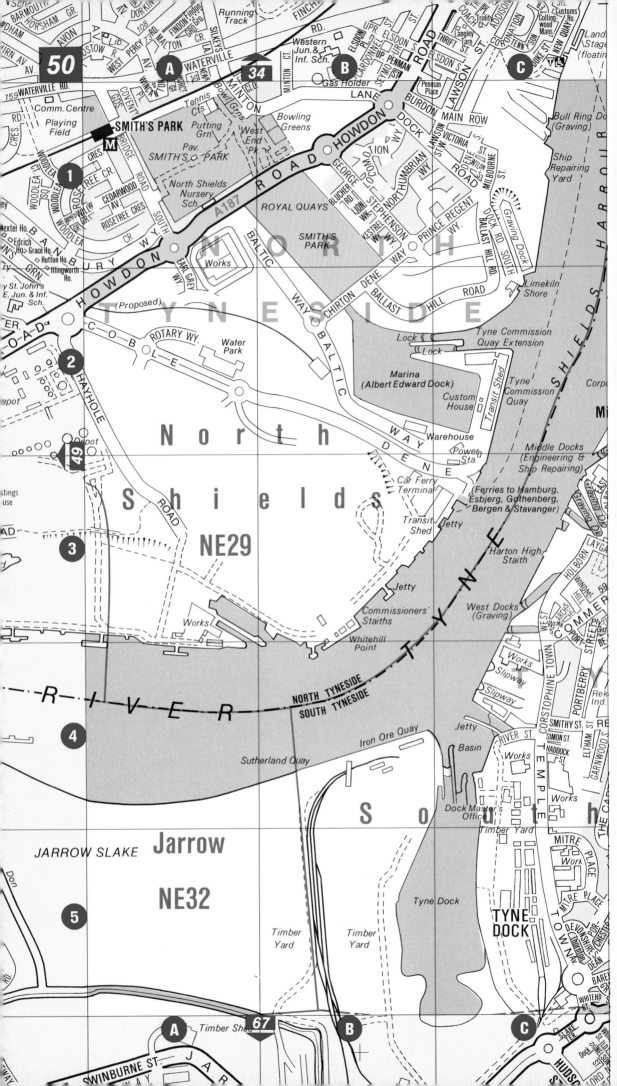

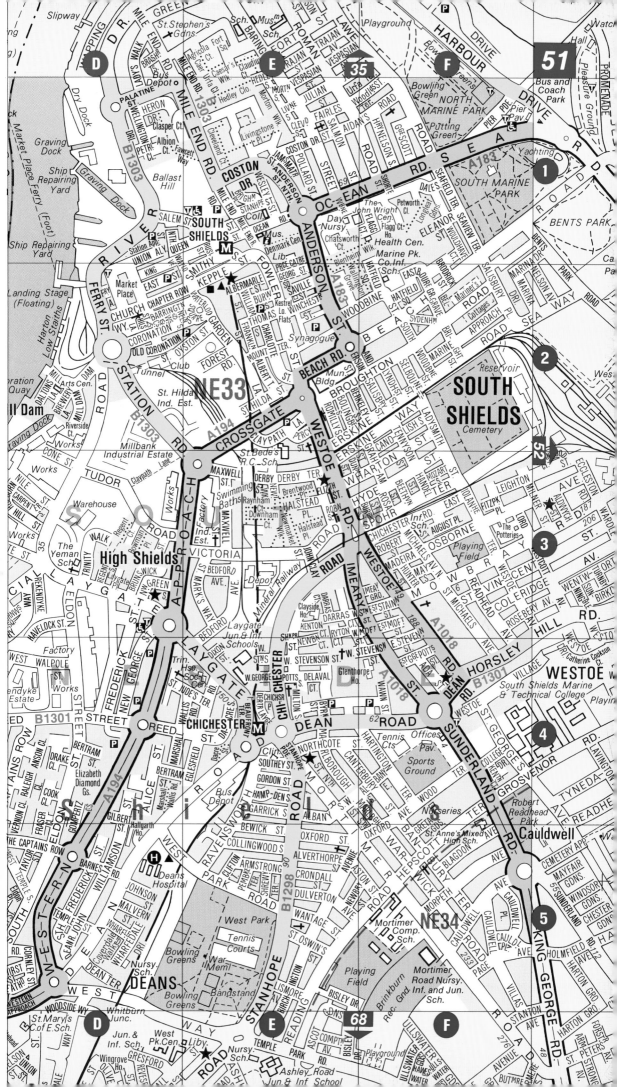

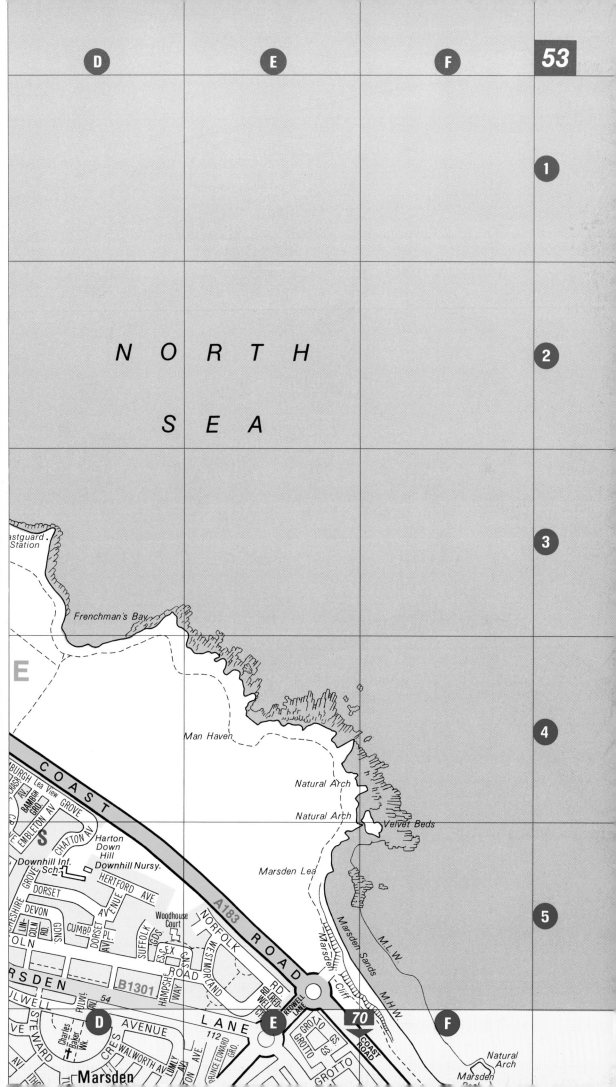

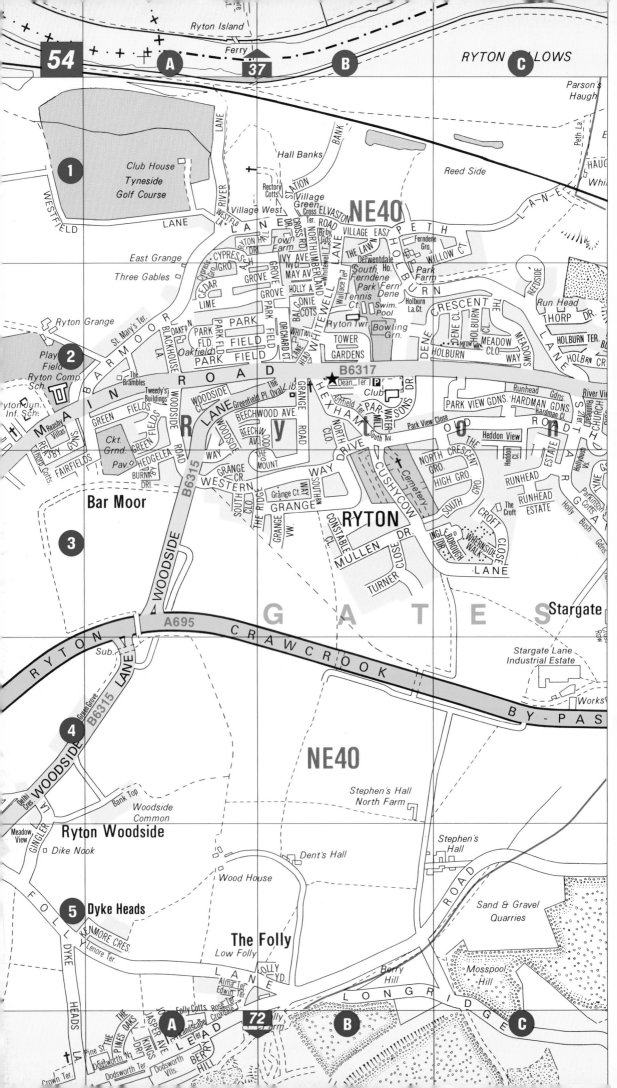

Ⓐ **37** Ⓑ RYTON WILLOWS Ⓒ

Ryton Island
Ferry
Parson's Haugh

1

Club House
Tyneside
Golf Course

Hall Banks
Reed Side
Peth La.
Whi

WESTFIELD LANE
RIVER LANE
WESTFIELD LA.
Village West
Rectory Cotts.

East Grange

Three Gables

Village Green
STATION RD.
CROSS RD.
ELVASTON
NE40

Town Farm
RYTON DR.
CYPRESS
CYPRESS GRO.
GROVE
CEDAR
LIME

IVY AVE.
IVY CT.
MAY AV.
GROVE
PARK FIELD
HOLLY A.
BALGONIE COTS.
Brby Gdns.
VILLAGE EAST
THE LAW
Derwentdale
South Ho.
Ferndene Park
Fern Dene
Tennis Ct.
Swim. Pool
Bowling Grn.

Ferndene Gro.
WILLOW CT.
Park Farm

HOLBURN
PETH LANE

DENE CRESCENT
Run Head
THORP DR.
HOLBURN TER.
HOLBURN CR.

Ryton Grange

2

Play Field
Ryton Comp. Sch.

Ryton Jun. Inf. Sch.

St. Mary's Ter.
BARMOOR
BLACKHOUSE LA.
OAKFN.
Oakfield
The Brambles
Tweedy's Buildings
Reasby Vilas
SNO.
Trood Cotts.
Fairfields
REASBY DRI.

PARK FLD.
PARK FIELD
PARK FIELD
PARK FIELD
WOODSIDE
WOODSIDE
ORCHARD CT.
WHITWELL LANE
WALLACE TER.
WHITWELL HEAD
Ryton Twr.
TOWER GARDENS

★ Dean Ter.
Library
B6317
Greenfield Pl.
Oval
HEXHAM
GRANGE RD.
Whitfield CLO.
NORTH CLO.
PARSONS DR.

ROAD
GREEN FIELDS
GREEN FIELDS
HEDGELEA
BURNS DRI.
Ckt. Grnd. Pav.
Woodside
Beechwood Ave.
BEECHW. AV.
THE MOUNT
WOODSIDE WAY
WESTERN
SOUTH CLO.
GRANGE CR.
Grange Ct.
GRANGE VW.
THE RIDGE
SOUTHERN WAY
GRANGE
WATER
MILL
South Av.
Park View Close
Heddon View

Bar Moor

B6315
WOODSIDE ROAD

3

DRIVE
CONSTABLE CL.
MULLEN DR.
TURNER CLO.
CUSHYCOW LANE
Cemetery
RYTON

PARK VIEW GDNS.
PARK VIEW GDNS.
HARDMAN GDNS.
Hardman Cl.
Runhead Gdns.
NORTH GRO.
HIGH GRO.
NORTH CRESCENT
SOUTH GRO.
INGLEBOROUGH
WHERNSIDE WALK
CROFT CLOSE
The Croft
Runhead
RUNHEAD ESTATE
LANE
River Vi.
CHURCH
Parkinson
Cotts.
Holly Bush Gdns.

G   **A**   **T**   **E**   **S**   **Stargate**

A695
RYTON
WOODSIDE ROAD
Sub.
CRAWCROOK
Stargate Lane
Industrial Estate
BY - PAS
Works

4

B6315 LANE
Green Grove
WOODSIDE LA.
Delh Cres.
GINGLER LA.

NE40

Bank Top
Woodside Common

Stephen's Hall
North Farm

Stephen's Hall

5

Meadow View
Dike Nook
Ryton Woodside

Dyke Heads

FOLLY DYKE LANE
KENMORE CRES.
Lenore Ter.

Wood House
Dent's Hall

The Folly
Low Folly

Sand & Gravel Quarries

LONGRIDGE ROAD
Berry Hill
Mosspool Hill

HEADS LA.
THE OAKS
THE PINES
Pine St.
Crown Ter.
JASPER AVE.
KINGS DRI.
Dodsworth Ter.
Dodsworth Vils.
LEA
Landscale
Folly Cotts.
Rose Ter.
Croftdale
BERRY HILL
Alma Ter.
Edwin Ter.
FOLLY LANE
FOLLY YD.
lly Farm

Ⓐ   **72**   Ⓑ   Ⓒ

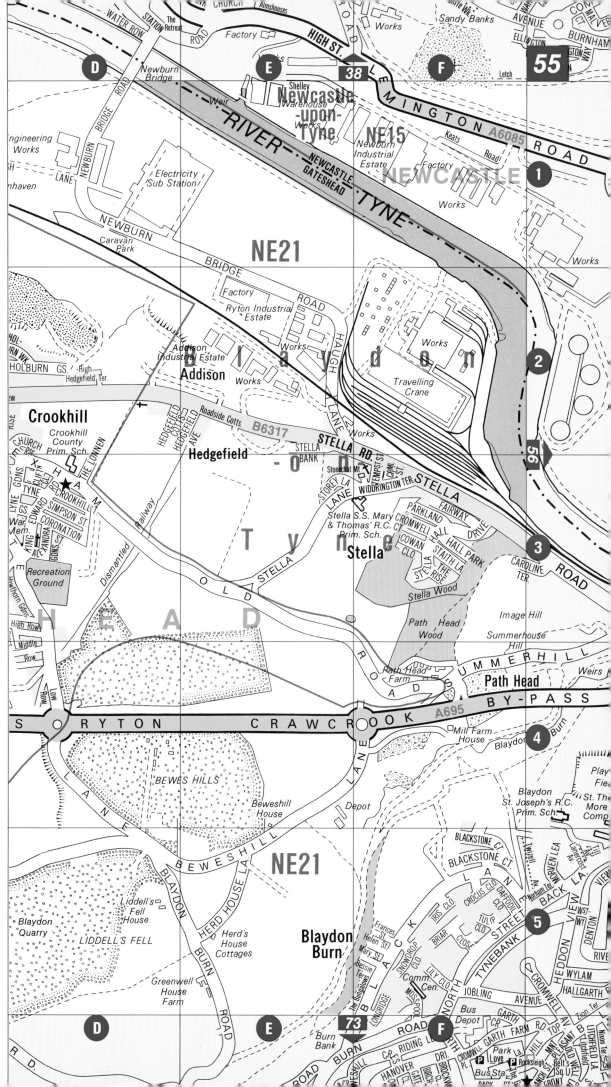

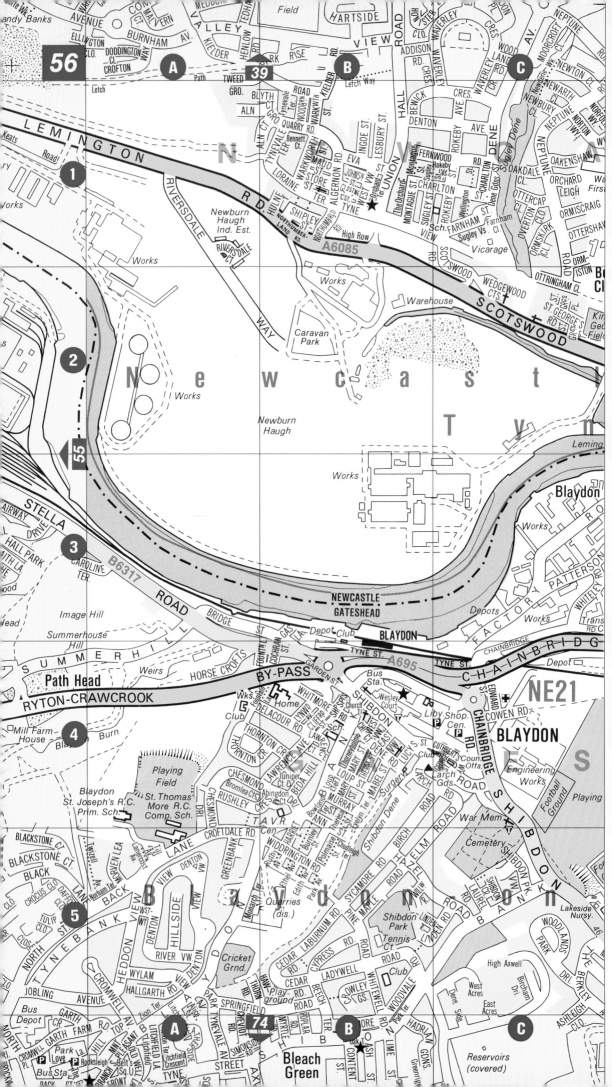

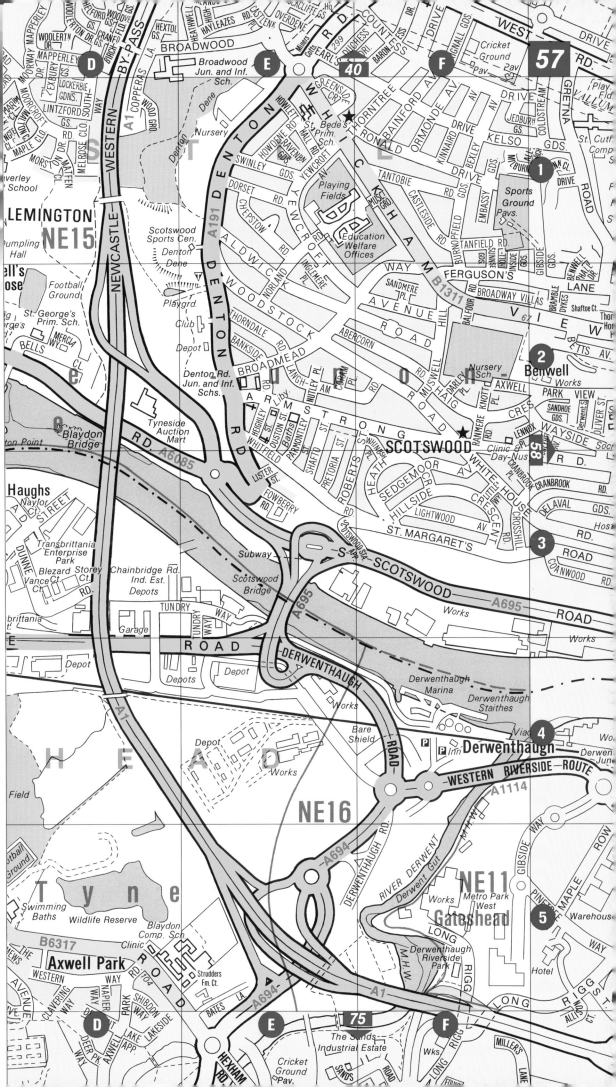

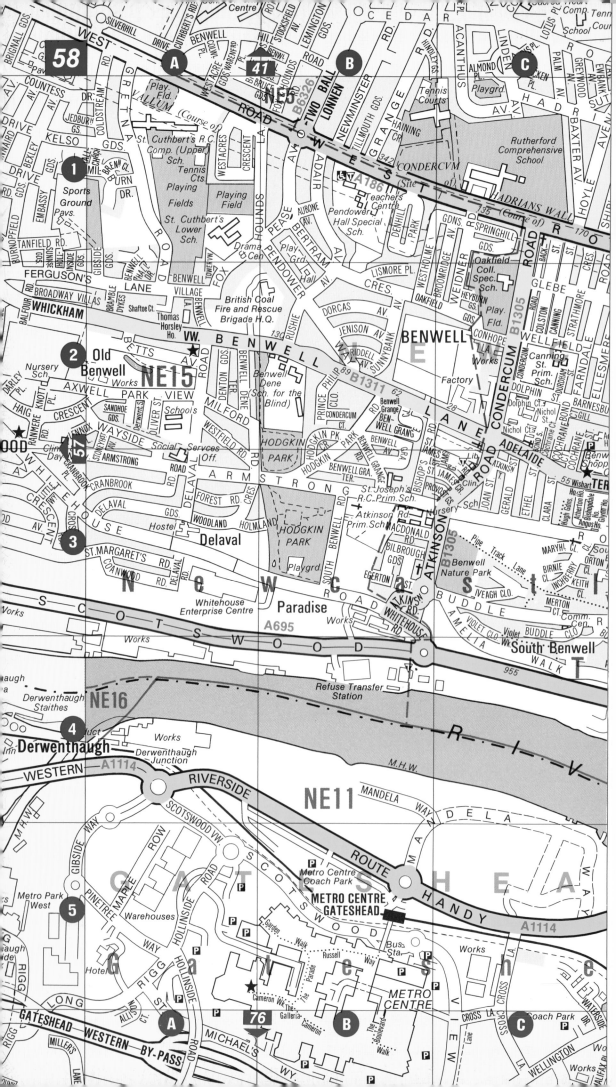

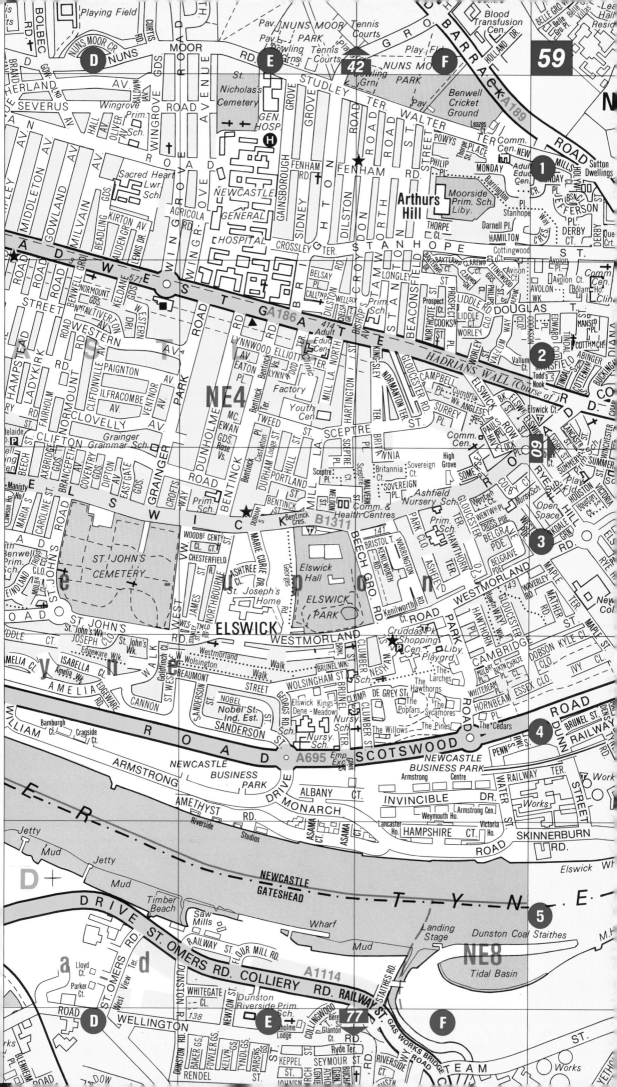

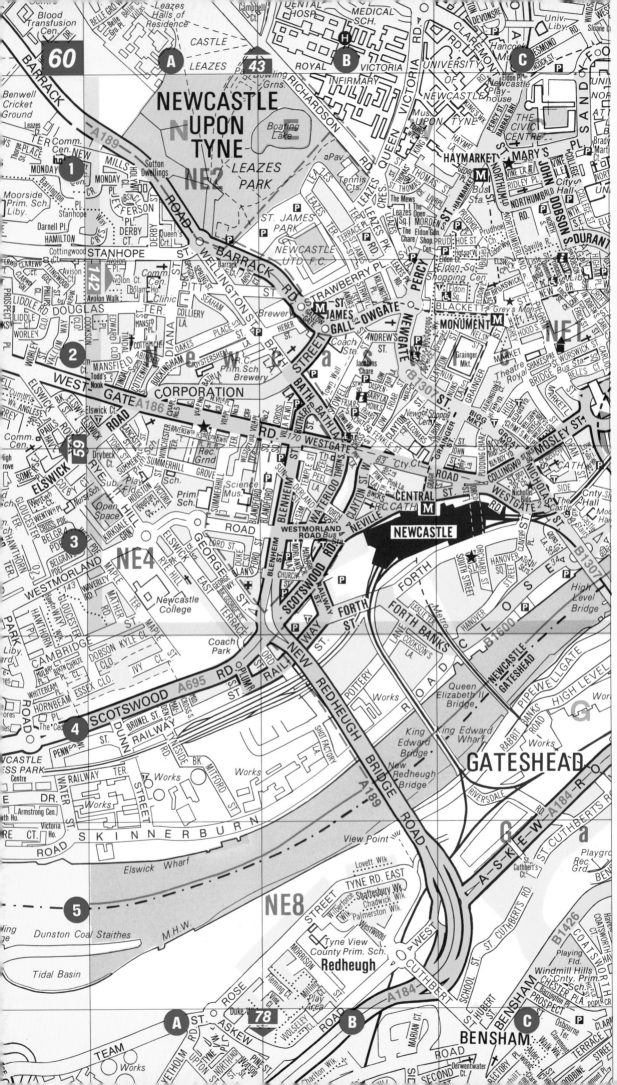

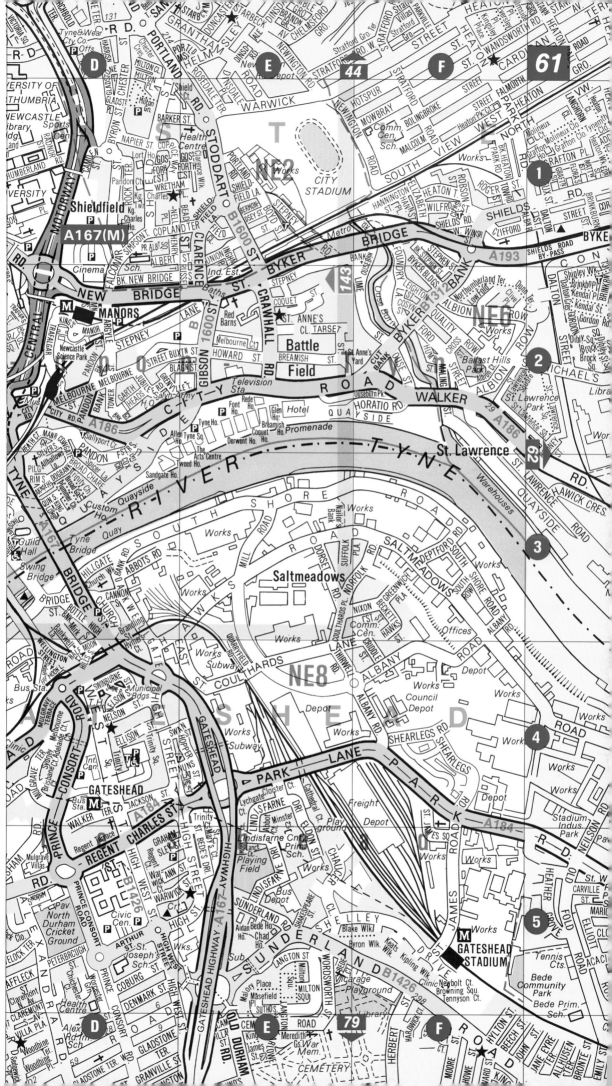

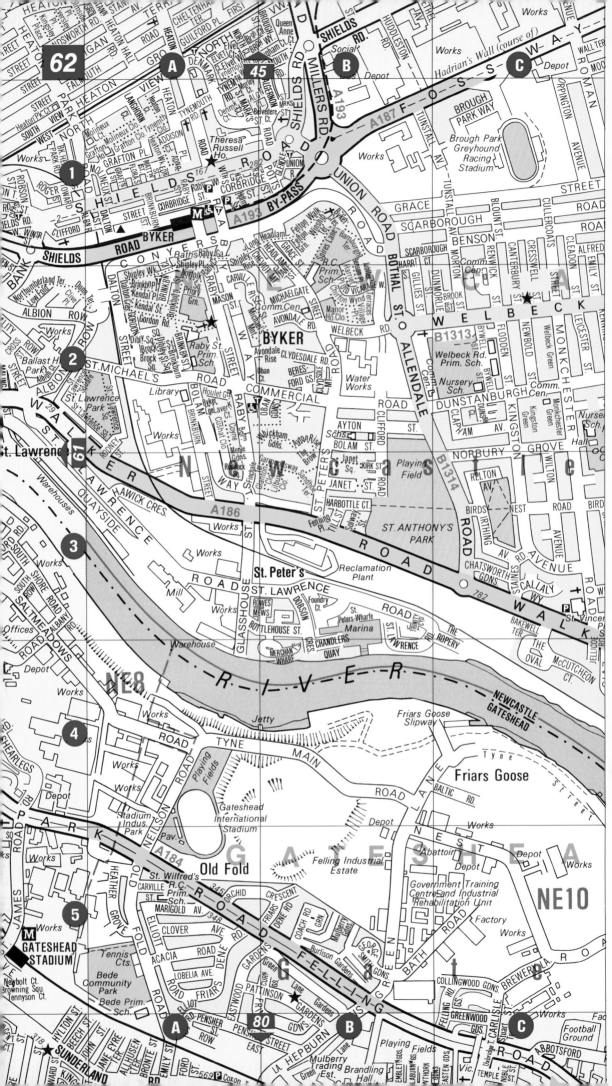

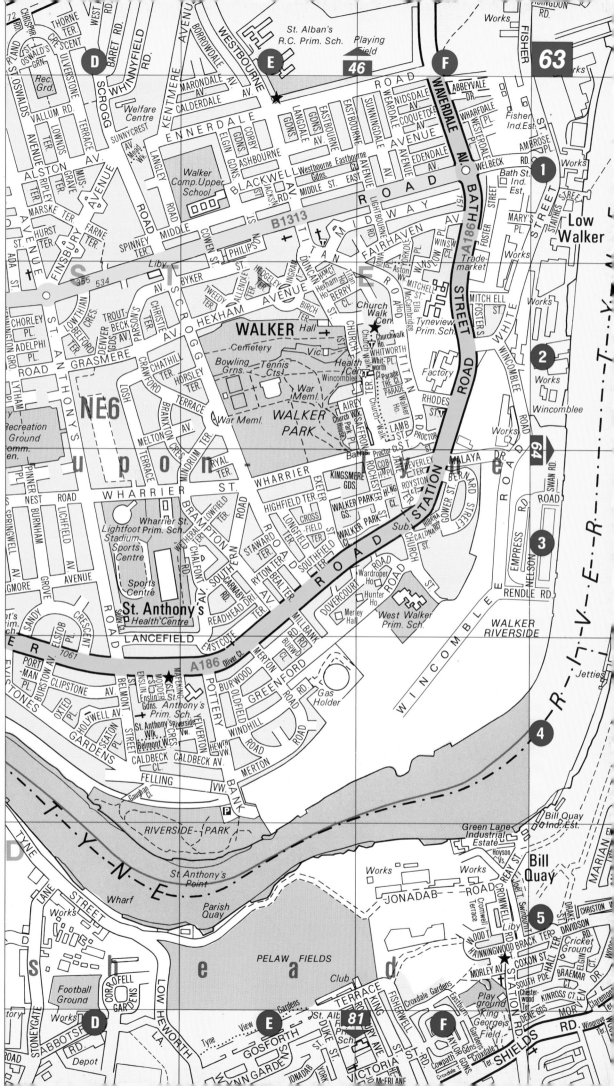

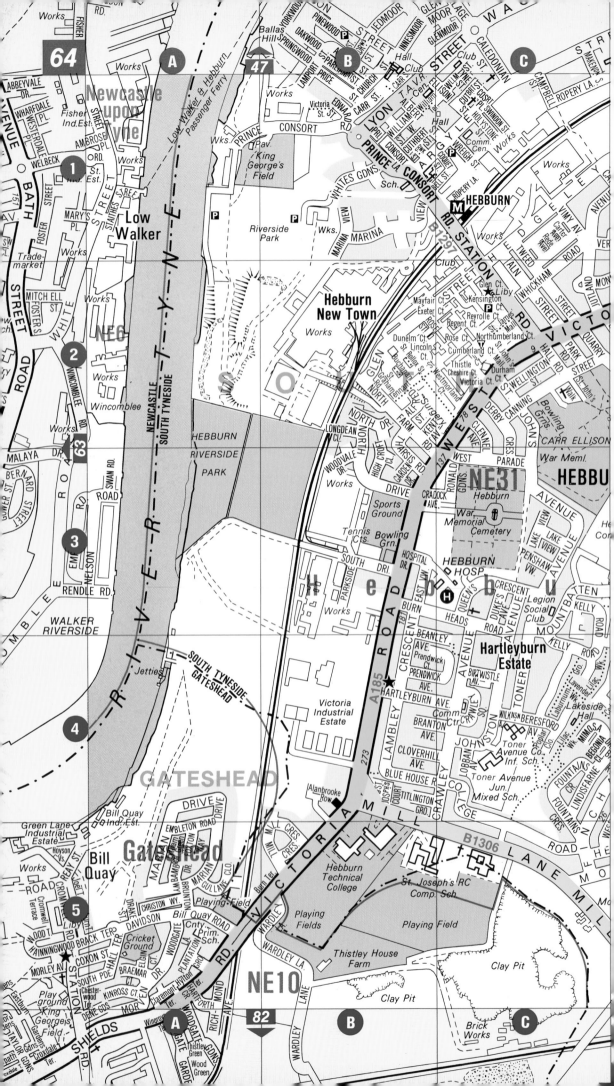

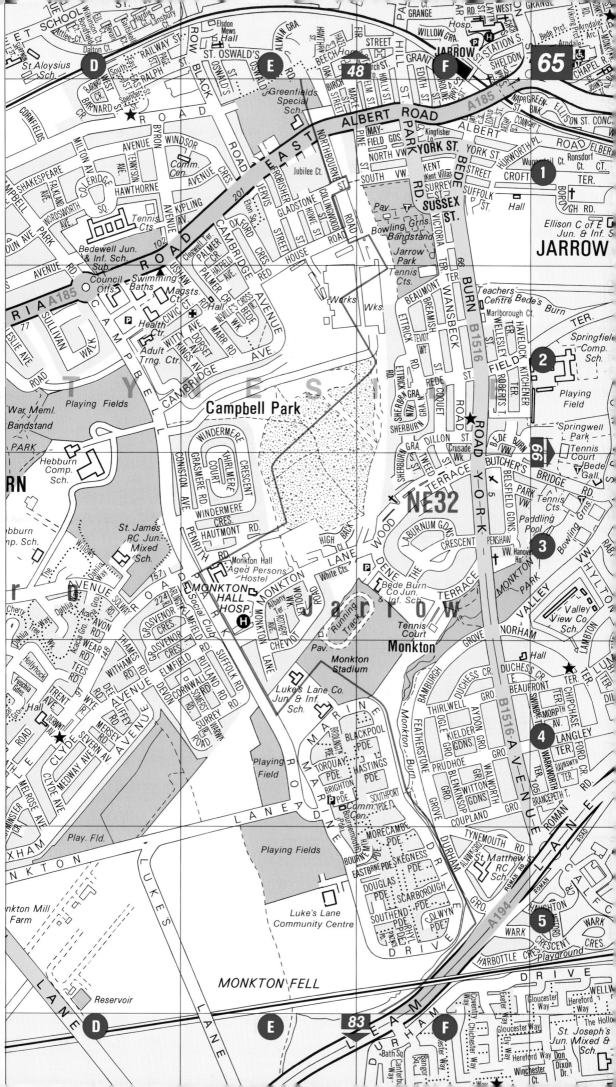

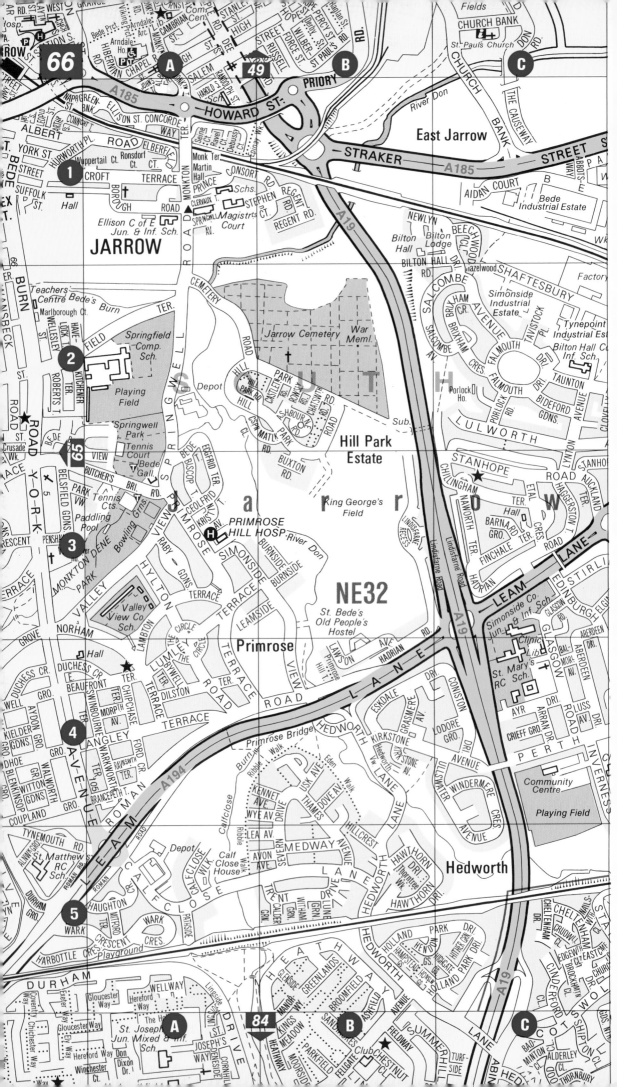

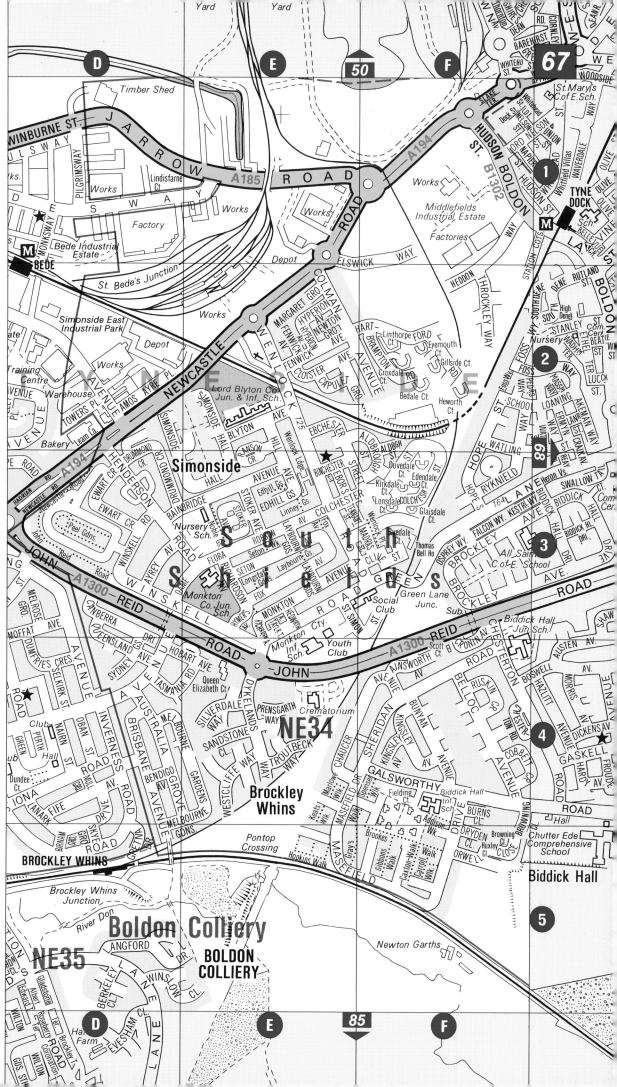

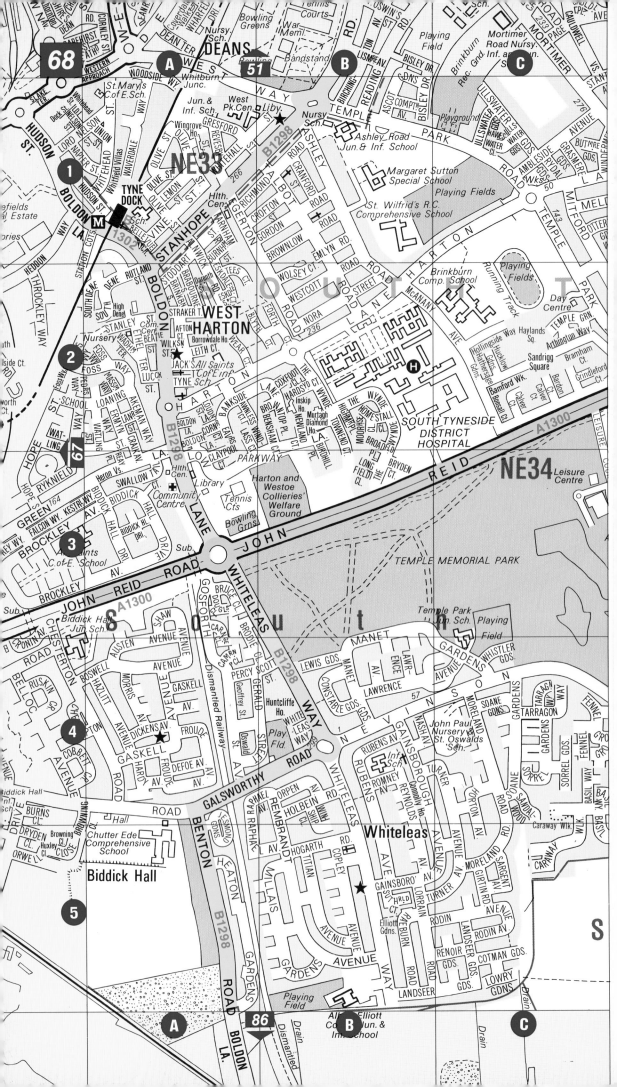

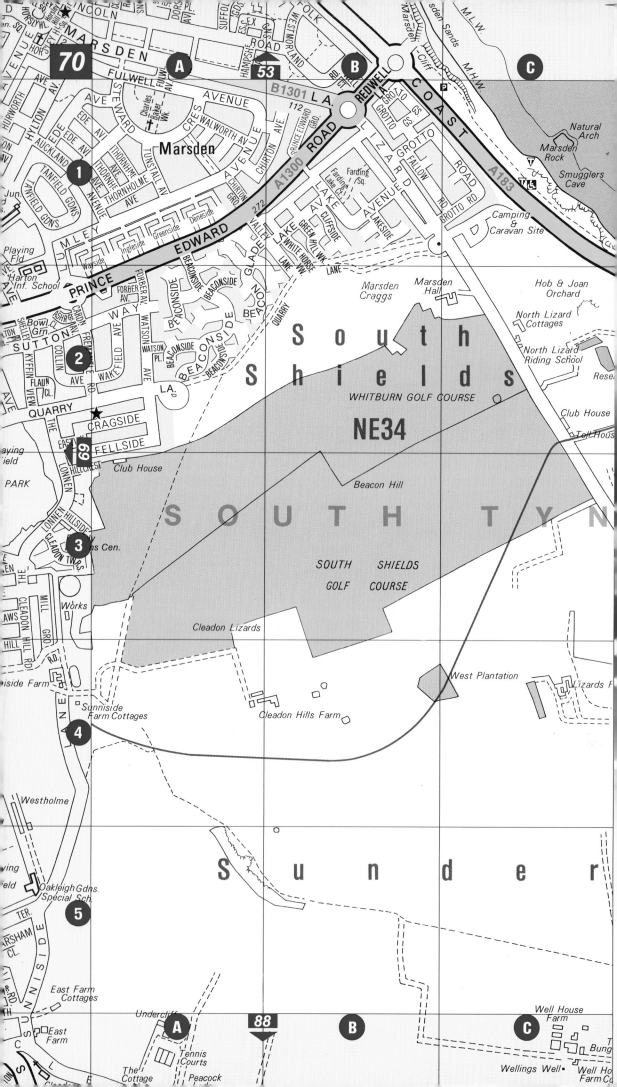

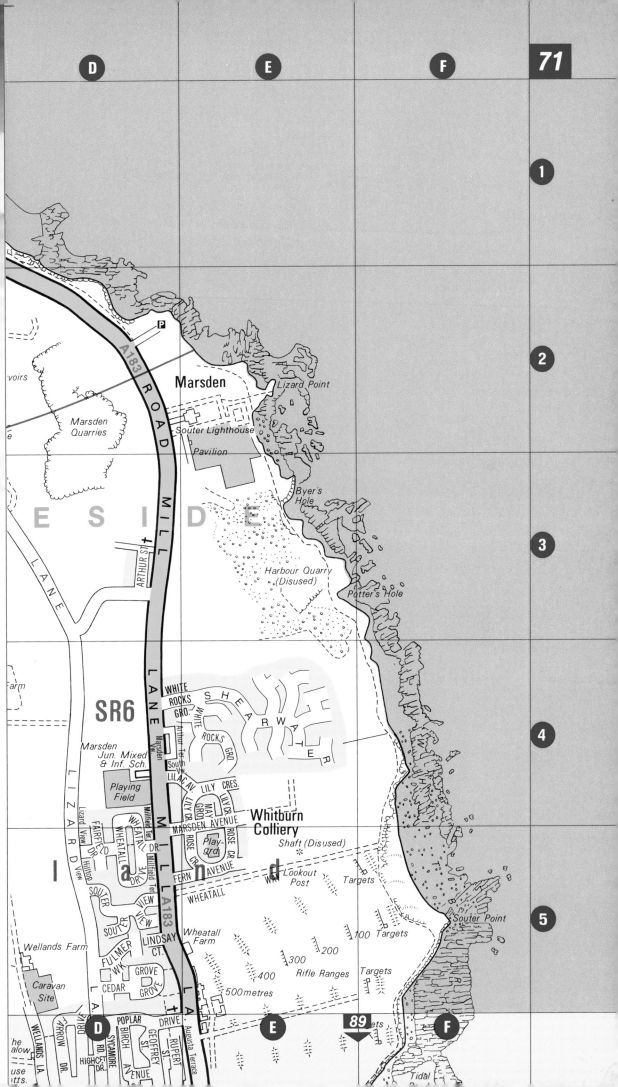

D E

F

1

2

Marsden

Lizard Point

A183 ROAD MILL

P

Marsden Quarries

Souter Lighthouse

Pavilion

Byer's Hole

3

E S I D E

LANE

ARTHUR ST.

Harbour Quarry (Disused)

Potter's Hole

SR6

WHITE ROCKS GRO.

S H E A R W A T E R

4

WHITE ROCKS

Marsden Jun. Mixed & Inf. Sch.

Arthur Ter. South Vw.

LILAC AV.

Playing Field

LILY CRES.

LILY GRO.

MAY GRO.

LILY CR.

Whitburn Colliery

LANE MILL A183

Marsden Vw.

Millfield Ter.

Lizard View

Hilltop View

FAIRFIELD DR.

WHEATALL DR.

MARSDEN AVENUE

ROSE CR.

ROSE CR.

Play- grd.

Shaft (Disused)

FERN AVENUE

Lookout Post

Targets

I

a

n

d

WHEATALL

SOUTER VIEW

SOUTER VIEW

WHEATALL

100 Targets

Souter Point

5

Wellands Farm

LINDSAY CT.

FULMER WK.

Wheatall Farm

200

300

Rifle Ranges

Targets

Caravan Site

CEDAR GRO.

GROVE

400

500 metres

WELLANDS LA.

D

POPLAR

DRIVE

E

89

F

ARROW DRIVE

HIGHCFT. DR.

BIRCH AVENUE

SYCAMORE

RD.

GEOFFREY ST.

RUPERT

Augusta Terrace

Tidal

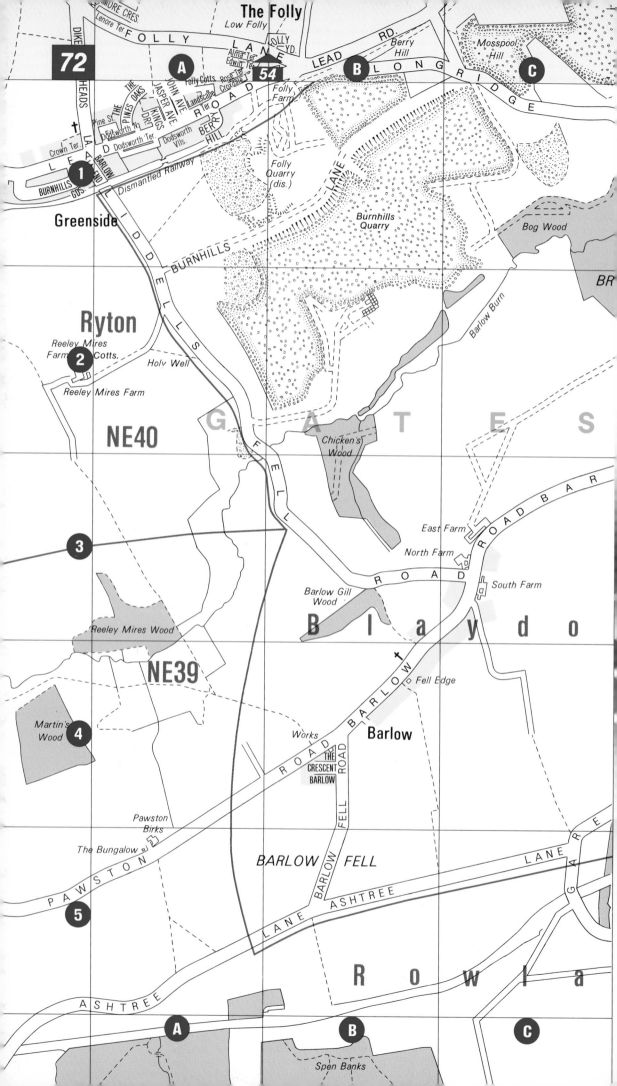

The Folly
Low Folly

LEAD RD.
Berry Hill

Mosspool Hill

MORE CRES.
Lenore Ter.
FOLLY LANE
FOLLY YD.
Alma Ter.
Edwin Ter.
Rose Ter.
Croxdale

A

54

B

LONGRIDGE

C

DIKE HEADS
THE PINES
JASPER AVE.
KINGS DRD.
JOHN AVE.
Landscape
Folly Cotts.

LEAD

Folly Farm

Pine St.
Dodsworth
Dodsworth Ter.
Dodsworth Vlls.
Crown Ter.
BERRY HILL
BARLOW

Folly Quarry (dis.)

Burnhills Quarry

Bog Wood

1

BURNHILLS GDS.

Dismantled Railway

BURNHILLS

BR

Greenside

LIDDELLS

Ryton

Reeley Mires Farm Cotts.
Holy Well

2

Reeley Mires Farm

FELL

GATES

Chicken's Wood

Barlow Burn

NE40

3

East Farm

North Farm

ROAD BAR

ROAD

South Farm

Reeley Mires Wood

Barlow Gill Wood

Blaydo

NE39

Martin's Wood

4

Works

THE CRESCENT BARLOW

ROAD
BARLOW
ROAD

Fell Edge

Barlow

Pawston Birks

The Bungalow

PAWSTON LANE

BARLOW FELL

BARLOW FELL
ASHTREE LANE

GARE LANE

5

R o w l a

ASHTREE

A

B

Spen Banks

C

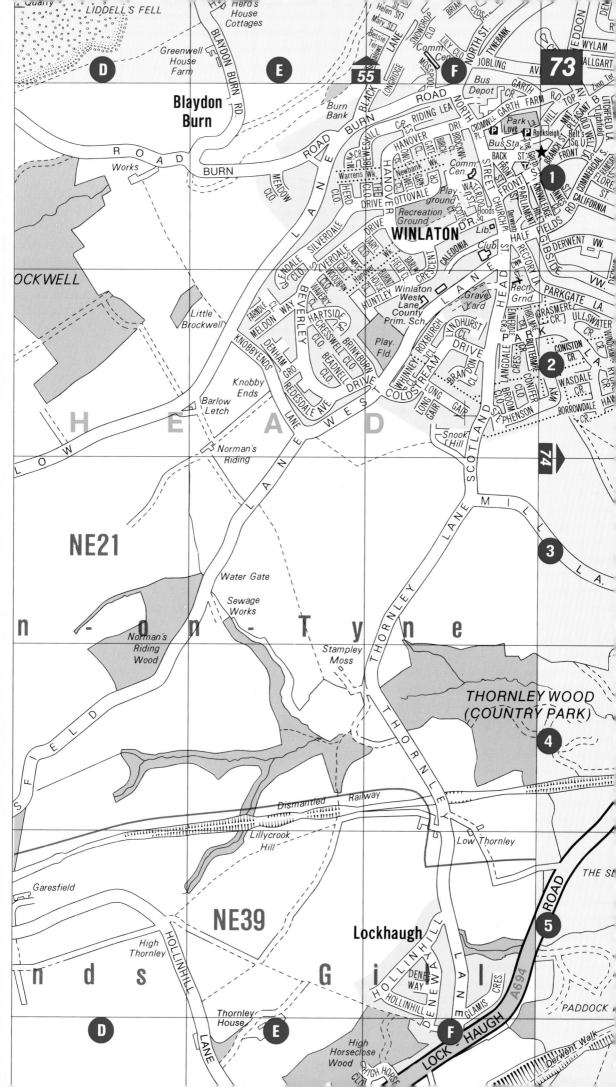

LIDDELL'S FELL

Herd's House Cottages

Quarry

Greenwell House Farm

D

E

Blaydon Burn

BLAYDON BURN RD.

Burn Bank

Helen ST.

Mary ST.

Bessie Ters.

SNOWDROP CLO.

Comm. Cen.

LILY CLO.

NORTH ST.

TYNEBANK

JOBLING AVE.

F

Bus Depot

GARTH CR.

EDDON

WYLAM

ALLGART

55

BURN

BLACK

ROAD

ROAD

RIDING LEA

CROMWELL PL.

GARTH FARM

Park Love

Rooksleigh

Belt's Sq. U.

NORTH

BACK

Bus Sta.

GARTH RD.

PLEASANT

Zion Ter.

1

WORKS

ROAD

BURN

LANE

MEADOW CLO.

HANOVER

HERD

HANOVER DRIVE

BREWSHILL CRES.

BIRCH

BROCKWL.

Newbank

OTTOVALE

Play ground

WATERLOO ST.

Comm. Cen.

Play ground

Recreation Ground

WINLATON

Hoods Sq.

Church

Lib.

Derwent

Half ST.

FRONT

PARLIAMENT ST.

KNOWLEDGE

COMMERCIAL

FIELDS

FLORE

CALIFORNIA

RD.

GIBSIDE

DERWENT VW.

VW.

BROCKWELL

Little Brockwell

Works

GLENDALE CLO.

SILVERDALE

SILVERDALE

FARNDALE CLO.

MELDON WAY

BEVERLEY

WAVERLY CLO.

WOODBN.

HUNTLEY

Winlaton West Lane County Prim. Sch.

CRESCENT

CALEDONIA

Play. Fld.

Grave Yard

HEAD

Recn. Grnd.

PARKGATE LA.

CRASMERE CR.

ULLSWATER CR.

VW.

Club

KNOBBYENDS

DENHAM GRO.

BRINKBURN

HARTSIDE

CRESSWELL CLO.

BEADNELL CLO.

COLDS

LANE

ROXBURGH

LYNDHURST CL.

CREAM

DRIVE

BRANDON CLO.

PARK

LANGDALE CRES.

BUTTERMR

BROOM CLO.

CONIFER

CONISTON CR.

WINDERMR

2

WASDALE CR.

BORROWDALE CR.

H   E   A   D

Knobby Ends

Barlow Letch

REDESDALE AVE.

DRIVE

WHINNEY CLS.

LONG GAIR

LONG GAIR

SCOTLAND

STEPHENSON

Snook Hill

74

Norman's Riding

LANE

WEST

LANE

MILL

LA.

NE21

3

Water Gate

Sewage Works

THORNLEY

n - o n - T y n e

Stampley Moss

Norman's Riding Wood

S F I E L D

THORNLEY

THORNLEY WOOD (COUNTRY PARK)

4

Dismantled   Railway

Lillycrook Hill

Low Thornley

THORNLEY

Garesfield

NE39

High Thornley

HOLLINHILL LANE

Lockhaugh

HOLLINHILL

DENEWAY

GLAMIS

DENEWAY

CRES.

ROAD

THE S

5

A694

PADDOCK

n   d   s

G i l l

D

E

Thornley House

HIGH HORSE CLO.

F

High Horseclose Wood

LOCKHAUGH LANE

Derwent Walk

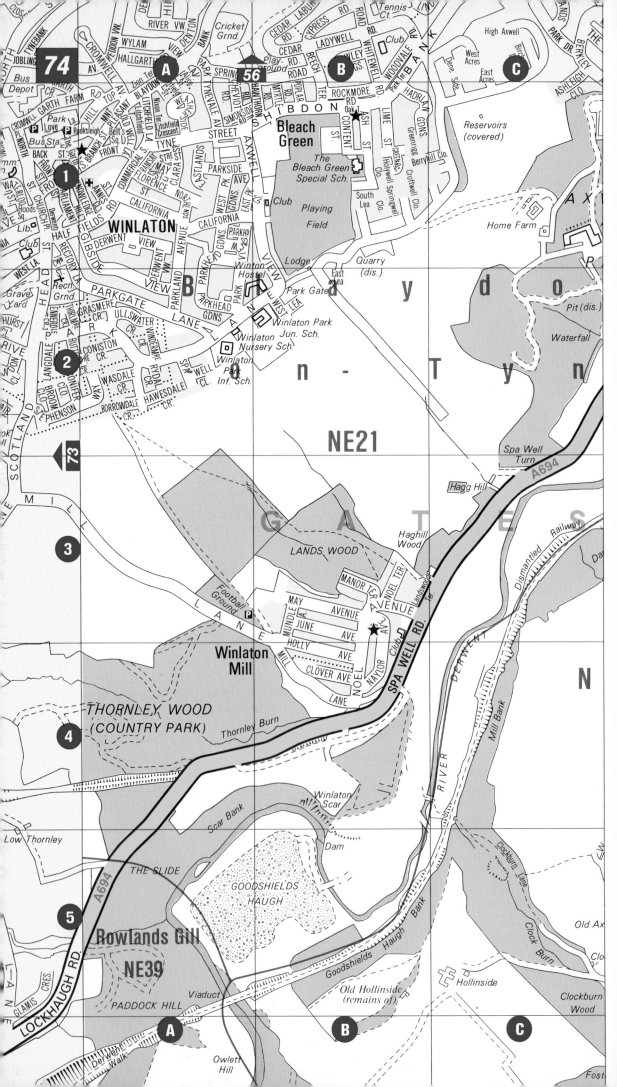

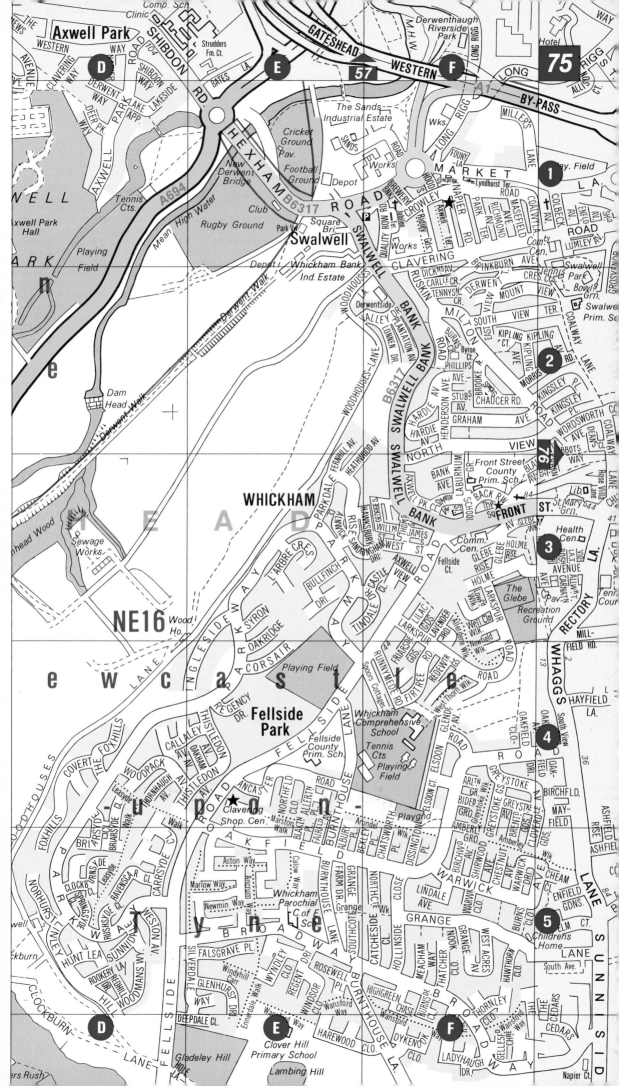

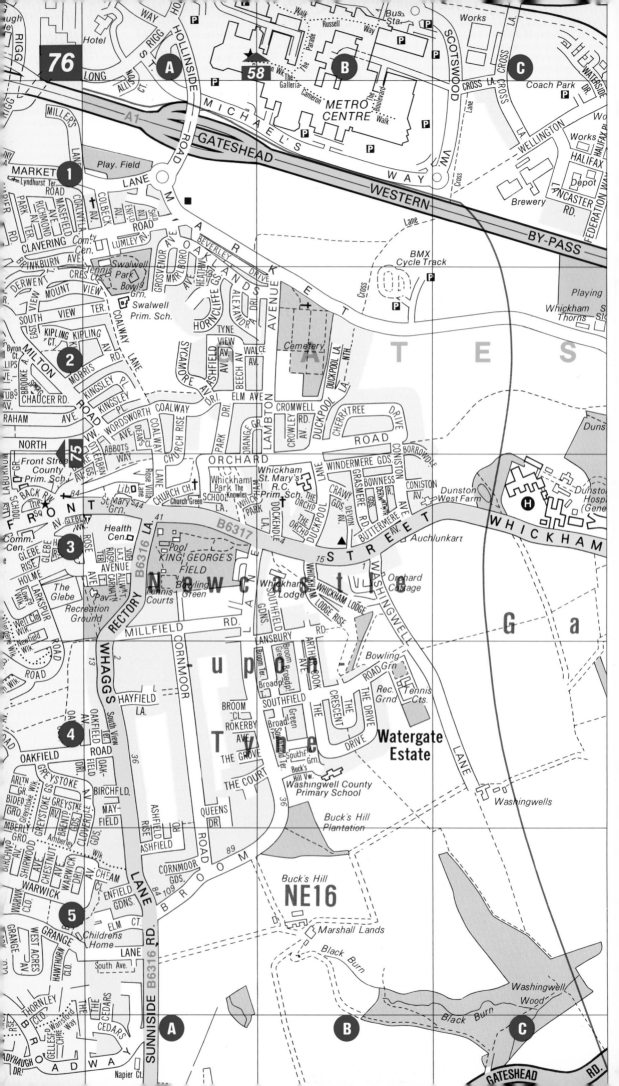

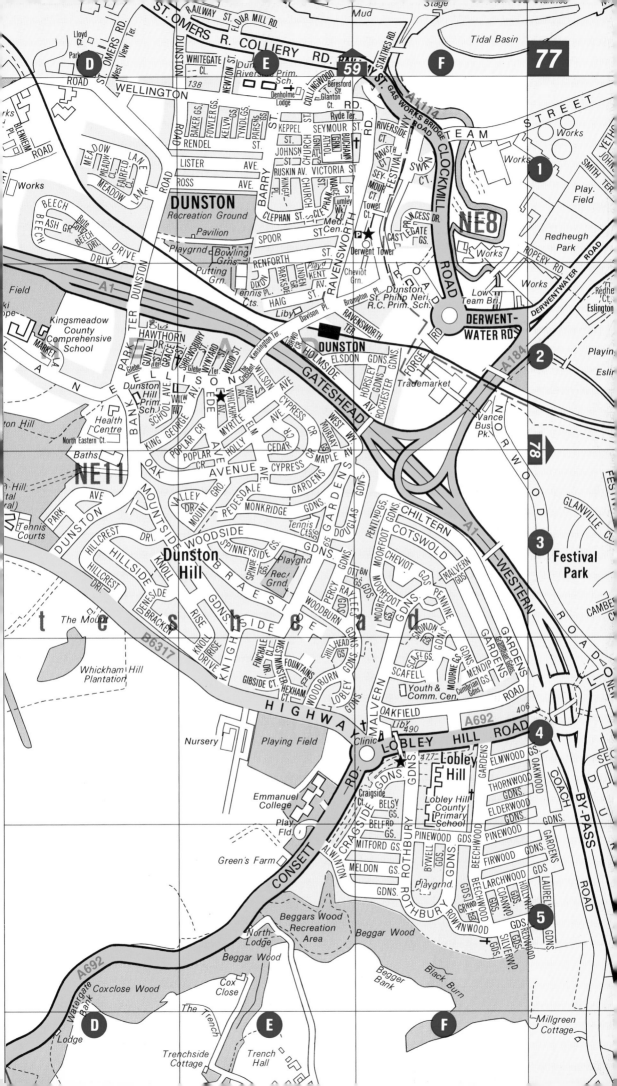

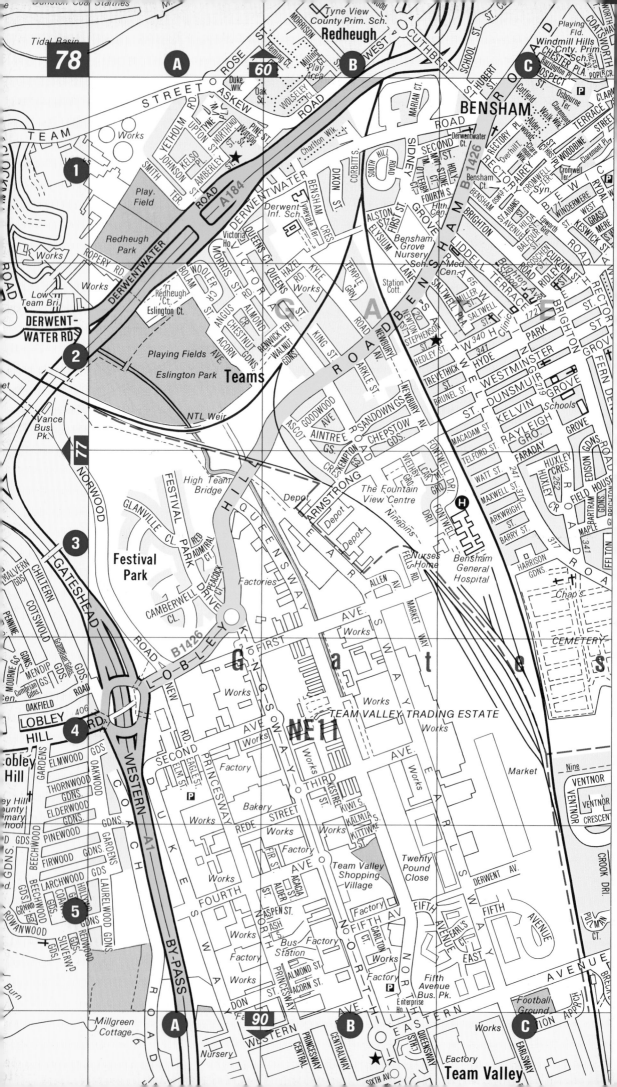

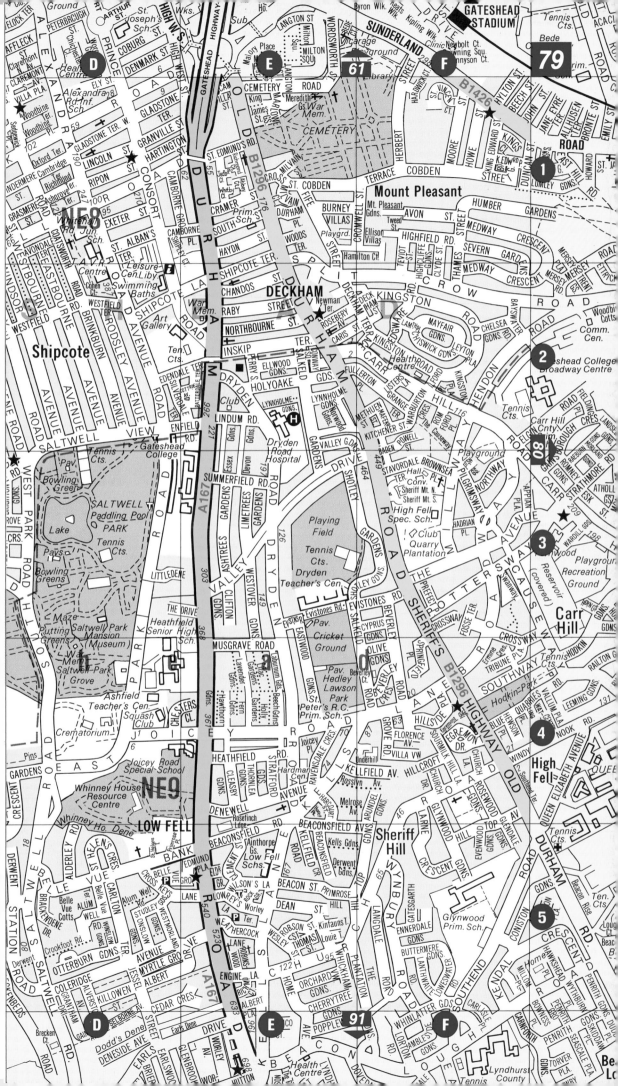

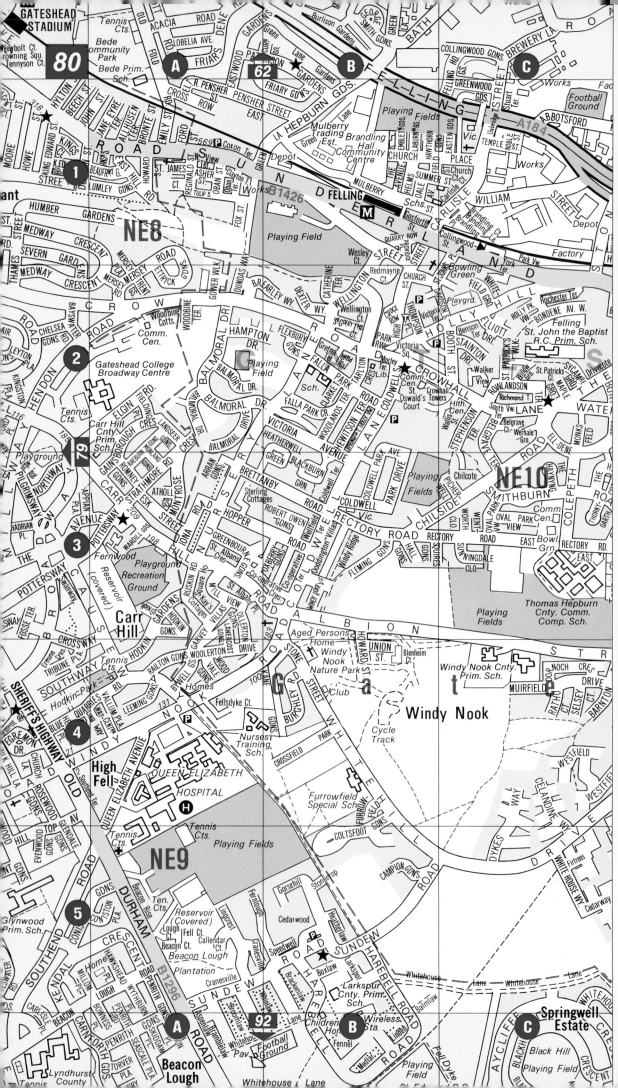

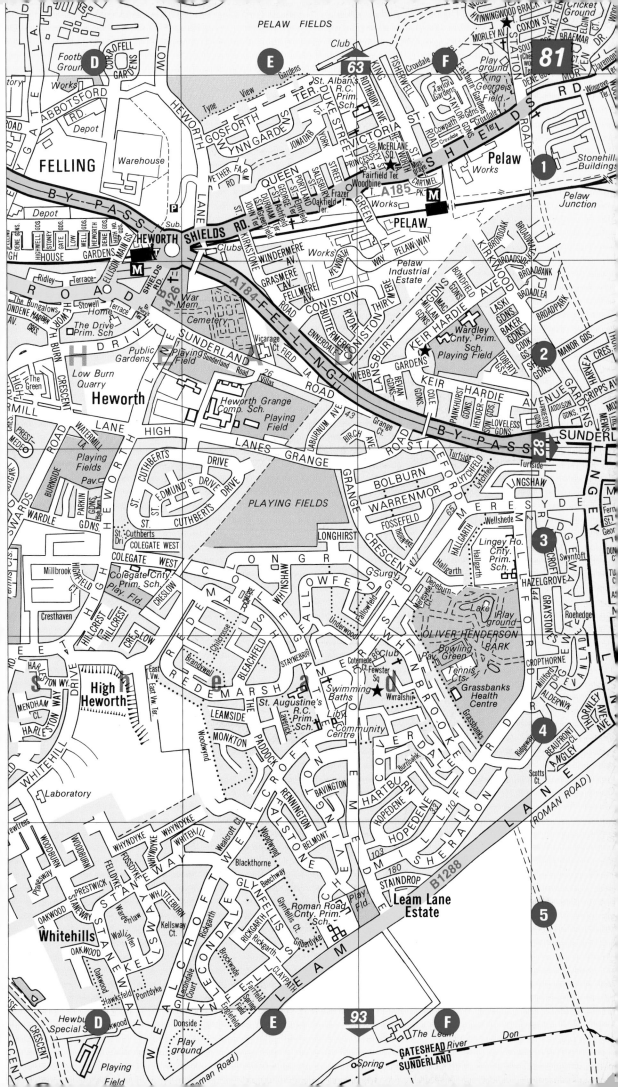

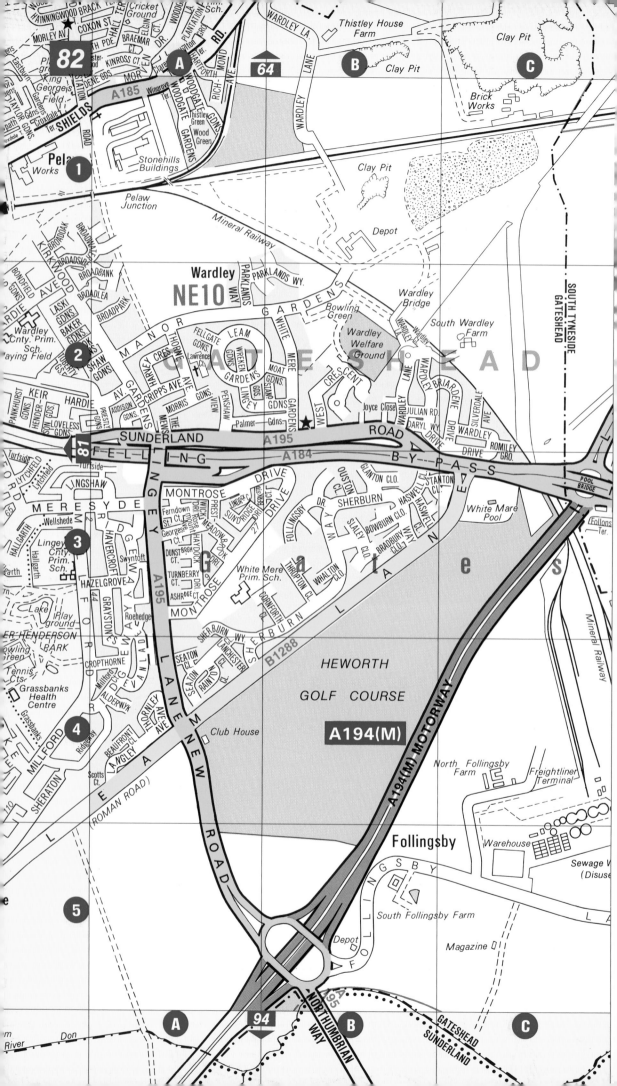

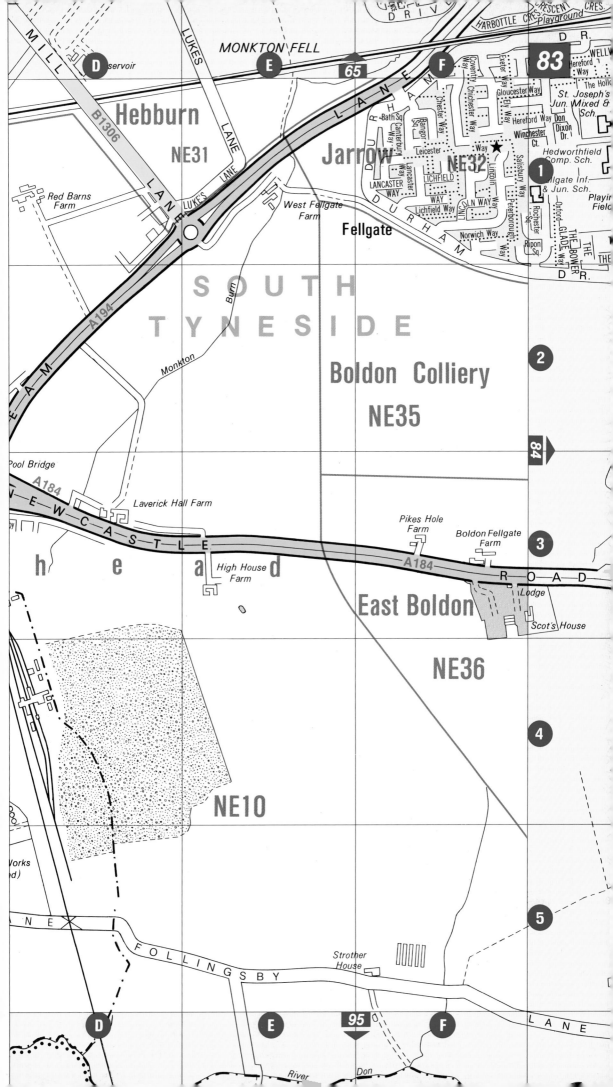

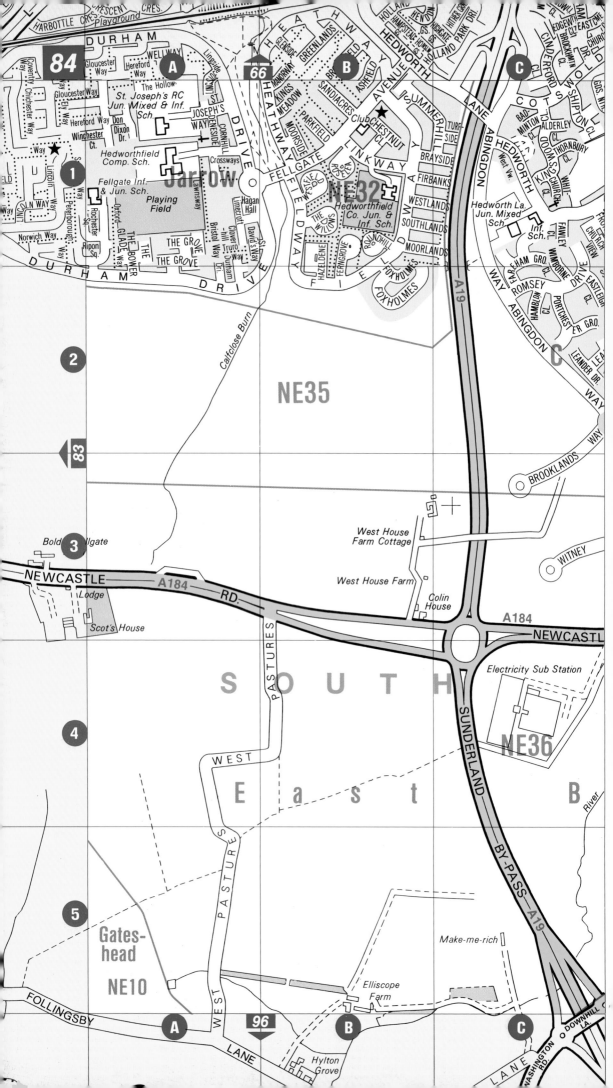

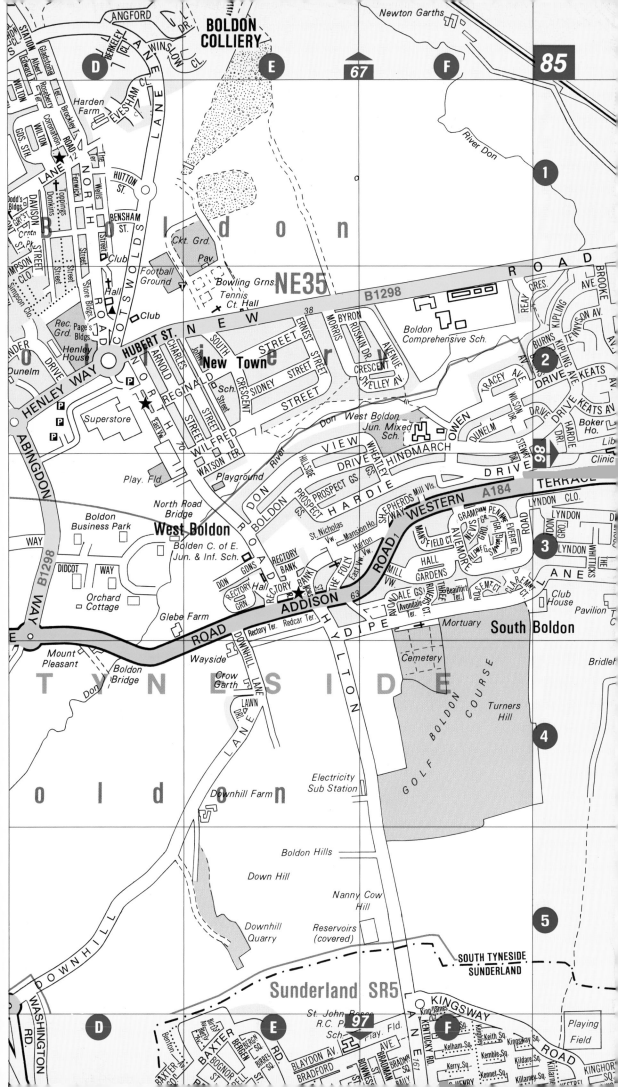

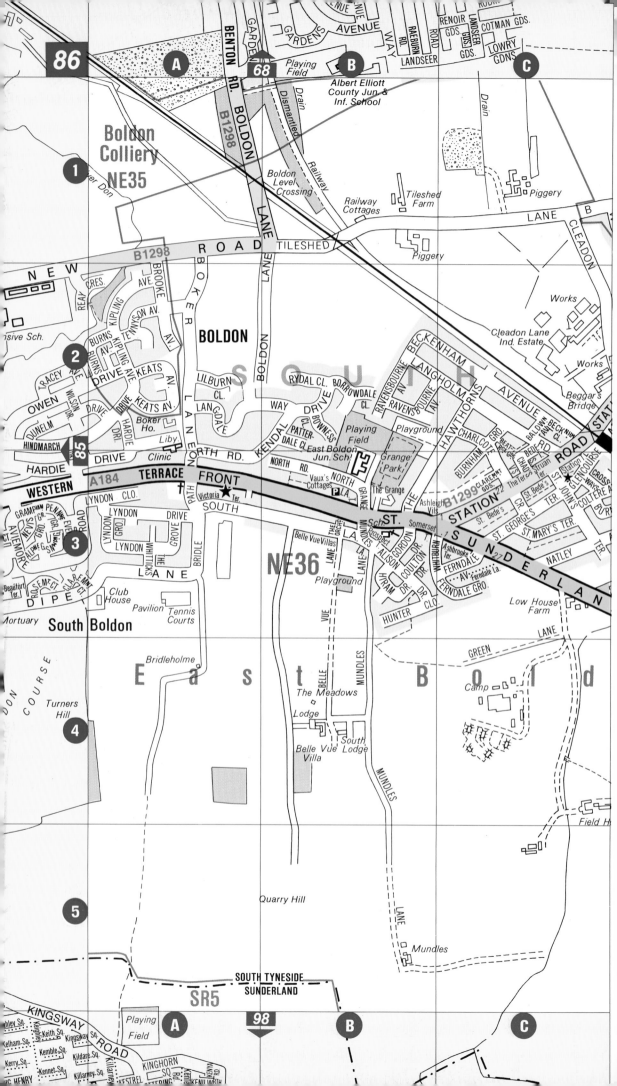

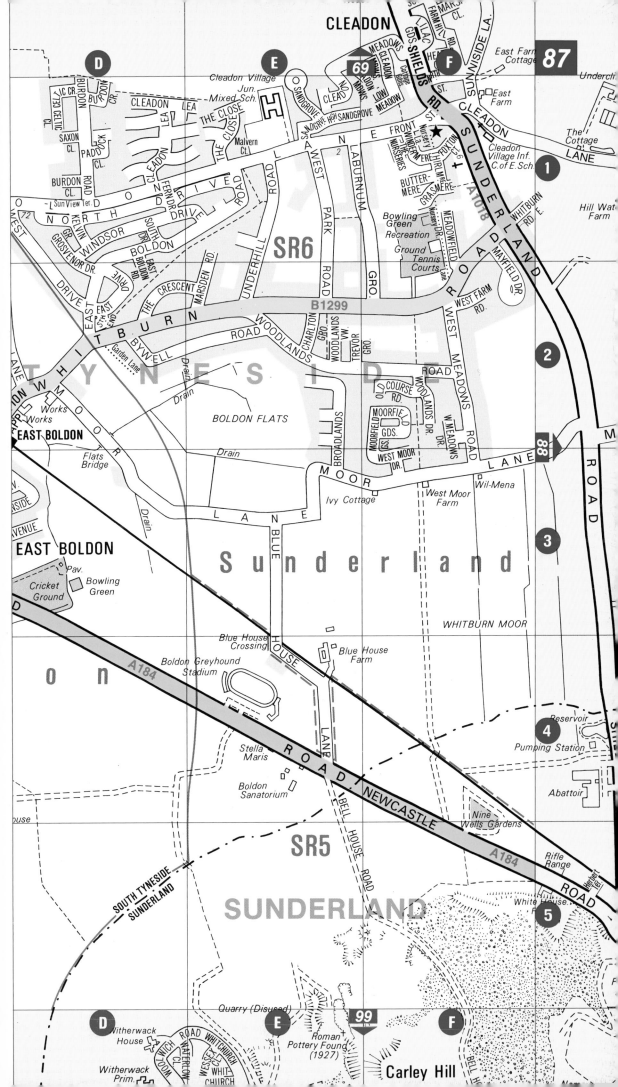

CLEADON

D **E** **69** **SHIELDS** **F**

East Farm
Cottage

Cleadon Village
Jun. - Mixed Sch.

SANDGROVE

East
Farm

Underch

Cleadon

The
Cottage

FRONT

Cleadon Village Inf.
C.of E. Sch.

1

Hill Wat
Farm

Bowling
Green
Recreation

Ground
Tennis
Courts

SR6

B1299

WOODLANDS

West Farm
Rd.

WEST MEADOWS

2

88

BOLDON FLATS

Drain

MOORFIELD
GDS.

WEST MOOR
DR.

Wil-Mena

West Moor
Farm

Ivy Cottage

3

EAST BOLDON

S u n d e r l a n d

WHITBURN MOOR

Cricket
Ground

Pav.

Bowling
Green

Blue House
Crossing

Blue House
Farm

Reservoir

4

o n

A184

Boldon Greyhound
Stadium

Pumping Station

Abattoir

Stella
Maris

Boldon
Sanatorium

NEWCASTLE

Nine
Wells Gardens

Rifle
Range

SR5

A184

SOUTH TYNESIDE
SUNDERLAND

SUNDERLAND

White House

5

D Witherwack
House

E **99** **F**

Witherwack
Prim.

Quarry (Disused)

Roman
Pottery Found
(1927)

Carley Hill

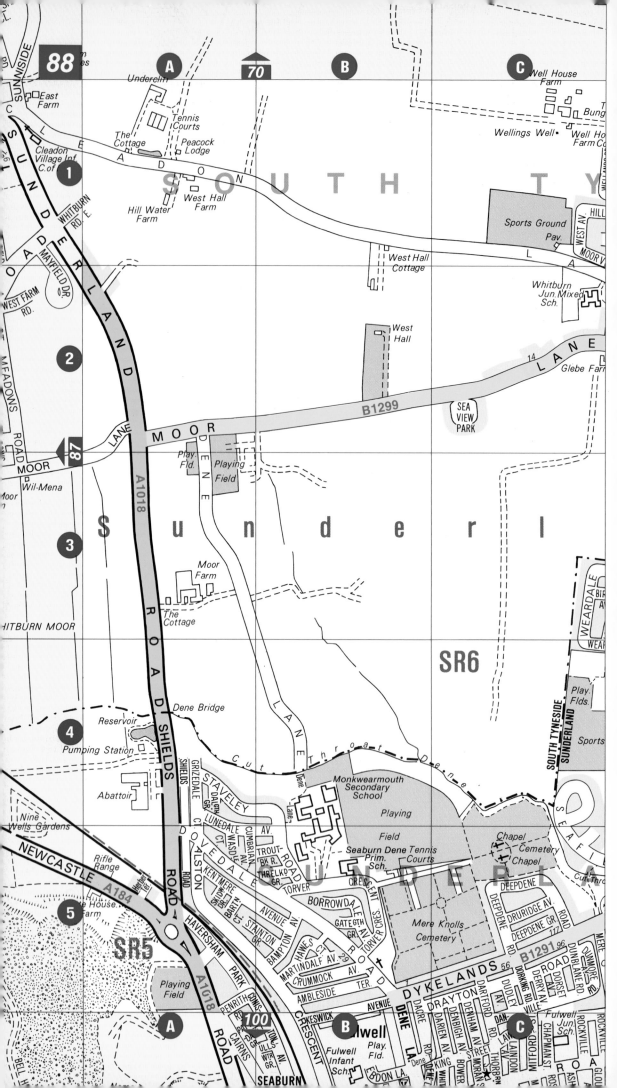

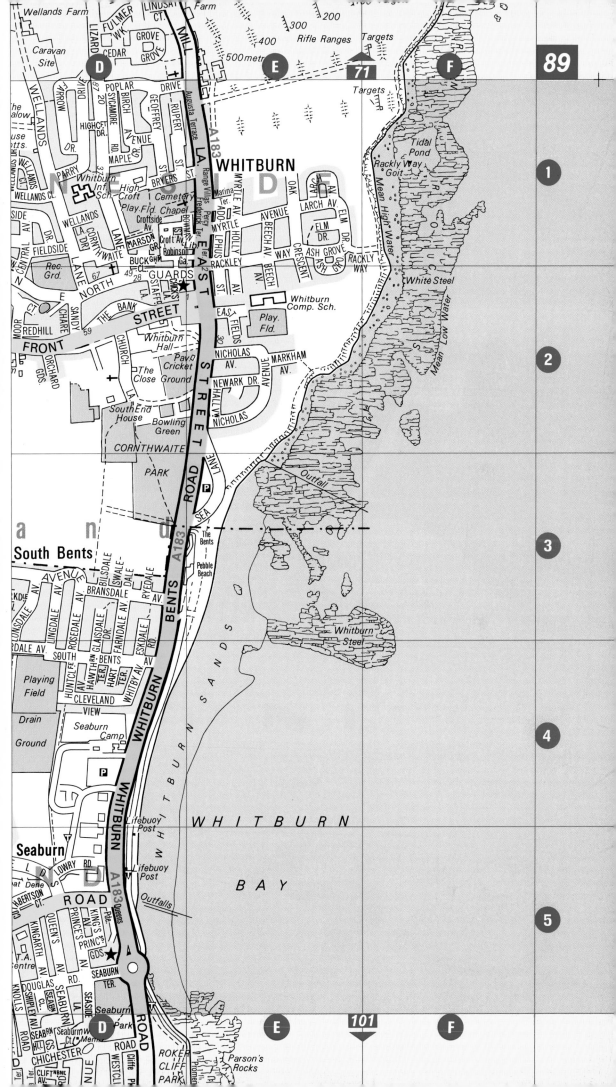

WHITBURN

South Bents

Seaburn

WHITBURN BAY

WHITBURN SANDS

Whitburn Steel

Whitburn Comp. Sch.

The Bents
Pebble Beach

Lifebuoy Post
Lifebuoy Post

Tidal Pond
Rackly Way Goit
White Steel
Mean High Water
Mean Low Water

Outfall
Outfalls

Rifle Ranges
Targets
Targets

71
101

Parson's Rocks

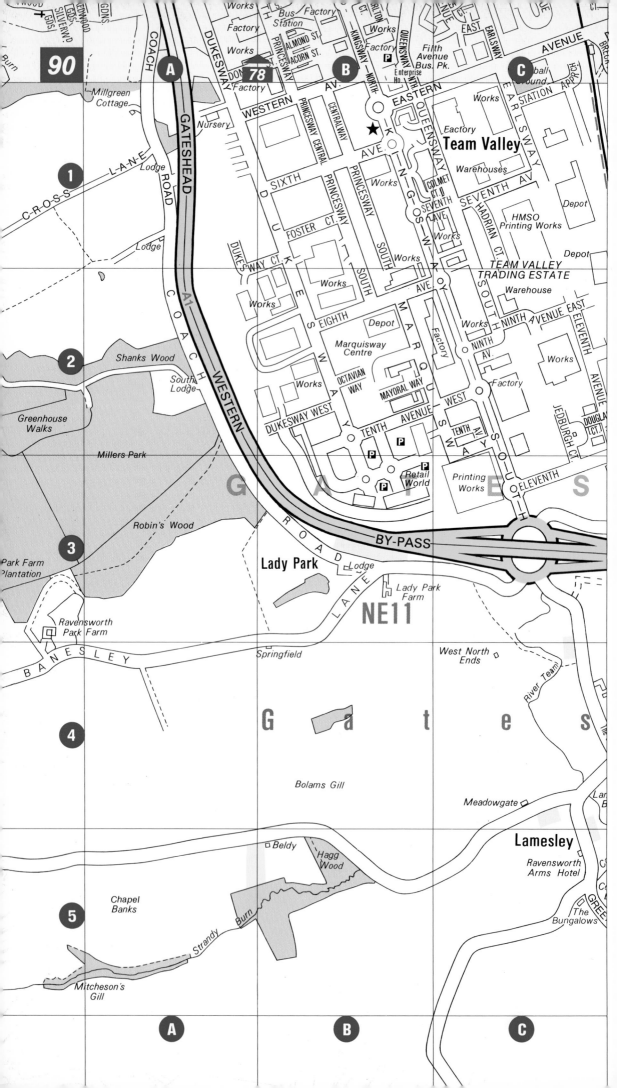

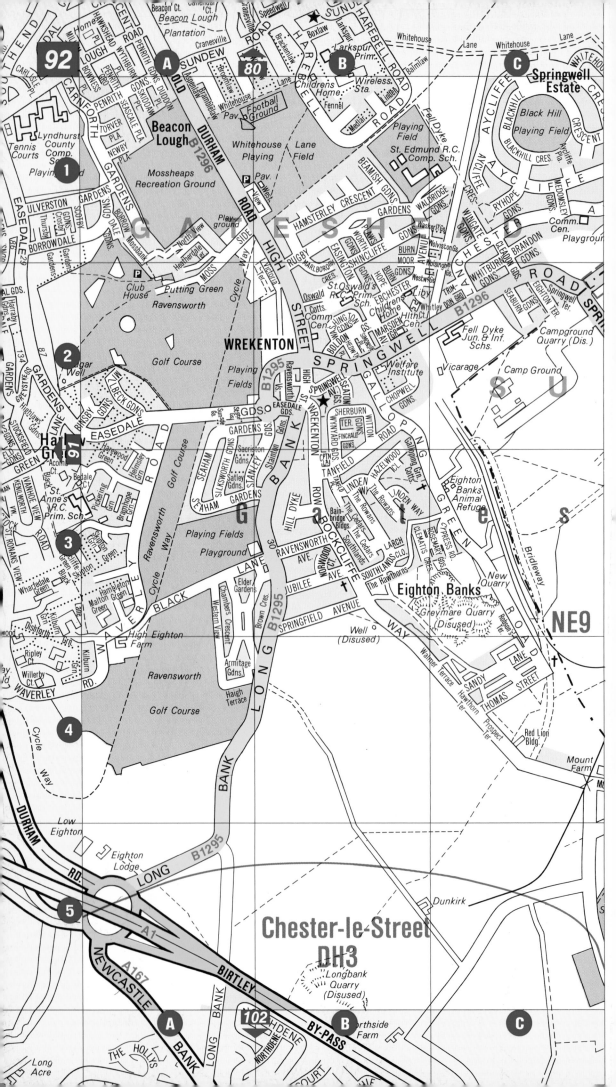

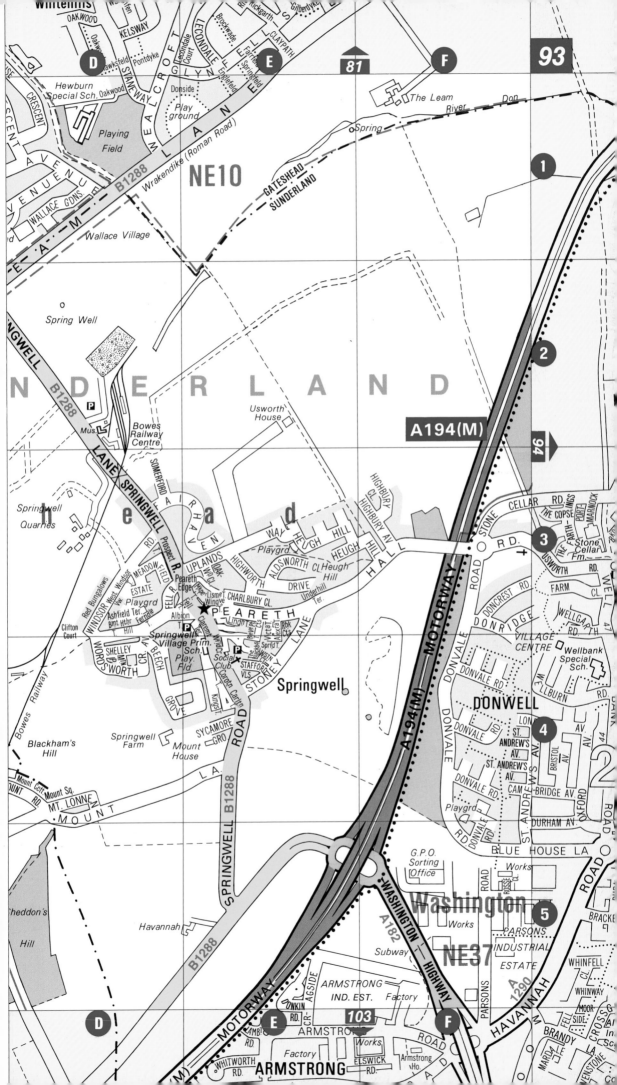

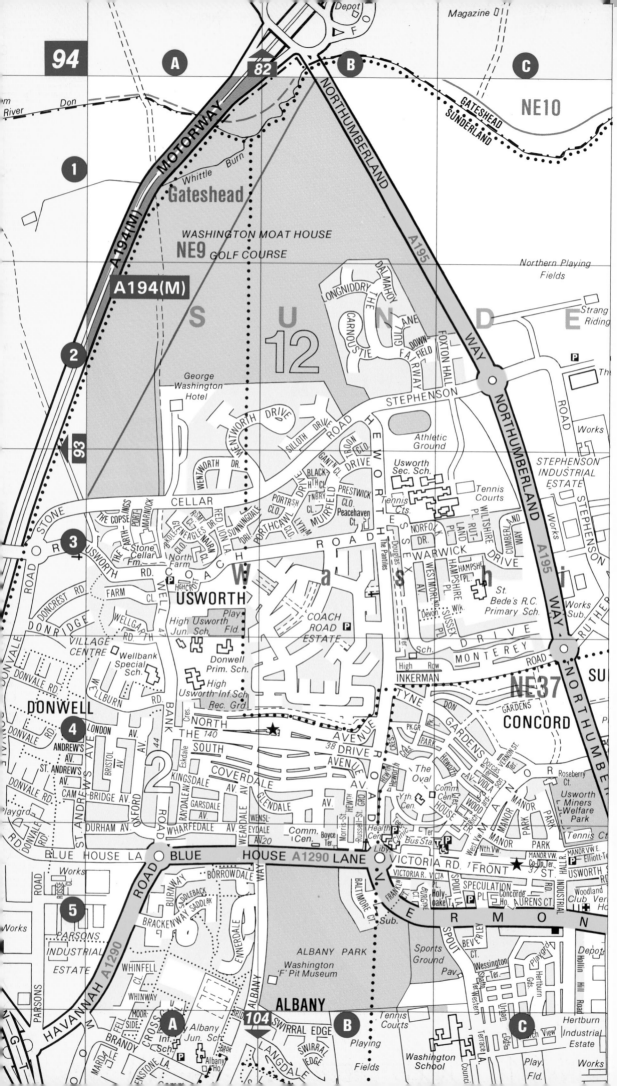

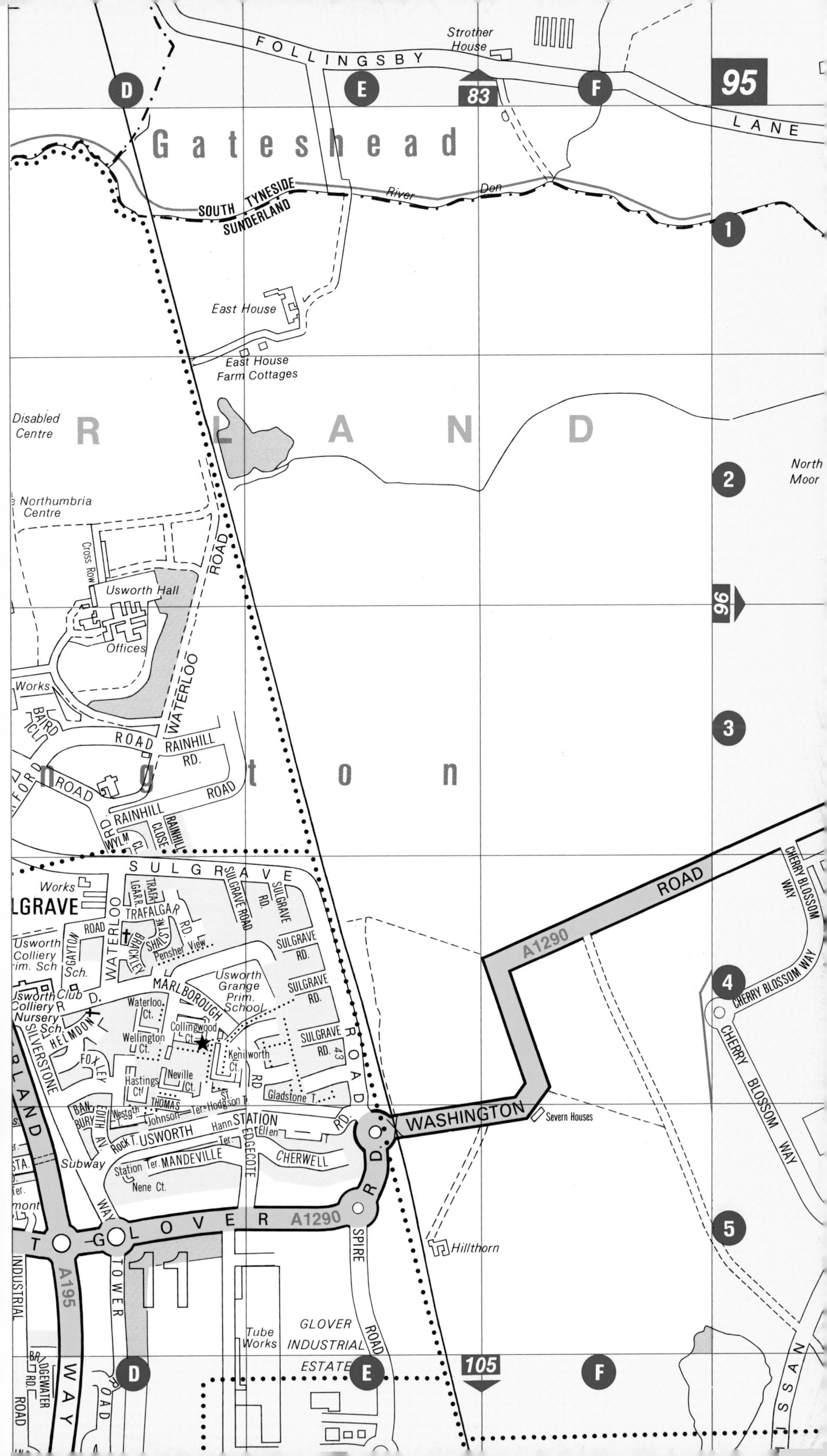

FOLLINGSBY

Strother House

LANE

Gateshead

SOUTH TYNESIDE
SUNDERLAND

River Don

1

East House

East House Farm Cottages

R **L** **A** **N** **D**

Disabled Centre

2

North Moor

Northumbria Centre

Cross Row

Usworth Hall

WATERLOO

ROAD

96

Offices

Works

BAIRD

CL.

ROAD

RAINHILL RD.

3

n g **t** o **n**

ROAD

RAINHILL ROAD

WYLM.

RAINHILL CLOSE

S U L G R A V E

Works

ROAD

ROAD

SULGRAVE

ROAD

SULGRAVE

TRAFALGAR

SULGRAVE ROAD

LGRAVE

WATERLOO

TRAFALGAR

SHAL

CALYTON

BRICKLE

RD.

Penshet View

Uworth Colliery Prim. Sch

Usworth Grange Prim. School

SULGRAVE RD.

ROAD

CHERRY BLOSSOM WAY

4

A1290

CHERRY BLOSSOM WAY

MARLBOROUGH

Usworth Club Colliery R D.

HELMDON

Waterloo Ct.

Collingwood Ct.

SULGRAVE RD. 43

Nursery Sch

Wellington Ct.

FOXLEY

SILVERSTONE

Kenilworth Ct.

Neville Ct.

Hastings Ct.

THOMAS

Hodgson T.

Gladstone T.

ROAD

BAN
BURY

EDITH AV.

Nest th.

Johnson Ter.

Rock T. USWORTH

Hann Ter.

STATION

Ellen

EDGECOTE

RD.

WASHINGTON

Severn Houses

R **L** **A** **N** **D**

Subway

Station Ter. MANDEVILLE

CHERWELL

Nene Ct.

SPIRE

ROAD

5

CHERRY BLOSSOM WAY

A1290

WAY

TOWER

GLOVER

A1290

Hillthorn

11

A195

ROAD

Tube Works

GLOVER INDUSTRIAL ESTATE

SSAN

BRIDGEWATER RD.

INDUSTRIAL

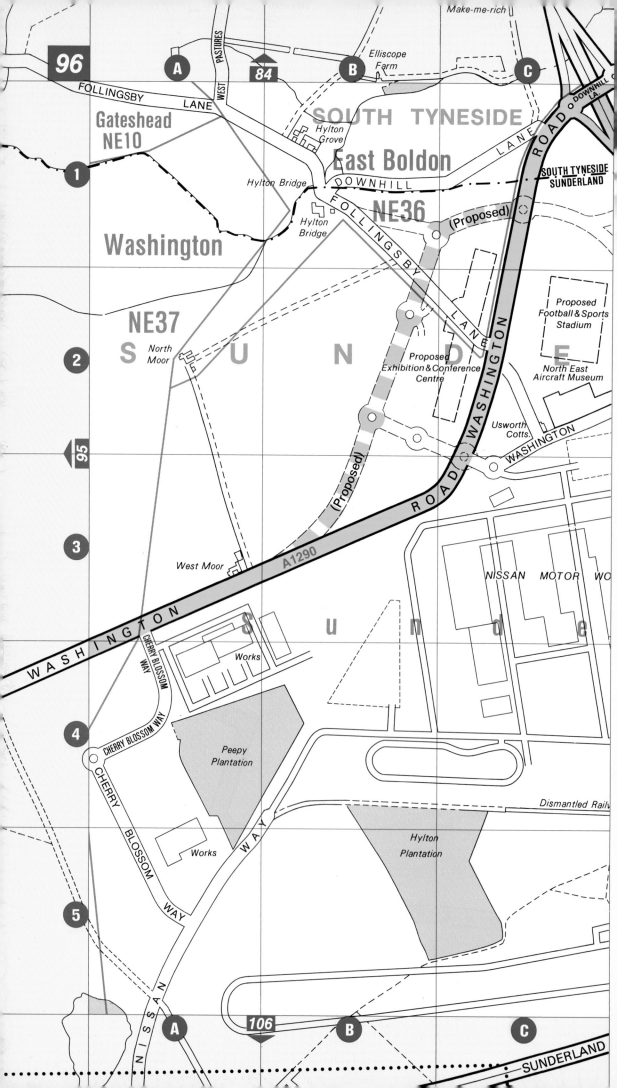

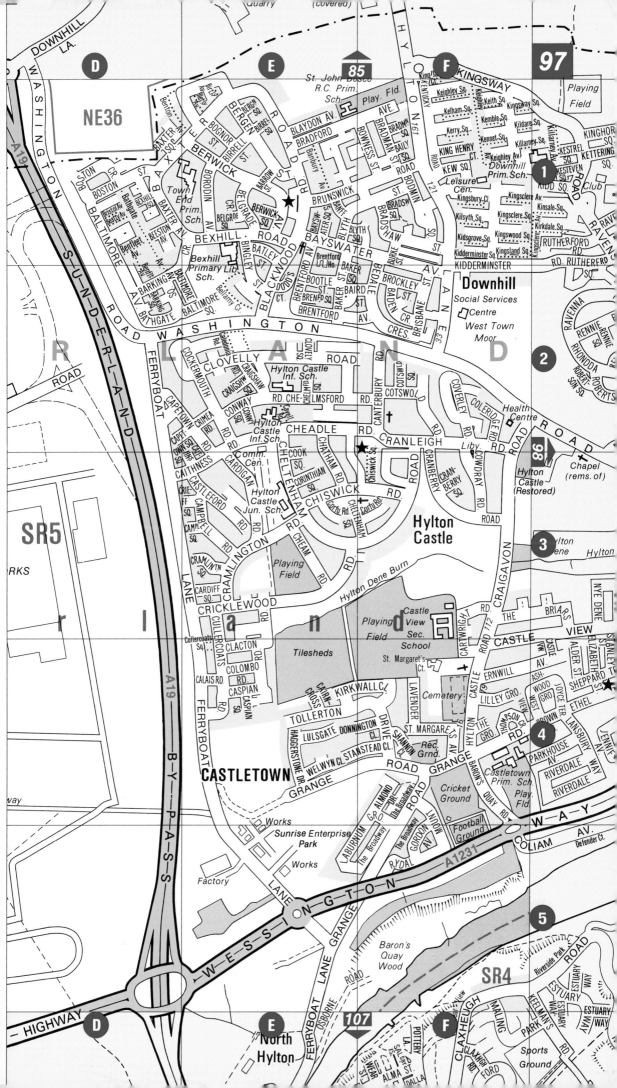

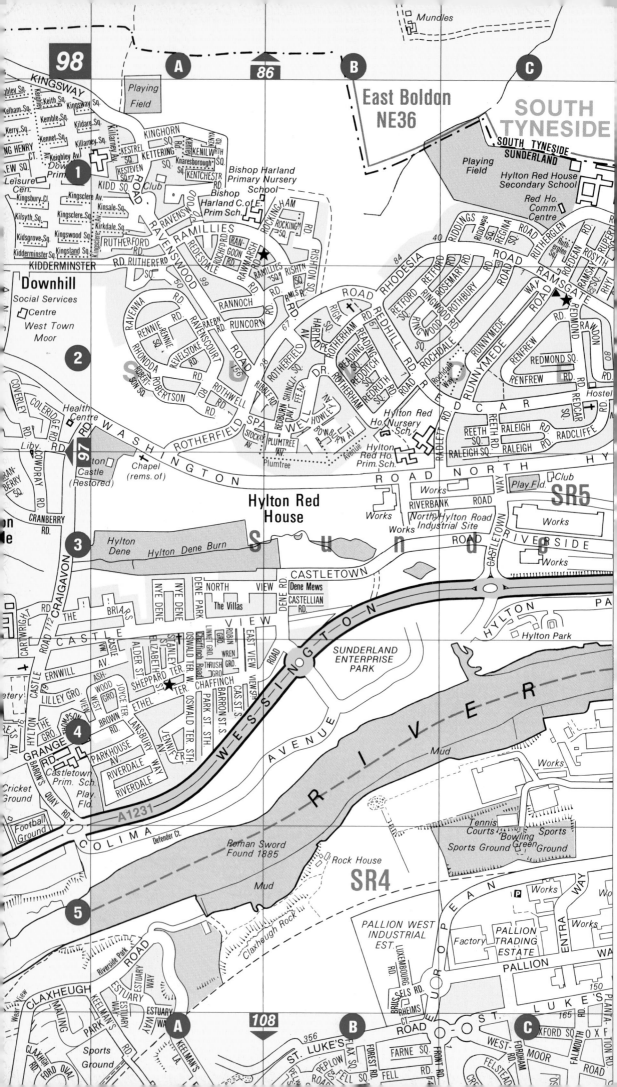

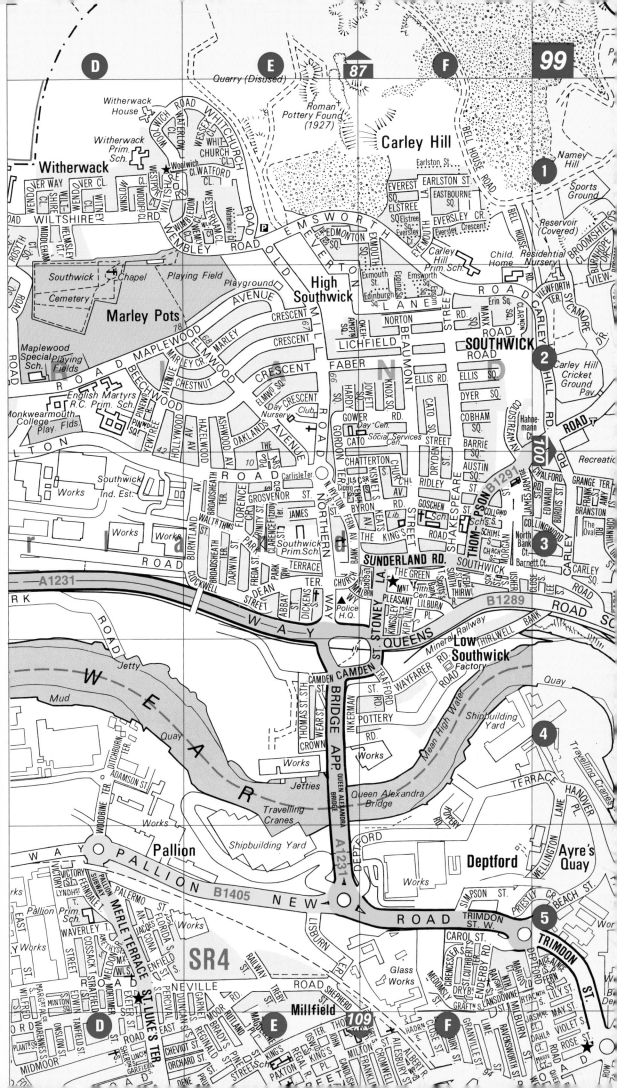

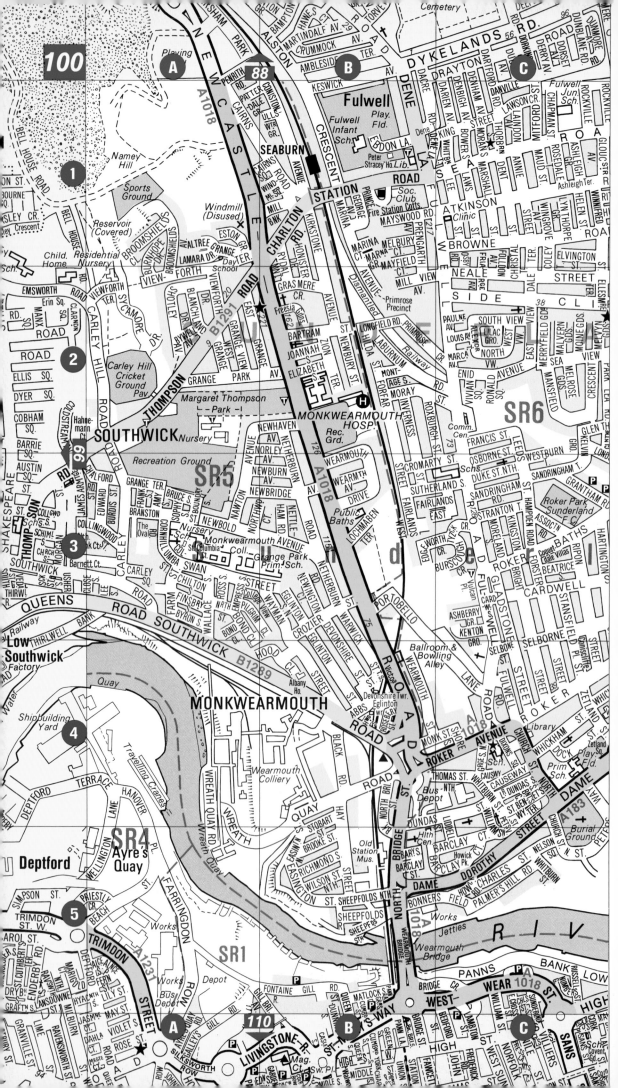

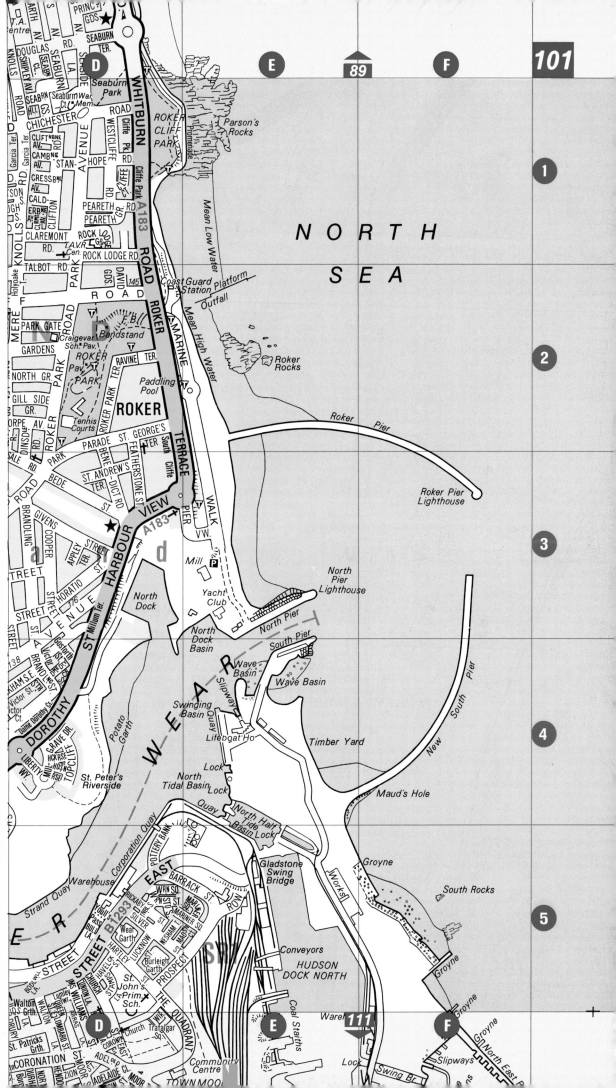

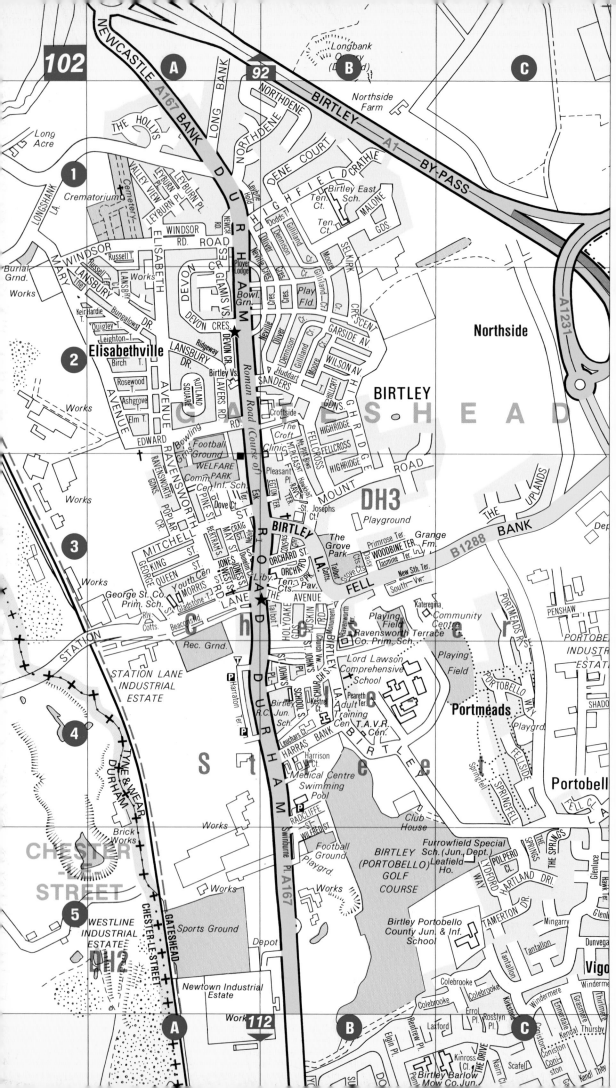

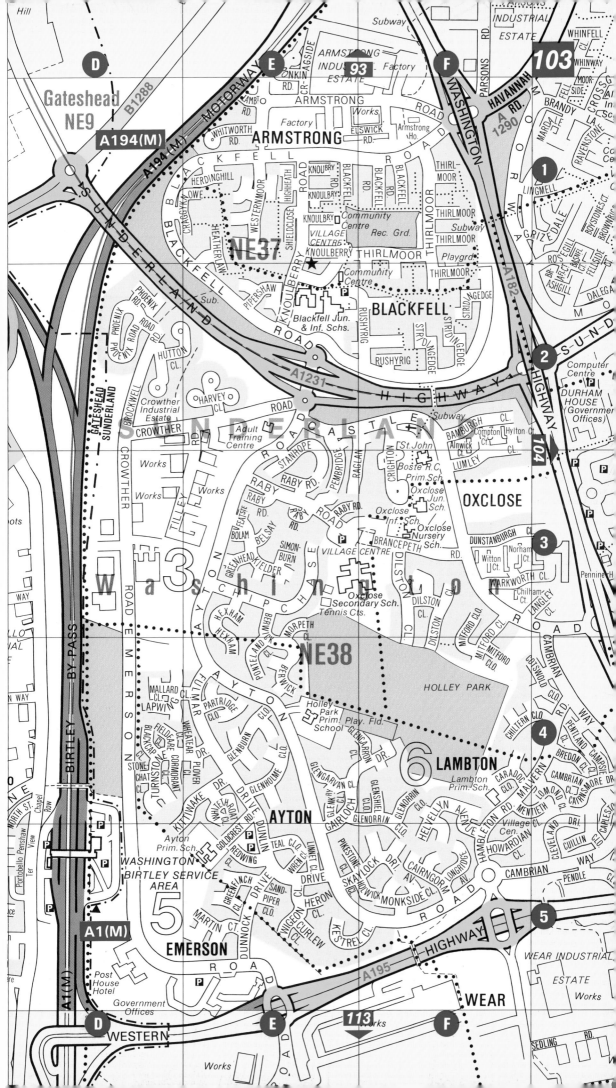

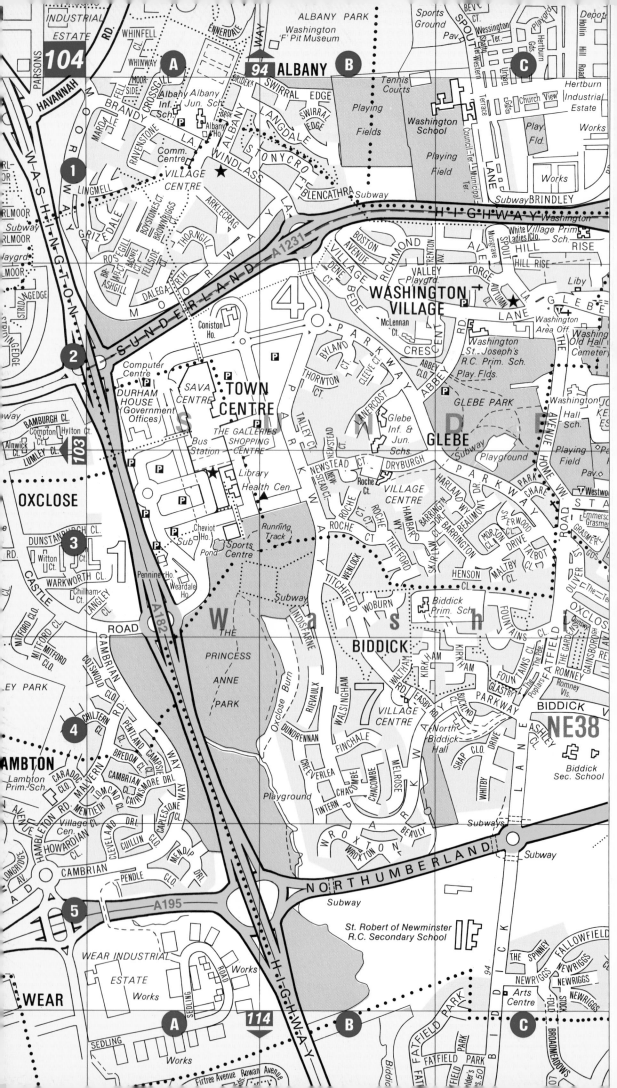

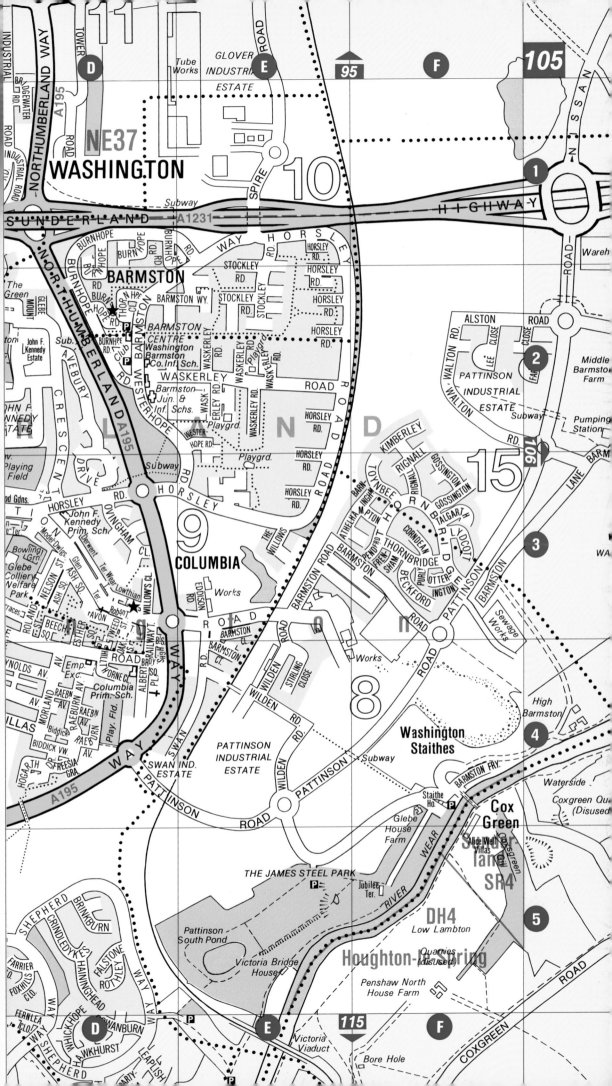

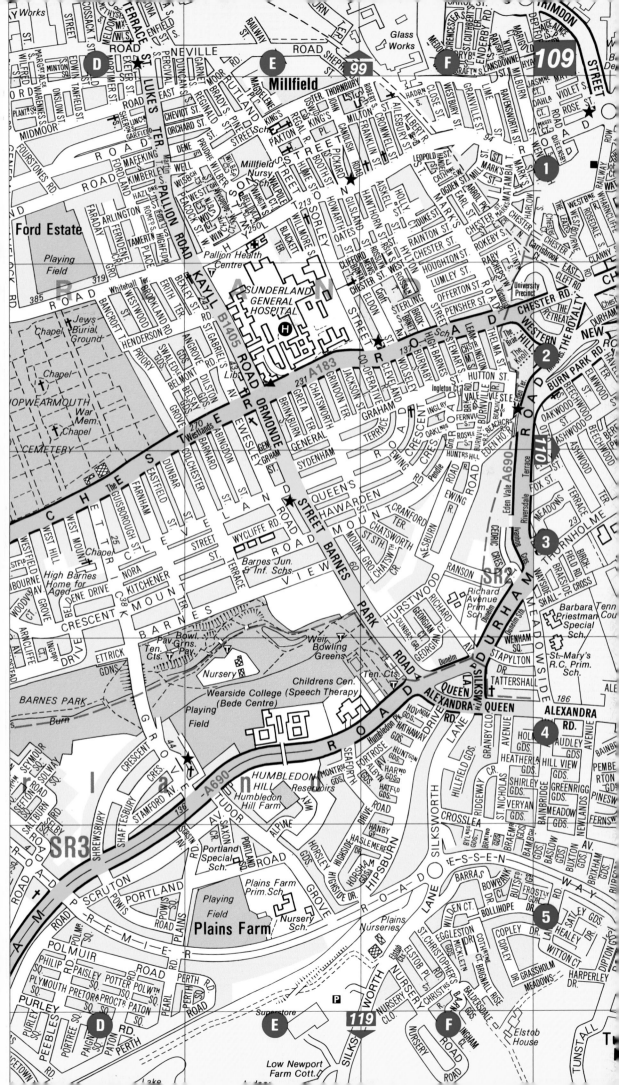

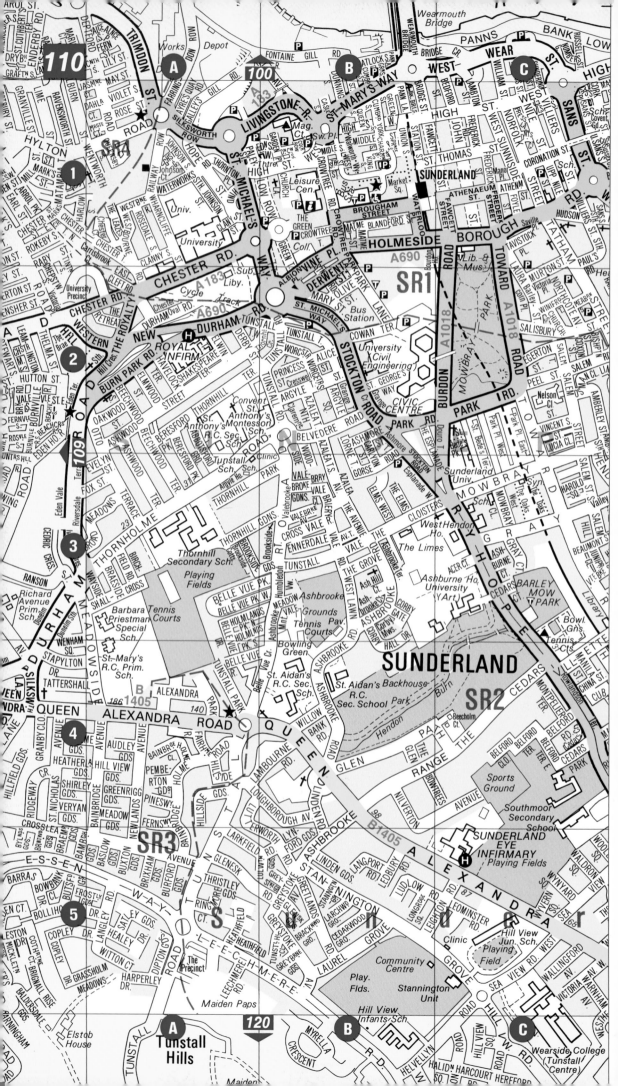

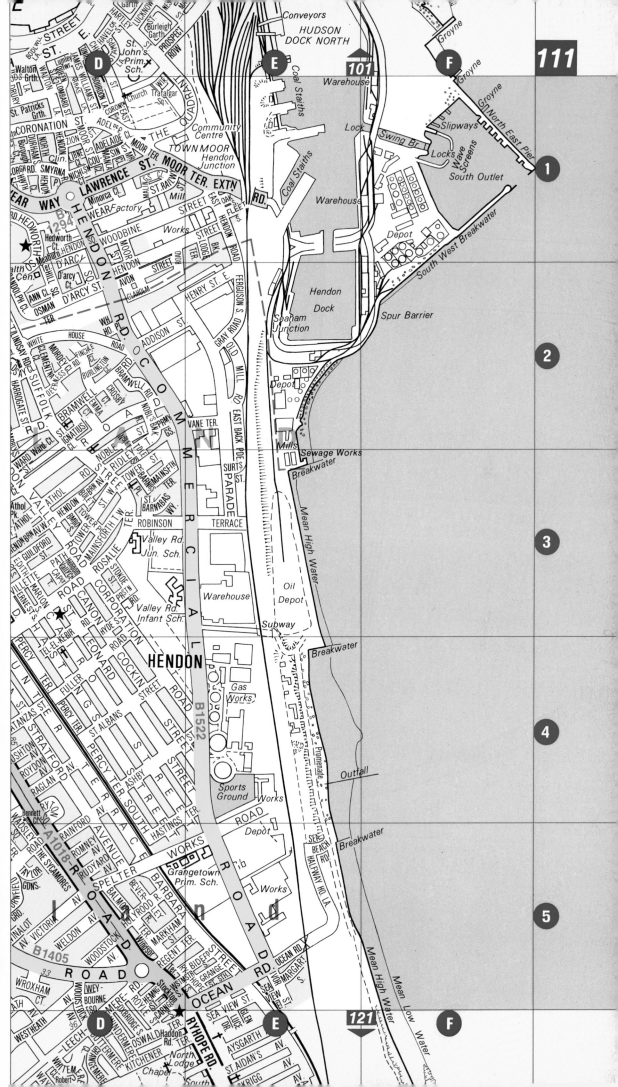

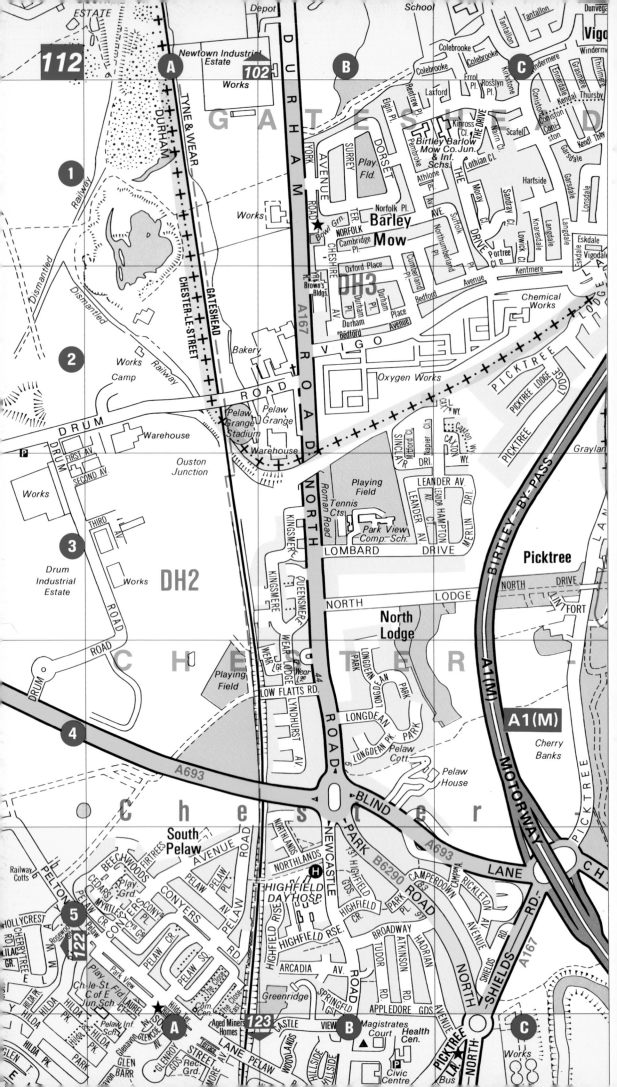

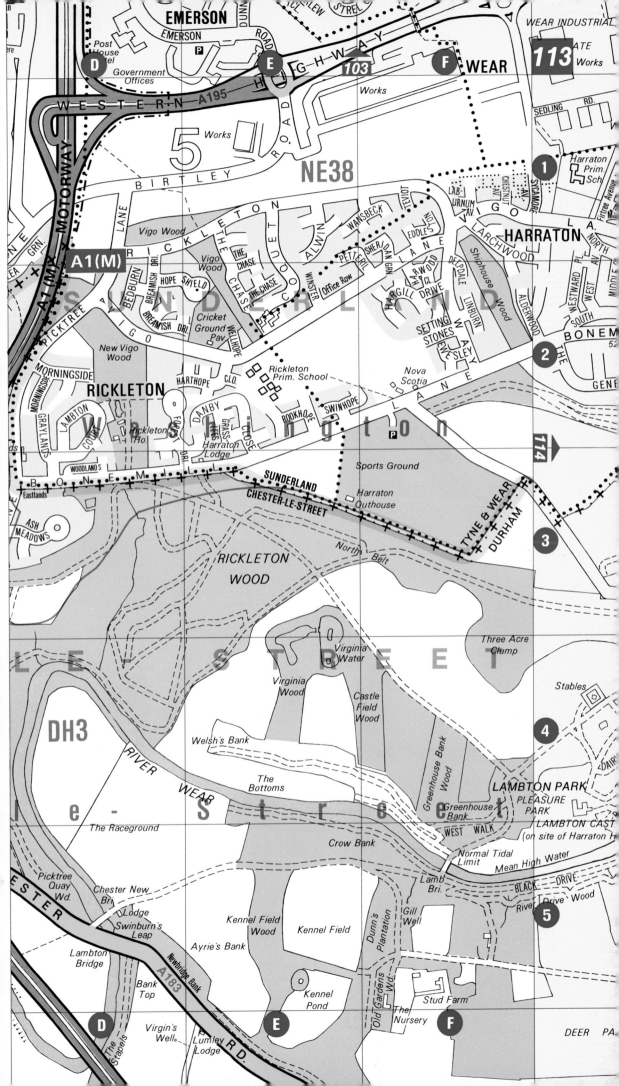

WEAR INDUSTRIAL ESTATE

Works

Works

Works

A

104

B

R.C. Secondary School

THE SPINNEY

FALLOWFIELD

NEWRIGGS

NEWRIGGS

NEWRIGGS

NEWRIGGS

C

SEDLING ROAD

SEDLING RD.

Firtree Avenue

Rowan Avenue

Lilac Gdns.

Crescent

Crescent

Avenue

Rowan Avenue

Harraton Prim. Sch.

Firtree Avenue

Hawthorn

Holly

Cedar

Hazelwood Gardens

Maplewood

Terrace

Crescent

Pinewood

Swiss Cottage

Rowan Avenue

1

SYCAMORE AV.

CHESTNUT AV.

LABURNUM AV.

LARCHWOOD

Shiphouse Wood

DEPDALE

LINBURN

ALDERWOOD

WESLEY

WESTWARD PL.

WEST

MIDDLE CL.

EAST AV.

NORTH CRES.

SOUTH CRES.

HARRATON

BONEMILL

New Rd.

New Road

THE GENERAL'S

WOOD

St. George's Estate

Hall Lane

★

Fatfield Ho.

WASHINGTON

A182

NE38

13

Biddick Burn

FATFIELD

Fatfield Prim. Sch.

BONEMILL

Play Fld.

Site of Fatfield Village

Comm. Cen.

Play Park

P

P

P

P

P

FATFIELD PARK

Fatfield Park

Fatfield Park

Fatfield Park

Fatfield Park

Calder's Cres.

Fatfield Park

Fatfield Park

PARK

BROOKSIDE WOOD

SOUTHCROFT

FALLOWFIELD

BRIARFIELD

94

LANE

BIDDICK

High Pasture

RIVERMEAD

LONGACRE

BROADMEADOWS

Worm Hill Ter.

VALLEY

Worm Hill

Worm Hill

JAMES War. Mem.

Club

Biddick Inn Ter.

Club

River Vw. Ter.

River Vw. Ter.

WEST BRIDGE

ST. PAUL'S DR.

STAITHES

The General's Wood

SUNDERLAND CHESTER-LE-STREET

2

THE GENERAL'S

113

TYNE & WEAR DURHAM

3

Pear Tree

Rec. Grd.

Carrshole Wood

Football Grd.

P

Harraton Ter.

Fatfield Lodge

Kennels

High Chartershaugh

Mean High Water

The Haugh Wood

Headley's House Plantation

CHESTER -LE- STREET

Three Acre Clump

Rickleton Wood

Stables

4

Chester-le-Str

LAMBTON PARK

PLEASURE PARK

Greenhouse Bank

LAMBTON CASTLE

(on site of Harraton Hall)

DAIRY WLK.

ROCK WALK

GASHOUSE DRIVE

HIGH WLK.

BLACK DRIVE

RIVER WEAR

New Bri.

Penshaw Lodge

Lambton Well

Old House Plantation

Shepherd's Gill

Sheep Wash

The Gill

Fence Plantat.

Normal Tidal Limit

Mean High Water

WEST WALK

BLACK DRIVE

River Drive Wood

5

Hedworth's Wood

Fox Cover Plantation

Scorer's Wood

DH3

Sheep Hill

Sheepfold

Sheep Hill

Bowes Ho. Cotts.

Bowes House Wood

Bowes House

FENCE ROAD

The Grange

The Paddocks

Shaft (Disused)

Sawmill Wood

Depot

Bowes House Farm

DEER PARK

A

124

B

C

Lodge

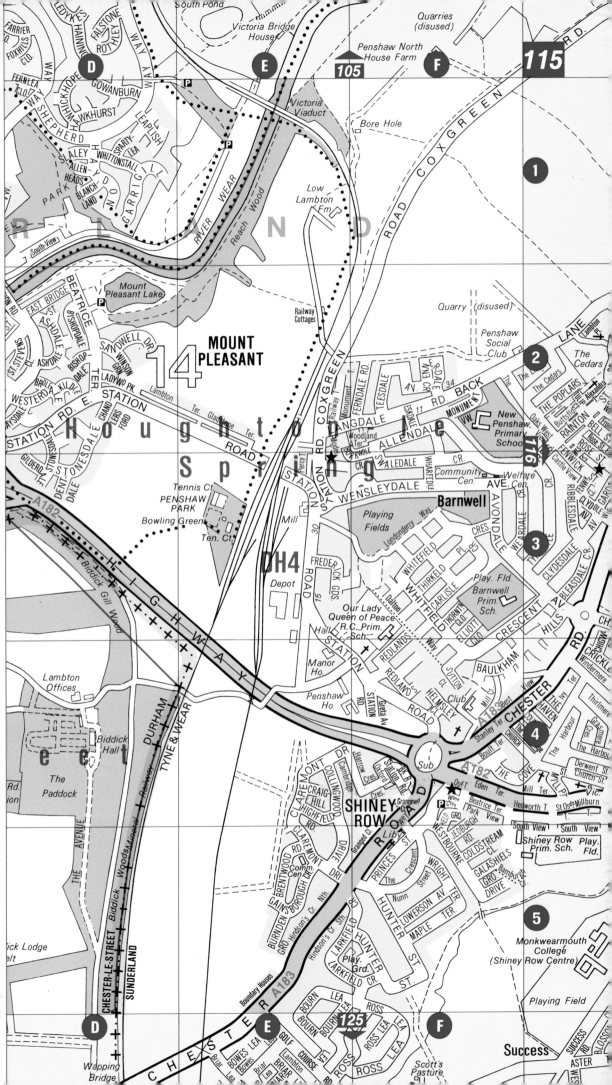

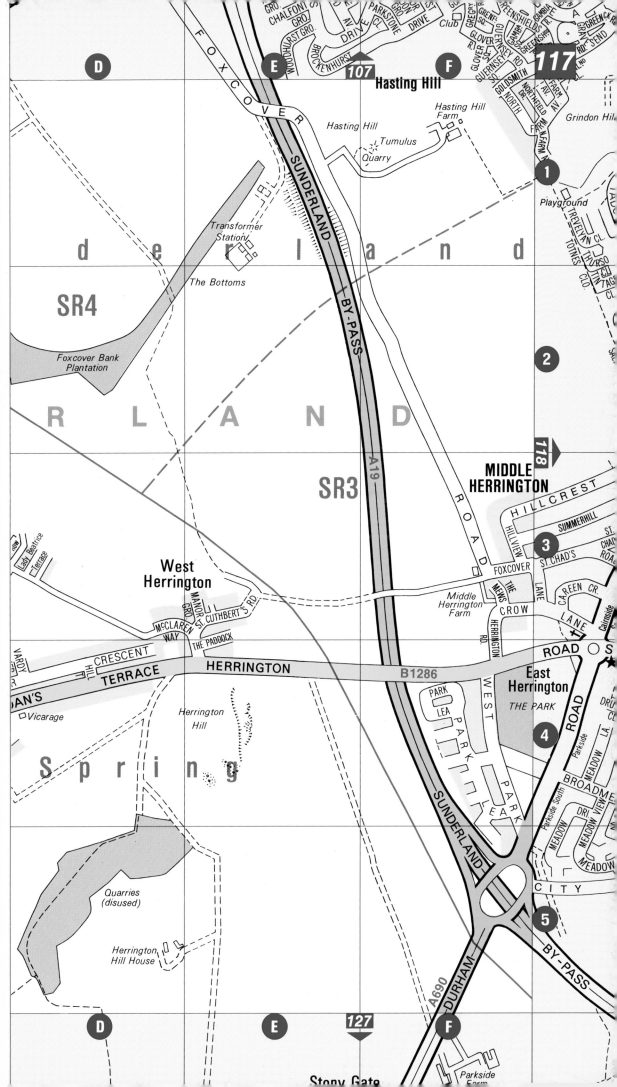

D **E** **107** **F**

Hasting Hill

CHALFONT GRO.
WOODHURST GRO.
CHALFONT GRO.
BROCKENHURST GRO.
PARKSTONE GRO.
PARKSTONE DRIVE
Club
GREGORY SQ.
GREGORY SQ.
GRENFELL SQ.
GUERNSEY RD.
GLOVER SQ.
GREENSHIELDS RD.
CAMBIA GREENS RD.
GRAVE END
GREEN CARD

FOXCOVER

1

Hasting Hill
Hasting Hill
Farm
Tumulus
Quarry

GOLDSMITH
NORTHFIELD FARM
NORTHFIELD FARM
Grindon Hill
Playground
TREVELYAN CL.
TOTNES CL.
THURSO CL.
TAGE CL.

SUNDERLAND

Transformer
Station

d **e** **r** **l** **a** **n** **d**

SR4

The Bottoms

BY-PASS

2

Foxcover Bank
Plantation

R **L** **A** **N** **D**

118

MIDDLE HERRINGTON

HILLCREST

SUMMERHILL

SR3

A19

HILLVIEW
FOXCOVER
ST. CHAD'S
ST. CHAD'S ROAD
Cairnside

3

CA REEN CR.

Lady Beatrice
Terrace
NOW

West Herrington

Middle
Herrington Farm

THE MEWS
CROW LANE
HERRINGTON RD.

MANOR GRO.
ST. CUTHBERT'S RD.
McCLAREN WAY
THE PADDOCK

4

East Herrington

THE PARK

VARDY
HILL CRESCENT
TERRACE
HERRINGTON
B1286
ROAD
PARK LEA
PARK LEA
WEST PARK
ROAD
BROADME

DAN'S
Vicarage

Herrington
Hill

PARK LEA

Parkside
Parkside South
MEADOW
MEADOW VIEW
MEADOW DRI
MEADOW

S **p** **r** **i** **n** **g**

Quarries
(disused)

CITY

SUNDERLAND

5

Herrington
Hill House

A690

DURHAM

BY-PASS

D **E** **127** **F**

Stony Gate

Parkside
Farm

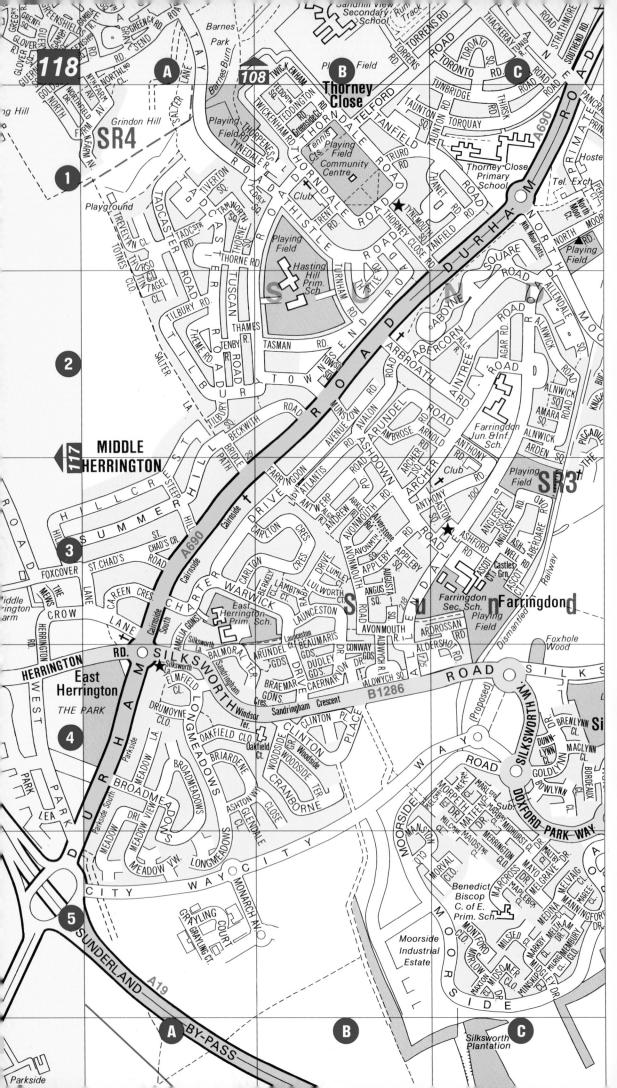

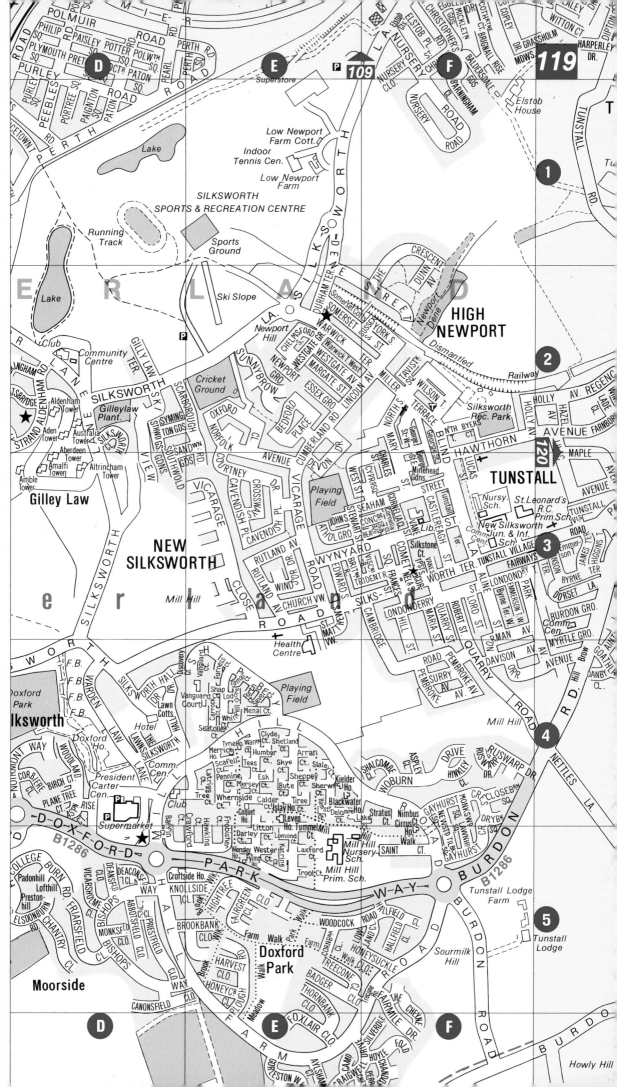

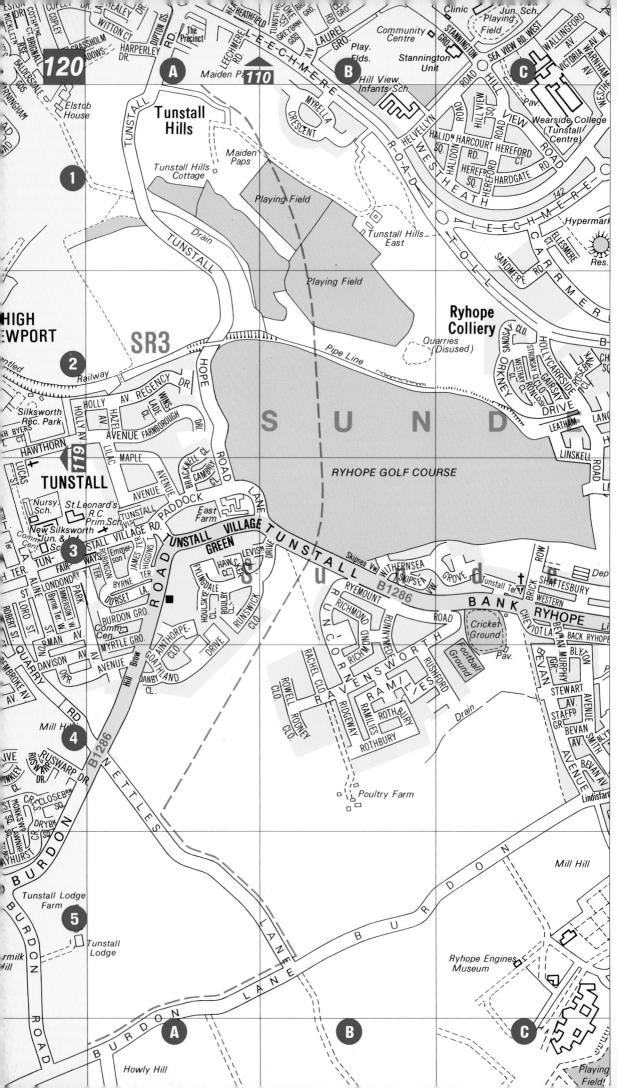

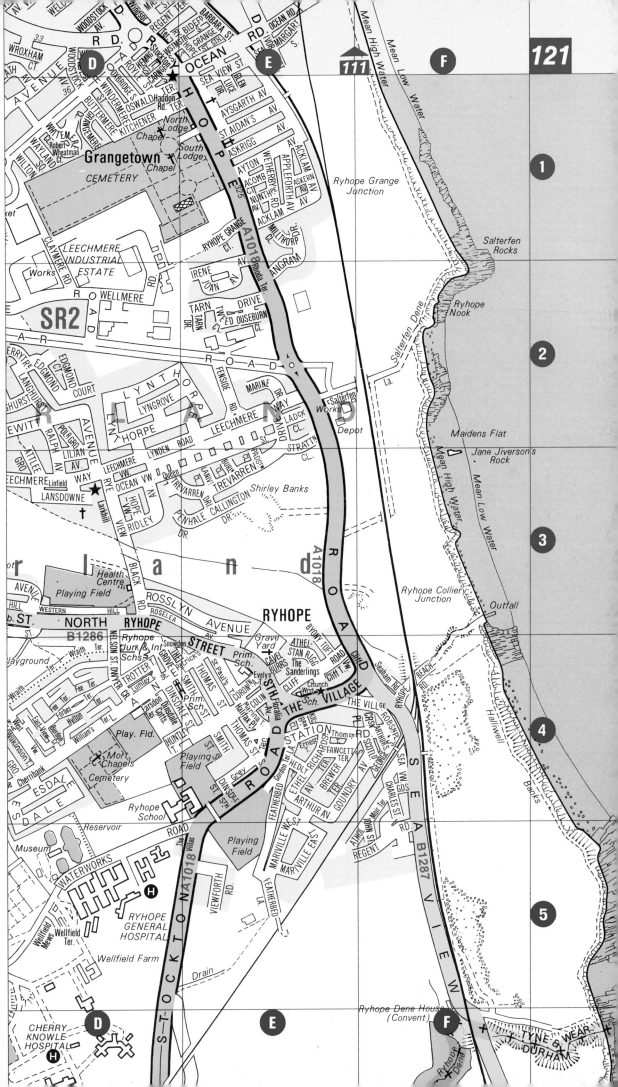

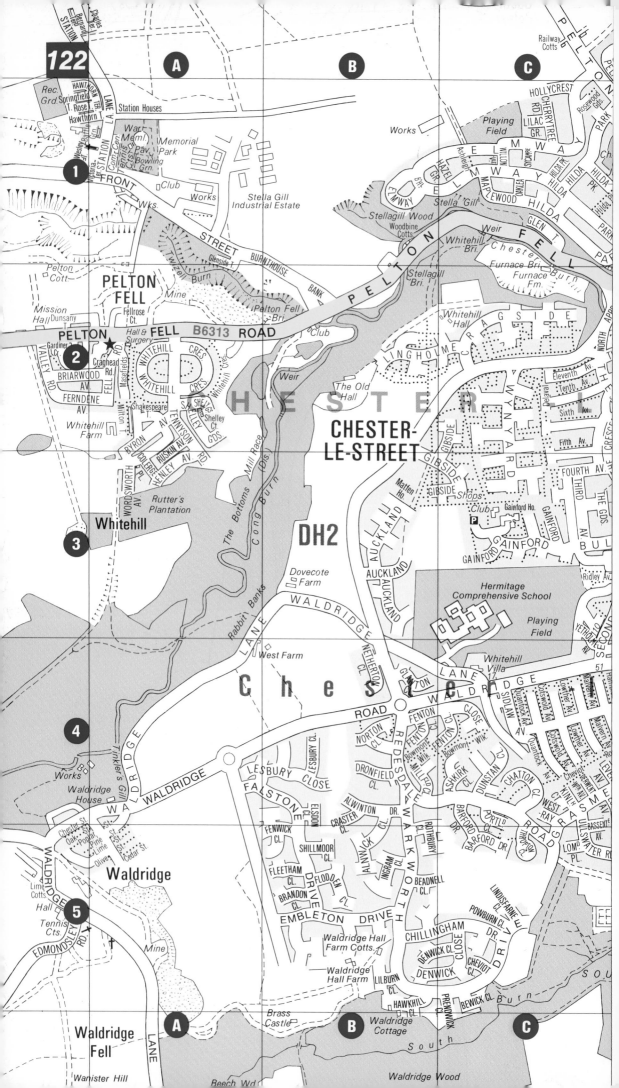

A   B   C

STATION

Rec. Grd. Springfield
HAWTHORN
T. Rose
Hawthorn
LANE LA.
Station Houses

War Meml.
Comm. Cen.
Pav
Memorial
Park

Tennis Cts.
Bowling Grn.

Club
Works
Stella Gill
Industrial Estate

Wks.
FRONT STREET

Pelton Cott.

Mission Hall Dunsany

PELTON FELL
Fellrose Ct.

BURNHOUSE BANK

Pelton Fell Bri.

Twizell Burn
Glenside T.
Mine
Club

Railway Cotts.
PELTON

HOLLYCREST
CHERRYTREE RD.
LILAC GR.
Playing Field
Rosewood Gdns.
PARK

HAZEL GR.
ASHLEIGH
WILLOW
SYCAMORE
HILDA PK.
HILDA PK.
HILDA
HILDA

ELM WAY
BRI.
Stella Gill
MAPLEWOOD
OAKLEA
HILDA

Stellagill Wood
Woodbine Cotts.
GLEN T.
FELL

Weir Bri.
Whitehill Bri.
Chester Burn

PELTON
FELL

Whitehill Hall
Furnace Bri.
Furnace Fm.
Stellagill Bri.

CRAGSIDE

PELTON

Gardiner Cr.
VALLEY RD.
BRIARWOOD AV.
FERNDENE AV.
Whitehill Farm

PELTON
FELL
B6313 ROAD

Craghead Rd.
Masefields
Milton T.
Shakespeare T.
BYRON
COLERIDGE
WORDSWORTH AV.

WHITEHILL CRES.
WHITEHILL CRES.
Whitehill Cres.

SHELLEY
SHELLEY
Shelley Ct.
GDS.
TENNYSON AV.
RUSKIN AV.
HENLEY AV.

CHESTER

Weir
The Old Hall

LINGHOLME
WYNYARD
GIBSIDE

CHESTER-LE-STREET

Eleventh Av.
Tenth. Av.
Sixth Av.
Fifth Av.

LEVEL
FELL

FOURTH AV.
THIRD AV.
THE GDS.
BUL

Whitehill
Rutter's Plantation

The Bottoms

Mill Race (Dis.)

Cong Burn

DH2

Dovecote Farm

AUCKLAND
Matten Ho.
GIBSIDE
GIBSIDE Shops
Club
Gainford Ho.

P
GAINFORD
GAINFORD
GAINFORD

Ridley Av.
YETHOLM

Hermitage Comprehensive School
Playing Field

Rabbit Banks

WALDRIDGE LANE

NETHERTON CL.
GLENTON

West Farm

Whitehill Villa
17.
51

Works

Waldridge House

Tinkler's Gill
WALDRIDGE

WALDRIDGE

Chester St.
Oak St.
Poplar St.
Pine St.
Lime St.
Olive St.
Cedar St.

Waldridge

Lime Cotts.
Hall
Tennis Cts.
EDMONDSLEY RD.
Mine

WELDRIDGE
Road

FENTON
FENTON CL.
FENTON
FENTON
SIDLAW

NORTON CL.
REDESDALE
BOWMONT WIK.
BOWMONT WIK.
MILFORD
DUNSTAN CL.
CHATTON CL.

LESBURY CL.
LESBURY CLOSE
DRONFIELD CL.
WARKWORTH
ASHKIRK CL.

FALSTONE
ELSDON CL.
CRASTER CL.
ALWINTON CL.
ALNWICK
INGRAM CL.
ROTHBURY
BARFORD DR.
BARFORD DR.
PORTLD
PL.
LOM.
PL.

COTSWOLD AV.
QUANTOCK AV.
LOWTHER AV.
MALVERN AV.
CHEVIOT
LEVE
AV.

FENWICK CL.
SHILLMOOR CL.
FLEETHAM CL.
BRANDON CL.
FLODDEN CL.
DRIVE
BEADNELL CL.
RAY
CL.
WEST
RASM
ULLSWATER RD.
BASSENTE
AV.

EMBLETON DRIVE

Waldridge Hall Farm Cotts.

CHILLINGHAM
DENWICK CLOSE
DENWICK
LINDISFARNE
POWBURN CL.
DRIVE

LILBURN CL.
HAWKHILL CL.
DENWICK CL.
PRENDWICK CL.
CHEVIOT CL.
BEWICK CL.
SOU
Burn

Waldridge Hall Farm

Waldridge Fell

Brass Castle

Waldridge Cottage

South

LANE

Wanister Hill
Beech Wd.
Waldridge Wood

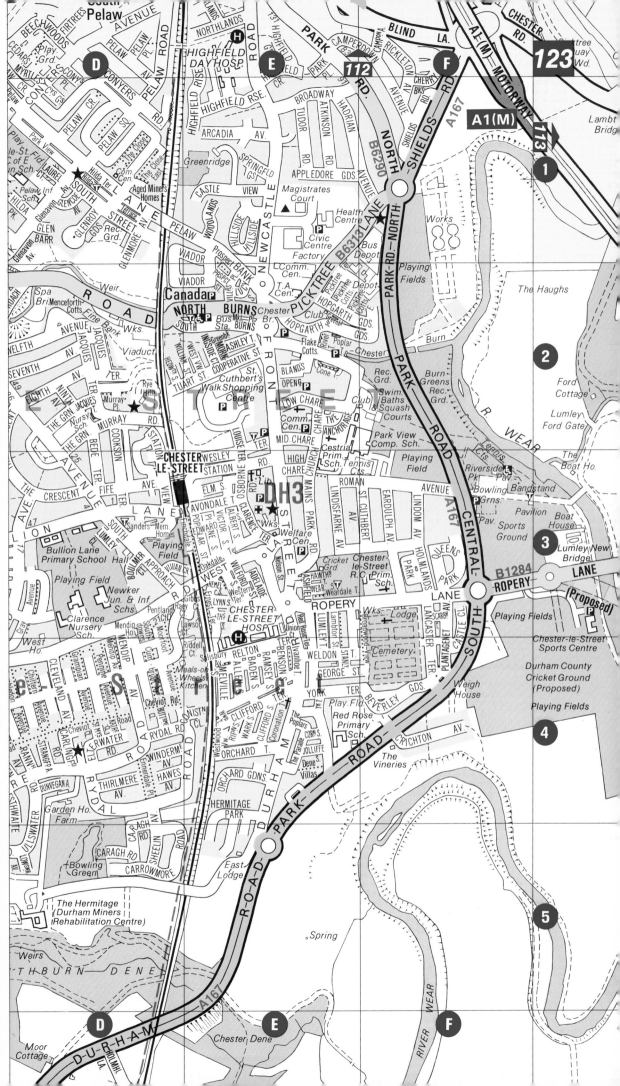

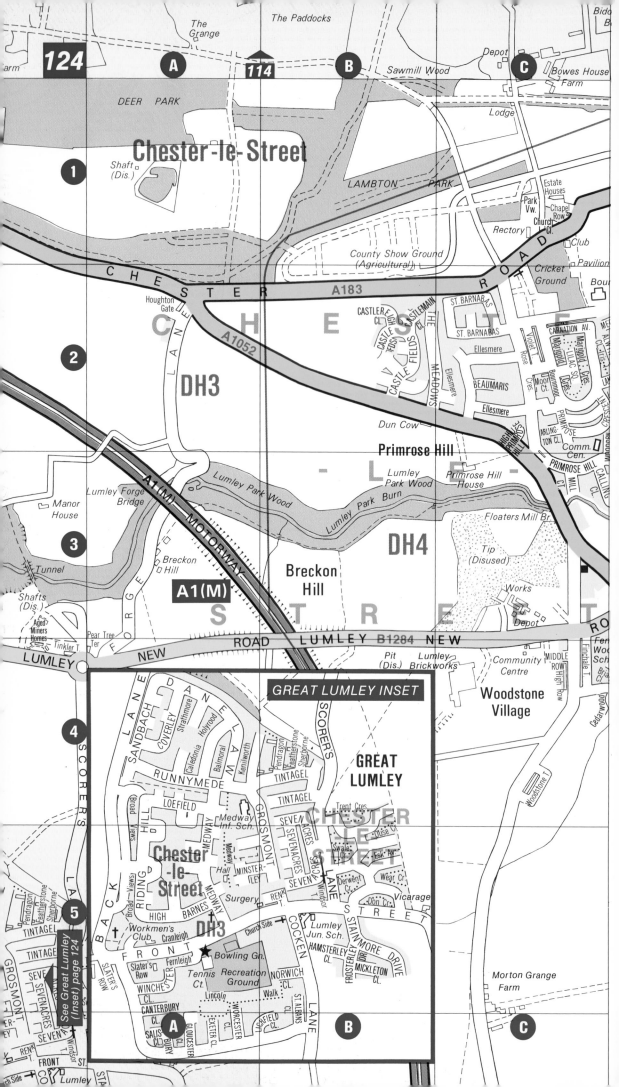

A 114 B C

Chester-le-Street

1

DEER PARK

Shaft (Dis.)

The Grange

The Paddocks

Sawmill Wood

Depot

Bowes House Farm

C

Lodge

LAMBTON PARK

Estate Houses

Park Vw.

Chapel Row

Rectory

Church Cl.

Club

Pavilion

Bou

Cricket Ground

CHESTER

A183

ROAD

Houghton Gate

A1052

CHE

STE

2

DH3

CASTLER.HIGH
CASTLE FDS.
CASTLEMAIN CL.
CASTLE FIELDS
CASTLE FDS.

ST. BARNABAS

ST. BARNABAS

THE MEADOWS

Ellesmere

Ellesmere

BEAUMARIS

Ellesmere

Violet Rose

CARNATION AV.

Marigold Cres.

Moor Ct.

LILAC SQ.
Bournmoor Cres.

Marigold

PRIMROSE

ARLING-TON CL.

Comm. Cen.

PRIMROSE HILL

CALLING

Dun Cow

Primrose Hill

HIGH PRIMROSE

PRIMROSE HILL

Lumley Park Wood

Lumley Park Wood

Primrose Hill House

-LE-

Lumley Forge Bridge

Manor House

A1(M)

MOTORWAY

3

Tunnel

Breckon Hill

Lumley Park Burn

Floaters Mill Br.

DH4

Tip (Dis.)

Breckon Hill

Works Depot

Shafts (Dis.)

FORGE

A1(M)

S

T

R

E

E

Aged Miners Homes

Tinkler T.

Pear Tree Ter.

NEW

ROAD

LUMLEY B1284 NEW

Pit (Dis.)

Lumley Brickworks

Community Centre

MIDDLE ROW

High Row

Finchale T.

Fern Woo Sch.

Bria Cl.

R

LUMLEY

4

SCORER'S

GREAT LUMLEY INSET

SCORER'S

GREAT LUMLEY

Woodstone Village

Woodstone T.

LANE

SANDBACH

COVERLEY

DANE
LAW

Strathmore
Holyrood

Caledonia
Balmoral

Kenilworth

Pendragon
Featherstone
Sherborne

TINTAGEL

TINTAGEL

SEVEN
ACRES

Trent Cres.

CHESTER
LE
STREET

RUNNYMEDE

LOEFIELD

MEDWAY
Medway Inf. Sch.

GROSMONT

SEVENACRES

SEVEN

Chise Cl.

RIDING
HILL
Broad Views
(peoɹ)

SEVEN

Swale

Esk Av.

Chester
-le-
Street

MEDWAY

Hall

MINSTER
LEY

Surgery

RENK
T.

Derwent T.

Wear Cr.

Vicarage

HIGH
BARNES

Don Cr.

LANE
Windsor

5

See Great Lumley (Inset) page 124

TINTAGEL

TINTAGE

BACK

Workmen's Club

Cranleigh

Church Side

Lumley Jun. Sch.

STAINMORE DRIVE

Morton Grange Farm

GROSMONT

SEVE

SEVENACRES

FRONT

Slater's Row

Fernleigh

DH3

Bowling Gn.

HAMSTERLEY CL.

SEVEN

RENK

WINCHESTER

Tennis Ct.

Recreation Ground

NORWICH CL.

COCKEN

FROSTERLEY

MICKLETON CL.

WINDSOR ST

CANTERBURY CL.

Lincoln Walk

ST. ALBANS

A

GLOUCESTER

SALIS
BURY

EXETER CL.

WORCESTER CL.

SCAFIELD CL.

B

LANE

C

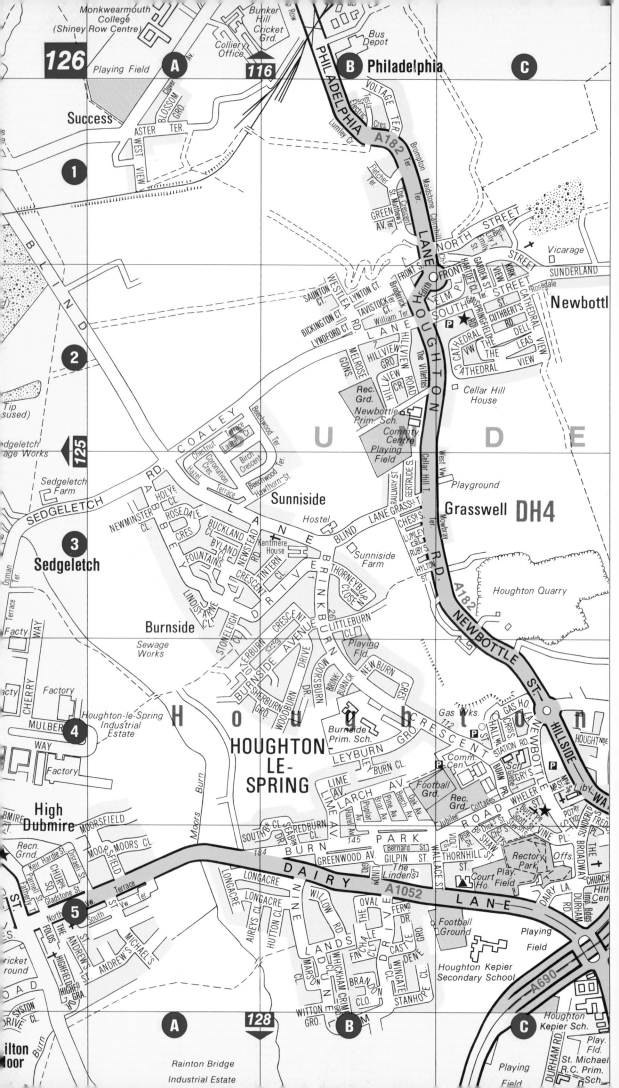

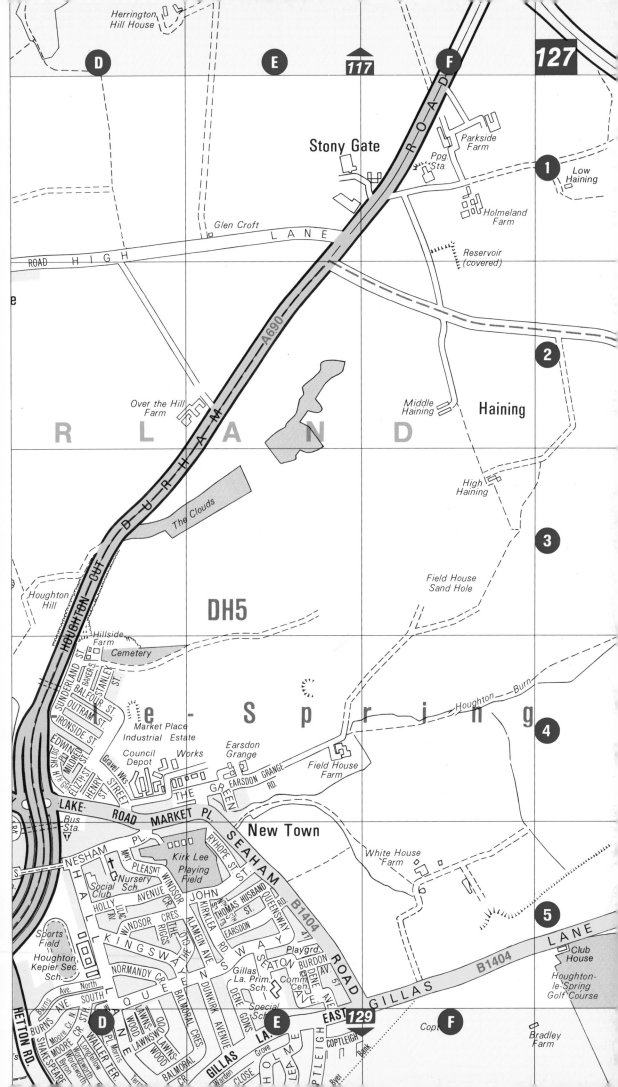

Herrington Hill House

D

E

↑ **117**

F

Stony Gate

Parkside Farm

Ppg. Sta.

1 Low Haining

Holmeland Farm

Glen Croft

LANE

ROAD HIGH

Reservoir (covered)

A 690

2

Middle Haining

Haining

Over the Hill Farm

D U R H A M

High Haining

R **L** **A** **N** **D**

The Clouds

3

Field House Sand Hole

Houghton Hill

DH5

HOUGHTON CUT

Hillside Farm

Cemetery

Houghton Burn

SUNDERLAND ST.

BAKER ST.

STANLEY ST.

BALFOUR ST.

OUTRAM ST.

IRONSIDE ST.

le - S p r i n g

4

EDWIN RD.

MILDRED ST.

ELIZTH ST.

HENRY ST.

Gravel Wks.

STREET

Market Place Industrial Estate

Earsdon Grange

Field House Farm

Council Depot

Works

EARSDON GRANGE RD.

THE GREEN

LAKE ROAD

MARKET PL.

New Town

White House Farm

Bus. Sta.

NESHAM PL.

MT PLEASNT

Kirk Lee Playing Field

RYHOPE ST.

SEAHAM

WINDSOR CR.

THE RIGGS

JOHN ST.

THOMAS HUSBAND ST.

QUEENSWAY

B1404 ROAD

Social Club

Nursery Sch.

HOLLY

LILAC AV.

WINDSOR CRES.

KIRKLEA RD.

EARSDON ST.

SEATON

Playgrd

BURDON

DENE AV.

5

White House Farm

Club House

Sports Field

Houghton Kepier Sec. Sch.

KINGSWAY

ALAMEIN AVE.

WAY

Gillas La. Prim. Sch.

Comm. Cen.

Special Sch.

Houghton-le-Spring Golf Course

NORMANDY CRES.

DUNKIRK AVE.

DENE GDNS.

GILLAS

B1404 LANE

HETTON RD.

SHAKESPEARE

BURNS AV. NORTH

MOORE CR. STH

WALLER TER.

LANE

LAWNSWOOD

LAWNSWOOD

BALMORAL CRES.

HOLME

LEA

COPTLEIGH

COPTLEIGH

D

E

EAST **129**

F

Copt

Bradley Farm

GILLAS

127

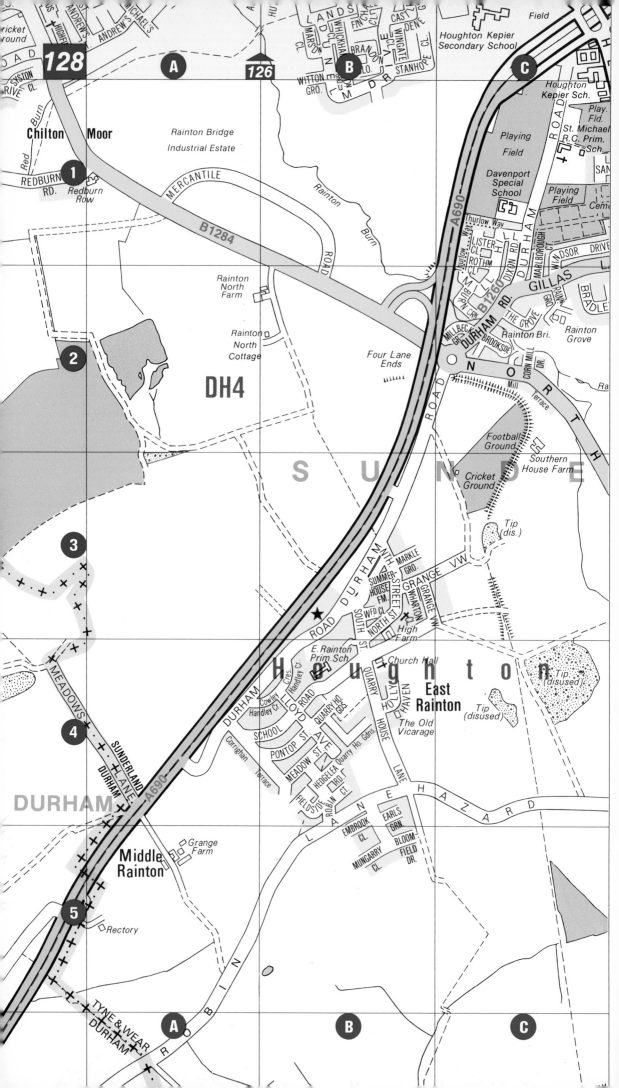

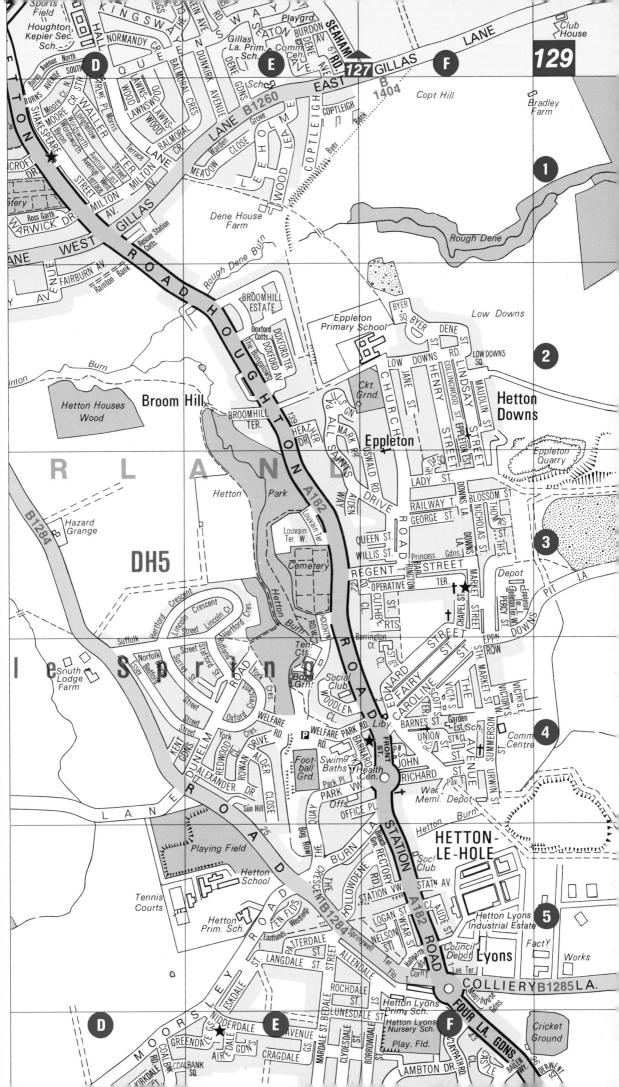

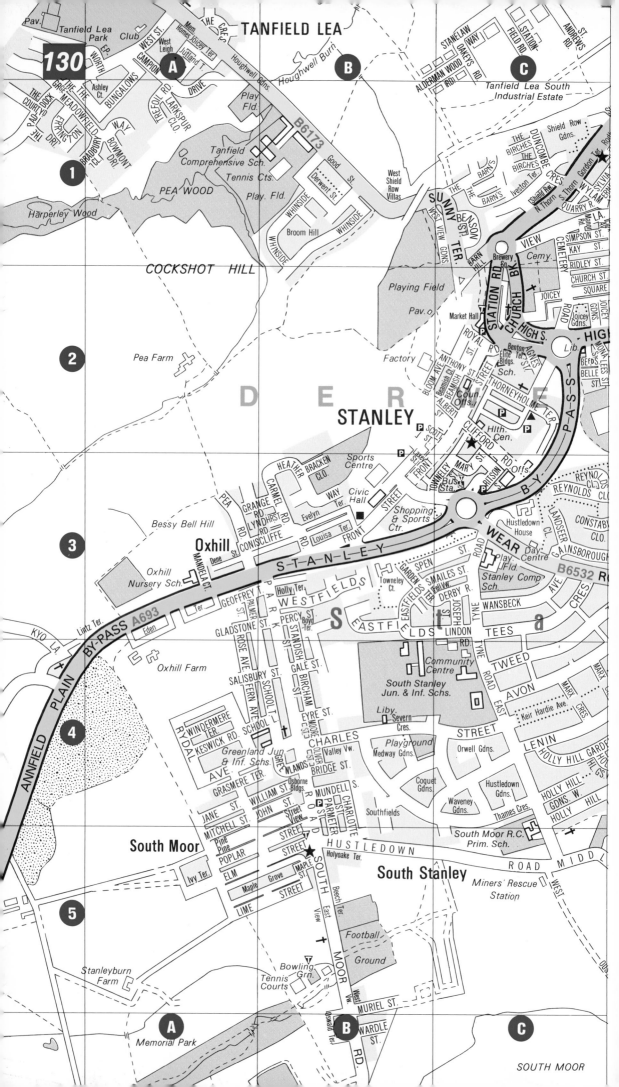

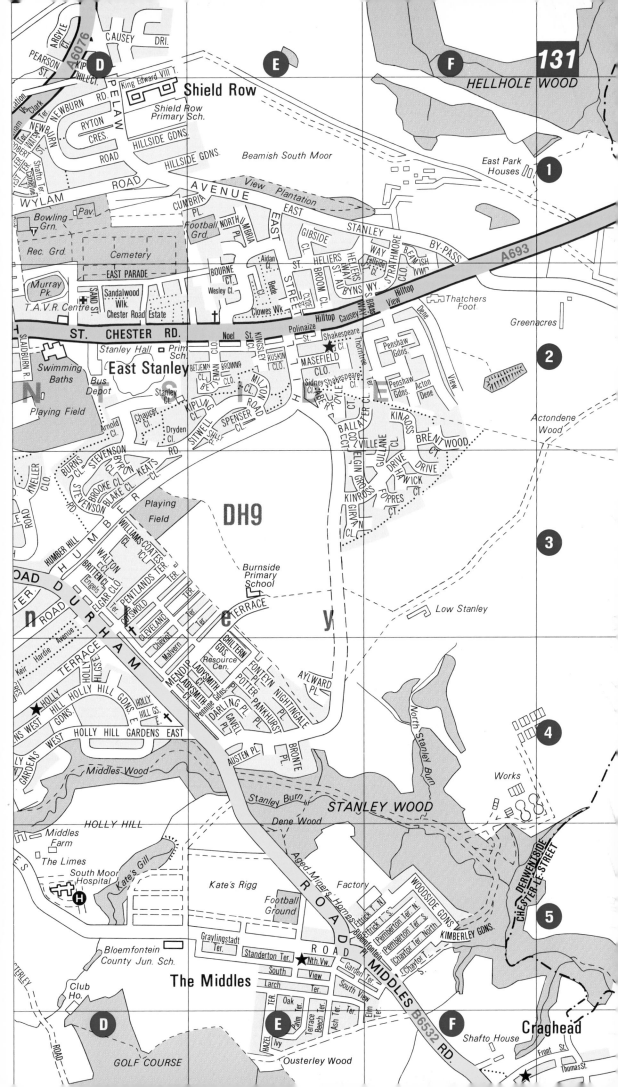

HELLHOLE WOOD

Shield Row

Beamish South Moor

East Park
Houses

1

Thatchers
Foot.

Greenacres

East Stanley

ST. CHESTER RD.

Masefield
CLO.

Penshaw
Gdns.

Actondene
Wood

2

DH9

Playing
Field

Burnside
Primary
School

Low Stanley

3

Works

4

Middles Wood

STANLEY WOOD

5

Dene Wood

HOLLY HILL

Middles
Farm

The Limes

South Moor
Hospital

H

Kate's Rigg

Factory

Bloemfontein
County Jun. Sch.

The Middles

Graylingstadt
Ter.

Ousterley Wood

GOLF COURSE

D   **E**   **F**

Shafto House

Craghead

Front St.

Thomas St.

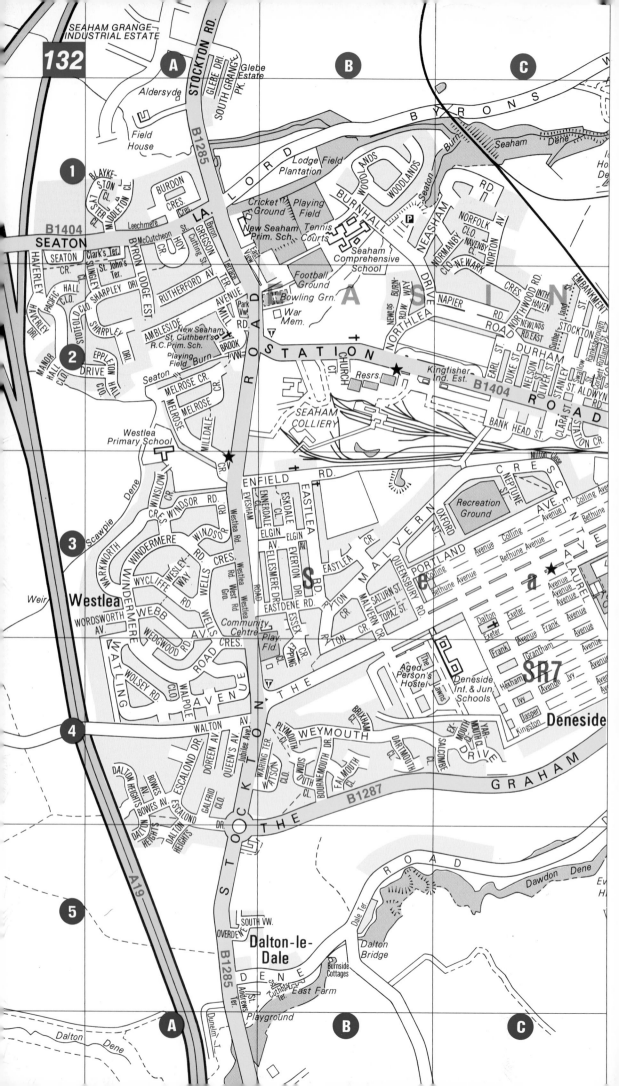

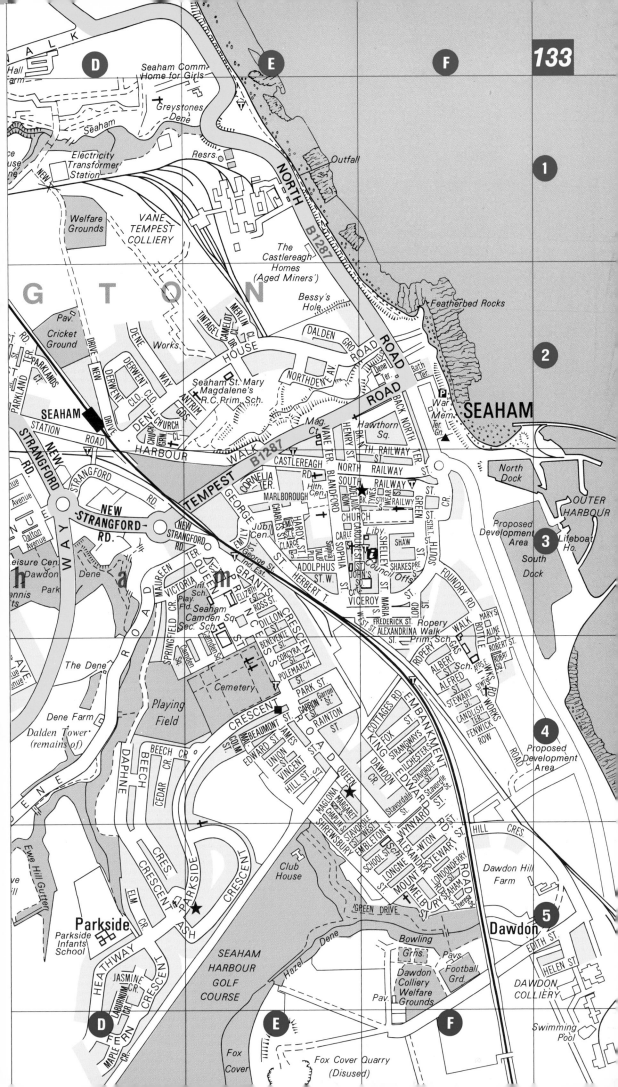

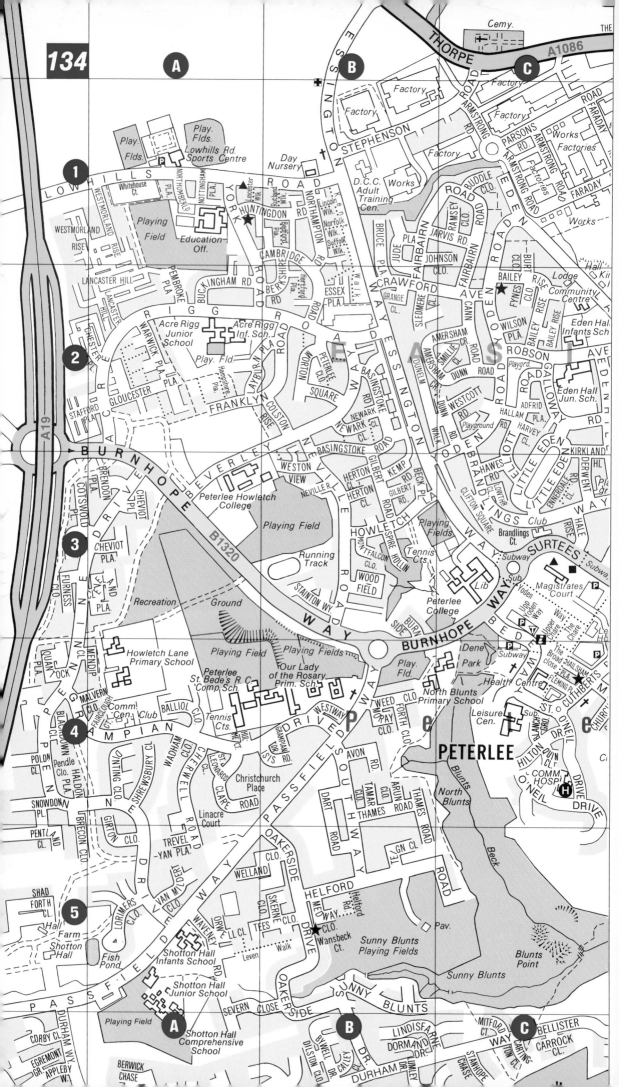

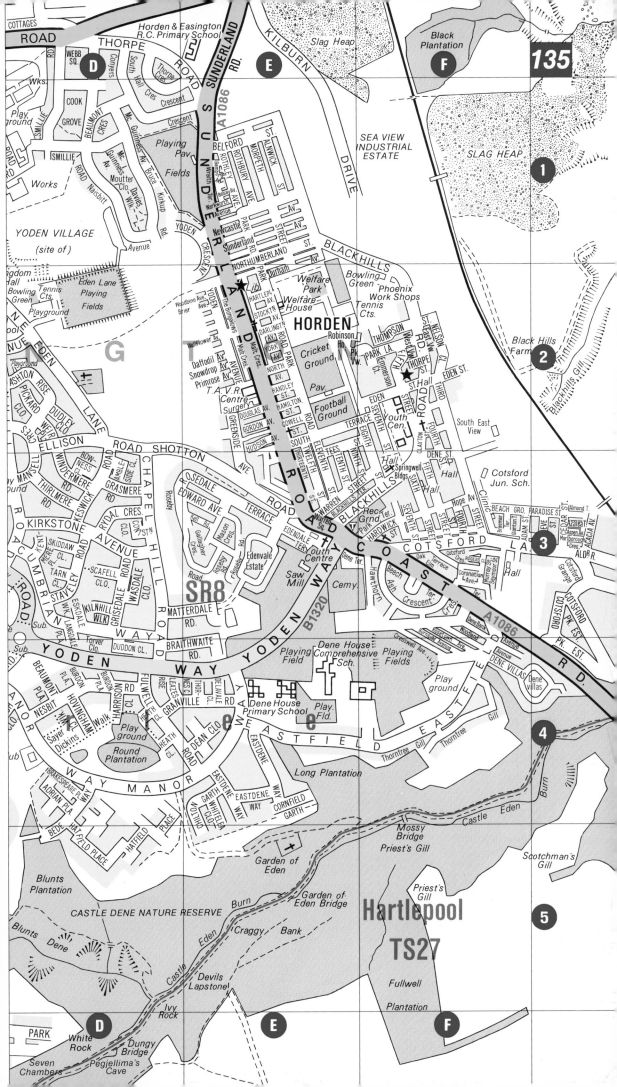

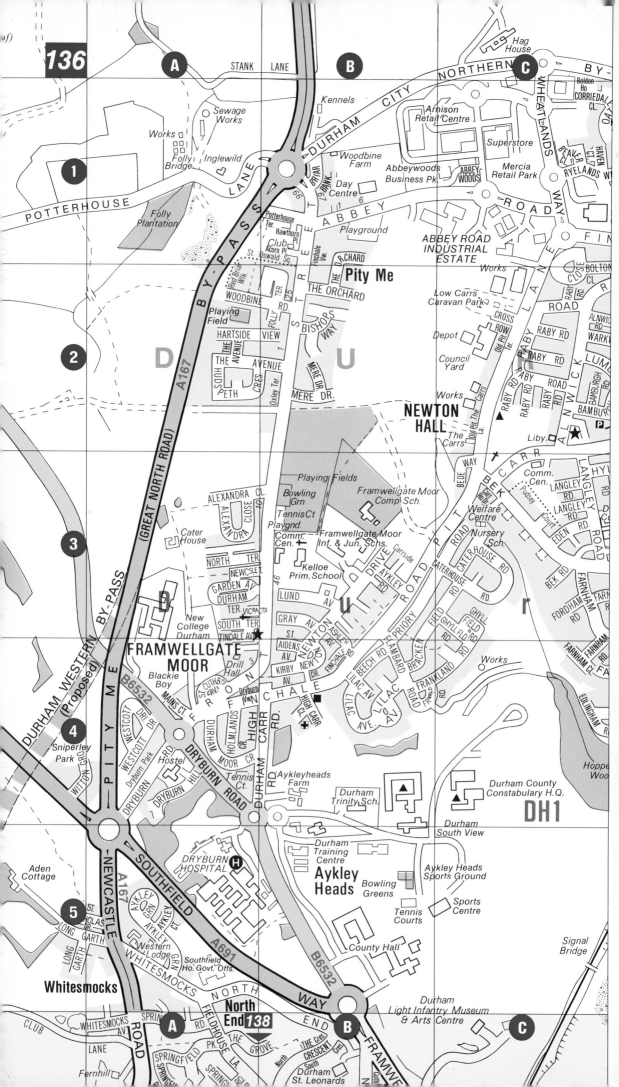

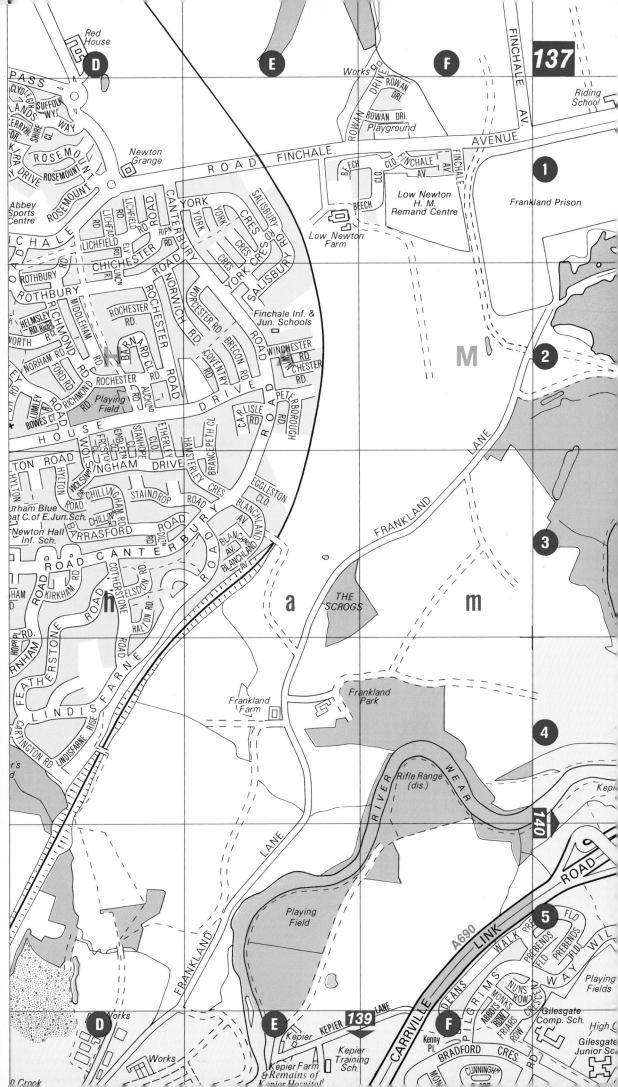

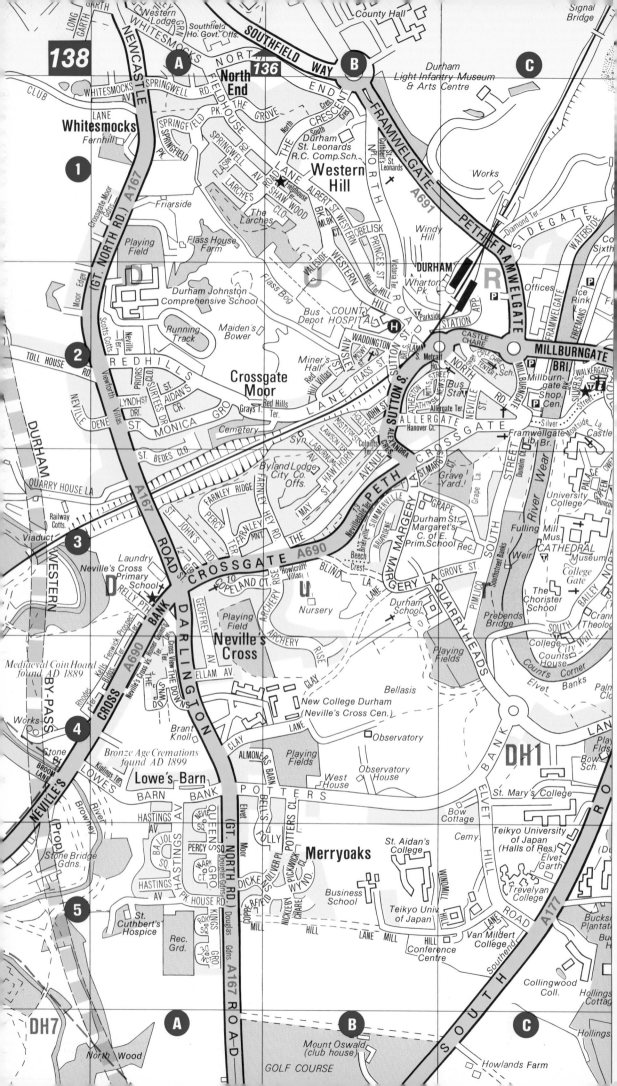

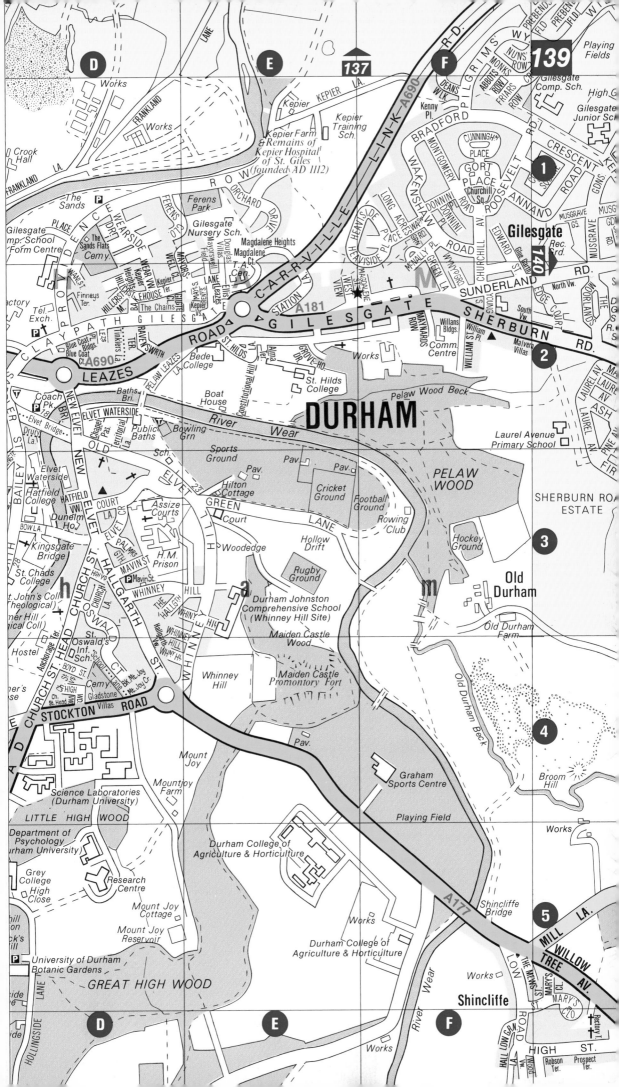

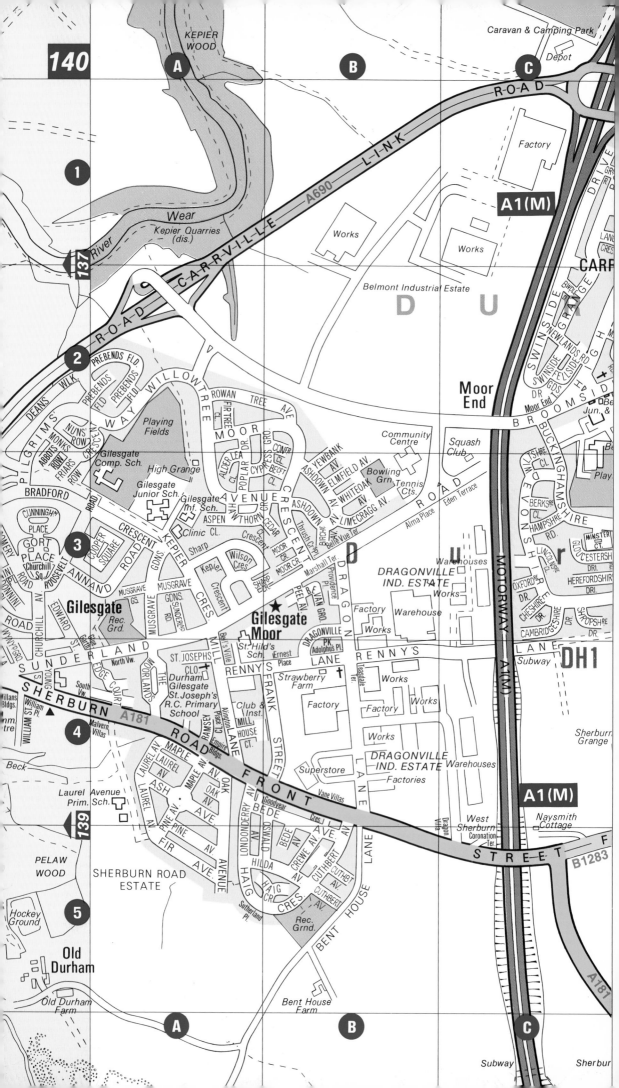

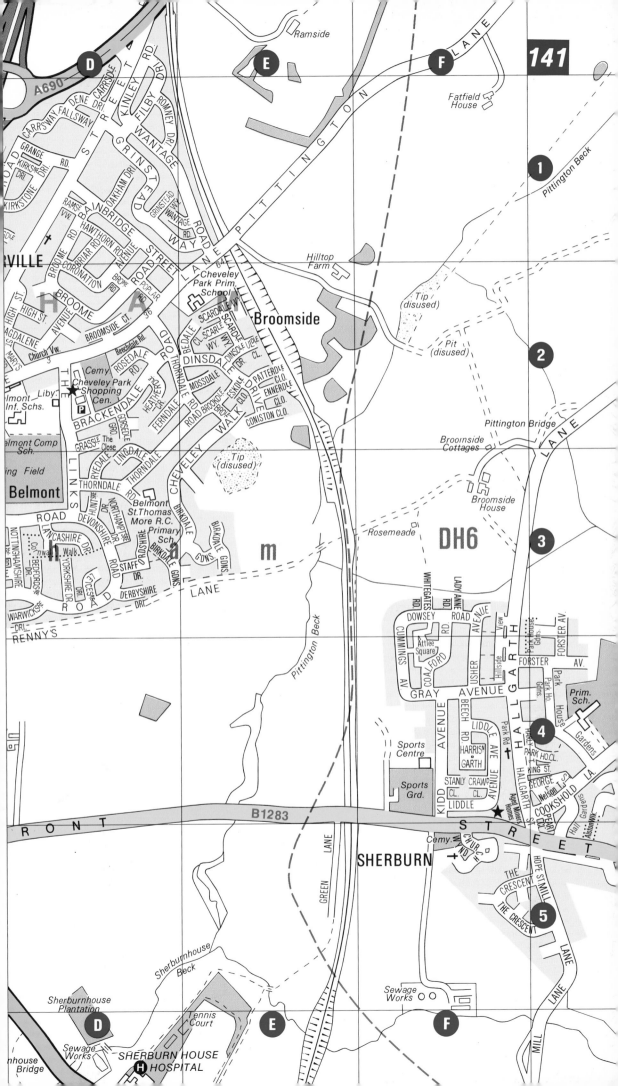

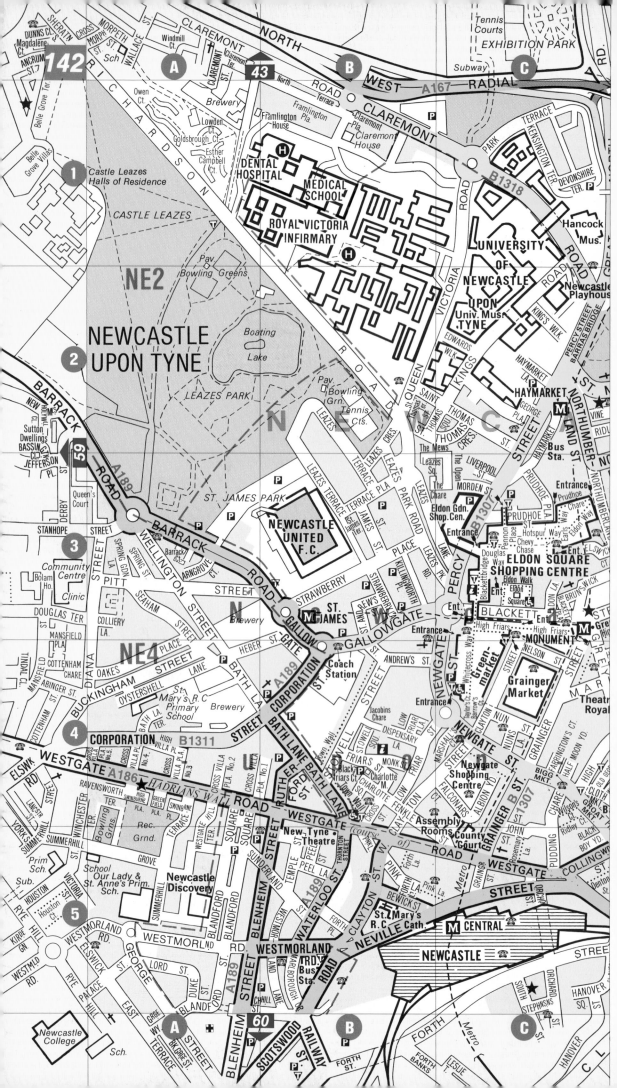

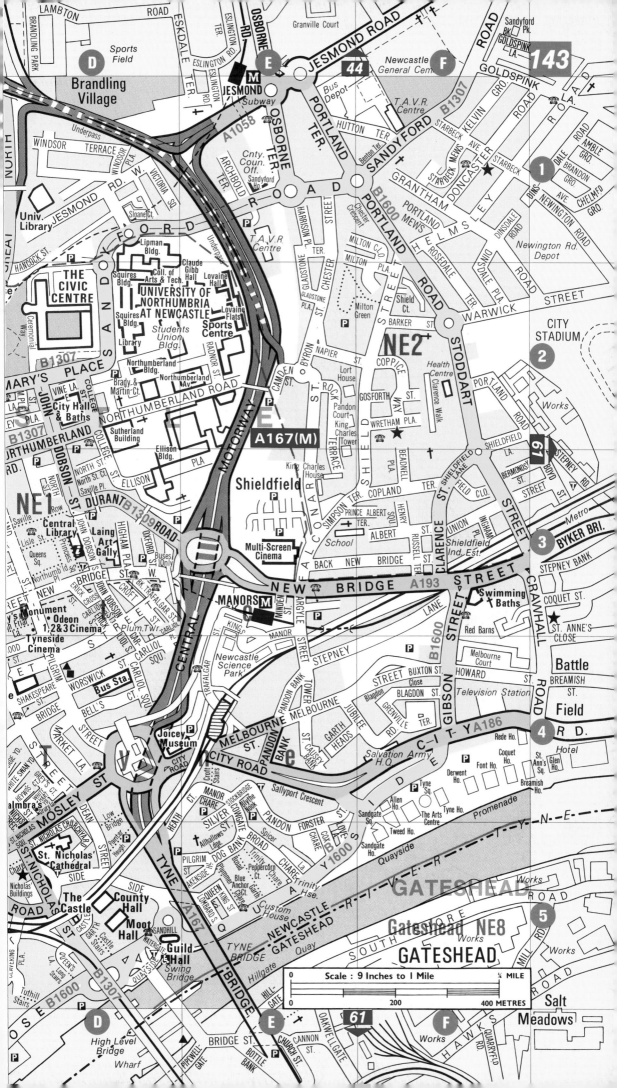

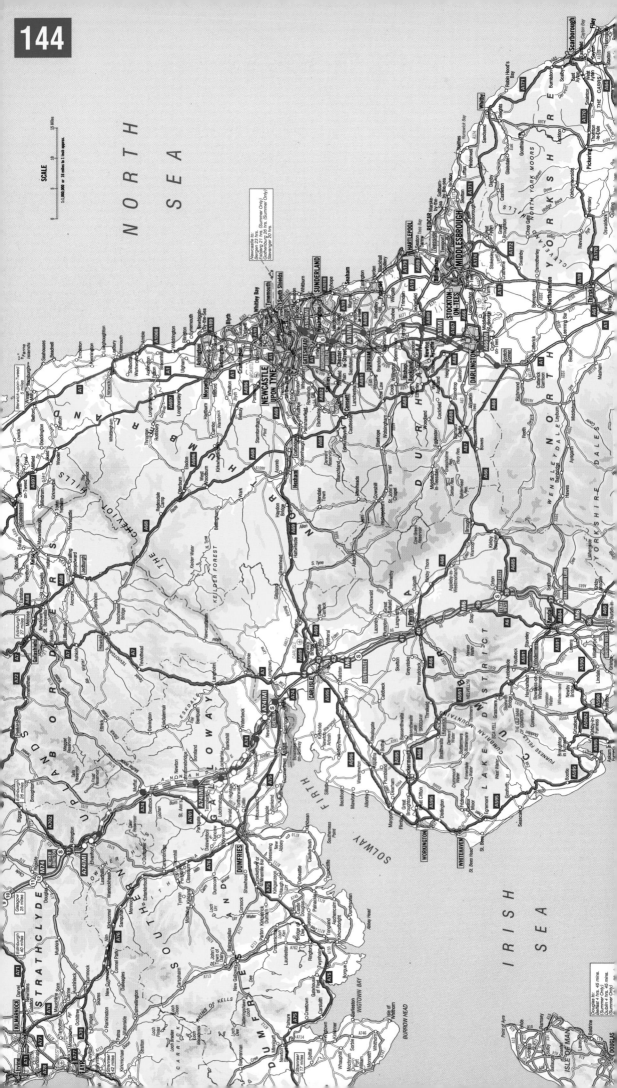

Index to Places & Areas

Names in this index shown in CAPITAL LETTERS, followed by their Postcode District(s), are Postal addresses.

Addison.-2E 55
Albany.-5B 94
Allerdene.-3E 91
ANNITSFORD. (NE23)-3A 8
ARMSTRONG. (NE37)-1E 103
ARTHURS HILL. (NE4)-1F 59
Axwell Park.-5D 57
AYKLEY HEADS. (DH1)-5B 136
Ayre's Quay.-5A 100
Ayton.-4E 103

BACKWORTH. (NE27)-2E 19
Bank Top.-2D 37
Barley Mow.-1B 112
BARLOW. (NE21)-4B 72
Bar Moor.-2A 54
Barmston.-2D 105
Barnwell.-2F 115
Battle Hill.-5E 31
Beaconhill.-3A 4
Beacon Lough.-1A 92
Bell's Close.-2D 57
BELMONT. (DH1)-3D 141
BENSHAM. (NE8)-1C 78
BENTON. (NE7 & NE12)-3F 29
Benton Square.-1D 30
BENWELL. (NE4 & NE15)-2B 58
Biddick.-4B 104
Biddick Hall.-4A 68
Bigges Main.-2B 46
Billy Mill.-3F 33
BIRTLEY. (DH2 & DH3)-2B 102
Blackfell.-2F 103
BLAYDON. (NE21)-4B 56
BLAYDON BURN. (NE21)-5E 55
Bleach Green.-1B 74
Boldon.-2A 86
BOLDON COLLIERY. (NE35)-1D 85
Boundary Houses.-1E 125
Bournmoor.-2C 124
Brandling Village.-5F 43
Breckon Hill.-3B 92
Brockley Whins.-4E 67
Broom Hill.-2E 129
Broomside.-2E 141
BRUNSWICK VILLAGE. (NE13)-1C 14
Burnside.-3A 126
BURRADON. (NE23)-1D 17
BYKER. (NE6)-2A 62

Campbell Park.-2E 65
CAMPERDOWN. (NE12)-2E 17
Carley Hill.-1F 99
CARR HILL. (NE9)-3A 80
CARRVILLE. (DH1)-2C 140
CASTLETOWN. (SR5)-4F 97
CHAPEL PARK. (NE5)-1E 39
CHESTER-LE-STREET. (DH2 & DH3)
-3E 123
CHILTON MOOR. (DH4)-5F 125
CHIRTON. (NE29)-4A 34
Chowdene.-2D 91
CLEADON. (SR6)-5F 69
Cleadon Park.-3E 69
COLLIERY ROW. (DH4)-5F 125
Columbia.-3D 105
Concord.-4C 94
Cox Green.-4F 105
COXLODGE. (NE3)-4C 26
CRAGHEAD. (DH9)-5F 131
CRAMLINGTON. (NE23)-3D 5
Crookhill.-3D 55
CROSSGATE MOOR. (DH1)-2A 138

DALTON-LE-DALE. (SR7)-5B 132
DAWDON. (SR7)-5F 133
Deans.-5D 51
Deneside.-4C 132
Deptford.-5F 99
Derwenthaugh.-4F 57
Donwell.-4F 93
Downhill.-1F 97
Doxford Park.-5E 119
DUDLEY. (NE23)-4E 7
DUNSTON. (NE11)-1E 77
DURHAM. (DH1, DH6 & DH7)-2C 138
Dyke Heads.-5A 54

EARSDON. (NE25)-2B 20
EAST BOLDON. (NE36)-3C 86
EAST DENTON. (NE5)-4C 40
EAST HERRINGTON. (SR3)-4A 118

East Howdon.-2E 49
EAST RAINTON. (DH5)-4B 128
EAST STANLEY. (DH9)-2E 131
EIGHTON BANKS. (NE9)-3C 92
Elisabethville.-2A 102
ELSWICK. (NE4)-3E 59
Emerson.-5E 103

FARRINGDON. (SR3)-3C 118
FATFIELD. (NE38)-2B 114
FAWDON. (NE3)-3A 26
Fellgate.-1F 83
FELLING. (NE10)-1B 80
Fellside Park.-4E 75
Fence Houses.-4E 125
FENHAM. (NE4)-5F 41
Festival Park.-3A 78
Follingsby.-5B 82
Folly, The.-5A 54
Ford Estate.-1D 109
Fordley.-4A 8
FOREST HALL. (NE12)-1F 29
FRAMWELLGATE MOOR. (DH1)-4A 136
Friars Goose.-4C 62
Fulwell.-1B 100

GATESHEAD. (NE8 to NE11)-4D 61
GILESGATE. (DH1)-3A 140
GILESGATE MOOR. (DH1)-3A 140
Gilley Law.-3D 119
Glebe.-2C 104
GOSFORTH. (NE3)-5E 27
GRASSWELL. (DH4)-3B 126
GREAT LUMLEY. (DH4)-5B 124
GREENSIDE. (NE40)-1A 72
Grindon.-5A 108

HARLOW GREEN. (NE9)-3F 91
HARRATON. (NE38)-1A 114
Hartley.-1C 12
Harton.-1E 69
Harton Nook.-2E 69
Hasting Hill.-5F 107
HAZLERIGG. (NE13)-3C 14
HEATON. (NE6)-4D 45
HEATON. (NE6) -4D 45
HEBBURN. (NE31)-1C 64
Hebburn Colliery.-5F 47
Hebburn New Town.-2C 64
HEDDON-ON-THE-WALL. (NE15)-2A 36
Hedgefield.-2E 55
Hedworth.-5B 66
HENDON. (SR2)-3D 111
HETTON-LE-HOLE. (DH5)-4F 129
Heworth.-2E 81
High Dubmire.-5F 125
High Fell.-4A 80
HIGH HEATON. (NE7)-2D 45
High Heworth.-4D 80
High Newport.-2F 119
High Shields.-3D 51
High Southwick.-2E 99
Hill Park Estate.-2B 66
Holy Cross.-1F 47
HOLYSTONE. (NE27)-5E 19
HOLYWELL. (NE25)-2E 11
HORDEN. (SR8)-2E 135
Horsley Hill.-4C 52
HOUGHTON-LE-SPRING. (DH4 & DH5)
-4C 126
Howdon.-1C 48
Hylton Castle.-3E 97
Hylton Red House.-3B 98

JARROW. (NE32)-5D 49
JESMOND. (NE2)-4A 44
Jesmond Vale.-5C 44

KENTON. (NE3)-1A 42
KENTON BANK FOOT. (NE13)-3D 25
Kenton Bar.-1B 41
Killingworth Township.-3F 17
KILLINGWORTH VILLAGE. (NE12)5F 17
KINGSTON PARK. (NE3)-4E 25

Lady Park.-3B 90
Lambton.-5F 103
LAMESLEY. (NE11)-5C 90
Lawe, The.-5E 35
Leam Lane Estate.-5F 81

LEMINGTON. (NE15)-1C 56
Lockhaugh.-5F 73
LONGBENTON. (NE7 & NE12)-4E 29
Lookout Hill.-4D 101
Lowe's Barn.-4A 138
LOW FELL. (NE9)-5E 79
Low Southwick.-4F 99
Lyndhurst.-1E 91

Marden.-4C 22
Marley Pots.-2D 99
Marsden.-1A 70 & 2E 71
Merryoaks.-5A 138
Middle Herrington.-3A 118
MIDDLE RAINTON. (DH4)-5A 128
MIDDLES, THE. (DH9)-5E 131
Millfield.-1E 109
MONKSEATON. (NE25 & NE26)-2F 21
Monkton.-4F 65
MONKWEARMOUTH. (SR5)-4B 100
Moor End.-2C 140
MOORSIDE. (SR3)-5C 118
Mount Pleasant.-1F 79
  (Gateshead)
Mount Pleasant.-2E 115
  (Sunderland)

NELSON VILLAGE. (NE23)-2A 4
Neville's Cross.-3A 138
Newbiggin Hall Estate.-5B 24
NEWBOTTLE. (DH4)-2C 126
NEWBURN. (NE15)-5B 38
NEWCASTLE UPON TYNE. (NE1 to NE7,
NE12, NE13, NE15, NE18 to NE20 &
NE27)-2C 60
NEW HERRINGTON. (DH4)-4C 116
NEW LAMBTON. (DH4)-3D 125
NEW SILKSWORTH. (SR3)-3D 119
Newton Hall.-2C 137
New Town.-2E 85
  (South Tyneside)
New Town.-5E 127
  (Sunderland)
New York.-1C 32
North End.-1A 138
NORTH HYLTON. (SR5)-1E 107
North Lodge.-3B 112
NORTH SHIELDS. (NE29 & NE30)-4C 34
Northside.-2C 102
Nuns Moor.-3A 42

Offerton.-4D 107
Old Durham.-3F 139
Old Fold.-5A 62
Oxclose.-3F 103
OXHILL. (DH9)-3B 130

Palmersville.-1B 30
Parkside.-5D 133
PELAW. (NE10)-1F 81
PELTON FELL. (DH2)-2A 122
Pennywell.-3F 107
PENSHAW. (SR4)-3A 116
PERCY MAIN. (NE29)-2F 49
PETERLEE. (SR8)-4C 134
PHILADELPHIA. (DH4)-5B 116
PICKTREE. (NE38)-3C 112
PITY ME. (DH1)-2B 136
Plains Farm.-5D 109
Portmeads.-4C 102
PRESTON. (NE29)-2B 34
Preston Grange.-5F 21
Primrose.-4A 66
Primrose Hill.-3C 124

Redheugh.-5B 60
RICKLETON. (NE38)-2D 113
Roker.-2D 101
RYHOPE. (SR2)-4E 121
Ryhope Colliery.-2C 120
RYTON. (NE40)-2B 54
RYTON WOODSIDE. (NE40)-4A 54

St Anthony's.-4D 63
St Lawrence.-2A 62
St Peter's.-3B 62
SCOTSWOOD. (NE15)-2F 57
SEAHAM. (SR7)-2F 133
SEATON BURN. (NE13)-4A 6
SEATON DELAVAL. (NE25)-1B 10

Seaton Terrace.-1C 10
SEDGELETCH. (DH4)-3F 125
SEGHILL. (NE23)-3E 9
SHERBURN. (DH6)-4F 141
SHERIFF HILL. (NE29)-4F 79
SHIELDFIELD. (NE2)-1D 61
SHIELD ROW. (DH9)-1D 131
SHINCLIFFE. (DH1)-5F 139
SHINEY ROW. (DH4)-4F 115
Shipcote.-2D 79
SHIREMOOR. (NE27)-4B 20
SILKSWORTH. (SR3)-4D 119
Simonside.-3E 66
South Bents.-3D 89
South Boldon.-3F 85
SOUTH GOSFORTH. (NE3)-5F 27
SOUTH HYLTON. (SR4)-1F 107
SOUTH MOOR. (DH9)-4A 130
SOUTH PELAW. (DH2)-5A 112
SOUTH SHIELDS. (NE33 & NE34)-1E 51
South Stanley.-4C 130
SOUTH WELLFIELD. (NE25)-2D 21
SOUTHWICK. (SR5)-3F 99
SPITAL TONGUES. (NE2)-5D 43
SPRINGWELL. (NE9)-4E 93
Springwell Estate.-1C 92
STANLEY. (DH9)-2C 130
Stargate.-3D 55
Stella.-3F 55
Success.-1A 126
Sulgrave.-4D 95
SUNDERLAND. (SR1 to SR6)-1B 110
SUNNISIDE. (DH4)-3B 126
SWALWELL. (NE16)-1F 75

TANFIELD LEA. (DH9)-1A 130
Teams.-2A 78
Team Valley.-1C 90
Thorney Close.-1B 118
THROCKLEY. (NE15)-2F 37
Town Centre.-2A 104
Town Moor.-4E 43
Tunstall.-3A 120
Tunstall Hills.-1A 120
Tyne Dock.-5C 50
TYNEMOUTH. (NE30)-2F 35

Usworth.-3A 94

Vigo.-5C 102

Waldridge.-5A 122
WALKER. (NE6)-2E 63
WALKERGATE. (NE6)-4A 46
Wallbottle.-3B 38
WALLSEND. (NE28)-3D 47
WARDLEY. (NE10)-2B 82
WASHINGTON. (NE37 & NE38)-1D 105
Washington Staithes.-4F 105
Washington Village.-2B 104
Watergate Estate.-4B 76
Wear.-5F 103
Welburn Park.-3B 44
WEST ALLOTMENT. (NE27)-5F 19
WEST BOLDON. (NE36)-3E 85
West Chirton.-5F 33
WEST DENTON. (NE5 & NE15)-3F 39
WESTERHOPE. (NE5)-2B 40
Western Hill.-1B 138
West Harton.-2A 68
WEST HERRINGTON. (DH4)-3E 117
West Monkseaton.-3E 21
Westoe.-4F 51
Whickham.-3F 75
WHITBURN. (SR6)-1D 89
Whitburn Colliery.-4E 71
Whitehill.-3A 122
Whitehills.-5D 81
Whiteleas.-5B 68
Whitesmocks.-5A 136
WHITLEY BAY. (NE25 & NE26)-2C 22
Wide Open.-1D 15
Willington.-1B 48
WILLINGTON QUAY. (NE28)-3C 48
WINDY NOOK. (NE10)-4B 80
WINLATON. (NE21)-1F 73
Witherwack.-1D 99
WOODSTONE VILLAGE. (DH4)-4C 124
WOOLSINGTON. (NE13)-2A 24
WREKENTON. (NE9)-2B 92

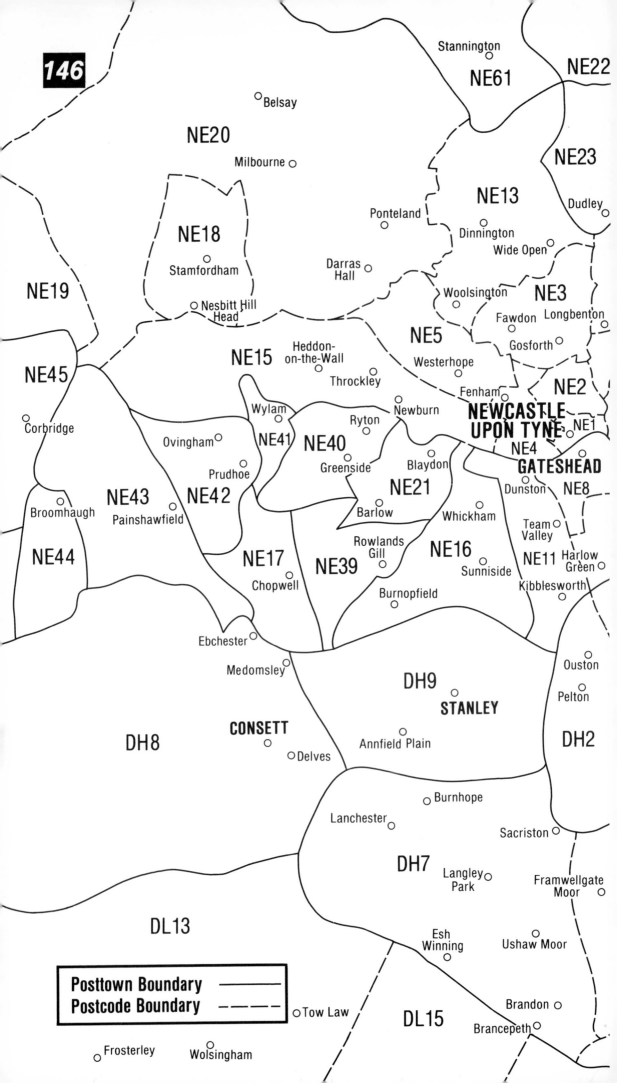

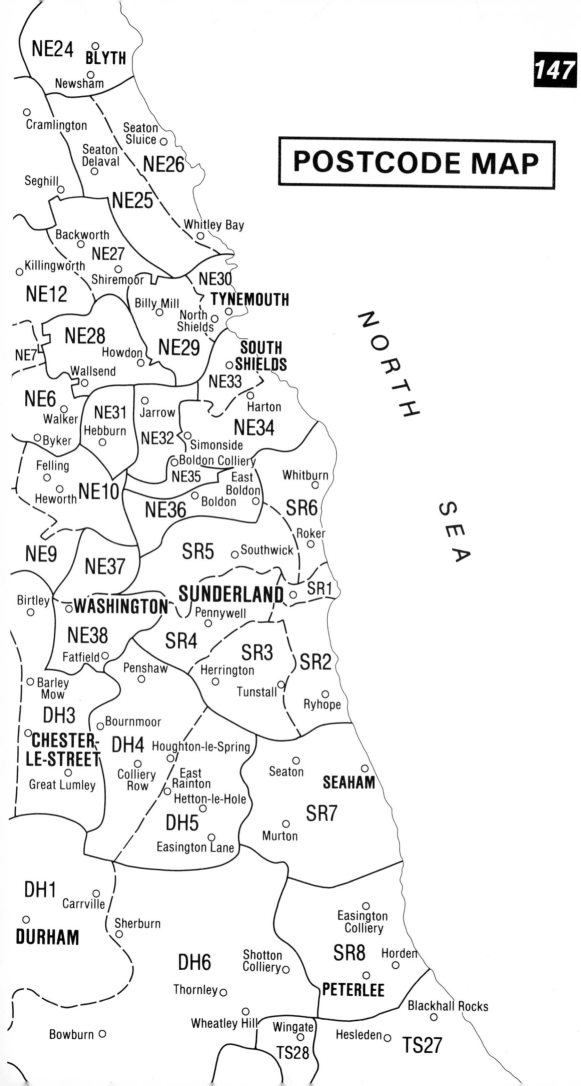

POSTCODE MAP

NE24 **BLYTH**
Newsham

Cramlington
Seaton Sluice
Seaton Delaval
NE26
Seghill
NE25
Whitley Bay
Backworth
NE27
Killingworth
Shiremoor
NE12
NE30
Billy Mill
TYNEMOUTH
North Shields
NE28
Howdon
NE29
SOUTH SHIELDS
NE7
Wallsend
NE33
NE6
Harton
Walker
NE31
Jarrow
NE34
Byker
Hebburn
NE32
Simonside
Felling
Boldon Colliery
NE10
NE35
East Boldon
Whitburn
Heworth
NE36
Boldon
SR6
NE9
SR5
Roker
NE37
Southwick
SR1
Birtley
WASHINGTON
SUNDERLAND
Pennywell
NE38
SR4
SR3
SR2
Fatfield
Penshaw
Herrington
Barley Mow
Tunstall
Ryhope
DH3
Bournmoor
CHESTER-LE-STREET
DH4
Houghton-le-Spring
Great Lumley
Colliery Row
East Rainton
Seaton
SEAHAM
Hetton-le-Hole
SR7
DH5
Murton
Easington Lane
DH1
Carrville
Easington Colliery
Sherburn
DURHAM
SR8
Horden
DH6
Shotton Colliery
Thornley
PETERLEE
Blackhall Rocks
Bowburn
Wheatley Hill
Wingate
Hesleden
TS27
TS28

NORTH SEA

INDEX TO STREETS

HOW TO USE THIS INDEX

1. Each street name is followed by its Postal District and then by its map page reference; e.g. Abbay St. SR5-3E 99 is in the Sunderland 5 Postal District and it is to be found in square 3E on page 99. However, with the now general usage of Postal Coding, it is not recommended that this index should be used as a means of addressing mail.

2. A strict alphabetical order is followed in which Av., Rd., St. etc. (even though abbreviated) are read in full and as part of the street name; e.g. Abbots Rd. appears after Abbotside Pl. but before Abbots Row.

3. Streets & Subsidiary names not shown on the Maps, appear in the Index in *Italics* with the thoroughfare to which it is connected shown in brackets; e.g. *Algernon Ct. NE6-5D 45 (off Algernon Rd.)*

4. The Postcode for any Town or locality used in Postal addresses can be found in the Index to Places on page 145.

GENERAL ABBREVIATIONS

All : Alley
App : Approach
Arc : Arcade
Av : Avenue
Bk : Back
Boulevd : Boulevard
Bri : Bridge
B'way : Broadway
Bldgs : Buildings
Bus : Business
Cen : Centre
Chu : Church
Chyd : Churchyard
Circ : Circle
Cir : Circus
Clo : Close
Comn : Common
Cotts : Cottages
Ct : Court
Cres : Crescent
Dri : Drive
E : East
Embkmt : Embankment
Est : Estate
Gdns : Gardens
Ga : Gate
Gt : Great
Grn : Green
Gro : Grove
Ho : House
Ind : Industrial
Junct : Junction
La : Lane
Lit : Little
Lwr : Lower
Mnr : Manor
Mans : Mansions
Mkt : Market
M : Mews
Mt : Mount
N : North
Pal : Palace
Pde : Parade
Pk : Park
Pas : Passage
Pl : Place
Rd : Road
S : South
Sq : Square
Sta : Station
St : Street
Ter : Terrace
Up : Upper
Vs : Villas
Wlk : Walk
W : West
Yd : Yard

Abbay St. SR5-3E 99
Abbey Clo. NE25-3F 21
Abbey Clo. NE38-2B 104
Abbey Ct. NE8-1E 79
Abbey Dri. DH4-3A 126
Abbey Dri. NE5-1C 38
Abbey Dri. NE30-1E 35
Abbey Dri. NE32-5E 49
Abbey Rd. DH1-1B 136
Abbey Rd. NE38-2C 104
Abbey Rd. Ind. Est. DH1 -1C 136
Abbey Ter. NE27-3A 20
Abbeyvale Dri. NE6-1F 63
Abbeywoods. DH1-1C 136
Abbeywoods Bus. Pk. DH1 -1C 136
Abbot Ct. NE8-4E 61
Abbotsfield Clo. SR3-5D 119
Abbotsford Gro. SR2-2A 110
Abbotsford Pk. NE25-3B 22
Abbotsford Rd. NE10-1C 80 (in two parts)
Abbotsford Ter. NE2-4F 43
Abbotside Pl. NE5-3E 39
Abbots Rd. NE8-3D 61
Abbots Row. DH1-1F 139
Abbots Way. NE16-2A 76
Abbots Way. NE29-1F 33
Abbotsway. NE32-1C 66
Abbs St. SR5-4B 100
Abemarle Av. NE2-1F 43
Abercorn Pl. NE28-4A 32
Abercorn Rd. NE15-2E 57
Abercorn Rd. SR3-2C 118
Abercrombie Pl. NE5-2D 41
Aberdare Rd. SR3-3C 118
Aberdeen Ct. NE3-2E 25
Aberdeen Dri. NE32-4C 66
Aberdeen Tower. SR3 -3D 119
Aberfoyle Ct. DH9-2E 131
Abersford Clo. NE5-1C 38
Abingdon Ct. NE3-3F 25
Abingdon Ct. NE21-4B 56
Abingdon Rd. NE6-5D 47
Abingdon Sq. NE23-1E 5
Abingdon St. SR4-2E 109
Abingdon Way. NE36 & NE35 -3D 85
Abinger St. NE4 -2A 60 & 4A 142
Aboyne Sq. SR3-2C 118
Acacia Av. DH4-4E 125
Acacia Av. SR8-3F 135
Acacia Gro. NE31-3D 65
Acacia Gro. NE34-2D 69
Acacia Rd. NE10-5A 62
Acacia St. NE11-5B 78
Acanthus Av. NE4-5F 41
Acer Ct. SR2-3C 110
Acklam Av. SR2-1E 121
Acomb Av. NE25-2B 10
Acomb Av. NE28-3F 31
Acomb Ct. NE9-3F 91
Acomb Ct. NE12-4E 17
Acomb Ct. SR2-1E 121
Acomb Cres. NE3-2B 26
Acomb Gdns. NE5-4E 41
Acorn Av. NE8-2A 78
Acorn Pl. DH1-1B 136
Acorn Rd. NE2-3A 44
Acorn St. NE11-5B 78
Acre Rigg Rd. SR8-2A 134
Acton Dene. DH9-2F 131
Acton Dri. NE29-2F 33
Acton Pl. NE7-2D 45
Acton Rd. NE5-4B 40
Adair Av. NE15-1B 58
Adamson St. SR4-4D 99
Adam St. SR8-3F 135
Ada St. NE6-1D 63
Ada St. NE33-4F 51
Adderstone Av. NE23-4D 5
Adderstone Cres. NE2-2A 44
Adderstone Gdns. NE29 -1D 33
Addington Cres. NE29-4A 34
Addington Dri. NE28-3F 31
Addison Clo. NE6-1A 62
Addison Ct. NE28-3C 48
Addison Gdns. NE10-2A 82
Addison Ind. Est. NE21 -2E 55
Addison Rd. NE6-1A 62
Addison Rd. NE15-5E 39
Addison Rd. NE36-3E 85
Addison St. NE29-5C 34
Addison St. SR2-2D 111
Addison Wlk. NE34-4F 67
Addycombe Ter. NE6-3E 45
Adelaide Clo. SR1-1D 111
Adelaide Ct. NE8-4D 61
Adelaide Ho. NE4-2D 59
Adelaide Pl. SR1-1D 111
Adelaide Row. SR7-3E 133
Adelaide St. DH3-3E 123
Adelaide Ter. NE4-3C 58
Adeline Gdns. NE3-2C 42
Adelphi Clo. NE29-2D 33
Adelphi Pl. NE6-2D 63
Aden Tower. SR3-2D 119
Adfrid Pl. SR8-2C 134
Admiral Ho. NE30-3E 35
Adolphus Pl. DH1-4B 140
Adolphus St. SR6-1E 89
Adolphus St. W. SR7-3E 133
Adrian Pl. SR8-4D 135
Affleck St. NE8-5D 61
Afton Ct. NE34-2A 68
Afton Way. NE3-4A 26
Agar Rd. SR3-2C 118
Aged Miners Homes. DH2 -1D 123
Aged Miners Homes. DH6 -4F 141
Aged Miners Homes. NE13 -1C 14
Aged Miners Homes. NE27 -2E 19
Agincourt. NE12-3E 17
Agincourt. NE31-5F 47
Agnes Maria St. NE3-4C 26
Agnes St. DH9-2C 130
Agricola Ct. NE33-5E 35
Agricola Gdns. NE28-3F 31
Agricola Rd. NE4-1E 59
Aidan Clo. DH9-2E 131
Aidan Clo. NE13-1C 14
Aidan Ct. NE32-1C 66
Aidan Ho. NE8-5E 61
Aidan Wlk. NE3-4F 27
Aiden Way. DH5-3E 129
Ailesbury St. SR4-1F 109
Ainderby Rd. NE15-2D 37
Ainsdale Gdns. NE5-3E 39
Ainsley St. DH1-2B 138
Ainslie Pl. NE5-3D 41
Ainsworth Av. NE34-4F 67
Ainthorpe Clo. SR3-4A 120
Ainthorpe Gdns. NE7-5D 29
Ainthorpe Gdns. NE9-5E 79
Aintree Clo. NE37-5C 94
Aintree Gdns. NE8-2B 78
Aintree Rd. SR3-2C 118
Ainwick Ct. NE38-2F 103
Airedale. NE28-5B 30
Airedale Gdns. DH5-5E 129
Aireys Clo. DH4-5A 126
Airey Ter. NE6-2E 63
Airport Ind. Est. NE3-4E 25
Airy Ter. NE8-1C 78
Aisgill Clo. NE23-3D 5
Aisgill Dri. NE5-3E 39
Aiskell St. SR4-1F 109
Akeld Clo. NE23-4D 5
Akeld Ct. NE3-1F 43
Akeman Way. NE34-2A 68
Akenside Hill. NE1 -3D 61 & 5E 143
Akenside Ter. NE2-4A 44
Alamein Av. DH5-5E 127
Alanbrooke Row. NE31 -4B 64
Albany Av. NE12-2E 29
Albany Ct. NE4-4E 59
Albany Gdns. NE26-2D 23
Albany Ho. NE37-1A 104
Albany Ho. SR5-4B 100
Albany M. NE3-2B 42
Albany Rd. NE8-4F 61
Albany St. E. NE33-4F 51
Albany St. W. NE33-4E 51
Albany Ter. NE32-3E 65
Albany Way. NE37-1A 104
Albemarle St. NE33-2E 51
Albert Av. NE28-2C 46
Albert Dri. NE9-5D 79
Albert Edward Ter. NE35 -5D 67
Albert Pl. NE9-5E 79
Albert Pl. NE38-4D 105
Albert Rd. NE32-1F 65
Albert Rd. SR4-1F 109
Albert Rd. Diversion. NE32 -1F 65
Albert St. DH1-1B 138
Albert St. DH3-3E 123
Albert St. DH9-2C 130
Albert St. NE2 -1D 61 & 3F 143
Albert St. NE31-1B 64 (in two parts)
Albert St. SR7-4F 133
Albert Ter. NE12-5E 17
Albert Ter. NE26-3D 23
Albert Ter. NE33-2E 51
Albion Ct. NE6-2F 61
Albion Ct. NE33-1D 51
Albion Pl. SR1-2B 110
Albion Rd. NE29 & NE30 -4B 34
Albion Rd. W. NE29-4B 34
Albion Row. NE6 -2F 61 & 1F 61
Albion St. NE10-3B 80
Albion St. SR4-1E 107
Albion Ter. NE9-3D 93
Albion Ter. NE29-4C 34
Albion Yd. NE1 -2B 60 & 4C 142
Albury Pk. Rd. NE30-2E 35
Albury Pl. NE16-5E 75
Albury Rd. NE2-1F 43
Albyn Gdns. SR3-4F 109
Alcroft Clo. NE5-1C 38
Aldbrough St. NE34-2F 67
Aldeburgh Av. NE15-4E 39
Aldenham Gdns. NE30-1E 35
Aldenham Rd. SR3-2D 119
Aldenham Tower. SR3 -2D 119
Alder Av. NE4-4F 41
Alder Clo. DH5-4E 129
Alder Ct. NE25-2A 22
Alder Gro. NE25-1A 22
Alder Lea Clo. DH1-3A 140
Alderley Clo. NE35-1C 84
Alderley Dri. NE12-3A 18
Alderley Rd. NE9-5D 79
Alderley Way. NE23-1E 5
Alderman Wood Rd. DH9 -1B 130
Alderney Gdns. NE5-3E 39
Alder Rd. NE28-4A 32
Alder Rd. NE29-2C 32
Alder Rd. SR8-3F 135
Aldershot Rd. SR3-4B 118
Aldershot Sq. SR3-4C 118
Alder St. NE11-5B 78
Alder St. SR5-4A 98
Alderwood. NE8-1C 78
Alderwood. NE38-2F 113
Alderwood Cres. NE6-3B 46
Alderwyk. NE10-4A 82
Aldsworth Clo. NE9-3E 93
Aldwick Rd. NE15-1B 56
Aldwych Dri. NE29-2D 33
Aldwych Rd. SR3-4B 118
Aldwych Sq. SR3-4B 118
Aldwych St. NE33-3A 52
Alexander Dri. DH5-4E 129
Alexander Ter. NE13-2C 14
Alexander Ter. SR6-2C 100
Alexandra Clo. DH1-3A 136
Alexandra Cres. DH1-3B 138
Alexandra Dri. NE16-2A 76
Alexandra Gdns. NE40-3D 55
Alexandra Pk. SR3-4A 110
Alexandra Rd. NE6-3D 45
Alexandra Rd. NE8-5D 61
Alexandra St. NE28-3E 47
Alexandra Ter. DH4-2A 116
Alexandra Ter. NE5-1B 40
Alexandra Ter. NE9-5E 93
Alexandra Ter. NE26-3D 23
Alexandra Way. NE23-4C 4
Alexandrina St. SR7-3F 133
Alford Grn. NE12-3E 29
Alfred St. NE6-1C 62
Alfred St. NE31-2B 64
Alfred St. SR7-4F 133
Alfred St. E. SR7-4F 133
Algernon Clo. NE6-1A 62
Algernon Ct. NE6-5D 45 (off Algernon Rd.)
Algernon Ind. Est. NE27 -1B 32
Algernon Pl. NE26-3D 23
Algernon Rd. NE6-1B 62
Algernon Rd. NE15-1B 56
Algernon Ter. NE30-2D 35
Algiers Rd. SR3-3B 118
Alice St. NE21-5A 56
Alice St. NE33-4D 51
Alice St. SR2-5E 121 (Ryhope)
Alice St. SR2-2B 110 (Sunderland)
Alice Well Vs. SR4-5F 105
Aline St. SR3-3F 119
Aline St. SR7-3F 133
Alington Pl. DH1-4A 140
Alison Dri. NE36-3B 86
Allandale Av. NE12-2E 29
Allanville. NE12-2D 17
Allchurch. NE15-1A 58
Allen Av. NE11-3B 78
Allendale Av. NE28-5D 31
Allendale Cres. DH4-2F 115
Allendale Cres. NE27-4B 20
Allendale Dri. NE34-4C 52
Allendale Pl. NE30-2F 35
Allendale Rd. NE6-2B 62
Allendale Rd. SR3-4B 118
Allendale Sq. SR3-2C 118
Allendale St. DH5-5E 129
Allendale Ter. NE6-2E 63
Allenheads. NE5-3A 40
Allenheads. NE38-1D 115
Allen Ho. NE1 -2D 61 & 4F 143
Allens Grn. NE23-3D 5
Allen St. DH3-4E 123
Allerdean Clo. NE15-5C 38
Allerdean Clo. NE25-2C 10
Allerdene Wlk. NE16-3F 75
Allergate. DH1-2B 138
Allergate Ter. DH1-2B 138
Allerhope. NE23-4D 5
Allerton Gdns. NE6-3F 45
Allerton Pl. NE16-4E 75
Allerwash. NE5-3A 40
All Hallows La. NE1-3D 61
Allhallows Lodge. NE1 -3D 61 & 5E 143
Allhusen Ter. NE8-1A 80
Alliance Pl. SR4-5A 100
Alliance St. SR4-5A 100
Allingham Ct. NE7-2F 45
Allison Ct. NE11-5A 58
Alloa Rd. SR3-2C 118
Allonby Way. NE5-4D 41
All Saints Ct. NE29-4E 33
All Saints Dri. DH5-2E 129
Allwork Ter. NE16-3A 76
Alma Pl. DH1-3B 140
Alma Pl. DH4-5A 116
Alma Pl. NE26-3D 23
Alma Pl. NE29-3B 34
Alma St. SR4-1F 107
Alma Ter. DH1-3A 138 (off Neville's Cross Bank)
Alma Ter. NE40-5A 54
Almond Cres. NE8-2A 78
Almond Dri. SR5-4F 97
Almond Pl. NE4-5F 41
Almond St. NE11-5B 78
Almond Ter. SR8-3F 135
Almoners Barn. DH1-4B 138
Almshouses. NE15-5B 38
Aln Av. NE3-3C 26
Aln Ct. NE15-1B 56
Aln Cres. NE3-3B 26
Aln Gro. NE15-1A 56
Alnham Ct. NE3-3A 26
Alnham Grn. NE5-3E 39
Alnmouth Av. NE29-5F 33
Alnmouth Dri. NE3-1F 43
Aln St. NE31-2C 64
Aln Wlk. NE3-3C 26
Alnwick Av. NE26-2B 22
Alnwick Av. NE29-5E 33
Alnwick Clo. DH2-5B 122
Alnwick Clo. NE16-3E 75
Alnwick Ct. NE38-2F 103
Alnwick Gro. NE32-5F 65
Alnwick Rd. DH1-2C 136
Alnwick Rd. NE34-1A 68
Alnwick Rd. SR3-2C 118
Alnwick Sq. SR3-2C 118
Alnwick St. NE15-4A 38
Alnwick St. NE28-2E 47
Alnwick St. SR8-1E 135
Alnwick Ter. NE13-5A 6
Alpine Gro. NE36-3F 85
Alpine Way. SR3-5E 109
Alresford. NE12-3F 17
Alston Av. NE6-1D 63
Alston Av. NE23-4F 5
Alston Clo. NE28-5C 32
Alston Clo. NE29-2D 33
Alston Cres. SR6-5A 88
Alston Gdns. NE15-2F 37
Alston Rd. NE38-2F 105
Alston St. NE8-1B 78
Alston Wlk. DH6-5F 141
Altan Pl. NE12-2D 29
Altree Grange. SR5-1A 100
Altrincham Tower. SR3 -3D 119
Alumwell Rd. NE9-5D 79 (in two parts)
Alverston Clo. NE15-4E 39
Alverstone Av. NE9-5D 79
Alverstone Rd. SR3-3B 118
Alverthorpe St. NE33-5E 51
Alwin. NE38-1E 113
Alwin Grange. NE31-5B 48
Alwinton Av. NE29-2F 33
Alwinton Clo. NE5-1C 40
Alwinton Dri. DH2-4B 122
Alwinton Gdns. NE11-5E 77
Alwinton Rd. NE27-4B 20
Alwinton Ter. NE3-4E 27
Alwyn Clo. DH4-2C 124
Amalfi Tower. SR3-3D 119
Amara Sq. SR3-2C 118
Ambassadors Way. NE29 -2D 33
Amberley. NE12-4F 17
Amberley Chase. NE12-3F 17
Amberley Ct. NE8-1A 78 (off Amberley St.)
Amberley Gdns. NE7-2E 45
Amberley Gro. NE16-4F 75
Amberley St. NE8-1A 78
Amberley St. SR2-2C 110
Amberley St. S. SR2-2D 111
Amberley Wlk. NE16-5F 75
Amble Av. NE25-3D 23
Amble Av. NE34-4C 52
Amble Gro. NE2 -5B 44 & 1F 143
Amble Pl. NE12-1A 30
Ambleside. NE15-2F 37
Ambleside Av. NE34-1C 68
Ambleside Av. SR7-2A 132
Ambleside Clo. NE25-1C 10
Ambleside Clo. SR8-3D 135
Ambleside Gdns. NE9-1F 91
Ambleside Grn. NE5-4C 40
Ambleside Ter. SR6-5B 88
Amble Tower. SR3-3D 119
Amble Way. NE3-3D 27
Ambridge Way. NE3-4A 26
Ambrose Pl. NE6-1A 64
Ambrose Rd. SR3-2B 118
Amec Way. NE28-3F 47
Amelia Clo. NE4-4D 59
Amelia Gdns. SR3-4A 118
Amelia Wlk. NE4-4C 58
Amersham Cres. SR8-2B 134
Amersham Pl. NE5-2D 41
Amesbury Clo. NE5-1C 38
Amethyst Rd. NE4-4E 59
Amethyst St. SR4-5D 99
Amherst Rd. NE3-3F 25
Amos Ayre Pl. NE34-2D 67
Amy St. SR5-3A 100
Ancaster Av. NE12-3C 28
Ancaster Rd. NE16-4E 75
Anchorage Ter. DH1-4D 139
Anchorage, The. DH3-2E 123
Anchorage, The. DH4-4A 116
Ancona St. SR4-5D 99
Ancroft Av. NE29-3B 34
Ancroft Pl. NE5-5D 41
Ancroft Rd. NE25-1A 10
Ancroft Way. NE3-2A 26
Ancrum St. NE2-5C 42
Ancrum Way. NE16-5E 75
Anderson St. N. NE33-1E 51
Anderson St. NE33-1E 51
Andover Pl. NE28-4A 32
Andrew Rd. SR3-3B 118
Anfield Ct. NE3-4A 26
Anfield Rd. NE3-4F 25
Angerton Av. NE27-4B 20
Angerton Av. NE30-1C 34
Angerton Gdns. NE5-4E 41
Angerton Ter. NE23-4E 7
Anglesey Gdns. NE5-3E 39
Anglesey Pl. NE4-2F 59
Anglesey Rd. SR3-3C 118
Anglesey Sq. SR3-3C 118
Angle Ter. NE28-2A 48
Angram Dri. SR2-1E 121
Angram Wlk. NE5-3E 39
Angrove Gdns. SR4-2E 109
Angus Clo. NE12-3D 17
Angus Ho. NE4-3C 58
Angus Rd. NE8-2A 78
Angus Sq. SR3-3B 118
Annard Rd. DH1-1F 139
Ann Clo. SR1-2D 111
Anne Dri. NE12-1B 30
Annfield Plain By-Pass. DH9 -5A 130
Annie St. SR6-1C 100
Annitsford Dri. NE23-4A 8
Ann St. NE8-5D 61
Ann St. NE21-4B 56
Ann St. NE27-3A 20
Ann St. SR7-3F 133
Ann Wlk. NE6-3F 63
Anscomb Gdns. NE7-2B 44
Anson Clo. NE33-4D 51
Anson Pl. NE5-1B 40
Anson St. NE8-1A 80
Anstead Clo. NE23-3D 5
Anthony Rd. SR3 -2C 118 & 3B 118
Anthony St. DH9-2C 130
Antonine Wlk. NE15-2B 36
Anton Pl. NE23-4D 5
Antrim Clo. NE5-1E 41
Antrim Gdns. SR7-2E 133
Antwerp Rd. SR3-3B 118
Apperley. NE5-3F 39
Apperley Av. NE3-1E 41
Appian Pl. NE9-3F 79
Appian Pl. NE15-3F 37 (in two parts)
Appleby Ct. NE29-4B 34
Appleby Gdns. NE9-1F 91
Appleby Gdns. NE28-5B 32
Appleby Pk. NE29-3A 34
Appleby Rd. SR3-3B 118
Appleby Sq. SR3-3B 118
Appleby St. NE29-1C 50
Appleby Way. SR8-5A 134
Apple Clo. NE15-4E 39
Appledore Gdns. DH3-1E 123
Appledore Gdns. NE9-1E 91
Appleforth Av. SR2-1E 121
Appletree Gdns. NE6-4A 46
Appletree Gdns. NE25 -3A 22 & 4A 22
Applewood. NE12-4B 18
Appley Ter. SR6-3D 101
Apsley Cres. NE3-4A 26
Aquila Dri. NE15-3A 36
Arbroath Rd. SR3-3C 118
Arcadia Av. DH3-1E 123
Archbold Ter. NE2 -5A 44 & 1E 143
Archer Rd. SR3-3B 118
Archer's Hill. NE33-3C 50
Archer Sq. SR3-3B 118
Archer St. NE28-2F 47
Archer St. E. NE28-2B 48
Archer Vs. NE28-2F 47
Archery Rise. DH1-3B 138
Archibald St. NE3-4D 27
Arcot Av. NE23-1A 4 & 2A 4
Arcot Av. NE25-4F 21
Arcot Dri. NE5-4A 40
Arcot Dri. NE25-4F 21
Arcot La. NE23-1B 6
Arden Av. NE3-5D 15
Arden Clo. NE28-2F 31
Arden Cres. NE5-3E 41
Arden Ho. NE3-4E 27
Arden Sq. SR3-2C 118
Ardrossan Rd. SR3-3C 118
Argyle Ct. DH9-1D 131
Argyle Ho. SR2-3A 110
Argyle Pl. NE29-2B 34
Argyle Sq. SR2-2B 110
Argyle St. NE1 -2D 61 & 3E 143
Argyle St. NE30-2F 35
Argyle St. NE31-1C 64
Argyle St. SR2-2B 110
Argyle Ter. NE29-2B 34
Arklecrag. NE37-1A 104
Arkle Rd. SR3-3B 118
Arkleside Pl. NE5-3E 39
Arkle St. NE8-2B 78
Arkle St. NE13-3C 14
Arkwright St. NE8-3C 78
Arlington Av. NE3-1B 42
Arlington Clo. DH4-2C 124
Arlington Gro. NE16-4F 75
Arlington Rd. NE31-3D 65
Arlington St. SR4-1D 109
Arlott Ho. NE29-1F 49
Armitage Gdns. NE9-4A 92
Armstrong Av. NE34-1D 69
Armstrong Av. NE6-3D 45
Armstrong Cen. NE4-4F 59
Armstrong Dri. NE12-5D 17
Armstrong Ho. NE37-1F 103
Armstrong Ind. Est. NE37 -5E 93
Armstrong Rd. NE15 & NE4 -2E 57 to 3D 59
Armstrong Rd. NE28-3C 48
Armstrong Rd. NE37-1E 103
Armstrong Rd. SR8-1C 134 (in three parts)
Armstrong St. NE8-3B 78
Armstrong Ter. NE33-5E 51
Arncliffe Av. SR4-4D 109
Arncliffe Gdns. NE5-3E 39
Arndale Arc. NE32-5D 49
Arndale Ho. NE3-5A 26
Arndale Ho. NE12-4C 28
Arndale Ho. NE32-5D 49
Arndale Sq. NE12-3C 28 (off Greyfriars La.)
Arngrove Ct. NE4 -2A 60 & 3A 142
Arnham Gro. SR4-5E 107
Arniston Retail Cen. DH1 -1C 136
Arnold Clo. DH9-2D 131
Arnold Rd. SR3-2B 118
Arnold St. NE35-2D 85
Arnside Wlk. NE5-3D 39
Arran Ct. SR3-4E 119
Arran Dri. NE32-4C 66
Arran Gdns. NE10-3A 80
Arran Pl. NE29-1D 33
Arras La. SR1-1D 111
Arrol Pk. SR4-1F 109
Arrow Clo. NE12-5D 17
Arthington Way. NE34-2C 68
Arthur Av. SR2-4E 121
Arthur Cook Av. NE16-4B 76
Arthur St. NE8-5D 61
Arthur St. NE32-1F 65
Arthur St. SR2-4F 121
Arthur St. SR6-3D 71
Arthur Ter. SR6-4D 71
Arts Cen., The. NE1 -2E 61 & 5F 143
Arun Clo. SR8-4B 134
Arundel Clo. NE13-2B 14
Arundel Ct. NE3-2E 25
Arundel Dri. NE15-5A 40
Arundel Dri. NE25-2D 21
Arundel Gdns. NE9-4F 79
Arundel Gdns. SR3-4B 118
Arundel Rd. SR3-2B 118
Arundel Wlk. NE16-4F 75
Asama Ct. NE4-5E 59
Ascot Clo. NE28-4F 31
Ascot Ct. NE3-2E 25
Ascot Ct. SR3-3C 118
Ascot Cres. NE8-2B 78
Ascot Gdns. NE34-1B 68
Ascot Wlk. NE3-2D 25
Ash Av. DH1-4A 140
Ashberry Gro. SR6-3C 100
Ashbourne Av. NE6-1E 63
Ashbourne Clo. NE27-2E 19
Ashbourne Rd. NE32-2B 66
Ashbridge Clo. NE34-2F 69
Ashbrooke. NE25-2F 21
Ashbrooke Clo. NE25-2F 21
Ashbrooke Cres. SR2-3B 110
Ashbrooke Gdns. NE28-2A 48
Ashbrooke Mt. SR2-3B 110
Ashbrooke Range. SR2 -5B 110
Ashbrooke Rd. SR2-4B 110
Ashbrooke St. NE3-1A 42
Ashbrooke Ter. NE36-3C 86
Ashbrooke Ter. SR2-3B 110
Ashburne Ct. SR2-3C 110
Ashburn Rd. NE28-3F 31
Ashburton Rd. NE3-1C 42
Ashbury. NE25-1E 21
Ashby St. SR2-4D 111
Ash Cres. SR7-5E 133
Ash Cres. SR8-3F 135
Ashcroft Dri. NE12-2A 30
Ashdale. DH4-2D 115
Ashdale Cres. NE5-3E 39
Ashdown Av. DH1-3B 140
Ashdown Clo. NE12-3D 29
Ashdown Rd. SR3-2B 118
Ashdown Way. NE12-3D 29
Asher St. NE10-1A 80
Ashfield. NE32-1B 84
Ashfield Av. NE16-2A 76
Ashfield Clo. NE4-3F 59
Ashfield Gdns. NE28-1B 46
Ashfield Gro. NE26-5E 13
Ashfield Gro. NE29-4B 34
Ashfield Rise. NE16-4A 76
Ashfield Rd. NE3-1C 42
Ashfield Rd. NE16-5A 76
Ashfield Ter. DH3-3E 123
Ashfield Ter. NE9-3D 93
Ashfield Ter. NE10-1E 81
Ashfield Ter. NE40-2B 54
Ashford. NE9-3E 91
Ashford Clo. NE29-1B 34
Ashford Gro. NE5-1C 38
Ashford Rd. SR3-3C 118
Ashgill. NE37-2A 104
Ash Gro. NE11-1D 77
Ash Gro. NE28-3E 47
Ash Gro. NE40-1B 54
Ash Gro. SR6-1E 89
Ashgrove Av. NE34-2D 69
Ashgrove Ter. DH3-2A 102
Ashgrove Ter. NE8-1D 79
Ash Hill Ct. SR2-3B 110
Ashkirk. NE23-4F 7
Ashkirk Clo. DH2-4C 122
Ashkirk Way. NE25-2B 10
Ashleigh. DH2-1C 122
Ashleigh Av. DH1-3B 136
Ashleigh Clo. NE21-1C 74
Ashleigh Cres. NE5-4B 40
Ashleigh Gdns. SR6-5F 69
Ashleigh Gro. NE2-3F 43
Ashleigh Gro. NE12-3E 29
Ashleigh Gro. NE30-2E 35
Ashleigh Gro. SR6-1C 100
Ashleigh Rd. NE5-5B 40
Ashleigh Ter. SR6-1C 100
Ashleigh Vs. E Bol. NE36 -3B 86
Ashley Clo. NE12-3A 18
Ashley Clo. NE38-4C 104
Ashley Ct. DH9-1A 130
Ashley Rd. NE34-1B 68
Ashley Ter. DH3-2E 123
Ashmead Clo. NE12-3A 18
Ash Meadows. NE38-3D 113
Ashmore St. SR2-2B 110
Ashmore Ter. SR2-2B 110
Asholme. NE5-3F 39
Ashridge Ct. NE10-3A 82
Ash Rd. NE29-5A 34
Ash Sq. NE38-3D 105
Ash St. NE11-5B 78

Ash St. NE21-1B 74
Ash Ter. DH9-5E 131
Ash Ter. NE13-2C 14
Ashton Clo. NE5-1C 38
Ashton Rise. SR8-2D 135
Ashton Way. NE26-5C 12
Ashton Way. SR3-4A 118
Ashtree Clo. NE4-3E 59
Ashtree Gdns. NE25-4A 22
Ashtree La. NE39 & NE21
-5A 72
Ashtrees Gdns. NE9-3E 79
Ash Way. DH4-4E 125
Ashwell Rd. SR3-3C 118
Ashwood Av. SR5-2E 99
Ashwood Clo. NE12-2A 30
Ashwood Cres. NE6-4A 46
Ashwood Gdns. NE9-2F 91
Ashwood Gro. NE13-2D 15
Ashwood Gro. SR5-4A 98
Ashwood Ho. NE7-5C 28
Ashwood St. SR2-2A 110
Ashwood Ter. SR2-3A 110
Askern Av. SR2-1E 121
Askew Rd. NE8-5C 60
Askew Rd. W. NE8-1B 78
Askrigg Av. NE28-2F 31
Askrigg Av. SR2-1E 121
Askrigg Wlk. NE5-3E 39
Aspen Av. NE8-3F 135
Aspen Clo. DH1-3A 140
Aspen Ct. SR3-4D 119
Aspenlaw. NE9-1A 92
Aspen St. NE11-5B 78
Aspley Clo. SR3-4F 119
Association Rd. SR6-3C 100
Aster Pl. NE4-5E 41
Aster Ter. DH4-1A 126
Astley Ct. NE12-4E 17
Astley Dri. NE26-3D 13
Astley Gdns. NE25-1B 10
Astley Rd. NE25-1A 10
Aston Sq. SR3-3C 118
Aston St. NE33-5F 51
Aston Wlk. NE6-2F 63
Aston Way. NE16-5E 75
Athelhampton. NE38-3F 105
Athelstan Rigg. SR2-4E 121
Athenaeum St. SR1-1C 110
Atherton Dri. DH4-5F 125
Atherton Ho. NE4-3C 58
Atherton St. DH1-2B 138
Atherton St. E. DH1-2B 138
Athlone Pl. DH3-1B 112
Athol Gdns. NE25-4F 21
Athol Gdns. SR2-5F 121
Athol Grn. NE11-1E 77
Athol Gro. SR3-3E 119
Atholl Gdns. NE9-3A 80
Athol Pk. SR2-3D 111
Athol Rd. SR2-3D 111
Athol St. NE11-1E 77
Athol Ter. SR2-3D 111
Atkinson Rd. DH3-1E 123
Atkinson Rd. NE4-3B 58
Atkinson Rd. SR6-1C 100
Atkinson St. NE28-3D 47
Atkinson Ter. NE4-3C 58
Atkinson Ter. NE28-3D 47
Atkin St. NE12-2D 17
Atlantis Rd. SR3-3B 118
Attlee Clo. NE23-2D 17
Attlee Ct. NE31-5A 48
Attlee Gro. SR2-3D 121
Attlee Sq. DH6-4F 141
Aubone Av. NE15-1B 58
Auburn Clo. NE28-3C 48
Auburn Ct. NE28-1A 48
Auburn Gdns. NE4-4A 42
Auckland. DH2-3B 122
Auckland Av. NE34-1F 69
Auckland Rd. DH1-2D 137
Auckland Rd. NE31-5A 48
Auckland Ter. NE32-3C 66
Auden Gro. NE4-1D 59
Audland Wlk. NE5-3E 39
Audley Ct. NE2-2B 44
Audley Gdns. SR3-4A 110
Audley Rd. NE3-5A 28
Augusta Ct. NE28-3A 32
Augusta Sq. SR3-3B 118
Augusta Ter. SR6-1E 89
August Pl. NE33-3F 51
Austen Av. NE34-4A 68
Austen Pl. DH9-4E 131
Austin Sq. SR5-3F 99
Australia Gro. NE34-4D 67
Australia Tower. SR3-2D 119
Austral Pl. NE13-1C 14
Austwick Wlk. NE5-3E 39
Autumn Clo. NE38-2C 104
Avalon Dri. NE15-4A 40
Avalon Rd. SR3-2B 118
Avebury Dri. NE38-2D 105
Avebury Pl. NE23-1E 5
Avenue Cres. NE25-1B 10
Avenue Rd. NE8-2D 79
Avenue Rd. NE25-1A 10
Avenues, The. NE11-2D 91
Avenue Ter. NE25-1C 10
Avenue Ter. SR2-3B 110
Avenue, The. DH1-3B 138
(Crossgate Moor)
Avenue, The. DH1-2A 136
(Pity Me)
Avenue, The. DH2-3D 123
Avenue, The. DH3-3B 102
Avenue, The. DH4-5D 115
Avenue, The. DH5-4F 129
Avenue, The. NE9-3F 79
Avenue, The. NE10-1B 80
Avenue, The. NE21-5D 57
Avenue, The. NE25-1B 10
Avenue, The. NE26-2B 22
Avenue, The. NE28 & NE6
-4C 46
Avenue, The. NE38-2C 104
Avenue, The. SR2-3B 110
Avenue, The. SR7-3C 132
Avenue Vivian. DH4-4E 125
Aviemore Rd. NE36-3F 85
Avison Ct. NE4-2F 59
Avolon Ct. NE4-2A 60
Avolon Pl. NE4
-2A 60 & 3A 142
Avolon Wlk. NE4-2A 60
Avon Av. NE29-5F 33
Avon Av. NE32-5B 66
Avon Clo. NE28-4F 31
Avon Cres. DH4-5F 125
Avondale. SR4-2E 107
Avondale Av. DH4-3F 115
Avondale Av. NE12-2E 29
Avondale Ct. NE3-1F 43
Avondale Gdns. NE36-3F 85
Avondale Rise. NE6-2A 62
Avondale Rd. NE6-2B 62
Avondale Ter. DH3-3E 123
Avondale Ter. NE8-1D 79
Avondale Ter. NE36-3F 85
Avonlea Way. NE5-2D 41
Avonmouth Rd. SR3-3B 118
Avonmouth Sq. SR3-3B 118
Avon Rd. DH9-4C 130
Avon Rd. NE31-3D 65
Avon Rd. SR8-4B 134
Avon St. NE8-1F 79
Avon St. SR1-2D 111
Avon Ter. NE38-3D 105
Awnless Ct. NE34-2A 68
Axbridge Gdns. NE4-3D 59
Axminster Clo. NE23-1E 5
Axwell Pk. Clo. NE16-3F 75
Axwell Pk. Rd. NE21-1D 75
Axwell Pk. View. NE15-2A 58
Axwell Ter. NE16-1F 75
Axwell View. NE16-3F 75
Axwell View. NE21-1A 74
Aycliffe Av. NE9-1C 92
Aycliffe Cres. NE9-1C 92
Aycliffe Pl. NE9-1C 92
Aydon Gro. NE32-4F 65
Aydon Rd. NE30-1E 35
Aydon Wlk. NE5-3A 40
Aykley Ct. DH1-5A 136
Aykley Grn. DH1-5A 136
Aykley Rd. DH1-3B 136
Aylesbury Pl. NE12-3D 29
Aylsham Clo. NE5-1C 38
Aylsham Ct. SR3-5E 119
Aylward Pl. DH9-4E 131
Aylyth Pl. NE3-1B 42
Ayr Dri. NE32-4C 66
Ayre's Quay Rd. SR1-1A 110
Ayre's Ter. NE29-4B 34
Ayrey Av. NE34-3D 67
Aysgarth Av. NE28-3F 31
Aysgarth Av. SR2-1E 121
Aysgarth Grn. NE3-1B 42
Ayton Av. SR2-1E 121
Ayton Clo. NE5-2A 40
Ayton Rise. NE6-2B 62
Ayton Rd. NE38
-3E 103 to 5F 103
Ayton St. NE6-2B 62
Azalea Av. SR2-3B 110
Azalea Ter. SR8-3F 135
Azalea Ter. N. SR2-2B 110
Azalea Ter. S. SR2-3B 110
Azalea Way. NE15-5A 38
Bk. Bridge St. SR1-1B 110
Bk. Buttsfield Ter. DH4
(off Rainton St.) *-2A 116*
Bk. Elswick St. NE4-2F 59
Bk. George St. NE4
-3A 60 & 5A 142
Bk. Goldspink La. NE2
-5B 44 & 1F 143
Bk. Hawthorn Rd. W. NE3
-1D 43
Bk. Heaton Pk. Rd. NE6-1F 61
Bk. High St. NE3-5E 27
Back La. DH3-5A 124
Back La. DH4-2F 115
Back La. NE21-5A 56
Back La. NE25-2A 22
Bk. Lodge Ter. SR1-1E 111
Bk. Maling St. NE6-2F 61
Bk. Maling St. NE6-2F 61
(off Walker Rd.)
Bk. Mitford St. NE4-4A 60
Bk. Mt. Joy. DH1-4D 139
Bk. New Bri. St. NE2
-2D 61 & 3E 143
Bk. N. Bridge St. SR6-4B 100
Bk. N. Railway St. SR7
-2F 133
Bk. North Ter. SR7-2F 133
Bk. Prudhoe Ter. NE30-2F 35
(off Percy Pk. Rd.)
Back Row. NE16-3F 75
Bk. Ryhope St. SR2-3C 120
Bk. Sandyford Pl. NE2-5F 43
Bk. Silver St. DH1-2C 138
Bk. S. Railway St. SR7-3F 133
Bk. Stephen St. NE6-1F 61
Back St. NE21-1F 73
Bk. Trafalgar St. NE1
-2D 61 & 3D 143
Bk. Western Hill. DH1-1B 138
Backworth La. NE23 & NE27
-3D 9 to 2D 19
Backworth Ter. NE27-1F 31
Baden Cres. SR5-2F 97
Baden Powell St. NE9-2F 79
Baden St. DH3-4E 123
Badger Clo. SR3-5E 119
Badminton Clo. NE35-1C 84
Baffin Ct. SR3-4D 119
Baildon Clo. NE28-5E 31
Bailey Ind. Est. NE32-5C 48
Bailey Rise. SR8-2C 134
Bailey Sq. SR5-1F 97
Bailey Way. DH5-5F 129
Bainbridge Av. NE34-3E 67
Bainbridge Av. SR3-4A 110
Bainbridge Bldgs. NE9-3B 92
Bainbridge Holme Clo. SR3
-4A 110
Bainbridge Holme Rd. SR3
-5A 110
Bainbridge St. DH1-1D 141
Bainford Av. NE15-1F 57
Baird Av. NE28-3E 49
Baird Clo. NE37-3D 95
Baird St. SR5-2E 97
Bakehouse La. DH1-2D 139
Baker Gdns. NE10-2F 81
Baker Gdns. NE11-1E 77
Baker Sq. SR5-2E 97
Baker St. DH5-4D 127
Baker St. SR5-2E 97
Bakewell Ter. NE6-3C 62
Baldersdale Gdns. SR3
-5F 109
Baldwin Av. NE4-1D 59
Baldwin Av. NE36-2C 86
Balfour Rd. NE15-2F 57
Balfour St. DH5-4D 127
Balfour St. NE8-1C 78
Balgonie Cotts. NE40-2B 54
Baliol Sq. DH1-5A 138
Balkwell Av. NE29-4F 33
Balkwell Grn. NE29-4F 33
Ballast Hill Rd. NE29-2B 50
Ballater Clo. DH9-2E 131
Balliol Av. NE12-1E 29
Balliol Clo. SR8-4A 134
Balliol Gdns. NE7-4D 29
Balmain Rd. NE3-5F 25
Balmlaw. NE9-5B 80
Balmoral. DH3-4A 124
Balmoral Av. NE3-5F 27
Balmoral Av. NE32-4C 66
Balmoral Cres. DH5-1D 129
Balmoral Dri. NE10-2A 80
Balmoral Gdns. NE26-1B 22
Balmoral Gdns. NE29-3B 34
Balmoral St. NE28-2C 46
Balmoral Ter. NE3-5F 27
Balmoral Ter. NE6-5D 45
Balmoral Ter. SR2-5D 111
Balmoral Ter. SR3-4A 118
Balroy Ct. NE12-2F 29
Baltic Rd. NE10-4C 62
Baltic Way. NE29-1B 50
Baltimore Av. SR5
-1D 97 & 2E 97
Baltimore Ct. NE37-5B 94
Baltimore Sq. SR5-2E 97
Bamborough Ct. NE23-4E 7
Bamborough Ter. NE30
-3C 34
Bambro' St. SR2-3D 111
Bamburgh Av. NE33 & NE34
-3B 52
Bamburgh Av. SR8-1E 135
Bamburgh Clo. NE38-2F 103
Bamburgh Ct. NE4-4D 59
Bamburgh Cres. DH4-5F 115
Bamburgh Cres. NE27-4A 20
Bamburgh Dri. NE10-5A 64
Bamburgh Dri. NE28-2A 48
Bamburgh Gdns. SR3-5F 109
Bamburgh Gro. NE32-4F 65
Bamburgh Gro. NE34-4D 53
Bamburgh Ho. NE5-2A 40
Bamburgh Rd. DH1-2C 136
Bamburgh Rd. NE5-2A 40
Bamburgh Rd. NE12-1B 30
Bamburgh Ter. NE6-1B 62
Bamburgh Tower. NE12
-3E 17
Bamburgh Wlk. NE3-4C 26
Bamford Ter. NE12-1B 30
Bamford Wlk. NE34-2C 68
Bampton Av. SR6-5B 88
Banbury. NE37-5D 95
Banbury Av. SR5-1E 97
Banbury Gdns. NE28-4F 31
Banbury Rd. NE3-4A 26
Banbury Ter. NE33 & NE34
-5F 51
Banbury Way. NE29-1F 49
Bancroft Ter. SR4-2D 109
Banesley La. NE11-4A 90
Banff St. SR5-1E 97
Bangor Sq. NE32-1F 83
Bank Av. NE16-3F 75
Bankhead Rd. NE15-3B 38
Bank Head St. SR7-2C 132
Bankhead Ter. DH4-4F 125
Bank Rd. NE8-3D 61
Banks Bldgs. DH4-4B 116
Bankside La. NE34-2A 68
Bankside Rd. NE15-2E 57
Bank, The. SR6-2D 89
Bank Top. NE25-1C 20
Bank Top. NE30-3E 23
Bank Top. NE40-4A 54
Bankwell La. NE8-3D 61
Bannister Dri. NE12-1B 30
Bannockburn. NE12-3E 17
Barass Av. NE23-3D 9
Barbara St. SR2-5D 111
Barbondale Lonnen. NE5
-3D 39
Barbour Av. NE34-5C 52
Barclay Ct. SR6-5C 100
Barclay Pl. NE5-3D 41
Barclay St. SR6-5B 100
Bardolph Rd. NE29-3E 33
Bardon Clo. NE5-1B 40
Bardon Ct. NE34-2C 68
Bardon Cres. NE25-2D 11
Bardsey Pl. NE12-3C 28
Barehirst St. NE33-5C 50
Barents Clo. NE5-2B 40
Baret Rd. NE6-4A 46
Barford Ct. NE9-3F 91
Barford Dri. DH2-5C 122
Baring St. NE33-5E 35
Barker St. NE2
-1D 61 & 2F 143
Barking Cres. SR5-2D 97
Barking Sq. SR5-2D 97
Barleycorn Pl. SR1-2C 110
Barlow Fell Rd. NE21-5B 72
Barlowfield Clo. NE21-1F 73
Barlow La. NE21-3C 72
Barlow La. End. NE40-1A 72
Barlow Rd. NE21-4B 72
Barmoor La. NE40-2A 54
Barmoor Wlk. NE8-5C 60
Barmouth Clo. NE28-4E 31
Barmouth Rd. NE29-4D 33
Barmouth Way. NE29-5F 33
Barmston Clo. NE38-3E 105
Barmston Ct. NE38-4E 105
Barmston Ferry. NE38-4F 105
Barmston La. NE38-3F 105
Barmston Rd. NE38-3E 105
Barmston Way. NE38-2D 105
Barnabas Pl. SR2-3D 111
Barnard Clo. DH1-2D 137
Barnard Cres. NE31-1D 65
Barnard Grn. NE3-3A 26
Barnard Gro. NE32-3C 66
Barnard Pk. DH5-4F 129
Barnard St. SR4-3E 109
Barnesbury Rd. NE4-2C 58
Barnes Pk. Rd. SR4-3E 109
Barnes Rd. NE33-5D 51
Barnes St. DH5-4F 129
Barnes View. SR4-3D 109
Barnett Clo. SR5-3F 99
Barn Hill. DH9-1C 130
Barningham. NE38-3F 105
Barningham Clo. SR3-1F 119
Barnstaple Clo. NE28-4E 31
Barnstaple Rd. NE29-1E 33
Barnton Rd. NE10-4C 80
Barnwood Clo. NE28-5E 31
Baroness Dri. NE15-5C 40
Baron's Quay Rd. SR5-4F 97
Barronswood. NE3-5D 27
Barrack Ct. NE4
-2A 60 & 3A 142
Barrack Rd. NE4 & NE2
-5C 42 & 2A 142
Barrack Row. DH4-4F 115
Barrack St. SR1-5D 101
Barras Av. NE23-3A 8
Barras Bri. NE1
-1C 60 & 2C 142
Barras Dri. SR3-5F 109
Barrasford Clo. NE3-5C 26
Barrasford Dri. NE13-1D 15
Barrasford Rd. DH1-3D 137
Barrasford Rd. NE23-4E 5
Barrasford St. NE28-3E 49
Barras Gdns. NE23-3A 8
Barr Clo. NE28-4F 31
Barrie Sq. SR5-2F 99
Barrington Av. NE30-4B 22
Barrington Ct. DH5-4F 129
Barrington Dri. NE38-3C 104
Barrington Pl. NE4-1F 59
Barrington Pl. NE8-5C 60
(off Bensham Rd.)
Barrington St. NE33-2D 51
Barrington Ter. DH5-3F 129
Barron St. S. SR5-4A 98
Barrowburn Pl. NE23-3E 9
Barrow's Ct. NE1
-2B 60 & 4C 142
Barrow St. SR5-1E 97
Barr's, The. DH9-1C 130
Barry St. NE8-3C 78
Barry St. NE11-1E 77
Barton Clo. NE28-5E 31
Barton Clo. NE30-1C 34
Barton Ct. SR6-5A 88
Bartram Gdns. NE8-3C 78
Bartram St. SR5-2B 100
Barwell Clo. NE28-4E 31
Basildon Gdns. NE28-5E 31
Basil Way. NE34-4C 68
Basingstoke Pl. NE12-2E 29
Basingstoke Rd. SR8-2B 134
Baslow Gdns. SR3-5A 110
Bassenfell Ct. NE37-1A 104
Bassenthwaite Av. DH2
-4C 122
Bassington Av. NE23-2A 4
Bassington Clo. NE4
-1A 60 & 2A 142
Bassington Dri. NE23-2A 4
Bassington Ind. Est. NE23
-2A 4
Bates La. NE21-5E 57
Bath Clo. NE28-4F 31
Bathgate Av. SR5-1D 97
Bathgate Clo. NE28-4A 32
Bathgate Sq. SR5-2D 97
Bath La. NE4-2B 60 & 4A 142
Bath La. Ter. NE4
-2A 60 & 4A 142
Bath Rd. NE10-5B 64
Bath Rd. NE31-4D 65
Bath Sq. NE32-1F 83
Bath St. NE6-1F 63
Bath St. Ind. Est. NE6-1F 63
Bath Ter. NE3-4E 27
Bath Ter. NE30-2F 35
Bath Ter. SR7-2F 133
Batley St. SR5-1E 97
Battery La. NE10-4B 80
Battle Grn. DH2-1A 122
Battle Hill Dri. NE28
-1D 47 to 4A 20
Battle Hill Est. NE28-3A 32
Baulkham Hills. DH4-4F 115
Bavington. NE10-4E 81
Bavington Dri. NE5-4E 41
Bavington Gdns. NE30-5C 22
Bavington Rd. NE25-2B 10
Bawtry Ct. NE28-4E 31
Bawtry Gro. NE29-5F 33
Baxter Av. NE4-1C 58
Baxter Av. SR5-1D 97
Baxter Pl. NE25-1B 10
Baxter Rd. SR5-1D 97
Baxter's Bldgs. NE25-1C 10
Baxter Sq. SR5-1D 97
Baxterwood Ct. NE4-1F 59
Baxterwood Gro. NE4-1F 59
Baybridge Rd. NE5-1A 40
Bayfield Gdns. NE8-1F 79
Baysdale. DH4-2D 115
Bayswater Av. SR5-1E 97
Bayswater Rd. NE2-2F 43
Bayswater Rd. NE8-2F 79
Bayswater Sq. SR5-1E 97
Baytree Gdns. NE25-4A 22
Baywood Gro. NE28-5E 31
Beach Av. NE26-2C 22
Beach Croft Av. NE30-5D 23
Beachcross Rd. SR4-2F 109
Beach Gro. SR8-3F 135
Beach Rd. NE29 & NE30
-3F 33 to 1E 35
Beach Rd. NE33-2E 51
Beach St. SR4-5A 100
Beachville St. SR4-2F 109
Beach Way. NE30-1B 34
Beacon Ct. NE9-5A 80
Beacon Ct. NE13-1C 14
Beacon Dri. NE13-1C 14
Beacon Glade. NE34-1A 70
Beacon Ho. NE26-4E 13
Beacon La. NE23-4A 4
Beacon Lough Rd. NE9-1E 91
Beacon M. NE23-3A 4
Beacon Rise. NE9-5A 80
Beaconsfield Av. NE9-5E 79
Beaconsfield Clo. NE25-5B 12
Beaconsfield Cres. NE9-5E 79
Beaconsfield Rd. NE9-5E 79
Beaconsfield St. DH9-2C 130
Beaconsfield St. NE4-2F 59
Beaconsfield Ter. DH3
-3A 102
Beaconside. NE34-2A 70
Beacon St. NE9-5E 79
Beacon St. NE30-4D 35
Beacon St. NE33-5E 35
Beadling Gdns. NE4-1D 59
Beadnell Av. NE29-5E 33
Beadnell Clo. DH2-5B 122
Beadnell Clo. NE21-2E 73
Beadnell Ct. NE28-4F 31
Beadnell Gdns. NE27-4B 20
Beadnell Pl. NE2
-1E 61 & 3F 143
Beadnell Way. NE3-4C 26
Beagle Sq. SR3-3F 119
Beal Dri. NE12-1A 30
Beal Gdns. NE28-5B 32
Beal Grn. NE3-5E 25
Beal Rd. NE27-4B 20
Beal Ter. NE6-3E 63
Beal Wlk. NE8-5C 60
Beal Way. NE3-4C 26
Beaminster Way. NE3-4D 25
Beamish Clo. NE28-5E 31
Beamish Ct. DH9-2C 130
Beamish Ct. NE25-4F 21
Beamish Gdns. NE9-1B 92
Beamish St. DH9-2C 130
Beamish View. DH9-1F 131
Beanley Av. NE15-1B 56
(off Shipley St.)
Beanley Av. NE31-4B 64
Beanley Cres. NE30-3E 35
Beanley Pl. NE7-2C 44
Beatrice Gdns. NE34-1D 69
Beatrice Gdns. NE36-2C 86
Beatrice Rd. NE6-3C 44
Beatrice St. SR6-3C 100
Beatrice Ter. DH4-2D 115
(Mount Pleasant)
Beatrice Ter. DH4-4F 115
(Shiney Row)
Beattie St. NE34-2A 68
Beatty Av. NE2-1F 43
Beatty Av. SR5-1D 97
Beaufort Clo. NE5-1F 41
Beaufort Gdns. NE28-5E 31
Beaufort Ter. NE33-4E 51
Beaufort Ter. NE36-3F 85
Beaufront Clo. NE10-4A 82
Beaufront Gdns. NE5-4E 41
Beaufront Gdns. NE8-1A 80
Beaufront Ter. NE32-4F 65
Beaufront Ter. NE33-4E 51
Beauly. NE38-5B 104
Beaumaris. DH4-2C 124
Beaumaris Gdns. SR3-3B 118
Beaumaris Way. NE5-1D 41
Beaumont Ct. NE25-1F 21
Beaumont Cres. SR8-1D 135
Beaumont Dri. NE25-5B 12
Beaumont Dri. NE38-3C 104
Beaumont Ho. NE5-2D 41
Beaumont Pl. SR8-4D 135
Beaumont St. NE4-4E 59
Beaumont St. NE29-4B 34
Beaumont St. SR2-3C 110
Beaumont St. SR5-2F 99
Beaumont St. SR7-4E 133
Beaumont Ter. NE3-4F 27
Beaumont Ter. NE5-2A 40
Beaumont Ter. NE13-1B 14
Beaumont Ter. NE32-2F 65
Beaver Clo. DH1-1C 136
Beckenham Av. NE36-2B 86
Beckenham Clo. NE36-2C 86
Beckenham Gdns. NE28
-5E 31
Beckett St. NE8-3F 61
Beckfoot Clo. NE5-3D 41
Beckford. NE38-3F 105
Beckford Clo. NE28-5E 31
Beck Pl. SR8-3B 134
Beckside Gdns. NE5-3D 39
Beckwith Rd. SR3-2A 118
Beda Hill. NE21-4B 56
Bedale Clo. DH1-2E 141
Bedale Clo. NE28-5E 31
Bedale Ct. NE9-3A 92
Bedale Ct. NE34-2F 67
Bedale Cres. SR5-2F 97
Bedale Dri. NE25-4B 22
Bedale Grn. NE5-1F 41
Bedale St. DH5-5E 129
Bedburn. NE38-2D 113
Bedburn Av. SR5-2B 98
Bede Av. DH1-4B 140
Bedeburn Rd. NE5-5B 24
Bede Burn Rd. NE32-2F 65
Bede Burn View. NE32-2F 65
Bede Clo. DH9-2E 131
Bede Ct. NE8-5E 61
Bede Cres. NE28-1F 47
Bede Cres. NE38-2B 104
Bede Ho. NE8-5E 61
Bede Ind. Est. NE32-1D 67
Bede Precinct. NE32-5D 49
Bede St. SR6-3D 101
Bedesway. NE32-1C 66
Bede Ter. DH2-2D 123
Bede Ter. NE32-3A 66
Bede Ter. NE36-3C 86
Bede Trading Est. NE34
-1D 67
Bede Wlk. NE3-5F 27
Bede Wlk. NE31-2E 65
Bede Way. DH1-3C 136
Bede Way. SR8
-3C 134 & 5D 135
Bedford Av. DH3-2B 112
Bedford Av. NE28-2B 46
Bedford Av. NE33-3E 51
Bedford Cen., The. NE29
-4C 34
Bedford Pl. NE5-3D 39
Bedford Pl. NE8-5C 60
(in two parts)
Bedford Pl. SR3-2E 119
Bedford Pl. SR8-1B 134
Bedfordshire Dri. DH1-3D 141
Bedford St. DH5-4D 129
Bedford St. NE29-4C 34
Bedford St. SR1-1C 110
Bedford Ter. NE29-4C 34
(off Bedford St.)
Bedford Way. NE29-4C 34
Beech Av. DH4-4B 126
Beech Av. NE3-3B 26
Beech Av. NE16-2A 76
Beech Av. SR6-1E 89
Beechburn Wlk. NE4-2F 59
Beech Clo. DH1-1F 137
Beech Clo. NE3-1E 27
Beech Ct. NE29-4B 34
Beech Cres. SR7-4D 133
Beech Crest. DH1-3B 138
Beechcroft Av. NE3-2C 42
Beechcroft Clo. DH1-3B 140
Beechdale Rd. DH1-2D 141
Beech Dri. NE11-1D 77
Beeches, The. NE4-4F 59
Beeches, The. NE12-4F 29
Beechfield Gdns. NE28-1B 46
Beechfield Rd. NE3-1D 43
Beech Gdns. NE9-4E 79
Beech Gro. NE9-4D 93
Beech Gro. NE12-3E 29
Beech Gro. NE26-2B 22
Beech Gro. NE28-3D 47
Beech Gro. NE34-3D 69
Beech Gro. Rd. NE4-3F 59
Beecholm Ct. SR2-4C 110
Beech Rd. DH1-4B 136
Beech Rd. DH6-4F 141
Beech Sq. NE38-3D 105
Beech St. NE4-3D 59
Beech St. NE8-1F 79
Beech St. NE32-5B 48
Beech Ter. DH9-5E 131
(Craghead)
Beech Ter. DH9-5B 130
(South Moor)
Beech Ter. NE21-5B 56
Beech Ter. SR8-3F 135
Beechway. NE10-5E 81
Beechwood Av. NE3-3F 27
Beechwood Av. NE9-2F 91
Beechwood Av. NE25-2F 21
Beechwood Av. NE40-2A 54
Beechwood Clo. NE32-1C 66
Beechwood Cres. SR5-2D 99
Beechwood Gdns. NE11
-5F 77
Beechwood Ho. NE7-5C 28
Beechwoods. DH2-5A 112
Beechwood St. SR2-2A 110
Beechwood Ter. DH4-3B 126
Beechwood Ter. SR2-2A 110
Beeston Av. SR5-1D 97
Beetham Cres. NE5-4B 40
Beethoven St. NE33-3F 51
Begonia Clo. NE31-4C 64
Bek Rd. DH1-3C 136
Beldene Dri. SR4-3D 109
Belford Av. NE27-4A 20
Belford Clo. NE28-5E 31
Belford Clo. SR2-4C 110
Belford Gdns. NE11-5F 77
Belford Rd. SR2-4C 110
Belford St. SR8-1E 135
Belford Ter. NE6-2D 63
Belford Ter. NE30-3C 34
Belford Ter. SR2-4C 110
Belford Ter. E. SR2-4C 110
Belgrade Cres. SR5-1E 97
Belgrade Sq. SR5-1E 97
Belgrave Ct. NE9-2C 80
Belgrave Ct. NE10-2C 80
Belgrave Gdns. NE34-1E 69
Belgrave Pde. NE4-3F 59
Belgrave Ter. NE10-2C 80
Belgrave Ter. NE33-2F 51
Bellamy Cres. SR5-2E 97
Bellburn Ct. NE23-1E 5
Belle Gro. Pl. NE2-5D 43
Belle Gro. Ter. NE2
-5D 43 & 1A 142
Belle Gro. Vs. NE2
-5D 43 & 1A 142
Belle Gro. W. NE2
-5D 43 & 1A 142
Belle St. DH9-2C 130
Belle Vue Av. NE3-5F 27
Belle Vue Bank. NE9-5D 79
Belle Vue Cotts. NE9-5D 79
Bellevue Cres. NE33-1A 68
Belle Vue Cres. SR2-4A 110
Belle Vue Dri. SR2-3A 110
Belle Vue Gro. NE9-5D 79
Belle Vue La. NE36-4B 86
Belle Vue Pk. SR2-3A 110
Belle Vue Pk. W. SR2-3A 110
Belle Vue Rd. SR2-4A 110
Belle Vue St. NE30-4E 23
Belle Vue Ter. DH1-3B 140
Belle Vue Ter. NE9-5D 79
(Low Fell)
Belle Vue Ter. NE9-3E 93
(Springwell)
Belle Vue Ter. NE29-5B 34
Belle Vue Vs. NE36-3B 86
Bellfield Av. NE3-4B 26
Bellgreen Av. NE3-1F 27
Bell Gro. NE12-2D 17
Bell Ho. Rd. SR5-4E 87
Bellingham Clo. NE28-5E 31
Bellingham Ct. NE3-4F 25
Bellingham Dri. NE12-2B 30
Bellister Gro. NE5-5D 41
Bellister Pk. SR8-5C 134
Bellister Rd. NE29-4E 33
Belloc Av. NE34-4F 67
Bells Clo. NE15-2D 56
Bell's Ct. NE1
-2C 60 & 4D 143
Bell's Folly. DH1-5B 138
Belshill Clo. NE28-3A 32
Belshill Wlk. NE8-5C 60
Bell St. DH4-2A 116
Bell St. NE30-4D 35
Bell St. NE31-1C 64
Bell St. NE38-3D 105
Bell St. SR4-1E 109
Bell's Ville. DH1-4A 140
Bellway Ind. Est. NE12-3B 30
Belmont. NE10-5E 81
Belmont Av. NE25-2F 21
Belmont Clo. NE28-5F 31
Belmont Cotts. NE5-1B 40
Belmont Ind. Est. DH1
-2B 140
Belmont Rd. SR4-2D 109
Belmont St. NE6-4D 63
Belmont Ter. NE9-3D 93
Belmont Wlk. NE6-4D 63
Belmount Av. NE3-1F 27
Belper Clo. NE28-5E 31
Belsay. NE38-3C 103
Belsay Av. NE13-3B 14
Belsay Av. NE25-3D 23
Belsay Av. NE34-5C 52
Belsay Av. SR8-1E 135
Belsay Clo. NE28-5E 31
Belsay Gdns. NE3-2B 26
Belsay Gdns. NE11-4F 77
Belsay Gdns. SR4-2E 109
Belsay Pl. NE4-2E 59
Belsfield Gdns. NE32-3F 65
Belsize Pl. NE6-4B 46
Beltingham. NE5-3A 40
Belt's Sq. NE21-1A 74
Belvedere. NE29-3A 34
Belvedere Av. NE25-3B 22
Belvedere Ct. NE6-1B 62
Belvedere Parkway. NE3
-4E 25
Belvedere Retail Pk. NE3
-4E 25
Belvedere Rd. SR2-2B 110
Bemersyde Dri. NE2-2A 44
Benbrake Av. NE29-1A 34
Bendigo Av. NE34-4D 67
Benedict Rd. SR6-3D 101
Benevente St. SR7-4E 133
Benfield Rd. NE6-3F 45
Benfleet Av. SR5-1D 97
Benjamin Rd. NE28-2B 48
Bennett Ct. NE15-1B 56
Bennett Ct. SR2-4D 111
Bennett Gdns. NE10-1C 80
Bensham Av. NE8-1C 78
Bensham Ct. NE8-1C 78
Bensham Ct. NE34-2B 68
Bensham Cres. NE8-1B 78
Bensham Rd. NE8-2B 78
Bensham St. NE35-1D 85
Benson Pl. NE6-2B 62
Benson Rd. NE6-1C 62
Benson St. DH3-4E 123
Benson St. DH9-1C 130
Benson Ter. NE10-2C 80
Bent Ho. La. DH1-5B 140
Bentinck Cres. NE4-3E 59
Bentinck Pl. NE4-3E 59
Bentinck Rd. NE4-3E 59
Bentinck St. NE4-3E 59
Bentinck Ter. NE4-2E 59
Bentinck Vs. NE4-2E 59
Benton Av. SR5-1D 97
Benton Bank. NE7-4C 44
Benton Clo. NE7-5D 29
Benton Hall Wlk. NE7-2E 45
Benton La. NE12-1D 29
Benton Lodge Av. NE7-4D 29
Benton Pk. Rd. NE7-5B 28
Benton Rd. NE7-5D 29
Benton Rd. NE27-5F 19
Benton Rd. NE34-5A 68
Benton Sq. Ind. Est. NE12
-1D 31
Benton Ter. DH9-2C 130
Benton Ter. NE2
-5A 44 & 1F 143
Benton View. NE12-2E 29
Benton Way. NE28-4D 47
Bents Cotts. NE33-3A 52
Bents Pk. Rd. NE33-1A 52
Bents, The. SR6-3E 89
Benwell Dene Ter. NE15
-2A 58
Benwell Grange. NE15-2B 58
Benwell Grange Av. NE15
-2B 58
Benwell Grange Clo. NE15
-2B 58
Benwell Grange Rd. NE15
-2B 58
Benwell Grange Ter. NE15
3B 58
Benwell Gro. NE4-2D 59
Benwell Hall Dri. NE15-2A 58
Benwell Hill Gdns. NE5-5E 41
Benwell Hill Rd. NE5-5D 41
Benwell La. NE15-2A 58
Benwell Shopping Cen. NE4
-3C 58
Benwell Village. NE15-2A 58
Berberis Way. NE15-5A 38
Beresford Av. NE31-4C 64
Beresford Gdns. NE6-2B 62
Beresford Pk. SR2-2A 110
Beresford Rd. NE30-4C 22
Beresford St. NE11-1F 77
Bergen Clo. NE29-5D 33
Bergen Sq. SR5-1E 97
Bergen St. SR5-1E 97
Berkdale Rd. NE9-2D 91
Berkeley Clo. NE12-3A 18
Berkeley Clo. NE35-5D 67
Berkeley Clo. SR3-3B 118
Berkeley Sq. NE3-3D 27
Berkeley St. NE15-4B 38
Berkeley St. NE33-2F 51
Berkeley Ter. NE15-4B 38
Berkhampstead Ct. NE10
-3B 82
Berkley Av. NE21-5C 56
Berkley Clo. NE28-5E 31
Berkley Rd. NE29-3F 33
Berkshire Clo. DH1-3C 140
Berkshire Clo. NE5-2B 40
Berkshire Rd. SR8-2B 134
Bermondsey St. NE2
-1E 61 & 3F 143
Bernard Shaw St. DH4
-5C 126
Bernard St. DH4-5B 126
Bernard St. NE6-3F 63
Bernard Ter. DH2-1A 122
Berrington Dri. NE5-1D 41
Berrishill Gro. NE25-1E 21
Berry Clo. NE6-2E 63
Berry Clo. NE28-5E 31
Berry Hill. NE40-1A 72
Berryhill Clo. NE21-1B 74

Bertha Ter. DH4-1C 126
Bertram Cres. NE15-1B 58
Bertram Pl. NE27-3B 20
Bertram St. DH3-3A 102
Bertram St. NE33-4D 51
Bertrams Yd. NE25-1B 20
Berwick. NE38-4E 103
Berwick Av. SR5-1E 97
Berwick Chase. SR8-5A 134
Berwick Clo. NE15-5C 38
Berwick Dri. NE28-4F 31
Berwicke St. NE28-3D 49
Berwick Sq. SR5-1E 97
Berwick St. NE31-1B 64
Berwick Ter. NE29-5E 33
Bessie Ter. NE21-5F 55
Best View. DH4-4F 115
Bethel Av. NE6-5E 45
Bethune Av. SR7-3C 132
Betjeman Clo. DH9-2E 131
Betts Av. NE15-2A 58
Bevan Av. SR2-4C 120
Bevan Ct. NE12-3B 28
Bevan Ct. NE31-5A 48
Bevan Gdns. NE10-2F 81
Bevan Gro. DH1-3B 140
Beverley Clo. NE3-5D 15
Beverley Ct. NE9-4F 79
Beverley Ct. NE32-5C 48
Beverley Ct. NE37-5C 94
Beverley Cres. NE9-4F 79
Beverley Dri. NE16-1A 76
Beverley Dri. NE21-2E 73
Beverley Gdns. DH3-4F 123
Beverley Gdns. NE30-4E 23
Beverley Pk. NE25-3A 22
Beverley Pl. NE28-2A 48
Beverley Rd. NE9-3F 79
Beverley Rd. NE25-3A 22
Beverley Rd. SR2-5D 111
Beverley Ter. NE6-3F 63
Beverley Ter. NE15-3B 38
Beverley Ter. NE30-4E 23
Beverley Vs. NE30-4E 23
Beverley Way. SR8-3A 134
Beweshill Cres. NE21-1F 73
Beweshill La. NE21-5E 55
Bewick Clo. DH2-5C 122
Bewick Ct. NE1-2C 60
(off Princess Sq.)
Bewick Cres. NE15-1B 56
Bewicke Lodge. NE28-2B 48
Bewicke Rd. NE28-3B 48
(in two parts)
Bewick Rd. NE8-1C 78
Bewick St. NE1 -3B 60 & 5B 142
Bewick St. NE33-5E 51
Bexhill Rd. SR5-1E 97
Bexhill Sq. SR5-1D 97
Bexley Av. NE15-1F 57
Bexley Gdns. NE28-5F 31
Bexley Pl. NE16-5F 75
Bexley St. SR4-2D 109
Bickerton Wlk. NE5-3A 40
Bickington Ct. DH4-2B 126
Biddick Hall Dri. NE34-3A 68
Biddick Inn Ter. NE38-2C 114
Biddick La. NE38-2C 114
Biddick Ter. NE38-4D 105
Biddick View. NE38-4D 105
Biddick Vs. NE38-4C 104
Biddlestone Cres. NE29-5F 33
Biddlestone Rd. NE6-3E 45
Bideford Gdns. NE9-2E 91
Bideford Gdns. NE26-1B 22
Bideford Gdns. NE32-2C 66
Bideford Gdns. NE34-4B 52
Bideford Gro. NE16-4F 75
Bideford Rd. NE3-1A 42
Bideford St. SR2-5E 111
Bigges Gdns. NE28-1B 46
Bigg Market. NE1 -2C 60 & 4C 142
Bilbrough Gdns. NE4-3B 58
Bill Quay. NE10-5A 64
Billy Mill Av. NE29-4A 34
Billy Mill La. NE29-1E 33
Bilsdale. SR6-3D 89
Bilsdale Pl. NE12-3B 28
Bilsmoor Av. NE7-3D 45
Bilton Hall Rd. NE32-1B 66
Binchester St. NE34-3E 67
Bingfield Gdns. NE5-4E 41
Bingley Clo. NE28-5F 31
Bingley St. SR5-1E 97
Binsby Gdns. NE9-2A 92
Binswood Av. NE5-3D 41
Bircham Dri. NE21-5C 56
Bircham St. DH9-4B 130
Birch Av. NE10-2E 81
Birch Av. SR6-1D 89
Birch Ct. SR3-4D 119
Birch Cres. DH4-3A 126
Birches, The. DH9-1C 130
Birchfield. NE16-4A 76
Birchfield Gdns. NE9-2F 91
Birchfield Gdns. NE15-5A 40
Birchfield Rd. SR2-3A 110
Birchgate Clo. NE21-1F 73
Birch Gro. NE28-5E 31
Birch Gro. NE32-5C 48
Birchgrove Av. DH1-3B 140
Birchington Av. NE33-1B 68
Birch Rd. NE21-5B 56
Birch St. NE32-1E 65
Birch Ter. DH3-2A 102
Birch Ter. NE6-2E 63
Birchtree Gdns. NE25-4A 22
Birchvale Av. NE5-3C 40
Birchwood Av. NE7-1D 45
Birchwood Av. NE13-2D 15
Birchwood Av. NE16-5F 75
Birchwood Clo. NE23-3D 9
Birdhill Pl. NE34-3B 68
Birds Nest Rd. NE6-3C 62
Bird St. NE30-4D 35
Birkdale. NE25-2E 21
Birkdale. NE33-3A 52
Birkdale Av. SR6-3C 88
Birkdale Clo. NE7-1E 45
Birkdale Clo. NE28-1D 47
Birkdale Clo. NE37-3A 94
Birkdale Gdns. DH1-3E 141
Birkshaw Wlk. NE5-3A 40
Birks Rd. NE15-1D 37
Birling Pl. NE5-3E 41
Birnam Gro. NE32-5D 67
Birnham Pl. NE3-2A 42
Birnie Clo. NE4-3C 58
Birrell Sq. SR5-1E 97
Birrell St. SR5-1E 97
Birtley Av. NE30-2E 35
(in two parts)
Birtley Av. SR5-1E 97
Birtley By-Pass. NE9 & DH3 -1B 102 to 3C 112
Birtley Clo. NE3-5C 26
Birtley La. DH3-3B 102
Birtley Rd. NE38-1D 113
Birtley Vs. DH3-2A 102
Birtwistle Av. NE31-4C 64
Biscop Ter. NE32-3A 66
Bishop Cres. NE32-5E 49
Bishopdale. DH4-2D 115
Bishopdale. NE28-4A 30
Bishopdale Ho. NE4-3C 58
Bishop Ramsay Ct. NE34 -1F 69
Bishop Rock Clo. NE12-3C 28
Bishop Rock Rd. NE12-3C 28
Bishop's Av. NE4-2F 59
Bishop's Rd. NE15-3B 58
Bishop's Way. DH1-2B 136
Bishops Way. SR3-5D 119
Bishopton St. SR2-2C 110
Bisley Ct. NE28-5E 31
Bisley Dri. NE34-1B 68
Bittern Clo. NE28-3B 32
Blackberries, The. NE9-4E 93
Black Boy Rd. DH4-5E 125
Black Boy Yd. NE1 -3C 60 & 5C 142
Blackburn Grn. NE10-3B 80
Blackcap Clo. NE38-4D 103
Blackdown Clo. NE12-4C 28
Blackdown Clo. SR8-4A 134
Black Dri. DH3 -5A 114 & 4A 114
Blackettbridge. NE1 -2C 60 & 3C 142
(off Eldon Sq.)
Blackett Pl. NE1 -2C 60 & 3C 142
Blackett St. NE1 -2C 60 & 3C 142
Blackett St. NE31-5B 48
Blackett Ter. SR4-1E 109
Blackfell Rd. NE37-1E 103
Blackfriars Ct. NE1 -2B 60 & 4B 142
Blackfriars Way. NE12-3C 28
Blackheath Clo. NE37-3B 94
Blackheath Ct. NE3-4D 25
Blackhill Av. NE28-3A 32
Blackhill Cres. NE9-1C 92
Blackhills Rd. SR8 -1E 135 to 3E 135
Blackhills Ter. SR8-3E 135
Blackhouse La. NE40-2A 54
Black La. NE5 & NE13-4B 24
Black La. NE9-3F 91 & 3A 92
Black La. NE21-5F 55
Blackpool Pde. NE31-4F 65
Black Rd. NE31-5B 48
Black Rd. SR2-3D 121
Black Rd. SR5-4B 100
Blackrow La. NE9-1F 91
Blackrow La. NE15-1B 36
Blackstone Ct. NE21-5F 55
Blackthorn Dri. NE28-5E 31
Blackthorne. NE10-5E 81
Blackthorn Pl. NE4-4F 59
Blackthorn Way. DH4-3F 125
Blackwater Ho. SR3-4E 119
Blackwell Av. NE6-1E 63
Blackwood Rd. SR5-2E 97
Bladen St. NE32-5C 48
Bladen St. Ind. Est. NE32 -5C 48
(off Bladen St.)
Blagdon Av. NE34-5F 51
Blagdon Clo. NE1 -2D 61 & 4F 143
Blagdon Cres. NE23-1A 4
Blagdon St. NE1 -2D 61 & 4F 143
Blagdon Ter. NE13-4A 6
Blagdon Ter. NE23-3D 5
Blake Av. NE16-3F 75
Blake Clo. DH9-3D 131
Blakelaw Rd. NE5 -2D 41 & 2E 41
Blakemoor Pl. NE5-3E 41
Blaketown. NE23-3E 9
Blake Wlk. NE8-5F 61
Blanchland. NE38-1D 115
Blanchland Av. DH1-3E 137
Blanchland Av. NE13-1D 15
Blanchland Av. NE15-5D 39
Blanchland Clo. NE28-5F 31
Blanchland Dri. NE25-2D 11
Blanchland Dri. SR5-2A 100
Blanchland Ter. NE30-3C 34
Blandford Pl. SR7-3E 133
Blandford Rd. NE29-1E 33
Blandford Sq. NE1 -3A 60 & 5A 142
Blandford St. NE1 -3A 60 & 5A 142
Blandford St. SR1-1B 110
Blandford Way. NE28-4E 31
Blands Opening. DH3-2E 123
Blaxton Pl. NE16-5E 75
Blaydon Av. SR5-1E 97
Blaydon Bank. NE21-5A 56
Blaydon Burn Rd. NE21 -5D 55
Blaydon Clo. NE1-2E 61
Blaykeston Clo. SR7-1A 132
Blayney Row. NE15-5E 37
Bleachfeld. NE10-4E 81
Bleach Grn. DH5-5F 129
Bleasdale Cres. DH4-3A 116
Blencartha. NE30-5B 22
Blencathra. NE37-1B 104
Blenheim. NE12-3E 17
Blenheim Ct. NE10-5B 80
Blenheim Pl. NE11-1D 77
Blenheim St. NE1 -3B 60 & 5A 142
Blenheim Wlk. NE33-1E 51
Blenkinsop Gro. NE32-4F 65
Blenkinsop St. NE28-3C 46
Bletchley Av. SR5-1E 97
Blezard Bus. Pk. NE13-3A 6
Blindburn St. NE31-1C 64
Blind La. DH1-3B 138
Blind La. DH3-4B 112
Blind La. DH4-1F 125
Blind La. SR3-2F 119
Bloemfontein Pl. DH9-5F 131
Bloom Av. DH9-2B 130
Bloomfield Dri. DH5-5B 128
Bloomsbury Ct. NE3-5D 27
Blossom Gro. DH4-1A 126
Blossom St. DH5-3F 129
Blount St. NE6-1C 62
Blucher Colliery Rd. NE15 -3D 39
Blucher Rd. NE12-5E 17
Blucher Rd. NE29-1B 50
Blucher Ter. NE15-4D 39
Blue Anchor Ct. NE1 -3D 61 & 5E 143
(off Quayside)
Bluebell Dene. NE5-4B 24
Blueburn Dri. NE12-3B 18
Blue Coat Bldgs. DH1-2D 139
Blue Coat Ct. DH1-2D 139
Blue Ho. La. NE37-5F 93
Blue Ho. La. SR6 & SR5 -3E 87
Blue Ho. Rd. NE31-4B 64
Blue Quarries Rd. NE9-4F 79
Blue Top Cotts. NE23-3E 5
Blumer St. DH4-5F 125
Blyth Clo. NE23-4E 7
Blyth Ct. NE15-1B 56
Blyth Ct. NE34-2A 68
Blythe Nook. NE1 -2D 61 & 4E 143
(off Stockbridge)
Blyth Rd. NE26-1C 12
Blyth Sq. SR5-1E 97
Blyth St. NE25-1A 10
Blyth St. SR5-1E 97
Blyton Av. NE34-2E 67
Blyton Av. SR2-4C 120
(in two parts)
Bodlewell La. SR1-5D 101
Bodley Clo. NE3-4F 25
Bodmin Clo. NE28-4F 31
Bodmin Ct. NE9-2E 91
Bodmin Rd. NE29-1E 33
Bodmin Sq. SR5-1F 97
Bodmin Way. NE3-4B 26
Bognor St. SR5-1E 97
Bog Row. DH5-5E 129
Boker La. NE36-2A 86
Bolam. NE38-3E 103
Bolam Av. NE30-5C 22
Bolam Ct. NE15-3F 37
Bolam Coyne. NE6-2A 62
Bolam Gdns. NE28-2C 48
Bolam Gro. NE30-5C 22
Bolam Ho. NE4 -2A 60 & 3A 142
Bolam Rd. NE12-4E 17
Bolam St. NE6-2B 62
Bolam St. NE8-2A 78
Bolam Way. NE6-2A 62
Bolam Way. NE25-1A 10
Bolbec Rd. NE4-5A 42
Bolburn. NE10-3F 81
Boldon Bus. Pk. NE35-3D 85
Boldon Clo. NE28-4F 31
Boldon Dri. NE36-3E 85
Boldon Gdns. NE9-2B 92
Boldon Ho. DH1-1C 136
Boldon La. NE34-1F 67
Boldon La. NE35 & NE36 -1A 86
Boldon La. SR6-1D 87
Bolingbroke Rd. NE29-3F 33
Bolingbroke St. NE6-1F 61
Bolingbroke St. NE33-2E 51
Bollihope Dri. SR3-5F 109
Bolton Clo. DH1-2C 136
Bonaventure. DH4-2A 116
Bonchester Ct. NE28-4A 32
Bonchester Pl. NE23-1E 5
Bond Clo. SR5-3A 100
Bond Ct. NE4-2C 58
Bondene Av. NE10-2D 81
Bondene Av. W. NE10-2C 80
(in two parts)
Bondfield Ct. NE31-5A 48
Bondfield Gdns. NE10-2F 81
Bondicarr Pl. NE5-3E 41
Bond St. NE4-2C 58
Bonemill La. NE38-3D 113
Bonners Field. SR6-5B 100
Bonnington Way. NE5-2D 41
Bonnivard Gdns. NE23-3E 9
Bonsall Ct. NE34-2C 68
Booth St. NE10-2C 80
Booth St. SR4-1E 109
Bootle St. SR5-2E 97
Border Rd. NE28-3C 46
Bordeux Clo. SR3-4C 118
Boreham Clo. NE28-5F 31
Borodin Av. SR5-1E 97
Borough Ct. SR1-1D 111
Borough Rd. NE29-5C 34
Borough Rd. NE32-1A 66
Borough Rd. NE34-2E 69
Borough Rd. SR1-1C 110
Borrowdale. NE16-2B 76
Borrowdale. NE37-5A 94
Borrowdale Av. NE6-5B 46
Borrowdale Av. SR6-5B 88
Borrowdale Clo. NE36-2B 86
Borrowdale Cres. DH4-3F 115
Borrowdale Cres. NE21 -2A 74
Borrowdale Dri. DH1-2C 140
Borrowdale Gdns. NE9-1F 91
Borrowdale Ho. NE34-2A 68
Borrowdale St. DH5-5F 129
Boscombe Dri. NE28-5E 31
Boston Av. NE7-5D 29
Boston Av. NE38-1B 104
Boston Clo. NE28-4F 31
Boston Ct. NE12-2B 30
Boston Cres. SR5-1D 97
Boston St. SR5-1D 97
Boswell Av. NE34-4A 68
Bosworth. NE12-3E 17
Bosworth Gdns. NE6-3E 45
Bothal St. NE6-2B 62
Botham Ho. NE29-1F 49
Bottle Bank. NE8 -3D 61 & 5E 143
Bottlehouse St. NE6-3B 62
Bottle Works Rd. SR7-3F 133
Boulby Clo. SR3-3A 120
Boulevard, The. NE16-1B 76
Boulmer Clo. NE3-2B 26
Boulmer Ct. DH2-3D 123
Boulmer Gdns. NE13-1D 15
Boulmer Wlk. NE8-5C 60
Boulsworth Rd. NE29-1A 34
Boult Ter. DH4-4F 115
Boundary Gdns. NE7-1C 44
Boundary Houses. DH4 -5E 115
Boundary St. SR5-3A 100
Bourdon Ho. SR1-1C 110
Bourdon La. SR1-1D 111
Bourne Av. NE4-5A 42
Bourne Ct. DH9-1E 131
Bournemouth Ct. NE28-4F 31
Bournemouth Dri. SR7 -4B 132
Bournemouth Gdns. NE5 -2B 40
Bournemouth Gdns. NE26 -1B 22
Bournemouth Pde. NE31 -4E 65
Bournemouth Rd. NE29 -4D 33
Bourn Lea. DH4-1E 125
Bournmoor. DH4-2C 124
Bourtree Clo. NE28-5D 31
Bowbank Clo. SR3-5F 109
Bowburn Av. SR5-2B 98
Bowburn Clo. NE10-3B 82
Bower St. SR6-1C 100
Bower, The. NE32-1A 84
Bowes Av. SR7-4A 132
Bowes Ct. DH1-2D 137
Bowes Ct. NE3-4A 28
Bowes Lea. DH4-1E 125
Bowes St. NE3-4A 28
Bowes Wlk. NE3-2E 29
(off Hailsham Av.)
Bowes Wlk. NE12-3E 29
Bowfell Av. NE5-1F 41
Bowfell Clo. NE5-1F 41
Bowfield Av. NE3-1E 27
Bowland Ter. NE21-4B 56
Bow La. DH1-3D 139
Bowlynn Clo. SR3-4C 118
Bowman Dri. NE23-4A 8
Bowman Pl. NE33-3D 51
Bowman St. SR6-1E 89
Bowmont Dri. DH9-1A 128
Bowmont Dri. NE23-1E 5
Bowmont Wlk. DH2-4B 122
Bowness Av. NE28-4A 32
Bowness Clo. NE36-2B 86
Bowness Clo. SR8-3D 135
Bowness Pl. NE9-1A 92
Bowness Rd. NE5-4C 40
Bowness Rd. NE16-3B 76
Bowness St. SR5-1F 97
Bowness Ter. NE28-4A 32
Bowsden Ct. NE3-4A 28
Bowsden Ter. NE3-5A 28
Bowtrees. SR2-4B 110
Boxlaw. NE9-5B 80
Boyce Ter. NE37-5B 94
Boyd Cres. NE28-2E 47
Boyd Rd. NE28-2E 47
Boyd St. DH1-4D 139
Boyd St. NE2-1E 61 & 3F 143
Boyd St. NE15-5A 38
Boyd Ter. DH9-3B 130
Boyd Ter. NE5-1A 40
Boyd Ter. NE15-3D 39
Boyne Gdns. NE27-3A 20
Boystones Ct. NE37-1A 104
Brabourne St. NE34-2A 68
Bracken Av. NE28-5E 31
Bracken Clo. DH9-3B 130
Brackendale Rd. DH1-2D 141
Brackendene Dri. NE9-5D 79
Bracken Dri. NE11-3D 77
Bracken Field Rd. DH1 -4B 136
Brackenfield Rd. NE3-5D 27
Brackenlaw. NE9-5B 80
Bracken Pl. NE4-5F 41
Brackenside. NE3-1E 27
Brackenway. NE37-5A 94
Brackenwood Gro. SR2 -5B 110
Brackley. NE37-4D 95
Brackley Gro. NE29-1F 49
Bracknell Clo. SR3-3A 120
Bracknell Gdns. NE5-3D 39
Brack Ter. NE10-5F 63
Bradbury Clo. DH9-1A 130
Bradbury Clo. NE10-3B 82
Bradford Av. NE28-4F 31
Bradford Av. SR5-1E 97
Bradford Cres. DH1-1F 139
Bradley Av. DH5-2C 128
Bradley Av. NE34-2F 69
Bradman Sq. SR5-1F 97
Bradman St. SR5-1F 97
Bradshaw Sq. SR5-1F 97
Bradshaw St. SR5-1F 97
Bradwell Rd. NE3-5F 25
Brady & Martin Ct. NE1 -1C 60 & 2D 143
Brady Sq. NE38-4D 105
Brady St. SR4-1E 109
Braebridge Pl. NE3-1B 42
Braefell Ct. NE37-2A 104
Braemar Ct. NE10-5A 64
Braemar Dri. NE34-4B 52
Braemar Gdns. NE25-3D 21
Braemar Gdns. SR3-4B 118
(East Herrington)
Braemar Gdns. SR3-5F 109
(Sunderland)
Braemar Ter. SR8-3F 135
Braeside. SR2-3A 110
Braeside Clo. NE30-4C 22
Braeside G'head NE11-3E 77
Braeside Ter. NE30-5B 22
Brae, The. SR2-2F 109
Braintree Gdns. NE3-5B 26
Braithwaite Rd. SR8-4D 135
Brakespeare Pl. SR8-4D 135
Bramble Dykes. NE15-2A 58
Bramblelaw. NE9-1A 92
Brambles, The. NE40-2A 54
Bramham Ct. NE34-2C 68
Bramhope Grn. NE9-3A 92
Bramley Clo. SR4-5E 107
Brampton Av. NE6-3E 63
Brampton Ct. NE23-1E 5
Brampton Gdns. NE9-1F 91
Brampton Gdns. NE15-2F 37
Brampton Gdns. NE28-5C 32
Brampton Pl. NE29-5F 33
Brampton Rd. NE34-2F 67
Bramwell Ct. NE3-4F 27
Bramwell Rd. SR2-2D 111
Brancepeth Av. DH4-4E 125
Brancepeth Av. NE4-3D 59
Brancepeth Clo. DH1-3E 137
Brancepeth Clo. NE15-5E 39
Brancepeth Rd. NE31-5A 48
Brancepeth Rd. NE38-3F 103
Brancepeth Ter. NE32-4A 66
Branch Gro. SR8-4C 134
Branch St. NE21-1A 74
Brand Av. NE4-5A 42
Brandling Ct. NE2-4A 44
Brandling Ct. NE10-1C 80
Brandling Ct. NE34-3E 69
Brandling Dri. NE3-5E 15
Brandling La. NE10-1C 80
Brandling M. NE3-5E 15
Brandling Pk. NE2 -4F 43 & 1D 143
Brandling Pl. NE3-5E 15
Brandling Pl. NE10-1C 80
Brandling Pl. S. NE2-4F 43
Brandlings Ct. SR8-3C 134
Brandling St. NE8-3D 61
Brandling St. SR6-3D 101
Brandling St. S. SR6-4D 101
Brandlings Way. SR8-3C 134
Brandling Ter. NE30-3C 34
Brandon Av. NE27-4A 20
Brandon Clo. DH2-5B 122
Brandon Clo. DH4-5B 126
Brandon Clo. NE21-2F 73
Brandon Gdns. NE9-1C 92
Brandon Gro. NE2 -5B 44 & 1F 143
Brandon Rd. NE3-3A 26
Brandon Rd. NE29-3E 33
Brandy La. NE37-1A 104
Brandywell. NE10-4E 81
Brannen St. NE29-5B 34
Bransdale. DH4-2D 115
Bransdale Av. SR6-3D 89
Branston St. SR5-3A 100
Branton Av. NE31-4B 64
Brantwood Av. NE25-3E 21
Branxton Cres. NE6-2D 63
Brasher St. NE33-5D 35
Bray Clo. NE28-5F 31
Brayside. NE32-1C 84
Breamish Dri. NE38-2D 113
Breamish Ho. NE1 -2E 61 & 4F 143
Breamish St. NE1 -2E 61 & 4F 143
Breamish St. NE32-2F 65
Brearley Way. NE10-2A 80
Breckenbeds Rd. NE9-5C 78
Brecken Ct. NE9-1D 91
Brecon Clo. NE5-1D 41
Brecon Clo. SR8-5A 134
Brecon Rd. DH1-2E 137
Bredon Clo. NE38-4A 104
Brendale Av. NE5-2F 39
Brendon Pl. SR8-3A 134
Brenkley Av. NE27-4A 20
Brenkley Ct. NE13-4A 6
Brenkley Way. NE13-3A 6
Brenlynn Clo. SR3-4C 118
Brennan Clo. NE15-1A 58
Brentford Av. SR5-2E 97
Brentford Ho. SR5-1E 97
Brentford Sq. SR5-2E 97
Brentwood Av. NE2-2F 43
Brentwood Clo. NE25-2C 10
Brentwood Ct. DH9-2F 131
Brentwood Gdns. NE2-2F 43
Brentwood Gdns. NE16-5F 75
Brentwood Gdns. SR3-5F 109
Brentwood Gro. NE28-3F 47
Brentwood Pl. NE33-3E 51
Brentwood Rd. DH4-5E 115
Brettanby Gdns. NE40-1B 54
Brettanby Rd. NE10-3A 80
Brett Clo. NE7-2F 45
Bretton Gdns. NE7-2E 45
Brewer Ter. SR2-4E 121
Brewery Bank. NE16-1F 75
Brewery La. NE10-5C 62
Brewery La. NE33-2D 51
Brewery Sq. DH9-1C 130
Brewhouse Bank. NE30-4E 35
Briar Av. DH4-4B 126
Briar Av. NE26-5E 13
Briar Bank. DH1-1B 136
Briar Clo. DH4-1E 125
(Shiney Row)
Briar Clo. DH4-4C 124
(Woodstone Village)
Briar Clo. NE21-5F 55
Briar Clo. NE28-5E 31
Briardene. DH1-3B 138
Briardene Clo. SR3-4A 118
Briardene Cres. NE3-1B 42
Briardene Dri. NE10-2C 82
Briardene View. NE26-4D 13
Briar Edge. NE12-1E 29
Briarfield. NE38-1C 114
Briarfield Rd. NE3-5D 27
Briarhill. DH2-1B 122
Briar La. NE15-3A 38
Briar Lea. DH4-1E 125
Briarmede Pk. NE9-1E 91
Briar Rd. DH1-1D 141
Briarside. NE5-2C 40
Briars, The. SR5-3A 98
Briarsyde. NE12-2A 30
Briarsyde Clo. NE16-4D 75
Briarwood. NE23-4A 8
Briarwood Av. DH2-2A 122
Briarwood Av. NE3-3F 27
Briarwood Cres. NE6-4B 46
Briarwood Cres. NE11-2E 77
Briarwood St. DH4-4D 125
Briary, The. NE15-3E 37
Brick Row. SR2-3C 120
Bridekirk. NE37-1A 104
(in two parts)
Bridge App. SR5-4E 99
Bridge Cotts. NE23-4A 8
Bridge Cres. SR1-5B 100
Bridge Pk. NE3-2D 27
Bridge Rd. S. NE29-1A 50
Bridges, The. SR1-1B 110
(off West St.)
Bridge St. DH1-2B 138
Bridge St. DH9-4B 130
Bridge St. NE8 -3D 61 & 5E 143
Bridge St. NE13-4A 6
Bridge St. NE21-3A 56
Bridge St. SR1-5B 100
Bridge Ter. NE27-3B 20
Bridgewater Clo. NE15-5D 39
Bridgewater Clo. NE28-5E 31
Bridgewater Rd. NE37 -1D 105
Bridle Path. NE36-3A 86
Bridle Path. SR3-2A 118
Bridleway, The. NE23-3F 7
Bridlington Av. NE9-2E 91
Bridlington Clo. NE28-4F 31
Bridlington Pde. NE31-4E 65
Bridport Rd. NE29-1F 33
Brier Av. SR8-2E 135
Brier Dene Clo. NE26-4E 13
Brierdene Ct. NE26-4D 13
Brier Dene Cres. NE26-4D 13
Brierdene Rd. NE26-3D 13
Brierdene View. NE26-4D 13
Brierfield Gro. SR4-3C 108
Briermede Av. NE9-1D 91
Brierville. DH1-3B 138
Brieryside. NE5-3F 41
Briery Vale Clo. SR2-3B 110
Briery Vale Rd. SR2-3B 110
Brigham Av. NE3-2A 42
Brigham Pl. NE33-1E 51
Brightman Rd. NE29-4B 34
Brighton Clo. NE28-4A 32
Brighton Gdns. NE8-3C 78
Brighton Gro. NE4-2E 59
Brighton Gro. NE26-5E 13
Brighton Gro. NE29-4A 34
Brighton Pde. NE31-4E 65
Brighton Rd. NE8 -1C 78 to 3C 78
Bright St. NE33-2F 51
Bright St. SR6-3C 100
Brignall Gdns. NE15-5C 40
Brignall Rise. SR3-5F 109
Brigside Cotts. NE13-4A 6
(in two parts)
Brindley Rd. NE37-1C 104
Brinkburn. NE38-5D 105
Brinkburn Av. NE3-4C 26
Brinkburn Av. NE8-1D 79
Brinkburn Av. NE16-1F 75
Brinkburn Av. NE23-4E 5
Brinkburn Clo. NE6-2A 62
Brinkburn Clo. NE21-2E 73
Brinkburn Ct. NE6-2A 62
Brinkburn Cres. DH4-3B 126
Brinkburn La. NE6-2A 62
(off Brinkburn Clo.)
Brinkburn Pl. NE6-2A 62
Brinkburn Sq. NE6-2A 62
Brinkburn St. NE6 -1A 62 & 2A 62
Brinkburn St. NE28-3D 49
Brinkburn St. NE34-2A 68
Brinkburn St. SR4-2E 109
Brisbane Av. NE34-4D 67
Brisbane Ct. NE8-4D 61
Brisbane St. SR5-2F 97
Brislee Av. NE30-2E 35
Brislee Gdns. NE3-1A 42
Bristol Av. NE37-4A 94
Bristol Av. SR5-1D 97
Bristol Dri. NE28-5E 31
Bristol Ter. NE4-3F 59
Bristol Way. NE32-1A 84
Britannia Ct. NE4-3F 59
Britannia Pl. NE4-2F 59
Britannia Rd. SR3-3E 119
Britannia Ter. DH4-5E 125
Britten Clo. DH9-3D 131
Brixham Av. NE9-1E 91
Brixham Clo. SR7-4B 132
Brixham Cres. NE32-2C 66
Brixham Gdns. SR3-5A 110
Broad Ash. NE2-5C 44
Broadbank. NE10-2F 81
Broad Chare. NE1 -3D 61 & 5E 143
Broadclose, The. SR8-4C 134
Broadfield Pl. NE34-3B 68
Broadfield Wlk. NE5-1B 40
Broad Garth. NE1 -3D 61 & 5E 143
Broadlands. SR6-2E 87
Broadlea. NE10-2F 81
Broadmayne Av. SR4-3C 108
Broadmayne Gdns. SR4 -3C 108
Broad Meadows. NE3-1A 42
Broadmeadows. NE38 -1C 114
Broad Meadows. SR2-3A 110
Broadmeadows. SR3-4A 118
Broadmead Way. NE15-2E 57
Broadoak. NE10-1F 81
Broadpark. NE10-2A 82
Broadpool Grn. NE16-4B 76
Broadpool Ter. NE16-4B 76
(in two parts)
Broadshaw Wlk. NE15-3E 37
Broadsheath Ter. SR5-3E 99
Broadside. NE10-1F 81
Broadstairs Ct. SR4-4B 108
Broadstone Gro. NE5-3E 39
Broadstone Way. NE28-5E 31
Broad Views. DH3-5A 124
(in two parts)
Broadwater. NE10-1F 81
Broadway. DH3-1E 123
Broadway. NE9-3F 79
Broadway. NE15-5F 39
Broadway. NE16-5E 75
Broadway Clo. NE30-4C 22
Broadway Ct. NE28-3A 32
Broadway E. NE3-2E 27
Broadway, The. DH4-5C 126
Broadway, The. NE30 -5D 23 to 2E 35
Broadway, The. NE33-3B 52
Broadway, The. SR4 -4A 108 & 3C 108
Broadway, The. SR5-5F 97
(in two parts)
Broadway Vs. NE15-2F 57
Broadway W. NE3-3C 26
Broadwell Ct. NE3-5B 28
Broadwood Rd. NE15-5A 40
Broadwood View. DH3 -3F 123
Brockdam Wlk. NE8-5C 60
Brockenhurst Dri. SR4 -5E 107
Brock Farm Ct. NE30-3C 34
Brockhampton Clo. NE35 -5C 66
Brockley Av. NE34-3F 67
Brockley St. SR5-2F 97
Brockley Ter. NE35-1D 85
Brock Sq. NE6-2A 62
Brock St. NE6-2A 62
Brockwade. NE10-5E 81
Brockwell Clo. NE21-1F 73
Brockwell Houses. NE5-2E 41
Brockwell Rd. NE38-2D 103
Broderick Ter. DH4-2B 126
Brodie Clo. NE34-3A 68
Brodrick Clo. NE3-4F 25
Brodrick St. NE33-2F 51
Brokenheugh. NE5-3A 40
Bromford Rd. NE3-5F 25
Bromlea Ct. NE21-4A 56
Bromley Av. NE25-4F 21
Bromley Ct. NE3-2F 25
Bromley Gdns. NE28-5F 31
Brompton Pl. NE11-2F 77
Brompton Ter. DH4-1B 126
Bromsgrove Clo. NE28-4F 31
Bronte Pl. DH9-4E 131
Bronte St. NE8-1A 80
Brookbank Clo. SR3-5E 119
Brookdale. DH1-2E 141
Brooke Av. NE16-2F 75
Brooke Av. NE35-2A 86
Brooke Clo. DH9-3D 131
Brooke St. SR5-5B 100
Brookes Wlk. NE34-5F 67
Brookfield. NE3-2D 43
Brookfield Cres. NE5-3D 39
Brook Gdns. NE26-1C 22
Brookland Dri. NE12-4A 18
Brookland Rd. SR4-2D 109
Brooklands Way. NE35-3C 84
Brookland Ter. NE29-1D 33
(in three parts)
Brook Rd. SR4-2F 109
Brookside. DH5-2C 128
Brookside. NE23-5F 7
Brookside. SR7-2A 132
Brookside Av. NE13-1C 14
Brookside Cotts. SR2-3A 110
Brookside Cres. NE5-3E 41
Brookside Gdns. SR2-3A 110
Brookside Ter. SR2-3B 110
Brookside Wlk. NE38-2C 114
Brooksmead. NE28-5B 30
Brook St. NE6-2C 62
Brook St. NE26-1C 22
Brookvale Av. NE3-1B 42
Brook View. SR7-2A 132
Brook Wlk. SR3-5E 119
Broom Clo. DH9-2E 131
Broom Clo. NE16-4A 76
Broom Clo. NE21-2F 73
Broome Clo. NE3-3B 26
Broome Rd. DH1-2D 141
Broomfield. NE32-5B 66
Broomfield Av. NE6-4A 46
Broomfield Av. NE28-4E 31
Broomfield Gro. NE29-1F 49
Broomfield Rd. NE3-5D 27
Broom Grn. NE16-4B 76
Broom Hill. DH9-1B 130
Broomhill Est. DH5-2E 129
Broomhill Gdns. NE5-3F 41
Broomhill Ter. DH5-2E 129
Broom La. DH1-4A 138
Broom La. NE16-5A 76
Broomlaw. NE9-1A 92
Broomlea. NE29-1D 33
Broomlee Rd. NE12-4E 17
Broomley Wlk. NE3-2B 26
Broomridge Av. NE15-2C 58
Broomshields Av. SR5 -1A 100
Broomshields Clo. SR5 -1A 100
Broomside Ct. DH1-2D 141
Broomside La. DH1-2C 140
Broom Ter. NE16-4B 76
Broomy Hill Rd. NE15-2E 37
Broomylinn Pl. NE23-1E 5
Brotherlee Rd. NE3-3A 26
Brougham St. SR1-1B 110
Brough Ct. NE6-5D 45
Brough Gdns. NE28-5C 32
Brough Pk. Way. NE6-1C 62
Brough St. NE6-5E 45
Broughton Rd. NE33-2E 51
Brough Way. NE6-5D 45
Brown Cres. NE9-3B 92
Browne Rd. SR6-1C 100
Browning Clo. DH9-2E 131
Browning Clo. NE34-4F 67
Browning Sq. NE8-5F 61
Brownlow Clo. NE7-2F 45
Brownlow Rd. NE34-1B 68
Brownrigg Dri. NE23-4E 5
Brownriggs Ct. NE37-1A 104
Brown's Bldgs. DH3-2B 112
Brownsea Pl. NE9-3F 79
Browntop Pl. NE34-2B 68
Brow, The. NE6-3B 62
Broxbourne Ter. SR4-2F 109
Broxburn Clo. NE28-4A 32
Broxburn Ct. NE5-1D 41
Broxholm Rd. NE6-4C 44
Bruce Clo. NE5-2A 40
Bruce Clo. NE34-3A 68
Bruce Gdns. NE5-5D 41
Bruce Kirkup Rd. SR8-1D 135
Bruce Pl. SR8-1B 134
Bruce St. SR5-3A 100

Brundon Av. NE26-5E 13
Brunel St. NE4-4A 60
Brunel St. NE8-2C 78
Brunel Ter. NE4-4E 59
(in two parts)
Brunel Wlk. NE4-4E 59
Brunswick Gro. NE13-1C 14
Brunswick Ind. Est. NE13 -1B 14
Brunswick Pl. NE1 -2C 60 & 3C 143
Brunswick Rd. NE27-5A 20
Brunswick Rd. SR5-1E 97
Brunswick Sq. NE27-5A 20
Brunswick St. NE33-3D 51
Brunton Av. NE3-3A 26
Brunton Av. NE28-2C 48
Brunton Clo. NE27-4A 20
Brunton Gro. NE3-3A 26
Brunton La. NE3 & NE13 -4E 25 to 5D 15
Brunton M. NE13-5B 14
Brunton Rd. NE13 & NE3 -3D 25
Brunton St. NE29-1E 49
Brunton Ter. SR4-2E 109
Brunton Wlk. NE3-3E 25
Brunton Wlk. NE8-5C 60
Brunton Way. NE10-5A 64
(in two parts)
Brussels Rd. NE28-4C 46
Brussels Rd. SR4-5B 98
Bryden Ct. NE34-3B 68
Bryers St. SR6-1D 89
Buchanan Grn. NE11-1E 77
Buchanan St. NE31-2B 64
Buckingham. SR3-2D 119
Buckingham Clo. SR6-1D 89
Buckingham Rd. SR8-2A 134
Buckinghamshire Rd. DH1 -2C 140
Buckingham St. NE4 -2A 60 & 4A 142
Buckland Clo. DH4-3A 126
Buckland Clo. NE38-4C 104
Bucks Hill View. NE16-4B 76
Buckthorne Gro. NE7-1D 45
Buckton Wlk. NE8-5C 60
Buddle Clo. NE4-3C 58
Buddle Clo. SR8-1C 134
Buddle Ct. NE4-3C 58
Buddle Ind. Est. NE28-4D 47
Buddle Rd. NE4-3C 58
Buddle St. NE28-4D 47
Buddle Ter. NE27-5F 19
Buddle Ter. SR2-3D 111
Bude Ct. NE28-5E 31
Bude Gdns. NE9-2E 91
Bude Gro. NE29-1F 33
Budle Clo. NE3-3C 26
Budleigh Rd. NE3-4A 26
Budle Wlk. NE8-5C 60
Bullfinch Dri. NE16-3E 75
Bullion La. DH2-3C 122
Bull La. SR1-5D 101
Bulman Ho. NE3-4E 27
Bulman's La. NE29-2B 34
Bulmer Ho. NE34-1E 69
Bulmer Rd. NE34-5B 52
Bungalows, The. DH3-2A 102
Bungalows, The. DH5-2E 129
Bungalows, The. DH9-1A 130
Bungalows, The. NE10-2D 81
Bungalows, The. NE21-5F 55
Bungalows, The. SR8-2E 135
(in two parts)
Bunyan Av. NE34-4F 67
Burdale Av. NE5-3C 40
Burdon Av. DH5-5E 127
Burdon Av. NE23-2A 4
Burdon Clo. SR6-1D 87
Burdon Cres. SR2-4D 121
Burdon Cres. SR6-1D 87
Burdon Cres. SR7-1A 132
Burdon Gro. SR3-3A 120
Burdon La. SR2-5A 120
Burdon Main Old Wagonway. NE29-1C 50
Burdon Main Row. NE29 -1B 50
Burdon Pl. NE2-4A 44
Burdon Pl. SR8-4D 135
(in two parts)
Burdon Rd. SR1 & SR2 -1C 110
Burdon Rd. SR3-5F 119
Burdon Rd. SR6-1D 87
Burdon St. NE29-1E 49
Burdon Ter. NE2-4F 43
Burford Ct. NE3-5B 28
Burford Gdns. SR3-5A 110
Burghley Rd. NE10-4B 80
Burgoyne Ct. NE37-5B 94
Burke St. SR5-1F 97
Burlawn Clo. SR2-3E 121
Burleigh Garth. SR1-5D 101
Burleigh St. NE33-3F 51
Burlington Clo. SR2-2D 111
Burlington Ct. NE2-2B 44
Burlington Ct. NE28-3A 32
Burlington Gdns. NE6-4D 45
Burlison Gdns. NE10-5B 62
Burnaby Dri. NE40-3A 54
Burnaby St. SR4-2F 109
Burn Av. NE12-1F 29
(in two parts)
Burn Av. NE28-2C 46
Burnbank. NE10-4F 81
Burnbank Av. NE25-2C 20
Burnbridge. NE13-4A 6
Burn Closes Cres. NE28 -2A 48
Burn Crook. DH5-2C 128
Burnden Gro. DH4-5E 115
Burnet Clo. NE28-4E 31
Burney Vs. NE8-1E 79
Burnfoot Ter. NE26-3D 23
Burnfoot Way. NE3-1A 42
Burnhall Dri. SR7-1B 132
Burnham Av. NE15-5C 38
Burnham Gro. NE6-3D 63
Burnham Gro. NE36-3C 86
Burnham St. NE34-1A 68
Burn Heads Rd. NE31-3B 64
Burnhills Gdns. NE40-1A 72
Burnhills La. NE40-1A 72
Burnhope Dri. SR5-2A 100
Burnhope Gdns. NE9-2B 92
Burnhope Rd. NE38-1D 105
Burnhope Way. SR8-3A 134
Burn La. DH5-5E 129
Burnlea Gdns. NE23-2F 9
Burnley St. NE21-5B 56
Burnmoor Gdns. NE9-1B 92
Burnopfield Gdns. NE15 -1F 57
Burn Pk. Rd. DH4-5B 126
Burn Pk. Rd. SR2-2A 110
Burn Prom. DH4-4C 126
(in two parts)
Burn Rd. NE21-1E 73
Burns Av. NE35-2A 86
Burns Av. N. DH5-5D 127
Burns Av. S. DH5-1D 129
Burns Clo. DH9-3D 131
Burns Clo. NE16-5F 75
Burns Clo. NE34-4F 67
Burns Cres. NE16-2F 75
Burnside. NE2-5D 43
(off Richardson Rd.)
Burnside. NE10-3D 81
Burnside. NE25-3D 11
Burnside. NE32-3B 66
Burnside. NE36-3C 86
Burnside. SR8-3B 134
Burnside Av. DH4-4A 126
Burnside Av. NE23-4A 8
Burnside Av. SR8-3F 135
Burnside Clo. NE16-5F 75
Burnside Clo. NE23-3C 8
Burnside Cotts. NE23-4A 8
Burnside Cotts. SR7-5B 132
Burnside Rd. NE3-2E 27
Burnside Rd. NE25 & NE30 -3D 23
Burnside, The. NE5-4A 40
Burnside View. NE23-3C 8
Burns St. NE32-5D 49
Burnstones. NE5-3A 40
Burn Ter. DH4-4A 116
Burn Ter. NE28-2B 48
Burn Ter. NE31-5B 64
Burnthouse Bank. DH2 -2B 122
Burnt Ho. Clo. NE21-2F 73
Burnthouse La. NE61-5F 75
Burnt Ho. Rd. NE25-4F 21
Burntland Av. SR5-3E 99
Burn View. NE23-4A 8
Burnville. NE6-5C 44
Burnville Rd. SR4-2F 109
Burnville Rd. S. SR4-2F 109
Burnway. NE37-5A 94
Burnway. SR7-2B 132
Burradon. NE23-2D 17
Burradon Rd. NE23 -4A 8 to 2D 17
Burrow St. NE33-2E 51
Burscough Cres. SR6-3C 100
Burstow Av. NE6-4D 63
Burt Av. NE29-4A 34
Burt Clo. SR8-1C 134
Burt Cres. NE23-4A 8
Burt Ter. NE15-3C 38
Burwell Av. NE5-4A 40
Burwood Clo. NE6-4E 63
Burwood Rd. NE6-4E 63
Burwood Rd. NE29-2E 33
Buston Ter. NE2-4B 44
Butcher's Bri. Rd. NE32-3F 65
Bute Cotts. NE11-1D 77
Bute Ct. SR3-4E 119
Buteland Rd. NE15-5B 40
Butsfield Gdns. SR3-5F 109
Buttermere. NE10-2E 81
Buttermere. SR6-1F 87
Buttermere Av. NE16-3B 76
Buttermere Clo. DH2-4D 123
Buttermere Clo. NE5-4D 41
Buttermere Cres. NE21-2F 73
Buttermere Gdns. NE9-5F 79
Buttermere Gdns. NE34 -1C 68
Buttermere Rd. NE30-5C 22
Buttermere St. SR2-1D 121
Buttsfield Ter. DH4-2A 116
Buxton Clo. NE28-4F 31
Buxton Gdns. NE5-1B 40
Buxton Gdns. SR3-5A 110
Buxton Grn. NE5-1B 40
Buxton Rd. NE32-3B 66
Buxton St. NE1 -2E 61 & 4F 143
Byer Bank. DH5-1E 129
Byers Ct. SR3-2F 119
Byer Sq. DH5-2F 129
Byer St. DH5-2F 129
Byeways, The. NE12-3D 29
Bygate Clo. NE3-1A 42
Bygate Rd. NE25-3A 22
Byker Bank. NE6-2F 61
Byker Bri. NE2 -1E 61 & 3F 143
Byker Bldgs. NE6-1F 61
Byker Cres. NE6-1B 62
Byker Lodge. NE6-2A 62
Byker St. NE6-2E 63
Byland Clo. DH4-3A 126
Byland Ct. NE38-2B 104
Byland Rd. NE12-3B 28
Bylands Gdns. SR3-5F 109
Byony Toft. SR2-4E 121
Byrness. NE5-3A 40
Byrness Clo. NE3-5E 25
Byrness Ct. NE28-4F 31
Byrness Row. NE23-1E 5
Byrne Ter. SR3-3A 120
Byrne Ter. W. SR3-3F 119
Byron Av. DH2-2A 122
Byron Av. NE28-3C 48
Byron Av. NE31-1D 65
Byron Av. NE35-2E 85
Byron Clo. DH9-3D 131
Byron Ct. NE5-2E 39
Byron Ct. NE16-2F 75
Byron Lodge Est. SR7-2A 132
Byron Rd. SR5-3F 99
Byron St. NE2 -1D 61 & 2E 143
Byron St. NE33-4E 51
Byron St. SR5-3A 100
Byron Ter. SR7-1A 132
Byron Wlk. NE8-5F 61
Byrton Ter. DH5-1D 129
By-Way, The. NE15-3F 37
Bywell Av. NE3-2B 26
Bywell Av. NE15-5A 40
Bywell Av. NE34-5C 52
Bywell Av. SR5-2A 100
Bywell Dri. SR8-5B 134
Bywell Gdns. NE10-4A 80
Bywell Gdns. NE11-5F 77
Bywell Gro. NE27-3B 20
Bywell Rd. SR6-2D 87
Bywell St. NE6-2C 62
(in two parts)
Bywell Ter. NE32-4A 66
Cadles Ct. NE23-1E 5
Caernarvon Clo. NE5-1D 41
Caernarvon Dri. SR3-4B 118
Caer Urfa Clo. NE33-5E 35
Caesar's Wlk. NE33-5E 35
Cairncross. SR5-4E 97
Cairnglass Grn. NE23-1E 5
Cairngorm Av. NE38-5F 103
Cairnhill Ter. DH4-1B 126
Cairnside. SR3-3A 118
Cairnside S. SR3-3A 118
Cairnsmore Clo. NE6-4C 46
Cairnsmore Clo. NE23-5D 5
Cairnsmore Dri. NE38-4A 104
Cairns Rd. SR5-1A 100
Cairns Sq. SR5-1B 100
Cairns Way. NE3-2B 26
Cairo St. SR2-4D 111
Caithness Rd. SR5-3E 97
Caithness Sq. SR5-3E 97
Calais Rd. SR5-4E 97
Caldbeck Av. NE6-4E 63
Caldbeck Clo. NE6-4D 63
Calderbourne Av. SR6 -1D 101
Calder Ct. SR3-4E 119
Calderdale. NE28-5B 30
Calderdale Av. NE6-1E 63
Calder Grn. NE32-5B 66
Calders Cres. NE38-1C 114
Calderwood Cres. NE9-2E 91
Calderwood Pk. NE9-2F 91
Caldew Cres. NE5-4B 40
Caldwell Rd. NE3-2B 26
Caledonia. DH3-4A 124
Caledonia. NE21-1F 73
Caledonian Rd. SR5-2E 97
Caledonian St. NE31-5F 47
Caledonia St. NE6-3F 63
Calfclose La. NE32-5A 66
Calfclose Wlk. NE32-5A 66
California. NE21-1A 74
(in two parts)
Callaley Av. NE16-4D 75
Callaly Av. NE23-4D 5
Callaly Way. NE6-3C 62
Callendar Ct. NE9-5A 80
Callerton Av. NE29-3E 33
Callerton Clo. NE23-4D 5
Callerton Pl. NE4-2E 59
Callerton Rd. NE15-3F 37
Calley Clo. SR8-5B 134
Callington Clo. DH4-3C 124
Callington Dri. SR2-3E 121
Calow Way. NE16-5E 75
Calver Ct. NE34-2C 68
Calvus Dri. NE15-2A 36
Cambell St. NE31-1C 64
Camberley Clo. SR3-3A 120
Camberley Rd. NE28-1B 48
Camberwell Clo. NE11-3A 78
Cambo Av. NE25-4F 21
Cambo Clo. NE3-4F 27
Cambo Clo. NE28-4F 31
Cambo Dri. NE23-4D 5
Cambo Grn. NE5-3E 41
Cambo Pl. NE30-1B 34
Camborne Gro. NE8-1D 79
Camborne Pl. NE8-1D 79
Cambourne Av. SR6-1D 101
Cambria Grn. SR4-2E 107
Cambrian Clo. NE38-4A 104
Cambrian St. NE32-5D 49
Cambrian Way. NE38-5A 104
Cambria St. SR4-2F 107
Cambridge Av. NE12-2E 29
Cambridge Av. NE26-2C 22
Cambridge Av. NE28-2B 46
Cambridge Av. NE31-1E 65
Cambridge Av. NE37-4F 93
Cambridge Cres. DH4-4E 115
Cambridge Pl. DH3-1B 112
Cambridge Rd. SR3-3F 119
Cambridge Rd. SR8-1B 134
Cambridgeshire Dri. DH1 -3C 140
Cambridge St. NE4-4F 59
Cambridge Ter. NE8-1D 79
Camden Sq. SR7-4E 133
Camden St. NE2 -1D 61 & 2E 143
Camden St. NE30-4C 34
Camden St. SR5-4E 99
Camelford Ct. NE15-5D 39
Camelot Clo. SR7-2E 133
Cameron Clo. NE34-4A 68
Cameron Wlk. NE11-5B 58
Camerton Pl. NE28-3A 32
Camilla Rd. NE15-2B 36
Camilla St. NE8-1F 79
Cammead. SR3-5E 119
Campbell Pk. Rd. NE31 -1D 65 to 4E 65
Campbell Pl. NE4-2F 59
Campbell Rd. SR5-3E 97
Campbell Sq. SR5-3E 97
Camperdown. NE5-3B 40
Camperdown Av. DH3-5B 112
Camperdown Av. NE12-2D 17
Camperdown Cen. NE12 -2C 16
Camperdown Ind. Est. NE12 -2C 17
Campion Dri. DH9-1A 130
Campion Gdns. NE10-5B 80
Campsie Clo. NE38-4A 104
Campsie Cres. NE30-1C 34
Camp Ter. NE29-3B 34
Campus Martius. NE15-3A 36
Campville. NE29-3B 34
Camsey Clo. NE12-3B 28
Camsey Pl. NE12-3B 28
Canberra Av. NE25-3F 21
Canberra Dri. NE34-3D 67
Canberra Rd. SR4-4C 108
Candelford Clo. NE7-2F 45
Candlish St. NE33-2F 51
Candlish Ter. SR7-4F 133
Canning St. NE4-2C 58
Canning St. NE31-2C 64
Cannock. NE12-3F 17
Cannock Dri. NE7-1C 44
Cannon St. NE4-4D 59
Cannon St. NE8 -3D 61 & 5E 143
Cann Rd. SR8-2C 134
Canonbie Sq. NE23-1E 5
Canon Cockin St. SR2 -3D 111
Canon Gro. NE32-5E 49
Canonsfield Clo. NE5-2C 38
Canonsfield Clo. SR3-5D 119
Canterbury Av. NE28-4F 31
Canterbury Clo. DH3-5A 124
Canterbury Rd. DH1 -3D 137 to 1D 137
Canterbury Rd. SR5-2F 97
Canterbury St. NE6 -1C 62 & 2C 62
Canterbury St. NE33-4F 51
Canterbury Way. NE13-1D 15
Canterbury Way. NE32-1F 83
Capercaille Lodge. NE23-3A 8
(in two parts)
Capetown Rd. SR5-2D 97
Capetown Sq. SR5-2D 97
Caplestone Clo. NE38-4A 104
Capstan Ct. NE9-2B 92
(off Capstan La.)
Capstan La. NE9-3B 92
Captains Row, The. NE33 -4D 51
Capulet Gro. NE34-2E 67
Capulet Ter. SR2-3D 111
Caradoc Clo. NE38-4F 103
Caragh Rd. DH2-5D 123
Caraway Wlk. NE34-5C 68
Carden Av. NE34-2F 69
Cardiff Sq. SR5-3E 97
Cardigan Gro. NE30-4B 22
Cardigan Rd. SR5-3E 97
Cardigan Ter. NE6-5C 44
Cardinal Clo. NE5-2C 38
Cardinals Clo. SR3-5D 119
Cardonnel St. NE29-5B 34
Cardwell St. SR6-3C 100
Careen Cres. SR3-3A 118
Carew Ct. NE23-4D 5
Carham Av. NE23-3E 5
Carham Clo. NE3-4F 27
Caris St. NE8-2E 79
Carlcroft Pl. NE23-4D 5
Carley Hill Rd. SR5-2A 100
Carley Rd. SR5-3A 100
Carley Sq. SR5-3A 100
Carlile Ho. NE4-2F 59
(off Northgate St.)
Carlingford Rd. DH2-4D 123
Carliol Pl. NE1 -2D 61 & 3D 143
Carliol Sq. NE1 -2C 60 & 4D 143
Carliol St. NE1 -2C 60 & 4D 143
Carlisle Ct. NE10-1C 80
Carlisle Cres. DH4-3F 115
Carlisle Pl. NE9-5F 79
Carlisle Rd. DH1-2E 137
Carlisle St. NE10-1C 80
Carlisle Ter. NE27-5F 19
Carlisle Ter. SR5-3E 99
Carlton Clo. NE3-1C 42
Carlton Ct. NE11-5B 78
Carlton Cres. SR3-3B 118
Carlton Gdns. NE15-5A 40
Carlton Rd. NE12-4E 29
Carlton Ter. NE9-5D 79
(Low Fell)
Carlton Ter. NE9-4E 93
(Springwell)
Carlton Ter. NE29-4A 34
Carlyle Ct. NE28-3C 48
Carlyle Cres. NE16-2F 75
Carlyle St. NE28-3C 48
Carlyon St. SR2-2B 110
Carmel Rd. DH9-3B 130
Carnaby Rd. NE6-3E 63
Carnation Av. DH4-2C 124
Carnation Ter. NE16-3A 76
Carnegie Clo. NE34-3A 68
Carnegie St. SR2-5D 111
Carnforth Clo. NE28-2F 31
Carnforth Gdns. NE9-1F 91
Carnforth Grn. NE3-5A 26
Carnoustie. NE37-2B 94
Carnoustie Clo. NE7-5D 29
Carnoustie Ct. NE10-4A 82
Carnoustie Dri. NE34-4E 69
Carol Gdns. NE7-1C 44
Caroline Cotts. NE5-4C 40
Caroline Gdns. NE28-1C 48
Caroline St. DH5-4F 129
Caroline St. NE4-3D 59
Caroline St. NE32-1F 65
Caroline St. SR7-3E 133
Caroline Ter. NE21-3F 55
Carol St. SR4-5F 99
Carolyn Clo. NE12-4E 29
Carolyn Cres. NE26-5C 12
Carolyn Way. NE26-5C 12
Carpenter St. NE33-3D 51
Carrfield Rd. NE3-4B 26
Carr Hill Rd. NE9 & NE10 -2F 79
Carr Ho. Dri. DH1-3C 136
Carrington Clo. NE23-2D 9
Carrisbrook Ct. SR1-1A 110
Carrmere Rd. SR2-1C 120
Carrock Clo. SR8-5C 134
Carrock Ct. SR3-4E 119
Carroll Wlk. NE34-5F 67
Carrowmore Rd. DH2-5D 123
Carrsdale. DH1-1D 141
Carrside. DH1-3B 136
Carrs, The. DH1-2C 136
Carr St. NE31-1B 64
Carrsway. DH1-1D 141
Carrsyde Clo. NE16-5E 75
(in two parts)
Carrville Link Rd. DH1 -2E 139 to 1C 140
Carsdale Rd. NE3-4F 25
Carter Av. NE31-1C 64
Cartington Av. NE27-4A 20
Cartington Clo. SR8-5C 134
Cartington Ct. NE3-3F 25
Cartington Rd. DH1-4D 137
Cartington Rd. NE29-5F 33
Cartington Ter. NE6-4D 45
Cartmel Grn. NE5-4C 40
Cartmel Gro. NE8-3B 78
Cartmel Pk. NE10-1F 81
Cartwright Rd. SR5-4F 97
Carville Gdns. NE28-4D 47
Carville Rise. NE6-2A 62
Carville Rd. NE28 -3D 47 & 4D 47
Carville Station Cotts. NE28 -3E 47
Carville St. NE10-5A 62
Carwarding Pl. NE5-3E 41
Caseton Clo. NE25-1E 21
Caspian Clo. NE32-2A 66
Caspian Rd. SR5-4E 97
Caspian Sq. SR5-4E 97
Castellian Rd. SR5-3B 98
Casterton Gro. NE5-2D 39
Castle Chare. DH1-2C 138
Castle Clo. DH3-4F 123
Castle Clo. DH5-5F 129
Castle Clo. NE3-4F 25
Castle Clo. NE16-3F 75
Castledene Ct. NE3-5B 28
Castle Dene Gro. DH4-5B 126
Castle Farm M. NE2-1A 44
Castle Farm Rd. NE3-1A 44
Castle Fields. DH4-2B 124
Castleford Rd. SR5-3E 97
Castle Garth. NE1 -3C 60 & 5D 143
Castlegate Gdns. NE8-1F 77
Castlemain Clo. DH4-2B 124
Castle M. SR3-3C 118
(off Ascot Ct.)
Castlenook Pl. NE15-5B 40
Castlereagh Rd. SR7-3E 133
Castlereagh St. SR3-3F 119
Castlereigh Clo. DH4-2B 124
Castle Rd. NE38-2E 103
Castles Grn. NE12-4A 18
Castles Grn. SR3-3C 118
Castleside Rd. NE15-1F 57
Castle Sq. NE27-2C 18
Castle Stairs. NE1 -3C 60 & 5D 143
Castle St. NE13-3C 14
Castle St. SR1-1B 110
Castle St. S. SR5-4A 98
Castleton Clo. NE2-2B 44
Castleton Gro. NE2-2B 44
Castleton Lodge. NE4-3E 59
Castleton Rd. NE32-2B 66
Castletown Rd. SR5-3B 98
Castletown Way. SR5-3C 98
Castle View. DH3-1E 123
Castle View. DH4-3A 116
Castle View. SR5-4F 97
Catcheside Clo. NE16-5F 75
Catchside. NE16-5F 75
Cateran Way. NE23-5D 5
Caterhouse Rd. DH1-3C 136
Catharine St. W. SR4-1F 109
Cathedral Ct. NE8-4E 61
Cathedral View. DH4-2C 126
Catherine Cookson Ct. NE33 -4A 52
Catherine Rd. DH4-4B 116
Catherine St. NE33-2E 51
Catherine Ter. DH9-1D 131
Catherine Ter. NE10-2B 80
Cato Sq. SR5-2F 99
Cato St. SR5-2E 99
Catrail Pl. NE23-1E 5
Catton Pl. NE28-3F 31
Caulderdale Wlk. NE3-4F 25
Cauldwell Av. NE25-4E 21
Cauldwell Av. NE34-5F 51
Cauldwell Clo. NE25-3F 21
Cauldwell La. NE25-3F 21
Cauldwell Pl. NE34-5F 51
Cauldwell Vs. NE34-5F 51
Causeway. NE9-3F 79
Causeway. SR6-4C 100
Causeway, The. NE9-2F 79
Causeway, The. NE15-3F 37
Causeway, The. NE32-1C 66
Causey Bank. NE1 -2D 61 & 4E 143
Causey Bldgs. NE3-1E 43
Causey Dri. DH9-1D 131
Causey St. NE3-1E 43
Causey View. DH9-2F 131
Cavel Burrs. SR2-4E 121
Cavell Pl. DH9-4E 131
Cavell Rd. SR5-2E 97
Cavendish Pl. NE2-3A 44
Cavendish Pl. SR3-3E 119
Cavendish Rd. NE2-3B 44
Caversham Rd. NE5-2D 39
Cawnpore Sq. SR4-1C 108
Cawthorne Ter. NE29-2B 34
(off Front St.)
Caxton Wlk. NE34-5F 67
Caxton Way. DH3-2C 112
(in three parts)
Caynham Clo. NE29-1A 34
Cayton Gro. NE5-2D 39
Cecil Ct. NE28-5C 46
Cecil St. NE29-4B 34
Cedar Clo. DH1-3B 140
Cedar Clo. NE25-4A 22
Cedar Cres. NE9-5D 79
Cedar Cres. NE11-2E 77
Cedar Cres. SR7-4D 133
Cedar Gro. NE28-3F 47
Cedar Gro. NE31-4D 65
Cedar Gro. NE34-2E 69
Cedar Gro. NE40-2A 54
Cedar Gro. SR6-5D 71
Cedar Rd. NE4-5E 41
Cedar Rd. NE21-5B 56
Cedars. DH2-5A 112
Cedars Ct. SR2-3C 110
Cedars Cres. SR2-4C 110
Cedars Grn. NE9-2F 91
Cedars Pk. SR2-4C 110
Cedars, The. DH4-2A 116
Cedars, The. NE4-4F 59
Cedars, The. NE9-3B 92
Cedars, The. NE16-5A 76
Cedars, The. SR2-4C 110
Cedar St. DH2-5A 122
Cedar St. SR8-3F 135
Cedar Ter. DH4-4F 125
Cedar Ter. NE38-1A 114
Cedartree Gdns. NE25-4A 22
Cedarway. NE10-5C 80
Cedar Way. NE12-1A 30
Cedarwood. DH4-4D 125
Cedarwood. NE9-5B 80
Cedarwood Av. NE6-3B 46
Cedarwood Av. NE29-1A 50
Cedarwood Gro. SR2-5B 110
Cedric Cres. SR4-3F 109
Celadon Clo. NE15-4E 39
Celandine Clo. NE3-2E 27
Celandine Way. NE10-4C 80
Cellar Hill Ter. DH4-3B 126
Celtic Clo. SR6-1D 87
Celtic Cres. SR6-1D 87
Cemetery App. NE34-5A 52
Cemetery Rd. DH9-1C 130
Cemetery Rd. NE8-1E 79
Cemetery Rd. NE32-2A 66
Centenary Av. NE34-2E 69
Centenary Ct. NE4-3E 59
Central Arc. NE1-2C 60
(off Market St.)
Central Av. NE29-4F 33
Central Av. NE34-1D 69
Central Av. SR6-1D 89
Central Gdns. NE34-2D 69
Central Lwr. Prom. NE26 -1C 22
Centralway. NE11-1B 90
Centurian Way. NE9-4A 80
Centurion Rd. NE15-5A 40
Centurion Way. NE15-2A 36
Ceolfrid Ter. NE32-3A 66
Ceremonial Way. NE1 -1C 60 & 2D 142
(off St Mary's Pl.)
Chacombe. NE38-4B 104
Chadderton Dri. NE5-2D 39
Chad Ho. NE8-5E 61
Chadlers Quay. NE6-4B 62
Chadwick St. NE28-3D 47
Chadwick Wlk. NE8-5B 60
Chaffinch Rd. SR5-4A 98
Chainbridge Rd. NE21 -4C 56 to 4E 57
Chainbridge Rd. NE21-3D 57
Chains, The. DH1-2D 139
Chalfont Gro. SR4-5E 107
Chalfont Rd. NE6-3E 63
Chalford Rd. SR5-3A 100
Chambers Cres. NE9-3A 92
Chandler Ct. NE2-2B 44
Chandlers Ford. DH4-2D 115
Chandlers Quay. NE6-4B 62
Chandos. SR3-5F 119
Chandos St. NE8-2E 79
Chandra Pl. NE5-2D 41
Chantry Clo. SR3-5D 119
Chantry Dri. NE13-5A 6
Chapel Clo. NE3-1E 27
Chapel Ct. NE13-4A 6
Chapel Hill Rd. SR8-3D 135
Chapel Ho. Dri. NE5-3E 39
Chapel Ho. Gro. NE5-3E 39
Chapel Ho. Rd. NE5-3E 39
Chapel La. NE25-2A 22
Chapel Pk. Shopping Cen. NE5-1E 39
Chapel Pas. DH1-2D 139
Chapel Pl. NE13-4A 6
Chapel Rd. NE32-5D 49
Chapel Row. DH3-4D 103
Chapel Row. DH4-1C 124
(Bournmoor)
Chapel Row. DH4-5B 116
(New Herrington)
Chapel Row. DH4-5B 116
(Shiney Row)
Chapel St. DH5-3F 129
Chapel St. NE29-4A 34
Chapel View. NE13-1C 14
Chapelville. NE13-4A 6
Chaplin St. SR7-4E 133
Chapman St. SR6-1C 100
Chapter Row. NE33-2D 51
Chare, The. NE1 -1B 60 & 3C 142
Chare, The. SR8-3C 134
Charlbury Clo. NE9-3E 93
Charlcote Cres. NE36-2C 86
Charles Av. NE3-3A 26
Charles Av. NE12-1E 29
Charles Av. NE26-1C 22
Charles Av. NE27-3A 20
Charles Baker Wlk. NE34 -1A 70
Charles Ct. NE6-5D 45
(off Elvet Clo.)
Charles Dri. NE23-4F 7
Charles St. DH4-1C 126
Charles St. DH9-4B 130
Charles St. NE8-5D 61
Charles St. NE13-2B 14
Charles St. NE35-2D 85
Charles St. SR1-5C 100
Charles St. SR2-4F 121
Charles St. SR3-3F 119
Charles St. SR6-5C 100
Charles St. SR7-3E 133
Charles Ter. DH2-1A 122
Charleswood. NE3-2E 27
Charlotte Clo. NE4-4F 59
Charlotte M. NE1 -2B 60 & 4B 142
Charlotte Sq. NE1 -2B 60 & 4B 142
Charlotte St. DH9-4B 130
Charlotte St. NE28-2E 47
Charlotte St. NE30-4D 35
Charlotte St. NE33-2E 51
Charlton Ct. NE25-4A 22
Charlton Gro. SR6-2E 87
Charlton Rd. SR5-1B 100
Charlton St. NE15-1C 56
Charlton Vs. NE40-1A 72
(off Lead Rd.)
Charlton Wlk. NE8-1B 78
Charman St. SR1-1B 110
Charminster Gdns. NE6-3E 45
Charnwood Av. NE12-4C 28
Charnwood Ct. NE33-3A 52
Charnwood Gdns. NE9-5F 79
Charter Dri. SR3-3A 118
Chase, The. NE12-3C 28
(Longbenton)
Chase, The. NE12-5C 16
(West Moor)
Chase, The. NE29-4B 34
Chase, The. NE38-2E 113
Chatham Clo. NE25-2C 10
Chatham Rd. SR5-3E 97
Chathill Clo. NE25-2E 21
Chathill Ter. NE6-2D 63
Chatsworth. NE3-2D 43
Chatsworth Ct. NE33-1E 51
Chatsworth Cres. SR4-3F 109
Chatsworth Gdns. NE5-1B 40
Chatsworth Gdns. NE6-3C 62
Chatsworth Gdns. NE25 -4F 21
Chatsworth Pl. NE16-5F 75
Chatsworth Rd. NE32-2B 66
Chatsworth St. SR4-2E 109
Chatsworth St. S. SR4-3F 109
Chatterton St. SR5-3E 99
Chatton Av. NE23-4E 5
Chatton Av. NE34-5D 53
Chatton Clo. DH2-4C 122
Chatton St. NE28-3E 49
Chatton Wynd. NE3-3C 26
Chaucer Av. NE34-4E 67
Chaucer Clo. DH9-2D 131
Chaucer Clo. NE8-5E 61
Chaucer Rd. NE16-2F 75
Chaucer St. DH4-5C 126
Chaucer St. NE8-5E 61
Chaytor Gro. NE32-5D 49
Chaytor Ter. N. DH9-5F 131
Chaytor Ter. S. DH9-5F 131
Cheadle Av. NE28-4F 31
Cheadle Rd. SR5-2E 97
Cheam Clo. NE16-5A 76
Cheam Rd. SR5-3E 97
Cheddar Gdns. NE9-2E 91
Cheeseburn Gdns. NE5-4E 41
Cheldon Clo. NE25-1E 21
Chelford Clo. NE28-2A 32
Chelmsford Gro. NE2 -5B 44 & 1F 143
Chelmsford Rd. SR5-2E 97
Chelmsford Sq. SR5-2E 97
Chelmsford St. SR3-2E 119
Chelsea Gdns. NE8-2F 79
Chelsea Gro. NE4-2E 59
Chelsea Ho. DH9-1C 130
(off Quarry Rd.)
Cheltenham Dri. NE35-5C 66
Cheltenham Rd. SR5-3E 97
Cheltenham Sq. SR5-3E 97
Cheltenham Ter. NE6-5D 45
Chelton Clo. NE13-3C 14
Chepstow Gdns. NE8-2B 78
Chepstow Rd. NE15-1E 57
Chepstow St. SR4-2F 109
Cherribank. SR2-4D 121
Cherry Banks. DH3-5C 112
Cherry Blossom Way. SR5 -4A 96
Cherryburn Gdns. NE4-4A 42
Cherrytree Clo. NE12-4B 18
Cherrytree Dri. NE16-2B 76
Cherrytree Gdns. NE9-5E 79
Cherrytree Gdns. NE25-4A 22
Cherrytree Rd. DH2-1C 122
Cherrytree Sq. SR2-2D 121
Cherry Tree Wlk. NE31-3D 65
Cherry Way. DH4-4F 125
Cherwell. NE37-5E 95
Cherwell Rd. SR8-4A 134
Cherwell Sq. NE12-1E 29
Chesham Gdns. NE5-2D 39
Chesham Grn. NE3-5B 26
Cheshire Ct. NE31-2C 64
Cheshire Dri. DH1-3C 140
Cheshire Gdns. NE28-2B 46
Cheshire Gro. NE34-5D 53
Chesils, The. NE12-4C 28
Chesmond Dri. NE21-4A 56
Chessar Av. NE5-2D 41
Chester Av. NE28-2A 48
Chester Cres. NE2 -5A 44 & 1F 143
Chester Cres. SR1-1A 110
Chesterfield Rd. NE4-3E 59
Chester Gdns. NE34-5A 52
Chester Gro. NE23-3D 9
Chesterhill. NE23-5D 5
Chester M. SR4-2F 109
Chester Oval. SR2-2A 110
Chester Pl. NE8-5C 60
Chester Pl. SR8-2A 134
Chester Rd. DH3 -5C 112 & 2A 124
Chester Rd. DH4-2B 124
Chester Rd. DH9-2D 131
Chester Rd. SR4, SR2 & SR1 -4A 116 to 2A 110
Chester Rd. Est. DH9-2D 131
Chesters Av. NE12-4B 28
Chesters Clo. NE9-4D 79
Chesters Ct. NE12-4D 29
Chesters, The. NE5-3D 39
Chesters, The. NE25-1F 21
Chester St. DH2-5A 122
Chester St. DH4-3B 126
Chester St. NE2 -1D 61 & 2E 143
Chester St. SR4-1F 109
Chester St. E. SR4-1F 109
Chester St. W. SR4-2F 109
Chester Ter. SR1-1A 110
Chester Ter. N. SR4-1F 109
Chesterton Rd. NE34-4F 67
Chester Way. NE32-1F 83
Chesterwood Dri. NE28-2C 46
Chesterwood Ter. NE10-5F 63
Chestnut Av. NE5-3F 41
Chestnut Av. NE16-5F 75
Chestnut Av. NE25-3B 22
Chestnut Av. NE38-1F 113
Chestnut Clo. NE32-1B 84
Chestnut Cres. SR5-2E 99
Chestnut Gdns. NE8-2A 78
Chestnut Gro. NE34-3D 69

Chestnut St. NE28-3D 47
Chestnut Ter. DH4-2A 126
Cheswick Dri. NE3-4E 27
Cheswick Rd. NE25-2C 10
Cheveley Pk. Shopping DH1
-2D 141
Cheveley Wlk. DH1-3D 141
Chevin Clo. NE6-4C 46
Chevington. NE10-5E 81
Chevington Gdns. NE5-3E 41
Chevington Gro. NE25-5C 12
Cheviot Clo. DH2-5C 122
Cheviot Clo. NE29-5A 22
Cheviot Ct. NE7-5C 28
Cheviot Ct. NE21-4B 56
Cheviot Ct. NE26-3E 23
Cheviot Gdns. NE11-3F 77
Cheviot Grange. NE23-1D 17
Cheviot Grn. NE11-2E 77
Cheviot Ho. NE38-3A 104
Cheviot La. SR2-3C 120
Cheviot Mt. NE6-1A 62
Cheviot Pl. SR8-3A 134
Cheviot Rd. DH2
-4C 122 & 4D 123
Cheviot Rd. NE21-1A 74
Cheviot Rd. NE32-4E 65
Cheviot Rd. NE34-4B 52
Cheviot St. SR4-1D 109
Cheviot Ter. DH9-4D 131
Cheviot View. NE12-4E 29
Cheviot View. NE13-1C 14
Cheviot View. NE23-3D 9
Cheviot View. NE26-2D 23
Cheviot View. NE27-1F 31
Chevy Chase. NE1
-1C 60 & 3C 142
(off Eldon Sq.)
Cheyne, The. SR3-5F 119
Chichester Av. NE23-2A 4
Chichester Clo. NE3-2E 25
Chichester Clo. NE8-5D 61
Chichester Pl. NE33-4E 51
Chichester Rd. DH1-1D 137
Chichester Rd. NE33-4E 51
Chichester Rd. SR6-1D 101
Chichester Rd. E. NE33-3F 51
Chichester Way. NE32-1F 83
Chicken Rd. NE28-1C 46
Chick's La. SR6-2D 89
Chigwell Clo. DH4-4A 116
Chilcote. NE10-3C 80
Chilcrosse. NE10-4E 81
Chilham Ct. NE29-2D 33
Chilham Ct. NE38-3F 103
Chillingham Ct. NE6-5E 45
Chillingham Dri. DH2-5B 122
Chillingham Rd. DH1-3D 137
Chillingham Rd. NE6-3D 45
Chillingham Ter. NE32-3C 66
Chilside Rd. NE10-3B 80
Chiltern Av. DH2-4D 123
Chiltern Clo. NE38-4F 103
Chiltern Dri. NE12-5D 17
Chiltern Gdns. DH9-4E 131
(in two parts)
Chiltern Gdns. NE11-3F 77
Chiltern Rd. NE29-5A 22
Chilton Gdns. DH4-5E 125
(in two parts)
Chilton Garth. SR8-4E 135
Chilton St. SR5-3A 100
China St. SR2-4C 110
Chingford Clo. DH4-4A 116
Chipchase. NE38-3E 103
Chipchase Av. NE23-4D 5
Chipchase Cres. NE5-1A 40
Chipchase Ter. NE32-4A 66
Chippendale Pl. NE2-5D 43
Chirnside. NE23-5D 5
Chirton Av. NE29-4A 34
Chirton Av. NE34-1B 70
Chirton Dene Way. NE29
-2B 50
Chirton Grn. NE29-4A 34
Chirton Gro. NE34-1A 70
Chirton Hill Dri. NE29-2E 33
Chirton La. NE29-4A 34
Chirton W. View. NE29-4B 34
Chirton Wynd. NE6-2B 62
Chislehurst Rd. DH4-3A 116
Chiswick Gdns. NE8-2F 79
Chiswick Rd. SR5-3E 97
Chiswick Sq. SR5-3F 97
Chollerford Av. NE25-3C 22
Chollerford Av. NE29-3E 33
Chollerford Clo. NE3-5C 26
Chollerford M. NE25-2D 11
Chollerton Dri. NE12-2C 30
Chopwell Gdns. NE9-2B 92
Chorley Pl. NE6-2D 63
Chowdene Bank. NE9-3D 91
Chowdene Ter. NE9-1E 91
Christal Ter. SR6-2C 100
Christchurch Pl. SR8-4A 134
Christie Ter. NE6-2D 63
Christon Clo. NE3-4F 27
Christon Rd. NE3-4E 27
Christon Way. NE10-5A 64
Christopher Rd. NE6-5A 46
Chudleigh Gdns. NE5-2D 39
Chudleigh Ter. NE21-5B 56
Church Av. NE3-5F 27
Church Bank. DH9-2C 130
Church Bank. NE15-5B 38
Church Bank. NE28-2F 47
Church Bank. NE32-5F 49
Church Bank. SR5-3E 99
Church Chare. DH3-3E 123
Church Chare. NE16-3A 76
Church Clo. DH4-1C 124
Church Clo. SR7-2D 133
Church Clo. SR8-4C 134
Church Ct. NE10-1C 80
Church Ct. SR7-2B 132
Churchdown Clo. NE35-5C 66
Church Dri. NE9-4F 79
Churcher Gdns. NE28-5C 30
Church Grn. NE16-3A 76
Church Grn. SR7-2D 133
Churchill Av. DH1-2F 139
Churchill Av. NE25-3A 22
Churchill Av. SR5-3F 99
Churchill Gdns. NE2
-4B 44 & 4C 44
Churchill Sq. DH1-1F 139
(off Gort Pl.)
Churchill Sq. DH4-5F 125
Churchill St. NE1
-3B 60 & 5A 142
Churchill St. NE28
-5A 32 to 2B 48
Churchill St. SR1-2C 110
Church La. DH1-3D 139
Church La. NE3-5F 27
Church La. NE9-4F 79
Church La. SR1-1B 110
Church La. SR6-2D 89
Church Pl. NE10-1B 80
Church Rise. NE16-3A 76
Church Rise. NE40-2C 54
Church Rd. DH5-2F 129
Church Rd. NE3-5E 27
Church Rd. NE9-5E 79
Church Rd. NE15-5B 38
Church Rd. NE27-2E 19
(in two parts)
Church Row. NE10-3B 80
(off Windy Nook Rd.)
Church Side. DH3-5B 124
Church St. DH1-3D 139
Church St. DH3-4B 102
Church St. DH4-4F 115
Church St. DH4-5C 126
(New Town)
Church St. DH4-4A 116
(Shiney Row)
Church St. DH9-2C 130
Church St. NE6
-2E 63 & 3F 63
Church St. NE8
-3D 61 & 5E 143
Church St. NE10-2B 80
Church St. NE11-1E 77
Church St. NE21-1F 73
Church St. NE23-3C 4
Church St. NE30-4D 35
Church St. NE31-1B 64
(in two parts)
Church St. NE32-5C 48
Church St. SR4-1F 107
Church St. SR5-3F 99
Church St. SR7-3E 133
Church St. E. SR1-5D 101
Church St. Head. DH1-4D 139
(in two parts)
Church St. N. SR6-4C 100
Church St. Vs. DH1-4D 139
Church Ter. NE21-4B 56
Church View. DH1-2D 141
Church View. DH3-4B 102
Church View. NE25-2B 20
Church View. NE35-1C 84
Church View. NE37-1C 104
Church View. SR3-3E 119
Church View Vs. DH5-3F 129
(off Co-operative Ter.)
Church Wlk. NE6-2E 63
(in two parts)
Church Wlk. NE8
-3D 61 & 5E 143
Church Wlk. NE8-3E 63
Church Wlk. SR1-1D 111
Churchwalk Ho. NE6-2F 63
Church Ward. SR2-4E 121
Church Way. NE25-1B 20
Church Way. NE29-4C 34
Church Way. NE33-2D 51
Church Wynd. DH6-5F 141
Cicero Ter. SR5-3E 99
Cinderford Clo. NE35-5C 66
Circle, The. NE32-3A 66
Cirencester St. SR4-5F 99
Cirrus Ho. SR3-5F 119
Citadel E. NE12-4F 17
Citadel W. NE12-4E 17
City Bank. NE1-2D 61
City Rd. NE1-2D 61 & 4D 143
City Way. SR3-5A 118
Civic Ct. NE31-2D 65
Clacton Rd. SR5-4E 97
Clanfield Ct. NE3-5B 28
Clanny St. SR1-1A 110
(in two parts)
Clapham Av. NE6-2C 62
Clara Av. NE27-3B 20
Clarabad Ter. NE12-1B 30
Clara St. NE4-3C 58
Clara St. NE21-1A 74
Clara St. SR7-2C 132
Claremont Av. NE15-4F 39
Claremont Av. SR6-1D 101
Claremont Ct. NE26-4D 13
(off Claremont Cres.)
Claremont Ct. NE36-3F 85
Claremont Cres. NE26-4D 13
Claremont Dri. DH4-4E 115
Claremont Gdns. NE26-1B 22
Claremont Gdns. NE36-3C 86
Claremont Ho. NE2-5E 43
Claremont N. Av. NE8-5D 61
Claremont Pl. NE2
-5E 43 & 1B 142
Claremont Pl. NE8-1C 78
Claremont Rd. NE2
-4C 42 & 1A 142
Claremont Rd. NE26
-4D 13 to 5E 13
Claremont Rd. SR6-1D 101
Claremont S. Av. NE8-1D 79
Claremont St. NE2
-5D 43 & 1A 142
Claremont St. NE8-1C 78
Claremont Ter. NE2
-5E 43 & 1A 142
Claremont Ter. NE9-3E 93
Claremont Ter. NE10-5A 64
Claremont Ter. SR2-2B 110
Claremont Wlk. NE8-1C 78
Claremount Ct. NE36-3F 85
Clarence Cres. NE26-3D 23
Clarence Pl. NE3-5A 28
Clarence St. NE2
-1E 61 & 3F 143
Clarence St. SR5-3E 99
(in two parts)
Clarence St. SR7-3E 133
Clarence Ter. DH3-3E 123
Clarence Wlk. NE2
-1E 61 & 2F 143
Clarendon Rd. NE6-3D 45
Clarendon Sq. SR5-2F 99
Clare Rd. SR8-4A 134
Clarewood Av. NE34-4C 52
Clarewood Ct. NE4-1F 59
Clarewood Grn. NE4-2F 59
Clarewood Pl. NE5-4E 41
Clarke's Ter. NE23-5F 7
Clarke Ter. NE10-2B 80
Clarks Hill Wlk. NE15-5B 38
Clark's Ter. SR7-1A 132
Clark Ter. DH9-1D 131
Clasper Ct. NE33-1D 51
Claude Gibb Hall. NE1-2D 143
Claude St. DH5-5F 129
Claudius Ct. NE33-5E 35
Claverdon St. NE5-1D 39
Clavering Pl. NE1
-3C 60 & 5D 143
Clavering Rd. NE16-1F 75
Clavering Rd. NE21-1B 74
Clavering Shopping NE16
-4E 75
Clavering Sq. NE11-2D 77
Clavering St. NE28-3C 48
Clavering Way. NE21-5D 57
Claverley Dri. NE27-2E 19
Claxheugh Rd. SR4-1F 107
Claxton St. SR8-2F 135
Clay La. DH1-4A 138
Claymere Rd. SR2-1D 121
Claypath. DH1-2D 139
Claypath. NE10-5E 81
Claypath La. NE33-3D 51
(in two parts)
Claypath Rd. DH5-5F 129
Claypath St. NE6-1F 61
Claypool Ct. NE34-2A 68
Clayside Ho. NE33-3E 51
Clayton Ho. NE3-4E 27
Clayton Pk. Sq. NE2-4F 43
Clayton Rd. NE2-4F 43
Clayton St. NE1
-2B 60 & 4B 142
Clayton St. NE23-4E 7
Clayton St. NE32-5C 48
Clayton St. W. NE1
-3B 60 & 5B 142
Clayton Ter. NE10-1A 80
Clayworth Rd. NE3-1D 27
Cleadon Ct. NE9-1C 92
Cleadon Gdns. NE28-5B 32
Cleadon Hill Dri. NE34-4F 69
Cleadon Hill Rd. NE34-3F 69
Cleadon La. NE36-3D 87
Cleadon La. SR6-1F 87
Cleadon La. Ind. Est. NE36
-2C 86
Cleadon Lea. SR6-1D 87
Cleadon Meadows. SR6
-1E 87 & 5F 69
Cleadon St. NE6-1C 62
Cleadon Towers. NE34-3F 69
Cleasby Gdns. NE9-4E 79
Cleaside Av. NE34-3E 69
Cleehill Dri. NE29-1A 34
Cleeve Ct. NE38-2B 104
Cleghorn St. NE6-4E 45
Clegwell Ter. NE31-1E 65
Clelands Way. NE28-3B 48
Clematis Cres. NE9-3B 92
Clementhorpe. NE29-2B 34
Clementina Clo. SR2-2D 111
Clement St. NE9-5E 79
Clennel Av. NE31-2C 64
Clent Way. NE12-4C 28
Clephan St. NE11-1E 77
Clervaux Ter. NE32-1A 66
Cleveland Av. DH2-4D 123
Cleveland Av. NE29-3B 34
Cleveland Ct. NE32-5C 48
Cleveland Ct. NE33-1E 51
Cleveland Cres. NE29-3B 34
Cleveland Dri. NE38-5A 104
Cleveland Gdns. NE7-1C 44
Cleveland Gdns. NE28-1C 48
Cleveland Pl. SR8-3A 134
Cleveland Rd. NE29-3B 34
Cleveland Rd. SR4-3D 109
Cleveland St. NE33-1E 51
Cleveland Ter. DH9-3D 131
Cleveland Ter. NE29-3B 34
Cleveland View. SR6-4D 89
Cliff Cotts. NE32-5F 49
Cliffe Ct. SR6-1D 101
Cliffe Pk. SR6-1D 101
Clifford Rd. DH9-2C 130
Clifford Rd. NE6-2B 62
Clifford's Fort Mount. NE30
-4E 35
Clifford St. DH3-4E 123
Clifford St. NE6-1F 61
Clifford St. NE21-4B 56
Clifford St. NE30-4E 35
Clifford St. SR4-2E 109
Clifford St. Bk. NE21-4B 56
Clifford Ter. DH3-4E 123
Cliff Rd. SR2-4E 121
Cliff Row. NE30-3E 23
Cliffside. NE34-1B 70
Cliff Ter. SR2-4E 121
Cliff View. SR2-4E 121
Clifton Av. NE28-2C 46
Clifton Av. NE34-5A 52
Cliftonbourne Av. SR6
-1D 101
Clifton Clo. NE40-3D 55
Clifton Ct. NE3-2F 25
Clifton Ct. NE9-3D 93
Clifton Ct. NE25-5C 12
Clifton Gdns. NE9-3E 79
Clifton Gro. NE25-1F 21
Clifton Rd. NE4-2D 59
Clifton Rd. NE23-4D 5
Clifton Rd. SR6-1D 101
Clifton Sq. SR8-3C 134
Clifton Ter. NE12-2F 29
Clifton Ter. NE26-2C 22
Clifton Ter. NE33-5E 51
Cliftonville Av. NE4-2D 59
Cliftonville Gdns. NE26-1B 22
Clifton Wlk. NE5-2D 39
Clintburn Ct. NE23-1E 5
Clinton Pl. NE3-5D 15
Clinton Pl. SR3-4B 118
Clipsham Clo. NE12-3D 29
Clipstone Av. NE6-4D 63
Clipstone Clo. NE15-2E 37
Clive Pl. NE6-2F 61
Clive St. NE29-5C 34
Clive St. NE34-3F 67
Clockburn La. NE16-5C 74
Clockburnsyde Clo. NE16
-5D 75
Clockmill Rd. NE8-1F 77
Clockwell St. SR5-3E 99
(in two parts)
Cloister Av. NE34-2E 67
Cloister Ct. NE8-4E 61
Cloister Garth. NE7-5C 28
Cloisters, The. NE7-5B 28
Cloisters, The. NE34-1D 69
Cloisters, The. SR2-3B 110
Cloister Wlk. NE32-5E 49
Close. NE1-3C 60
Closeburn Sq. SR3-4F 119
Close E., The. DH2-1D 123
Closefield Gro. NE25-3A 22
Close St. SR4-1F 109
Close St. SR5-3F 99
Close, The. DH1-2D 141
Close, The. DH2-1D 123
Close, The. DH5-5D 127
Close, The. NE5-4F 39
Close, The. NE21-1F 73
Close, The. NE23-3E 9
Close, The. SR6-1E 87
Cloth Mkt. NE1
-2C 60 & 4C 142
Clousden Dri. NE12-1A 30
Clousden Grange. NE12
-5F 17
Clovelly Av. NE4-2D 59
Clovelly Gdns. NE26-1B 22
Clovelly Pl. NE32-2C 66
Clovelly Rd. SR5-2E 97
Clovelly Sq. SR5-2E 97
Clover Av. DH4-1A 126
Clover Av. NE10-5A 62
Clover Av. NE21-4B 74
Cloverdale Gdns. NE7-1C 44
Cloverdale Gdns. NE16-5F 75
Cloverfield Av. NE3-4B 26
Cloverhill. NE32-1A 84
Cloverhill Av. NE31-4B 64
Cloverhill Clo. NE23-1F 7
Clowes Wlk. DH9-2E 131
Club La. DH1-1A 138
Clumber St. NE4-4F 59
(in two parts)
Clyde Av. NE31-4D 65
Clyde Ct. SR3-4E 119
Clydedale Av. NE12-2E 29
Clydesdale Av. DH4-3A 116
Clydesdale Garth. DH1
-1D 137
Clydesdale Mt. NE6-2B 62
Clydesdale Rd. NE6-2B 62
Clydesdale St. DH5-5E 129
Clyde St. DH9-2E 131
Clyde St. NE8-2F 79
Clyvedon Rise. NE34-4E 69
Coach La. NE12 & NE7
-4E 29
Coach La. NE13
-2A 14 & 2C 14
Coach La. NE29-4B 34
Coach Open. NE28-3D 49
Coach Rd. NE11-4A 78
Coach Rd. NE15-2E 37
Coach Rd. NE28-3E 47
Coach Rd. NE37-3A 94
Coach Rd. Est. NE37-3B 94
Coach Rd. Grn. NE10-5B 62
Coalbank Rd. DH5-5D 129
Coalbank Sq. DH5-5D 129
Coaley La. DH4-2A 126
Coalford Rd. DH6-4F 141
Coalway Dri. NE16-2A 76
Coalway La. NE16
-1A 76 to 3A 76
Coanwood Bungalows. NE23
-4D 5
Coanwood Dri. NE23-4D 5
Coanwood Gdns. NE11-5F 77
Coanwood Rd. NE15-3A 58
Coast Rd. NE28 & NE29
-3E 45 to 3F 33
Coast Rd. NE33 & NE34
-3B 52 to 2D 71
Coast Rd. SR8-3F 135
Coates Clo. DH9-3D 131
Coatsworth Ct. NE8-5C 60
Coatsworth Rd. NE8-5C 60
Cobalt Clo. NE15-4E 39
Cobbett Cres. NE34-4F 67
Cobden Rd. NE23-5E 5
Cobden St. NE8-1F 79
Cobden St. NE28-3C 46
Cobden Ter. NE8-1E 79
Cobham Pl. NE6-3F 63
Cobham Sq. SR5-2F 99
Coble Dene Rd. NE29-2A 50
Coburg St. NE8-5D 61
Coburg St. NE30-3D 35
Coburn Clo. NE23-2E 17
Cochrane Ct. NE4-2C 58
(in two parts)
Cochrane Pk. Av. NE7-2E 45
Cochrane St. NE4-3C 58
Cochran St. NE21-4B 56
Cockburn Ter. NE29-1F 49
Cocken La. DH3-5B 124
Cockermouth Rd. SR5-2E 97
Cohen Ct. NE8-2D 79
Colbeck Av. NE16-1A 76
Colbeck Ter. NE30-2F 35
Colby Ct. NE4-3F 59
Colchester St. NE34-3E 67
Colchester Ter. SR4-3E 109
Coldingham Gdns. NE5-3F 41
Coldside Gdns. NE5-2D 39
Coldstream Av. SR5-2F 99
Coldstream Clo. DH4-5F 115
Coldstream Dri. NE21-2F 73
Coldstream Gdns. NE28
-2B 48
Coldstream Rd. NE15-1A 58
Coldstream Way. NE29-1E 33
Coldwell La. NE10-3B 80
Coldwell Pk. Av. NE10-3B 80
Coldwell Pk. Dri. NE10-3B 80
Coldwell St. NE10-2B 80
Coldwell Ter. NE10-3B 80
Colebridge Clo. NE5-1E 41
Colebrooke. DH3-5C 102
Cole Gdns. NE10-2F 81
Colegate. NE10-3E 81
Colegate W. NE10-3D 81
(in two parts)
Colepeth. NE10-3C 80
Coleridge Av. NE5-1C 40
Coleridge Av. NE9-5D 79
Coleridge Av. NE33-3F 51
Coleridge Pl. DH2-3A 122
Coleridge Rd. SR5-2F 97
Coleridge Sq. NE31-1D 65
Coley Grn. NE5-1D 39
Coley Hill Clo. NE5-1D 39
Coley Ter. SR6-1C 100
Colgrove Pl. NE3-4A 26
Colgrove Way. NE3-4A 26
(in two parts)
Colima Av. SR5-5F 97
Colin Pl. NE6-5C 46
Colin Ter. SR2-4E 121
College Burn Rd. SR3-5D 119
College Dri. NE33-4F 51
College La. NE12-4E 29
College of Art & Technology.
NE1-2D 143
College Rd. NE31-4C 64
College St. NE1
-1C 60 & 2D 143
(in two parts)
College View. SR5-3A 100
Collier Row. SR1-1B 100
Colliery La. DH5-5F 129
Colliery La. NE4
-2A 60 & 3A 142
Colliery Rd. NE11-5E 59
Collin Av. NE34-2F 69
Colling Av. SR7-3C 132
Collingwood Av. NE28-1C 46
Collingwood Clo. NE23-2A 4
Collingwood Ct. NE37-4D 95
Collingwood Dri. DH4-4E 115
Collingwood Gdns. NE10
-5C 62
Collingwood Mans. NE29
-5C 34
Collingwood Rd. NE25-2C 20
Collingwood St. DH5-2F 129
Collingwood St. NE1
-3C 60 & 5C 142
Collingwood St. NE10-1C 80
Collingwood St. NE31-1E 65
Collingwood St. NE33-5E 51
Collingwood St. SR5
-3F 99 & 3A 100
Collingwood Ter. NE2-3B 44
Collingwood Ter. NE11-1E 77
Collingwood Ter. NE26-3D 23
Collingwood Ter. NE30-3F 35
Collingwood View. NE29
-4B 34
Collingwood Wlk. NE37
-4D 95
(off Marlborough Rd.)
Colman Av. NE34-2E 67
Colmet Ct. NE11-1C 90
Colnbrook Clo. NE3-3F 25
Colombo Rd. SR5-4E 97
Colpitts Ter. DH1-2B 138
Colston Pl. NE12-2E 29
Colston Rise. SR8-2B 134
Colston St. NE4-2C 58
Colston Way. NE25-5C 12
Coltere Av. NE36-3C 86
Colton Gdns. NE9-1F 91
Coltpark. NE5-4B 40
Coltpark Pl. NE23-4D 5
Coltsfoot Gdns. NE10-5B 80
Columba St. SR5-3A 100
Columba Wlk. NE3-4F 27
Columbia Grange. NE3-4F 25
Colville Ct. DH9-2E 131
Colwell Pl. NE5-5D 41
Colwell Rd. NE27-5A 20
Colwell Rd. NE29-1A 34
Colwyne Pl. NE5-2D 41
Colwyn Pde. NE31-5F 65
Combe Dri. NE15-5D 39
Comet Row. NE12-5D 17
Comet Sq. SR3-3F 119
Commercial Rd. NE3-5A 28
Commercial Rd. NE6-2B 62
Commercial Rd. NE32-4D 49
Commercial Rd. NE33-3C 50
Commercial Rd. SR2-2D 111
Commercial St. NE21-1A 74
Commercial Way. NE23-3C 4
Compton Av. NE34-1B 68
Compton Ct. NE38-2F 103
Compton Rd. NE29-5A 34
Concorde Ho. NE25-3C 10
Concorde Ho. NE37-5C 94
Concorde Sq. SR3-3F 119
Concorde Way. NE32-1A 66
Condercum Ct. NE15-2B 58
Condercum Rd. NE4-2C 58
Condercum Rd. Bk. NE4
-2C 58
Cone St. NE33-3D 51
Cone Ter. DH3-2E 123
Conewood Ho. NE3-3B 26
Conhope La. NE4-2C 58
Conifer Clo. DH1-2B 140
Conifer Clo. NE21-2F 73
Conifer Ct. NE12-2B 30
Coniscliffe Av. NE3-1B 42
Coniscliffe Pl. SR6-4C 100
Coniscliffe Rd. DH9-3A 130
Coniston. DH3-1C 112
Coniston Av. NE2-3A 44
Coniston Av. NE16-3B 76
Coniston Av. NE31-3E 65
Coniston Av. SR5-1B 100
Coniston Clo. DH1-2E 141
Coniston Clo. DH2-4E 123
Coniston Clo. NE15-5A 38
Coniston Clo. SR8-3D 135
Coniston Ct. NE5-4D 41
Coniston Cres. NE21-2A 74
Coniston Dri. NE32-4C 66
Coniston Gdns. NE9-5F 79
Coniston G'head NE10-2E 81
Coniston Ho. NE38-2A 104
Coniston Pl. NE9-5A 80
Coniston Rd. NE28-5B 32
Coniston Rd. NE30-5B 22
Connaught Gdns. NE12-2E 29
Connaught Ter. NE32-1F 65
Connolly Ho. NE34-4B 68
Consett Rd. NE11-5E 77
Constable Clo. DH9-3C 130
Constable Clo. NE40-3B 54
Constable Gdns. NE34-4B 68
Constables Garth. DH3
-3B 102
Constitutional Hill. DH1
-2E 139
Content St. NE21-1B 74
Convent Rd. NE4-5F 41
Conway Dri. NE7-1C 44
Conway Gdns. NE28-5C 30
Conway Gdns. SR3-4B 118
Conway Rd. SR5-2E 97
Conway Sq. NE9-2E 79
Conway Sq. SR5-2E 97
Conyers Av. DH2-1D 123
Conyers Cres. SR8-1D 135
Conyers Gdns. DH2-1D 123
Conyers Pl. DH2-1D 123
Conyers Rd. DH2-5A 112
Conyers Rd. NE6-1A 62
Cook Clo. NE33-4D 51
Cook Gdns. NE10-2F 81
Cook Gro. SR8-1D 135
Cookshold La. DH6-4F 141
Cookson Clo. NE4-2A 60
Cookson's La. NE1-4B 60
Cookson St. NE4-2F 59
Cookson Ter. DH2-2D 123
Cook Sq. SR5-3E 97
Coomside. NE23-5D 5
Co-operative Bldgs. NE25
-1C 10
Co-operative Cres. NE10
-3B 80
Cooperative St. DH3-2E 123
Cooperative Ter. DH4-4D 125
Co-operative Ter. DH5-3F 129
Co-operative Ter. NE10-3B 80
Co-operative Ter. NE12-1B 30
Co-operative Ter. NE13-1C 14
Co-operative Ter. NE27-4F 19
(Shiremoor)
Co-operative Ter. NE27-1F 31
(West Allotment)
Co-operative Ter. NE37-5C 94
Co-operative Ter. SR4-2F 109
Cooper Sq. DH1-3A 140
Cooper St. SR6-3D 101
Copeland Ct. DH1-3A 138
Copland Ter. NE2
-1D 61 & 3F 143
Copley Av. NE34-5B 68
Copley Dri. SR3-5F 109
Copperas La. NE15-1D 57
Copperfield. DH1-5A 138
Coppice Way. NE2
-1D 61 & 2F 143
Copse, The. NE37-3A 94
Coptleigh. DH5-1F 129
Coquet. NE38-2E 113
Coquet Av. NE3-3D 27
Coquet Av. NE26-2B 22
Coquet Av. NE34-5C 52
Coquet Bldgs. NE15-3D 39
Coquetdale Av. NE6-1F 63
Coquetdale Vs. SR6-3C 100
Coquet Gdns. DH9-4B 130
Coquet Gro. NE15-3E 37
Coquet Ho. NE1
-2E 61 & 4F 143
Coquet Ho. SR3-4E 119
Coquet St. NE1
-2E 61 & 3F 143
Coquet St. NE31-1C 64
Coquet St. NE32-2F 65
Coquet Ter. NE6-4D 45
Coquet Ter. NE23-4E 7
Coram Pl. NE15-2E 57
Corbett St. SR7-2C 132
Corbiere Clo. SR3-4D 119
Corbitt St. NE8-1B 78
Corbridge Av. NE13-1D 15
Corbridge Clo. NE28-4F 31
Corbridge St. NE6-1A 62
Corby Clo. SR8-5A 134
Corby Gdns. NE6-1E 63
Corby Ga. SR2-3B 110
Corby Hall Dri. SR2-3B 110
Corby M. SR2-3B 110
Corchester Wlk. NE7-1D 45
Corcyra St. SR7-4E 133
Corfu Rd. SR5-3E 97
Corinthian Sq. SR5-3E 97
Cork St. SR1-1C 110
Cormorant Clo. NE38-4D 103
Cornbank Clo. SR3-5E 119
Corndean. NE38-3F 105
Cornelia Clo. SR3-3F 119
Cornelia St. SR3-3F 119
Cornelia Ter. SR7-3E 133
Cornel M. NE7-1D 45
Cornel Rd. NE7-2D 45
Corney St. NE33-5D 51
Cornfield Garth P'lee SR8
-4E 135
Cornfields. NE31-1D 65
Cornforth Clo. NE10-3B 82
Cornhill. NE5-3B 40
Cornhill. NE32-1A 84
Cornhill Av. NE3-2A 26
Cornhill Clo. NE29-3F 33
Cornhill Cres. NE29-3F 33
Cornhill Rd. NE23-3D 5
Cornhill Rd. SR5-3A 100
Corn Mill Dri. DH5-2C 128
Cornmoor Gdns. NE16-5A 76
Cornmoor Rd. NE16-4A 76
Cornthwaite Dri. SR6-1D 89
Cornwallis Sq. NE33-3D 51
Cornwallis St. NE33-2D 51
Cornwall Rd. NE31-4E 65
Cornwall Wlk. DH1-3D 141
Cornwell Ct. NE3-5B 28
Coronation Av. DH1-2D 141
Coronation Av. SR2-4E 121
Coronation Av. SR8-3F 135
Coronation Bungalows. NE3
-5F 27
Coronation Clo. SR1-1D 111
Coronation Cres. DH4-3A 126
Coronation Cres. NE25-2A 22
Coronation Rd. NE5-1C 38
Coronation Rd. NE25-1A 10
Coronation St. DH3-4E 123
Coronation St. NE23-3A 8
Coronation St. NE28-3D 47
Coronation St. NE29-5C 34
Coronation St. NE33-2D 51
Coronation St. NE40-3D 55
Coronation St. SR1-1C 110
Coronation Ter. DH1-5C 140
Coronation Ter. DH3-4E 123
Coronation Ter. DH5-5F 129
Coronation Ter. NE9-4E 93
Coronation Ter. NE29-1D 33
Coronation Ter. NE35-1D 85
Coronation Ter. SR4-1F 107
Corporation Rd. SR2-3D 111
Corporation St. NE4
-2A 60 & 4A 142
Corriesdale Clo. DH1-1C 136
Corrighan Ter. DH5-4A 128
Corrofell Gdns. NE10-5D 63
Corry Ct. SR4-3C 108
Corsair. NE16-4E 75
Corsenside. NE5-3B 40
Corstorphine Town. NE33
-4C 50
Cortina Av. SR4-3C 108
Cosford Ct. NE3-3D 25
Cossack Ter. SR4-5D 99
Cosserat Pl. NE31-1C 64
Coston Dri. NE33-1E 51
Cosyn St. NE6-2F 61
Cotehill Rd. NE5-4C 40
Cotemede. NE10-4E 81
Cotemede Ct. NE10-4F 81
Cotfield Wlk. NE8-1C 78
Cotgarth, The. NE10-3C 80
Cotherstone Ct. SR3-5F 109
Cotherstone Rd. DH1-3D 137
Cotman Gdns. NE34-5C 68
Cotsford Cres. SR8-3F 135
Cotsford Grange. SR8-3F 135
Cotsford La. SR8-3F 135
Cotsford Pk. Est. SR8-3F 135
Cotswold Av. DH2-4C 122
Cotswold Av. NE12-1D 29
Cotswold Clo. NE38-4A 104
Cotswold Dri. NE25-4B 22
Cotswold Gdns. NE7-1B 44
Cotswold Gdns. NE11-3F 77
Cotswold La. NE35-1C 84
Cotswold Pl. SR8-3A 134
Cotswold Rd. NE29-5A 22
Cotswold Rd. SR5-2F 97
Cotswold Sq. SR5-2F 97
Cotswold Ter. DH9-3D 131
Cottage Gdns. SR6-5F 69
Cottage La. NE5-3F 41
Cottages Rd. SR7-4F 133
Cottages, The. NE11-4D 91
Cottages, The. SR8-1D 135
Cottenham Chare. NE4
-2A 60 & 4A 142
Cottenham St. NE4
-2A 60 & 4A 142
Cotterdale. NE28-5B 30
Cotterdale Av. NE8-2E 79
Cotterdale Gdns. NE5-2D 39
Cotter Riggs Pl. NE5-2D 39
Cotter Riggs Wlk. NE5-2D 39
Cottersdale Gdns. NE5-2D 39
Cottingwood Ct. NE4-1F 59
Cottingwood Gdns. NE4
-2F 59
Coulthards La. NE8-4E 61
Coulthards Pl. NE8-3E 61
Coulton Dri. NE36-3B 86
Council Av. DH4-4A 116
Council Ter. NE37-1C 104
Counden Rd. NE5-2A 40
Countess Av. NE26-2B 22
Countess Dri. NE15-5C 40
Coupland Gro. NE32-4F 65
Courtfield Rd. NE6-4B 46
Court La. DH1-3D 139
Courtney Ct. NE3-3E 25
Courtney Dri. SR3-3E 119
Court, The. NE16-4A 76
Courtyard, The. DH9-1A 130
Cousin St. SR1-1D 111
Coutts Rd. NE6-5A 46
Covent Garden. SR1-1C 110
Coventry Gdns. NE4-3D 59
Coventry Gdns. NE29-1A 50
Coventry Rd. DH1-2E 137
Coventry Way. NE32-5F 65
Coverdale. NE10-4F 81
Coverdale. NE28-5B 30
Coverdale Av. NE37-4A 94
Coverdale Wlk. NE33-5D 51
Coverley. DH3-4A 124
Coverley Rd. SR5-2F 97
Covers, The. NE12-3F 29
Cove, The. DH4-4A 116
Cowan Clo. NE21-3F 55
Cowans Av. NE12-2D 17
Cowan Ter. SR2-2B 110
Cowden Rd. NE21-4C 46
Cowdray Ct. NE3-3E 25
Cowdray Rd. SR5-3F 97
Cowdrey Ho. NE29-1F 49
Cowell St. SR8-2E 135
Cowen Gdns. NE9-4F 91
Cowen St. NE6-1E 63
Cowen St. NE21-1F 73
Cowgate. NE1
-2D 61 & 4E 143
Cowley Cres. DH5-4B 128
Cowpath Gdns. NE10-1F 81
Cowper Ter. NE12-5E 17
Cox Chare. NE1
-3D 61 & 5E 143
Coxfoot Clo. NE34-2B 68
Coxgreen Rd. DH4 & SR4
-3E 115
Coxlodge Rd. NE3-4C 26
Coxlodge Ter. NE3-4C 26
Coxon St. NE10-5F 63
Coxon St. SR2-2C 110
Coxon Ter. NE10-1A 80
Cradock Av. NE31-3B 64
Cragdale Gdns. DH5-5E 129
Craggyknowe. NE37-1E 103
Craghall Dene. NE3-1A 44
Craghall Dene Av. NE3-1A 44
Craghead Rd. DH2-2A 122
Cragside. DH2-2B 122
Cragside. NE7-2C 44
Cragside. NE13-1C 14
Cragside. NE23-5D 5
Cragside. NE26-5D 13

Cragside. NE34-2A 70
Cragside Av. NE29-2E 33
Cragside Ct. NE4-4D 59
Cragside Ct. NE11-4F 77
Cragside Gdns. NE11-5E 77
Cragside Gdns. NE28-1A 48
Cragside Rd. NE37-1E 103
Cragston Av. NE5-2D 41
Cragston Clo. NE5-2E 41
Cragston Ho. NE5-2E 41
Cragavon Rd. SR5-3F 97
Craig Cres. NE23-4F 7
Craigend. NE23-5D 5
Craighill. DH4-4E 115
Craiglands, The. SR2-4A 110
(off Tunstall Rd.)
Craigmillar Av. NE5-1D 41
Craigmillar Clo. NE5-1D 41
Craigshaw Rd. SR5-2E 97
Craigshaw Sq. SR5-2E 97
Craig St. DH3-3A 102
Craigwell Dri. SR3-5F 119
Craik Av. NE34-2A 68
Cramer St. NE8-1E 79
Cramlington Rd. SR5-3E 97
Cramlington Sq. SR5-3E 97
Cramlington Ter. NE27-1F 31
Cramond Ct. NE9-2D 91
Cramond Way. NE23-5D 5
Cranberry Rd. SR5-3F 97
Cranberry Sq. SR5-3F 97
Cranborne. SR3-4B 118
Cranbourne Gro. NE30-4C 22
Cranbrook Av. NE3-3D 27
Cranbrook Ct. NE3-3F 25
Cranbrook Pl. NE15-3F 57
Cranbrook Rd. NE15-3A 58
Cranesville. NE9-5A 80
(in two parts)
Craneswater Av. NE26-3D 13
Cranfield Pl. NE15-5D 39
Cranford Gdns. NE15-5A 40
Cranford St. NE34-1B 68
Cranford Ter. SR4-3F 109
Cranham Clo. NE12-3A 18
Cranleigh. DH3-5A 124
Cranleigh Av. NE3-3D 25
Cranleigh Pl. NE25-5C 12
Cranleigh Rd. SR5-2F 97
Cranshaw Pl. NE23-5D 5
Cranston Pl. SR2-4F 121
Crantock Rd. NE3-5B 26
Cranwell Ct. NE3-3D 25
Cranwell Dri. NE13-1C 14
Craster Av. NE12-1B 30
Craster Av. NE27-4A 20
Craster Av. NE34-4D 53
Craster Clo. DH2-4B 122
Craster Clo. NE25-5C 12
Craster Gdns. NE28-1A 48
Craster Rd. NE29-4E 33
Craster Sq. NE3-4C 26
Craster Ter. NE7-2D 45
Crathie. DH3-1B 102
Crawford Av. SR8-2B 134
Crawford Clo. DH6-4F 141
Crawford Ct. SR3-5E 119
Crawford Pl. NE25-3F 21
Crawford St. NE28-2B 48
Crawford Ter. NE6-2D 63
Crawhall Rd. NE1
-2E 61 & 3F 143
Crawley Av. NE31-4C 64
Crawley Gdns. NE16-3B 76
Crawley Rd. NE28-4D 47
Crawley Sq. NE31-4C 64
Craythorne Gdns. NE6-3E 45
Creeverlea. NE38-4B 104
Creighton Av. NE3-1A 42
Creland Way. NE5-1E 41
Crescent Barlow, The. NE21
-4B 72
Crescent, The. DH1-1B 138
Crescent, The. DH2-3D 123
Crescent, The. DH4-1B 126
(Newbottle)
Crescent, The. DH4-5F 115
(Shiney Row)
Crescent, The. DH5-5E 129
Crescent, The. DH6-5F 141
Crescent, The. DH9-1A 130
Crescent, The. NE7-5D 29
Crescent, The. NE13-3D 25
Crescent, The. NE15-2F 37
Crescent, The. NE16-4B 76
Crescent, The. NE23-3E 9
Crescent, The. NE26-2C 22
Crescent, The. NE28-1D 47
Crescent, The. NE30-2E 35
Crescent, The. NE32-3F 65
Crescent, The. NE34-2E 69
Crescent, The. NE40-3C 54
Crescent, The. SR3-1F 119
Crescent, The. SR6-2D 87
Crescent, The G'head NE11
-2E 77
Crescent Vale. NE26-2C 22
(off Marden Rd.)
Crescent Way. NE12-1A 30
Crescent Way. N. NE12-1F 29
Crescent Way. S. NE12-1A 30
Creslow. NE10-4D 81
Cressbourne Av. SR6-1D 101
Cresswell Av. NE12-1A 30
Cresswell Av. NE29-3B 34
Cresswell Av. SR8-4F 135
Cresswell Clo. NE21-2E 73
Cresswell Clo. NE25-4F 21
Cresswell Dri. NE3-2A 26
Cresswell Rd. NE28-3C 46
Cresswell St. NE6-1C 62
Cresswell Ter. SR2-2B 110
Cresthaven. NE10-3D 81
Crewe Av. DH1-5B 140
Crichton Av. DH3-4F 123
Cricklewood Dri. DH4-4A 116
Cricklewood Rd. SR5-3E 97
Criddle St. NE8-4F 61
Crieff Gro. NE32-4C 66
Crieff Sq. SR5-3E 97
Crigdon Hill. NE5-3B 40
Crighton. NE38-3F 103
Crimdon Gro. DH4-5B 126
Crimea Rd. SR5-2E 97
Crindledykes. NE38-5D 105
Cripps Av. NE10-2A 82
Criston Way. NE10-5A 64
Crocus Clo. NE21-5F 55
Croft Av. NE12-2F 29
Croft Av. NE28-3D 47
Croft Av. SR4-2F 109
Croft Av. SR6-1D 89
Croft Clo. NE40-3C 54
Croftdale Rd. NE21-5A 56
Crofters Clo. NE23-3F 7
Crofthead Dri. NE23-5D 5
Crofton St. NE34-1B 68
Crofton Way. NE15-5D 39
Croftside. DH3-2B 102
Croftside Av. SR6-1D 89
Croftside Ho. SR3-5D 119
Croft Stairs. NE1
-2D 61 & 4E 143
(off City Rd.)
Croft St. NE1-2C 60 & 3D 143
Croftsway. NE4-3D 59
Croft Ter. NE32-1F 65
Croft, The. NE3-1B 42
Croft, The. NE40-3C 54
Croft View. NE12-4A 18
Croftwell Clo. NE21-1B 74
Cromarty St. SR6-3B 100
Cromdale Pl. NE5-3C 40
Cromer Av. NE9-2E 91
Cromer Ct. NE9-2E 91
Cromer Gdns. NE2-1F 43
Cromer Gdns. NE26-1B 22
Crompton Rd. NE6-4D 45
Cromwell Av. NE21-5A 56
Cromwell Ct. NE21-3F 55
Cromwell Rd. NE10-5F 63
Cromwell Rd. NE16-2B 76
Cromwell St. NE8-1F 79
Cromwell St. NE21-3F 55
Cromwell St. SR4-1F 109
Cromwell Ter. NE8-1C 78
Cromwell Ter. NE10-5F 63
Cromwell Ter. NE29-3B 34
Crondall St. NE33-5E 51
Cronin Av. NE34-4F 67
Crookham Way. NE23-5E 5
Crookhill Ter. NE40-3D 55
Cropthorne. NE10-4A 82
Crosby Ct. SR2-2D 111
Crosby Gdns. NE9-1F 91
Cross Av. NE28-1B 46
Crossbank Rd. NE5-2F 41
Crossbrook Rd. NE5-3E 41
Cross Camden La. NE30
-4C 34
Cross Carliol St. NE1
-2C 60 & 3D 143
Cross Dri. NE40-1B 40
Crossfield Pk. NE10-4B 80
Crossfield Ter. NE6-3E 63
Crossgate. DH1-2C 138
Crossgate. NE33-2E 51
Crossgate Moor Gdns. DH1
-1A 138
Crossgate Peth. DH1-3A 138
Crossgill. NE37-1A 104
Crosshill Rd. NE15-3F 57
Cross Keys La. NE9-5D 79
Cross La. NE11-5C 58
(Dunston)
Cross La. NE11-1A 90
(Team Valley)
Crosslaw. NE5-3B 40
Crosslea Av. SR3-4F 109
Crossley Ter. NE4-1E 59
Crossley Ter. NE12-1A 30
Cross Morpeth St. NE2
-5D 43 & 1A 142
Cross Pde. NE4-3F 59
Cross Pl. SR1-1C 110
Cross Row. DH1-2C 136
Cross Row. NE10-1A 80
Cross Row. NE37-2D 95
Cross Row. NE40-3C 54
Cross Sheraton St. NE2
(off Sheraton St.) -5D 43
Cross St. DH4-5F 125
(High Dubmire)
Cross St. DH4-4C 126
(Houghton-le-Spring)
Cross St. NE1
-2B 60 & 4B 142
Cross St. NE6-2F 61
Cross St. NE8-1E 79
Cross Ter. NE40-1B 54
Cross Vale Rd. SR2-3B 110
Cross View Ter. DH1-4A 138
Cross Villa Pl. No. 1. NE4
-2B 60 & 4A 142
Cross Villa Pl. No. 2. NE4
-2A 60 & 4A 142
Cross Villa Pl. No. 3. NE4
-2A 60 & 4A 142
Cross Villa Pl. No. 4. NE4
-2A 60 & 4A 142
Cross Villa Pl. No. 5. NE4
-2A 60 & 4A 142
Crossway. NE2-2F 43
Crossway. NE9-3F 79
(in two parts)
Crossway. NE30-2E 35
Cross Way. NE34-2E 69
Crossways. NE32-1A 84
Crossways. NE36-3C 86
Crossways. SR3-3E 119
Crossways, The. NE13-3B 14
Cross Way, The. NE3-1B 42
Crossway, The. NE15-5F 39
Croudace Row. NE10-2B 80
Crowhall La. NE10-2B 80
Crow Hall La. NE23-1B 4
Crowhall Towers. NE10-2B 80
Crow La. SR3-3F 117
Crowley Av. NE16-2B 76
Crowley Gdns. NE21-5B 56
Crowley Rd. NE16-1F 75
Crown Bank. NE28-2E 47
Crown Rd. SR5-4E 99
Crown Ter. NE40-1A 72
Crowther Ind. Est. NE38
-2D 103
Crowther Rd. NE38
-3D 103 to 2E 103
Crowtree Rd. SR1-1B 110
Crowtree Ter. SR1-1B 110
Croxdale Ct. NE34-2F 67
Croxdale Gdns. NE10-5F 63
Croxdale Ter. NE10-1F 81
Croxdale Ter. NE40-1A 72
Croydon Rd. NE4-2F 59
Crozier St. SR5-3B 100
Cruddas Pk. Shopping Cen.
NE4-3F 59
Crudwell Clo. NE35-5C 66
Crummock Av. SR6-5B 88
Crummock Ct. NE28-5B 32
Crummock Rd. NE5-4C 40
Crumstone Ct. NE12-3A 18
Crusade Wlk. NE32-2F 65
Cuba St. SR2-4C 110
Cuillin Clo. NE38-5A 104
Culford Pl. NE28-3A 32
Cullercoats Rd. SR5-3E 97
Cullercoats Sq. SR5-4E 97
Cullercoats St. NE6-1C 62
Culloden Wlk. NE12-3E 17
Cumberland Ct. NE31-2C 64
Cumberland Pl. DH3-2B 112
Cumberland Pl. NE34-5D 53
Cumberland Rd. NE29-2D 33
Cumberland Rd. SR3-2E 119
Cumberland St. NE28-2E 47
(Wallsend)
Cumberland St. NE28-3D 49
(Willington Quay)
Cumberland St. SR1-1B 110
(in two parts)
Cumberland Wlk. NE7-1D 45
Cumberland Way. NE37
-3C 94
Cumbrian Av. DH2-4D 123
Cumbrian Av. SR6-5A 88
Cumbrian Gdns. NE11-4F 77
Cumbrian Way. SR8-3D 135
Cumbria Pl. DH9-1D 131
Cumbria Wlk. NE4-2F 59
Cummings Av. DH6-4F 141
Cunningham Pl. DH1-1F 139
Curlew Clo. NE12-3C 28
Curlew Clo. NE38-5E 103
Curlew Rd. NE32
-4D 49 & 4E 49
Curran Ho. NE32-5E 49
Curren Gdns. NE10-5B 62
Curtis Rd. NE4-5A 42
Curzon Pl. NE5-2D 41
Curzon Rd. W. NE28-4C 46
Curzon St. NE8-1C 78
Cushat Clo. NE6-2A 62
Cushycow La. NE40-3B 54
Customs Ho. NE29-5C 34
Cut Bank. NE1-2F 61
Cuthbert Av. DH1-5B 140
Cuthbert Ct. NE32-1D 67
Cuthbertson Ct. SR6-5D 89
Cuthbert St. NE8-5B 60
Cuthbert St. NE31
-1B 64 & 1C 64
Cuthbert Wlk. NE3-5F 27
Cutting St. SR7-1A 132
Cygnet Clo. NE5-1F 39
Cyncopa Way. NE5-2F 41
Cypress Av. NE4-4F 41
Cypress Cres. NE11-2E 77
Cypress Gro. DH1-3A 140
Cypress Gro. NE40-1A 54
Cypress Rd. NE9-3C 92
Cypress Rd. NE21-5B 56
Cypress Sq. SR3-3F 119
Cyprus Gdns. NE9-3F 79

Dacre Rd. SR6-5B 88
Dacre St. NE33-4E 51
Daffodil Av. SR8-2E 135
Daffodil Clo. NE21-5F 55
Dahlia Ct. SR4-1A 110
Dahlia Pl. NE4-5E 41
Dahlia Way. NE31-3D 65
Dairy La. DH4-5B 126
Dairy Wlk. DH3-4A 114
Daisy Cotts. DH3-3B 102
Dalden Gro. SR7-2E 133
Dalegarth. NE37-2A 104
Dalegarth Gro. SR6-4A 88
Dale Rd. NE25-3F 21
Dales, The. NE5-2F 41
Dale St. NE33-1F 51
Dale Ter. SR6-2C 100
Dale Ter. SR7-5B 132
Dale Top. NE25-3D 11
Dalla St. SR4-1F 107
Dalmahoy. NE37-2B 94
Dalton Av. SR7
-3C 132 & 3D 133
Dalton Clo. NE23-4D 5
Dalton Ct. NE28-5A 30
Dalton Ct. NE31-5A 48
Dalton Cres. NE6-2A 62
Dalton Heights. SR7-4A 132
Dalton Pl. NE5-1E 39
Daltons La. NE33-2D 51
Dalton St. NE6-1A 62 & 2A 62
Dalton Way. DH4-3F 115
Dame Dorothy Cres. SR6
(in two parts) -4D 101
Dame Dorothy St. SR6
-5B 100
Dame Flora Robson Av. NE34
-3E 67
Danby Clo. NE38-2E 113
Danby Clo. SR3-4A 120
Danby Gdns. NE6-3E 45
Danelaw. DH3-4A 114
Dannatis Ct. SR1-1C 110
Danville Rd. SR6-1C 110
Daphne Cres. SR7-4D 133
D'Arcy Ct. SR1-2D 111
D'Arcy Sq. SR1-1D 111
D'Arcy St. SR2-2D 111
Darden Clo. NE12-3B 18
Darden Lough. NE5-3B 40
Darenth St. NE34-2A 68
Darien Av. SR6-1C 100
Darley Ct. SR3-5E 119
Darley Pl. NE15-2F 57
Darling Pl. DH9-4E 131
Darlington Av. SR8-2E 135
Darlington Rd. DH1-4A 138
Darnell Pl. NE4-1F 59
Darras Ct. NE33-3E 51
Darras Dri. NE29-3D 33
Darrell St. NE13-1C 14
Dartford Rd. NE33-3A 52
Dartford Rd. SR6-5C 88
Dartmouth Av. NE9-2D 91
Dartmouth Clo. SR7-4B 132
Dartmouth Rd. NE29-4D 33
Dart Rd. SR8-4B 134
Darvall Clo. NE25-5C 12
Darwin Cres. NE3-2B 42
Darwin St. SR5-3E 99
Daryl Clo. NE21-1F 73
Daryl Way. NE10-2B 82
Datchet Rd. NE25-5C 12
Davenport Dri. NE3-1D 27
David Gdns. SR6-2D 101
Davidson Cotts. NE2-1F 43
Davidson Rd. NE10-5A 64
Davidson St. NE10-2C 80
David St. NE28-3C 46
Davies Wlk. SR8-1D 135
Davison Av. NE26-1A 22
Davison Av. SR3-4F 119
Davison Pl. NE11-2E 77
Davison St. NE15-5A 38
Davison St. NE35-1D 85
Davison Ter. SR5-3E 99
(off Fern Av.)
Davy Bank. NE28-3E 47
Dawdon Cres. SR7-4F 133
Dawlish Clo. NE29-2F 33
Dawlish Gdns. NE9-2E 91
Dawlish Pl. NE5-2E 39
Dawson Sq. NE30-2F 35
Dawson Ter. SR4-1F 107
Daylesford Dri. NE3-5B 28
Dayshield. NE5-3B 40
Deacon Clo. NE5-2C 38
Deaconsfield Clo. SR3
(in two parts) -5D 119
Dean Clo. SR8-4E 135
Deanham Gdns. NE5-4E 41
Dean Ho. NE6-4C 46
Dean Rd. NE33
-5C 50 to 4F 51
Deans Clo. NE16-2A 76
Deansfield Clo. SR3-5D 119
Deansfield Gro. NE5-2C 38
Dean St. NE1-3C 60 & 4D 142
Dean St. NE9-5E 79
Deans Wlk. DH1-5F 137
Dean Ter. NE33-5D 51
Dean Ter. NE40-2B 54
Dean Ter. SR5-3E 99
Debdon Gdns. NE6-3E 45
Debdon Pl. NE23-4C 4
Debussy Ct. NE32-1A 66
Deckham St. NE8-2F 79
Deckham Ter. NE8-2E 79
Deepbrook Rd. NE5-3E 41
Deepdale. NE28-5A 30
Deepdale. NE38-2F 113
Deepdale Clo. NE16-5E 75
Deepdale Cres. NE5-2F 41
Deepdale Grn. NE5-2F 41
Deepdale Rd. NE30-5C 22
Deepdale Rd. SR6-5C 88
Deepdene Gro. SR6-5C 88
Deepdene Rd. SR6-5C 88
Deerbolt Pl. NE12-3E 29
Deerbush. NE5-3B 40
Deerness Rd. SR2-2D 111
Dee Rd. NE31-4D 65
Deer Pk. Way. NE21-1D 75
Dees Av. NE28-2D 47
Dee St. NE32-5D 49
Defender Ct. SR5-5A 98
Defoe Av. NE34-4A 68
De Grey St. NE4-4F 59
Deighton Wlk. NE5-3B 40
Delacour Rd. NE21-4B 56
Delamere Ct. SR3-4E 119
Delamere Rd. NE3-4B 26
Delaval. DH2-2C 122
Delaval Av. NE25-1B 10
Delaval Av. NE29-4A 34
Delaval Ct. NE33-4E 51
Delavale Clo. SR8-4E 135
Delaval Gdns. NE15-3A 58
Delaval Rd. NE12-1F 29
Delaval Rd. NE15-3A 58
(in two parts)
Delaval Rd. NE26-2D 23
Delaval Ter. NE3-1C 42
Delhi Cres. NE40-4A 40
Dell, The. DH4-2C 126
Denbeigh Pl. NE12-3E 29
Denbigh Av. NE28-1C 48
Denbigh Av. SR6-1C 100
Denby Wlk. NE5-1E 39
Dene Av. DH5-5E 127
Dene Av. NE3-5A 28
Dene Av. NE12-5C 16
Dene Av. NE13-1C 14
Dene Av. NE15-1C 56
Denebank. NE25-2F 21
Dene Bank Av. SR8-3F 135
Dene Bank View. NE3-1A 42
Deneburn. NE10-3F 81
Dene Clo. NE7-3C 44
Dene Clo. NE40-2C 54
Dene Ct. DH3-1B 102
Dene Ct. NE7-3C 44
Dene Ct. NE15-4A 40
Dene Ct. NE38-2B 104
Dene Cres. NE3-1A 44
Dene Cres. NE26-1A 22
Dene Cres. NE28-2E 47
Dene Cres. NE40-2B 54
Dene Dri. DH1-1D 141
Dene Gdns. DH5-5E 127
Dene Gdns. NE10-1F 81
Dene Gdns. NE15-1C 56
Dene Gdns. NE25-2A 22
Dene Gro. NE3-1A 44
Dene Gro. NE23-2F 9
Deneholm. NE25-1F 21
Deneholm. NE28-1F 47
Dene Ho. Rd. SR7-2D 133
Dene La. SR6
-3A 88 & 1B 100
Dene M. SR5-3B 98
Dene Pk. SR5-3A 98
Dene Rd. NE21-4B 56
Dene Rd. NE30-2D 35
Dene Rd. SR5-3B 98
Dene Rd. SR7-5B 132
Deneside. NE5-5B 24
Deneside. NE11-3D 77
Deneside. NE15-5B 40
Dene Side. NE21-5C 56
Deneside. NE23-2F 9
Deneside. NE32-1A 84
Deneside. NE34-1A 70
Deneside Av. NE9-1D 91
Deneside Ct. NE2-4C 44
Dene St. DH5-2F 129
Dene St. DH9-3A 130
Dene St. NE25-2D 11
Dene St. NE29-1C 50
Dene St. SR3-2E 119
Dene St. SR4-1D 109
Dene St. SR8-3F 135
Dene Ter. NE3-1A 44
Dene Ter. NE15-4B 38
Dene Ter. NE21-5A 56
Dene Ter. NE32-3F 65
Dene Ter. SR4-1D 109
Dene Ter. SR6-1B 100
Dene Ter. SR7-2F 133
Dene Ter. SR8-3E 135
Dene, The. NE25-2A 22
Dene View. DH9-2F 131
Dene View. NE3-1A 44
Dene View. NE25-3D 11
Dene View Cres. SR4-2F 107
Dene Vs. DH3-4E 123
Dene Vs. SR8-4F 135
Deneway. NE39-5F 73
Deneway Way. SR7-2D 133
Denewell Av. NE7-2C 44
Denewell Av. NE9-4E 79
Denewood. NE12-5F 17
Denewood Ct. NE28-3C 48
Denham Av. SR6-1C 100
Denham Dri. NE25-2B 10
Denham Gro. NE21-2E 73
Denham Wlk. NE5-1D 39
Denhill Pk. NE15-1B 58
Denholme Lodge. NE11
-1E 77
Denmark Cen. NE33-1E 51
Denmark Ct. NE6-1A 62
Denmark St. NE6-5D 45
Denmark St. NE8-5D 61
Dennison Cres. DH3
-1B 102 & 2B 102
Dentdale. DH4-3D 115
Denton Av. NE15-1B 56
Denton Av. NE29-4E 33
Denton Chare. NE1
-3C 60 & 5C 142
Denton Ct. NE5-5C 40
Denton Gdns. NE15-2A 58
Denton Ga. NE5-1B 40
Denton Gro. NE5-2B 40
Denton Pk. Shopping NE5
-3A 40
Denton View. NE21-5A 56
Dent St. SR6-1C 100
Denver Gdns. NE6-2D 63
Denwick Av. NE15-1B 56
(off Shipley St.)
Denwick Clo. DH2-5B 122
Denwick Ter. NE30-2E 35
Depot Rd. NE6-5E 45
Deptford Rd. NE8-3F 61
Deptford Rd. SR4-5A 100
Deptford Ter. SR4-5E 99
Derby Ct. NE4-1A 60
Derby Cres. NE31-2C 64
Derby Gdns. NE28-2B 46
Derby Rd. DH9-3C 130
Derbyshire Dri. DH1-3D 141
Derby St. NE4
-1A 60 & 3A 142
Derby St. NE32-5E 49
Derby St. NE33-3E 51
Derby St. SR2-1A 110
Derby Ter. NE33-3E 51
Dereham Ct. NE5-5D 25
Dereham Way. NE29-2D 33
Derry Av. SR6-5C 88
Derwent Av. NE11-5C 78
Derwent Av. NE15-5A 38
Derwent Av. NE31-4D 65
Derwent Clo. SR7-2D 133
Derwent Ct. NE7-5C 28
Derwent Cres. DH3-5B 124
Derwent Cres. NE16-2F 75
Derwent Crook Dri. NE9
-5D 79
Derwent Crook Foot Rd. NE9
-5D 79
Derwentdale Gdns. NE7
-1D 45
Derwentdale Ho. NE40-1B 54
Derwent Gdns. NE9-1E 91
Derwent Gdns. NE28-5B 32
Derwenthaugh Riverside Pk.
NE21-5F 57
Derwenthaugh Rd.
NE21 & NE16-4E 57
Derwent Ho. NE1
-2E 61 & 4F 143
Derwent Pl. NE21-1F 73
Derwent Rd. NE30-5C 22
Derwent Rd. SR8-3C 134
Derwentside. NE16-2F 75
Derwent St. DH4-4A 116
Derwent St. DH5-5F 129
Derwent St. DH9-1B 130
Derwent St. NE15-2A 58
Derwent St. SR1-2B 110
Derwent Ter. NE38-3D 105
Derwent Tower. NE11-1F 77
Derwent View. NE21-1A 74
Derwentwater Av. DH2
-4C 122
Derwentwater Ct. NE8-1C 78
Derwentwater Gdns. NE16
-3B 76
Derwentwater Rd. NE8-2F 77
Derwentwater Ter. NE33
-4E 51
Derwent Way. NE21-1D 75
Deuchar St. NE2-4B 44
Devon Av. NE16-3B 76
Devon Cres. DH3-2A 102
Devon Dri. SR3-3E 119
Devon Gdns. NE9-3E 79
Devon Gdns. NE34-5D 53
Devon Rd. NE29-1F 33
Devon Rd. NE31-4D 65
Devonshire Dri. NE27-1D 31
Devonshire Gdns. NE28
-2B 46
Devonshire Pl. NE2-3A 44
Devonshire Rd. DH1-3C 140
Devonshire St. NE33-5C 50
Devonshire St. SR5-3B 100
Devonshire Ter. NE2
-5F 43 & 1C 142
Devonshire Ter. NE26-3D 23
Devonshire Tower. SR5
-4B 100
Devon St. DH4-5B 116
Devon St. DH5-4D 129
Devon Wlk. NE37-3B 94
Dewley. NE23-4D 5
Dewley Ct. NE23-4D 5
Dewley Pl. NE5-1A 40
Dewley Rd. NE5-3C 40
Dewsgreen. NE23-3C 4
Dexter Ho. NE29-1F 49
Dexter Way. NE10-2B 80
Deyncourt. DH1-5A 138
Diamond Ct. NE3-4E 25
Diamond St. NE28-3C 46
Diamond Ter. DH1-1C 138
Diana St. NE4
-2A 60 & 4A 142
Dibley Sq. NE6-2A 62
Dibley St. NE6-2A 62
Dickens Av. NE16-2F 75
Dickens Av. NE34-4A 68
Dickens St. DH4-4C 126
Dickens St. SR5-3E 99
Dickens Wlk. NE5-2D 39
Dickens Wynd. DH1-5A 138
Dickins Wlk. SR8-4D 135
Didcot Av. NE29-5A 34
Didcot Way. NE35-3D 85
Dillon St. NE32-2F 65
Dillon St. SR7-3E 133
Dilston Av. NE25-3C 22
Dilston Clo. NE27-4B 20
Dilston Clo. NE38-3F 103
Dilston Clo. SR8-5B 134
Dilston Dri. NE5-2A 40
Dilston Gdns. SR4-2E 109
Dilston Rd. DH1-3D 137
Dilston Rd. NE4
-2E 59 & 1E 59
Dilston Ter. NE3-5F 27
Dilston Ter. NE32-4A 66
Dimbula Gdns. NE7-2F 45
Dinmont Pl. NE23-4C 4
Dinnington Rd. NE29-3E 33
Dinsdale Av. NE28-5D 31
Dinsdale Cotts. SR2-4D 121
Dinsdale Dri. DH1-2E 141
Dinsdale Pl. NE2
-1E 61 & 1F 143
Dinsdale Rd. NE2
-5B 44 & 1F 143
(in two parts)
Dinsdale Rd. SR6-2D 101
Dinsdale St. SR2-4D 121
Dinsdale St. S. SR2-4E 121
Dinting Clo. SR8-4A 134
Dipe La. NE36-3F 85
Dipton Av. NE4-3D 59
Dipton Gdns. SR3-5A 110
Dipton Gro. NE23-3D 5
Dipton Rd. NE25-5C 12
Discovery Ct. SR3-4D 119
Dishforth. NE9-3F 91
Dishforth Grn. NE9-4F 91
Dispensary La. NE1
-2B 60 & 4B 142
Disraeli St. DH4-5F 125
Dissington Pl. NE5-4E 41
Dissington Pl. NE16-5F 75
Ditchburn Ter. SR4-4D 99
Dixon Pl. NE11-2E 77
Dixon Rd. DH5-2C 128
Dixon's Sq. SR6-4C 100
Dixon St. NE8-1B 78
Dixon St. NE33-4E 51
Dobson Clo. NE4-4A 60
Dobson Cres. NE6-3B 62
Dobson Ho. NE3-4D 27
Dobson Ho. NE12-5D 17
Dockendale La. NE16-3B 76
Dock Rd. NE29-1B 50
Dock Rd. S. NE29-1C 50
Dock St. NE33-1F 67
Dock St. SR6-4C 100
Dockwray Sq. NE30-4D 35
Dr. Winterbottom Hall. NE33
-4A 52
Doddington Clo. NE15-5D 39
Doddington Dri. NE23-3C 4
Doddington Vs. NE10-3B 80
Dodd's Bldgs. NE35-1D 85
Dodds Ct. SR5-2E 97
Dodds Ter. DH3-1B 102
Dodsworth N. NE40-1A 72
Dodsworth Ter. NE40-1A 72
Dodsworth Vs. NE40-1A 72
Dog Bank. NE1
-3D 61 & 5E 143
Dolphin Ct. NE4-2C 58
Dolphin Quay. NE29-5D 35
Dolphin St. NE4-2C 58
Dolphin Vs. NE13-3C 14
Donald St. NE3-5A 28
Doncaster Rd. NE2
-5B 44 & 1F 143
Don Cres. DH3-5B 124
Doncrest Rd. NE37-3F 93
Don Dixon Dri. NE32-1A 84
Don Gdns. NE36-3E 85
Don Gdns. NE37-4C 94
Donington Clo. SR6-4F 97
Donkin Rd. NE37-5E 93
Donkins St. NE35-1D 85
Donkin Ter. NE30-3D 35
Donnington Ct. NE3-5B 28
Donnini Pl. DH1-1F 139
Donridge. NE37-3F 93
Don Rd. NE32-5F 49
Donside. NE10-1E 93
Don St. NE11-5A 78
Donvale Rd. NE37-4F 93
Don View. NE36-3E 85
Dorcas Av. NE15-2B 58
Dorcas Ter. NE37-4C 94
Dorchester Clo. NE5-1D 39
Dorchester Gdns. NE9-2E 91
Doreen Av. SR7-4A 132
Dorking Av. NE29-5A 34
Dorking Rd. SR6-5C 88
Dormond Dri. SR8-5B 134
Dornoch Cres. NE10-4C 80
Dorrington Rd. NE3-3F 25
Dorset Av. DH3-1B 112
Dorset Av. NE28-2B 46
Dorset Av. NE31-2E 65
Dorset Av. NE34-5D 53
Dorset Av. SR6-5C 88
Dorset Gro. NE29-1F 33
Dorset La. SR3-3A 120
Dorset Rd. NE8-3E 61
Dorset Rd. NE15-1E 57
Douglas Av. NE3-1C 42
Douglas Av. SR8-2E 135
Douglas Clo. NE34-3A 68
Douglas Ct. NE11-2C 90
Douglas Gdns. DH1-5A 138
(in two parts)
Douglas Gdns. NE11-3E 77
Douglas Pde. NE31-5F 65
Douglas Rd. SR6-5D 89
Douglas St. NE28-3C 46
(Wallsend)
Douglas St. NE28-3C 48
(Willington Quay)
Douglas Ter. DH4-3A 116
Douglas Ter. NE4
-2F 59 & 3A 142
Douglas Ter. NE37-3B 94
Douglas Vs. DH1-1E 139
Douglas Way. NE1
-2C 60 & 3C 142
(off Eldon Sq.)
Doulting Clo. NE12-3D 29
Douro Ter. SR2-2C 110
Dove Av. NE32-4B 66
Dovecote Clo. NE25-1E 21
Dovecote Rd. NE12-2A 30
Dove Ct. DH3-3A 102
Dove Ct. NE30-3E 23
Dovecrest Ct. NE28-1A 48
Dovedale Ct. NE34-3F 67
Dovedale Gdns. NE7-1C 44
Dovedale Gdns. NE9-1F 91
Dovedale Rd. SR6-5A 88
Dove Ho. NE5-1D 39
Dovercourt Rd. NE6-3E 63
Dove Row. NE30-3E 23
Dowling Av. NE25-3B 22
Downend Rd. NE5-2F 39
Downfield. NE37-2B 94
Downham. NE5-3B 40
Downham Ct. NE33-3E 51
Downhill La. NE36
-1B 96 to 4E 85
Downs La. DH5-3F 129
Downs Pit La. DH5-4F 129
Downs, The. DH1-4A 138
Downswood. NE12-4B 18
Dowsey Rd. DH6-3F 141
Doxford Av. DH5-2E 129
Doxford Cotts. DH5-2E 129
Doxford Gdns. NE5-3E 41
Doxford Pk. Way. SR3
-4C 118
Doxford Pl. NE23-4C 4
Doxford Ter. DH5-2E 129
Dragon La. DH1-3B 140
Dragon Villa. DH1-5C 140
Dragonville Ind. Est. DH1
-4B 140
Dragonville Pk. DH1-4B 140
Drake Clo. NE33-4D 51
Drake St. NE10-5A 64
Drayton Rd. NE3-5A 26
Drayton Rd. SR6-5C 88
Drivecote. NE10-2C 80
Drive, The. DH3-1C 112
Drive, The. NE3-1E 43
Drive, The. NE5-4B 40
Drive, The. NE7-5D 29
Drive, The. NE9-3E 79
Drive, The. NE10-2D 81
Drive, The. NE16-4B 76
Drive, The. NE28-2C 46
Drive, The. NE30-1E 35
Drive, The. NE37-4B 94
Dronfield Clo. DH2-4B 122
Drove Rd. NE15-1D 37
Drum Ind. Est. DH3-3A 112
Drummond Cres. NE34-3D 67
Drummond Rd. NE3-1A 42
Drummond Ter. NE30-3C 34
Drumoyne Clo. SR3-4A 118
Drumoyne Gdns. NE25-4E 21
Drum Rd. DH2 & DH3-2A 112
Drumsheugh Pl. NE5-2D 41
Druridge Av. SR6-5C 88
Druridge Cres. NE34-4C 52
Druridge Dri. NE5-3E 41
Drury La. DH1-2D 139
Drury La. NE1
-2C 60 & 4D 143
(off Mosley St.)
Drury La. NE29-2D 33
Drury La. NE32-5D 49
Drury La. SR1-1D 111
Drybeck Ct. NE4-3A 60
Drybeck Sq. SR3-4F 119
Dryborough St. SR4-5F 99
Dryburgh. NE38-3B 104
Dryburgh Clo. NE29-2F 33
Dryburn Hill. DH1-4A 136
Dryburn Pk. DH1-4A 136
Dryburn Rd. DH1-4A 136
Dryburn View. DH1-4A 136
Dryden Clo. DH9-2D 131
Dryden Clo. NE34-5F 67
Dryden Rd. NE9-2E 79
Dryden St. SR5-3F 99
Drysdale Ct. NE13-1C 14
Drysdale Cres. NE13-1C 14
Dubmire Cotts. DH4-5E 125
Dubmire Ct. DH4-4F 125
Duchess Cres. NE32-4F 65
Duchess Cres. E. NE32-4F 65
Duchess Dri. NE15-5C 40
Duchess St. NE26-2B 22
Duckpool La. NE16-3B 76
Duckpool La. N. NE16-2B 76
Duddon Clo. SR8-4D 135
Duddon Pl. NE9-1A 92
Dudley Av. SR6-5C 88
Dudley Clo. SR8-2D 135
Dudley Ct. NE23-3C 4
Dudley Dri. NE23-4F 7
Dudley Gdns. SR3-4B 118
Dudley La. NE13 & NE23
-4A 6 to 3C 4
Dugdale Rd. NE3-5F 25

Duke of Northumberland. NE28-5F 31
Duke's Av. NE31-3C 64
Dukes Cotts. NE15-5A 38
Dukes Cotts. NE27-2D 19
Dukes Dri. NE3-5D 15
Dukesfield. NE23-4C 4
Dukes Meadow. NE13-1A 24
Duke St. NE1-3A 60 & 5A 142
Duke St. NE10-1E 81
Duke St. NE26-2B 22
Duke St. NE29-5C 34
Duke St. SR4-1F 109
Duke St. SR7-2C 132
Duke St. N. SR6-3C 100
Dukes Wlk. NE26-5E 13
Dukesway. NE11-5A 78
Dukesway Ct. NE11-1A 90
Dukesway W. NE11-2B 90
Duke Wlk. NE8-1A 78
Dulverston Clo. NE5-2E 39
Dulverton Av. NE33-5E 51
Dulverton Ct. NE2-2B 44
Dumas Wlk. NE5-2D 39
Dumfries Cres. NE32-4D 67
Dunbar Clo. NE5-1D 39
Dunbar Gdns. NE28-1B 48
Dunbar St. SR4-3D 109
Dunblane Cres. NE5-4B 40
Dunblane Rd. SR6-5C 88
Dunbreck Gro. SR4-3F 109
Duncairn. DH9-1C 130 (off View La.)
Duncan St. NE6-2E 63
Duncan St. NE8-1F 79
Duncan St. SR4-5D 99
Duncombe Cres. DH9-1C 130
Duncow La. DH1-3C 138
Dun Cow St. SR1-1B 110
Dundas St. SR6-4B 100
Dundas Way. NE10-2A 80
Dundee Clo. NE5-1D 39
Dundee Ct. NE32-4D 67
Dundrennan. NE38-4B 104
Dunelm. SR2-4F 109
Dunelm Clo. DH3-3A 102
Dunelm Ct. DH1-3C 138
Dunelm Ct. NE31-2B 64
Dunelm Dri. DH4-5B 126
Dunelm Dri. NE36-2F 85
Dunelm Rd. DH5-4E 129
Dunelm S. SR2-4F 109
Dunelm St. NE33-3E 51
Dunelm Ter. SR7-5A 132
Dunelm Wlk. SR8-2B 134
Dunford Gdns. NE5-1F 39
Dunholme Rd. NE4-3E 59
Dunira Clo. NE2-3A 44
Dunkirk Av. DH5-5E 127
Dunlin Dri. NE38-5E 103
Dunlop Clo. NE7-5E 29
Dunlop Cres. NE34-2E 69
Dunmoor Clo. NE3-5C 26
Dunmore Av. SR6-5C 88
Dunmorlie St. NE6-2C 62
Dunn Av. SR3-2F 119
Dunne Rd. NE21-3D 57
Dunning St. SR1-1B 110
Dunnlynn Clo. SR3-4C 118
Dunnock Dri. NE38-5E 103
Dunn Rd. SR8-2C 134
Dunns Clo. NE2 -5D 43 & 1A 142
Dunn's Ter. NE2-5D 43
Dunn St. NE4-4A 60
Dunn Ter. NE6-2F 61
Dunnykirk Av. NE3-4F 25
Dunsany Ter. DH2-2A 122
Dunsdale Rd. NE25-2C 10
Dunsmuir Gro. NE8-2C 78
Dunstable Pl. NE5-1D 39
Dunstanburgh Clo. NE6 -2C 62
Dunstanburgh Clo. NE38 -3F 103
Dunstanburgh Ct. NE10 -3A 82
Dunstanburgh Rd. NE6-2C 62
Dunstanburgh Wlk. NE8 -5C 60
Dunstan Clo. DH2-4C 122
Dunstan Tower. NE12-3E 17
Dunstan Wlk. NE5-3B 40
Dunston Bank. NE11-3D 77
Dunston Rd. NE11 -2D 77 & 5E 59
Dunvegan. DH3-5C 102
Dunvegan Av. DH2-4D 123
Durant Rd. NE1 -1C 60 & 3D 143
Durdham St. NE4-2C 58
Durham Av. NE37-5A 94
Durham Av. SR8-2E 135 (in two parts)
Durham City Northern By-Pass. DH1-1B 136
Durham Ct. NE31-2C 64
Durham Dri. NE32-1F 83
Durham Gro. NE32-5F 65
Durham Moor Cres. DH1 -4A 136
Durham Pl. DH3-2B 112 (in two parts)
Durham Pl. DH4-2C 126 (off Front St.)
Durham Pl. NE8-1E 79
Durham Rd. DH1-4A 136
Durham Rd. DH2 & DH3 -5D 123
Durham Rd. DH3-1A 102
Durham Rd. DH4-5C 126
Durham Rd. DH5 & DH4 -3D 127
Durham Rd. DH9-3D 131
Durham Rd. NE8 & NE9 -1E 79 to 4F 91
Durham Rd. NE23-1D 5
Durham Rd. SR3 & SR2 -4A 118 to 2A 110
Durham St. DH4-5E 125
Durham St. NE4-3E 59 (in two parts)
Durham St. NE10-1E 81
Durham St. NE28-3E 47
Durham St. SR7-2C 132
Durham St. W. NE28-3E 47
Durham Ter. DH1-3A 136
Durham Ter. SR3-2E 119
Durham Way. SR8-5B 134
Duxfield Rd. NE7-2C 44
Dwyer Cres. SR2-4D 121
Dyer Sq. SR5-2F 99
Dykefield Av. NE3-3A 26
Dyke Heads La. NE40-5A 54
Dykelands Rd. SR6-5B 88
Dykelands Way. NE34-4E 67
Dykenook Clo. NE16-5F 75
Dykes Way. NE10-5C 80
Dymock Ct. NE3-4D 25

Eaglescliffe Dri. NE7-2F 45
Eagle St. NE11-4A 78
Ealing Ct. NE3-3D 25
Ealing Dri. NE30-1D 35
Ealing Sq. SR5-1E 99
Eardulph Av. DH3-3F 123
Earl Grey Way. NE29-1A 50
Earlington Ct. NE12-1A 30
Earl's Ct. NE11-5C 78
Earls Dene. NE9-1D 91
Earl's Dri. NE9-1D 91
Earl's Dri. NE15-5B 40
Earls Grn. DH5-4B 128
Earlston St. SR5-1F 99
Earl St. SR4-1F 109
Earl St. SR7-2C 132
Earls Way. NE1 -1C 60 & 3C 143 (off Eldon Sq.)
Earlsway. NE11-3B 78
Earlswood Av. NE9-1D 91
Earlswood Pk. NE9-1D 91
Earnshaw Way. NE25-5B 12
Earsdom Rd. DH5-5E 127
Earsdon Clo. NE5-3B 40
Earsdon Grange Rd. DH5 -4E 127
Earsdon Rd. NE3-1A 42
Earsdon Rd. NE27 & NE25 -5F 19 to 3F 21
Earsdon Ter. NE27-1F 31
Earsdon Ter. SR2-4D 121
Earsdon View. NE27-3B 20
Easby Rd. NE38-4B 104
Easedale Av. NE3-5E 15
Easedale Gdns. NE9-1F 91
Easington Av. NE9-1B 92
Easington St. SR5-5B 100
Easington St. N. SR5-5B 100
E. Acres. NE21-5C 56
East Av. NE12-3F 29
East Av. NE25-2F 21
East Av. NE34-1F 69
East Av. NE38-2A 114
E. Back Pde. SR2-2E 111
E. Bailey. NE12-3F 17
E. Bank Pde. SR2-2E 111
E. Boldon Rd. SR6-2D 87
Eastbourne Av. NE6-1E 63
Eastbourne Av. NE8-2D 79
Eastbourne Ct. NE6-1E 63
Eastbourne Gdns. NE6-1E 63
Eastbourne Gdns. NE26 -1B 22
Eastbourne Gro. NE33-2F 51
Eastbourne Pde. NE31-5F 65 (in two parts)
Eastbourne Sq. SR5-1F 99
E. Bridge St. DH4-2D 115
Eastburn Gdns. NE10-5F 63
Eastcheap. NE6-3E 45
E. Cleft Rd. SR2-2A 110
Eastcliffe Av. NE3-2C 42
East Clo. NE34-1F 69
Eastcombe Clo. NE35-5C 66
Eastcote Ter. NE6-4E 63
E. Cross St. SR1-5C 100
Eastdene Rd. SR7-2B 132
Eastdene Way. SR8-4E 135
East Dri. SR6-2D 87
Easten Gdns. NE10-1C 80
Easten Ter. NE28-3E 49
Eastern Av. NE11 & NE9 -1B 90
Eastern Way. NE5-2F 41
E. Farm Ct. NE23-3D 5
E. Farm Ter. NE23-3D 5
Eastfield. SR8-4E 135
Eastfield Av. NE6-4C 46
Eastfield Av. NE25-3F 21
Eastfield Ho. NE6-4C 46
Eastfield Rd. NE12-4E 29
Eastfield Rd. NE34-4B 52
Eastfields. DH9-3B 130
E. Fields. SR6-2E 89
Eastfield St. SR4-3D 109
Eastfield Ter. NE12-3F 29
E. Forest Hall Rd. NE12-1F 29
E. Front. NE2-4F 43
Eastgarth. NE5-5B 24
Eastgate Gdns. NE4-3D 59
E. George Potts St. NE33 -4F 51
E. George St. NE30-3D 35
E. Grange. NE25-2E 11
E. Grange. SR5-2A 100
East Gro. SR4-2F 107
E. Hendon Rd. SR1-2E 111
E. Hill Rd. NE8-1A 80
E. Holborn. NE33-3C 50
E. Howden By-Pass. NE28 & NE29-3D 49
Eastlands. DH5-5E 129
Eastlands. NE7-2C 44
Eastlands. NE21-1A 74
E. Lea. NE21-1B 74
Eastlea Cres. SR7-3B 132
Eastlea Rd. SR7-3B 132
Eastleigh Clo. NE35-2C 84
E. Moffett St. NE33-3F 51
E. Moor Rd. SR4-1D 109
E. Norfolk St. NE30-4C 34
East Pde. DH9-2D 131
East Pde. NE26-1C 22
E. Park Gdns. NE21-1A 74
E. Park Rd. NE9-4D 79
E. Percy St. NE30-4D 35
E. Stainton St. NE33-3F 51
E. Stanley By-Pass. DH9 -1E 131
E. Stevenson St. NE33-4F 51
East St. DH9-1E 131
East St. NE8-4E 61
East St. NE30-2F 35
East St. NE31-5A 48 (in two parts)
East St. NE33-2D 51
East St. SR4-5D 99
East St. SR6-2E 89
E. Thorp. NE5-5B 24
E. View. DH9-5B 130
E. View. NE13-5A 6
E. View. NE21-4B 56
E. View. NE23-3E 9
E. View. NE31-3B 64
E. View. NE35-2D 85
E. View. NE36-3E 85
E. View. SR2-4D 121
E. View. SR5-4A 98
E. View. SR6-2C 100
E. View. SR7-1A 132
E. View. SR8-2F 135
E. View Av. NE23-3D 5
E. View S. SR5-4A 98
E. View Ter. NE10-4D 81
E. View Ter. NE16-2F 75
E. View Ter. NE23-4E 7
Eastward Grn. NE25-3E 21
Eastway. NE34-2F 69
E.W. Link Rd. NE23-2C 4
Eastwood Clo. NE23-2E 17
Eastwood Ct. NE12-3F 29
Eastwood Gdns. NE3-5B 26
Eastwood Gdns. NE9-3E 79
Eastwood Gdns. NE10-5A 62
Eaton Pl. NE4-2E 59
Eavers Ct. NE34-2A 68
Ebba Wlk. NE3-4F 27
Ebchester Av. NE9-2B 92
Ebchester Ct. NE3-4E 25
Ebchester St. NE34-2E 67
Ebdon La. SR6-1B 100
Ebor St. NE6-4E 45
Ebor St. NE34-3E 67
Eccles Ct. NE27-2E 19
Eccles Ter. NE27-5F 19
Eccleston Clo. NE27-3F 19
Eccleston Rd. NE33-3A 52
Ecgfrid Ter. NE32-3A 66
Eddison Rd. NE38-3E 105
Eddleston. NE38-1F 113
Eddleston Av. NE3-2B 42
Eddrington Gro. NE5-2E 39
Ede Av. NE11-2E 77
Ede Av. NE34-1F 69
Edenbridge Cres. NE12-2D 29
Eden Clo. NE5-2E 39
Eden Ct. NE28-3D 47
Edendale Av. NE6-1F 63
Edendale Av. NE12-2E 29
Edendale Ct. NE34-3F 67
Edendale Ter. NE8-2D 79
Edendale Ter. SR8-3E 135
Edengarth. NE30-5B 22
Edenhill Rd. SR8-2C 134
Eden Ho. Rd. SR4-2F 109
Eden La. SR8-1C 134
Eden Pl. NE30-5B 22
Eden Rd. DH1-3C 136
Eden St. NE28-3D 47
Eden St. SR8-2F 135
Eden St. W. SR1-1A 110
Eden Ter. DH1-3C 140
Eden Ter. DH4-4F 115
Eden Ter. DH9-3A 130
Eden Ter. SR2-2F 109
Eden Vale. SR2-3F 109
Eden Vale. SR8-3E 135
Edenvale Est. SR8-3E 135
Eden Wlk. NE32-4B 66
Edgar St. NE3-5B 28
Edge Ct. DH1-4A 140
Edgefield Av. NE3-5B 26
Edgemount. NE12-2F 17
Edgeware Rd. NE4-4D 59
Edgeware Wlk. NE4-4D 59
Edgeworth Clo. NE35-5C 66
Edgeworth Cres. SR6-3B 100
Edgmond Ct. SR2-2D 121
Edgware Rd. NE8-2F 79
Edhill Av. NE34-2E 67
Edhill Gdns. NE34-3E 67 (in two parts)
Edinburgh Ct. NE3-2E 25
Edinburgh Rd. NE32-3C 66
Edinburgh Sq. SR5-2F 99
Edington Gro. NE30-1C 34
Edington Rd. NE30-5B 22
Edison Gdns. NE8-3C 78
Edith Av. NE21-5B 56
Edith Av. NE37-5D 95
Edith Moffat Ho. NE29-4C 34 (off Albion Rd.)
Edith St. NE30-2D 35
Edith St. NE32-5C 48
Edith St. SR2-3D 111
Edith St. SR7-5F 133
Edith Ter. DH4-2B 126
Edlingham Clo. NE3-1B 44
Edlingham Rd. DH1-4C 136
Edmondsley Rd. DH2-5A 122
Edmonton Sq. SR5-1E 99
Edmund Pl. NE9-5E 79
Edna Ter. NE5-2B 40
Edrich Ho. NE29-1F 49
Edward Av. SR8-3E 135
Edward Burdis St. SR5 -3A 100
Edward Pl. NE4-2A 60
Edward Rd. DH3-2A 102
Edward Rd. NE28-1A 48
Edwards Rd. NE26-2D 23
Edward St. DH1-1F 139
Edward St. DH3-3E 123
Edward St. DH5-4F 129
Edward St. NE3-5D 27
Edward St. NE21-4C 56
Edward St. NE31-1B 64
Edward St. SR3-3E 119
Edward St. SR7-4E 133
Edward's Wlk. NE1 -1B 60 & 2C 142
Edwina Gdns. NE29-3F 33
Edwin Gro. NE28-2C 48
Edwin's Av. NE12-1F 29
Edwin's Av. S. NE12-1F 29
Edwin St. DH5-4D 127
Edwin St. NE6-1A 62
Edwin St. NE13-1B 14
Edwin St. SR4-5D 99
Edwin Ter. NE40-5A 54
Egerton Rd. NE34-1A 68
Egerton St. NE4-3B 58 (in two parts)
Egerton St. SR2-2C 110
Eggleston Clo. DH1-3E 137
Eggleston Dri. SR3-5F 109
Egham Rd. NE5-2E 39
Eglesfield Rd. NE33-4E 51
Eglingham Av. NE30-5E 23
Eglinton St. SR5-4B 100
Eglinton St. N. SR5-3B 100
Eglinton Tower. SR5-4B 100
Egremont Dri. NE9-4F 79
Egremont Gdns. NE9-4F 79
Egremont Gro. SR8-5A 134
Egremont Pl. NE26-3D 23
Egton Ter. DH3-3B 102
Eight Av. NE11-2B 90
Eighth Av. DH2-2D 123
Eighth Av. NE6-5D 45
Eighth St. SR8-2F 135
Eighton Ter. NE9-2C 92
Eishort Way. NE12-3D 29
Eland Clo. NE3-4F 25
Elberfield Ct. NE32-1A 66
Elder Gdns. NE9-3A 92
Elder Gro. NE9-5E 79
Elder Gro. NE34-4D 69
Elderwood Gdns. NE11-4F 77
Eldon Ct. NE1-1C 60
Eldon Ct. NE28-3C 48 (off Eldon St.)
Eldon Garden Shopping Cen. NE1-1B 60 & 3C 142
Eldon Ho. NE3-4D 27
Eldon La. NE1 -2C 60 & 3C 142
Eldon Pl. NE1-1C 60
Eldon Pl. NE15-5F 39
Eldon Pl. NE33-5D 51
Eldon Rd. NE15-5F 39
Eldon Sq. NE1 -2C 60 & 3C 142
Eldon Sq. Shopping Cen. NE1 -1C 60 & 3C 142
Eldon St. NE8-5E 61
Eldon St. NE28-3C 48
Eldon St. NE33-3D 51
Eldon St. SR4-2F 109
Eldon Wlk. NE1 -2C 60 & 3C 142
Eldon Way. NE1 -1C 60 & 3C 142
Eldston Clo. SR8-5B 134
Eleanor St. NE30-3D 23
Eleanor St. NE33-1F 51
Electric Cres. DH4-1B 126
Eleventh Av. DH2-2C 122
Eleventh Av. NE11-3C 90
Eleventh Av. N. NE11-2D 91
Eleventh St. SR8-2E 135
Elford Clo. NE25-2E 21
Elgar Av. NE5-2E 39
Elgar Clo. DH9-3D 131
Elgin Av. NE28-1B 48
Elgin Av. SR7-3B 132
Elgin Clo. NE29-1E 33
Elgin Ct. NE10-5A 64
Elgin Gdns. NE6-1E 63
Elgin Gro. DH9-3E 131
Elgin Pl. DH3-1B 112
Elgin Rd. NE9-2F 79
Elgin St. NE32-3C 66
Elgy Rd. NE3-1C 42
Elisabeth Av. DH3-1A 102
Elite Bldgs. DH9-2C 130
Elizabeth Ct. NE12-1C 30
Elizabeth Cres. NE23-4F 7
Elizabeth Diamond Gdns. NE33-4D 51
Elizabeth Dri. NE12-1C 30
Elizabeth Rd. NE28-2B 48
Elizabeth St. DH5-4D 127
Elizabeth St. NE6-1F 61
Elizabeth St. NE33-3E 51
Elizabeth St. SR5-4A 98 (Castletown)
Elizabeth St. SR5-2B 100 (Southwick)
Elizabeth St. SR7-3E 133
Ellam Av. DH1-4A 138
Ella McCambridge Ho. NE6 -2F 63
Elldene Cres. NE10-2C 80
Ellen Ct. NE32-5D 49
Ellen Ter. NE37-5E 95
Ellen Wilkinson Ct. NE31 -5A 48
Ellersmere Gdns. NE30 -4C 22
Ellesmere. DH4-2C 124
Ellesmere Av. NE3-5A 28
Ellesmere Av. NE5-2F 41
Ellesmere Av. NE6-5A 46
Ellesmere Ct. SR2-1C 120
Ellesmere Dri. SR7-3B 132
Ellesmere Rd. NE4-2C 58
Ellesmere Ter. SR6-2C 100
Ellie Bldgs. DH9-2C 130 (off Royal Rd.)
Ellington Clo. NE15-5D 39
Elliot Rd. NE10-5A 62
Elliot Rd. NE10-1A 80
Elliott Clo. DH4-3F 115
Elliott Dri. NE10-2C 80
Elliott Gdns. NE28-5C 30
Elliott Gdns. NE34-5B 68
Elliott Rd. SR8-3C 134
Elliott Ter. NE4-2E 59
Elliott Ter. NE37-5C 94
Elliott Wlk. NE13-2B 14
Ellis Leazes. DH1-2E 139
Ellison Building. NE1-2D 143
Ellison Main Gdns. NE10 -2D 81
Ellison Pl. NE1 -1C 60 & 3D 143
Ellison Pl. NE9-1E 91
Ellison Pl. NE32-5C 48
Ellison Rd. NE11 & NE8 -2D 77
Ellison Rd. SR8-2D 135
Ellison St. NE8-4D 61
Ellison St. NE31 -5E 47 to 1C 64
Ellison St. NE32 -5C 48 & 1A 66
Ellison Vs. NE8-1F 79
Ellis Rd. SR5-2F 99
Ellis Sq. SR5-2F 99
Ellwood Gdns. NE9-2E 79
Elm Av. NE11-2E 77
Elm Av. NE16-2A 76
Elm Av. NE34-3D 69
Elm Ct. NE16-5A 76
Elm Cres. SR7-5D 133
Elm Croft Rd. NE12-2A 30
Elm Dri. SR6-1E 89
Elmfield App. NE3-1E 43
Elmfield Av. DH1-3B 140
Elmfield Clo. SR3-4A 118
Elmfield Gdns. NE3-1C 42
Elmfield Gdns. NE25-3F 21
Elmfield Gdns. NE28-1B 46
Elmfield Gro. NE3-1C 42
Elmfield Pk. NE3-1C 42
Elmfield Rd. NE3-1D 43
Elmfield Rd. NE15-3F 37
Elmfield Rd. NE31-4D 65
Elmfield Ter. NE10-1E 81
Elmfield Ter. NE31-3E 65
Elm Gro. NE3-3B 26
Elm Gro. NE12-5F 17
Elm Gro. NE34-3E 69
Elm Pl. DH4-2C 126
Elm Rd. NE21-5B 56
Elm Rd. NE29-2C 32
Elmsford Gro. NE12-3D 29
Elmsleigh Gdns. SR6-5F 69
Elms, The. NE3-1D 43
Elms, The. SR2-3B 110
Elm St. DH3-3E 123
Elm St. DH9-5A 130
Elm St. NE11-4A 78
Elm St. NE13-4B 6
Elm St. NE32-1F 65
Elms W. SR2-3B 110
Elm Ter. DH3-2A 102
Elm Ter. DH9-5F 131
Elm Ter. NE13-2C 14
Elm Ter. NE28-2D 47
Elm Ter. SR8-3F 135
Elmtree Gdns. NE25-4A 22
Elmtree Gro. NE3-1D 43
Elmway. DH2 -1B 122 & 1C 122
Elmwood Av. NE13-2D 15
Elmwood Av. NE28-2B 48
Elmwood Av. SR5-2E 99
Elmwood Cres. NE6-4A 46
Elmwood Gdns. NE11-4F 77
Elmwood Gro. NE26-1C 22
Elmwood Rd. NE25-2F 21
Elmwood Sq. SR5-2E 99
Elmwood St. DH4-4D 125
Elmwood St. SR2-2A 110
Elrick Clo. NE5-2E 39
Elrington Gdns. NE5-4D 41
Elsdon Av. NE25-1B 10
Elsdonburn Rd. SR3-5D 119
Elsdon Clo. DH2-4B 122
Elsdon Clo. SR8-5B 134
Elsdon Ct. NE16-4F 75
Elsdon Dri. NE12-2A 30
Elsdon Gdns. NE11-2E 77
Elsdon M. NE31-5B 48
Elsdon Pl. NE29-5B 34
Elsdon Rd. DH1-3D 137
Elsdon Rd. NE3-4E 27
Elsdon Rd. NE16-4F 75
Elsdon St. NE29-5C 34
Elsdon Ter. NE28-3C 46
Elsdon Ter. NE29-5E 33
Elsham Grn. NE3-3A 26
Elsing Clo. NE5-5D 25
Elstob Cotts. SR3-5F 109
Elstob Pl. NE6-4D 63
Elstob Pl. SR3-5F 109
Elston Clo. NE5-2E 39
Elstree Ct. NE3-3D 25
Elstree Sq. SR5-1F 99
Elswick Ct. NE1 -2C 60 & 3C 142
Elswick Ct. NE4-2F 59
Elswick Dene. NE4-4E 59
Elswick E. St. NE4-3A 60
Elswick E. Ter. NE4 -3A 60 & 5A 142
Elswick Rd. NE4 -3D 59 & 4A 142
Elswick Rd. NE37-1E 103
Elswick Row. NE4-2F 59
Elswick St. NE4-2F 59
Elswick Way. NE34-1E 67
Elsworth Grn. NE5-1E 41
Elterwater Rd. DH2-4D 123
Eltham St. NE33-4C 50
Elton St. E. NE28-3C 46
Elton St. W. NE28-3C 46
Eltringham Clo. NE28-2C 46
Elvaston Rd. NE40-1B 54
Elvet Bri. DH1-2D 139
Elvet Clo. NE6-5D 45
Elvet Clo. NE13-1C 14
Elvet Ct. NE6-5D 45
Elvet Cres. DH1-3D 139
Elvet Hill Rd. DH1-4C 138
Elvet Moor. DH1-4A 138
Elvet Waterside. DH1-2D 139
Elvet Way. NE6-5D 45
Elvington St. SR6-1C 100
Elwin Ter. SR2-2A 110
Elwood Ho. NE7-1C 44
Ely Clo. NE7-5E 29
Ely Rd. DH1-1D 137
Elysium La. NE8-1B 78
Ely St. NE8-1D 79
Ely Way. NE32-1F 83
Embankment Rd. SR7-4F 133 (Dawdon)
Embankment Rd. SR7-2C 132 (Seaham)
Embassy Gdns. NE15-1F 57
Emblehope Dri. NE3-5C 26
Embleton Av. NE3-4C 26
Embleton Av. NE28-5B 32
Embleton Av. NE34-5D 53
Embleton Clo. DH1-2D 137
Embleton Cres. NE29-2E 33
Embleton Dri. DH2-5B 122
Embleton Gdns. NE5-3E 41
Embleton Gdns. NE10-1B 80
Embleton Rd. NE10-5A 64
Embleton Rd. NE29-2E 33
Embleton St. SR7-5F 133
Embleton Wlk. NE8-5C 60 (off St Cuthbert's Rd.)
Embrook Clo. DH5-4B 128
Emden Rd. NE3-4A 26
Emerson Rd. NE38-4D 103
Emily St. DH4-1C 126
Emily St. NE6-2C 62
Emily St. NE8-1A 80
Emily St. SR7-3E 133
Emily St. E. SR7-3E 133
Emlyn Rd. NE34-1B 68
Emma Ct. SR2-2D 111
Emmerson Ct. SR8-2F 135
Emmerson Pl. NE27-4A 20
Emmerson Ter. NE38-3C 104
Emmerson Ter. SR3-3A 120
Emmerson Ter. W. SR3 -3F 119
Empire Bldgs. DH1-4A 140
Empress Rd. NE6-3F 63
Empress St. SR5-3A 100
Emsworth Rd. SR5-1E 99
Emsworth Sq. SR5-2F 99
Enderby Rd. SR4-5F 99
Enfield Av. NE16-1A 76
Enfield Gdns. NE16-5A 76
Enfield Rd. NE8-2E 79
Enfield Rd. SR7-3B 132
Enfield St. SR4-5D 99
Engels Ter. DH9-3D 131
Engine Inn Rd. NE28-5A 32
Engine La. NE9-5E 79
Englefeld. NE10-1E 93
Englefield Clo. NE3-2F 25
Enid Av. SR6-2C 100
Enid St. NE13-2B 14
Ennerdale. DH3-5C 102
Ennerdale. NE10-2E 81
Ennerdale. NE37-5A 94
Ennerdale. SR2-3B 110
Ennerdale Clo. DH1-2E 141
Ennerdale Clo. SR7-3B 132
Ennerdale Clo. SR8-3C 134
Ennerdale Cres. DH4-2F 115
Ennerdale Cres. NE21-2F 73
Ennerdale Gdns. NE9-5F 79
Ennerdale Gdns. NE28-5B 32
Ennerdale Pl. DH2-4D 123
Ennerdale Rd. NE6-1E 63
Ennerdale Rd. NE30-5C 22
Ennerdale Wlk. NE16-5E 75
Ennismore Ct. NE12-3F 29
Ensign Ho. NE30-3E 35
Enslin Gdns. NE6-4D 63
Enslin St. NE6-4D 63
Entra Way. SR4-5C 98
Epinay Wlk. NE32-1A 66
Epping Clo. SR7-4B 132
Epping Sq. SR5-2F 99
Eppleton Est. DH5-3F 129
Eppleton Hall Clo. SR7 -2A 132
Eppleton Row. DH5-4F 129
Eppleton Ter. E. DH5-3F 129
Eppleton Ter. W. DH5-3F 129
Epsom Clo. NE29-5A 34
Epsom Ct. NE3-2E 25
Epsom Sq. SR5-2F 99
Epworth. DH9-1A 130
Epworth Gro. NE8-1C 78
Equitable St. NE28-3C 46
Erick St. NE1-2C 60 & 3D 143 (in two parts)
Erin Sq. SR5-2F 99
Erith Ter. SR4-2D 109
Ermine Cres. NE9-4F 79
Ermyn Way. NE34-2A 68
Ernest Pl. DH1-4B 140
Ernest St. NE35-2E 85
Ernest St. SR2-3D 111
Ernest Ter. DH3-3E 123
Ernest Ter. DH9-1C 130
Ernest Ter. SR2-4E 121
Ernwill Av. SR5-4F 97
Errington Dri. DH9-1A 130
Errington Ter. NE12-1A 30
Errol Pl. DH3-5C 102
Erskine Ct. NE2-2B 44
Erskine Rd. NE33-2E 51
Erskine Way. NE33-3E 51
Escalond Dri. SR7-4A 132
Escombe Ter. NE6-3B 62 (off St Peter's Rd.)
Esdale. SR2-4D 121
Esher Ct. NE3-2E 25
Eshmere Cres. NE5-2E 39
Eshott Clo. NE3-4C 26
Eshott Clo. NE5-3B 40
Eshott Ct. NE5-3B 40
Esk Av. DH3-5B 124
Esk Ct. SR3-4E 119
Eskdale. DH3-1C 112
Eskdale. DH4-2F 115
Eskdale Av. NE28-5D 31
Eskdale Clo. DH1-2E 141
Eskdale Clo. SR7-3B 132
Eskdale Ct. NE34-2A 68
Eskdale Cres. NE37-4A 94
Eskdale Dri. NE32-4B 66
Eskdale Gdns. NE9-1F 91
Eskdale Rd. SR6-4D 89
Eskdale St. DH5-5E 129
Eskdale St. NE34-2A 68
Eskdale Ter. NE2 -4A 44 & 1E 143
Eskdale Ter. NE26 & NE30 -3E 23
Eskdale Wlk. SR8-3D 135
Esk St. NE9-3A 80
Esk Ter. DH3-3A 102
Eslington Ct. NE8-2A 78
Eslington Rd. NE2 -5A 44 & 1E 143
Eslington Rd. NE8-2F 77
Eslington Ter. NE2 -4A 44 & 1E 143
Esmeralda Gdns. NE23-3E 9
Esplanade. NE26-2D 23
Esplanade Av. NE26-2D 23
Esplanade Pl. NE26-2D 23
Esplanade, The. SR2-2B 110
Esplanade W. SR2-3B 110
Espley Clo. NE12-2C 30
Essen Way. SR3-5F 109
Essex Clo. NE4-4F 59
Essex Cres. SR7-3B 132
Essex Dri. NE37-3B 94
Essex Gdns. NE9-3E 79
Essex Gdns. NE28-1F 47
Essex Gdns. NE34-5D 53
Essex Gro. SR3-2E 119
Essex Pl. SR8-2B 134
Essex St. DH5-4D 129
Essington Way. SR8-1B 134
Estate Houses. DH4-1C 124
Esther Campbell Ct. NE2 -5D 43 & 1A 142
Esther Sq. NE38-3D 105
Esthwaite Av. DH2-4D 123
Eston Ct. NE28-5A 30
Eston Gro. SR5-1A 100
Estuary Way. SR4-5A 98
Etal Av. NE25-3C 22
Etal Av. NE29-5F 33
Etal Clo. NE27-3A 20
Etal Ct. NE29-4B 34
Etal Cres. NE27-3A 20
Etal Cres. NE32-3C 66
Etal La. NE5-1C 40
Etal Pl. NE3-3B 26
Etal Way. NE5-1D 41
Ethel Av. NE21-5B 56
Ethel Av. SR2-4E 121
Ethel St. NE4-3C 58
Ethel St. NE23-1C 16
Ethel Ter. NE34-2A 68
Ethel Ter. SR5-4A 98
Etherley Clo. DH1-2D 137
Etherley Rd. NE6-5F 45
Etherstone Av. NE7-2D 45
Eton Sq. NE31-1E 65
Ettrick Clo. NE12-3E 17
Ettrick Gdns. NE8-2A 80
Ettrick Gdns. SR4-4D 109
Ettrick Gro. SR4 & SR3 -3D 109
Ettrick Rd. NE32-2F 65
Ettrick Ter. N. DH9-5E 131
Ettrick Ter. S. DH9-5F 131
European Way. SR4-5B 98
Euryalus Ct. NE33-3A 52
Eustace Av. NE29-4A 34
Evanlade. NE10-4B 82
Eva St. NE15-1B 56
Evelyn St. SR2-3A 110
Evelyn Ter. DH9-3B 130
Evelyn Ter. NE21-4B 56
Evelyn Ter. SR2-4E 121
Evenwood Gdns. NE9-5F 79
Everest Gro. NE36-3F 85
Everest Sq. SR5-1F 99
Eversleigh Pl. NE15-3A 38
Eversley Cres. SR5-1F 99 (in three parts)
Eversley Pl. NE6-5C 44
Eversley Pl. NE28-2A 48
Everton Dri. SR7-3B 132
Everton La. SR5-1E 99
Evesham. SR4-2E 107
Evesham Av. NE26-5E 13
Evesham Clo. NE35-1D 85
Evesham Garth. NE3-1A 42
Evesham Rd. SR7-3A 132
Eve St. SR8-3F 135
Evistones Gdns. NE6-4D 63
Evistones Rd. NE9-3E 79
Ewart Ct. NE3-3B 26
Ewart Cres. NE34-3D 67
Ewbank Av. NE4-5F 41
Ewe Hill Ter. DH4-4E 125
Ewe Hill Ter. W. DH4-4E 125
Ewen Ct. NE29-2D 33
Ewesley. NE38-2F 113
Ewesley Clo. NE5-3C 40
Ewesley Gdns. NE13-1D 15
Ewesley Rd. SR4-2E 109
Ewing Rd. SR4-3F 109 (in two parts)
Exchange Bldgs. NE1 -3D 61 & 5E 143 (off King St.)
Exchange Bldgs. NE26-2C 22
Exelby Clo. NE3-2F 27
Exeter Av. SR7-3C 132
Exeter Clo. DH3-5A 124
Exeter Ct. NE31-2B 64
Exeter Rd. NE28-5B 30
Exeter Rd. NE29-1E 33
Exeter St. NE6-3E 63
Exeter St. NE8-1D 79
Exeter St. SR4-5D 99
Exeter Way. NE32-5F 65
Exmouth Clo. SR7-4C 132
Exmouth Rd. NE29-4D 33
Exmouth Sq. SR5-1F 99
Exmouth St. SR5-2F 99
Extension Rd. SR1-1E 111
Eyemouth Ct. NE34-2F 67
Eyemouth La. SR5-1F 99
Eyemouth Rd. NE29-4D 33
Eyre St. DH9-4B 130

Faber Rd. SR5-2E 99
Factory Rd. NE21-3C 56
Fairbairn Rd. SR8-1B 134
Fairburn Av. DH5-2D 129
Fairburn Av. NE7-5E 29
Fairclough Ct. SR8-4A 134
Fairdale Av. NE7-1E 45
Fairfield. NE12-4B 28
Fairfield Av. NE12-1F 29
Fairfield Av. NE16-5E 75
Fairfield Clo. NE11-1D 77
Fairfield Dri. NE25-3E 21
Fairfield Dri. NE30-4D 23
Fairfield Dri. SR6-5D 71
Fairfield Grn. NE25-3E 21
Fairfield Rd. NE2-3F 43
Fairfields. NE40-3A 54
Fairfield Ter. NE10-1F 81
Fair Grn. NE25-3E 21
Fairgreen Clo. SR3-5E 119
Fairhaven. NE9-3D 93
Fairhaven Av. NE6-1F 63
Fairhill Clo. NE7-5E 29
Fairholme Av. NE34-1E 69
Fairholme Rd. SR3-4A 110
Fairholm Rd. NE4-2D 59
Fairlands E. SR6-3B 100
Fairlands W. SR6-3B 100

Fairlawn Gdns. SR4-4C 108
Fairlees Garden. NE6-1B 62
Fairless Gdns. NE6-1B 62
(off Grace St.)
Fairles St. NE33-1E 51
Fairmead Way. SR4-2E 107
Fairmile Dri. SR3-5F 119
Fairmont Way. NE7-5E 29
Fairnley Wlk. NE5-3B 40
Fairspring. NE5-2B 40
Fairview Av. NE34-1E 69
Fairview Grn. NE7-5E 29
Fairville Cres. NE7-5D 29
Fairway. NE21-3F 55
Fairway. NE25-3A 22
Fairway Clo. NE3-1D 27
Fairways. NE25-2E 21
Fairways. SR3-3F 119
Fairways Av. NE7-5E 29
Fairway, The. NE3-2D 27
Fairway, The. NE37-2B 94
Fairy St. DH5-4F 129
Falconars Ct. NE1
-2B 60 & 4C 142
Falconar St. NE2
-2D 61 & 3E 143
Falcon Pl. NE12-3C 28
Falcon Way. NE34-3F 67
Faldonside. NE6-3F 45
Falkirk. NE12-3E 17
Falkland Av. NE3-1B 42
Falkland Av. NE31-1D 65
Falkland Rd. SR4-1C 108
Falla Pk. Cres. NE10-2B 80
Falla Pk. Rd. NE10-2B 80
Falloden Av. NE3-2B 26
Fallodon Gdns. NE5-3F 41
Fallodon Rd. NE29-5F 33
Fallowfeld. NE10-3E 81
Fallowfield Av. NE3-4B 26
Fallowfield Way. NE38
-1C 114
Fallow Rd. NE34-1B 70
Fallsway. DH1-1D 141
Falmouth Clo. SR7-4B 132
Falmouth Dri. NE32-2C 66
Falmouth Rd. NE6-1F 61
Falmouth Rd. NE29-1E 33
Falmouth Rd. SR4-1C 108
Falmouth Sq. SR4-1C 108
Falmouth Wlk. NE23-2C 4
Falsgrave Pl. NE16-5E 75
Falstaff Rd. NE29-3F 33
Falston Clo. NE12-2C 30
Falstone. NE10-5E 81
Falstone. NE38-5D 105
Falstone Av. NE15-4A 40
Falstone Av. NE34-1E 69
Falstone Dri. DH2-4A 122
Falstone Sq. NE3-3B 26
Faraday Clo. NE38-2A 106
Faraday Gro. NE8-3C 78
Faraday Gro. SR4-1D 109
Faraday Rd. SR8-1C 134
Farding Lake Ct. NE34-1B 70
Farding Sq. NE34-1B 70
Fareham Gro. NE35-2C 84
Fareham Way. NE23-2C 4
Farlam Av. NE30-5B 22
Farlam Rd. NE5-4C 40
Farleigh Ct. NE29-1D 33
Farm Clo. NE37-3A 94
Farm Hill Rd. SR6-5F 69
Farm St. SR5-3A 100
Farm Wlk. SR3-5E 119
Farnborough Clo. NE23-1D 5
Farnborough Dri. SR3-2A 120
Farn Ct. NE3-2F 25
Farndale. NE28-5B 30
Farndale Av. SR6-4D 89
Farndale Clo. NE21-2E 73
Farndale Rd. NE4-2C 58
Farne Av. NE3-2B 26
Farne Av. NE34-5C 52
Farne Rd. NE12-1A 30
Farne Rd. NE27-4A 20
Farne Sq. SR4-1B 108
Farne Ter. NE6-1D 63
Farnham Clo. DH1-4C 136
Farnham Clo. NE15-1C 56
Farnham Lodge. NE12-3C 28
Farnham Rd. DH1-3C 136
Farnham Rd. NE29-1F 49
Farnham Rd. NE34-1A 68
Farnham St. NE15-1C 56
Farnham Ter. SR4-3D 109
Farnley Hey Rd. DH1-3B 138
Farnley Mt. DH1-3A 138
Farnley Ridge. DH1-3A 138
Farnley Rd. NE6-3D 45
Farnon Rd. NE3-4C 26
Farnsworth Ct. NE2-2B 44
Farquhar St. NE2-4B 44
Farrfeld. NE10-5E 81
Farrier Clo. NE38-5D 105
Farringdon Av. SR3-3B 118
Farringdon Rd. NE30-4B 22
Farringdon Row. SR1-5A 100
Farrington's Ct. NE1
-2C 60 & 4C 142
Farrow Dri. SR6-1D 89
Farthings, The. NE37-3A 94
Fatfield Pk. NE38-1B 114
Fatfield Rd. NE38-4C 104
Fatherly Ter. DH4-5F 125
Faversham Ct. NE3-2E 25
Faversham Pl. NE23-1C 4
Fawcett St. SR1-1B 110
Fawcett Ter. SR2-4E 121
Fawcett Ter. SR5-4A 98
Fawcett Way. NE33-1E 51
Fawdon Clo. NE3-2A 26
Fawdon Ho. NE3-2A 26
Fawdon Pk. Cen. NE3-3B 26
Fawdon Pk. Ho. NE3-3B 26
(off Fawdon Pk. Rd.)
Fawdon Pk. Rd. NE3-3A 26
Fawdon Pl. NE29-4E 33
Fawdon Wlk. NE3-2E 25
Fawlee Grn. NE3-1E 41
Fawley Clo. NE35-1C 84
Fawn Rd. SR4-1B 108
Featherbed La. SR2
-4E 121 & 5E 121
Featherstone. DH3-4B 124
Featherstone. NE38-3E 103
Featherstone Gro. NE32-4F 65
Featherstone Rd. DH1-4D 137
Featherstone St. SR6-3D 101
Featherstone Vs. SR6-3D 101
Federation Way. NE11-1C 76
Fee Ter. SR2-4D 121
Feetham Av. NE12-2B 30
Feetham Ct. NE12-1B 30
Felixstowe Dri. NE7-2E 45
Fell Bank. DH3-3B 102
Fell Clo. DH3-4C 102
Fell Clo. NE37-1A 104
Fell Cotts. NE9-3D 93
(off Fell Rd.)
Fell Ct. NE9-5A 80
Fellcross. DH3-2B 102
Felldyke. DH10-5D 81
Fellgate Av. NE32-1B 84
Fellgate Gdns. NE10-2A 82
Felling By-Pass. NE10
-5B 62 to 3C 82
Felling Dene Gdns. NE10
-1D 81
Felling Ho. Gdns. NE10-1C 80
Felling View. NE6-4D 63
Fellmere Av. NE10-2E 81
Fell Pl. NE9-3E 93
Fell Rd. DH2-2A 122
Fell Rd. NE9-3D 93
Fell Rd. SR4-1B 108
Fellrose Ct. DH2-2A 122
Fellsdyke Ct. NE10-4A 80
Fellside. DH3-4C 102
Fellside. NE34-2A 70
Fellside Clo. DH9-2F 131
Fellside Ct. NE16-3F 75
Fellside Ct. NE37-2A 104
Fellside Gdns. DH1-2C 140
Fellside Rd. NE16-5D 75
Fell Side, The. NE3-1A 42
Fell Sq. SR4-1B 108
Fells Rd. NE11-3B 78
Fell View. DH9-3C 130
Fell Way, The. NE5-4F 39
Felsham Sq. SR4-1C 108
Felstead Cres. SR4-1C 108
Felstead Sq. SR4-1C 108
Felthorpe Ct. NE5-1D 41
Felton Av. NE3-4B 26
Felton Av. NE25-3C 22
Felton Av. NE34-1E 69
Felton Clo. NE27-4A 20
Felton Cres. NE8-3C 78
Felton Dri. NE12-1A 30
Felton Grn. NE6-1B 62
Felton Ter. NE30-2F 35
(off Hotspur St.)
Felton Wlk. NE6-1B 62
Fencer Ct. NE3-2E 27
Fencer Hill Pk. NE3-1D 27
Fence Rd. DH4-4C 114
Fenham Chase. NE4-5F 41
Fenham Ct. NE4-5F 41
Fenham Hall Dri. NE4-5F 41
Fenham Rd. NE4-1E 59
(in two parts)
Fenkle St. NE1
-2B 60 & 4B 142
Fennel. NE9-1B 92
Fennel Gro. NE34-4C 68
Fenning Pl. NE6-3B 62
Fenside Rd. SR2-2E 121
Fenton Clo. DH2-4B 122
Fenton Sq. SR4-1C 108
Fenton Ter. DH4-4B 116
Fenton Wlk. NE5-2B 40
Fenwick Av. NE34-2E 67
Fenwick Clo. DH2-5B 122
Fenwick Clo. DH4-3A 116
Fenwick Clo. NE2-4B 44
Fenwick Row. SR7-4F 133
Fenwick St. DH4-3A 116
Fenwick St. NE35-1D 85
Fenwick Ter. DH1-4A 138
Fenwick Ter. NE2-4B 44
Fenwick Ter. NE29-3C 34
Fenwick Wlk. NE8-5C 60
(off St Cuthbert's Rd.)
Ferens Clo. DH1-1D 139
Ferguson Cres. NE13-2C 14
Ferguson's La. NE15-4F 57
Ferguson St. SR2-2E 111
Fern Av. DH9-4A 130
Fern Av. NE2-3A 44
Fern Av. NE3-3B 26
Fern Av. NE26-2C 22
Fern Av. NE29-3A 34
Fern Av. SR5-3E 99
Fern Av. SR6-5D 71
Fern Cres. SR7-5D 133
Ferndale. DH1-2D 141
Ferndale Av. NE3-1F 27
Ferndale Av. NE28-3D 47
Ferndale Av. NE36-3C 86
Ferndale Ct. NE3-1E 43
Ferndale Gro. NE36-3C 86
Ferndale La. NE36-3C 86
Ferndale Rd. DH4-2F 115
Ferndale Ter. NE9-3D 93
Ferndale Ter. SR4-5D 99
Fern Dene. NE28-1A 48
Ferndene Av. DH2-2A 122
Ferndene Cres. SR4-1D 109
Ferndene Gro. NE7-1D 45
Ferndene Gro. NE40-1B 54
Fern Dene Rd. NE8-2C 78
Ferndown Ct. NE10-3A 82
Fern Dri. NE23-4F 7
Fern Dri. SR6-1D 87
Fern Gdns. NE9-4E 79
Ferngrove. NE32-1B 84
Fernhill Av. NE16-3E 75
Fernlea. NE23-4A 8
Fernlea Clo. NE38-1D 115
Fernlea Grn. NE3-4B 26
Fernleigh. DH3-5A 124
Fernley Vs. NE23-3E 5
Fernlough. NE9-5A 80
Fern St. SR4-5A 100
Fernsway. SR3-4A 110
Fernville Rd. NE3-2D 43
Fernville St. SR4-2F 109
Fernwood Av. NE3-3F 27
Fernwood Ho. NE33-3D 51
Fernwood Rd. NE2-5A 44
Fernwood Rd. NE15-1C 56
Ferrand Dri. DH4-5B 126
Ferriby Clo. NE3-1F 27
Ferrisdale Way. NE3-3A 26
Ferry App. NE33-2D 51
Ferryboat La. SR5
-2D 97 to 1E 107
Ferrydene Av. NE3-1B 42
Ferry St. NE32-4D 49
Ferry St. NE33-2D 51
Festival Cotts. NE12-2D 17
Festival Pk. Dri. NE11-3A 78
Festival Way. NE11-1F 77
Fetcham Ct. NE3-2E 25
Fewster Sq. NE10-4F 81
Field Clo. NE2
-1E 61 & 3F 143
Fieldfare Clo. NE38-4D 103
Field Ho. NE33-4A 52
Fieldhouse La. DH1-1A 138
Field Ho. Rd. NE8-3C 78
Fieldhouse Ter. DH1-1B 138
Fielding Ct. NE5-1B 40
Fielding Ct. NE34-4F 67
Fielding Pl. NE9-2A 80
Field La. NE10-2E 81
Fieldside. DH5-4B 128
Fieldside. SR6-1D 89
Field Sq. SR4-1B 108
Field St. NE3-5A 28
Field St. NE10-1B 80
Field Ter. NE15-2F 37
Field Ter. NE32-2F 65
Fieldway. NE32-1B 84
Fife Av. DH2-3D 123
Fife Av. NE32-4D 67
Fife St. NE8-1E 79
Fifth Av. DH2-2C 122
Fifth Av. NE6-5D 45
Fifth Av. NE11-5B 78
Fifth Av. Bus. Pk. NE11-5C 79
Fifth Av. E. NE11-5B 78
Fifth St. SR8-2F 135
Filby Dri. DH1-1D 141
Filey Clo. NE23-2C 4
Filton Clo. NE23-2D 5
Finchale. NE38-4B 104
Finchale Av. DH1-1E 137
Finchale Clo. DH4-5B 126
Finchale Clo. NE11-4E 77
Finchale Clo. SR2-2D 111
Finchale Gdns. NE9-2B 92
Finchale Gdns. NE15-2F 37
Finchale Rd. DH1-4A 136
(Framwellgate Moor)
Finchale Rd. DH1-1C 136
(Newton Hall)
Finchale Rd. NE31-5C 64
Finchale Ter. DH4-4C 124
Finchale Ter. NE6-3A 62
Finchale Ter. NE32-3C 66
Finchale View. DH1-1B 136
Finchdale Clo. NE29-5B 34
Finchdale Ter. DH3-3E 123
Finchley Ct. NE6-4C 46
Finchley Cres. NE6-4B 46
Findon Gro. NE29-5A 34
Finney's Ter. DH1-2D 139
Finsbury Av. NE6-2D 63
Finsbury St. SR5-3A 100
Finsmere Pl. NE5-3D 41
Fins, The. NE3-5C 26
Finstock Ct. NE3-5B 28
Fir Av. DH1-5A 140
Firbank Av. NE30-5D 23
Firbanks. NE32-1B 84
Fire Sta. Cotts. SR6-1B 100
Firfield Rd. NE5-2E 41
Fir Gro. NE34-2E 69
First Av. DH2-3A 112
First Av. NE6-5D 45
First Av. NE11-4B 78
First Av. NE29-5D 33
Fir St. NE11-5B 78
Fir St. NE32-5C 48
First St. NE8-1B 78
Firth Sq. SR4-1B 108
Firtree Av. NE6-4B 46
Firtree Av. NE12-1E 29
Firtree Av. NE38-1A 114
Fir Tree Clo. DH2-2A 140
Firtree Cres. NE12-1E 29
Firtree Gdns. NE25-4A 22
Firtree Rd. NE16-4F 75
Firtrees. DH2-5A 112
Firtrees. NE10-5C 80
Firtrees Av. NE28-2D 49
Firwood Gdns. NE11-5F 77
Fisher Ind. Est. NE6-1F 63
Fisher La. NE13 & NE23-2A 6
Fisher Rd. NE27-2D 19
Fisher St. NE6-5C 46
Fisherwell Rd. NE10-5F 63
Fish Quay. NE30-4E 35
Fitzpatrick Pl. NE33-3F 51
Fitzroy Ter. SR5-3E 99
Fitzsimmons Av. NE28-1C 46
Flagg Ct. NE33-1F 51
Flagg Ct. Ho. NE33-1F 51
Flake Cotts. DH3-2E 123
Flambard Rd. DH1-4B 136
Flassburn Rd. DH1-1A 138
Flass St. DH1-2B 138
Flaunden Clo. NE34-2F 69
Flax Sq. SR4-1B 108
Fleetham Clo. DH2-5B 122
Fleet St. SR1-1E 111
Fleming Ct. NE8-5B 60
Fleming Gdns. NE10-3B 80
Fleming Pl. SR8-4C 134
Fletcher Cres. DH4-4C 116
Fletcher Ter. DH4-1B 126
Flexbury Gdns. NE9-2F 91
Flexbury Gdns. NE10-2B 80
Flexbury Gdns. NE15-1D 57
Flock Sq. SR4-1B 108
Flodden. NE12-3F 17
Flodden Clo. DH2-5B 122
Flodden Rd. SR4-2B 108
Flodden St. NE6-2C 62
Floral Dene. SR4-2F 107
Floralia Av. SR2-4E 121
Flora St. NE6-1A 62
Florence Av. NE9-4F 79
Florence Cres. SR5-3E 99
Florence St. NE21-1A 74
Florence Ter. DH5-5F 129
Florida St. SR4-5D 99
Flotterton Gdns. NE5-5D 41
Flour Mill Rd. NE11-5E 59
Folds, The. DH4-5F 125
Fold, The. NE6-4C 46
Fold, The. NE25-2A 22
Folldon Av. SR6-1C 100
Follingsby Dri. NE10-3B 82
Follingsby La. NE10-5B 82
Follingsby La. SR5-1B 96
Follonsby Ter. NE10-3C 82
Folly Cotts. NE40-1A 72
Folly La. NE40-5A 54
Folly Ter. DH1-2B 136
Folly, The. NE36-3E 85
Folly Yd. NE40-5B 54
Fontaine Rd. SR1-5B 100
Fontburn Pl. NE7-4C 28
Fontburn Rd. NE25-1C 10
Fontburn Ter. NE30-3C 34
Fonteyn Pl. DH9-4E 131
Font Ho. NE1-2E 61 & 4F 143
Fontwell Dri. NE8-3C 78
Forbeck Rd. SR4-1B 108
(in two parts)
Forber Av. NE34-2A 70
Forbes Ter. SR2-4D 121
Ford Av. NE29-5F 33
Ford Av. SR4-1F 107
Ford Cres. NE27-3A 20
Ford Cres. NE32-4A 66
Ford Cres. SR4-1F 107
Fordenbridge Cres. SR4
-2C 108
Fordenbridge Rd. SR4
-2C 108
Fordenbridge Sq. SR4-2C 108
Fordfield Rd. SR4-2A 108
Ford Gro. NE3-3C 26
Fordham Rd. DH1-1C 136
Fordham Rd. SR4-1C 108
Fordham Sq. SR4-2C 108
Fordland Pl. SR4-1D 109
Fordmoss Wlk. NE5-3C 40
Ford Oval. SR4-1F 107
Ford Rd. DH1-2D 137
Ford St. NE6-2F 61
Ford St. NE8-1A 80
Ford Ter. NE28-3A 48
Ford Ter. SR4-1D 109
Ford Tower. NE12-3E 17
Ford View. NE23-3E 7
Forest Av. NE12-2F 29
Forestborn Ct. NE5-3B 40
Forest Dri. NE38-2D 113
Forest Hall Rd. NE12-1F 29
Fore St. NE6-5C 44
Forest Rd. NE15-3A 58
Forest Rd. NE33-2E 51
Forest Rd. SR4-1B 108
Forest Way. NE23-3E 9
Forfar St. SR6-2B 100
Forge La. DH3-3A 124
Forge Rd. NE8-2F 77
Forge Wlk. NE15-3B 38
Forres Ct. DH9-3F 131
Forres Pl. NE23-2C 4
Forrest Pl. NE27-3A 20
Forrest Rd. NE28-3B 46
Forster Av. DH6-4F 141
Forster Av. NE34-1D 69
Forster St. NE1
-3D 61 & 5E 143
Forster St. SR6-3C 100
Forsyth Rd. NE2-3F 43
Forsyth St. NE29-1D 33
Forth Banks. NE1
-3B 60 & 5B 142
Forth Clo. SR8-4B 134
Forth Ct. NE34-2B 68
Forth Ct. SR3-4E 119
Forth La. NE1
-3B 60 & 5B 142
(in two parts)
Forth Pl. NE1-3B 60 & 5B 142
Forth St. NE1-3B 60 & 5B 142
Fortrose Av. SR3-4F 109
Fort Sq. NE33-5E 35
Fort St. NE33-5E 35
Forum, The. NE15-5B 40
Forum, The. NE28-3D 47
Forum Way. NE23-3B 4
Fossdyke. NE10-5D 81
Fossefeld. NE10-3F 81
Fosse Law. NE15-3A 38
Fosse Ter. NE9-3F 79
Fossway. NE6-1B 62 to 5C 46
Foss Way. NE34-2A 68
Foster Ct. NE11-1B 90
Foster St. NE6-1F 63 & 2F 63
Foundry Ct. NE6-3B 62
Foundry La. NE6-1F 61
Foundry La. NE16-1F 75
Foundry Rd. SR7-3F 133
Fountain Gro. NE34-4B 52
Fountain La. NE21-4B 56
Fountain Row. NE2-5C 42
Fountains Clo. NE11-4E 77
Fountains Clo. NE38
-3C 104 & 4C 104
Fountains Cres. DH4-3A 126
Fountains Cres. NE31-4C 64
Fouracres Rd. NE5-2A 42
Four La. Ends. DH5-5F 129
Fourstones. NE5-3B 40
Fourstones Clo. NE3-4F 25
Fourstones Rd. SR4-1D 109
Fourth Av. DH2-3C 122
Fourth Av. NE6-5D 45
Fourth Av. NE11-5A 78
Fourth St. NE8-1B 78
Fourth St. SR8-2F 135
Fowberry Cres. NE4-5A 42
Fowberry Rd. NE15-3E 57
Fowler Gdns. NE11-1E 77
Fowler St. NE33-1E 51
Fox Av. NE34-3E 67
(in two parts)
Foxcover La. SR3-3F 117
Foxcover Rd. SR4 & SR3
-5D 107
Foxhills Clo. NE38-5D 105
Foxhills Covert. NE16-5D 75
Foxhills, The. NE16-4D 75
Foxholmes. NE32-2B 84
Fox & Hounds La. NE15
-2A 58
Fox & Hounds Rd. NE5-1B 58
Foxhunters Rd. NE25-4B 22
Foxlair Clo. SR3-5E 119
Fox Lea Wlk. NE23-3C 8
Foxley. NE37-4D 95
Foxley Clo. NE12-3A 18
Fox St. NE10-1A 80
Fox St. SR2-3A 110
Fox St. SR7-4F 133
Foxton Av. NE3-2B 26
Foxton Av. NE30-3D 23
Foxton Ct. SR6-1F 87
Foxton Grn. NE3-5A 26
Foxton Hall. NE37-2C 95
Foxton Way. NE10-5A 64
Foyle St. SR1-1C 110
Framlington Ho. NE2
-5E 43 & 1B 142
Framlington Pl. NE2
-5E 43 & 1B 142
Framwelgate. DH1-2C 138
Framwelgate Peth. DH1
-1B 138
Framwelgate Waterside. DH1
-2C 138
Frances St. NE21-5F 55
Frances St. SR3-3F 119
Francis St. SR6-2C 100
Frank Av. SR7-4C 132
Frankham St. NE5-2A 40
Frankland Dri. NE25-4F 21
Frankland La. DH1-1D 139
Frankland Mt. NE25-4F 21
Frankland Rd. DH1-4B 136
Franklin Ct. NE37-5B 94
Franklin St. NE33-2E 51
Franklin St. SR4-1F 109
Franklyn Rd. SR8-2A 134
Frank Pl. NE29-4C 34
Frank St. DH1-4B 140
Frank St. NE28-3D 47
Frank St. SR5-3A 100
Frater Ter. NE28-2E 49
Frazer Clo. NE33-4D 51
Frazer Ter. NE10-1E 81
Freda St. SR5-3E 99
Frederick Gdns. DH4-3E 115
Frederick Pl. DH4-4C 126
Frederick Rd. SR1-1C 110
Frederick St. NE33-4D 51
Frederick St. SR1-1C 110
(in two parts)
Frederick St. SR4-1F 107
Frederick St. SR7-3F 133
Frederick Ter. SR6-1E 89
Freeman Rd. NE3 & NE7
-5A 28
Freemans Pl. DH1-2C 138
Freeman Way. NE26-5C 12
Freesia Gdns. SR5-2B 100
Freesia Grange. NE38-4D 105
Freezemoor Rd. DH4-4B 116
Fremantle Rd. NE34-2F 69
Frenchmans Way. NE34
-5C 52
Frensham. NE38-3F 105
Frenton Clo. NE5-2D 39
Friarage Av. SR6-1C 100
Friar Rd. SR4-2B 108
Friars Ct. NE1-2B 60
Friars Dene Rd. NE10-5A 62
Friarsfield Clo. SR3-5D 119
Friarside Gdns. NE16-4F 75
Friarside Rd. NE4-4A 42
Friar Sq. SR4-2C 108
Friars Row. DH1-1F 139
Friars St. NE1
-2B 60 & 4B 142
(in two parts)
Friar Way. NE32-5D 49
Friary Gdns. NE10-1B 80
Friday Fields La. NE2-2A 44
Frobisher Ct. SR3-5E 119
Frobisher St. NE31-1E 65
Frome Gdns. NE9-2E 91
Frome Pl. NE23-1C 4
Frome Sq. SR4-1B 108
Front Rd. SR4-1C 108
Front St. DH1 & DH6
-4B 140 to 5F 141
Front St. DH1-4A 136
(Framwellgate Moor)
Front St. DH2-1A 122
Front St. DH3-2E 123
(Chester-le-Street)
Front St. DH3-5A 124
(Great Lumley)
Front St. DH4-5F 125
(High Dubmire)
Front St. DH4
-2B 126 & 1C 126
(Newbottle)
Front St. DH4-2A 116
(Penshaw)
Front St. DH5-4F 129
Front St. DH9-5F 131
(Craghead)
Front St. DH9-3B 130
(Tanfield Lea)
Front St. NE7-4D 29
Front St. NE12-2D 17
Front St. NE13-3A 6
Front St. NE16-3F 75
Front St. NE21-1F 73
Front St. NE23-3A 8
(Annitsford)
Front St. NE23-3C 4
(Cramlington)
Front St. NE23-4E 5
(E. Cramlington)
Front St. NE23-3D 9
(Seghill)
Front St. NE25-1B 20
(Earsdon)
Front St. NE25-2A 22
(Monkseaton)
Front St. NE29-2B 34
(Preston)
Front St. NE29-5A 34
(West Chirton)
Front St. NE30-2F 35
Front St. NE35-1D 85
Front St. NE36-3B 86
Front St. NE36-3B 86
Front St. NE37-5C 94
Front St. SR6-1F 87
(Cleadon)
Front St. SR6-2D 89
(Whitburn)
Front St. E. DH4-2A 116
Front St. W. DH4-2A 116
Frosterley Clo. DH1-2D 137
Frosterley Dri. DH3-5B 124
Frosterley Gdns. SR3-5F 109
Froude Av. NE34-4A 68
Fuchsia Gdns. NE31-4D 65
Fuchsia Pl. NE5-2E 41
Fulbrook Rd. NE3-4B 26
Fuller Rd. SR2-4D 111
Fullerton Pl. NE9-2F 79
Fulmar Dri. NE38-4E 103
Fulmar Lodge. NE33-2A 52
Fulmer Wlk. SR6-5D 71
Fulton Pl. NE5-2D 41
Fulwell Av. NE34-5D 53
Fulwell Grn. NE5-3D 41
Fulwell Rd. SR6-1C 100
Fulwell Rd. SR8-4D 135
Furness Clo. SR8-3A 134
Furness Ct. SR3-4E 119
Furrowfield. NE10-4B 80
Furzefield Rd. NE3-1D 43
Fylingdale Dri. SR3-3A 120
Fyling Ho. SR3-5E 119
Fynes Clo. SR8-2C 134

Gables Ct. SR4-4B 108
Gables, The. NE13-3C 24
Gables, The. NE38-4C 104
(off Fatfield Rd.)
Gainers Ter. NE28-4D 47
Gainford. DH2-3C 122
Gainford. NE9-3E 91
(in three parts)
Gainford Ho. DH2-3C 122
Gainsborough Av. NE34
-4B 68
Gainsborough Av. NE38
-4C 104
Gainsborough Clo. NE25
-5B 12
Gainsborough Cres. DH4
-5E 115
Gainsborough Cres. NE9
-3A 80
Gainsborough Gro. NE4
-1E 59
Gainsborough Pl. NE23-1A 8
Gainsborough Rd. DH9
-3C 130
Gainsborough Rd. SR4
-5A 108
Gainsborough Sq. SR4
-5A 108
Gainsford Av. NE9-1D 91
Gairloch Dri. NE38-4E 103
Gairloch Rd. SR4-5A 108
Gairsay Clo. SR2-2C 120
Gaitskell Ct. NE31-5A 48
Galashiels Gro. DH4-5F 115
Galashiels Rd. SR4-4A 108
Galashiels Sq. SR4-4A 108
Gale St. DH9-4B 130
Galfrid Clo. SR7-4A 132
Gallagher Cres. SR8-3E 135
Gallalaw Ter. NE3-4A 28
Gallant Ter. NE28-3D 49
Galleria, The. NE11-5B 58
Galleries Shopping NE38
-2A 104
Galley's Gill Rd. SR1-1A 110
Galloping Grn. Cotts. NE9
-3B 92
Galloping Grn. Rd. NE9-2B 92
Galloway Rd. SR8-2C 134
Gallowgate. NE1
-2B 60 & 3B 142
Galsworthy Rd. NE34-4F 67
Galsworthy Rd. SR4-4B 108
Galway Rd. SR4-5A 108
Galway Sq. SR4-5A 108
Gambia Rd. SR4-5A 108
Gambia Sq. SR4-5F 107
Ganton Av. NE23-5C 4
Ganton Clo. NE37-3B 94
Ganton Ct. NE34-4E 69
Garcia Ter. SR6-1D 101
Garden Av. DH1-3A 136
Garden Clo. NE13-4A 6
Garden Croft. NE12-2A 30
Garden Dri. NE31-3B 64
Gardener St. NE4-4E 59
Garden Est. DH5-4F 129
Garden La. NE33-2E 51
Garden La. SR6-2D 87
Garden Pl. DH4-3A 116
Garden Pl. SR1-1B 110
Gardens, The. DH2-3C 122
Gardens, The. NE25-3A 22
Gardens, The. NE38-4C 104
Garden St. DH4-2C 126
Garden St. NE3-5E 27
Garden St. NE21-4B 56
Garden St. NE29-3F 33
Garden Ter. DH4-2C 126
Garden Ter. DH9-5E 131
(Craghead)
Garden Ter. DH9-3B 130
(Stanley)
Garden Ter. NE25-2B 20
Garden Ter. NE40-4A 40
Garden Wlk. NE11-5B 58
Gardiner Cres. DH2-2A 122
Gardiner Rd. SR4-5F 107
Gardiner Sq. SR4-4F 107
Gardner Pl. NE29-5C 34
Garesfield La. NE39-5C 72
Garfield St. SR4-1D 109
Garforth Clo. NE23-5C 4
Garland Ter. DH4-4F 125
Garleigh Clo. NE12-3B 18
Garmondsway. NE6-3B 62
Garner Clo. NE5-1F 39
Garnet St. SR4-5E 99
Garnwood St. NE33-4C 50
Garrick Clo. NE29-2D 33
Garrick St. NE33-4E 51
Garrigill. NE38-1D 115
Garrigill Pl. NE12-3C 28
Garron St. SR7-4E 133
Garsdale. DH3-1C 112
Garsdale Av. NE37-4A 94
Garsdale Rd. NE26-3D 13
Garside Av. DH3-2B 102
Garstin Clo. NE7-2A 46
Garth 4. NE12-4E 17
Garth 6. NE12-4E 17
Garth 7. NE12-4D 17
Garth 9. NE12-4D 17
Garth 11. NE12-3D 17
Garth 12. NE12-3D 17
Garth 13. NE12-3D 17
Garth 16. NE12-3E 17
Garth 20. NE12-3F 17
Garth 21. NE12-3A 18
Garth 22. NE12-4A 18
Garth 24. NE12-4A 18
Garth 25. NE12-3B 18
Garth 27. NE12-4B 18
Garth 32. NE12-4F 17
Garth 33. NE12-4F 17
Garth Cres. NE21-1F 73
Garth Cres. NE34-4B 52
Garth Farm Rd. NE21-1F 73
Garthfield Clo. NE5-2C 40
Garthfield Corner. NE5-2C 40
Garthfield Cres. NE5-2C 40
Garth Heads. NE1
-2D 61 & 4E 143
Garth, The. NE3-1A 42
Garth, The. NE5-4F 39
Garth, The. NE21-1F 73
Gartland Rd. SR4-5F 107
Garvey Vs. NE10-3A 80
Gashouse Dri. DH3-4A 114
Gas Ho. La. DH4-4C 126
Gaskell Av. NE34-4A 68
Gas La. NE21-3B 56
Gas Works Bri. Rd.
NE11 & NE8-1F 77
Gas Works Rd. SR7-4F 133
Gatesgarth. NE9-5F 79
Gatesgarth Gro. SR6-5B 88
Gateshead Highway. NE8
-4E 61
Gateshead Ter. NE36-3E 85
(off Addison Rd.)
Gateshead Western By-Pass.
NE16 & NE11-1A 76 to 5F 91
Gatwick Ct. NE3-3D 25
Gatwick Rd. SR4-5F 107
Gaughan Clo. NE6-4D 63
Gaweswell Ter. DH4-1C 126
(off North St.)
Gayhurst Cres. SR3-4F 119
Gayton Rd. NE37-4D 95
Geddes Rd. SR4-4A 108
Gellesfield Chare. NE16-5F 75
General Graham St. SR4
-3E 109
General Havelock Rd. SR4
-1C 108
General's Wood, The. NE38
-2A 114
Geneva Rd. SR4-5F 107
Genister Pl. NE4-4F 41
Geoffrey Av. DH1-3A 138
Geoffrey St. NE34-4A 68
Geoffrey St. SR6-1D 89
Geoffrey Ter. DH9-3A 130
George Pl. NE1
-1C 60 & 2C 142
George Rd. NE6 & NE28
-4C 46
George Scott St. NE33-1F 51
George Smith Gdns. NE10
-5B 62
George Sq. NE30-4D 35
Georges Rd. NE4
-3E 59 & 4E 59
George Stephenson Way.
NE29-1B 50
George St. DH1-3A 138
George St. DH3-3A 102
(Birtley)
George St. DH3-4E 123
(Chester-le-Street)
George St. DH5-3F 129
George St. DH6-4F 141
George St. NE3-4B 26
George St. NE4
-3A 60 & 5A 142
George St. NE10-1E 81
George St. NE13-1B 14
George St. NE15-3B 38
George St. NE16-3F 75
George St. NE21-4C 26
George St. NE28-3C 48
George St. NE30-4D 35
George St. SR1-1C 110
George St. SR2-4F 121
George St. SR3-2F 119
George St. SR7-3E 133
George St. E. SR3-3F 119
George St. Ind. Est. SR7
-3E 133
George St. N. SR6-4C 100
George St. W. SR3-2F 119
George's View. NE23-5F 7
George Way. NE4
-3A 60 & 5A 142
Georgian Ct. NE12-5D 17
Georgian Ct. SR4-4F 109
Gerald St. NE4-3C 58
Gerald St. NE34-4A 68
Gerrard Clo. NE23-1A 8
Gerrard Clo. NE26-3D 13
Gerrard Rd. NE26-3D 13
Gerrard Rd. SR4-5F 107
Gertrude St. DH4-3B 126
Ghyll Field Rd. DH1-3C 136
Gibbons Walk. NE34-5F 67
Gibbs Ct. DH2-3E 123
Gibside. DH2-3C 122
Gibside Clo. DH9-1E 131
Gibside Ct. NE11-4E 77
Gibside Gdns. NE15-2A 58
Gibside View. NE21-1A 74
Gibside Way. NE21-5F 57
Gibson St. NE1
-2E 61 & 4F 143
Gibson St. NE28-5A 32
Gifford Sq. SR4-4B 108
Gilberdyke. NE10-5E 81
Gilbert Rd. SR4-5A 108
Gilbert Rd. SR8-3B 134
Gilbert Sq. SR4-5A 108
Gilbert St. NE33-4D 51
Gilderdale. DH4-3D 115
Gilderdale Way. NE23-1F 7
Gilesgate. DH1-2D 139
Gilesgate Clo. DH1-2E 139
Gillas La. DH5-5F 127

Gillas La. E. DH5-1D 129
Gillas La. W. DH5-2C 128
Gill Bri. Av. SR1-5B 100
Gill Cres. N. DH4-3D 125
Gill Cres. S. DH4-3D 125
Gillhurst Grange. SR1-1A 110
Gillies St. NE6-2B 62
Gilliland Cres. DH3-1B 102
Gillingham Rd. SR4-5A 108
Gill Rd. SR1-5B 100
Gillside Ct. NE34-2F 67
Gill Side Gro. SR6-2D 101
Gill St. NE4-2C 58
Gill Ter. SR4-1F 107
(off Pottery La.)
Gilly Law Ter. SR3-2D 119
Gilmore Clo. NE5-2F 39
Gilpin St. DH4-5B 126
Gilsland Av. NE28-1B 48
Gilsland St. SR4-1E 109
Gingler La. NE40-5A 54
Girtin Rd. NE34-5C 68
Girton Clo. SR8-5A 134
Girvan Clo. DH9-3E 131
Gishford Way. NE5-3D 41
Givens St. SR6-3D 101
Glade, The. NE5-2C 38
Glade, The. NE32-1A 84
Gladstonbury Pl. NE12-3E 29
Gladstone Av. NE26-1B 22
Gladstone Pl. NE2
-1D 61 & 2E 143
Gladstone St. DH4-5F 125
Gladstone St. DH9-3A 130
Gladstone St. NE15-1B 56
Gladstone St. NE28-3C 48
Gladstone St. NE31-1E 65
Gladstone St. SR6-3C 100
Gladstone Ter. DH3-3A 102
Gladstone Ter. DH4-2E 115
Gladstone Ter. NE2
-1D 61 & 2E 143
Gladstone Ter. NE8-1D 79
Gladstone Ter. NE26-3D 23
Gladstone Ter. NE35-5D 67
Gladstone Ter. NE37-4E 95
Gladstone Ter. W. NE8-1D 79
Gladstone Vs. DH1-4D 139
Gladwyn Rd. SR4-5A 108
Gladwyn Sq. SR4-5A 108
Glaholm Rd. SR1-2D 111
Glaisdale Ct. NE34-3F 67
Glaisdale Dri. SR6-4D 89
Glaisdale Rd. NE7-4C 28
Glamis Av. NE3-5E 15
Glamis Av. SR4-4B 108
Glamis Ct. NE34-4E 69
Glamis Cres. NE39-5F 73
Glamis Vs. DH3-2A 102
Glanmore Rd. SR4-4F 107
Glantlees. NE5-2C 40
Glanton Av. NE25-1A 10
Glanton Clo. DH2-4B 122
Glanton Clo. NE6-3B 62
Glanton Clo. NE10-3B 82
Glanton Ct. NE11-1E 77
Glanton Rd. NE29-3F 33
Glanton Sq. SR4-4B 108
Glanton Ter. SR8-3F 135
Glanton Wynd. NE3-3D 27
Glanville Clo. NE11-3A 78
Glasbury Av. SR4-3B 108
Glasgow Rd. NE32-4C 66
Glasshouse St. NE6-3A 62
Glastonbury. NE38-4C 104
Glastonbury Gro. NE2-2B 44
Glebe Av. NE12-3F 29
Glebe Av. NE16-3F 75
Glebe Clo. NE5-2F 39
Glebe Cres. NE12-1E 29
Glebe Cres. NE38-2C 104
Glebe Dri. SR7-1A 132
Glebe Mt. NE38-2D 105
Glebe Rise. NE16-3F 75
Glebe Rd. NE12-5E 17
Glebe St. NE4-2C 58
Glebe Ter. DH4-4C 126
Glebe Ter. NE11-2E 77
Glebe Ter. NE12-1E 29
Glebe Vs. NE12-1E 29
Glebe Wlk. NE16-3F 75
Glenallen Gdns. NE30-5E 23
Glenavon Av. DH2-1D 123
Glen Barr. DH2-1D 123
Glenbrooke Ter. NE9-1E 91
Glenburn Clo. NE38-4E 103
Glencarron Clo. NE38-4F 103
Glencoe. NE12-3E 17
Glencoe Av. DH2-1D 123
Glencoe Av. NE23-1F 7
Glencoe Rd. SR4-5F 107
Glencoe Sq. SR4-5F 107
Glencourse. NE36-3C 86
Glen Ct. NE31-2C 64
Glendale Av. NE3-1C 42
Glendale Av. NE16-4F 75
Glendale Av. NE26-5E 13
Glendale Av. NE28-5D 31
Glendale Av. NE29-3A 34
Glendale Av. NE37-4B 94
Glendale Clo. NE5-1F 39
Glendale Clo. NE21-2E 73
Glendale Clo. SR3-4A 118
Glendale Gdns. NE9-5F 79
Glendale Gro. NE29-4A 34
Glendale Rd. NE27-4B 20
Glendale Ter. NE6-1B 62
Glendower Av. NE29-4F 33
Glendyn Clo. NE7-3C 44
Gleneagle Clo. NE5-1F 39
Gleneagles. NE33-3A 52
Gleneagles Clo. NE7-4E 29
Gleneagles Ct. NE25-1E 21
Gleneagles Dri. NE37-3A 94
Gleneagles Rd. NE9-2D 91
Gleneagles Rd. SR4-5F 107
Gleneagles Sq. SR4-5F 107
Glenesk Gdns. SR2-5B 110
Glenesk Rd. SR2-5A 110
Glenfield Rd. NE12-3D 29
(in two parts)
Glengarvan Clo. NE38-4E 103
Glenholme Clo. NE38-4E 103
Glen Ho. NE1-2E 61 & 4F 143
Glenhurst Dri. NE5-1F 39
Glenhurst Dri. NE16-5E 75
Glenhurst Gro. NE34-1D 69
Glenkerry Clo. NE38-4E 103
Glenleigh Dri. SR4-4B 108
Glenluce. DH3-5C 102
Glenluce Dri. NE23-1F 7
Glen Luce Dri. SR2-1E 121
Glenmoor. NE31-5F 47
Glenmore Av. DH2-1D 123
Glenmuir Av. NE23-1F 7
Glenorrin Clo. NE38-4F 103
Glen Path. SR2-4B 110
Glenridge Av. NE6-4D 45
Glenroy Gdns. DH2-1D 123
Glenshiel Clo. NE38-4F 103
Glenside. NE32-5B 66
Glenside Ter. DH2-1A 122
Glen St. NE31-2B 64
Glen Ter. DH2-1C 122
Glen Ter. DH4-2A 116
(off Rainton St.)
Glen Ter. NE38-3D 105
Glen, The. SR2-4B 110
Glenthorne Rd. SR6-2C 100
Glenthorn Rd. NE2-2F 43
Glen Thorpe Av. SR6-2C 100
Glenthorpe Ho. NE33-4F 51
Glenwood Wlk. NE5-1F 39
Gloucester Av. SR6-1C 100
Gloucester Clo. DH3-5A 124
Gloucester Ct. NE3-2E 25
Gloucester Pl. NE34-2E 69
Gloucester Pl. SR8-2A 134
Gloucester Rd. NE4-2F 59
Gloucester Rd. NE29-3C 32
Gloucestershire Dri. DH1
-3C 140
Gloucester Ter. NE4-3F 59
Gloucester Way. NE4-3F 59
Gloucester Way. NE32-5A 66
Glover Ind. Est. NE37-5E 95
Glover Rd. NE37-5D 95
Glover Rd. SR4-5F 107
Glover Sq. SR4-5F 107
Glue Garth. DH1-2F 139
Glynfellis. NE10-5E 81
Glynfellis Ct. NE10-5E 81
Glynn Ho. NE4-3C 58
Glynwood Gdns. NE9-4F 79
Goathland Av. NE12-3D 29
Goathland Dri. SR3-4A 120
Godfrey Rd. SR4-4F 107
Gofton Wlk. NE5-2C 40
Goldcrest Rd. NE38-5E 103
Goldfinch Clo. NE4-4D 59
Goldlynn Dri. SR3-4C 118
Goldsbrough Ct. NE2
-5D 43 & 1A 142
Goldsmith Rd. SR4-1F 117
Goldspink La. NE2
-5B 44 & 1F 143
Goldstone Ct. NE12-3A 18
Golf Course Rd. DH4-1E 125
Gompertz Gdns. NE33-4D 51
Good St. DH9-1B 130
Goodwood. NE12-4A 18
Goodwood Av. NE8-2B 78
Goodwood Clo. NE5-1F 39
Goodwood Rd. SR4-5F 107
Goodwood Sq. SR4-5F 107
Goodyear Cres. DH1-4B 140
Goole Rd. SR4-5B 108
Gordon Av. NE3-1E 43
Gordon Av. SR5-5F 97
Gordon Av. SR8-2E 135
Gordon Ct. NE10-1C 80
(off Church Pl.)
Gordon Dri. NE36-4B 86
Gordon Rd. NE6-2A 62
Gordon Rd. NE34-1B 68
Gordon Rd. SR4-5F 107
Gordon Sq. NE6-2A 62
Gordon Sq. NE26-2D 23
Gordon St. NE33-4E 51
Gordon Ter. DH4-2A 116
Gordon Ter. DH9-1C 130
Gordon Ter. NE26-2D 23
Gordon Ter. SR2-4E 121
Gordon Ter. SR5-2E 99
Gorleston Way. SR3-5E 119
Gorse Av. NE34-2E 69
Gorsedale Gro. DH1-2D 141
Gorsedene Av. NE26-3D 13
Gorsedene Rd. NE26-3D 13
Gorsehill. NE9-5B 80
Gorse Hill Way. NE5-1E 41
Gorse Rd. SR2-3B 110
Gort Pl. DH1-1F 139
Goschen St. NE8-1C 78
Goschen St. SR5-5F 99
Gosforth Av. NE34-3A 68
Gosforth Cen., The. NE3
-5E 27
Gosforth Ind. Est. NE3-4A 28
Gosforth Pk. Vs. NE13-2D 15
Gosforth St. NE2
-1D 61 & 2F 143
(in two parts)
Gosforth St. NE10-1B 80
Gosforth St. SR6-4D 101
Gosforth Ter. NE3-5A 28
Gosforth Ter. NE10-1E 81
Gossington. NE38-3F 105
Goswick Av. NE7-2D 45
Goswick Dri. NE3-2B 26
Goundry Av. SR2-4E 121
Gourock Sq. SR4-4F 107
Gowanburn. NE23-1F 7
Gowanburn. NE38-1D 115
Gowan Ter. NE2-4A 44
Gower Rd. SR5-2E 99
Gower St. NE6-3F 63
Gower Wlk. NE8-2A 80
Gowland Av. NE4-1D 59
Gracefield Clo. NE5-1E 39
Grace Gdns. NE28-1C 46
Grace Ho. NE29-1F 49
Grace St. NE6-1B 62
(in two parts)
Grace St. NE11-2D 77
Grafton Clo. NE6-1A 62
Grafton Ho. NE6-1A 62
Grafton Pl. NE6-1A 62
Grafton Rd. NE26-3D 23
Grafton St. NE6-1A 62
Grafton St. SR4-5F 99
Graham Av. NE16-2F 75
Graham Pk. Rd. NE3-1D 43
Graham Rd. NE31-2B 64
Grahamsley St. NE8-5D 61
Graham St. NE33-3F 51
Graham Way, The. SR7
-5B 132
Grainger Mkt. NE1-2C 60
Grainger Pk. Rd. NE4-3D 59
Grainger St. NE1
-3B 60 & 5C 142
Graingerville N. NE4-2E 59
(off Westgate Rd.)
Graingerville S. NE4-2E 59
(off Westgate Rd.)
Grampian Av. DH2-4D 123
Grampian Clo. NE29-1A 34
Grampian Dri. SR8-4A 134
Grampian Gdns. NE11-4F 77
Grampian Gro. NE36-3F 85
Grampian Pl. NE12-1D 29
Granby Clo. SR3-4F 109
Grand Pde. NE30
-5E 23 to 1F 35
Grandstand Rd. NE4 & NE2
-4B 42
Grange Av. DH4-4F 125
Grange Av. NE12-4F 29
Grange Av. NE27-3B 20
Grange Clo. NE25-3E 21
Grange Clo. NE28-2D 47
Grange Clo. NE30-5D 23
Grange Clo. SR8-2B 134
Grange Ct. NE10-2F 81
Grange Ct. NE32-5D 49
Grange Ct. NE40-3B 54
Grange Cres. NE10-3E 81
Grange Cres. NE40-3A 54
Grange Cres. SR2-2B 110
Grange Dri. NE40-3B 54
Grange Farm Dri. NE16-5E 75
Grange La. NE16-5F 75
Grangemere Clo. SR2-1D 121
Grange Nook. NE16-5F 75
Grange Pk. NE25-3E 21
Grange Pk. Av. SR5-2A 100
Grange Pl. NE32-5C 48
Grange Rd. DH1-2C 140
Grange Rd. DH9-3A 130
Grange Rd. NE3-3E 27
Grange Rd. NE4-1B 58
Grange Rd. NE10-3E 81
Grange Rd. NE15-5A 38
Grange Rd. NE32-5D 49
Grange Rd. NE40-2B 54
Grange Rd. SR5-4E 97
Grange Rd. W. NE32-5C 48
Grange St. S. SR2-5E 111
Grange Ter. NE9-2F 79
Grange Ter. NE36-3B 86
Grange Ter. SR2-2B 110
Grange Ter. SR5-3A 100
Grange, The. DH9-1A 130
Grange, The. NE25-3E 21
Grange, The. NE36-3B 86
Grange View. DH5-3B 128
Grange View. NE40-3B 54
Grange View. SR5-2A 100
Grange Vs. NE28-2D 47
Grange Wlk. NE16-5E 75
Grangeway. NE29-1B 34
Grangewood Clo. DH4
-5F 115
Grangewood Ct. DH4-4F 115
Grantham Av. SR7-4C 132
Grantham Dri. NE9-5D 79
Grantham Pl. NE23-1F 7
Grantham Rd. NE2
-5B 44 & 1F 143
Grantham Rd. SR6-3C 100
Grants Cres. SR7-3E 133
Grant St. NE32-5C 48
Grant St. SR8-2F 135
Granville Av. NE12-1F 29
Granville Ct. NE2
-5A 44 & 1E 143
Granville Cres. NE12-3F 29
Granville Dri. NE5-2E 39
Granville Dri. NE12-2A 30
Granville Gdns. NE2-4C 44
Granville Rd. NE2-5A 44
Granville Rd. NE3-2E 27
Granville Rd. SR8-4D 135
Granville St. NE8-1D 79
Granville St. SR4-1F 109
Grape La. DH1-3C 138
(in two parts)
Grasmere. DH3-5C 102
Grasmere. SR6-1F 87
Grasmere Av. NE6-2D 63
Grasmere Av. NE10-2E 81
Grasmere Av. NE32-4B 66
Grasmere Ct. NE15-5A 38
Grasmere Cres. DH4-4A 116
Grasmere Cres. NE21-2A 74
Grasmere Cres. NE26-5D 13
Grasmere Cres. SR5-2B 100
Grasmere Gdns. NE34-1C 68
Grasmere Gdns. NE38
-3C 104
Grasmere Pl. NE3-2D 27
Grasmere Rd. DH2-4C 122
Grasmere Rd. NE16-3B 76
Grasmere Rd. NE28-3C 46
Grasmere Rd. NE31-3E 65
Grasmere Rd. SR8-3D 135
Grasmere St. NE8-1C 78
Grasmere St. W. NE8-1D 79
Grasmere Ter. DH9-4A 130
Grasmere Ter. NE38-3C 104
Grasmoor Pl. NE15-5D 39
Grassbanks. NE10-4F 81
Grassdale. DH1-2D 141
Grassholm Meadows. SR3
-5F 109
Grassholm Pl. NE12-3B 28
Grassington Dri. NE23-1F 17
Grasslees. NE38-2E 113
Grasswell Dri. NE5-2F 41
Grasswell Ter. DH4-3B 126
Gravel Walks. DH5-4D 127
Gravesend Rd. SR4-5A 108
Gravesend Sq. SR4-5A 108
Gray Av. DH1-3B 136
Gray Av. DH2-3D 123
Gray Av. DH6-4F 141
Gray Av. NE13-5A 6
Gray Ct. SR2-3C 110
Graylands. NE38-2D 113
Grayling Ct. SR3-5A 18
Graylingstadt Ter. DH9
-5E 131
Gray Rd. SR2
-3C 110 & 2E 111
Grays Ter. DH1-2A 138
Gray's Ter. NE35-1D 85
Graystones. NE10-3A 82
Gray St. NE32-5D 49
Gray's Wlk. NE34-5E 67
Greathead St. NE33-5D 51
Gt. Lime Rd. NE12-4B 16
Gt. North Rd. DH1
-5A 138 to 2A 13
Gt. North Rd. NE2
-2E 43 & 1D 143
Gt. North Rd. NE3-1E 27
Greely Rd. NE5-2A 40
Greenacre Pk. NE9-2D 91
Green Av. DH4-1B 126
Greenbank. NE21-5A 56
Greenbank. NE32-1A 66
Greenbank Dri. SR4-2F 107
Greenbank St. DH3-2E 123
Greenbank Ter. DH3-2E 123
Greenbourne Gdns. NE10
-3A 80
Green Clo. NE25-3E 21
Green Clo. NE30-1D 35
Green Cres. NE23-4D 7
Greencroft Av. NE6-4B 46
Greendale Gdns. DH5-5E 129
Green Dri. SR7-5F 133
Greendyke Ct. NE5-4C 24
Greenfield Av. NE5-2C 40
Greenfield Pl. NE4
-2A 60 & 4A 142
Greenfield Pl. NE40-2B 54
Greenfield Rd. NE3-5D 15
Grn. Fields. NE40-2A 54
Greenfield Ter. NE10-1E 81
Greenfinch Clo. NE38-5E 103
Greenford La. NE11-5C 90
Greenford Rd. NE6-4E 63
Green Gro. NE40-4A 54
Greenhall View. NE5-3A 42
Greenhaugh. NE12-1D 29
Greenhaugh Rd. NE25-2D 21
Greenhead. NE38-3E 103
Greenhill View. NE5-3F 41
Green Hill Wlk. NE34-1B 70
Greenlands. DH9-4B 130
Greenlands. NE32-5B 66
Greenlands Ct. NE25-1B 10
Green La. DH1-3E 139
(Durham)
Green La. DH1-1F 139
(Gilesgate)
Green La. DH6-5E 141
Green La. NE10
-1B 80 & 5B 62
(Low Felling)
Green La. NE10-1F 81
(Pelaw)
Green La. NE12
-3F 17 & 4F 17
Green La. NE13-2B 24
Green La. NE23-4D 7
Green La. NE34-3F 67
Green La. NE36-3C 86
Green La. SR8-2A 134
Green La. Gdns. NE10-5B 62
Green La. Ind. Est. NE10
-5F 63
Greenlaw. NE5-4A 40
Greenlaw Rd. NE23-1F 7
Greenlea. NE29-1C 32
Greenlea Clo. SR4-4B 108
Greenock Rd. SR4-5A 108
Green Pk. NE28-1A 46
Greenrigg. NE21-1B 74
(in two parts)
Greenrigg Gdns. SR3-4A 110
Greenriggs Av. NE3-1F 27
Greenshields Rd. SR4-5F 107
Greenshields Sq. SR4-5F 107
Greenside. NE34-1A 70
Greenside Av. NE13-1C 14
Greenside Av. NE28-1B 48
Greenside Av. SR8-2E 135
Greenside Ct. SR3-1B 118
Greenside Cres. NE15-1E 57
Green's Pl. NE33-5D 35
Green Sq. NE25-3E 21
Green St. SR1-1B 110
(in two parts)
Green St. SR7-3F 133
Green Ter. SR1-1B 110
Green, The. DH2-2D 123
Green, The. DH5-4E 127
Green, The. NE3-1B 42
Green, The. NE10-2D 81
Green, The. NE15-3B 38
Green, The. NE25-1F 21
Green, The. NE28-2D 47
Green, The. SR1-1B 110
Green, The. SR5-3F 99
Greentree Sq. NE5-3C 40
Greenway. NE4-4F 41
Greenway. NE5-1E 39
Green Way. NE25-3E 21
Greenway Ho. SR4-3B 108
Greenway, The. SR4-4A 108
Greenwell Clo. NE21-1F 73
Greenwich Pl. NE8-3F 61
Greenwood. NE12-4B 18
Greenwood Av. DH4-5B 126
Greenwood Av. NE6-3B 46
Greenwood Gdns. NE10
-1C 80
Greenwood Gdns. NE11
-5F 77
Greenwood Rd. SR4-4A 108
Greenwood Sq. SR4-5A 108
Greetlands Rd. SR2-5B 110
Gregory Rd. SR4-5F 107
Gregory Ter. DH4-4F 125
Gregson Ter. SR7-1A 132
Grenada Clo. NE26-4E 13
Grenada Dri. NE26-4D 13
Grenada Pl. NE26-4D 13
Grenfell Sq. SR4-5F 107
Grenville Dri. NE3-5D 15
Grenville Ter. NE1
-2D 61 & 4F 143
Grenville Way. NE26-5C 12
Gresford St. NE33-1A 68
Gresham Clo. NE23-5C 4
Greta Av. DH4-4F 115
Greta Gdns. NE33-5F 51
Greta Ter. SR4-2E 109
Gretna Dri. NE32-5D 67
Gretna Rd. NE15-1A 58
Gretna Ter. NE10-2B 80
Gretton Pl. NE7-1C 44
Grey Av. NE23-1F 7
Greybourne Gdns. SR2
-5B 110
Greyfriars La. NE12-3C 28
Grey's Ct. NE1
-2C 60 & 4D 143
Greystead Clo. NE5-1F 39
Greystead Rd. NE25-2C 20
Greystoke Av. NE2-5B 44
Greystoke Av. NE16-4F 75
(in two parts)
Greystoke Av. SR2-5B 110
Greystoke Gdns. NE2-5C 44
Greystoke Gdns. NE9-2F 91
(in two parts)
Greystoke Gdns. NE16-4F 75
Greystoke Gdns. SR2-5B 110
Greystoke Pk. NE3-2D 27
Greystoke Pl. NE23-1F 7
Greystoke Wlk. NE16-4F 75
Grey St. DH4-4C 126
Grey St. NE1-2C 60 & 4C 142
Grey St. NE13-1C 14
Grey St. NE28-2E 47
Grey St. NE30-3D 35
Grey Ter. SR2-4E 121
Greywood Av. NE4-5F 41
Grieves Bldgs. DH4-4B 116
Grieves' Row. NE23-3E 7
Griffith Ter. NE27-1F 31
Grindleford Ct. NE34-2C 68
Grindon Av. SR4-2F 107
Grindon Clo. NE23-1F 7
Grindon Clo. NE25-4F 21
Grindon Ct. SR4-4A 108
Grindon Gdns. SR4-4A 108
Grindon La. SR3 & SR4
-4B 108
Grindon La. SR4-2A 108
Grindon Pk. SR4-4A 108
Grindon Ter. SR4-2E 109
Grinstead Clo. NE34-5B 52
Grinstead Way. DH1-1D 141
Grisedale Gdns. NE9-1F 91
Grisedale Rd. SR8-3D 135
Grizedale. NE37-1A 104
Grizedale Ct. SR6-4A 88
Groat Mkt. NE1
-2C 60 & 4C 142
Grosmont. DH3-5B 124
Grosvenor Av. NE2-3B 44
Grosvenor Av. NE16-2A 76
Grosvenor Clo. NE23-1F 7
Grosvenor Ct. NE5-2E 39
Grosvenor Cres. NE31-3D 65
Grosvenor Dri. NE26-2B 22
Grosvenor Dri. NE34-4A 52
Grosvenor Dri. SR6-1D 87
Grosvenor Gdns. NE2-4C 44
Grosvenor Gdns. NE28-1C 48
Grosvenor Gdns. NE34-2E 69
Grosvenor M. NE29-3B 34
Grosvenor Pl. NE2-3A 44
Grosvenor Pl. NE29-3B 34
Grosvenor Rd. NE2-3A 44
Grosvenor Rd. NE33-4A 52
Grosvenor St. SR5-3E 99
Grosvenor Vs. NE2-3A 44
Grosvenor Way. NE5-2E 39
Grotto Gdns. NE34-1B 70
Grotto Rd. NE34-1B 70
Grove Av. NE3-1E 43
Grove Cotts. DH3-3B 102
Grove Ho. Dri. DH1-2E 139
Grove Rd. NE9-4F 79
Grove Rd. NE15-3B 38
Grove St. DH1-3C 138
Grove, The. DH1-1A 138
Grove, The. DH5-2C 128
Grove, The. NE2-3B 44
(in two parts)
Grove, The. NE3-5F 27
Grove, The. NE5-4F 39
Grove, The. NE12-3F 29
Grove, The. NE16-4A 76
Grove, The. NE25-3A 22
Grove, The. NE32-1A 84
Grove, The. SR2-4D 121
(Ryhope)
Grove, The. SR2-3B 110
(Sunderland)
Grove, The. SR5-4F 97
Guelder Rd. NE7-1D 45
Guernsey Rd. SR4-5F 107
Guernsey Sq. SR4-5F 107
Guildford St. SR2-3D 111
Guilford Pl. NE6-5D 45
Guisborough Dri. NE29-1D 33
Guisborough St. SR4-3D 109
Gullane. NE37-2B 94
Gullane Clo. DH9-3F 131
Gullane Clo. NE10-5A 64
Gunnerston Gro. NE3-4F 25
Gunnerton Clo. NE23-1A 8
Gunnerton Pl. NE29-3E 33
Gunn St. NE11-2D 77
Gut Rd. NE28-3B 48
Guyzance Av. NE3-4C 26

Haddington Rd. NE25-5B 12
Haddock St. NE33-4C 50
Haddon Clo. NE25-2D 21
Haddon Grn. NE25-2D 21
Haddon Rd. SR2-1D 121
Haddricksmill Ct. NE3-5A 28
Haddricksmill Rd. NE3-1A 44
Hadleigh Rd. SR4-2C 108
Hadrian Av. DH3-1E 123
Hadrian Bus. Pk. NE28-3B 32
Hadrian Ct. NE11-1C 90
Hadrian Ct. NE15-4A 40
Hadrian Gdns. NE21-1B 74
Hadrian Pk. Est. NE28-3F 31
Hadrian Pl. NE9-3F 79
Hadrian Pl. NE15-2F 37
Hadrian Rd. NE4-1C 58
Hadrian Rd. NE28-3E 47
Hadrian Rd. NE32
-4B 66 to 3D 67
Hadrian St. SR4-1F 109
Hadstone Pl. NE5-3E 41
Hagan Hall. NE32-1A 84
Haggerston Clo. NE5-1C 40
Haggerston Ct. NE5-1C 40
Haggerston Cres. NE5-1C 40
Haggerstone Dri. SR5-3C 98
Haggerston Ter. NE32-3C 66
Haggerston Wlk. NE8-4C 60
Haggie Av. NE28-1F 47
Hahnemann Ct. SR5-2A 100
Haig Av. NE25-3A 22
Haig Cres. DH1-5A 140
Haig Cres. NE15-2F 57
Haigh Ter. NE9-4A 92
Haig St. NE11-2E 77
Hailsham Av. NE12-2E 29
Hailsham Pl. SR8-4C 134
Haining Cres. NE4-1B 58
Haininghead. NE38-5D 105
Hainingwood Ter. NE10-5F 63
Haldane Ct. NE2-4A 44
Haldane Ter. NE2-4A 44
Haldon Pl. SR8-4A 134
Hale Rise. SR8-3C 134
Halewood Av. NE3-5A 26
Half Fields Rd. NE21-1F 73
Half Moon La. NE8-4D 61
(in two parts)
Half Moon La. NE30-2F 35
Half Moon La. NE30-2F 35
(off Front St.)
Half Moon Yd. NE1
-2C 60 & 4C 142
Halfway Ho. La. SR2-5E 111
Halidon Rd. SR2-1C 120
Halidon Sq. SR2-1C 120
Halifax Pl. NE11-1C 76
Halifax Pl. SR2-4E 121
Halifax Rd. NE11-1C 76
Hallam Rd. SR8-2C 134
Hall Av. NE4-1D 59
Hall Cres. SR8-1D 135
Hall Dri. NE12-2D 17
Hall Farm Rd. SR3-5D 119
Hallfield Clo. SR3-5F 119
Hall Gdns. DH6-5F 141
Hall Gdns. NE10-3B 80
Hall Gdns. NE36-3F 85
Hallgarth. NE10-3F 81
(in three parts)
Hallgarth Bungalows. DH5
-5F 129
Hallgarth Ho. NE33-5D 51
Hallgarth La. DH6-4F 141
Hallgarth Rd. NE21-5A 56
Hallgarth St. DH1-3D 139
Hallgarth St. DH6-4F 141
Hallgarth, The. DH1-3D 139
Hallgarth View. DH1-4D 139
Halling Clo. NE6-3F 63
Hallington Dri. NE25-1C 10
Hallington M. NE12-4D 17
Halliwell St. DH4-4C 126
Hall La. DH1-5F 139
Hall La. DH5-5D 127
Hallow Dri. NE15-3E 37
Hall Pk. NE21-3F 55
Hall Rd. NE31-2C 64
Hall Rd. NE37-5C 94
Hall Ter. NE10-5A 64
Hall View. SR6-2E 89
Halstead Pl. NE33-3E 51
Halstead Sq. SR4-2C 108
Halterburn Clo. NE3-5C 26
Halton Dri. NE13-1D 15
Halton Dri. NE27-4F 19
Halton Rd. DH1-3D 137
Hamar Clo. NE29-5D 33
Hambard Way. NE38-3B 104
Hambledon Av. DH2-4D 123
Hambledon Av. NE30-4C 22
Hambledon Clo. NE35-2C 84
Hambledon Gdns. NE7-2B 44
Hambledon Pl. SR8-4A 134
Hambleton Grn. NE9-3A 92
Hambleton Rd. NE38-5F 103
Hamilton Ct. NE8-1E 79
Hamilton Cres. NE4-1F 59
Hamilton Cres. NE29-1D 33
Hamilton Dri. NE26-4D 13
Hamilton St. SR8-2E 135
Hamilton Ter. NE36-3F 85
(off Dipe La.)
Hamilton Way. NE26-4D 13
Hampden Rd. SR6-3C 100
Hampden St. NE33-4E 51
Hampshire Ct. NE4-5F 59
Hampshire Gdns. NE28-1F 47
Hampshire Pl. NE37-3C 94
Hampshire Pl. SR8-2A 134
Hampshire Rd. DH1-3C 140
Hampshire Way. NE34-5D 53
Hampstead Gdns. NE32
-5B 66
Hampstead Rd. NE4-2D 59
Hampstead Rd. SR4-3B 108
Hampstead Sq. SR4-3B 108
Hampton Clo. NE23-2E 5
Hampton Ct. DH3-3C 112
Hampton Dri. NE10-2A 80
Hampton Dri. NE25-3D 21
Hampton Rd. NE30-4B 22
Hamsterley Clo. DH3-5B 124
Hamsterley Ct. SR3-4E 119
Hamsterley Cres. DH1-3E 137
Hamsterley Cres. NE9-1B 92
Hamsterley Cres. NE15-5D 39
Hamsterley Dri. NE12-3E 17
Hanby Gdns. SR3-5F 109
Hancock St. NE2
-5F 43 & 2D 143
Handel St. NE33-3F 51
Handel St. SR4-1F 109
Handley Cres. DH5-4B 128
Handley St. SR8-2E 135
Handy Dri. NE11-5B 58
Hanlon Ct. NE32-5B 48
Hannington Pl. NE6-1F 61
Hannington St. NE6-1F 61
Hann Ter. NE37-5D 95
Hanover Clo. NE5-2E 39
Hanover Ct. NE9-2E 91
Hanover Dri. NE21-1F 73
Hanover Gdns. NE28-3C 48
(off Station Rd.)
Hanover Ho. NE32-3F 65
Hanover Pl. SR4-4A 100
Hanover Sq. NE1
-3C 60 & 5C 142
Hanover Sq. NE21-1F 73
(off Waterloo St.)
Hanover St. NE1
-3C 60 & 5C 142
Hanover Wlk. NE5-2E 39
Hanover Wlk. NE21-2E 73
Harbottle Av. NE3-4C 26
Harbottle Av. NE27-4B 20
Harbottle Ct. NE6-3B 62
Harbottle Cres. NE32-5F 65
Harbour Dri. NE33-5F 35
Harbour, The. DH4-4A 116
Harbour View. SR6-3D 101
Harbour Wlk. SR7-3D 133
Harcourt Pk. NE9-4F 79
Harcourt Rd. SR2-1C 120
Harcourt St. NE9-4E 79
Hardgate Rd. SR2-1C 120
Hardie Av. NE16-2F 75
Hardie Ct. NE31-5A 48
Hardie Dri. NE36-3E 85
Hardman Clo. NE40-2C 54
Hardman Gdns. NE40-2C 54
Hardwick Ct. NE8-1F 78
Hardwick Pl. NE3-2B 42
Hardwick Rise. SR6-4D 101
Hardwick St. SR8-3F 135
Hardyards Ct. NE34-2B 68
Hardy Av. NE34-4A 68
Hardy Gro. NE28-5B 30
Hardy Sq. SR5-2E 99
Hardy St. SR7-3E 133
Harebell Rd. NE9-5B 80
Harehills Av. NE5-2F 41
Harehills Tower. NE3-1A 42
Harelaw Gro. NE5-3F 39
Hareshaw Rd. NE25-2C 20
Hareshaw Ter. NE6-3B 62
(off St Peter's Rd.)
Hareside. NE23-4C 4
Hareside Clo. NE15-4B 38
Hareside Ct. NE15-5B 38
Hareside Path. NE15-5B 38
Hareside Wlk. NE15-5B 38
Harewood Clo. NE16-5E 75
Harewood Clo. NE25-3D 21
Harewood Ct. NE25-3D 21
Harewood Cres. NE25-3D 21
Harewood Gdns. SR3-4F 109
Harewood Grn. NE9-3A 92
Harewood Rd. NE3-3E 27
Hareydene. NE5-4B 24
Hargill Dri. NE38-2F 113
Harland Way. NE38-3C 104
Harle Cres. NE5-4A 40
Harle Rd. NE27-3F 19
Harleston Way. NE10-4D 81
Harle St. NE28-2C 46
Harley Ter. DH6-4F 141
Harley Ter. NE3-4F 27
Harlow Av. NE3-2B 26
Harlow Av. NE27-3F 19
Harlow Grn. La. NE9-3F 91
Harlow Pl. NE7-2D 45
Harlow St. SR4-1F 109
Harnham Av. NE29-5E 33
Harnham Gdns. NE5-4E 41
Harnham Gro. NE23-4C 4
Harold Sq. SR2-3C 110
Harold St. NE32-1A 66
Harperley Dri. SR3-5A 110
Harraby Gdns. NE9-2F 91
Harras Bank. DH3-4B 102
Harraton Ter. DH3-4A 102
Harriet Pl. NE6-2B 62
Harriet St. NE9-2B 62
Harriet St. NE21-5B 56
Harrington St. NE26-3C 46
(off North Rd.)
Harriot Dri. NE12-5C 16
Harrison Clo. SR8-4D 135
Harrison Ct. NE23-4A 8
Harrison Ct. NE23-4A 8
Harrison Gdns. NE8-3C 78
Harrison Garth. DH6-4F 141
Harrison Pl. NE2
-5A 44 & 1E 143
Harrison Rd. NE28-1B 48
Harrogate St. SR2-2D 111
Harrow Cres. DH4-4F 115
Harrow Gdns. NE13-2D 15
Harrow Sq. SR4-2C 108
Harrow St. NE27-3A 20
Hartburn. NE10-4F 81
Hartburn Dri. NE5-1E 39
Hartburn Pl. NE4-5A 42
Hartburn Rd. NE30-1B 34
Hartburn Ter. NE25-1C 10
Hartburn Wlk. NE3-5F 25
(in two parts)
Hartford Rd. NE3-3E 27
Hartford Rd. NE34-2F 67
Hartford Rd. SR4-2C 108
Hartford St. NE6-5E 45
Hartforth Cres. NE10-5A 64
Harthope Av. SR5-2B 98
Harthope Clo. NE38-2E 113
Hartington Rd. NE30-5C 22
Hartington St. NE4-2E 59
Hartington St. NE8-1D 79
Hartington St. SR6-3C 100
Hartington Ter. NE33-4F 51
Hartland Dri. DH3-5C 102
Hartlepool Av. SR8-2E 135
Hartley Av. NE26-1A 22
Hartleyburn Av. NE31-4B 64
Hartley Gdns. NE25-1B 10
Hartley La. NE25 & NE26
-1C 20
Hartley Sq. NE26-1C 12
Hartley St. NE25-1B 10
Hartley St. SR1-5D 101
Hartley St. N. NE25-1B 10
Hartoft Clo. DH4-2C 126
Harton Ho. Rd. NE34-5A 52
Harton Ho. Rd. E. NE34
-5B 52
Harton La. NE34-2A 68
Harton Rise. NE34-5B 52
Harton View. NE36-3F 85
Hartside. DH3-1C 112
Hartside. NE15-5E 39
Hartside Cres. NE21-2E 73
Hartside Cres. NE27-3F 19
Hartside Gdns. NE2-3B 44

Hartside Pl. NE3-5E 15
Hartside Rd. SR4-3B 108
Hartside Sq. SR4-3B 108
Hartside View. DH1-2A 136
Hart Sq. SR4-3C 108
Hartswood. NE9-3F 91
Hart Ter. SR6-4D 89
Harvard Rd. NE3-4A 26
Harvest Clo. SR3-5E 119
Harvey Clo. NE38-2E 103
Harvey Clo. SR8-2C 134
Harvey Combe. NE12-4D 17
Harvey Cres. NE10-2A 82
Harvey Garden. NE6-1B 62
Harwood Clo. NE23-4C 4
Harwood Clo. NE38-2F 113
Harwood Ct. NE23-4C 4
Harwood Dri. NE12-3B 18
Harwood Grn. NE3-4A 26
Hascombe Clo. NE25-1E 21
Haslemere Dri. SR3-5F 109
Hastings Av. DH1-5A 138
Hastings Av. NE3-2F 25
Hastings Av. NE12-3F 29
Hastings Av. NE26-4D 13
Hastings Ct. NE37-4D 95
Hastings Dri. NE30-1E 35
Hastings Ho. NE28-3F 49
Hastings Pde. NE31-4F 65
Hastings St. NE23-4E 5
Hastings St. SR2-4D 111
Hastings Ter. SR2-5D 111
Hastings Wlk. NE37-4D 95
(off Edith Av.)
Haswell Clo. NE10-3B 82
Haswell Ho. NE30-3F 35
Hatfield Av. NE31-2E 65
Hatfield Dri. NE23-2E 9
Hatfield Gdns. NE25-2D 21
Hatfield Gdns. SR3-4F 109
Hatfield Pl. SR8-5D 135
Hatfield Sq. NE33-2F 51
Hatfield View. DH1-3D 139
Hathaway Gdns. SR3-4F 109
Hathersage Gdns. NE34 -2C 68
Hatherton Av. NE30-4D 23
Hatton Gro. NE34-5A 52
Haugh La. NE21-2E 55
Haugh La. NE40-1C 54
Haughton Ct. NE4-4E 59
(off Wolsingham St.)
Haughton Cres. NE5-4A 40
Haughton Cres. NE32-5A 66
Hautmont Rd. NE31-3E 65
Hauxley Dri. NE3-2A 26
Hauxley Gdns. NE5-3F 41
Havannah Rd. Wash 2. NE37 -1F 103
Havant Gdns. NE13-5A 6
Havelock Clo. NE8-5D 61
Havelock Ct. SR4-1C 108
Havelock Pl. NE4-2F 59
Havelock Rd. NE27-3F 19
Havelock St. NE4-3F 59
Havelock St. NE33-3D 51
(in two parts)
Havelock St. SR1-5D 101
Havelock Ter. DH9-2C 130
(off High St.)
Havelock Ter. NE8-5D 61
Havelock Ter. NE32-2F 65
Havelock Ter. SR2-2A 110
Haven Ct. DH1-1C 136
Haven, The. DH4-4A 116
Havercroft. NE10-3A 82
Haverley Dri. SR7-2A 132
Haversham Clo. NE7-5C 28
Haversham Pk. SR5-5A 88
Hawarden Cres. SR4-3E 109
Hawes Av. DH2-4D 123
Hawes Ct. SR6-5B 88
Hawesdale Cres. NE21-2A 74
Hawes Rd. SR8-3C 134
Haweswater Clo. NE34-1C 68
Hawick Ct. DH9-3F 131
Hawick Cres. NE6-3A 62
Hawkesley Rd. SR4-3B 108
Hawkey's La. NE29-4B 34
Hawkhill Clo. DH2-5B 132
Hawkhills Ter. DH3-3B 102
Hawkhurst. NE38-1D 115
Hawkins Ct. SR3-5E 119
Hawksbury. NE16-3F 75
Hawksfield. NE10-5D 81
Hawkshead Ct. NE3-2F 25
Hawkshead Pl. NE9-5A 80
Hawksley. NE5-3B 40
Hawks Rd. NE8 -3E 61 & 5F 143
Hawks St. NE8-3F 61
Hawk Ter. DH3-5D 103
Hawkwell Rise. NE15-3E 37
Hawsker Clo. SR3-3A 120
Hawthorn Av. NE13-2C 14
Hawthorn Av. NE34-3E 69
Hawthorn Av. SR3-2F 119
Hawthorn Clo. NE16-5F 75
Hawthorn Cres. DH1-3A 140
Hawthorn Cres. NE38-1A 114
Hawthorn Cres. SR8-3F 135
Hawthorn Dri. NE11-2D 77
Hawthorn Dri. NE32-5B 66
Hawthorne Av. NE31-1D 65
Hawthorn Gdns. NE3-5A 26
Hawthorn Gdns. NE9-4E 79
Hawthorn Gdns. NE10-1B 80
Hawthorn Gdns. NE26-2B 22
Hawthorn Gdns. NE29-3B 34
Hawthorn Gdns. NE40-3D 55
Hawthorn Gro. NE28-3D 47
Hawthorn M. NE3-1E 43
Hawthorn Pl. DH1-1B 136
Hawthorn Pl. NE4-3F 59
Hawthorn Rd. DH1-1D 141
Hawthorn Rd. NE3-1E 43
Hawthorn Rd. NE21-5A 56
Hawthorn Rd. W. NE3-1D 43
Hawthorn Sq. SR7-2F 133
Hawthorns, The. NE4-4F 59
Hawthorns, The. NE9-3B 92
Hawthorns, The. NE36-2C 86
Hawthorn St. DH4-3B 126
Hawthorn St. NE15-3B 38
Hawthorn St. NE32-5B 48
Hawthorn St. SR4-1F 109
Hawthorn Ter. DH1-3B 138
Hawthorn Ter. DH2-1A 122
Hawthorn Ter. DH3-3E 123
Hawthorn Ter. NE4-3F 59
Hawthorn Ter. NE9-4C 92
Hawthorn Ter. NE15-3B 38
Hawthorn Ter. SR6-4D 89
Hawthorn Vs. NE23-3E 5
Hawthorn Vs. NE28-2D 47
Hawthorn Wlk. NE4-3F 59
Haydn St. NE8-1E 79
Haydock Dri. NE10-3A 82
Haydon. NE38-1D 115
Haydon Clo. NE3-2A 26
Haydon Dri. NE25-4A 22
Haydon Gdns. NE27-3F 19
Haydon Pl. NE5-4C 40
Haydon Sq. SR4-2C 108
Hayes Wlk. NE13-1C 14
Hayfield La. NE16-4A 76
Hayhole Rd. NE29-2F 49
Haylands Sq. NE34-2C 68
Hayleazes Rd. NE15-5B 40
Haymarket. NE1 -1C 60 & 2C 142
Haymarket La. NE1 -1C 60 & 2C 142
Haynyng, The. NE10-3C 80
Hay St. SR5-4B 100
Hayton Av. NE34-2F 69
Hayton Clo. NE23-2E 5
Hayton Rd. NE30-5B 22
Hayward Av. NE25-1B 10
Hayward Pl. NE5-2D 41
Hazard La. DH5-4C 128
Hazel Av. DH4-4B 126
Hazel Av. NE29-3A 34
Hazel Av. SR3-2A 120
Hazeldene. NE25-2F 21
Hazeldene. NE32-1B 84
Hazeldene Av. NE3-5E 25
Hazeldene Ter. SR4-1D 109
Hazeley Gro. NE3-5E 25
Hazeley Way. NE3-5E 25
Hazel Gro. DH2-1C 122
Hazelgrove. NE10-3A 82
Hazel Gro. NE12-5D 17
Hazel Gro. NE34-3D 69
Hazelmere Av. NE3-1F 27
Hazelmere Cres. NE23-2E 5
Hazelmoor. NE31-5E 47
Hazel Rd. NE8-2B 78
Hazel Rd. NE21-5B 56
Hazel St. NE32-5B 48
Hazel Ter. DH4-3A 126
Hazel Ter. DH9-5E 131
Hazelwood. NE12-4B 18
Hazelwood. NE32-1C 66
Hazelwood Av. NE2-2A 44
Hazelwood Av. SR5-2E 99
Hazelwood Clo. NE9-3B 92
Hazelwood Gdns. NE38 -1A 114
Hazelwood Ter. NE28-2C 48
Hazlitt Av. NE34-4A 68
Hazlitt Pl. NE23-3E 9
Headlam Garden. NE6-1B 62
Headlam Gdns. NE6-1B 62
(off Grace St.)
Headlam Grn. NE6-2B 62
Headlam St. NE6 -1A 62 & 1B 62
Headlam View. NE28-2B 48
Healey Dri. SR3-5A 110
Heartsbourne Dri. NE34 -4E 69
Heath Clo. SR8-4D 135
(in two parts)
Heathcote Grn. NE5-1D 41
Heath Ct. NE1 -2D 61 & 5D 143
Heath Cres. NE15-3F 57
Heathdale Gdns. NE7-1C 44
Heather Clo. SR6-5F 69
Heatherdale Cres. DH1 -2D 141
Heatherdale Ter. NE9-1A 92
Heather Dri. DH5-2E 129
Heather Gro. NE10-5A 62
Heather Hill. NE9-3D 93
Heatherlaw. NE9-5B 80
Heatherlaw. NE37-1E 103
Heatherlea Gdns. SR3-4F 109
Heather Pl. NE4-4F 41
Heatherslaw Rd. NE5-4E 41
Heather Way. DH7-3B 130
Heatherwell Grn. NE10-2B 80
Heathery La. NE3-3A 28
Heathfield. SR2-5A 110
Heathfield Cres. NE5-2F 41
Heathfield Pl. NE3-1E 27
Heathfield Rd. NE9-4E 79
Heath Grange. DH5-4D 127
Heath Sq. SR4-3C 108
Heathway. NE32-5B 66
Heathway. SR7-5D 133
Heathwell Gdns. NE16-2A 76
Heathwell Rd. NE15-5B 40
Heathwood Av. NE16-3E 75
Heaton Clo. NE6-1A 62
Heaton Gdns. NE34-5A 68
Heaton Gro. NE6-1A 62
Heaton Hall Rd. NE6-5D 45
Heaton Pk. Ct. NE6-1F 61
Heaton Pk. Rd. NE6-5C 44
Heaton Pk. View. NE6-5C 44
Heaton Pl. NE6-1A 62
Heaton Rd. NE6-3D 45
Heaton Ter. NE6-1F 61
Heaton Ter. NE29-3F 33
Heaton Wlk. NE6-1A 62
Heaviside Pl. DH1-1F 139
Hebburn Village. NE31-5E 47
Heber St. NE4 -2B 60 & 4A 142
Hebron Way. NE23-4C 4
Hector St. NE27-3B 20
Heddon Av. NE13-3B 14
Heddon Banks. NE15-3A 36
Heddon Clo. NE3-3B 26
Heddon Clo. NE40-3C 54
Heddon View. NE21-5A 56
Heddon View. NE40-2C 54
Heddon Way. NE34-2F 67
Hedgefield Av. NE21-2E 55
Hedgefield Cotts. NE21-2D 55
Hedgefield View. NE23-3F 7
Hedgehope Rd. NE5-5C 24
Hedgelea. NE40-3A 54
Hedgelea Rd. DH5-4B 128
Hedgeley Rd. NE5-4A 40
Hedgeley Rd. NE29-3F 33
Hedgeley Rd. NE31-1C 64
Hedgeley Ter. NE6-2E 63
Hedley Clo. NE33-1E 51
Hedley Pl. NE28-3C 46
Hedley Rd. NE25-2D 11
Hedley St. NE3-4E 27
Hedley St. NE8-2B 78
Hedley St. NE33-1E 51
Hedley Ter. NE3-4E 27
Hedley Ter. SR2-4E 121
Hedworth Av. NE34-3E 67
Hedworth Ct. SR1-1D 111
Hedworth La. NE32 & NE35 -4B 66
Hedworth Pl. NE9-2B 92
Hedworth Sq. SR1-1D 111
Hedworth St. DH3-2D 123
Hedworth Ter. DH4-4A 116
Hedworth Ter. SR1-1D 111
Hedworth View. NE32-4B 66
Heighley St. NE15-2E 57
Helena Av. NE26-2D 23
Helen St. NE21-5F 55
Helen St. SR6-1C 100
Helen St. SR7-5F 133
Helford Rd. SR8-5B 134
Helmdon. NE37-4D 95
Helmsdale Av. NE10-1B 80
Helmsdale Rd. SR4-3C 108
Helmsley Clo. DH4-4F 115
Helmsley Dri. NE28-2D 47
Helmsley Grn. NE9-3A 92
Helmsley Rd. DH1-2D 137
Helmsley Rd. NE2 -5B 44 & 1F 143
Helston Ct. NE15-5D 39
Helvellyn Av. NE38-5F 103
Helvellyn Rd. SR2-1B 120
Hemel St. DH3-3E 123
Hemming St. SR2-5D 111
Hemsley Rd. NE34-4B 52
Henderson Av. NE16-2F 75
Henderson Gdns. NE10-2F 81
Henderson Rd. NE28-1C 46
Henderson Rd. NE34-3D 67
Henderson Rd. SR4-2D 109
Hendon Burn Av. SR2-3D 111
Hendon Burn Av. W. SR2 -3D 111
Hendon Clo. SR1-1D 111
Hendon Ct. SR1-1D 111
(off Hendon Clo.)
Hendon Gdns. NE32-5B 66
Hendon Rd. NE8-2F 79
Hendon Rd. SR1 & SR2 -1D 111
Hendon Sq. SR1-1D 111
Hendon St. SR1-2D 111
Hendon Valley Ct. SR2 -3D 111
Hendon Valley Rd. SR2 -3C 110
Henley Av. DH2-3A 122
Henley Clo. NE23-2E 5
Henley Gdns. NE28-1C 48
Henley Rd. NE30-5D 23
Henley Rd. SR4-3B 108
Henley St. NE6-5E 45
Henley Way. NE35-2D 84
Henlow Rd. NE15-5D 39
Henry Nelson St. NE33-1F 51
Henry Sq. NE2 -1D 61 & 3F 143
Henry St. DH4-5A 116
Henry St. DH5-2F 129
(Hetton-le-Hole)
Henry St. DH5-4D 127
(New Town)
Henry St. NE3-4E 27
Henry St. NE15-3B 38
Henry St. NE29-5B 34
Henry St. NE33-5E 35
Henry St. SR7-2E 133
Henry St. E. SR2-2E 111
Henry Ter. DH4-3D 125
Hensby Ct. NE5-1D 41
Henshaw Gro. NE32-2D 11
Henshaw Pl. NE5-5C 40
Henshelwood Ter. NE2-3A 44
Henson Clo. NE38-3C 104
Hepburn Gdns. NE10-1B 80
Hepple Way. NE3-3C 26
Hepscott Dri. NE25-1F 21
Hepscott Ter. NE33-5F 51
Herbert St. NE8-1F 79
Herbert Ter. SR5-5A 88
Herbert Ter. SR7-3E 133
Herd Clo. NE21-1E 73
Herd Ho. La. NE21-5E 55
Herdinghill. NE37-1E 103
Herdlaw. NE23-4C 4
Hereford Ct. NE3-2F 25
Hereford Ct. SR2-1C 120
Hereford Rd. SR2-1C 120
Herefordshire Dri. DH1 -3C 140
Hereford Sq. SR2-1C 120
Hereford Way. NE32 -1F 83 & 5A 66
Hermiston. NE25-1F 21
Hermitage Pk. DH3-4E 123
Heron Clo. NE38-5E 103
Heron Dri. NE33-1D 51
Heron Pl. NE12-3C 28
Heron Vs. NE34-3A 68
Herrick St. NE5-1C 40
Herrington M. DH4-4C 116
Herrington Rd. DH4 & SR3 -4E 117
Hersham Clo. NE3-3E 25
Hertburn Gdns. NE37-5C 94
Hertburn Ind. Est. NE37 -5C 94
Hertford. NE9-3E 91
Hertford Av. NE34-5D 53
Hertford Clo. NE25-1E 21
Hertford Cres. DH5-3D 129
Hertford Gro. NE23-2E 5
Hertford Pl. SR8-2B 134
Hertford Rd. SR8-3B 134
(in two parts)
Hesket Ct. NE3-2F 25
Hesleyside Dri. NE5-4D 41
Hesleyside Rd. NE25-2D 21
Hetton Lyons Ind. Est. DH5 -5F 129
Hetton Rd. DH5-1D 129
Heugh Hill. NE9-3E 93
Hewitson Ter. NE10-2B 80
Hewitt Av. SR2-2D 121
Hewley Cres. NE15-3F 37
Heworth Av. NE10-1F 81
Heworth Burn Cres. NE10 -2D 81
Heworth Ct. NE34-2F 67
Heworth Cres. NE37-4B 94
Heworth Dene Gdns. NE10 -1D 81
Heworth Gro. NE37-4B 94
Heworth Rd. NE37-3B 94
Heworth View. NE6-4E 63
Heworth Way. NE10-2E 81
Hewson Pl. NE9-4F 79
Hexham. NE38-3E 103
Hexham Av. NE6-2E 63
Hexham Av. NE23-2E 5
Hexham Av. NE31-5D 65
Hexham Av. SR7-4C 132
Hexham Clo. NE29-2E 33
Hexham Ct. NE6-2E 63
Hexham Ct. NE11-4E 77
Hexham Ho. NE6-2E 63
Hexham Old Rd. NE40 & NE21-2B 54
Hexham Rd. NE15-2A 36
Hexham Rd. NE16-1E 75
Hexham Rd. SR4-3C 108
Hexham Wlk. NE8-4C 60
Hextol Gdns. NE15-5A 40
Heybrook Av. NE29-1A 34
Heyburn Gdns. NE15-2C 58
Heywood's Ct. NE1 -2C 60 & 4D 143
Hibernian Rd. NE32-5D 49
Hibernia Rd. NE6-3F 63
Hickling Ct. NE5-5D 25
Hickstead Clo. NE28-3A 32
Hickstead Gro. NE23-2E 5
Hiddleston Av. NE7-5C 28
Higgins Ter. SR3-3A 120
Higham Pl. NE1 -2C 60 & 3D 143
High Axwell. NE21-5C 56
High Back Clo. NE32-3E 65
High Barnes. DH3-5A 124
High Barnes Ter. SR4-2F 109
High Bri. NE1 -2C 60 & 4C 142
Highburn. NE23-5B 4
Highburn Av. NE9-3F 93
High Burn Ter. NE10-3D 81
Highbury. NE2-3F 43
Highbury. NE10-2C 80
Highbury. NE25-2F 21
Highbury Clo. NE9-3F 93
Highbury Pl. NE29-4A 34
High Carr Clo. DH1-4B 136
High Carr Rd. DH1-4B 136
High Chapel Row. DH4 -3B 114
High Chare. DH3-3E 123
Highcliffe Gdns. NE8-2F 79
High Croft. NE37-3A 94
High Croft Dri. NE31-3B 64
Highcroft Dri. SR6-1D 89
Highcross Rd. NE30-4C 22
High Dene. NE7-3C 44
High Dene. NE34-2A 68
High Downs Sq. DH5-3F 129
Highfield. DH3-1B 102
Highfield Av. NE12-1F 29
Highfield Ct. NE10-3D 81
Highfield Cres. DH3-5B 112
Highfield Dri. DH4-5F 125
Highfield Dri. NE34-4B 52
Highfield Gdns. DH3-5B 112
Highfield Grange. DH4-5F 125
Highfield Pl. NE13-2C 14
Highfield Pl. SR4-1D 109
Highfield Rise. DH3-5B 112
Highfield Rd. DH4-4E 115
Highfield Rd. NE5-2B 40
Highfield Rd. NE8-1F 79
Highfield Rd. NE33 & NE34 -4A 52
Highfield Ter. NE6-3E 63
High Flatworth. NE29-4C 32
High Friar La. NE1 -2C 60 & 3C 142
High Friars. NE1
-2C 60 & 3C 142
(off Blackett St.)
High Garth. SR1-5C 100
(off High St. E.)
Highgate Gdns. NE32-5C 66
Highgate Rd. SR4-2C 108
High Ga., The. NE3-1A 42
Highgreen Chase. NE16-5F 75
High Grindon Ho. SR4 -4B 108
High Gro. NE4-3F 59
Highgrove. NE5-2E 39
High Gro. NE40-3C 54
Highheath. NE37-1E 103
High Hedgefield Ter. NE21 -2D 55
High Hedgefield Ter. NE40 -2D 55
High Heworth La. NE10 -3D 81
High Horse Clo. NE39-5F 73
High Ho. Gdns. NE10-1D 81
(in two parts)
Highland Rd. NE5-2F 41
High La. DH4-1D 127
High La. Row. NE31-5A 48
High Lanes. NE10-2D 81
High Laws. NE3-1A 44
Highlaws Gdns. NE9-2F 91
High Level Rd. NE8-4C 60
High Meadow. NE34-4B 52
High Meadows. NE3-1A 42
High Moor Ct. NE5-3F 41
High Moor Pl. NE34-2B 68
High Pk. NE2-5B 44
High Pasture. NE38-1C 114
High Pit Rd. NE23-4E 5
High Primrose Hill. DH4 -2C 124
Highridge. DH3-2B 102
High Ridge. NE13-3C 14
High Rd., The. NE34-1E 69
High Row. DH4-4C 124
High Row. NE15-1B 56
High Row. NE37-4B 94
High Row. NE40-3D 55
High Sandgrove. SR6-1E 87
Highside Dri. SR3-5E 109
High St. Carrville, DH1 -2C 140
High St. E. NE28-3D 47
High St. E. SR1-5C 100
High St. Felling, NE10-2B 80
High St. Gateshead, NE8 -3D 61 to 5D 61
High St. Gosforth, NE3-5E 27
High St. Jarrow, NE32-5D 49
High St. Newburn, NE15 -5B 38
High St. Shincliffe, DH1 -5F 139
High St. South Hylton, SR4 -1E 107
High St. Stanley, DH9-2C 130
(in two parts)
High St. W. NE28-3C 46
High St. W. SR1-1B 110
High St. Wrekenton, NE9 -2B 92
High Swinburne Pl. NE4 -2A 60 & 4A 142
Hightree Clo. SR3-5E 119
High View. NE28-1C 46
High View. N. NE28-1C 46
High Villa Pl. NE4 -2A 60 & 4A 142
High Wlk. DH3-4A 114
Highwell Gdns. NE10-1D 81
Highwell La. NE5-3F 39
High West St. NE8-5D 61
Highwood Rd. NE15-5B 40
High Wood Ter. DH1-4D 139
(off Stockton Rd.)
High Wood View. DH1 -4D 139
Highworth Dri. NE7-2F 45
Highworth Dri. NE9-3E 93
High Yd. DH1-3D 139
Hilda Av. DH1-5B 140
Hilda Pk. DH2-1C 122
Hilda St. NE8-1C 78
Hilda St. SR6-2B 100
Hilda Ter. DH2-1D 123
Hilda Ter. NE15-2F 37
Hilden Bldgs. NE7-3D 45
Hilden Gdns. NE7-3D 45
Hillary Av. NE12-2A 30
Hillary Pl. NE5-1B 40
Hill Av. NE23-2F 9
Hill Brow. SR3-4A 120
Hill Cres. SR7-5F 133
Hill Crest. DH1-2D 139
Hillcrest. NE10-3D 81
Hillcrest. NE25-2F 21
Hillcrest. NE32-5B 66
Hillcrest. NE34-3F 69
Hillcrest. SR3-3A 118
Hillcrest Dri. NE11-3D 77
Hill Crest Gdns. NE2-1A 44
Hillcrest M. DH1-2D 139
Hillcroft. DH3-2B 102
Hillcroft. NE9-4F 79
Hill Dyke. NE9-3B 92
Hillfield. NE25-2F 21
Hillfield Gdns. SR3-4F 109
Hillfield St. NE8-5C 60
Hillgate. NE8 -3D 61 & 5E 143
Hill Head Dri. NE5-3F 39
Hillhead Gdns. NE11-4E 77
Hillhead Parkway. NE5-2D 39
Hill Head Rd. NE5-3E 39
Hill Heads Rd. NE25-4B 22
Hillhead Way. NE5-1F 39
Hill Ho. Rd. NE15-3D 57
Hillingdon Gro. SR4-5F 107
Hill La. DH4-2A 116
Hill Pk. Rd. NE32-2A 66
Hill Rise. NE37-1C 104
Hillsden Rd. NE25-5B 12
Hillside. DH3-1E 123
Hillside. NE11-3D 77
Hillside. NE12-4F 17
Hillside. NE21-5A 56
Hillside. NE34-3F 69
Hillside. NE36-3E 85
Hillside. SR3-4A 110
Hillside Av. NE15-5A 40
Hillside Cres. NE15-3F 57
Hillside Dri. SR6-1C 88
Hillside Gdns. DH9-1D 131
(in two parts)
Hillside Gdns. SR2-4A 110
Hillside Pl. NE9-4F 79
Hillside View. DH6-4F 141
Hillside Way. DH4-4C 126
Hillsleigh Rd. NE5-2F 41
Hill Sq. SR1-2D 111
Hills St. NE8-4D 61
Hill St. NE32-5C 48
Hill St. NE33-3D 51
Hill St. SR3-3F 119
Hill St. SR7-4E 133
Hillsview Av. NE3-5F 25
Hill Ter. DH4-4D 117
Hillthorne Clo. NE38-4D 105
Hill Top. DH3-3C 102
Hilltop. DH9-2E 131
Hill Top. NE21-1A 74
Hill Top Av. NE9-5F 79
Hill Top Gdns. NE9-5F 79
Hilltop Ho. NE5-3C 40
Hilltop View. SR6-5D 71
Hillview. SR3-3F 117
Hillview Cres. DH4-2B 126
Hill View Gdns. SR3-4A 110
Hillview Gro. DH4-2B 126
Hillview Rd. DH4-2B 126
Hill View Rd. SR2-1C 120
Hill View Sq. SR2-1C 120
Hilton Av. NE5-2D 41
Hilton Dri. SR8-4C 134
Hindley Gdns. NE4-5E 41
Hindmarch Dri. NE36 & NE35 -2F 85
Hindson's Cres. N. DH4 -5E 115
Hindson's Cres. S. DH4 -5E 115
Hind St. SR1-1A 110
Hinkley Clo. SR3-4F 119
Hipsburn Dri. SR3-5F 109
Hiram Dri. NE36-3B 86
Histon Ct. NE5-2D 41
Histon Way. NE5-2D 41
Hither Grn. NE32-5C 66
Hobart. NE26-5D 13
Hobart Av. NE34-4E 67
Hobart Gdns. NE7-4C 28
Hodgkin Gdns. NE9-4A 80
Hodgkin Pk. Cres. NE15 -2B 58
Hodgkin Pk. Rd. NE15-3B 58
Hodgson Ter. NE37-4D 95
Hogarth Dri. NE38-4D 105
Hogarth Rd. NE34-5B 68
Holbein Rd. NE34-4B 68
Holborn Pl. NE5-3F 39
Holborn Rd. SR4-3B 108
Holborn Sq. SR4-3B 108
Holburn Clo. NE40-2C 54
Holburn Ct. NE40-2C 54
Holburn Cres. NE40-2C 54
Holburn Gdns. NE40-2D 55
Holburn La. NE40-1B 54
Holburn La. Ct. NE40-2B 54
Holburn Ter. NE40-2C 54
Holburn Wlk. NE40-2C 54
Holburn Way. NE40-2C 54
Holden Pl. NE5-2E 41
Holder Ho. Way. NE34-4D 69
Holderness Rd. NE6-3D 45
Holderness Rd. NE28-1C 48
Hole La. NE16-5E 75
Holeyn Rd. NE15-3E 37
Holland Dri. NE2-5C 42
Holland Pk. NE28-1A 46
Holland Pk. Dri. NE32-5B 66
Hollinghill Rd. NE25-2D 11
Hollings Cres. NE28-1C 46
Hollingside La. DH1-5D 139
Hollingside Way. NE34-2C 68
Hollington Av. NE12-3C 28
Hollington Clo. NE12-4C 28
Hollinhill. NE39-5F 73
Hollinhill La. NE39-5D 73
Hollin Hill Rd. NE37-5C 94
Hollinside Clo. NE16-5F 75
Hollinside Gdns. NE15-1F 57
Hollinside Rd. NE11-5A 58
Hollinside Rd. SR4-3B 108
Hollinside Sq. SR4-3B 108
Hollowdene. DH5-5E 129
Hollow, The. NE32-1A 84
Holly Av. DH5-5D 127
Holly Av. NE2-4A 44
Holly Av. NE3-3B 26
Holly Av. NE11-2E 77
Holly Av. NE12-1E 29
Holly Av. NE21-4B 74
Holly Av. NE25-2C 20
Holly Av. NE26-2B 22
Holly Av. NE28-3D 47
Holly Av. NE34-2F 69
Holly Av. NE40-2B 54
Holly Av. SR3-2F 119
Holly Av. SR6-1E 89
Holly Av. W. NE2-4A 44
Holly Bush Gdns. NE40-3C 54
Hollybush Vs. NE40-3C 54
Hollycarrside Rd. SR2-2C 120
Holly Ct. NE5-3D 41
Holly Ct. SR4-1F 109
Hollycres. DH2-1C 122
Holly Cres. NE38-1A 114
Holly Gdns. NE9-4E 79
Holly Haven. DH5-4B 128
Holly Hill. NE10-2C 80
Holly Hill Gdns. DH9-4D 131
Holly Hill Gdns. E. DH9
(in four parts) -4D 131
Holly Hill Gdns. W. DH9
(in four parts) -4C 130
Hollyhock Heb NE31-4D 65
Holly M. NE26-2C 22
Hollyoake Ter. DH9-5B 130
Holly Pk. View. NE10-2C 80
Holly Rd. NE29-3A 34
Hollys, The. DH3-1A 102
Holly St. DH1-2B 138
Holly St. NE32-1F 65
Holly Ter. DH9-3B 130
Holly View. NE10-2B 80
Hollywell Gro. NE13-2A 24
Hollywell Rd. NE29-3F 33
Hollywood Av. NE3-4E 27
Hollywood Av. NE6-3C 46
Hollywood Av. SR5-2D 99
Hollywood Cres. NE3-4E 27
Hollywood Gdns. NE11-5F 77
Holme Av. NE6-4B 46
Holme Av. NE16-3F 75
Holme Gdns. NE28-2B 48
Holme Gdns. SR3-4F 109
Holme Rise. NE16-3F 75
Holmesdale Rd. NE5-3F 41
Holmeside. SR1-1B 110
Holmfield Av. NE34-5A 52
Holm Grn. NE25-3E 21
Holmhill La. DH2-5D 123
Holmland. NE15-3A 58
Holmlands. NE25-2A 22
Holmlands Clo. NE25-2A 22
Holmlands Cres. DH1-4A 136
Holmlands Pk. DH3-3F 123
Holmlands Pk. N. SR2 -3A 110
Holmlands Pk. S. SR2-3A 110
Holmside Av. NE11-2E 77
Holmside Pl. NE6-5C 44
Holmwood Av. NE25-3F 21
Holmwood Gro. NE2-2F 43
Holwick Clo. NE38-5F 103
Holylake Sq. SR4-3C 108
Holyoake Gdns. DH3-3B 102
Holyoake Gdns. NE9-2E 79
Holyoake Ter. NE37-5C 94
Holyoake Ter. SR6-2D 101
Holyrood. DH3-4A 124
Holyrood Rd. SR2-5D 111
Holystone Av. NE3-4C 26
Holystone Av. NE25-3C 22
Holystone Clo. DH4-3A 126
Holystone Ct. NE8-1C 78
Holystone Cres. NE7-2C 44
Holystone Dri. NE27-5D 19
Holystone Gdns. NE29-2F 33
Holystone St. NE31-1C 64
Holywell Av. NE6-4D 63
Holywell Av. NE25-2E 11
Holywell Av. NE26-1A 22
Holywell Clo. NE4 -1A 60 & 2A 142
Holywell Clo. NE21-1B 74
Holywell Clo. NE25-2E 11
Holywell Dene Rd. NE25 -2E 11
Holywell Ter. NE27-1F 31
Home Av. NE9-5E 79
Homedowne Ho. NE3-4E 27
Homeforth Ho. NE3-4E 27
Homelea. DH4-1D 125
Home Pk. NE28-2A 46
Homeprior Ho. NE25-2A 22
Homer Ter. DH1-4A 138
Homestall Clo. NE34-2B 68
Home View. NE38-3C 104
Honeycomb Clo. SR3-5E 119
Honeysuckle Clo. SR3-5F 119
Honister Av. NE2-1F 43
Honister Clo. NE15-5E 39
Honister Dri. SR5-1B 100
Honister Rd. NE30-5C 22
Honiton Ct. NE3-4D 25
Honiton Way. NE29-1D 33
Hood Clo. SR5-4B 100
Hoods Sq. NE21-1F 73
Hood St. NE1 -2C 60 & 4D 143
Hood St. NE16-1F 75
Hope Av. SR8-3F 135
Hopedene. NE10-4F 81
Hope Shield. NE38-2D 113
Hope St. DH6-5F 141
Hope St. NE32-5E 49
Hope St. NE34-3F 67
Hope St. SR1-1A 110
Hope View. SR2-3D 121
Hopgarth Gdns. DH3-2E 123
Hopkins Wlk. NE34-5E 67
Hopper Pl. DH1-4D 137
Hopper Pl. NE8-4E 61
Hopper Rd. NE10-3A 80
Hopper St. NE8-4E 61
Hopper St. NE28-3C 46
Hopper St. NE29-4B 34
Hopper St. W. NE29-4B 34
Horatio Ho. NE30-3F 35
Horatio St. NE1-2F 61
Horatio St. SR6-3D 101
Hornbeam Pl. NE4-4F 59
Horncliffe Gdns. NE16-2A 76
Horncliffe Pl. NE15-2D 37
Horncliffe Wlk. NE15-5C 38
Horning Ct. NE5-1D 41
Hornsea Clo. NE13-1C 14
Horse Crofts. NE21-4A 56
Horsham Gdns. SR3-5E 109
Horsham Gro. NE29-5F 33
Horsley Av. NE27-4B 20
Horsley Ct. NE3-3F 25
Horsley Gdns. NE11-2F 77
Horsley Gdns. NE25-2D 11
Horsley Gdns. SR3-5E 109
Horsley-Heddon By-Pass. NE15-1F 37
Horsley Hill Rd. NE33-4F 51
Horsley Hill Sq. NE33-5C 52
Horsley Hill Sq. NE34-5C 52
Horsley Ho. NE3-4D 27
Horsley Rd. NE7-3D 45
Horsley Rd. NE38 -1E 105 to 3D 105
Horsley Ter. NE6-2E 63
Horsley Ter. NE30-3E 35
Horsley Vale. NE34-5B 52
Horton Av. NE27-5A 20
Horton Av. NE34-4C 68
Horton Dri. NE23-1C 4
Horwood Av. NE5-2F 39
Hospital Dri. NE31-3B 64
Hospital La. NE15-5C 38
Hotch Pudding Pl. NE5-4A 40
Hotspur Av. NE25-3B 22
Hotspur Av. NE34-1D 69
Hotspur Rd. NE28-5B 30
Hotspur St. NE6-1F 61
Hotspur St. NE30-1F 35
Hotspur Way. NE1 -1C 60 & 3C 142
Houghton Av. NE5-2F 41
Houghton Av. NE30-4D 23
Houghton Cut. DH4 & DH5 -3D 127
Houghton Ga. DH3-2A 124
Houghton-le-Spring. Ind. DH4 -4A 126
Houghton Rd. DH4-2B 126
Houghton Rd. DH5-2E 129
Houghton Rd. W. DH5 -3E 129
Houghtonside. DH4-4C 126
Houghton St. SR4-2F 109
Houghwell Gdns. DH9-1A 130
Houlet Garth. NE6-2A 62
Houlskye Clo. SR3-3A 120
Houndelee Pl. NE5-3E 41
Hounslow Gdns. NE32-5B 66
House Ter. NE37-4C 94
Houston Ct. NE4 -3A 60 & 5A 142
Houston St. NE4 -3A 60 & 5A 142
Houxty Rd. NE25-2C 20
Hovingham Clo. SR8-4D 135
Hovingham Gdns. SR3 -4F 109
Howardian Clo. NE38-5F 103
Howard Pl. NE3-5E 27
Howard St. NE1 -2E 61 & 4F 143
Howard St. NE8-1A 80
Howard St. NE10-4B 80
Howard St. NE30-4C 34
Howard St. NE32-1A 66
Howard St. SR5-4B 100
Howarth St. SR4-1E 109
Howat Av. NE5-3F 41
Howdene Rd. NE15-1E 57
Howden Grn. Ind. Est. NE28 -3C 48

Howdon La. NE28-2C 48
Howdon Rd. NE28 & NE29
-3E 49 to 5C 34
Howe Sq. SR4-3B 108
Howe St. NE8-1F 79
Howe St. NE31-1E 65
Howick Av. NE3-3B 26
Howick Pk. SR6-5C 100
Howick Rd. SR6-5C 100
Howlcroft Vs. DH1-3B 138
Howletch La. SR8-3B 134
Howlett Hall Rd. NE15-1E 57
Howley Av. SR5-2B 98
Hownam Clo. NE3-5C 26
Hoy Cres. SR7-1A 132
Hoylake Av. NE7-4E 29
Hoyle Av. NE4-1C 58
Hoyle Fold. SR3-5F 119
Hoyson Vs. NE10-5F 63
Hubert St. NE35-2D 85
Hubert Ter. NE8-1C 78
Hucklow Gdns. NE34-2C 68
Huddart Ter. DH3-2B 102
Huddleston. NE30-3D 23
Huddleston Rd. NE6-5E 45
Hudleston Rise. SR6-4D 101
Hudson Av. NE23-4A 8
Hudson Av. SR8-2E 135
Hudson Rd. SR1-1C 110
(in two parts)
Hudson St. NE8-4D 61
Hudson St. NE30-4D 35
Hudson St. NE34-1F 67
Hudspeth Cres. DH1-2A 136
Hugh Av. NE27-3A 20
Hugh Gdns. NE4-3C 58
Hugh St. NE28-3D 47
Hugh St. NE38-4D 105
Hugh St. SR6-1D 101
Hull St. NE4-3E 59
Hulme Ct. SR8-4A 134
Hulne Av. NE30-3E 35
Hulne Ter. NE15-1B 56
Humber Ct. SR3-4E 119
Humber Gdns. NE8-1F 79
Humber Hill. DH9-3D 131
Humber St. NE32-1F 65
Humbledon Pk. SR3-4F 109
Humbledon View. SR2
-3B 110
Hume St. NE6-2F 61
Hume St. SR4-1E 109
Humford Gro. NE23-2E 5
Humshaugh Clo. NE12-2C 30
Humshaugh Rd. NE29-4E 33
Hunstanton Ct. NE9-2D 91
Huntcliffe Av. SR6-4D 89
Huntcliffe Gdns. NE6-3E 45
Huntcliffe Ho. NE34-4B 68
Hunter Clo. NE36-3B 86
Hunter Ho. NE6-3F 63
Hunters Clo. NE29-1E 49
Hunters Ct. NE3-4A 28
Hunters Hall Rd. SR4-3F 109
Hunter's Moor Clo. NE2
-5C 42
Hunters Pl. NE2-5D 43
Hunter's Rd. NE2
-5C 42 & 1A 142
Hunter's Rd. NE3-5A 28
Hunter's Ter. NE9-3E 93
(off Peareth Hall Rd.)
Hunter's Ter. NE33-3F 51
(off Chichester Rd. E.)
Hunter St. DH4-5F 115
Hunter St. NE28-4D 47
Hunter St. NE33-3F 51
Hunter Ter. SR2-4D 111
Huntingdon Clo. NE3-2E 25
Huntingdon Dri. NE23-2E 5
Huntingdon Gdns. SR3
-4F 109
Huntingdon Pl. NE30-2E 35
Huntingdon Rd. SR8-1A 134
Huntingdonshire Dri. DH1
-3D 141
Hunt Lea. NE16-5D 75
Huntley Cres. NE21-2F 73
Huntley Sq. SR4-2C 108
Huntley Ter. SR2-4D 121
Huntly Rd. NE25-5B 12
Hurst Ter. NE6-1D 63
Hurstwood Rd. SR4-3F 109
Hurworth Av. NE34-1F 69
Hurworth Pl. NE32-1F 65
Hustledown Gdns. DH9
-4C 130
Hustledown Ho. DH9-3C 130
Hustledown Rd. DH9-5B 130
Hutton Clo. DH4-5B 126
Hutton Clo. NE38-2D 103
Hutton Ho. NE29-1F 49
Hutton St. NE3-4B 26
Hutton St. NE35-1D 85
Hutton St. SR4-2F 109
Hutton Ter. NE2
-5A 44 & 1E 143
Hutton Ter. NE9-1E 91
Huxley Clo. NE34-5F 67
Huxley Cres. NE8-3C 78
Hyacinth St. SR4-5F 99
Hyde Pk. NE28-1A 46
Hyde Pk. St. NE8-2C 78
Hyde St. NE33-3F 51
Hyde St. SR2-3D 111
Hyde Ter. NE3-4F 27
Hylton Av. NE34-1F 69
Hylton Bank. SR4-2F 107
Hylton Castle Rd. SR5-4F 97
Hylton Ct. NE38-1F 103
Hylton La. NE36 & SR5-3E 85
Hylton Pk. Rd. SR5-3C 98
Hylton Rd. DH1-3D 137
Hylton Rd. NE32-3A 66
Hylton Rd. SR4
-3F 107 to 1F 109
Hylton St. DH4-3B 126
Hylton St. NE8-1F 79
Hylton St. NE29-5B 34
Hylton St. SR4-1F 109
Hylton Ter. NE10-5A 64
Hylton Ter. NE29-5B 34
Hylton Ter. SR2-4D 121
Hylton Wlk. SR4-2F 107
Hymers Av. NE34-3E 67
Hymers Ct. NE8-4D 61
Hyperion Av. NE34-2E 67

Ilchester St. SR7-4F 133
Ilderton Pl. NE5-4A 40
Ilford Av. NE23-1C 4
Ilford Pl. NE8-2F 79
Ilford Rd. NE2-2F 43
Ilford Rd. NE28-1B 48
Ilfracombe Av. NE4-2D 59
Ilfracombe Gdns. NE9-2E 91
Ilfracombe Gdns. NE26-1B 22
Illingworth Ho. NE29-1F 49
Ilminster Ct. NE3-4E 25
Imeary Gro. NE33-3F 51
Imeary St. NE33-3E 51
Imperial Bldgs. DH4-5C 126
Inchberry Clo. NE4-3C 58
Inchcliffe Cres. NE5-2E 41
Industrial Rd. NE37
-5C 94 to 1D 105
Industry Rd. NE6-2F 45
Ingham Gro. NE23-1C 4
Ingham Pl. NE2
-1E 61 & 3F 143
Ingleborough Dri. NE40
-3C 54
Ingleby Ter. SR4-2F 109
Inglemere Pl. NE15-2E 57
Ingleside. NE16-4E 75
Ingleside. NE34-1A 70
Ingleside Rd. NE29-2B 34
Ingleton Ct. SR4-2F 109
Ingleton Dri. NE15-2D 37
Inglewood Pl. NE3-5E 15
Ingoe Av. NE3-2A 26
Ingoe St. NE15-1B 56
Ingoe St. NE28-3E 49
Ingoldsby Ct. SR4-4D 109
Ingram Av. NE3-2B 26
Ingram Clo. DH2-5B 122
Ingram Clo. NE28-5B 32
Ingram Dri. NE5-1E 39
(in two parts)
Ingram Ter. NE6-2E 63
Inkerman Rd. NE37-4B 94
Inkerman St. SR5-4E 99
Innesmoor. NE31-5E 47
Inskip Ho. NE34-2B 68
Inskip Ter. NE8-2E 79
Inverness Rd. NE32-4C 66
Inverness St. SR6-2B 100
Invincible Dri. NE4-4F 59
Iolanthe Cres. NE6-5F 45
Iolanthe Ter. NE33-3F 51
Iona Ct. NE28-5B 32
Iona Pl. NE6-1F 63
Iona Rd. NE10-3A 80
Iona Rd. NE32-4D 67
Irene Av. SR2-2E 121
Iris Clo. NE21-5F 55
Iris Pl. NE4-5F 41
Iris Ter. DH4-2C 124
Ironside St. DH5-4D 127
Irthing Av. NE6-3C 62
Irton St. NE3-4E 27
Irwin Av. NE28-2D 47
Isabella Clo. NE4-4D 59
Isis Rd. SR8-4B 134
Islay Ho. SR3-4E 119
Ivanhoe. NE25-1F 21
Ivanhoe Cres. SR2-3F 109
Ivanhoe Ter. DH3-4E 123
Ivanhoe View. NE9-3F 91
Iveagh Clo. NE4-3C 58
Iveston Ter. DH9-1C 130
Ivor St. SR2-5E 111
Ivy Av. NE40-1B 54
Ivy Av. SR7-4C 132
Ivy Clo. NE4-4A 60
Ivy Clo. NE40-2B 54
Ivy La. NE9-1E 91
Ivymount Rd. NE6-3C 44
Ivy Rd. NE3-5E 27
Ivy Rd. NE6-4A 46
Ivy Rd. NE12-1F 29
Ivy St. NE13-4A 6
Ivy Ter. DH4-4A 116
Ivy Ter. DH9-5E 131
(Craghead)
Ivy Ter. DH9-5A 130
(South Moor)

Jackson St. NE6-1E 63
Jackson St. NE8-4D 61
Jackson St. NE30-3D 35
Jackson St. SR4-2E 109
Jackson St. W. NE30-3C 34
Jack's Ter. NE34-2A 68
Jacobins Chare. NE1
-2B 60 & 4B 142
Jacques St. SR4-5D 99
Jacques Ter. DH2-2D 133
Jade Clo. NE15-4E 39
James Armitage St. SR5
-3F 99
James Av. NE27-3A 20
James Clydesdale Ho. NE15
-5B 40
James Mather St. NE33-1E 51
James Pl. NE6-1F 61
James St. DH4-5E 125
James St. NE4-3E 59
James St. NE5-2A 40
James St. NE16-3F 75
James St. SR5-3E 99
(in two parts)
James Ter. DH4-5E 125
James Ter. NE28-3D 47
James Ter. SR3-3A 120
Jame St. SR7-4E 133
James Williams St. SR1
-5D 101
Jane Eyre Ter. NE8-1A 80
Jane St. DH5-2F 129
Jane St. DH9-4A 130
Jane St. NE6-2B 62
Jane Ter. NE6-3F 63
Janet Sq. NE6-3B 62
Janet St. NE6-3B 62
Janus Clo. NE5-1E 39
Jarrow Rd. NE34-1D 67
Jarvis Rd. SR8-1C 134
Jasmin Av. NE5-1E 39
Jasmine Clo. NE6-4A 46
Jasmine Ct. SR4-1A 110
Jasmine Cres. SR7-5D 133
Jasmine Ter. DH3-3B 102
Jasper Av. NE40-1A 72
Jasper Av. SR7-4C 132
Jedburgh Clo. NE5-1E 39
Jedburgh Clo. NE8-1E 79
Jedburgh Clo. NE29-2A 34
Jedburgh Ct. NE11-2C 90
Jedburgh Gdns. NE15-1F 57
Jedburgh Rd. DH4-5F 115
Jedburgh Rd. NE4-3A 42
Jedmoor. NE31-5E 47
Jefferson Pl. NE4
-1A 60 & 3A 142
Jellicoe Rd. NE6-4C 62
Jenifer Gro. NE7-1C 44
Jenison Av. NE15-2B 58
Jennifer Av. SR5-4A 98
Jervis St. NE31-1E 65
Jesmond Dene Rd. NE2
-2F 43 to 4B 44
Jesmond Dene Ter. NE2
-3B 44
Jesmond Gdns. NE2-3B 44
Jesmond Gdns. NE34-5A 68
Jesmond Pk. Ct. NE7-3C 44
Jesmond Pk. E. NE7-3C 44
Jesmond Pk. W. NE7-2B 44
Jesmond Pl. NE2-3A 44
Jesmond Rd. NE2
-5A 44 & 1E 143
Jesmond Rd. W. NE2-5F 43
Jesmond Ter. NE26-2C 22
Jesmond Vale. NE2-5C 44
Jesmond Vale La. NE6-4C 44
Jesmond Vale Ter. NE6-4D 45
(in two parts)
Jessel St. NE9-5D 79
Joan Av. SR2-2E 121
Joannah St. SR5-2B 100
Joan St. NE4-3C 58
Jobling Av. NE21-5F 55
Joel Ter. NE10-5F 63
John Av. NE40-1A 72
John Candlish Rd. SR4
-1E 109
John Clay St. NE33-3E 51
John Dobson St. NE1-2C 60
John Dobson St. NE1
-1C 60 & 2D 143
(in two parts)
John F. Kennedy Est. NE38
-2D 105
John Reid Rd. NE34
-3D 67 to 2D 69
Johnson Clo. SR8-1C 134
Johnson Ct. SR1-1A 110
Johnson St. NE8-1A 78
Johnson St. NE11-1E 77
Johnson St. NE15-1B 56
Johnson St. NE33-5D 51
Johnson St. SR1-1A 110
Johnson Ter. NE37-5D 95
Johnston Av. NE31-4C 64
John St. DH1-2B 138
John St. DH4-5E 125
John St. DH5-4F 129
(Hetton-le-Hole)
John St. DH5-5E 127
(New Town)
John St. DH9-4B 130
John St. NE3-4B 26
(Coxlodge)
John St. NE3-4A 28
(South Gosforth)
John St. NE8-1F 79
John St. NE10-1E 81
John St. NE25-2B 20
John St. NE28-3C 46
John St. NE30-3D 23
John St. NE35-2E 85
John St. SR1-1C 110
John St. SR2-5F 121
John St. SR3-3E 119
John St. SR4-1F 107
John Williamson St. NE33
-5D 51
Joicey Gdns. DH9-2C 130
(in two parts)
Joicey Pl. NE9-4E 79
Joicey Rd. NE9-4D 79
Joicey Sq. DH9-2C 130
Joicey St. NE10-1F 81
Joicey Ter. DH9-1A 130
Jolliffe St. DH3-4E 123
Jonadab Rd. NE10-5F 63
Jonadab St. NE10-1E 81
Jones St. DH3-3A 102
Jonquil Clo. NE5-1E 39
Joseph Clo. NE4-4D 59
Joseph Hopper Memorial NE9
-4A 80
Joseph St. DH9-3C 130
Jowett Sq. SR5-2F 99
Joyce Clo. NE10-2B 82
Joyce Ter. SR5-4A 98
Jubilee Av. NE9-3B 92
Jubilee Av. SR7-4A 132
Jubilee Cotts. DH4-4C 126
Jubilee Ct. NE23-3A 8
Jubilee Ct. NE31-1E 65
Jubilee Cres. NE3-4C 26
Jubilee M. NE3-5D 27
Jubilee Rd. NE1
-2D 61 & 4E 143
Jubilee Rd. NE3-4B 26
Jubilee St. NE28-3C 46
Jubilee Ter. NE6-2B 62
Jubilee Ter. NE13-4A 6
Jubilee Ter. NE16-1F 75
Jubilee Ter. NE38-5F 105
Jude Pl. SR8-1B 134
Julian Av. NE6-5A 46
Julian Av. NE33-5E 35
Julian Rd. NE10-2B 82
Julian St. NE33-1E 51
Juliet Av. NE29-3F 33
Julius Caesar St. SR5-3E 99
June Av. NE21-3B 74
Juniper Clo. NE3-5E 15
Juniper Clo. SR2-3C 110
Juniper Ct. NE21-4B 56
Juniper Wlk. NE5-1E 39
Jutland Av. NE31-2C 64
Jutland Ter. DH9-1A 130

Kalmia St. NE11-4B 78
Kane Gdns. NE10-4B 80
Kateregina. DH3-3B 102
Katrine Clo. DH2-4D 123
Katrine Ct. SR3-5E 119
Kayll Rd. SR4-2E 109
Kay's Cotts. NE10-3A 80
Kay St. DH9-1C 130
Kearsley Clo. NE25-1B 10
Kearton Av. NE5-1E 39
Keats Av. NE35-2A 86
Keats Av. SR5-3F 99
Keats Clo. DH9-3D 131
Keats Rd. NE15-1F 55
Keats Wlk. NE8-5F 61
Keats Wlk. NE34-4E 67
Keebledale Av. NE6-5A 46
Keelman's La. SR4-1A 108
Keelman's Rd. SR4-5A 98
Keighley Av. SR5-1F 97
Keighley Sq. SR5-1F 97
Keir Hardie Av. DH9-4C 130
Keir Hardie Av. NE10-2F 81
Keir Hardie St. DH4-5F 125
Keir Hardie Ter. DH3-2A 102
Keith Clo. NE4-3C 58
Keith Sq. SR5-1F 97
Keldane Gdns. NE4-2D 59
Kelham Sq. SR5-1F 97
Kellfield Av. NE9-4F 79
Kellfield Rd. NE9-5E 79
Kell Rd. SR8-3E 135
Kells Bldgs. DH1-4A 138
Kells Gdns. NE9-5E 79
Kells La. NE9-5E 79
Kellsway. NE10-5D 81
Kellsway Ct. NE10-5D 81
Kelly Rd. NE31-4C 64
Kelso Clo. NE5-1E 39
Kelso Dri. NE29-2F 33
Kelso Gdns. NE15-1F 57
Kelso Gdns. NE28-1C 48
Kelso Gro. DH4-4F 115
Kelson Way. NE5-1E 39
Kelso Pl. NE8-1A 78
Kelston Way. NE5-2E 41
Kelvin Gdns. NE11-1E 77
Kelvin Gro. NE2
-5B 44 & 1F 143
Kelvin Gro. NE8-2C 78
Kelvin Gro. NE29-2B 34
Kelvin Gro. NE33-3B 52
Kelvin Gro. SR6-1D 87
(Cleadon)
Kelvin Gro. SR6-2C 100
(Roker)
Kelvin Pl. NE12-1C 30
Kemble Sq. SR5-1F 97
Kemp Rd. SR8-3B 134
Kempton Gdns. NE8-3B 78
Kendal. DH3-1C 112
(in two parts)
Kendal Av. NE30-4C 22
Kendal Cres. NE9-5F 79
Kendal Dri. NE23-2E 5
Kendal Dri. NE36-2B 86
Kendale Wlk. NE5-2F 39
Kendal Gdns. NE28-5C 32
Kendal Grn. NE6-2A 62
(off Brinkburn Clo.)
Kendal Ho. NE6-2A 62
Kendal St. NE6-2A 62
Kenilworth. DH3-4A 124
Kenilworth. NE12-3F 17
Kenilworth Ct. NE4-3F 59
Kenilworth Ct. NE37-4D 95
Kenilworth Rd. NE4-3F 59
Kenilworth Rd. NE25-2A 22
Kenilworth Sq. SR5-1A 98
Kenilworth View. NE9-3F 91
Kenley Rd. NE5-5C 40
Kenley Rd. SR5-1A 98
Kenmore Cres. NE40-5A 54
Kenmorr Way. NE5-1E 39
Kennersdene. NE30-1E 35
Kennet Av. NE32-4B 66
Kennet Sq. SR5-1F 97
Kennford. NE9-3E 91
Kennington Gro. NE6-2D 63
Kenny Pl. DH1-1F 139
Kensington Av. NE3-3D 27
Kensington Clo. NE25-2A 22
Kensington Ct. NE31-2C 64
Kensington Ct. NE33-4F 51
Kensington Gdns. NE25
-2A 22
Kensington Gdns. NE28
-1A 46
Kensington Gdns. NE30
-3C 34
Kensington Gro. NE30-3C 34
Kensington Ter. NE2
-5F 43 & 1C 142
Kensington Ter. NE11-2E 77
Kensington Vs. NE5-1A 40
Kenswith Wlk. NE8-5C 60
Kent Av. NE11-2E 77
Kent Av. NE28-2B 48
Kent Av. NE31-2B 64
Kentchester Rd. SR5-1A 98
Kent Ct. NE3-2E 25
Kent Gdns. DH5-4D 129
Kentmere. DH3-2C 112
Kentmere Av. NE6-1D 63
Kentmere Av. SR6-5A 88
Kentmere Clo. NE23-2F 9
Kentmere Ho. DH4-3B 126
Kentmere Pl. SR8-3D 135
Kenton Av. NE3-1C 42
Kenton Ct. NE33-3E 51
Kenton Cres. NE3-5B 26
Kenton Gro. SR6-3C 100
Kenton La. NE3-1E 41
Kenton Pk. Shopping NE3
-1B 42
Kenton Rd. NE3-5B 26
Kenton Rd. NE29-3E 33
Kent Pl. NE34-2E 69
Kent St. NE32-1F 65
Kentucky Rd. SR5-1F 97
Kent Vs. NE32-1F 65
Kent Wlk. SR8-1B 134
Kenwood Gdns. NE9-2F 91
Kenya Rd. SR5-1A 98
Kepier Cres. DH1-3A 140
(in two parts)
Kepier Gdns. SR4-2E 107
Kepier Heights. DH1-2D 139
Kepier La. DH1-1E 139
Kepier Ter. DH1-2D 139
Kepier Vs. DH1-2E 139
Keppel St. NE11-1E 77
Keppel St. NE33-2E 51
Kerryhill Dri. DH1-1D 136
Kerry Sq. SR5-1F 97
Kesteven Sq. SR5-1A 98
Kestrel Clo. NE38-5E 103
Kestrel Ct. DH3-4B 102
Kestrel Lodge Flats. NE33
-2E 51
Kestrel Pl. NE12-3C 28
Kestrel Sq. SR5-1A 98
Kestrel St. NE11-4B 78
Kestrel Way. NE29-1B 50
Kestrel Way. NE34-3F 67
Keswick Av. SR6-1B 100
Keswick Dri. NE30-4D 23
Keswick Gdns. NE28-1C 48
Keswick Gro. NE5-4C 40
Keswick Rd. DH9-4A 130
Keswick Rd. SR8-3D 135
Keswick St. NE8-1C 78
Kettering Pl. NE23-1D 5
Kettering Sq. SR5-1A 98
Kettlewell Ter. NE30-4D 35
Ketton Clo. NE12-3D 29
Kew Gdns. NE26-1B 22
Kew Sq. SR5-1F 97
Keyes Gdns. NE2-1A 44
Kidd Av. DH6-4F 141
Kidderminster Dri. NE5-1E 39
Kidderminster Rd. SR5-2F 97
Kidderminster Sq. SR5-1F 97
Kidd Sq. SR5-1A 98
Kidlandlee Grn. NE5-1C 40
Kidlandlee Pl. NE5-1C 40
Kidsgrove Sq. SR5-1F 97
Kielder. NE38-3E 103
Kielder Clo. NE5-1B 40
Kielder Clo. NE12-3E 17
Kielder Gdns. NE32-4F 65
Kielder Ho. SR3-4E 119
Kielder Pl. NE25-2C 20
Kielder Rd. NE15-5D 39
Kielder Rd. NE25-2C 20
Kielder Ter. NE30-3C 34
Kielder Way. NE3-3D 27
Kilburn Clo. SR2-4E 121
Kilburn Dri. SR8-1E 135
Kilburne Clo. NE7-2F 45
Kilburn Grn. NE9-3F 91
Kildale. DH4-2D 115
Kildare Sq. SR5-1F 97
Killarney Av. SR5-1A 98
Killarney Sq. SR5-1F 97
Killiebrigs. NE15-3A 36
Killin Clo. NE5-1E 39
Killingworth Av. NE27-3C 18
Killingworth Dri. NE12-5C 16
Killingworth Dri. SR4-4C 108
Killingworth La.
NE12 & NE27-4A 18
Killingworth La. NE27-2C 18
Killingworth Pl. NE1
-2B 60 & 3B 142
Killingworth Rd. NE3-5A 28
Killingworth Rd. NE12-5A 18
Killowen St. NE9-5D 79
Kilnhill Wlk. SR8-3D 135
Kiln Rise. NE16-5F 75
Kilnshaw Pl. NE3-1E 27
Kilsyth Av. NE29-5A 22
Kilsyth Sq. SR5-1F 97
Kimberley. NE38-3F 105
Kimberley Av. NE29-3A 34
Kimberley Gdns. DH9-5F 131
Kimberley Gdns. NE2-4C 44
Kimberley St. SR4-1D 109
Kinfauns Ter. NE9-5E 79
Kingarth Av. SR6-5D 89
King Charles Ho. NE2
-1D 61 & 3E 143
King Charles Tower. NE2
-1D 61 & 2E 143
King Edward VIII Ter. DH9
-1D 131
King Edward Pl. NE8-1F 79
King Edward Rd. NE6-3D 45
King Edward Rd. NE30-2D 35
King Edward Rd. NE40-3D 55
King Edward Rd. SR4-1F 107
King Edward Rd. SR7-4F 133
King Edward St. NE8-1F 79
Kingfisher Lodge. NE32-1F 65
Kingfisher Rd. NE12-3C 28
Kingfisher Way. NE28-3B 32
King George Av. NE11-2D 77
King George Rd. NE3-3A 26
King George Rd. NE34
-5A 52 to 4D 69
Kingham Ct. NE3-5B 28
King Henry Ct. SR5-1F 97
Kinghorn Sq. SR5-1A 98
King James Ct. SR5-1F 97
King James St. NE8-1E 79
King John St. NE6-5D 45
King John Ter. NE6-5D 45
King's Av. NE31-2E 65
King's Av. SR6-5D 89
Kingsbridge. NE12-3B 28
Kingsbury Clo. SR5-1F 97
Kingsclere Av. SR5-1F 97
Kingsclere Sq. SR5-1F 97
Kings Clo. NE8-1F 79
King's Clo. NE30-4D 35
Kings Ct. Ind. Pk. NE32-5B 48
Kingsdale Av. NE37-4A 94
Kingsdale Rd. NE12-3B 28
King's Dri. NE26-2C 22
Kings Dri. NE40-1A 72
Kings Gro. DH1-5A 138
Kingsland. NE2-4A 44
Kingsland Sq. SR5-1F 97
Kingsley Av. NE3-1E 27
Kingsley Av. NE25-3B 22
Kingsley Av. NE34-4F 67
Kingsley Clo. DH9-2E 131
Kingsley Clo. SR5-3F 99
Kingsley Pl. NE6-5C 44
Kingsley Pl. NE11-1E 77
Kingsley Pl. NE16-2A 76
Kingsley Pl. NE28-2A 48
Kingsley Ter. NE4-2F 59
(in two parts)
Kings Mnr. NE1
-2D 61 & 3E 143
Kings Meadow. NE32-1B 84
Kings Meadows. NE4-4E 59
Kingsmere. DH3-3B 112
Kingsmere Gdns. NE6-3E 63
King's Pl. SR4-1E 109
King's Rd. NE1
-1B 60 & 2C 142
Kings Rd. NE12-5E 17
King's Rd. NE26-1B 22
Kings Rd. NE28-1D 47
King's Rd., The. SR5-3F 99
Kings Ter. NE9-4E 93
King's Ter. SR4-1E 109
Kingston Av. NE6-2C 62
Kingston Av. SR7-4C 132
Kingston Clo. NE26-4E 13
Kingston Ct. NE26-4E 13
(off Kingston Dri.)
Kingston Dri. NE26-4D 13
Kingston Grn. NE6-2C 62
Kingston Pk. Av. NE3-3E 25
Kingston Pk. Cen. NE3-3E 25
Kingston Pk. Rd. NE3
-2E 25 to 3C 26
Kingston Pl. NE8-2F 79
Kingston Rd. NE8-2F 79
Kingston Ter. SR6-3C 100
Kingston Way. NE26-4E 13
King St. DH3-3A 102
King St. DH6-4F 141
King St. NE1-3D 61 & 5E 143
King St. NE8-2B 78
King St. NE10-5F 63
King St. NE30-4D 35
King St. NE33-2D 51
King St. SR1-1B 110
King St. SR6-1C 100
King's Wlk. NE1
-1C 60 & 2C 142
Kings Wlk. NE5-1D 39
Kingsway. DH5-5D 127
Kingsway. NE4-4A 42
Kingsway. NE30-1E 35
Kingsway. NE33-3A 52
Kingsway Av. NE3-3D 27
Kingsway Ho. NE11-1B 90
Kingsway Interchange. NE9
-3D 91
Kingsway N. NE11-3A 78
Kingsway Rd. SR5-5F 85
Kingsway S. NE11-1B 90
Kingsway Sq. SR5-1F 97
Kingswood Av. NE2-1F 43
Kingswood Clo. NE35-1C 84
Kingswood Gro. SR4-5E 107
Kingswood Rd. NE23-1D 5
Kingswood Sq. SR5-1F 97
Kinley Rd. DH1-1D 141
Kinloch Ct. DH2-4C 122
Kinloss Sq. NE23-1E 5
Kinnaird Av. NE15-1F 57
Kinross Clo. DH3-1C 112
Kinross Ct. NE10-5A 64
Kinross Dri. DH9
-3E 131 & 2F 131
Kinross Dri. NE3-4A 26
Kinsale Sq. SR5-1A 98
Kinver Dri. NE5-1E 39
Kip Hill Ct. DH9-1D 131
Kipling Av. NE16-2F 75
Kipling Av. NE31-1E 65
Kipling Av. NE35-2A 86
Kipling Clo. DH9-2E 131
Kipling Ct. NE16-2F 75
Kiplings Ter. DH1-4A 138
Kipling St. SR5-3F 99
Kipling Wlk. NE8-5F 61
Kira Dri. DH1-1D 137
Kirby Av. DH1-4B 136
Kirkbride Pl. NE23
-1E 5 & 2E 5
Kirkdale Ct. NE23-2D 17
Kirkdale Ct. NE34-3F 67
Kirkdale Grn. NE4
-3A 60 & 5A 142
Kirkdale Sq. SR5-1A 98
Kirkdale St. DH5-5D 129
Kirkham. NE38
-4B 104 to 4C 104
Kirkham Av. NE3-3D 25
Kirkham Rd. DH1-3D 137
Kirkheaton Pl. NE5-4E 41
Kirkland Hill. SR8-2C 134
Kirklands. NE23-2E 17
Kirkland Wlk. NE27-4A 20
Kirklea Rd. DH5-5E 127
Kirkleatham Gdns. NE6-3F 45
Kirkley Av. NE34-1F 69
Kirkley Clo. NE3-3C 26
Kirkley Clo. Flats. NE3-3C 26
Kirkley Rd. NE27-5A 20
Kirklinton Rd. NE30-5C 22
Kirkside. DH4-4C 116
Kirkston Av. NE15-5E 39
Kirkstone. DH3-5C 102
Kirkstone Av. NE30-4C 22
Kirkstone Av. NE32-4B 66
Kirkstone Av. SR5-1B 100
Kirkstone Av. SR8-3D 135
Kirkstone Dri. DH1-1D 141
Kirkstone Gdns. NE7-1B 44
Kirkstone Rd. NE10-1E 81
Kirk St. NE6-3B 62
Kirk View. DH4-2C 126
Kirkwall Clo. SR5-4F 97
Kirkwood. NE23-1D 17
Kirkwood Av. SR4-5E 107
Kirkwood Dri. NE3-5A 26
Kirkwood Gdns. NE10-1F 81
Kirkwood Pl. NE3-1D 27
Kirton Av. NE4-1D 59
Kirton Pk. Ter. NE29-3C 34
Kirton Way. NE23-1D 5
Kismet St. SR5-3F 99
Kitchener St. NE9-2F 79
Kitchener St. SR4-3D 109
Kitchener Ter. DH4-4C 116
Kitchener Ter. NE30-3D 35
Kitchener Ter. NE32-2F 65
Kitchener Ter. SR2-1D 121
Kittiwake Clo. NE28-3C 32
Kittiwake Dri. NE38-4E 103
Kittiwake Ho. NE26-2D 23
Kittiwake St. NE11-5B 78
Kiwi St. NE11-4B 78
Knaresborough Sq. SR5
-1A 98
Knaresdale. DH3-1C 112
Knarsdale Av. NE29-4E 33
Knarsdale Pl. NE5-3F 39
Kneller Clo. DH9-3D 131
Knightsbridge. NE3-3E 27
Knightsbridge. SR3-2D 119
Knightside Gdns. NE11-4E 77
Knightside Wlk. NE5-1E 39
Knivestone Ct. NE12-3F 17
Knobbyends La. NE21-2E 73
Knoll Rise. NE11-3D 77
Knollside Clo. SR3-5D 119
Knoll, The. SR2-2F 109
Knott Flats. NE30-3E 35
Knott Pl. NE15-2F 57
Knoulberry. NE37-1E 103
Knoulberry Rd. NE37-2E 103
Knowledge Hill. NE21-1F 73
Knowle Pl. NE12-4D 29
Knowles, The. NE16-3A 76
Knowsley Ct. NE3-4D 25
Knox Sq. SR5-2F 99
Knutsford Wlk. NE23-1D 5
Kristin Av. NE32-3A 66
Kyffin View. NE34-2F 69
Kyle Clo. NE4-4A 60
Kyle Rd. NE8-2B 78
Kyloe Av. NE25-2C 10
Kyloe Clo. NE3-2A 26
Kyloe Pl. NE5-1C 40
(in two parts)
Kyloe Vs. NE5-1C 40
Kyloe Wlk. NE8-5C 60
Kyo La. DH9-3A 130

Laburmum Gro. NE34-2D 69
Laburnham Clo. SR4-1E 107
Laburnum Av. DH1-3B 138
Laburnum Av. NE6-4B 46
Laburnum Av. NE10-2E 81
Laburnum Av. NE26-2C 22
Laburnum Av. NE28-2D 47
Laburnum Av. NE38-1F 113
Laburnum Clo. SR4-1E 107
Laburnum Cres. SR7-5D 133
Laburnum Gdns. NE9-4E 79
Laburnum Gdns. NE10-1B 80
Laburnum Gdns. NE32-3F 65
Laburnum Gro. NE16-3F 75
Laburnum Gro. NE31-4C 64
Laburnum Gro. SR5-5E 97
Laburnum Gro. SR6-1E 87
Laburnum Ho. NE28-3D 47
Laburnum Rd. NE21-5B 56
Laburnum Rd. SR6-2B 100
Ladock Clo. SR2-2E 121
Lady Anne Rd. DH6-3F 141
Ladybank. NE5-1D 39
Lady Beatrice Ter. DH4
-3D 117
Ladyhaugh Dri. NE16-5F 75
Ladykirk Rd. NE4-2D 59
Ladykirk Way. NE23-3A 4
Ladysmith Ct. DH9-4E 131
Ladysmith St. NE33-2F 51
Lady St. DH5-3F 129
Lady's Wlk. NE33-1D 51
Ladywell Rd. NE21-5B 56
Ladywell Way. DH4-2D 115
Laet St. NE29-5C 34
Laing Gro. NE28-1C 48
Laith Rd. NE3-4A 26
Lake App. NE21-1D 75
Lake Av. NE34-1B 70
Lake Ct. SR3-4F 119
Lake Rd. DH5-4D 127
Lakeside. NE21-1D 75
Lakeside. NE34-1B 70
Lake View. NE31-3C 64
Laleham Ct. NE3-4E 25
Lamara Dri. SR5-1A 100
Lambert Rd. NE37-1E 103
Lambert Sq. NE3-5C 26
Lambeth Pl. NE8-2F 79
Lambley Av. NE30-5D 23
Lambley Cres. NE31-4B 64
Lambourn Av. NE29-5F 33
Lambourne Av. NE12-3D 29
Lambourne Clo. DH4-2D 125
Lambourne Rd. SR2-4A 110
Lamb St. NE6-2F 63
Lamb Ter. NE27-1F 31
Lambton Av. NE16-2B 76
Lambton Ct. NE38-2D 113
Lambton Ct. SR3-3B 118
Lambton Dri. DH5-5F 129
Lambton La. DH4-3E 125
Lambton Lea. DH4-1E 125
Lambton Pl. DH4-2A 116
Lambton Rd. NE2-5F 43
Lambton Rd. NE31-5A 48
Lambton St. DH1-2B 138
Lambton St. DH3-3E 123
Lambton St. SR1-1C 110
Lambton Ter. DH4-2D 115
Lambton Ter. NE32-3A 66
Lambton Tower. SR1-5D 101
(off High St. E.)
Lambton Wlk. DH1-2C 138
(off Silver St.)
Lampeter Clo. NE5-1D 41
Lamport St. NE31-5E 47
Lanark Clo. NE29-1D 33
Lanark Dri. NE32-4D 67
Lancashire Dri. DH1-3D 141
Lancaster Ct. NE3-3F 25
Lancaster Dri. NE28-3F 31
(in two parts)
Lancaster Hill. SR8-2A 134
Lancaster Ho. NE4-5F 59
Lancaster Ho. NE23-4E 5
Lancaster Rd. NE11-1C 76
Lancaster St. NE4
-2A 60 & 4A 142
Lancaster Ter. DH3-3F 123
Lancaster Way. NE32-1F 83
(in two parts)
Lancastrian Rd. NE23-4B 4
Lancefield Av. NE6-4D 63
Lancet Ct. NE8-5E 61
Lanchester Av. NE9-2C 92
Lanchester Clo. NE10-4A 82
Lanchester St. NE34-2A 68
Lancing Ct. NE3-3D 25
Landon Av. SR6-1C 100
Landscape Ter. NE40-1A 72
Landseer Clo. DH9-3C 130

Landseer Gdns. NE9-2A 80
Landseer Gdns. NE34-5B 68
Landswood Ter. NE21-3B 74
Lane Corner. NE34-2A 68
Lane Head. NE40-2B 54
Lanercost. NE38-2B 104
Lanercost Av. NE21-5A 56
Lanercost Dri. NE5-4D 41
Lanercost Gdns. NE10-3A 80
Lanercost Gdns. NE15-2F 37
Lanercost Pk. NE23-4F 5
Lanercost Rd. NE29-5F 33
Langdale. DH3-1C 112
Langdale. NE25-1A 22
Langdale. NE37-1B 104
Langdale Clo. NE12-4C 28
Langdale Cres. DH1-1C 140
Langdale Cres. NE21-2F 73
Langdale Dri. NE23-3A 4
Langdale Gdns. NE6-1E 63
Langdale Gdns. NE28-5B 32
Langdale Pl. NE12-4C 28
Langdale Pl. SR8-3D 135
Langdale Rd. DH4-2E 115
Langdale Rd. NE9-5F 79
Langdale St. DH5-5E 129
Langdale Way. NE36-2A 86
Langdon Clo. NE29-1B 34
Langdon Rd. NE5-2F 39
Langford Dri. NE35-5D 67
Langham Rd. NE15-2E 57
Langholm Av. NE29-1D 33
Langholm Ct. NE36-2C 86
(off Station Rd.)
Langholm Rd. NE3-3E 27
Langholm Rd. NE36-2B 86
Langhorn Clo. NE6-1A 62
Langhurst. SR2-2D 121
Langleeford Rd. NE5-1C 40
Langley Av. NE10-4A 82
Langley Av. NE25-3F 21
Langley Av. NE27-4B 20
Langley Clo. NE38-3A 104
Langley Mere. NE12-2E 29
Langley Rd. DH1-3C 136
Langley Rd. NE5-4A 40
Langley Rd. NE6-1D 63
Langley Rd. NE29-4E 33
Langley Rd. SR3-5A 110
Langley St. DH4-4C 116
Langley Tarn. NE29-5C 34
Langley Ter. NE32-4A 66
Langport Rd. SR2-5B 110
Langton St. NE8-5E 61
(in two parts)
Langton Ter. DH4-3D 125
Langton Ter. NE7-3D 45
Lanivet Clo. SR2-3E 121
Lannerwood. NE29-5C 34
(off Coach La.)
Lansbury Clo. DH3-2A 102
Lansbury Ct. NE31-5A 48
Lansbury Dri. DH3-2A 102
Lansbury Gdns. NE10-2F 81
Lansbury Rd. NE16-3B 76
Lansbury Way. SR5-4A 98
Lansdowne. SR2-3D 121
Lansdowne Cres. NE3-4E 27
Lansdowne Gdns. NE2-4C 44
Lansdowne Pl. NE3-5E 27
Lansdowne Rd. NE12-1F 29
Lansdowne St. SR4-5F 99
Lansdowne Ter. NE3-4E 27
(in two parts)
Lansdowne Ter. NE29-4B 34
Lansdowne Ter. E. NE3-4E 27
Lansdowne Ter. W. NE29
-4A 34
Lanthwaite Rd. NE9-5F 79
Lanton St. DH4-4B 116
Lapwing Clo. NE38-4D 103
L'Arbre Cres. NE16-3E 75
Larch Av. DH4-4B 126
Larch Av. NE34-2F 69
Larch Av. SR6-1E 89
Larch Clo. NE9-3B 92
Larches Rd. DH1-1A 138
Larches, The. NE4-4F 59
Larch Rd. NE21-4B 56
Larch Ter. DH9-5E 131
Larchwood. NE38-1F 113
Larchwood Av. NE3-3B 26
Larchwood Av. NE6-4A 46
Larchwood Av. NE13-2D 15
Larchwood Gdns. NE11-5F 77
Larchwood Gro. SR2-5B 110
Larkfield Cres. DH4-5E 115
Larkfield Rd. SR2-5A 110
Larkhill. SR2-3D 121
Larkrise Clo. NE7-2F 45
Larkspur. NE9-5B 80
Larkspur Clo. DH9-1A 128
Larkspur Rd. NE16-3F 75
Larkspur Ter. NE2-3A 44
Larne Cres. NE9-4F 79
Larriston Pl. NE23-3A 4
Lartington Gdns. NE3-5A 28
Lascelles Av. NE34-2D 69
Laski Gdns. NE10-2F 81
Latimer St. NE30-2F 35
Latrigg Ct. SR3-4E 119
Lauderdale Av. NE28-5D 31
Launceston Clo. NE3-2E 25
Launceston Ct. SR3-3B 118
Launceston Dri. SR3-3B 118
Laura St. SR1-2C 110
Laurel Av. DH1-4A 140
Laurel Av. NE3-3B 26
Laurel Av. NE12-1B 30
Laurel Av. SR7-3C 132
Laurel Ct. DH2-1D 123
Laurel Ct. NE30-4D 35
Laurel Cres. DH4-2A 126
Laurel Cres. NE6-4A 46
Laurel End. NE12-1C 30
Laurel Gro. SR2-5B 110
Laurel Pl. NE12-1B 30
Laurel Rd. NE21-5C 56
Laurels, The. SR3-2E 119
(off Chelmsford St.)
Laurel St. NE15-2F 37
Laurel St. NE28-3D 47
Laurel Ter. NE25-2D 11
Laurel Wlk. NE3-4E 27
Laurelwood Gdns. NE11
-5A 78
Laurens Ct. NE37-5C 94
Lavender Gdns. NE2-3F 43
Lavender Gdns. NE9-4E 79
Lavender Gro. SR5-4F 97
Lavender Rd. NE16-3F 75
Lavender St. SR4-1E 107
Lavender Wlk. NE31-4C 64
Laverick. NE10-4E 81
Laverock Ct. NE6-2A 62
Laverock Pl. NE3-5F 25
(in two parts)
Lavers Rd. DH3-2A 102
Lavington Rd. NE34-4A 52
Lawe Rd. NE33-5E 35
Lawmill Way. NE5-2D 41
Lawn Cotts. SR3-4D 119
Lawn Dri. NE36-4E 85
Lawnhead Sq. SR3-5F 119
Lawns, The. SR3-4D 119
Lawnsway. NE32-1A 84
Lawnswood. DH5-1D 129
Lawn, The. NE40-1B 54
Lawrence Av. NE21-4B 56
Lawrence Av. NE34-4B 68
Lawrence Ct. NE10-2A 82
Lawrence Ct. NE21-4B 56
Lawrence St. DH3-3E 123
Lawrence St. SR1-1D 111
Lawson Av. NE32-4B 66
Lawson Ct. DH2-3E 123
Lawson Cres. SR6-1C 100
Lawson Ho. NE4-3D 59
Lawson St. NE28-3E 47
Lawson St. NE29-1C 50
Lawson St. W. NE29-1C 50
Lawson Ter. DH1-2B 138
Laws St. SR6-1C 100
Laxey St. DH9-3B 130
Laxford Ches-le-S DH3
-1C 112
Laxford Ct. SR3-5E 119
Laybourn Gdns. NE34-3E 67
(in three parts)
Layburn Gdns. NE15-5A 40
Layburn Pl. SR8-2A 134
Laycock Gdns. NE23-3D 9
Layfield Rd. NE3-1D 27
Laygate. NE33-3D 51
Laygate Pl. NE33-3D 51
Laygate St. NE33-3C 50
Lea Av. NE32-5A 66
Leabank. NE15-5E 39
Lead Rd. NE40-1A 72
Leafield Cres. NE34-5B 52
Lea Grn. DH3-1D 113
Leagreen Ct. NE3-4C 26
Lealholm Rd. NE7-4B 28
Leam Gdns. NE10-2A 82
Leamington St. SR4-2F 109
Leam La. NE9 & NE10
-1D 93 to 3C 82
Leam La. NE10 & NE32
-2C 82 to 3C 66
Leam La. NE32-2D 67
Leamside. NE10-4E 81
Leamside. NE32-3A 66
Leander Av. DH3-3B 112
Leander Dri. NE35-2C 84
Leaplish. NE38-1D 115
Leas, The. DH4-2C 126
Leasyde Wlk. NE16
-5D 75 to 4E 75
Leatham. SR2-2C 120
Lea View. NE34-4D 53
Leazes Ct. NE4-1F 59
Leazes Cres. NE1
-1B 60 & 3B 142
Leazes La. NE1
-1B 60 & 3B 142
Leazes Pk. Rd. NE1
-1B 60 & 3B 142
Leazes Parkway. NE15-3E 37
Leazes Pl. DH1-2D 139
Leazes Rise. SR8-4D 135
Leazes Rd. DH1-2D 139
Leazes Sq. NE1
-1B 60 & 3B 142
Leazes Ter. NE1
-1B 60 & 2B 142
Leazes, The. NE15-3E 37
Leazes, The. NE34-1D 69
Leazes, The. SR1-1A 110
Lecondale. NE10-5E 81
Lecondale Ct. NE10-5E 81
Ledbury Rd. SR2-5B 110
Leechmere Cres. SR7-1A 132
Leechmere Ind. Est. SR2
-1D 121
Leechmere Rd. SR2
-5A 110 to 5D 111
Leechmere View. SR2-3D 121
Leechmere Way. SR2
-3D 121 & 2E 121
Lee Clo. NE38-2F 105
Leeds St. SR6-2C 100
Leeholme. DH5-1E 129
Leeming Gdns. NE9-4A 80
Lees St. DH9-2C 130
Lee St. SR5-3A 100
Lee St. SR6-1C 100
Lee Ter. DH5-5F 129
Legion Gro. NE15-5B 40
Legion Rd. NE15-5B 40
Leicester Clo. NE28-4B 30
Leicestershire Dri. DH1
-3D 141
Leicester St. NE6-2C 62
Leicester Wlk. SR8-1A 134
Leicester Way. NE32-1F 83
Leighton Rd. SR2-5B 110
Leighton St. NE6-2F 61
Leighton St. NE33-3F 51
Leighton Ter. DH3-2A 102
Leisure Ct. NE34-2C 68
Leith Ct. NE34-2A 68
Lemington Gdns. NE5-5E 41
Lemington Rd. NE15-1F 55
Lemon St. NE33-1A 68
Lena Av. NE25-3F 21
Lenin Ter. DH9-4C 130
Lennox Pl. NE15-2F 57
Lenore Ter. NE40-5A 54
Leominster Rd. SR2-5C 110
Leopold St. NE32-1F 65
Leopold St. SR4-1F 109
Lesbury Av. NE27-4A 20
Lesbury Av. NE28-1B 48
Lesbury Chase. NE3-3C 26
Lesbury Clo. DH2-4B 122
Lesbury Gdns. NE13-1D 15
Lesbury Rd. NE6-4D 45
Lesbury St. NE15-1B 56
Lesbury St. NE28-3E 49
Leslie Av. NE31-2D 65
Leslie Cres. NE3-1E 43
Leslie Ter. NE1
-3B 60 & 5C 142
Letch Path. NE15-5D 39
Letch Way. NE15-1B 56
Letchwell Vs. NE12-1F 29
Leuchars Ct. DH3-4B 102
Leven Av. DH2-4C 122
Leven Ho. SR3-4E 119
Levens Wlk. NE23-3A 4
Leven Wlk. SR8-5A 134
Levisham Clo. SR3-3A 120
Lewis Dri. NE4-1D 59
Lewis Gdns. NE34-4B 68
Leybourne Av. NE12-5F 17
Leybourne Dene. NE12-5F 17
Leybourne Hold. DH3-1A 102
Leyburn Clo. DH4-4B 126
Leyburn Dri. NE7-1C 44
Leyburn Gro. DH4-4B 126
Leyburn Pl. DH3-1A 102
Leyton Pl. NE8-2F 79
Liberty Way. SR6-4D 101
Lichfield Av. NE6-3D 63
Lichfield Clo. DH3-5B 124
Lichfield Clo. NE3-2F 25
Lichfield Rd. DH1-1D 137
Lichfield Rd. SR5-2F 99
Lichfield Way. NE32-1F 83
(in two parts)
Liddells Fell Rd. NE21-1A 72
Liddell St. NE30-5D 35
Liddell St. SR6-4C 100
Liddell Ter. NE8-1C 78
Liddle Av. DH6-4F 141
Liddle Ct. NE4-2F 59
Liddle Rd. NE4-2F 59
Lieven St. NE13-2B 14
Liffey Rd. NE31-4D 65
Lightbourne Rd. NE6-1F 63
Lightwood Av. NE15-3F 57
Lilac Av. DH1-4B 136
Lilac Av. DH5-5D 127
Lilac Av. NE12-2A 30
Lilac Av. NE34-2E 69
Lilac Av. SR3-2A 120
Lilac Av. SR6-4D 71
Lilac Clo. NE5-1D 39
Lilac Gdns. NE9-4E 79
Lilac Gdns. NE16-3F 75
Lilac Gdns. NE38-1A 114
Lilac Gdns. SR6-5F 69
Lilac Gro. DH2-1C 122
Lilac Gro. SR6-2C 100
Lilac Rd. NE6-3C 46
Lilac Sq. DH4-2C 124
Lilac St. SR4-1E 107
Lilac Wlk. NE31-4C 64
(in two parts)
Lilburn Clo. DH2-5B 122
Lilburn Clo. NE6-3B 62
Lilburn Clo. NE36-2A 86
Lilburne Clo. SR1-1D 111
Lilburn Gdns. NE3-5B 28
Lilburn Pl. SR5-3F 99
Lilburn Rd. NE27-5A 20
Lilburn St. NE29-4A 34
Lilian Av. NE28-3B 46
Lilian Av. SR2-3D 121
Lilley Gro. SR5-4F 97
Lily Av. NE2-3A 44
Lily Bank. NE28-2D 47
Lily Clo. NE21-5F 55
Lily Cres. NE2-3A 44
Lily Cres. SR6-4E 71
Lily St. SR4-5A 100
Lily Ter. DH4-1C 126
Lily Ter. NE5-2B 40
Lime Av. DH4-4B 126
Lime Cotts. DH2-5A 122
Limecragg Av. DH1-3B 140
Limecroft. NE32-1A 84
Lime Gro. NE40-2A 54
Limekiln Rd. NE28-3F 47
Limes St. NE21-1B 74
Limes, The. DH4-2A 116
Limes, The. SR6-2D 89
(off Front St.)
Lime St. DH2-5A 122
Lime St. DH9-5A 130
Lime St. NE1-2F 61
Lime St. NE15-2F 37
Lime St. SR4-1F 109
Limetrees Gdns. NE9-3E 79
Limewood Ct. NE4-5D 43
Limewood Gro. NE13-2D 15
Linacre Clo. NE3-4D 25
Linacre Ct. SR8-4A 134
Linbridge Dri. NE5-3F 39
Linburn. NE38-2F 113
Lincoln Av. NE28-2C 46
Lincoln Av. SR3-2E 119
Lincoln Ct. NE31-2B 64
Lincoln Cres. DH5-3E 129
Lincoln Grn. NE3-1D 27
Lincoln Rd. DH1-2D 137
Lincoln Rd. NE34-5C 52
Lincolnshire Clo. DH1-3C 140
Lincoln St. NE8-1D 79
Lincoln St. SR4-1D 109
Lincoln Wlk. DH3-5A 124
Lincoln Wlk. SR8-1B 134
Lincoln Way. NE32-1F 83
(in two parts)
Lindale Av. NE16-5F 75
Lindale Rd. NE4-4A 42
Lindean Pl. NE23-3A 4
Linden. NE9-1B 92
Linden Av. NE3-5D 27
Linden Av. NE4-5F 41
Linden Gdns. SR2-5B 110
Linden Gro. DH4-5B 126
Linden Gro. NE11-2E 77
Linden Rd. NE3-5D 27
Linden Rd. NE12-3F 29
Linden Rd. NE21-5B 56
Linden Rd. NE25-1A 10
Linden Ter. NE9-3E 93
Linden Ter. NE12-3F 29
Linden Ter. NE26-2C 22
Linden Way. NE9-3B 92
Lindfield Av. NE5-3D 41
Lindisfarne. NE38-3B 104
Lindisfarne. SR2-4C 120
Lindisfarne. SR8-5B 134
Lindisfarne Av. DH3-3E 123
Lindisfarne Clo. DH2-5C 122
Lindisfarne Clo. DH4-3A 126
Lindisfarne Clo. NE2-2B 44
Lindisfarne Clo. NE5-4A 40
Lindisfarne Ct. NE34-1D 67
Lindisfarne Dri. NE8
-5E 61 to 4E 61
Lindisfarne Pl. NE28-2F 47
Lindisfarne Recess. NE32
-3B 66
Lindisfarne Rd. DH1-4D 137
Lindisfarne Rd. NE2-2A 44
Lindisfarne Rd. NE31-4C 64
Lindisfarne Rd. NE32-3C 66
Lindisfarne Ter. NE30-3C 34
Lindom Av. DH3-3F 123
Lindon Mnr. NE12-3E 17
Lindon Rd. DH9-3C 130
Lindrick Ct. NE10-3A 82
Lindsay Clo. SR2-2D 111
Lindsay Ct. SR6-5D 71
Lindsay Rd. SR2-2D 111
Lindsay St. DH5-2F 129
Lindsey Clo. NE23-3A 4
Lindum Rd. NE9-2E 79
Linfield. SR2-3D 121
Lingcrest. NE9-5A 80
Lingdale. DH1-3D 141
Lingdale Av. SR6-3D 89
Lingey Gdns. NE10-2A 82
Lingey La. NE10-3A 82
Lingholme. DH2-2B 122
Lingmell. NE37-1A 104
Lingshaw. NE10-3F 81
Lingside. NE32-5A 66
(in two parts)
Linhope Av. NE3-3B 26
Linhope Rd. NE5-3B 40
Link Rd. NE5-3A 42
Link Rd. NE13-3C 14
Links Av. NE26-5D 13
Links Av. NE30-5D 23
Links Ct. NE26-5E 13
Links Grn. NE3-3E 27
Links Grn. Wlk. NE3-3E 27
Links Rd. NE30-4D 23
Links, The. DH3-3D 141
Links, The. NE26-4E 13
Links Wlk. NE5-3B 40
Linkway. NE32-1B 84
Linley Hill. NE16-5D 75
Linnel Dri. NE15-5F 39
Linnet Clo. NE38-5E 103
Linnet Gro. SR5-3A 98
Linney Gdns. NE34-3E 67
Linskell. SR2-2C 120
Linskill Pl. NE3-1A 42
Linskill Pl. NE30-3D 35
Linskill St. NE30-4D 35
Linskill Ter. NE30-3C 34
Linslade Wlk. NE23-4A 4
Lintfort. DH3-3C 112
Linthorpe Ct. NE34-2F 67
Linthorpe Rd. NE3-3E 27
Linthorpe Rd. NE30-1C 34
Linton Rd. NE9-2D 91
Linton Rd. NE26-3D 13
Lintzford Gdns. NE15-1D 57
Lintz Ter. DH9-3A 130
Linum Pl. NE4-4F 41
Linwood Pl. NE3-5E 15
Lion Wlk. NE29-1B 50
Lipman Building. NE1-1D 143
Lisa Av. SR4-2F 107
Lisburn Ter. SR4-5E 99
Lish Av. NE26-3D 23
Lisle Ct. NE28-3D 47
Lisle Gro. NE28-1B 48
Lisle Rd. NE34-5B 52
Lisle St. NE1-1C 60 & 3D 143
Lisle St. NE28-3C 46
Lismore Av. NE33-5E 51
Lismore Pl. NE15-2B 58
Lismore Ter. NE9-3E 93
Lister Av. NE11-1E 77
Lister Clo. DH5-1C 128
Listers La. NE9-2F 79
Lister St. NE15-3E 57
Litchfield Cres. NE21-1A 74
Litchfield La. NE21-1A 74
Litchfield St. NE21-1A 74
Litchfield Ter. NE21-1A 74
Lit. Bedford St. NE29-4C 34
Littleburn Clo. DH4-3B 126
Lit. Dene. NE2-1E 43
Littledene. NE9-3D 79
Lit. Eden. SR8-3C 134
Lit. Villiers St. SR1-1C 110
Little Way. NE15-3F 57
Litton Ct. SR3-5E 119
Littondale. NE28-5B 30
Liverpool St. NE1
-1B 60 & 3C 142
Livingstone Pl. NE33-1E 51
Livingstone Rd. SR1-1A 110
Livingstone St. NE33-1E 51
Livingstone View. NE30
-2D 35
Lizard La. NE34 & SR6-1B 70
Lizard La. SR6-4D 71
Lizard View. SR6-4D 71
Lloyd Av. DH5-4B 128
Lloyd Ct. NE11-5D 59
Lobban Av. NE31-4C 64
Lobelia Av. NE10-5A 62
Lobelia Clo. NE5-1D 39
Lobley Gdns. NE11-4E 77
Lobley Hill Rd. NE11 & NE8
-4F 77 to 2B 78
Lochmaben Ter. SR5-3B 100
Lochraig Pl. NE23-3A 4
Lockerbie Gdns. NE15-1D 57
Lockerbie Rd. NE23-3A 4
Lockhaugh Rd. NE39-5F 73
Locksley Clo. NE29-1C 32
Locomotion Way. NE12
-2D 17
Locomotion Way. NE29
-1B 60
Lodges Rd., The. NE9-2D 91
Lodge Ter. NE28-3F 47
Lodore Ct. SR3-4E 119
Lodore Gro. NE32-4C 66
Lodore Rd. NE2-1F 43
Loefield. DH3-4A 124
Lofthill. SR3-5D 119
Logan Rd. NE6-3B 46
Logan St. DH5-5F 129
Lola St. NE13-2B 14
Lombard Dri. DH3-3B 112
Lombard St. NE1
-3D 61 & 5E 143
Lombard St. SR1-1D 111
Lomond Clo. NE38-4A 104
Lomond Ct. SR3-5E 119
Lomond Pl. DH2-5C 122
London Av. NE37-4F 93
Londonderry Av. DH1-5A 140
Londonderry St. SR3-3F 119
Londonderry St. SR7-5F 133
Londonderry Ter. SR3-3F 119
Londonderry Way. DH4
-3F 115
Londsale Rd. SR6-3C 100
Longacre. DH4-5A 126
Longacre. NE38-1C 114
Long Acres. DH1-1F 139
Long Bank. DH3-1A 102
Long Bank. NE9
-1A 102 & 5A 92
Longbenton Ind. Est. NE12
-3B 30
Longborough Ct. NE3-5B 28
Longdean Clo. NE31-2B 64
Longdean Pk. DH3-4B 112
Longfellow St. DH5-1D 129
Longfield Clo. NE34-3B 68
Longfield Rd. SR6-2B 100
Longfield Ter. NE6-3E 63
Long Gair. NE21-2F 73
Long Garth. DH1-5A 136
Long Headlam. NE6-1A 62
Longhirst. NE5-3B 40
Longhirst. NE10-3E 81
Longhirst Dri. NE13-2D 15
Longleat Gdns. NE33-1F 51
Longley St. NE4-2F 59
Longmeadows. SR3-4A 118
Longnewton St. SR7-5F 133
Longniddry. NE37-2B 94
Longniddry Ct. NE9-2D 91
Longridge. NE21-5F 55
Longridge Av. NE7-2E 45
Longridge Av. NE38-5F 103
Longridge Dri. NE26-5D 13
Longridge Rd. NE40 & NE21
-5B 54
Longridge Sq. SR2-5B 110
Longridge Way. NE23-3A 4
Longrigg. NE10-3E 81
Long Rigg. NE16-1F 75
Longshank La. DH3-1A 102
Longstaff Gdns. NE34-3E 67
Long Stairs. NE1
-3C 60 & 5D 143
Longston Av. NE30-4D 23
Longstone Ct. NE12-3F 17
Longstone Sq. NE5-3F 39
Lonnen Av. NE4-5E 41
Lonnen Dri. NE16-2F 75
Lonnen, The. NE34-3F 69
Lonnen, The. NE40-3D 55
Lonsdale. DH3-1C 112
Lonsdale Av. SR6-3D 89
Lonsdale Ct. NE2-3F 43
Lonsdale Ct. NE34-3F 67
Lonsdale Gdns. NE28-5C 32
Lonsdale Ter. NE2-2F 43
Loraine Ter. NE15-1B 56
Lord Byrons Wlk. SR7
-1A 132
Lordenshaw. NE5-3A 40
Lord Gort Clo. SR5-3F 99
Lord Nelson St. NE33-1F 67
Lord St. NE1-3A 60 & 5A 142
Lord St. NE33-3F 51
Lord St. SR3-3F 119
Lord St. SR7-3F 133
Lorimers Clo. SR8-5A 134
Lorne Ter. SR2-2B 110
Lorrain Rd. NE34-5B 68
Lort Ho. NE2-1D 61 & 2E 143
Lorton Av. NE30-5B 22
Lorton Rd. NE9-1F 91
Losh Ter. NE6-2D 63
Lossiemouth Rd. NE29-4D 33
Lothian Clo. DH3-1C 112
Lothian Ct. NE5-1D 41
Lotus Clo. NE5-1D 39
Lotus Pl. NE4-5F 41
Loudon St. NE34-2A 68
Loughborough Av. NE30
-1E 35
Loughborough Av. SR2
-4B 110
Lough Ct. NE9-5A 80
Loughrigg Av. NE23-3A 4
Louie Ter. NE9-5E 79
Louisa Ter. DH9-3B 130
Louis Av. SR6-2C 100
Louise Ter. DH3-2E 123
Loup St. NE21-4B 56
Loup Ter. NE21-4B 56
Louvain Ter. DH5-3E 129
Louvain Ter. W. DH5-3E 129
Lovaine Av. NE25-3B 22
Lovaine Av. NE29-4B 34
Lovaine Flats. NE1-2E 143
Lovaine Hall. NE1-2E 143
Lovaine Pl. NE29-4B 34
Lovaine Pl. W. NE29-5B 34
Lovaine Row. NE30-2F 35
Lovaine St. NE15-5A 38
Lovaine Ter. NE29-4B 34
Love Av. NE23-4F 7
Love Av. Cotts. NE23-4F 7
Lovelady Ct. NE30-2F 35
(off St Oswin's Pl.)
Love La. NE1-3D 61 & 5E 143
Love La. NE21-1F 73
Loveless Gdns. NE10-2F 81
Lovett Wlk. NE8-5B 60
Lowbiggin. NE5-4A 24
Low Bri. NE1-3C 60 & 4D 143
Low Carrs Caravan Pk. DH1
-2C 136
Low Chare. DH3-2E 123
Lowden Ct. NE2
-5D 43 & 1A 142
Lowdham Av. NE29-5F 33
Low Downs Rd. DH5-2F 129
Low Downs Sq. DH5-2F 129
Lwr. Crone St. NE27-3B 20
(off Up. Crone St.)
Lwr. Dundas St. SR6-4C 100
Lwr. Main Pl. NE23-3C 4
Lwr. Rudyerd St. NE29-5C 34
Lowerson Av. DH4-5F 115
Lowe's Barn Bank. DH1
-4A 138
Loweswater Av. DH2-5D 123
Loweswater Rd. NE5-4D 41
Loweswater Rd. NE9-5F 79
Loweswood Clo. NE7-3C 44
Lowfield Ter. NE6-3E 63
Lowfield Wlk. NE16-3F 75
Low Flatts Rd. DH3-4B 112
Low Fold. NE6-2F 61
Low Friar La. NE1
-2B 60 & 4B 142
Low Friar St. NE1
-2B 60 & 4B 142
Lowgate. NE15-3F 37
Low Gosforth Ct. NE3-1E 27
Low Grn. DH1-5F 139
Low Heworth La. NE10-5D 63
Lowhills Rd. SR8-1A 134
Lowick Clo. DH3-1C 112
Lowick Ct. NE3-1A 44
Lowland Clo. SR3-5F 119
Low Leam Ct. NE5-3A 40
Low Meadow. SR6-1F 87
Lownds Ter. NE6-1D 63
Lowrey's La. NE9-5E 79
Low Rd. DH1-5F 139
Low Row. NE40-4D 55
Low Row. SR1-1B 110
Lowry Gdns. NE34-5C 68
Lowry Rd. SR6-5D 89
Low St. SR1-5C 100
Lowther Av. DH2-4C 122
Lowther Clo. SR8-3C 134
Lowther Sq. NE23-4A 4
Lowthian Cres. NE6-2D 63
Lowthian Ter. NE38-3D 105
Low Well Gdns. NE10-1D 81
Lucas St. SR3-3F 119
Lucknow St. SR1-5D 101
Lucock St. NE34-2A 68
Lucy St. DH3-2E 123
Lucy St. NE21-4B 56
Ludlow Av. NE29-2A 34
Ludlow Ct. NE3-2F 25
Ludlow Dri. NE25-2D 21
Ludlow Rd. SR2-5B 110
Luffness Dri. NE34-4D 69
Luke Ct. SR8-5C 134
Luke's La. NE31-5D 65
Lulsgate. SR5-4E 97
Lulworth Av. NE32-2C 66
Lulworth Ct. SR3-3B 118
Lulworth Gdns. SR2-5B 110
Lumley Av. NE16-1A 76
Lumley Av. NE34-1F 69
Lumley Clo. DH2-3D 123
Lumley Clo. NE38-3F 103
Lumley Ct. SR3-3B 118
Lumley Cres. DH4-1B 126
Lumley Dri. SR8-5B 134
Lumley Gdns. NE8-1A 80
Lumley New Rd. DH3 & DH4
-4A 124
Lumley Rd. DH1-2C 136
Lumley St. DH4-3B 126
Lumley St. SR4-2F 109
Lumley Ter. DH3-3E 123
Lumley Ter. NE32-4A 66
Lumley Ter. SR2-4D 121
Lumley Tower. SR1-5D 101
Lumley Wlk. NE11-1E 77
Lund Av. DH1-3B 136
Lunedale Av. SR6-4A 88
Lune Grn. NE32-5B 66
Lunesdale St. DH5-5E 129
Lupin Clo. NE5-1D 39
Luss Av. NE32-4C 66
Luton Cres. NE29-1F 49
Lutterworth Clo. NE12-4C 28
Lutterworth Dri. NE12-4C 28
(in two parts)
Lutterworth Pl. NE12-4C 28
Lutterworth Rd. SR2-4A 110
Luxembourg Rd. SR4-5B 98
Lyall Ho. NE23-3E 9
Lychgate Ct. NE8-4E 61
Lydcott. NE38-3F 105
Lyden Ga. NE9-2E 91
Lydford Ct. NE3-4D 25
Lydford Way. DH3-5C 102
Lydney Clo. NE15-3E 37
Lyncroft Rd. NE29-4A 34
Lynden Gdns. NE5-2B 40
Lyndford Ct. DH4-2B 126
Lyndhurst Av. DH3-4B 112
Lyndhurst Av. NE2-2F 43
Lyndhurst Av. NE9-1E 91
Lyndhurst Clo. NE21-2F 73
Lyndhurst Cres. NE9-1E 91
Lyndhurst Dri. DH1-2A 138
Lyndhurst Dri. NE9-1E 91
Lyndhurst Gdns. NE2-2F 43
Lyndhurst Grn. NE9-1E 91
Lyndhurst Gro. NE9-1E 91
Lyndhurst Rd. DH9-3A 130
Lyndhurst Rd. NE12-3F 29
Lyndhurst Rd. NE25-2A 22
Lyndhurst St. NE33-2F 51
Lyndhurst Ter. NE16-1F 75
Lyndhurst Ter. SR4-5D 99
Lyndon Clo. NE36-3A 86
Lyndon Dri. NE36-3A 86
Lyndon Gro. NE36-3A 86
Lynfield. NE26-4D 13
Lynfield Ct. NE5-2D 41
Lynfield Pl. NE5-2D 41
Lynford Gdns. SR2-5B 110
Lyngrove. SR2-2D 121
Lynholm Gro. NE12-2F 29
Lynmouth Pl. NE7-2D 45
Lynmouth Rd. NE9-2E 91
Lynmouth Rd. NE29-4E 33
Lynnholme Gdns. NE9-2E 79
(in two parts)
Lynn Rd. NE28-3C 46
Lynn Rd. NE29-2E 33
Lynn St. DH3-3E 123
Lynnwood Av. NE4-2E 59
Lynnwood Ter. NE4-2E 59
Lynthorpe. SR2-2D 121
Lynthorpe Gro. SR6-1C 100
Lynton Av. NE32-3C 66
Lynton Ct. DH4-2B 126
Lynton Ct. NE5-2D 41
Lynton Pl. NE5-2D 41
Lynton Way. NE5-2D 41
Lynwood Av. NE21-4B 56
Lynwood Av. SR4-5E 107
Lyon St. NE31-1B 64
Lyric Pl. NE29-2D 33
Lyster Clo. SR7-1A 132
Lytchfeld. NE10-3F 81
(in two parts)
Lytham Clo. NE23-3A 4
Lytham Clo. NE28-3F 31
Lytham Clo. NE37-3B 94
Lytham Grn. NE10-5A 64
Lytham Pl. NE6-2D 63
Lythe Way. NE12-4D 29

Mabel St. NE21-4B 56
Macadam St. NE8-2C 78
McAnany Av. NE34-2B 68
McClaren Way. DH4-3D 117
McCracken Dri. NE13-5A 6
McCutcheon Ct. NE6-4C 62
McCutcheon St. SR7-1A 132
Macdonald Rd. NE4-3B 58
McErlane Sq. NE10-1F 81
McEwan Gdns. NE4-2E 59
McGuinness Av. SR8-1D 135
(in two parts)
McIntyre Hall. NE31-5A 48
McKendrick Vs. NE5-3F 41
McLennan Ct. NE38-2B 104
McIlvenna Gdns. NE28-5C 30
Maclynn Clo. SR3-4C 118
MacMillian Gdns. NE10-2F 81
McNally Pl. DH1-1F 139
McNamara Rd. NE28-1A 48
Maddison Ct. SR1-5D 101
Maddison Gdns. NE23-3D 9
Maddox Rd. NE12-3E 29
Maderia Av. NE26-5D 13
Maderia Clo. NE5-1D 39
Maderia Ter. NE33-3F 51
Madras St. NE34-3F 67
Mafeking Pl. NE29-1D 33
Mafeking St. NE6-4D 63
Mafeking St. NE9-2F 79
Mafeking St. SR4-1D 109
Magdalene Av. DH1-2D 141
Magdalene Ct. DH1-1E 139
Magdalene Ct. NE2
-5D 43 & 1A 142
Magdalene Heights. DH1
-1E 139
Magdalene St. DH1-2F 139
Magdelene Pl. SR4-1E 109
Magenta Cres. NE5-1E 39
Maglona St. SR7-4E 33
Maiden Law. DH4-5F 125
Maiden St. NE4-4A 60
Maidstone Clo. SR3-5C 118
Maidstone Ter. DH4-1B 126
Main Cres. NE28-1B 46
Main Rd. NE13-3D 25
Main Rd. NE40-2A 54
Mains Ct. DH1-4A 136
Mainsforth Ter. SR2-3D 111
Mainsforth Ter. W. SR2
-3D 111
Mains Pk. Rd. DH3-3E 123
Mainstone Clo. NE23-4B 4
Main St. NE23-3D 9
Makendon St. NE31-5F 47
Makepeace Ter. NE9-3E 93
Malaburn Way. SR5-3F 99
Malaga Clo. NE5-1D 39
Malaya Dri. NE6-3F 63
Malcolm St. NE6-1F 61
Malcom Ct. NE25-3E 21
Malcom St. SR7-4E 133
Malden Clo. NE23-3B 4
Maling Pk. SR4-1F 107
Malings Clo. SR1-1D 111
Maling St. NE6-2F 61
Mallard Clo. NE38-4D 103
Mallard Way. NE28-4C 32
Mallowburn Cres. NE3-5E 25
Malmo Clo. NE29-5D 33
Malone Gdns. DH3-1B 102
Malory Pl. NE8-5E 61
Maltby Clo. NE38-3C 104
Maltby Clo. SR3-5C 118
Malt Cres. SR8-2E 135
Malthouse Way. NE5-5D 25
Malton Clo. NE15-1D 57
Malton Ct. NE32-5C 48
Malton Cres. NE29-5A 34
Malton Gdns. NE28-1C 46
Malton Grn. NE9-3A 92
Malvern Av. DH2-4C 122
Malvern Clo. SR8-4A 134
Malvern Ct. NE15-5D 39
Malvern Ct. SR6-1E 87
Malvern Cres. SR7-3B 132
Malvern Gdns. NE11-4F 77
Malvern Gdns. SR6-2C 100
Malvern Rd. NE28-1B 48
Malvern Rd. NE29-1F 33
Malvern Rd. NE38-4A 104
Malvern St. NE4-3F 59
Malvern St. NE33-5D 51
Malvern Ter. DH9-4D 131
Malvern Vs. DH1-4A 140
Malver Ter. DH9-4D 131
Mandale Cres. NE30-4C 22
Mandela Clo. SR1-1D 111
Mandela Ct. DH9-3A 130
Mandela Way. NE11-4B 58
Mandeville. NE37-5D 95
Manet Gdns. NE34-4B 68
Mangrove Clo. NE5-1D 39
Manila St. SR2-4C 110
Manisty Ho. NE4-3D 59
Manners Gdns. NE25-1B 10
Manningford Clo. NE23-4B 4
Manningford Dri. SR3-5C 118
Manor Av. NE7-5D 29
Manor Av. NE15-4B 38
Manor Chare. NE1
-2D 61 & 4E 143

Manor Clo. NE3-5F 27
Manor Ct. NE33-4A 52
Manor Dri. NE7-4E 29
Manor Gdns. NE7-5D 29
Manor Gdns. NE10-2A 82
Manor Gro. DH4-3E 117
Manor Gro. NE7-5D 29
Manor Gro. NE15-5B 38
Manor Hall Clo. SR7-2A 132
Manor Ho. Clo. NE6-2B 62
Manor Ho. Farm Cotts. NE3 -1F 41
Manor Ho. Rd. NE2-4B 44
Manor Pk. NE37-5C 94
Manor Pl. NE7-4D 29
Manor Pl. SR1-1C 110
Manor Rd. DH9-1C 130
Manor Rd. NE7-5D 29
Manor Rd. NE30-2E 35
Manor Rd. NE37-4C 94
Manor Ter. NE21-3B 74
Manor View. NE37-5C 94
Manor View. E. NE37-5C 94
Manor Wlk. NE7-4D 29
Manorway. NE30-2E 35
Manorway. NE32-5B 66
Manor Way. SR8-4D 135
Mansell Cres. SR8-3D 135
Mansell Pl. NE3-1A 42
Mansfield Ct. NE36-3F 85
Mansfield Cres. SR6-2C 100
Mansfield Pl. NE4 -2A 60 & 3A 142
Mansfield St. NE4 -2A 60 & 4A 142
Mansion Ho. NE36-3E 85
Manston Clo. SR3-5B 118
Manx Sq. SR5-2F 99
Maple Av. DH1-4A 140
Maple Av. NE11-3E 77
Maple Av. NE25-3A 22
Maple Av. SR3-3A 120
Maplebeck Clo. SR3-5C 118
Maple Clo. NE15-1D 57
Maple Cres. SR7-5D 133
Mapledene Rd. NE3-3B 26
Maple Gro. DH9-5A 130
Maple Gro. NE8-3C 78
Maple Gro. NE10-2C 80
Maple Gro. NE34-3E 69
Maple Gro. SR6-1D 89
Maple Rd. NE21-5B 56
Maple Row. NE11-5A 58
Maple St. DH9-5B 130
Maple St. NE4-3A 60
Maple St. NE32-1E 65
Maple Ter. DH4-5F 115
Maple Ter. NE4-3A 60
Maplewood. DH2-1C 122
Maplewood Av. SR5-2D 99
Maplewood Cres. NE38 -1A 114
Maplewood St. DH4-4D 125
Mapperley Dri. NE15-5A 40
Marbury Clo. SR3-4C 118
March Rd. NE23-4F 7
Marcia Av. SR6-2C 100
Marcross Clo. NE5-2C 38
Marcross Dri. SR3-5C 118
Mardale. NE37-1A 104
Mardale Gdns. NE9-2F 91
Mardale Rd. NE5-4D 41
Mardale St. DH5-5E 129
Marden Av. NE30-4D 23
Marden Cres. NE26-3D 23
Marden Farm Dri. NE30 -4C 22
Marden Rd. NE26-2C 22 (in two parts)
Marden Rd. S. NE25-3C 22
Marden Ter. NE30-4D 23
Mareburn Cres. NE10-2D 81
Mare Clo. NE23-1F 9
Maree Clo. SR3-5C 118
Margaret Alice St. SR4-5D 99
Margaret Cotts. NE25-4A 22
Margaret Dri. NE12-1B 30
Margaret Gro. NE34-2E 67
Margaret Rd. NE26-3D 23
Margaret St. SR2-5E 111
Margaret St. SR7-4E 133
Margaret Ter. DH4-4B 116
Margate St. SR3-2E 119
Margery La. DH1-3B 138
Marguerite Ct. SR4-1A 110
Marian Ct. NE8-1B 78
Marian Dri. NE10-5A 64
Marian Way. NE34-4D 69
Maria St. NE4-3D 59
Maria St. SR3-3F 119
Maria St. SR7-3F 133
Marie Curie Dri. NE4-3E 59
Marigold Av. NE10-5A 62
Marigold Ct. SR4-5F 99
Marigold Cres. DH4-2C 124
Marina Av. SR6-1B 100
Marina Ct. SR6-1B 100
Marina Dri. NE25-3D 21
Marina Dri. NE33-2F 51
Marina Gro. SR6-1B 100
Marina Ter. SR2-4E 121
Marina Ter. SR6-1E 89
Marina View. NE28-3B 48
Marina View. NE31-1B 64
Marine App. NE33-2F 51
Marine Av. NE26-2A 22
Marine Ct. E. NE26-1B 22 (off Marine Av.)
Marine Ct. W. NE26-1B 22 (off Marine Av.)
Marine Dri. NE31-4E 65
Marine Dri. SR2-2E 121
Marine Gdns. NE26-1B 22
Mariners' Cotts. NE33-2F 51
Mariners' La. NE30-2E 35
Mariners Point. NE30-3F 35
Mariner Sq. SR1-5E 101
Marine Wlk. SR6-2E 101
Marion St. SR2-3D 111
Maritime St. SR1-1B 110
Maritime Ter. SR1-1B 110
Marius Av. NE15-2A 36
Mariville E. SR2-5E 121
Mariville W. SR2-5E 121
Markby Clo. SR3-5C 118
Market Cres. DH4-4B 116
Market Hall. DH9-2C 130
Market La. NE1 -2C 60 & 4D 143
Market La. NE16 & NE11 -1F 75
Market Pl. DH1-2C 138 (off Silver St.)
Market Pl. DH3-2E 123
Market Pl. DH5-4D 127
Market Pl. NE33-2D 51
Market Sq. NE32-5D 49
Market Sq. SR1-1B 110
Market St. DH5-3F 129
Market St. NE1 -2C 60 & 4C 142
Market St. NE23-4E 7
Market Way. NE11-3B 78
Markham Av. SR6-2E 89
Markham St. SR2-5D 111
Markle Gro. DH5-3B 128
Mark Rise. DH5-2E 129
Marlborough. SR7-3E 133
Marlborough App. NE3-3D 27
Marlborough Av. NE3-3D 27
Marlborough Av. NE16-2A 76
Marlborough Ct. DH5-2C 128
Marlborough Ct. NE3-3F 25
Marlborough Ct. NE32-2F 65
Marlborough Cres. NE1 -3B 60 & 5B 142
Marlborough Cres. NE9 -2B 92
Marlborough Cres. SR8 -3F 135
Marlborough Rd. NE37-4D 95
Marlborough Rd. SR4-5E 107
Marlborough St. N. NE33 -4E 51
Marlborough St. S. NE33 -4F 51
Marleen Av. NE6-4E 45
Marleen Ct. NE6-4E 45
Marlesford Clo. SR3-4C 118
Marley Cres. SR5-2D 99
Marlfield Ct. NE5-1D 41
Marlow Dri. SR3-5C 118
Marlowe Gdns. NE8-1E 79
Marlowe Pl. DH5-1D 129
Marlowe Wlk. NE34-4E 67
Marlow Pl. NE12-3E 29
Marlow Way. NE16-5E 75
Marmion Rd. NE6-4B 46
Marmion Ter. NE25-2B 22
Marne St. DH4-4A 116
Marondale Av. NE6-1E 63
Marquis Av. NE5-1E 39
Marquis Clo. NE12-4F 29
Marquisway. NE11-2B 90
Marr Rd. NE31-2E 65
Marsden Av. SR6-5D 71
Marsden Clo. DH4-5B 126
Marsden Gro. NE9-2B 92
Marsden Gro. SR8-1D 89
Marsden La. NE5-1C 40
Marsden La. NE34-5D 53
Marsden Rd. NE34-1D 69
Marsden Rd. SR6-2E 87
Marsden View. SR6-4D 71
Marshall's Ct. NE1 -2B 60 & 4C 142
Marshall St. SR6-1C 100
Marshall Ter. DH1-3B 140
Marshall Wallis Rd. NE33 -4D 51
Marsham Clo. NE15-1D 57
Marsham Clo. SR6-5F 69
Marsham Rd. NE5-2F 39
Marshmont Av. NE30-1D 35
Marske Ter. NE6-1D 63
Marston. NE12-2E 17
Marston Wlk. NE16-4E 75
Martello Gdns. NE7-2E 45
Martin Ct. NE38-5E 103
Martindale Av. SR6-5B 88
Martindale Pl. NE25-1C 10
Martin Hall. NE32-1A 66
Martin Rd. NE28-2B 48
Martin Ter. SR4-1D 109
Martin Way. NE13-1C 14
Marwood Ct. NE25-1E 21
Marx Cres. DH9-4C 130 (in two parts)
Mary Agnes St. NE3-4C 26
Mary Av. DH3-2A 102
Maryhill Clo. NE4-3C 58
Maryside Pl. NE40-5A 36
Mary's Pl. NE6-1F 63
Mary St. DH9-3C 130
Mary St. NE21-5F 55 (Blaydon Burn)
Mary St. NE21-4B 56 (Blaydon in two parts)
Mary St. SR1-2B 110
Mary St. SR3-2F 119
Mary St. SR7-3F 133
Mary Ter. NE5-2B 40
Masefield Av. NE16-1F 75
Masefield Clo. DH9-2E 131
Masefield Dri. NE34-5E 67
Masefield Pl. NE8-5E 61
Masefields. DH2-2A 122
Mason Av. NE26-2C 22
Mason Cres. SR8-3E 135
Mason Rd. NE28-5C 30
Mason St. NE6-1A 62
Mason St. NE13-1B 14
Mason View. NE13-4A 6
Massingham Way. NE34 -2A 68
Master Mariners' Homes. NE30-3E 35
Mast La. NE30-4D 23
Matambia Ter. SR4-1F 109
Matanzas St. SR2-4D 111
Matfen Av. NE13-3C 14
Matfen Av. NE27-4B 20
Matfen Clo. NE15-1D 57
Matfen Dri. SR3-4C 118
Matfen Gdns. NE28-5B 32
Matfen Ho. DH2-3B 122
Matfen Pl. NE3-4B 26
Matfen Pl. NE4-5A 42
Mather Rd. NE4-3A 60
Matlock Gdns. NE5-1B 40
Matlock Rd. NE32-2A 66
Matlock St. SR1-5B 100
Matterdale Rd. SR8-3D 135
Matthew Bank. NE2-1A 44
Matthew St. NE6-1A 62
Maude Gdns. NE28-4D 47
Maudlin Pl. NE5-3E 41
Maudlin St. DH5-2F 129
Mauds La. SR1-1C 110
Maud St. NE15-1B 56
Maud St. SR6-1C 100
Maud Ter. NE27-5F 19
Maureen Ter. SR7-3E 133
Maurice Rd. NE28-4C 46
Maurice Rd. Ind. Est. NE28 -5C 46
Mautland Sq. DH4-4C 126
Mautland St. DH4-4C 126
Mavin St. DH1-3D 139 (in two parts)
Maxstoke Pl. NE12-3C 28
Maxton Clo. SR3-5C 118
Maxwell Rd. SR4-5D 99
Maxwell St. NE8-3C 78
Maxwell St. NE33-3E 51
May Av. NE21-3B 74
May Av. NE40-2B 54
Mayfair Ct. NE31-2B 64
Mayfair Gdns. NE8-2F 79
Mayfair Gdns. NE34-5A 52
Mayfair Rd. NE2-3F 43
Mayfield. NE16-4A 76
Mayfield Av. NE15-3F 37
Mayfield Av. NE23-3E 5
Mayfield Ct. SR6-1B 100
Mayfield Dri. SR6-1F 87
Mayfield Gdns. NE15-3A 38
Mayfield Gdns. NE28-1B 46
Mayfield Gdns. NE32-1F 65
Mayfield Gro. SR4-5E 107
Mayfield Pl. NE13-2C 14
Mayfield Rd. NE3-5D 27
Mayfield Rd. SR4-2E 107
Mayfield Ter. NE5-3F 41
May Gro. SR6-4E 71
Maynards Row. DH1-2F 139
Mayo Dri. SR3-5C 118
Mayoral Rd. NE11-2B 90
Mayorswell Clo. DH1-1E 139
Mayorswell Field. DH1 -1E 139
Mayorswell St. DH1-2E 139
May St. DH1-3B 138
May St. DH3-3A 102
May St. NE21-1A 74
May St. NE33-3F 51
May St. SR4-5A 100
Mayswood Rd. SR6-1B 100
Maywood Clo. NE3-5A 26
Meaburn St. SR1-2C 110
Meaburn Ter. SR1-1D 111
Meacham Way. NE16-5F 75
Mead Av. NE12-2A 30
Mead Cres. NE12-2A 30
Meadowbrook Dri. NE10 -3A 82
Meadow Clo. DH5-1E 129
Meadow Clo. NE11-1D 77
Meadow Clo. NE12-3D 29
Meadow Clo. NE21-1E 73
Meadow Clo. NE23-3C 8
Meadow Clo. NE40-2C 54
Meadowcroft M. NE8-1B 78
Meadowdale Cres. NE5-2F 41
Meadow Dri. NE13-4A 6
Meadow Dri. SR3-5A 118
Meadow Dri. SR4-2F 107
Meadowfield. NE25-2E 21
Meadowfield Av. NE3-4B 26
Meadowfield Dri. DH9-1A 130
Meadowfield Dri. SR6-1F 87
Meadowfield Est. NE9-3D 93
Meadowfield Gdns. NE6 -4C 46
Meadowfield Rd. NE3-1D 43
Meadowfield Ter. NE12-1B 30
Meadowfield Way. DH9 -1A 130
Meadow Gdns. SR3-4A 110
Meadow Grange. DH4-3D 125
Meadow Gro. SR4-2F 107
Meadow La. NE11-1D 77
Meadow La. SR3-4A 118
Meadow Laws. NE34-3F 69
Meadow Rise. NE5-1D 41
Meadow Rd. NE15-5F 39
Meadow Rd. NE25-3F 21
Meadow Rd. NE28-3A 48
Meadowside. SR2-3A 110
Meadows La. DH4-4A 128
Meadows, The. DH4-2B 124
Meadows, The. NE3-3B 26
Meadows, The. NE40-2C 54
Meadow St. DH5-4B 128
Meadow Ter. DH4-4B 116
Meadow Vale. SR2-3B 110
Meadow View. NE40-5A 40
Meadow View. SR3-5A 118
Meadow Wlk. NE40-2C 54
Meadow Wlk. SR3-5E 119
Mead Wlk. NE6-1D 63
Mead Way. NE12-2A 30
Meadway Dri. NE12-2B 30
Meadway Ho. NE12-2A 30
Means Ct. NE23-1D 17
Means Dri. NE23-1D 17
Medburn Av. NE30-5D 23
Medburn Rd. NE15-5D 39
Medburn Rd. NE25-2D 11
Medina Clo. SR3-5C 118
Medlar. NE9-1B 92
Medomsley Gdns. NE9-1C 92
Medomsly St. SR4-5F 99
Medway. DH3-5A 124
Medway. NE32-5B 66
Medway Av. NE31-4D 65
Medway Clo. SR8-5B 134
Medway Cres. NE8-1F 79
Medway Gdns. DH9-4B 130
Medway Gdns. NE30-2C 34
Medway Gdns. SR4-3C 108
Medwyn Clo. DH4-2D 125
Megstone Av. NE23-4B 4
Megstone Ct. NE12-3A 18
Melbourne Ct. NE1 -2E 61 & 4F 143
Melbourne Ct. NE8-4D 61
Melbourne Cres. NE25-3F 21
Melbourne Gdns. NE34 -4D 67
Melbourne Pl. SR4-3C 108
Melbourne St. NE1 -2D 61 & 4E 143
Melbury. NE25-1E 21
Melbury Ct. SR6-1B 100
Melbury Rd. NE7-3C 44
Melbury St. SR7-5F 133
Meldon Av. NE3-2B 26
Meldon Av. NE34-1C 68
Meldon Clo. NE28-1A 48
Meldon Gdns. NE11-5F 77
Meldon Rd. SR4-5D 99
Meldon St. NE4-3E 59
Meldon St. NE28-3D 49
Meldon Ter. NE6-4D 45
Meldon Way. NE21-2E 73
Melgrave Dri. SR3-5C 118
Melkington Ct. NE5-1D 41
Melkridge Pl. NE23-4B 4
Melling Rd. NE23-3B 4
Melmerby Clo. NE3-2F 27
Melness Rd. NE13-2C 14
Melock Ct. NE13-2C 14
Melrose. NE38-4B 104
Melrose Av. NE9-4E 79
Melrose Av. NE25-2B 22 (Monkseaton)
Melrose Av. NE25-3B 10 (Seaton Delaval)
Melrose Av. NE27-2E 19
Melrose Av. NE30-4B 22
Melrose Av. NE31-4D 65
Melrose Clo. NE3-5D 15
Melrose Clo. NE15-1D 57
Melrose Cres. SR7-2A 132
Melrose Gdns. DH4-2B 126
Melrose Gdns. NE28-5C 32
Melrose Gdns. SR6-2C 100
Melrose Gro. NE32-3D 67
Melsonby Clo. SR3-4C 118
Meltham Ct. NE5-2C 38
Meltham Dri. SR3-5C 118
Melton Av. NE6-2D 63
Melvaig Clo. SR3-5C 118
Melville Gdns. NE25-3E 21
Melville Gro. NE7-1B 44
Melville St. DH3-4E 123
Melvin Pl. NE5-2D 41
Melvyn Gdns. SR6-2C 100
Membury Clo. SR3-5C 118
Memorial Homes. DH9 -1A 130
Menai Ct. SR3-4E 119
Menceforth Cotts. DH2 -2D 123
Mendham Clo. NE10-4D 81
Mendip Av. DH2-4D 123 (in two parts)
Mendip Clo. NE29-5A 22
Mendip Clo. SR8-4A 134
Mendip Dri. NE38-5A 104
Mendip Gdns. NE11-4F 77
Mendip Ho. DH2-3D 123
Mendip Ter. DH9-4D 131
Mendip Way. NE12-3B 28
Mentieth Clo. NE38-4F 103
Mercantile Rd. DH4-1A 128
Merchants Wharf. NE6-3B 62
Mercia Retail Pk. DH1-1C 136
Mercia Way. NE15-2D 56
Meredith Gdns. NE8-1E 79
Mere Dri. DH1-2B 136
Mere Knolls Rd. SR6 -5C 88 to 2D 10
Meresyde. NE10-3F 81
Meresyde Ct. NE10-3F 81
Meridian Way. NE7-2F 45
Merle Gdns. NE6-2A 62
Merle Ter. SR4-5D 99
Merley Hall. NE6-3E 63
Merlin Clo. SR7-2E 133
Merlin Ct. NE10-1B 80 (off High St. Felling,)
Merlin Cres. NE28-2B 48
Merlin Dri. DH3-3C 112
Merlin Pl. NE12-3B 28
Merrick Ho. SR3-4E 119
Merrington Clo. SR3-5C 118
Merrion Clo. SR3-4C 118
Merryfield Gdns. SR6-2C 100
Mersey Ct. SR3-4E 119
Mersey Pl. NE8-1A 80
Mersey Rd. NE8-2A 80
Mersey Rd. NE31-4D 65
Merton Ct. NE4-3C 58
Merton Rd. NE6-4E 63
Metcalf Ho. DH1-2B 138
Methuen St. NE9-2F 79
Metro Cen. NE11-5B 58
Metro Pk. W. NE21-5F 57
Mews, The. DH1-5F 139
Mews, The. DH4-3F 117
Mews, The. NE1 -1B 60 & 2C 142
Mews, The. NE10-2A 82
Mews, The. NE21-5D 57
Mews, The. NE30-3C 34
Michaelgate. NE6-2B 62
Mickleton Clo. DH3-5B 124
Mickleton Gdns. SR3-5F 109
Middle Chare. DH3-2E 123
Middle Clo. NE38-2A 114
Middle Cross St. NE4-4A 60
Middle Dri. NE13-1A 24
Middle Engine La. NE28 & NE29-4A 32
Middlegarth. NE5-2F 41
Middle Ga. NE5-4F 39
Middle Grn. NE25-3E 21
Middleham Ct. SR5-1D 99
Middleham Rd. DH1-2D 137
Middle Row. DH4-4C 124
Middle Row. NE40-4D 55
Middles Rd. DH9-5C 130
Middle St. NE6-1E 63
Middle St. NE30-2F 35
Middle St. SR1-1B 110 (in two parts)
Middle St. E. NE6-1E 63
Middleton Av. NE4-1D 59
Middleton Clo. SR7-1A 132
Middlewood Pk. NE4-5F 41
Midgley Dri. SR3-5C 118
Midhurst Av. NE34-4B 52
Midhurst Clo. SR3-5C 118
Midhurst Rd. NE12-3F 29
Midmoor Rd. SR4-1D 109
Midsomer Clo. SR3-5C 118
Midway. NE6-1F 63
Milbourne St. NE29-1C 50
Milburn Dri. NE15-1F 57
Milburngate Cen. DH1-2C 138
Milburn Ho. NE5-2F 41
Milburn St. SR4-1F 109
Milcombe Clo. SR3-4C 118
Mildmay Rd. NE2-2F 43
Mildred St. DH5-4D 127
Milecastle Ct. NE5-3F 39
Mile End Rd. NE33-5D 35
Milfield Av. NE27-3B 20
Milfield Av. NE28-5D 31
Milford Gdns. NE3-1C 26
Milford Rd. NE15-2A 58
Military Rd. NE30-3C 34
Millais Gdns. NE34-5B 68
Mill Bank. SR5-1B 100
Millbank Ct. DH1-1B 138
Millbank Ind. Est. NE33 -2D 51
Millbank Rd. NE6-3E 63
Millbeck Gdns. NE9-2A 92
Millbeck Gro. DH5-2C 128
Millbrook. NE10-3D 81
Millburngate. DH1-2C 138
Millburngate Bri. DH1-2C 138
Millburngate Shopping DH1 -2C 138
Millburn Ter. DH4-4A 116
Mill Clo. NE29-4A 34
Mill Ct. DH4-3C 124
Mill Cres. DH4-4F 115
Mill Cres. NE31-5B 64
Milldale. SR7-2A 132
Mill Dam. NE33-2D 51
Milldene Av. NE30-2D 35
Mill Dyke Clo. NE25-1E 21
Miller's Bank. NE28-2B 48
Millers Hill. DH4-4A 116
Miller's La. NE16-1F 75
Millers Rd. NE6-5E 45
Miller St. NE8-2C 78
Miller Ter. SR3-2F 119
Millfield Av. NE3-1A 42
Millfield Clo. DH2-4B 122
Millfield Clo. NE15-5B 38
Millfield Gdns. NE10-2B 80
Millfield Gdns. NE30-2D 35
Millfield Gro. NE30-1D 35
Millfield La. NE15-4B 38
Millfield Rd. NE16-3A 76
Millfield Ter. SR6-4D 71 (in two parts)
Millford. NE10-5F 81 to 3F 81
Millford Ct. NE10-4A 82
Mill Gro. NE30-2E 35
Mill Gro. NE34-3F 69
Millgrove View. NE3-1B 42
Mill Hill. DH5-2C 128
Mill Hill La. DH1-5B 138
Mill Hill Rd. NE5-4A 40
Mill Hill Rd. SR3-4D 119
Mill Hill Wlk. SR3-4E 119
Mill Ho. Ct. DH1-4A 140
Mill Houses. NE2-5D 43 (off Morpeth St.)
Milling Ct. NE8-5B 60
Mill La. DH1-4A 140 (Gilesgate Moor)
Mill La. DH1-5F 139 (Shincliffe)
Mill La. DH6-5F 141
Mill La. NE4-3E 59
Mill La. NE15-1B 36
Mill La. NE21-3F 73
Mill La. NE23-3A 8
Mill La. NE31-4B 64
Mill La. SR6-3D 71
Mill La. N. NE4-2E 59
Millom Pl. NE9-5F 79
Mill Pit. DH4-4A 116
Mill Rise. NE3-5A 28
Mill Rd. NE8-3E 61 & 5F 143
Mill Rd. SR7-2A 132
Mills Gdns. NE28-1C 46
Mill St. SR4-1F 109
Mill Ter. DH4-4A 116
Mill Ter. DH5-2C 128
Millthorp Clo. SR2-1E 121
Millum Ter. SR6-3D 101
Mill View. NE10-3A 80
Mill View. NE36-3F 85
Mill View Av. SR6-2B 100
Millview Dri. NE30-1D 35
Mill Vs. NE36-3F 85
Millway. NE9-3F 79
Milner Cres. NE21-1E 73
Milner St. NE33-3A 52
Milne Way. NE3-4B 26
Milrig Clo. SR3-5C 118
Milsted Clo. SR3-5C 118
Milsted Ct. NE5-2C 38
Milton Av. DH5-1D 129 (in two parts)
Milton Av. NE31-1D 65
Milton Clo. DH9-2E 131
Milton Clo. NE2 -5A 44 & 1F 143
Milton Clo. SR7-3C 132
Milton Grn. NE2 -1D 61 & 2F 143
Milton Gro. NE29-3B 34
Milton Pl. DH2-2A 122
Milton Pl. NE2 -1D 61 & 1E 143
Milton Pl. NE9-4D 93
Milton Pl. NE29-3B 34
Milton Rd. NE16-2F 75
Milton Sq. NE8-5E 61 (in two parts)
Milton St. NE32-5D 49
Milton St. NE33-4E 51
Milton St. SR4-1E 109
Milton Ter. DH2-2A 122
Milton Ter. NE29-3B 34
Milvain Av. NE4-1D 59
Milvain Clo. NE8-1E 79
Milvain St. NE8-1E 79
Milverton Ct. NE3-4E 25
Mimosa Dri. NE31-4C 64
Mimosa Pl. NE4-5F 41
Minden St. NE1 -2D 61 & 3E 143
Mindrum Ter. NE6-3E 63
Mindrum Ter. NE29-1E 49
Mindrum Way. NE25-1C 10
Minehead Gdns. SR3-3F 119
Miners' Cotts. NE15-5B 40
Mingarry. DH3-5C 102
Minorca Clo. SR1-1D 111
Minorca Pl. NE3-1B 42
Minskip Clo. SR3-5C 118
Minstarley. DH3-5B 124
Minster Ct. DH1-3C 140
Minster Ct. NE8-4E 61
Minster Gro. NE5-2C 38
Minster Pde. NE32-5D 49
Minting Pl. NE23-4B 4
Minton Ct. NE29-5B 34
Minton La. NE29-1A 50
Minton Sq. SR4-5D 99
Mirk La. NE8-3D 61
Mirlaw Rd. NE23-4B 4
Mistletoe Rd. NE2-3A 44
Mistletoe St. DH1-2B 138
Mitcham Cres. NE7-1C 44
Mitchell Av. NE2-2F 43
Mitchell Av. NE25-3F 21
Mitchell Gdns. NE34-5A 52
Mitchell St. DH1-2B 138
Mitchell St. DH3-3A 102
Mitchell St. DH9-5A 130
Mitchell St. NE6-2F 63
Mitford Av. NE25-1A 10
Mitford Clo. DH3-2B 112
Mitford Clo. NE38-4F 103
Mitford Ct. SR8-5C 134
Mitford Dri. NE5-1A 40
Mitford Gdns. NE11-5F 77
Mitford Gdns. NE13-5A 6
Mitford Gdns. NE28-5B 32
Mitford Pl. NE3-4B 26
Mitford Rd. NE34-1C 68
Mitford St. NE28-3D 49
Mitford St. SR6-5C 88
Mitford Ter. NE32-5A 66
Mithras Gdns. NE15-2A 36
Mitre Pl. NE33-5C 50
Moat Gdns. NE10-2B 82
Moatside La. DH1-2C 138
Modder St. NE6-4D 63
Model Dwellings. NE38 -3D 105
Model Ter. DH4-2E 115
Moffat Av. NE32-3D 67
Moffat Clo. NE29-1D 33
Moine Gdns. SR6-2C 100
Moir Ter. SR2-5F 121
Molesdon Clo. NE30-1C 34
Molineux Clo. NE6-1A 62
Molineux Ct. NE6-1A 62
Molineux St. NE6-1A 62
Monarch Av. SR3-5A 118
Monarch Rd. NE4-4E 59
Monarch Ter. NE21-5A 56
Monastery Ct. NE32-5D 49
Mona St. DH9-2C 130
Monday Cres. NE4-1F 59
Monday Pl. NE4-1A 60
Monkbridge Ct. NE3-1F 43 (off Alnmouth Dri.)
Monkchester Grn. NE6-2C 62
Monkchester Rd. NE6-2C 62
Monk Ct. NE8-5E 61
Monkhouse Av. NE30-1C 34
Monkridge. NE5-2C 38
Monkridge. NE26-5D 13
Monkridge Ct. NE3-1F 43
Monkridge Gdns. NE11-3E 77
Monks Av. NE25-3E 21
Monks Cres. DH1-5F 137
Monkseaton Dri. NE25 & NE26-2E 21
Monkseaton Rd. NE25-2C 20
Monks Feld. NE10-2C 80
Monks Field. NE10-2C 80
Monksfield Clo. SR3-5D 119
Monkside. NE23-5B 4
Monkside Clo. NE38-5F 103
Monks Pk. Way. NE12-3B 28
Monks Rd. NE25-3E 21
Monkstone Av. NE30-1D 35
Monkstone Clo. NE30-1D 35
Monkstone Cres. NE30-1D 35
Monk St. NE1 -2B 60 & 4B 142
Monk St. SR6-4B 100
Monks Way. NE30-1D 35
Monksway. NE32-1D 67
Monkswood Sq. SR3-4F 119
Monk Ter. NE32-1A 66
Monkton. NE10-4E 81 (in two parts)
Monkton Av. NE34-3E 67
Monkton Hall. NE31-3E 65
Monkton La. NE31-5D 65
Monkton La. NE32-3E 65
Monkton Rd. NE32-5D 49 (in two parts)
Monkton Ter. NE32-1A 66 (in two parts)
Monmouth Gdns. NE28 -1C 48
Monroe Pl. NE5-2E 41
Mons Av. NE31-2C 64
Mons Cres. DH4-4A 116
Montagu Av. NE3-2B 42
Montagu Ct. NE3-2C 42
Montague St. NE15-1B 56
Montague St. SR6-2B 100
Monterey. NE37-4C 94
Montfalcon Clo. SR8-3B 134
Montford Clo. SR3-5C 118
Montgomery Rd. DH1-1F 139
Montpelier Ter. SR2-4C 110
Montpellier Pl. NE3-1A 42
Montrose Cres. NE9-3A 80
Montrose Dri. NE10-3A 82
Montrose Gdns. SR3-4E 109
Monument Mall. NE1 -2C 60 & 3C 142 (off Blackett St.)
Monument Ter. DH3-3B 102
Monument Ter. DH4-2E 115
Monument View. DH4 -2F 115
Moor Clo. NE29-2D 33
Moor Clo. SR1-1D 111
Moor Ct. DH4-2C 124
Moor Ct. NE3-2D 43
Moor Ct. SR6-2D 89
Moor Cres. DH1-2A 140
Moor Cres. NE3-2E 43
Moor Crest Ter. NE29-2B 34 (off Front St.)
Moorcroft Clo. NE15-5F 39
Moorcroft Rd. NE15-1D 57
Moore Av. NE11-2E 77
Moore Av. NE34-1D 69
Moore Ct. NE15-5D 37
Moore Cres. DH3-1B 102
Moore Cres. N. DH5-1D 129
Moore Cres. S. DH5-1D 129
Moor Edge. DH1-2A 138
Moor Edge Rd. NE27-3F 19
Moor End Ter. DH1-2C 140
Moore St. DH9-4B 130
Moore St. NE8-1F 79
Moorfield. NE2-1F 43
Moorfield Gdns. SR6-2F 67
Moorfoot Av. DH2-4D 123
Moorfoot Gdns. NE11-3F 77
Moor Gdns. NE29-2D 33
Moorhead. NE5-3A 42
Moorhead M. NE5-3A 42
Moorhouse Clo. NE34-2B 68
Moorhouses Rd. NE29-2E 33
Moorland Cres. NE6-5F 45
Moorlands. NE32-1B 84
Moorlands, The. DH1-4A 140
Moor La. NE3-1F 41
Moor La. NE34-1D 69
Moor La. NE36 & SR6 -2D 87 to 2C 88
Moor La. E. NE34-1D 69
Moor Pk. Ct. NE12-5C 16
Moor Pk. Ct. NE29-2D 33
Moor Pk. Rd. NE29-2D 33
Moor Pl. NE3-1E 43
Moor Rd. N. NE3-5E 27
Moor Rd. S. NE3-1E 43
Moorsburn Dri. DH4-4B 126
Moors Clo. DH4-5A 126
Moorsfield. DH4-5A 126
Moorside. NE12-5C 16
Moorside. NE32-1B 84
Moorside. NE37-1A 104
Moorside Ct. NE5-3A 42 (in two parts)
Moorside Ind. Est. SR3 -5B 118
Moorside N. NE4-4A 42
Moorside Pl. NE4-4A 42
Moorside Rd. SR3 -4B 118 to 5C 11
Moorside S. NE4-5B 42
Moorsley Rd. DH5-5D 129
Moor St. SR1-1D 111 (in two parts)
Moor Ter. SR1-1D 111
Moorvale La. NE5-2A 42
Moor View. NE3-1F 41
Moor View. NE12-2E 17
Moor View. SR6-1C 88
Moorview Cres. NE5-2F 41
Moor View Wlk. NE12-2D 17
Moorway. NE37-1F 103
Moorway Dri. NE15-5A 40
Moran St. SR6-1C 100
Moray Clo. DH3-1C 112
Moray Clo. SR8-4B 134
Moray St. SR6-2B 100
Morcott Gdns. NE29-1A 50
Morden St. NE1 -1B 60 & 3C 142
Mordey Clo. SR2-2D 111
Morecambe Pde. NE31-5F 65
Moreland Rd. NE34-4C 68
Moreland St. SR6-3C 100
Morgan St. SR5-3F 99
Morland Av. NE38-4D 105
Morland Gdns. NE9-2A 80
Morley Av. NE10-5F 63
Morley Ct. NE6-1A 62
Morley Hill Rd. NE5-4D 40
Morley Pl. NE27-3A 20 (off Earsdon Rd.)
Morley Ter. DH4-4F 125
Morningside. NE38-2D 113
Morningside Ct. DH3-2E 123
Mornington Av. NE3-1B 42
Morpeth Av. NE13-5A 6
Morpeth Av. NE32-4A 66
Morpeth Av. NE34-5F 51
Morpeth Clo. NE38-3E 103
Morpeth Dri. SR3-4C 118
Morpeth St. NE2 -5D 43 & 1A 142
Morpeth St. SR8-1E 135
Morpeth Ter. NE29-5E 33
Morris Av. NE34-4A 68
Morris Ct. NE23-4A 8
Morris Cres. NE35-2E 85
Morris Gdns. NE10-2A 82
Morrison St. NE8-5B 60
Morris Rd. NE16-2F 75
Morris St. DH3-3A 102
Morris St. NE8-1A 78
Morris St. NE37-5B 94
Morris Ter. DH5-1D 129
Morrit Ct. NE7-4D 29
Morston Dri. NE15-1D 57
Mortimer Av. NE5-1B 40
Mortimer Av. NE29-4F 33
Mortimer Rd. NE33 & NE34 -4E 51
Mortimer St. SR4-5D 99
Mortimer Ter. NE25-2D 11 (off Laurel Ter.)
Morton Clo. NE38-3C 104
Morton Cres. DH4-4D 125
Morton Grange Ter. DH4 -4D 125
Morton Sq. SR8-2B 134
Morton St. NE6-1C 62
Morton St. NE33-1E 51
Morton Wlk. NE33-1E 51
Morval Clo. SR3-5C 118
Morven Dri. NE10-5A 64
Morven Lea. NE21-5A 56
Morwick Clo. NE23-4B 4
Morwick Pl. NE5-3E 41
Morwick Rd. NE29-2F 33
Mosley St. NE1 -2C 60 & 4D 143
Mossbank. NE9-1A 92
Moss Clo. NE15-4E 39
Mossdale. DH1-2E 141
Mosspool. NE21-5F 55
Moss Side. NE9-2A 92

Mostyn Grn. NE3-5A 26
Moulton Ct. NE5-2D 41
Moulton Pl. NE5-2D 41
Mountbatten Av. NE31-3C 64
Mount Clo. NE12-3E 17
Mount Clo. NE25-4F 21
Mount Clo. SR4-2F 107
Mount Cotts. NE9-4F 93
Mountfield Gdns. NE3-5A 26
Mountfield St. NE28-3D 49
Mount Gro. NE11-3E 77
Mount Gro. SR4-3E 109
Mt. Joy Cres. DH1-4D 139
Mount La. NE9-4D 93
Mt. Lonnen. NE9-4D 93
Mt. Pleasant. DH3-3B 102
Mt. Pleasant. DH5-5D 127
Mt. Pleasant. NE6-1B 62
Mt. Pleasant. NE21-1A 74
Mt. Pleasant. SR5-3F 99
Mt. Pleasant Bungalows. DH3 -3B 102
Mt. Pleasant Ct. NE15-3F 37
Mt. Pleasant Gdns. NE8-1F 79
Mount Rd. DH3-3B 102
Mount Rd. NE9-4C 92
Mount Rd. SR4-3D 109
Mountside Gdns. NE11-3D 77
Mount Sq. NE9-4D 93
Mt. Stewart St. SR7-5F 133
Mount Ter. NE33-2E 51
Mount, The. NE15-2D 37
Mount, The. NE40-3B 54
Mt. View. NE16-2F 75
Mourne Gdns. NE11-4F 77
Moutter Clo. SR8-1D 135
Mowbray Clo. SR2-3C 110
Mowbray Rd. NE12-1F 29
Mowbray Rd. NE29-3F 33
Mowbray Rd. NE33-3F 51
Mowbray Rd. SR2-3C 110
Mowbray St. DH1-2B 138
Mowbray St. NE6-1F 61
Mowbray Ter. DH4-3C 126
Mozart St. NE33-3F 51
Muirfield. NE25-2E 21
Muirfield. NE33-3A 52
Muirfield Dri. NE10-4C 80
Muirfield Dri. NE37-3B 94
Muirfield Rd. NE7-5E 29
Mulben Clo. NE4-3D 59
Mulberry Gdns. NE10-5B 62
Mulberry Pl. NE4-4F 59
Mulberry St. NE10-1B 80
Mulberry Trading Est. NE10 -1B 80
Mulberry Way. DH4-4F 125
Mulcaster Gdns. NE28-1C 46
Mulgrave Dri. SR6-4D 101
Mulgrave Ter. NE8-4D 61
(in two parts)
Mulgrave Vs. NE8-5D 61
Mullen Dri. NE40-3B 54
Mullen Gdns. NE28-5C 30
Mullen Rd. NE28-5C 30
Mull Gro. NE32-4D 67
Mundella Ter. NE6-5D 45
Mundell St. DH9-4B 130
Mundle Av. NE21-3B 74
Mundles La. NE36 -3B 86 to 5B 86
Mungarry Clo. DH5-5B 128
Municipal Ter. NE37-1C 104
Munslow Rd. SR3-2B 118
Muriel St. DH9-5B 130
Murphy Gro. SR2-4C 120
Murray Av. DH4-4F 125
Murrayfield. NE23-2E 9
Murrayfield Rd. NE5-2F 41
Murray Gdns. NE11-2E 77
Murray Pl. DH2-2D 123
Murray Rd. DH2-2D 123
Murray Rd. DH3-2D 123
Murray Rd. NE28-2B 48
Murray St. NE21-4B 56
Murray St. SR8-3F 135
Murtagh Diamond Ho. NE34 -2B 68
Murton La. NE27 & NE29 -5C 20
Murton St. SR1-2C 110
Muscott Gro. NE15-1F 57
Musgrave Gdns. DH1-3A 140
Musgrave Rd. NE9-4E 79
Musgrave Ter. NE6-1D 63
Musgrave Ter. NE10-1F 81
Musgrave Ter. NE38-1C 104
Muswell Hill. NE15-2F 57
Mutual St. NE28-3C 46
Mylord Cres. NE12-2C 16
Myrella Cres. SR2-1B 120
Myreside Pl. NE12-3D 29
Myrtle Av. NE11-2E 77
Myrtle Av. SR6-1E 89
Myrtle Cres. NE12-1E 29
Myrtle Gro. NE2-2F 43
Myrtle Gro. NE9-5D 79
Myrtle Gro. NE28-3E 47
Myrtle Gro. NE34-3E 69
Myrtle Gro. SR3-3A 120
Myrtle Rd. NE21-1B 74
Myrtles. DH2-5A 112

Nafferton Pl. NE5-4E 41
Nailor's Bank. NE8-3E 61
Nailsworth Clo. NE35-5C 66
Nairn Clo. DH3-1C 112
Nairn Clo. NE37-3A 94
Nairn Rd. NE23-2C 4
Nairn St. NE32-4D 67
Naisbitt Av. SR8-1D 135
Nansen Clo. NE5-2B 40
Napier Clo. DH3-2B 112
Napier Rd. NE16-1F 75
Napier Rd. SR7-2C 132
Napier St. NE2 -1D 61 & 2E 143
Napier St. NE32 -5C 48 & 1F 65
Napier St. NE33-1F 67
Napier Way. NE21-5D 57
Narvik Way. NE39-5D 33
Nash Av. NE34-4B 68
Naters St. NE26-3E 23
Natley Av. NE36-3C 86
Navenby Clo. NE3-1F 27
Navenby Clo. SR7-1C 132
Naworth Av. NE30-5B 22
Naworth Dri. NE5-1F 39
Naworth Ter. NE32-3C 66
Nawton Av. SR5-3A 100
Nayland Rd. NE23-2C 4
Naylor Av. NE21-4B 74
Nazareth M. NE2-4B 44
Neale St. SR6-2C 100
Neale Ter. DH3-3A 102
Neale Wlk. NE3-1F 41
Nearlane Clo. NE13-4B 6
Neasdon Cres. NE30-1C 34
Neasham Rd. SR7-1B 132
Nedderton Clo. NE5-1D 39
Needham Pl. NE23-2C 4
Neilson Rd. NE10-5A 62
Nelson Av. NE3-4C 26
Nelson Av. NE23-1A 4
Nelson Av. NE33-2A 52
Nelson Clo. SR2-2C 110
Nelson Clo. SR8-2F 135
Nelson Cres. NE29-2F 49
Nelson Dri. NE23-1A 4
Nelson Ho. NE30-3F 35
Nelson Ind. Est. NE23-1A 4
Nelson Rd. NE6-2F 63
Nelson Rd. NE25-2C 20
Nelson Sq. SR6-5C 100
Nelson St. DH3-3E 123
Nelson St. DH5-5F 129
Nelson St. NE1 -2C 60 & 4C 142
Nelson St. NE8-4D 61
Nelson St. NE29-4B 34
Nelson St. NE33-2D 51
Nelson St. NE38-3D 105
Nelson St. SR2-4D 121
Nelson St. SR7-2C 132
Nelson Ter. DH6-4F 141
Nelson Ter. NE29-2F 49
Nelson Way. NE23-1A 4
Nene Ct. NE37-5D 95
Neptune Rd. NE15-5F 39
Neptune Rd. NE28-4D 47
Neptune St. SR7-3C 132
Nesbit Rd. SR8-4D 135
Nesburn Rd. SR4-3F 109
Nesham Pl. DH5-5D 127
Nesham St. NE4-4F 59
Nesham Ter. SR1-5D 101
Nest Rd. NE10-5C 62
Netherburn Rd. SR5-3B 100
Netherby Dri. NE5-4E 41
Nether Farm Rd. NE10-1E 81
Netherton Av. NE29-2E 33
Netherton Clo. DH2-4B 122
Netherton Gdns. NE13-1D 15
Netherton Gro. NE29-2F 33
Nettleham Rd. SR5-3B 100
Nettles La. SR3-4A 120
Neville Ct. NE37-4D 95
Neville Cres. DH3-2B 102
Nevilledale Ter. DH1-3B 138
Neville Dene. DH1-2A 138
Neville Rd. NE15-5F 39
Neville Rd. SR4-5E 99
Neville Rd. SR8-3B 134
Neville's Cross Bank. DH1 -4A 138
Neville's Cross Rd. NE31 -2E 65
Neville's Cross Vs. DH4 -4A 138
Neville Sq. DH1-4A 138
Neville St. DH1-2C 138
Neville St. NE1 -3B 60 & 5B 142
Neville Ter. DH1-2A 138
Neville Wlk. NE37-4D 95
(off Marlborough Rd.)
Nevinson Av. NE34-4B 68
Nevis Clo. NE26-4C 12
Nevis Ct. NE26-4C 12
Nevis Gro. NE36-3F 85
Nevis Way. NE26-4C 12
Newark Clo. SR8-2B 134
Newark Cres. SR7-1C 132
Newark Dri. SR6-2E 89
Newark Sq. NE29-5A 34
Newarth Clo. NE15-1C 56
Newbank Wlk. NE21-1F 73
Newbiggin Hall Cen. NE5
(off Trevelyan Dri.) -1B 40
Newbiggin La. NE5-1B 40
Newbold Av. SR5-3A 100
Newbold St. NE6-2C 62
Newbolt Ct. NE8-5F 61
Newbottle La. DH4-5D 125
Newbottle St. DH4-3C 126
Newbridge Av. SR5-3B 100
Newbridge Bank. DH3 -5D 113
New Bri. St. NE1 -2D 61 & 3E 143
New Bri. St. W. NE1 -2C 60 & 3D 143
Newbrough Cres. NE2-2A 44
Newburgh Av. NE25-2B 10
Newburn Av. SR5-3B 100
Newburn Bri. Rd. NE40 & NE21-1D 55
Newburn Ct. NE33-4E 51
Newburn Cres. DH4-4B 126
Newburn Haugh Ind. Est. NE15-1A 56
Newburn Ind. Est. NE15 -1F 55
Newburn Rd. DH9-1D 131
Newburn Rd. NE15-3F 37
Newbury. NE12-3F 17
Newbury Av. NE8-2B 78
Newbury Clo. NE15-1C 56
Newbury St. NE33-5E 51
Newbury St. SR5-2B 100
Newby Pl. NE9-1A 92
Newcastle Av. SR8-1E 135
Newcastle Bank. DH3-5A 92
Newcastle Pk. NE4 -4E 59 & 4F 59
Newcastle Rd. DH1-5A 136
Newcastle Rd. DH3-1A 102
(Birtley)
Newcastle Rd. DH3-5B 112
(South Pelaw)
Newcastle Rd. NE10 & NE36 -3D 83
Newcastle Rd. NE34 -3D 67 & 2E 67
Newcastle Rd. SR5 -4F 87 to 4B 100
Newcastle Science Pk. NE1 -2D 61 & 4E 143
Newcastle St. NE29-4B 34
Newcastle Ter. DH1-3A 136
Newcastle Ter. NE30-2F 35
Newcastle Western By-Pass. NE13, NE3, NE5, NE15, NE21 & NE16-5B 14 to 5E 57
Newdene Wlk. NE15-1C 56
New Dri. SR7-1D 133
New Durham Rd. SR2 & SR1 -2A 110
New Elvet. DH1-3D 139
New Elvet Bri. DH1-2D 139
Newfield Wlk. NE16-4F 75
Newgate Shopping Cen. NE1 -2B 60 & 4C 142
Newgate St. NE1 -2B 60 & 4C 142
New George St. NE33-4D 51
New Green St. NE33-3D 51
Newham Av. NE13-3B 14
Newhaven Av. SR5-2B 100
New Herrington Ind. Est. DH4 -4B 116
Newington Ct. SR5-3B 100
Newington Rd. NE2 & NE6 -5B 44 & 1F 143
Newland Ct. NE34-2B 68
Newlands. NE30-5B 22
Newlands Av. NE3-1E 27
Newlands Av. NE25-4F 21
Newlands Av. SR3-4A 110
Newlands Rd. DH1-2C 140
Newlands Rd. NE2-1F 43
Newlands Rd. E. SR7-2C 132
Newlands Rd. W. SR7-2B 132
Newlyn Cres. NE29-4A 34
Newlyn Dri. NE23-2C 4
Newlyn Dri. NE32-1B 66
Newlyn Rd. NE3-5A 26
Newman Ter. NE8-2E 79
Newmarch St. NE32-5B 48
Newmarket Wlk. NE33-3E 51
(in two parts)
New Mills. NE4-1F 59
Newminster Clo. DH4-3A 126
Newminster Rd. NE4-1B 58
Newmin Way. NE16-5E 75
Newport Gro. SR3-2E 119
New Quay. NE29-5C 34
Newquay Gdns. NE9-2E 91
New Rainton. DH4-2A 116
(off Rainton St.)
New Redheugh Bri. Rd. NE1 & NE8-4B 60
Newriggs. NE38-5C 104
New Rd. NE10-4A 82
New Rd. NE11-4A 78
New Rd. NE35 & NE36-2F 85
New Rd. NE38-2A 114
Newsham Clo. NE5-1D 39
New S. Ter. DH3-3B 102
Newstead Ct. NE38-3B 104
Newstead Rd. DH4-3A 126
Newsteads Clo. NE25-2E 21
Newsteads Dri. NE25-2E 21
Newsteads Sq. SR3-4F 119
New Strangford Rd. SR7 -2D 133
New St. DH1-2C 138
New St. SR4-2E 107
Newton Av. NE28-1A 48
Newton Av. NE30-4D 23
Newton Clo. NE15-5F 39
Newton Dri. DH1-4B 136
Newton Gro. NE34-2E 67
Newton Hall. NE7-2C 44
Newton Pl. NE7-2C 44
Newton Rd. NE7-2C 44
(in two parts)
Newton St. NE8-2B 78
Newton St. NE11-1E 77
Newtown Ind. Est. DH3 -5A 102
New York By-Pass. NE29 -1C 32
New York Ind. Est. NE27 -1C 32
New York Rd. NE27 -4F 19 to 1C 32
New York Rd. NE29-1C 32
New York Way. NE27-1C 33
(in two parts)
Nicholas Av. SR6-2E 89
Nicholas St. DH5-3F 129
Nichol Ct. NE4-2C 58
Nicholson Ct. SR1-1D 111
Nicholson St. SR2-3D 121
Nicholson Ter. NE12-5A 18
Nichol St. NE4-2C 58
Nickleby Chare. DH1-5B 138
Nidderdale Av. DH5-5E 129
Nidsdale Av. NE6-1F 63
Nightingale Pl. DH9-4E 131
Nile Clo. NE15-4E 39
Nile St. NE29-4C 34
Nile St. NE33-3D 51
Nile St. SR1-1C 110
Nilverton Av. SR2-4B 110
Nimbus Ct. SR3-4F 119
Nine Lands. DH4-5B 126
Nine Pins. NE9-4C 78
Ninth Av. DH2-2D 123
Ninth Av. NE6-4D 45
Ninth Av. NE11-2C 90
Ninth Av. E. NE11-2C 90
Ninth St. SR8-3E 135
Nissan Way. SR5-1A 106
Nithdale Clo. NE6-4C 46
Nixon St. NE8-3F 61
Nixon Ter. NE21-1A 74
Nobel St. NE4-4E 59
Nobel St. Ind. Est. NE4 -4E 59
Noble Gdns. NE34-3E 67
Noble's Bank Rd. SR2 -2D 111
Noble St. NE10-1C 80
Noble St. SR2-3D 111
Noble Ter. SR2-2D 111
Noel Av. NE21-4B 74
Noel St. DH9-2E 131
Noel Ter. NE21-3B 74
Noirmont Way. SR3-4D 119
Nook Cotts., The. SR4 -3B 108
Nookside. SR4-3B 108
Nookside Ct. SR4-4B 108
Nook, The. NE25-3B 22
Nook, The. NE29-4B 34
Nora St. NE34-2B 68
Nora St. SR4-3D 109
Norbury Gro. NE6-3C 62
Norfolk Av. DH3-1B 112
Norfolk Av. SR3-2E 119
Norfolk Clo. SR7-1C 132
Norfolk Dri. NE37-3B 94
Norfolk Gdns. NE28-1F 47
Norfolk M. NE30-3C 34
Norfolk Pl. DH3-1B 112
Norfolk Rd. NE8-3F 61
Norfolk Rd. NE34-5E 53
Norfolk Sq. NE6-2A 62
Norfolk St. DH5-4D 129
Norfolk St. NE30-4C 34
Norfolk St. SR1-1C 110
Norfolk Wlk. SR8-1B 134
Norfolk Way. NE15-1C 56
Norham Av. N. NE34-4C 52
Norham Av. S. NE34-4C 52
Norham Clo. NE13-2C 14
Norham Ct. NE38-3F 103
Norham Dri. NE5-2A 40
Norham Pl. NE2-3A 44
Norham Rd. DH1-2D 137
Norham Rd. NE3-3D 27
Norham Rd. NE26-2B 22
Norham Rd. NE29-4E 33
Norham Rd. N. NE29-1C 32
Norham Ter. NE21-5A 56
Norham Ter. NE32-3F 65
Norhurst. NE16-5D 75
Norland Rd. NE15-2E 57
Norley Av. SR5-2B 100
Norma Cres. NE26-3E 33
Norman Av. SR3-4F 119
Normanby Clo. SR7-1C 132
Normandy Cres. DH5-5D 127
Norman Ter. NE28-3C 48
Normanton Ter. NE4-2F 59
Normount Av. NE4-2D 59
Normount Gdns. NE4-2D 59
Normount Rd. NE4-2D 59
Northampton Rd. SR8 -1B 134
Northamptonshire Dri. DH1 -3D 141
North App. DH2-2C 122
North Av. NE3-5D 27
North Av. NE5-2B 40
North Av. NE12-3F 29
North Av. NE34-1D 69
North Av. NE37-4A 94
North Av. SR8-2E 135
N. Bailey. DH1-3D 139
N. Bank Ct. SR5-3A 100
Northbourne Rd. NE32-1E 65
Northbourne St. NE4-3E 59
Northbourne St. NE8-2E 79
N. Bridge St. SR5-5B 100
N. Burns. DH3-2E 123
N. Church St. NE30-3C 34
North Clo. NE6-5D 45
North Clo. NE34-2E 69
North Clo. NE40-2B 54
Northcote. NE16-5F 75
Northcote Av. NE5-3E 39
Northcote Av. NE25-2F 21
Northcote Av. SR1-2C 110
Northcote St. NE4-2F 59
Northcote St. NE33-4E 51
Northcott Gdns. NE23-3D 9
North Ct. NE32-5D 49
North Cres. DH1-1B 138
North Cres. NE38-1A 114
North Croft. NE12-3A 30
N. Cross St. NE3-5E 27
Northdene. DH3-1A 102
Northdene Av. SR7-2E 133
North Dri. DH3-3C 112
North Dri. NE31-2B 64
North Dri. SR6-1D 87
N. Durham St. SR1-1D 111
N. Eastern Ct. NE11-2D 77
North End. DH1-5A 136
Northern Prom. NE26-4E 13
Northern Ter. NE23-3E 7
Northern Way. SR5-3E 99
N. Farm Av. SR4-1F 117
N. Farm Rd. NE31-2B 64
Northfield Clo. NE16-4E 75
Northfield Dri. NE12-5D 17
Northfield Dri. SR4-1F 117
Northfield Gdns. NE34-4B 52
Northfield Rd. NE3-5D 27
Northfield Rd. NE33-4B 52
Northgate. NE12-3F 17
North Gro. NE40-3B 54
North Gro. SR6-2D 101
N. Guards. SR6-2D 89
N. Hall Rd. SR4-3C 108
N. Haven. SR7-2C 132
N. Hylton Rd. SR5-3C 98
N. Jesmond Av. NE2-2A 44
N. King St. NE30-3D 35
Northland Clo. SR4-5A 108
Northlands. DH3-5B 112
Northlands. NE21-1A 74
Northlands. NE30-1D 35
North La. NE36-3B 86
Northlea. NE15-5A 40
Northlea Rd. SR7-1B 132
N. Lodge. DH3-3B 112
N. Moor Ct. SR3-1C 118
N. Moor La. SR3-1C 118
Northmoor Rd. NE6-4A 46
N. Moor Rd. SR3-1C 118
Northolt Av. NE23-2C 4
North Pde. NE26-2C 22
N. Park View. NE12-1F 29
N. Railway. St. SR7-3E 133
N. Ravensworth St. SR4 -5F 99
N. Ridge. NE25-1D 21
North Rd. DH1-1B 138
North Rd. DH3-3B 112
North Rd. DH5-2C 128
North Rd. NE28-3C 46
North Rd. NE29-2B 34
North Rd. NE35 & NE36 -1D 85
North Rd. NE36-3A 86
North Rd. SR7-1E 133
North Row. NE27-5C 10
Northside Pl. NE25-2D 11
North St. DH3-4D 103
North St. DH4-1C 126
North St. DH5-3B 128
North St. DH5-5E 127
(New Town)
North St. NE1 -1C 60 & 3D 143
North St. NE21-5F 55
North St. NE32-5D 49
North St. NE33-1D 51
North St. SR3-2F 119
North St. SR5-3A 100
North St. SR6-1F 87
North St. Ct. NE1 -1C 60 & 3D 143
(off North St.)
North St. E. NE1-1C 60
North Ter. DH1-3A 136
North Ter. NE2 -5E 43 & 1B 142
North Ter. NE27-5F 19
North Ter. NE28-3F 47
North Ter. SR3-2F 119
North Ter. SR7-2F 133
N. Thorn. DH9-1C 130
N. Tyne Ind. Est. NE12-2C 30
Northumberland Av. NE1 -2D 143
Northumberland Av. NE3 -1C 42
Northumberland Av. NE12 -2F 29
Northumberland Av. NE28 -2B 48
Northumberland Building. NE1-2D 143
Northumberland Ct. NE1 -2C 60 & 3C 142
Northumberland Ct. NE31 -2C 64
Northumberland Dock Rd. NE28-3E 49
Northumberland Gdns. NE2 -4C 44
Northumberland Gdns. NE5 -1C 38
Northumberland Ho. NE23 -3E 5
Northumberland Pl. DH3 -1C 112
Northumberland Pl. NE1 -2C 60 & 3D 143
Northumberland Pl. NE30 -4C 34
Northumberland Pl. SR8 -1A 134
Northumberland Rd. NE1 -1C 60 & 3D 143
Northumberland Rd. NE15 -1B 56
Northumberland Rd. NE40 -1B 54
Northumberland Sq. NE26 -2C 22
Northumberland Sq. NE30 -4C 34
Northumberland St. NE1 -1C 60 & 2C 142
(in two parts)
Northumberland St. NE8 -1A 78
Northumberland St. NE15 -1B 56
Northumberland St. NE28 -2E 47
Northumberland St. NE30 -4D 35
Northumberland St. SR8 -1E 135
Northumberland Ter. NE6 -2F 61
Northumberland Ter. NE28
(off Tynemouth Rd.) -2B 48
Northumberland Ter. NE30 -3F 35
Northumberland Vs. NE28 -2A 48
Northumberland Way. NE37 -1B 94
Northumberland Way. NE38 -5B 104 to 1D 105
Northumbria Ho. NE3-4D 27
Northumbria Lodge. NE5 -3A 42
Northumbrian Rd. NE23 -5C 4 to 1B 4
Northumbrian Way. NE12 -4D 17
Northumbrian Way. NE29 -1B 50
Northumbria Pl. DH9-1E 131
Northumbria Wlk. NE5-3B 40
North View. DH1-4A 140
N. View. DH4-3D 125
N. View. DH9-5E 131
N. View. NE6-1F 61 & 5D 45
N. View. NE9-1A 92
N. View. NE12-1F 29
North View. NE13-2C 14
N. View. NE16-2F 75
N. View. NE28-2D 47
North View. NE29-2B 34
N. View. NE30-3D 23
N. View. NE32-1F 65
N. View. NE34-4B 52
N. View. NE37-5C 94
N. View. NE40-5A 36
North View. SR2-4E 121
(off Grey Ter.)
N. View. SR4-3F 107
N. View. SR5-3A 98
N. View. SR6-2C 100
N. View Ter. DH4-5F 125
N. View Ter. NE10-1A 80
North Vs. NE23-3E 7
N. Walbottle Rd. NE15 & NE5 -3C 38
Northway. NE9-3F 79
Northway. NE15-2F 37
N. W. Radial. -4D 43 & 1B 142
Northwood Ct. SR5-3A 100
Northwood Rd. SR7-2C 132
Norton Av. SR7-1C 132
Norton Clo. DH2-4B 122
Norton Rd. SR5-2F 99
Norton Way. NE15-1C 56
Norway Av. SR4-4C 108
Norwich Av. NE13-2D 15
Norwich Clo. DH3-5B 124
Norwich Rd. DH1-2D 137
Norwich Way. NE23-2C 4
Norwich Way. NE32-1F 83
Norwood Av. NE3-1D 27
Norwood Av. NE6-3D 45
Norwood Ct. NE9-3B 92
Norwood Ct. NE12-4F 29
Norwood Gdns. NE9-2E 79
Norwood Rd. NE11-2F 77
Norwood Rd. NE15-4F 39
Nottingham Pl. SR8-1A 134
Nottinghamshire Rd. DH1 -3D 141
Numbers Garth. SR1-5C 100
Nuneaton Way. NE5-1D 39
Nunn St. DH4-5F 115
Nuns La. NE1 -2C 60 & 4C 142
Nuns La. NE8-4E 61
Nuns Moor Cres. NE4-5A 42
Nuns Moor Rd. NE4-5A 42
Nuns' Row. DH1-5F 137
Nun St. NE1-2C 60 & 4C 142
Nunthorpe Av. SR2-1E 121
Nunwick Gdns. NE29-4E 33
Nurseries, The. SR6-1F 87
Nursery Clo. SR3-5F 109
Nursery La. NE10-3A 80
Nursery La. SR6-1F 87
Nursery Rd. SR3-5F 109
Nutley Pl. NE15-2E 57
Nyedene. SR5-3A 98

Oak Av. DH1-4A 140
Oak Av. DH4-4B 126
Oak Av. NE11-3D 77
Oak Av. NE34-2E 69
Oak Cres. SR6-1E 89
Oakdale Clo. NE15-1C 56
Oakdale Ter. DH3-3E 123
Oakenshaw. NE15-1C 56
Oakerside Dri. SR8-5B 134
Oakes Pl. NE4 -2A 60 & 4A 142
Oakeys Rd. DH9-1C 130
Oakfield Av. NE16-4A 76
Oakfield Clo. NE16-4F 75
Oakfield Clo. SR3-4A 118
Oakfield Ct. SR3-4B 118
Oakfield Dri. NE12-4B 18
Oakfield Dri. NE16-4A 76
Oakfield Gdns. NE15-2B 58
Oakfield Gdns. NE28-1B 46
Oakfield N. NE40-2A 54
Oakfield Rd. NE3-2D 43
Oakfield Rd. NE11-4F 77
Oakfield Rd. NE16-5E 75
Oakfield Ter. NE3-1C 42
Oakfield Ter. NE10-1E 81
Oakfield Ter. NE12-1A 30
Oakfield Way. NE23-3D 9
Oak Gro. NE12-1F 29
Oak Gro. NE28-3E 47
Oakham Av. NE16-4E 75
Oakham Dri. DH1-1D 141
Oakham Gdns. NE29-5A 34
(in two parts)
Oakhurst Dri. NE3-2C 42
Oakhurst Ter. NE12-3F 29
Oakland Rd. NE2-3F 43
Oakland Ter. NE25-2F 21
Oaklands. NE3-2E 43
Oaklands. NE16-1A 76
Oaklands Av. NE3-2D 43
Oaklands Cres. SR5-2E 99
Oaklands Ter. SR4-2F 109
Oaklea. DH2-1C 122
Oakleigh Gdns. SR6-5F 69
Oakley Clo. NE23-4F 7
Oakley Dri. NE23-2E 5
Oakridge. NE16-3E 75
Oak Rd. NE29-2C 32
Oak Sq. NE8-1A 78
Oaks, The. DH4-2A 116
Oaks, The. NE40-1A 72
Oaks, The. SR2-3C 110
Oak St. DH2-5A 122
Oak St. DH4-4D 125
Oak St. NE13-4A 6
Oak St. NE15-2F 37
Oak St. NE32-5B 48
Oak St. NE38-4D 105
Oak St. SR1-1E 111
Oaks W., The. SR2-3C 110
Oak Ter. DH9-5E 131
Oak Ter. NE21-1B 74
Oak Ter. SR8-3F 135
Oaktree Av. NE6-3B 46
Oaktree Gdns. NE25-4A 22
(in two parts)
Oakwellgate. NE8 -3D 61 & 5E 143
Oakwood. NE10-5D 81
(in four parts)
Oakwood. NE31-5E 47
Oakwood Av. NE9-2E 91
Oakwood Av. NE13-2D 15
Oakwood Clo. NE9-3E 93
Oakwood Gdns. NE11-4A 78
Oakwood Pl. NE5-3E 41
Oakwood St. SR2-2A 110
Oakwood Ter. NE28-3F 49
Oates St. SR4-1E 109
Oatlands Rd. SR4-3C 108
Oatlands Way. DH1-1C 136
Oban Av. NE28-1B 48
(in two parts)
Oban Ct. NE6-2B 62
Oban Gdns. NE6-2B 62
Oban St. NE10-1A 80
Oban St. NE32-4D 67
Oban Ter. NE10-1A 80
Obelisk La. DH1-1B 138
Occupation Rd. NE34-4E 69
Ocean Rd. NE33-1E 51
Ocean Rd. SR2-5E 111
Ocean Rd. N. SR2-5E 111
(off Ocean Rd.)
Ocean Rd. S. SR2-5E 111
(off Ocean Rd.)
Ocean View. NE26-2C 22
Ocean View. SR2-3C 121
Octavia Ct. NE28-5A 32
Octavian Way. NE11-2B 90
Offerton Clo. SR4-2E 107
Offerton La. SR4-5A 106
Offerton St. SR4-2F 109
Office Pl. DH5-4E 129
Office Row. DH4-3C 116
Office Row. NE23-1E 17
Office Row. NE38-2E 113
Ogden St. SR4-1F 109
Ogle Av. NE13-3B 14
Ogle Gro. NE32-4F 65
O'Hanlon Cres. NE28-5C 30
Oil Mill Rd. NE6-5D 47
Okehampton Ct. NE9-2E 91
Okehampton Sq. SR5-2F 99
Old Coronation St. NE33 -2D 51
Old Course Rd. SR6-2F 87
Old Crow Hall La. NE23-2B 4
Old Durham Rd. NE8 & NE9 -1E 79 to 2B 92
Old Elvet. DH1-2D 139
Oldfield Rd. NE6-4E 63
Old Fold Rd. NE10-5A 62
Old George Yd. NE1 -2C 60 & 4C 142
Old Harbour Dri. NE33-5F 35
Old Mill Rd. SR2-2E 111
Old Mill Rd. SR5-2E 99
Old Newbiggin La. NE5-4B 24
Old Pit La. DH1-2C 136
Old Pit Ter. DH1-2C 136
Oldstead Gdns. SR4-4C 108
Old Vicarage Wlk. NE6-2B 62
Oldwell Av. NE21-1A 74
(off Oldwell La.)
Old Well La. NE21-1A 74
Olive Gdns. NE9-4F 79
Olive Pl. NE4-5F 41
Oliver Av. NE4-1D 59
Oliver Ct. NE6-4E 63
Oliver Cres. DH3-2B 102
Oliver Pl. DH1-5B 138
Oliver St. DH9-4B 130
Oliver St. NE15-2A 58
Oliver St. NE38-3C 104
Oliver St. SR7-2C 132
Olive St. DH2-5A 122
Olive St. NE33-1A 68
Olive St. SR1-2B 110
Ollerton Dri. NE15-2D 37
Ollerton Gdns. NE10-3A 80
Olney Clo. NE23-3E 5
O'Neil Dri. SR8-4C 134
Ongar Way. NE12-3D 29
Onslow Gdns. NE9-5D 79
Onslow St. SR4-1D 109
Open, The. NE1 -1B 60 & 3C 142
Orange Gro. NE16-2A 76
Orange Gro. NE23-3A 8
Orchard Clo. NE12-4F 18
Orchard Ct. NE40-2B 54
Orchard Dri. DH1-1E 139
Orchard Gdns. DH3-4E 123
Orchard Gdns. NE9-5E 79
Orchard Gdns. NE28-1B 46
Orchard Gdns. SR6-2D 89
Orchard Grn. NE5-1F 41
Orchard Leigh. NE15-1C 56
Orchard Pk. DH3-3B 102
Orchard Pl. NE2-3B 44
Orchard Rd. NE16-3A 76
Orchard St. DH3-3B 102
Orchard St. NE1 -3C 60 & 5C 142
(in two parts)
Orchard St. SR4-1D 109
Orchard Ter. DH3-4E 123
Orchard Ter. NE15-1B 56
(Lemington)
Orchard Ter. NE15-2F 37
(Throckley)
Orchard, The. DH1-2B 136
Orchard, The. NE15-1B 25
Orchard, The. NE16-3B 76
(in two parts)
Orchard, The. NE29-4B 34
Orchard, The. NE36-3B 86
Orchid Cres. NE10-5A 62
Orde Av. NE28-2A 48
Ord St. NE4-4B 60
Orkney Dri. SR2-2C 120
Orlando Rd. NE29-4F 33
Ormesby Rd. SR6-1C 100
Ormiscraig. NE15-1C 56
Ormiston. NE15-1C 56
Ormonde Av. NE15-1F 57
Ormonde St. NE32-5D 49
Ormonde St. SR4-2E 109
Ormsby Grn. NE5-4B 40
Ormskirk Clo. NE15-1C 56
Ormskirk Gro. NE23-2E 5
Orpen Av. NE34-4F 68
Orpington Av. NE6-1C 62
Orpington Rd. NE23-2E 5
Orr Av. SR3-4F 119
Orton Clo. NE4-3C 58
Orwell Clo. NE34-5F 67
Orwell Clo. SR8-5A 134
Orwell Gdns. DH9-4C 130
Orwell Grn. NE3-1F 41
Osbaldeston Gdns. NE3 -2C 42
Osborne Av. NE2-4A 44
Osborne Av. NE33-3F 51
Osborne Bldgs. DH9-4B 130
Osborne Ct. NE2-4A 44
Osborne Gdns. NE26-2B 22
Osborne Gdns. NE29-3B 34
Osborne Pl. NE12-1B 30
Osborne Rd. DH3-3E 123
Osborne Rd. NE2 -2F 43 & 1E 143
Osborne Rd. SR5-1E 107
Osborne St. SR6-3C 100
Osborne Ter. NE2 -5A 44 & 1E 143
Osborne Ter. NE8-1C 78

Osborne Ter. NE23-3B 4
Osborne Vs. NE2-4A 44
Oslo Clo. NE29-5D 33
Osman Clo. SR2-2C 110
Osman Ter. DH4-3F 125
Osman Ter. SR1-2D 111
Osmond Ter. DH4-4F 115
Osprey Way. NE34-3F 67
Oswald Av. DH1-5B 140
Oswald Cotts. NE9-2B 92
Oswald Ct. DH1-3D 139
Oswald Rd. DH5-3F 129
Oswald St. NE34-4A 68
Oswald St. SR4-1E 109
Oswald Ter. DH9-5B 130
Oswald Ter. NE8-1C 78
Oswald Ter. SR2-1D 121
Oswald Ter. S. SR5-4A 98
Oswald Ter. W. SR5-4A 98
Oswald Wlk. NE3-4F 27
Oswestry Pl. NE23-2E 5
Oswin Av. NE12-1F 29
Oswin Ct. NE12-1F 29
Oswin Rd. NE12-1F 29
Oswin Ter. NE29-4F 33
Otley Clo. NE23-2E 5
Otterburn Av. NE3-1C 42
Otterburn Av. NE25-3C 20
Otterburn Clo. NE12-2B 30
Otterburn Ct. NE8-1B 78
Otterburn Ct. NE25-3C 20
Otterburn Cres. DH4-4A 126
Otterburn Gdns. NE9-5D 79
Otterburn Gdns. NE11-3F 77
Otterburn Gdns. NE16-3A 76
Otterburn Gdns. NE34-1C 68
Otterburn Rd. NE29-2B 34
Otterburn Ter. NE2-4A 44
Otterburn Vs. NE2-4A 44 (off Otterburn Ter.)
Otterburn Vs. N. NE2-4A 44 (off Otterburn Ter.)
Otterburn Vs. S. NE2-4A 44 (off Otterburn Ter.)
Ottercap Clo. NE15-1C 56
Otterington. NE38-3F 105
Ottershaw. NE15-1C 56
Otto Ter. SR2-2A 110
Ottovale Cres. NE21-1F 73
Ottringham Clo. NE15-2C 56
Oulton Clo. NE5-5D 25
Oulton Clo. NE23-2E 5
Ousby Ct. NE3-2F 25
Ouseburn Clo. SR2-2E 121
Ouseburn Pk. NE1 -2F 61 & 4F 143
Ouseburn Rd. NE6-2F 61 (Byker)
Ouseburn Rd. NE6-5C 44 (Heaton)
Ouse Cres. DH3-5B 124
Ouse St. NE1-2F 61
Ouston Clo. NE10-3B 82
Ouston St. NE15-2E 57
Outram St. DH5-4D 127
Oval Pk. View. NE10-3C 80
Oval, The. DH4-5B 126
Oval, The. NE6-4C 62
Oval, The. NE12-3F 29
Oval, The. NE13-1A 24
Oval, The. NE40-2B 54
Oval, The. SR5-3A 100
Overdene. NE15-5B 40
Overdene. SR7-5A 132
Overfield Rd. NE3-4B 26
Overhill Ter. NE8-1C 78
Overton Clo. NE15-1C 56
Overton Rd. NE29-1A 34
Ovingham Clo. NE38-3D 105
Ovingham Gdns. NE13-1D 15
Ovington Gro. NE5-5E 41
Owen Brannigan Dri. NE23 -4A 8
Owen Ct. NE2 -5D 43 & 1A 142
Owen Dri. NE36 & NE35 -2F 85
Owengate. DH1-3C 138
Owlet Clo. NE21-1F 73
Oxberry Gdns. NE10-3B 80
Oxbridge St. SR2-1D 121
Oxclose Rd. NE38-3C 104
Oxford Av. NE12-1E 29
Oxford Av. NE23-3E 5
Oxford Av. NE28-2B 46
Oxford Av. NE33-5F 51
Oxford Av. NE37-5A 94
Oxford Clo. SR3-2E 119
Oxford Cres. DH5-4E 129
Oxford Cres. NE31-1E 65
Oxford Pl. DH3-2B 112
Oxfordshire Dri. DH1-3C 140
Oxford Sq. SR4-1C 108
Oxford St. NE1 -2D 61 & 3D 143
Oxford St. NE26-1C 22
Oxford St. NE30-3F 35
Oxford St. NE33-5E 51
Oxford St. SR4-1C 108
Oxford St. SR7-3C 132
Oxford Ter. DH4-4F 115
Oxford Ter. NE8-1D 79
Oxford Way. NE32-1A 84
Oxley Ter. DH1-2B 136
Oxnam Cres. NE2-5D 43
Oxted Clo. NE23-2E 5
Oxted Pl. NE6-4D 63
Oystershell La. NE4 -2A 60 & 4A 142
Oyston St. NE33-2E 51
Ozanan Clo. NE23-5F 7

Pacific Hall Clo. SR7-2A 132
Packham Rd. SR4-2A 108
Paddock Clo. SR6-1D 87
Paddock La. SR3-3A 120
Paddock, The. DH4-4E 117
Paddock, The. DH9-1A 130
Paddock, The. NE10-4E 81
Paddock, The. NE12-4F 17
Paddock, The. NE13-1B 24
Paddock, The. NE15-3B 38
Paddock, The. NE23-4F 5
Padgate Rd. SR4-2A 108
Padgham Rd. SR4-3F 107
Padonhill. SR3-5D 119
Padstow Clo. SR2-3E 121
Padstow Ct. NE9-2D 91
Padstow Rd. NE29-5A 34
Page Av. NE34-5F 51
Page's Bldgs. NE35-2D 85
Page St. NE31-5A 48
Paignton Av. NE4-2D 59
Paignton Av. NE25-3F 21
Paignton Sq. SR3-1D 119
Painter Heugh. NE1 -3C 60 & 5D 143
Paisley Sq. SR3-5D 109
Palace Grn. DH1-3C 138
Palace St. NE4 -3A 60 & 5A 142
Palatine St. NE33-1D 51
Palatine View. DH1-3B 138 (off Margery La.)
Palermo St. SR4-5D 99
Paley St. SR1-1A 110
Palgrove Rd. SR4-3A 108
Palgrove Sq. SR4-3B 108
Palinsburn Ct. NE5-2D 41
Pallion New Rd. SR4-5D 99
Pallion Rd. SR4-1D 109
Pallion Subway. SR4-5D 99
Pallion Trading Est. SR4 -5C 98
Pallion Way. SR4-5C 98
Pallion W. Ind. Est. SR4 -5B 98
Palm Av. NE4-5F 41
Palm Av. NE34-2E 69
Palm Ct. NE12-1B 30
Palmer Cres. NE31-1E 65
Palmer Gdns. NE10-2A 82 (in two parts)
Palmers Garth. DH1-3D 139
Palmers Grn. NE12-1A 30
Palmer's Hill Rd. SR6-5C 100
Palmerston Av. NE6-5A 46
Palmerston Rd. SR4-4F 107
Palmerston Sq. SR4-4A 108
Palmerston Wlk. NE8-5B 60
Palmer St. DH9-3A 130
Palmer St. NE32-5C 48
Palmersville. NE12 -1A 30 & 1B 30
Palmstead Rd. SR4-2A 108
Palmstead Sq. SR4-3A 108
Palm Ter. DH9-5E 131
Pancras Rd. SR3-1C 118
Pandon. NE1-2D 61 & 4E 143
Pandon Bank. NE1 -2D 61 & 4E 143 (in two parts)
Pandon Ct. NE2 -1D 61 & 2E 143
Panfield Ter. DH4-3D 125
Pangbourne Clo. NE15-5E 39
Pankhurst Gdns. NE10-2F 81
Pankhurst Pl. DH9-4E 131
Pan La. SR1-1B 100 (in two parts)
Panns Bank. SR1-5C 100
Pantiles, The. NE37-3B 94
Parade Clo. NE6-2F 63
Parade, The. DH3-4E 123
Parade, The. NE6-2F 63
Parade, The. NE11-5B 58
Parade, The. NE28-5F 31
Parade, The. NE38-4C 104
Parade, The. SR2-3E 111
Paradise Row. NE23-3D 5
Paradise St. SR8-3F 135
Park Av. DH9-1C 130
Park Av. NE3-3B 26 (Fawdon)
Park Av. NE3-3C 26 to 3E 27 (Gosforth)
Park Av. NE11-3D 77
Park Av. NE21-5A 56 & 5B 56
Park Av. NE26-2C 22
Park Av. NE27-3B 20
Park Av. NE28-2C 46
Park Av. NE30-3D 35
Park Av. NE34-3D 69
Park Av. NE37-4B 94
Park Av. SR3-3F 119
Park Av. SR6-2D 101
Park Chare. NE38-3C 104
Park Clo. NE4-3F 59
Park Ct. NE6-3C 46
Park Ct. NE8-4E 61 (off Hopper St.)
Park Cres. NE27-4B 20
Park Cres. NE30-3D 35
Park Cres. E. NE30-3D 35
Parkdale Rise. NE16-3E 75
Park Dri. NE3-1E 27
Park Dri. NE12-2F 29
Park Dri. NE16-2A 76
Parker Av. NE3-1D 43
Parker Ct. NE11-5D 59
Parkfield. NE32-1B 84
Park Field. NE40-2A 54
Park Gdns. NE26-2C 22
Park Ga. SR6-2D 101
Parkgate La. NE21-2A 74
Park Gro. NE27-4B 20
Park Gro. NE37-4B 94
Park Head. NE7-3C 44
Parkhead Gdns. NE21-2A 74
Park Head Rd. NE7-3C 44
Parkhead Sq. NE21-1A 74
Park Ho. NE6-2E 63
Parkhouse Av. SR5-4A 98
Park Ho. Clo. DH6-4F 141
Park Ho. Gdns. DH6-4F 141 (in three parts)
Park Ho. Rd. DH1-5A 138
Parkhurst Rd. SR4-3F 107
Parkin Gdns. NE10-3D 81
Parkinson Cotts. NE40-3C 54
Parkland. NE12-4E 29
Parkland. NE21-3F 55
Parkland Av. NE21-2A 74
Parklands Ct. SR7-2D 133
Parklands Way. NE10-2A 82
Parkland Ter. SR7-2D 133
Park La. NE8-4E 61
Park La. NE21-2F 73
Park La. NE27-5B 20
Park La. SR1-2B 110
Park La. SR8-2F 135
Park Lea. SR3-4F 117
Park Lea Rd. SR6-2C 100
Parkmore Rd. SR4-4F 107
Park Pde. NE26-2C 22
Park Pde. SR6-3D 101
Park Pl. DH3-5B 112
Park Pl. DH5-4E 129
Park Pl. E. SR2-2C 110
Park Pl. W. SR2-2C 110
Park Rise. NE15-5E 39
Park Rd. DH5-4E 129
Park Rd. DH6-4F 141
Park Rd. DH9-3B 130
Park Rd. NE4-3F 59
Park Rd. NE8 & NE10-4F 61
Park Rd. NE15-4A 38
Park Rd. NE25-1B 10
Park Rd. NE26-1C 22
Park Rd. NE27-4B 20
Park Rd. NE28-2D 47
Park Rd. NE31-2C 64
Park Rd. NE32-1F 65
Park Rd. SR2-2B 110
Park Rd. SR8-1E 135
Park Rd. Central. DH3 -2F 123
Park Rd. N. DH3 -2F 123 to 4B 112
Park Rd. S. DH3-4E 123
Park Row. NE10-2B 80
Park Row. SR5-3E 99
Parkshiel. NE34-3E 69
Parkside. DH1-2B 138
Parkside. NE11-2E 77
Parkside. NE12-5C 16
Parkside. NE15-3A 38
Parkside. NE28-2F 47
Parkside. NE30-1E 35
Parkside. NE31-3B 64
Parkside. SR3-4A 118
Parkside Av. NE7-5D 29
Parkside Av. NE21-1A 74
Parkside Cres. NE30-1E 35
Parkside Cres. SR7-5D 133
Parkside S. SR3-4A 118
Parkside Ter. NE28-5D 32
Parkstone Clo. SR4-5F 107
Park St. SR7-4E 133
Park St. S. SR5-4A 98
Park Ter. NE2 -5F 43 & 1C 142
Park Ter. NE11-2D 77
Park Ter. NE12-5C 16
Park Ter. NE16-1F 75
Park Ter. NE21-1B 74
Park Ter. NE26-1C 22
Park Ter. NE28-2D 47
Park Ter. NE30-3D 35
Park Ter. NE37-4B 94
Park Ter. SR5-3E 99
Park Ter. SR8-3F 135
Park View. DH2-1D 123 (Chester-le-Street)
Park View. DH2-1A 122 (Pelton Fell)
Park View. DH4-1C 124 (Bournmoor)
Park View. DH4-4F 115 (Shiney Row)
Park View. DH5-4E 129
Park View. NE10-1C 80
Park View. NE12-1F 29
Park View. NE13-1D 15
Park View. NE16-1E 75
Park View. NE21-2A 74
Park View. NE25-1B 10 (in two parts)
Park View. NE26-1B 22
Park View. NE28-2D 47
Park View. NE32-3F 65
Park View. SR7-2A 132
Park View. SR8-2F 135
Park View Clo. NE40-2B 54
Park View Ct. NE3-5A 26
Park View Ct. NE26-1B 22
Pk. View Gdns. NE40-2C 54
Park Vs. NE3-2D 43
Park Vs. NE28-2D 47
Parkville. NE6-5C 44
Park Wlk. SR3-5E 119
Parkway. NE16 -5D 75 to 3E 75
Parkway. NE38 -2B 104 to 4C 104
Parliament St. NE21-1F 73
Parliament St. NE31-5E 47
Parmeter St. DH9-4B 130
Parmontley St. NE15-2E 57
Parnell St. DH4-5F 125
Parry Dri. SR6-1D 89
Parson Ind. Est. NE37-5F 93
Parson's Av. NE6-2D 63
Parsons Dri. NE40-2B 54
Parson's Gdns. NE11-1E 77
Parsons Rd. NE37-5F 93
Parsons Rd. SR8-1C 134
Partick Rd. SR4-3A 108
Partick Sq. SR4-4A 108
Partridge Clo. NE38-4E 103
Passfield Way. SR8-5A 134
Paston Rd. NE25-2C 10
Pathside. NE32-5A 66
Path, The. NE9-1E 91
Patience Av. NE13-4A 6
Patina Clo. NE15-4E 39
Paton Rd. SR3-1D 119
Paton Sq SR3-5D 109
Patrick Cain Ho. NE33-4D 51
Patrick's Ter. SR2-4E 121
Patrick Ter. NE23-5A 8
Patterdale Clo. DH1-2E 141
Patterdale Clo. NE36-2B 86
Patterdale Gdns. NE7-1C 44
Patterdale Gro. SR5-1A 100
Patterdale St. DH5-5E 129
Patterdale Ter. NE8-2E 79
Patterson St. NE21-3C 56
Pattinson Gdns. NE9-3F 79
Pattinson Gdns. NE10-5A 62
Pattinson Ind. Est. NE38 -2F 105 & 4E 105
Pattinson Rd. NE38-4D 105
Pauline Av. SR6-2C 100
Pauline Gdns. NE15-5B 40
Pauls Grn. DH5-2E 129
Paul's Rd. SR1-1C 110
Paulsway. NE32-1C 66
Pavilion Ct. NE2-4A 44
Pavilion Ter. DH5-4F 129
Pawston Rd. NE39 & NE21 -5A 72
Paxford Clo. NE7-4B 28
Paxton Ter. SR4-1E 109
Peacehaven Ct. NE37-3B 94
Peacock Ct. NE11-3A 78
Peacock St. W. SR4-1E 109
Peareth Ct. NE8-4E 61 (off Hopper St.)
Peareth Edge. NE9-3E 93
Peareth Gro. SR6-1D 101
Peareth Hall Rd. NE9 & NE37 -3E 93
Peareth Rd. SR6-1D 101
Peareth Ter. DH3-4B 102
Pearl Rd. SR3-5D 109
Pea Rd. DH9-3A 130
Pearson Ct. NE30-4D 35
Pearson Pl. NE30-4D 35
Pearson Pl. NE32-5D 49
Pearson St. DH9-1D 131
Pearson St. NE33-5E 35
Peart Clo. DH6-4F 141
Peartree Gdns. NE6-3B 46
Pear Tree Ter. DH3-3A 124
Peary Clo. NE5-2B 40
Pease Av. NE15-1B 58
Peasemore Rd. SR4-3F 107
Pebble Beach. SR6-3E 89
Peddars Way. NE34-2F 67
Peebles Clo. NE29-1D 33
Peebles Rd. SR3-1D 119
Peel Av. DH1-3B 140
Peel Gdns. NE34-3D 67
Peel La. NE1-3B 60 & 5B 142
Peel St. NE1-3B 60 & 5B 142
Peel St. SR2-2C 110
Pegwood Rd. SR4-3B 108
Pelaw Av. DH2-5A 112
Pelaw Av. DH9-1D 131
Pelaw Bank. DH3-1E 123
Pelaw Cres. DH2-1D 123 (in two parts)
Pelaw Ind. Est. NE10-2E 81
Pelaw Leazes La. DH1-2D 139
Pelaw Pl. DH2-5A 112
Pelaw Rd. DH2-1D 123
Pelaw Sq. DH2-1D 123
Pelaw Sq. SR4-1B 108
Pelaw Ter. DH2-1C 122
Pelaw Way. NE10-1F 81
Peldon Clo. NE7-4B 28
Pelham Ct. NE3-2F 25
Pelton Fell Rd. DH2-2A 122
Pelton La. DH2-1C 122
Pelton Rd. SR4-4A 108
Pemberton Gdns. SR3 -4A 110
Pemberton St. DH5-4F 129
Pemberton Ter. N. DH9 -5F 131
Pemberton Ter. S. DH9 -5F 131
Pembridge. NE38-3E 103
Pembroke Av. DH3-1B 112
Pembroke Av. NE6-5F 45
Pembroke Av. SR5-4D 99
Pembroke Ct. NE3-3F 25
Pembroke Gdns. NE28-1C 48
Pembroke Pl. SR8-2B 134
Pembroke Ter. NE33-5E 51
Pendeford. NE38-3F 105
Pendle Clo. NE38-5A 104
Pendle Clo. SR8-4A 134
Pendle Grn. SR4-3F 109
Pendower Way. NE15-2B 58
Pendragon. DH3-4B 124
Penfold Clo. NE7-5E 29
Penhale Dri. SR2-3E 121
Penistone Rd. SR4-3F 107
Penman Pl. NE29-1B 50
Penman Sq. SR4-4A 108
Pennant Sq. SR4-1B 108
Pennine Av. DH2-4D 123
Pennine Ct. SR3-4E 119
Pennine Dri. SR8-4A 134
Pennine Gdns. DH9-4E 131
Pennine Gdns. NE11-3E 77
Pennine Gro. NE36-3F 85
Pennine Ho. NE38-3A 104
Pennine Way. NE12-3B 28
Pennon Pl. NE1 -1C 60 & 3C 142 (off Eldon Sq.)
Penn Sq. SR4-2B 108
Penn St. NE4-4F 59 (in two parts)
Pennycross Rd. SR4-3F 107
Pennycross Sq. SR4-3F 107
Pennyfine Clo. NE29-2B 34
Pennygate Sq. SR4-3F 107
Pennygreen Sq. SR4-3F 107
Pennymore Sq. SR4-3F 107
Pennywell Ind. Est. SR4 -4E 107
Pennywell Rd. SR4-3A 108
Penrith Av. NE30-5B 22
Penrith Gdns. NE9-5A 80
Penrith Gro. NE9-1A 92
Penrith Rd. NE31-3E 65
Penrith Rd. SR6-5A 88
Penrose Grn. NE3-5A 26
Penrose Rd. SR4-3A 108
Pensford Ct. NE3-4D 25
Penshaw Gdns. DH9-2F 131 (in two parts)
Penshaw Grn. NE5-2F 41
Penshaw La. DH4-2A 116
Penshaw View. DH3-5D 103
Penshaw View. NE10-2A 82
Penshaw View. NE31-3C 64
Penshaw View. NE32-3F 65
Penshaw Way. DH3-3C 102
Pensher St. NE10-1A 80
Pensher St. SR4-2F 109
Pensher St. E. NE10-1A 80
Pensher View. NE37-4D 95
Pentland Clo. NE29-1A 34
Pentland Clo. NE38-4A 104
Pentland Clo. SR8-5A 134
Pentland Ct. DH2-3D 123
Pentland Gdns. NE11-3F 77
Pentland Gro. NE12-1D 29
Pentlands Ter. DH9-3D 131
Pentridge Clo. NE23-2E 5
Penwood Rd. SR4-3A 108
Penzance Pde. NE31-5F 65
Penzance Rd. SR4-4F 107
Peplow St. SR4-1B 108
Peppercorn Ct. NE1 -3D 61 & 5E 143 (off Trinity Chare)
Percival St. SR4-5D 99
Percy Av. NE26-2B 22
Percy Av. NE30-3D 23
Percy Cotts. NE25 -1C 10 & 2C 10
Percy Ct. NE29-1E 49
Percy Cres. NE29-1F 49
Percy Gdns. NE11-3E 77
Percy Gdns. NE12-1F 29
Percy Gdns. NE25-3C 22
Percy Gdns. NE30-1F 35
Percy Gdns. Cotts. NE30 -1F 35 (off Percy Gdns.)
Percy Pk. NE30-2E 35
Percy Pk. Rd. NE30-1F 35
Percy Rd. NE26-2D 23
Percy Scott St. NE34-4A 68
Percy Sq. DH1-5A 138
Percy St. DH5-3F 129
Percy St. DH9-3B 130
Percy St. NE1 -1B 60 & 3C 142
Percy St. NE12-1B 30
Percy St. NE23-4E 5
Percy St. NE28-2E 47
Percy St. NE30-2F 35
Percy St. NE32-5E 49
Percy St. NE33-2E 51
Percy Ter. DH1-3A 138
Percy Ter. DH4-3E 115
Percy Ter. NE3-5A 28
Percy Ter. NE15-5A 38
Percy Ter. NE25-2A 22
Percy Ter. SR2-4D 111
Percy Ter. SR6-1F 89
Percy Ter. S. SR2-4D 111
Percy Way. NE15-3B 38
Peregrine Ct. NE29-4A 34
Peregrine Pl. NE12-3B 28
Perivale Rd. SR4-4F 107
Perrycoats. SR3-5F 119
Perry St. NE9-2E 79
Perth Av. NE32 & NE34 -4C 66
Perth Clo. NE28-5B 32
Perth Clo. NE29-2E 33
Perth Ct. NE11-2D 91
Perth Ct. SR3-1C 118
Perth Gdns. NE28-5B 32
Perth Grn. NE32-4D 67
Perth Rd. SR3-1D 119
Perth Sq. SR3-5E 109
Peterborough Clo. NE8-5D 61
Peterborough Rd. DH1 -2E 137
Peterborough St. NE8-5D 61
Peterborough Way. NE32 -1F 83
Peterlee Clo. SR8-2B 134
Petersfield Rd. SR4-3A 108
Petersham Rd. SR4-2A 108
Peter Stracey Ho. SR6-1B 100
Petherton Ct. NE3-4E 25
Peth La. NE40-1B 54
Petrel Clo. NE33-1D 51
Petteril. NE38-1E 113
Petworth Clo. NE33-1F 51
Pevensey Clo. NE29-1A 34
Pexton Way. NE5-4B 40
Philadelphia La. DH4-5B 116
Philiphaugh. NE28-4C 46
Philip Pl. NE4-1F 59
Philipson St. NE6-1E 63
Philip Sq. SR3-5D 109
Phillips Av. NE16-2F 75
Phoenix Chase. NE29-2D 33
Phoenix Ct. NE29-2D 33
Phoenix Rd. NE38-2D 103
Phoenix Rd. SR4-1B 108
Piccadilly. SR3-2C 118
Picherwell. NE10-3C 80
Pickard Clo. SR8-2D 135
Pickard St. SR4-1E 109
Pickering Ct. NE32-5C 48
Pickering Grn. NE9-3A 92
Pickering Rd. SR4-4F 107
Pickering Sq. SR4-4F 107
Pickhurst Rd. SR4-4F 107
Pickhurst Sq. SR4-4A 108
Picktree Cotts. DH3-2E 123
Picktree Cotts. E. DH3-2F 123
Picktree La. DH3-2E 123
Picktree Lodge. DH3-2C 112
Picktree Ter. DH3-2E 123
Pickwick Clo. DH1-5B 138
Pier Pde. NE33-1F 51
Pier Rd. NE30-2F 35
Pier View. SR6-3E 101
Pikestone Clo. NE38-5E 103
Pilgrim Clo. SR5-3A 100
Pilgrim St. NE1 -2C 60 & 4D 143
Pilgrim St. NE1 -3D 61 & 5E 143
Pilgrim's Way. DH1-1F 139
Pilgrimsway. NE9-3F 79
Pilgrimsway. NE32-1D 67
Pilton Rd. NE5-1B 40 (in two parts)
Pilton Wlk. NE5-1B 40
Pimlico. DH1-3C 138
Pimlico Ct. NE9-1E 91
Pimlico Rd. SR4-4F 107
Pine Av. DH1-5A 140
Pine Av. DH4-4B 126
Pine Av. NE3-3B 26
Pine Av. NE34-2E 69
Pine Rd. NE21-5B 56
Pines, The. NE4-4F 59
Pines, The. NE40-1A 72
Pine St. DH2-5A 122
Pine St. DH3-3A 102 (Birtley)
Pine St. DH3-3E 123 (Chester-le-Street)
Pine St. DH9-5A 130
Pine St. NE8-1A 78
Pine St. NE13-4A 6
Pine St. NE15-2F 37
Pine St. NE32-1F 65
Pine St. NE40-1A 72
Pine St. SR4-1E 109
Pinesway. SR3-4A 110
Pinetree Gdns. NE25-4A 22
Pinetree Way. NE11-5A 58
Pine View. DH9-5A 130
Pinewood. NE31-5E 47
Pinewood Av. NE13-2D 15
Pinewood Av. NE38-1A 114
Pinewood Clo. NE3-3D 25
Pinewood Clo. NE6-4A 46
Pinewood Gdns. NE11-5F 77
Pinewood Rd. SR5-2D 99
Pinewood Sq. SR5-2D 99
Pinewood St. DH4-4D 125
Pinewood Vs. NE34-1E 69
Pink La. NE1-3B 60 & 5B 142 (in three parts)
Pinner Pl. NE6-3D 63
Pinner Rd. SR4-2B 108
Pipershaw. NE37-2E 103
Pipe Track La. NE4-3C 58
Pipewellgate. NE8 -4C 60 & 5E 143
Pitcairn Rd. SR4-2A 108
Pit La. DH1-3C 136
Pittington La. DH1 & DH6 -1E 141
Pitt La. NE23-3D 9
Pitt St. NE4-2A 60 & 3A 142
Pity Me By-Pass. DH1-4A 136
Plains Rd. SR3-5D 109
Plaistow Sq. SR4-1B 108
Planesway. NE10-5D 81
Planet Pl. NE12-5D 17
Planetree Av. NE4-4F 41
Plane Tree Ct. SR3-4D 119
Plantagenet Av. DH3-4F 123
Plantation Av. NE16-2F 75
Plantation Gro. NE10-5A 64
Plantation Rd. SR4-5C 98
Plantation Sq. SR4-1D 109
Plantation, The. NE9-5F 79
Plawsworth Gdns. NE9-1B 92
Plawsworth Rd. SR4-3F 107
Plawsworth Sq. SR4-3F 107
Pleasant Pl. DH3-3B 102
Plessey Cres. NE25-3C 22
Plessey Gdns. NE29-4E 33
Plessey Ter. NE7-3D 45
Plough Rd. SR3-5E 119
Plover Clo. NE38-4E 103
Plover Lodge. DH3-1A 102
Plover Rd. SR4-4F 107
Plummer Chare. NE1 -3D 61 & 5E 143 (off Quayside)
Plummer St. NE4-4A 60
Plumpton Rd. SR4-3F 107
Plumtree Av. SR5-2B 98
Plymouth Clo. SR7-4B 132
Plymouth Rd. NE29-4D 33
Plymouth Sq. SR3-5D 109
Point Pleasant Ind. Est. NE28 -3A 48
Point Pleasant Ter. NE28 -3A 48
Polden Clo. SR8-4A 134
Polden Cres. NE29-5A 22
Polebrook Rd. SR4-2A 108
Polemarch St. SR7-4E 133
Polinaize St. DH9-2E 131
Pollard St. NE33-1E 51
Polmaise St. NE21-5B 66
Polmuir Rd. SR3-5D 109
Polmuir Sq. SR3-5D 109
Polperro Clo. DH3-5C 102
Polsham Rd. SR4-3F 107
Polton Sq. SR4-1B 108
Polwarth Cres. NE3-1D 27
Polwarth Dri. NE3-1D 27
Polwarth Pl. NE3-1D 27
Polwarth Rd. NE3-5D 15
Polworth Sq. SR3-5D 109
Polytechnic Precinct. SR2 -2F 109
Pontdyke. NE10-5D 81
Pontefract Rd. SR4-4F 107
Ponteland Clo. NE29-3E 33
Ponteland Clo. NE38-4E 103
Ponteland Rd. NE3 NE5, NE4 -4D 25 to 5C 42
Ponteland Rd. NE13-1A 24
Ponteland Rd. NE15-1F 37
Pontop Sq. SR4-1B 108
Pontop St. DH5-4B 128
Pool Bri. NE10-3C 82
Poole Clo. NE23-2D 5
Poole Rd. SR4-2B 108
Pooley Clo. NE5-3D 41
Pooley Rd. NE5-4C 40
Poplar Av. DH4-4B 126
Poplar Av. NE6-4B 46
Poplar Clo. NE31-4C 64
Poplar Cres. DH3-3A 102
Poplar Cres. NE8-5C 60
Poplar Cres. NE11-3E 77
Poplar Dri. DH1-3A 140
Poplar Dri. SR6-1D 89
Poplar Gro. NE34-2D 69
Poplar Gro. SR2-2D 121
Poplar Pl. NE3-4E 27
Poplar Rd. DH1-2D 141
Poplar Rd. NE21-1B 74
Poplars, The. DH3-4E 123
Poplars, The. DH4-2A 116
Poplars, The. NE3-1E 43
Poplars, The. NE4-4F 59
Poplars, The. NE38-4C 104
Poplars, The. SR4-1F 107
Poplars, The. SR5-3E 99
Poplar St. DH2-5A 122
Poplar St. DH3-3E 123
Poplar St. DH9-5A 130
Poplar St. NE15-2F 37
Poplar Ter. DH3-2E 123
Popplewell Gdns. NE9-1E 91
Popplewell Ter. NE29-2B 34
Porchester Dri. NE23-2D 5
Porchester St. NE33-5C 50
Porlock Ho. NE32-2C 66
Porlock Rd. NE32-2C 66
Portadown Rd. SR4-4F 107
Portberry St. NE33-4C 50
Portberry Way. NE33-4C 50
Portchester Gro. NE35-2C 84
Portchester Rd. SR4-3A 108
Portchester Sq. SR4-3A 108
Porthcawl Dri. NE37-3B 94
Portland Av. SR7-3C 132
Portland Clo. DH2-4C 122
Portland Clo. NE28-5B 32
Portland Gdns. NE9-2E 91
Portland Gdns. NE23-2E 5
Portland Gdns. NE30-2C 34
Portland M. NE2 -5A 44 & 2F 143
Portland Rd. NE2 -5A 44 & 1F 143
Portland Rd. NE15-3F 37
Portland Rd. SR3-5D 109
Portland Sq. SR3-5E 109
Portland St. NE4-3E 59
Portland St. NE10-1E 81
Portland Ter. NE2 -5A 44 & 1E 143
Portman Pl. NE6-4D 63
Portman Sq. SR4-3A 108
Portmarnock. NE37-3A 94
Portmeads Rise. DH3-3C 102
Portobello Ind. Est. DH3 -3C 102
Portobello La. SR5 & SR6 -3B 100
Portobello Ter. DH3-5D 103
Portobello Way. DH3-4C 102
Portree Clo. DH3-1C 112
Portree Sq. SR3-1D 119
Portrush Clo. NE37-3B 94
Portrush Rd. SR4-2A 108
Portrush Way. NE7-5E 29
Portslade Rd. SR4-3A 108
Portsmouth Rd. NE29-4E 33
Portsmouth Rd. SR4-3A 108
Portsmouth Sq. SR4-3F 107
Portugal Pl. NE28-3C 46
Post Office La. NE29-2B 34
Potterhouse La. DH1-1A 136
Potterhouse Ter. DH1 -1B 136
Potteries, The. NE33-3F 51
Potter Pl. DH9-4E 131
Potters Bank. DH1-4B 138
Potters Clo. DH1-4B 138
Potter Sq. SR3-5D 109
Potter St. NE28-3B 48
Potter St. NE32-5B 48
Pottersway. NE9-3F 79
Pottery Bank. NE6-4E 63
Pottery Bank. SR1-5D 101
Pottery La. NE1-4B 60
Pottery La. SR4-1F 107
Pottery Rd. SR5-4F 99
Pottery Yd. DH4-4C 126
Potts St. NE6-1B 62
Poultry Farm. DH4-4B 116
Powburn Clo. DH2-5C 122
Powburn Gdns. NE4-4A 42
Powis Rd. SR3-5D 109
Powis Sq. SR3-5D 109
Powys Pl. NE4-1F 59
Poynings Clo. NE3-4D 25
Poynings Rd. NE3-4D 25
Prebends Field. DH1-2A 140
Prebends Fields. DH1-2A 140
Precinct, The. SR2-5A 110
Prefect Pl. NE9-3F 79
Premier Rd. SR3-5D 109
Prendwick Av. NE31-4B 64
Prendwick Clo. DH2-5C 122
Prendwick Ct. NE31-4B 64
Prengarth Av. SR6-1B 100
Prensgarth Way. NE34-4E 67
Prescot Rd. SR4-2A 108
President Carter Cen. SR3 -4D 119
Press La. SR1-1C 110
Prestbury Rd. NE29-5A 34 (in two parts)
Prestbury Rd. SR4-4F 107
Presthope Rd. SR4-4F 107
Prestmede. NE10-2D 81
Preston Av. NE30-3C 34
Preston Ga. NE29-5B 22
Prestonhill. SR3-5D 119
Preston N. Rd. NE29-5A 22
Preston Pk. NE29-2B 34
Preston Rd. NE29-2C 34
Preston Rd. SR2-3D 111
Preston Ter. NE27-1F 31
Preston Ter. NE29-2B 34
Preston Wood. NE30-1B 34
Prestwick. NE10-5D 81
Prestwick Av. NE29-3E 33
Prestwick Clo. NE37-3B 94
Prestwick Dri. NE10-3A 82
Prestwick Gdns. NE3-5B 26
Prestwick Rd. SR4-1A 108
Pretoria Sq. SR3-5D 109
Pretoria St. NE15-3E 57
Price St. NE31-1B 64
Priestfield Clo. SR3-5D 119
Priestley Gdns. NE10-2A 82
Priestly Cres. SR4-5F 99
Priestman Ct. SR4-2B 108
Primary Gdns. SR2-2D 111
Primate Rd. SR3-1C 118
Primrose Av. SR8-2E 135
Primrose Clo. NE23-4F 7
Primrose Cres. DH4-2C 124
Primrose Cres. SR6-2B 100
Primrose Gdns. NE28-1C 46
Primrose Hill. DH4-3C 124
Primrose Hill. NE9-5E 79
Primrose Hill Ter. NE32 -4B 66
Primrose Pl. NE9-5D 79
Primrose Precinct. SR6 -2B 100
Primrose St. SR4-1F 107
Primrose Ter. DH3-3B 102
Primrose Ter. NE32-3A 66
Prince Albert Ter. NE2 -1D 61 & 3E 143
Prince Consort La. NE31 -1B 64
Prince Consort Rd. NE8 -4D 61
Prince Consort Rd. NE31 -1A 64
Prince Consort Rd. NE32 -1A 66
Prince Edward Ct. NE34 -2F 69
Prince Edward Gro. NE34 -1B 70

Prince Edward Rd. NE34
-2D 69
Prince George Av. SR6
-1B 100
Prince George Sq. NE33
-2E 51
Prince of Wales Clo. NE34
-2D 69
Prince Philip Clo. NE15-2B 58
Prince Regent Way. NE29
-1B 50
Prince Rd. NE28-2C 46
Princes Av. NE3-3D 27
Prince's Av. SR6-5D 89
Princes Clo. NE3-1D 27
Princes Gdns. NE25-2A 22
Prince's Gdns. SR6-5D 89
Princes Rd. NE3-1D 27
Princess Gdns. DH5-3F 129
Princess Rd. SR7-3E 133
Princess Sq. NE1
-2C 60 & 3D 143
Princess St. NE10-1F 81
Princess St. SR2-2B 110
Princes St. DH1-1B 138
Princes St. DH4-5F 115
Princes St. NE30-3D 35
Prince St. SR1-1B 110
Princesway Central. NE11
-1B 90
Princesway N. NE11-4A 78
Princesway S. NE11-1B 90
Princetown Ter. SR3-1C 118
Princeway. NE30-2E 35
Prior's Clo. DH1-2A 138
Prior's Ter. NE30-3F 35
Priory Av. NE25-3B 22
Priory Cotts. NE26-1C 22
Priory Ct. NE8-4E 61
(off Hopper St.)
Priory Grn. NE6-2A 62
Priory Gro. SR4-2D 109
Priory M. NE30-3F 35
Priory Pl. NE13-2C 14
Priory Rd. DH1-3B 136
Priory Rd. NE32-5E 49
Priory Way. NE5-5B 24
Proctor Ct. NE6-3F 63
Proctor Sq. SR3-5D 109
Proctor St. NE6-2F 63
Promenade. NE26-1C 22
Promenade. NE33-1A 52
Promenade Ter. NE30-2F 35
Promendade. SR2-4E 111
Promontory Ter. NE26-3E 23
Prospect Av. NE25-1A 10
Prospect Av. NE28-1D 47
Prospect Av. N. NE28-5D 31
Prospect Cotts. NE9-3E 93
Prospect Ct. NE4-2F 59
Prospect Gdns. NE36-3E 85
Prospect Pl. NE4-2F 59
Prospect Row. SR1-5D 101
Prospect St. DH3-2E 123
Prospect St. NE8-5C 60
Prospect Ter. DH1-3A 138
(Neville's Cross)
Prospect Ter. DH1-5F 139
(Shincliffe)
Prospect Ter. DH3-2E 123
Prospect Ter. NE9-4C 92
(Eighton Banks)
Prospect Ter. NE9-3D 93
(Springwell)
Prospect Ter. NE30-3D 35
Prospect Ter. NE36-3B 86
Providence Pl. DH1-3B 140
Providence Pl. NE10-1B 80
Providence Row. DH1-2D 139
Provident Ter. NE28-3C 46
Provost Gdns. NE15-3C 58
Prudhoe Chare. NE1
-1C 60 & 3C 142
Prudhoe Ct. NE3-3A 26
Prudhoe Gro. NE32-4F 65
Prudhoe Pl. NE1
-1C 60 & 3C 142
Prudhoe St. NE1
-1C 60 & 3C 142
Prudhoe St. NE29-5C 34
Prudhoe St. SR4-1E 109
Prudhoe Ter. NE29-5C 34
Prudhoe Ter. NE30-2F 35
Pudding Chare. NE1
-3C 60 & 5C 142
Pudsey Ct. DH1-3C 136
Pullman Ct. NE9-5C 78
Pump La. NE33-5C 50
Purbeck Clo. NE29-5A 22
Purbeck Gdns. NE23-2D 5
Purbeck Rd. NE12-3D 29
Purley. NE38-3F 105
Purley Clo. NE28-5B 32
Purley Gdns. NE3-5B 26
Purley Rd. SR3-5D 109
Purley Sq. SR3-1D 119
Putney Sq. SR4-4A 108
Pykerley M. NE25-2A 22
Pykerley Rd. NE25-2F 21

Quadrant, The. NE29-4F 33
Quadrant, The. SR1-1D 111
Quality Row. NE6-2F 61
Quality Row Rd. NE16-1F 75
Quantock Av. DH2-4C 122
Quantock Clo. NE12-4B 28
Quantock Clo. NE29-5A 22
Quantock Pl. SR8-4A 134
Quarry Cotts. NE23-5B 8
Quarryfield Rd. NE8
-3E 61 & 5F 143
Quarryheads La. DH1-3C 138
Quarry Ho. Gdns. DH5
(in two parts) -4B 128
Quarry Ho. La. DH1-3A 138
Quarry Ho. La. DH5-4B 128
Quarry La. NE34-3E 69
Quarry Rd. DH9-1C 130
Quarry Rd. NE15-1B 56
Quarry Rd. NE31-2C 64
Quarry Rd. SR3-4F 119
Quarry Row. NE10-1B 80
Quarry St. SR3-3F 119
Quayside. NE1 & NE6
-3C 60 & 5D 143
Quayside Ct. NE30-4D 35
Quay, The. DH5-4E 129
Quay View. NE28-3B 48
Queen Alexandra Bri. SR5
-4E 99
Queen Alexandra Rd. NE29
-3B 34
Queen Alexandra Rd.
SR3 & SR2-4A 110
Queen Alexandra Rd. SR7
-4E 133
Queen Alexandra Rd. W.
NE29-3A 34
Queen Anne Ct. NE6-5E 45
Queen Anne St. NE6-5E 45
(off Shields Rd.)
Queen Elizabeth Av. NE9
-4A 80
Queen Elizabeth Ct. NE34
-4E 67
Queen's Av. SR6-5D 89
Queen's Av. SR7-4A 132
Queensberry St. SR4-1A 110
Queensbridge. NE12-3B 28
Queensbury Dri. NE5-2C 38
Queensbury Rd. SR7-3B 132
Queens Ct. NE3-5D 15
Queen's Ct. NE4
-1A 60 & 3A 142
Queens Ct. NE8-1A 78
Queen's Ct. NE15-3C 38
Queen's Cres. NE28-1C 46
Queen's Cres. NE31-3C 64
Queen's Cres. SR4-3E 109
Queens Dri. NE16-4A 76
Queen's Dri. NE26-2B 22
Queen's Gdns. NE12-3F 29
Queens Gdns. NE23-3A 8
Queens Gro. DH1-5A 138
Queensland Av. NE34-4D 67
Queen's La. NE1
-3C 60 & 5D 143
Queensmere. DH3-3B 112
Queens Pde. SR6-5D 89
Queens Pk. DH3-3F 123
Queen's Rd. NE2-3A 44
(in two parts)
Queens Rd. NE5-2B 40
Queens Rd. NE15-3B 38
Queens Rd. NE23-3A 8
Queen's Rd. NE26-1A 22
Queen's Rd. SR5-4F 99
Queens Sq. NE1
-2C 60 & 3D 143
Queen's Ter. NE2-3A 44
Queens Ter. NE28-2D 47
Queen St. DH3-1A 102
Queen St. DH5-3F 129
Queen St. NE1
-3D 61 & 5E 143
Queen St. NE8-2B 78
Queen St. NE30-4D 35
Queen St. NE33-1E 51
Queen St. SR1-1B 110
(in two parts)
Queen st. SR7-3E 133
Queen St. E. SR1-1D 111
Queensway. DH5-5D 127
Queensway. NE3-5D 15
Queensway. NE4-4F 41
Queensway. NE30-2E 35
Queensway. NE38-3C 104
Queensway. N. NE11-3A 78
Queensway. S. NE11-1B 90
Queen Victoria Rd. NE1
-1B 60 & 2B 142
Queen Victoria St. NE10
-1E 81
Quentin Av. NE3-4F 25
Quigley Ter. DH3-2A 102
Quin Clo. SR8-4C 134
Quinn's Ter. DH1-3A 138

Rabbit Banks Rd. NE8-4C 60
Raby Clo. DH4-4E 125
Raby Cres. NE6-2A 62
Raby Cross. NE6-2A 62
Raby Dri. SR3-3B 118
Raby Gdns. NE32-3A 66
Raby Ga. NE6-1A 62
Raby Rd. DH1-2C 136
Raby Rd. NE38-3E 103
Raby St. NE6-1A 62
(in two parts)
Raby St. NE8-2E 79
Raby St. SR4-1F 109
Raby Wlk. NE6-1A 62
Raby Way. NE6-1A 62
Rachel Clo. SR2-4B 120
Rackley Way. SR6-1E 89
(in two parts)
Radcliffe Pl. NE5-3F 41
Radcliffe Rd. SR5-2C 98
Radcliffe St. DH3-4B 102
Radlett Rd. SR5-2C 98
Radnor Gdns. NE28-1C 48
Radnor St. NE1
-1D 61 & 2E 143
Radstock Pl. NE12-3E 29
Rae Av. NE28-5D 31
Raeburn Av. NE38-4D 105
Raeburn Gdns. NE9-3A 80
Raeburn Rd. NE34-5B 68
Raeburn Rd. SR5-2A 98
Raey Ct. DH2-3E 123
Raglan. NE38-3F 103
Raglan Av. SR2-4D 111
Raglan Row. DH4-5B 116
Raglan St. NE32-5E 49
Railton Gdns. NE9-4A 80
Railway Cotts. DH1-3A 138
Railway Cotts. DH2-1C 122
Railway Cotts. DH3-3A 102
(Birtley)
Railway Cotts. DH4-5E 125
(High Dubmire)
Railway Cotts. DH4-2E 115
(Penshaw)
Railway Cotts. NE27-4F 19
Railway Row. SR1-1A 110
Railway St. DH4-3B 126
Railway St. DH5-4F 129
Railway St. NE4 & NE1
-4A 60 & 5B 142
Railway St. NE11-5E 59
(in two parts)
Railway St. NE29-4C 34
Railway St. NE31-5A 48
Railway St. NE32-1F 65
Railway St. SR1-1D 111
Railway St. SR4-5E 99
Railway Ter. DH4-4C 116
(New Herrington)
Railway Ter. DH4-2E 115
(Penshaw)
Railway Ter. DH5-3F 129
Railway Ter. NE4-4F 59
Railway Ter. NE28-3F 47
Railway Ter. NE29-4C 34
Railway Ter. NE38-4D 105
Railway Ter. SR4-1F 107
Railway Ter. N. DH4-4C 116
Rainford Av. SR2-5D 111
Rainhill Clo. NE37-3D 95
Rainhill Rd. NE37-3D 95
Rainton Bank. DH5-2D 129
Rainton Bri. Ind. Est. DH4
-1A 128
Rainton Clo. NE10-4A 82
Rainton Gro. DH5-2C 128
Rainton St. DH4-2A 116
Rainton St. SR4-1F 109
Rainton St. SR7-4E 133
Rake La. NE29-1E 33
Raleigh Clo. NE33-4D 51
Raleigh Rd. SR5-2C 98
Raleigh Sq. SR5-2C 98
Ralph Av. SR2-2D 121
Ralph St. NE31-5A 48
Ramilies. SR2-4B 120
Ramillies Rd. SR5-1A 98
Ramillies Sq. SR5-2A 98
Ramparts, The. NE15-4A 40
Ramsay Sq. SR5-2C 98
Ramsay St. NE21-1A 74
Ramsey Clo. DH1-4A 140
Ramsey Clo. SR8-1C 134
Ramsey St. DH3-4E 123
Ramsgate Rd. SR5-2C 98
Ramside View. DH1-1D 141
Randolph Clo. SR1-2D 111
Randolph St. NE32-1A 66
Range Vs. SR6-1E 89
Rangoon Rd. SR5-1A 98
Ranksborough St. SR7
-2C 132
Ranmere Rd. NE15-2F 57
Ranmore Clo. NE23-2D 5
Rannoch Av. DH2-4D 123
Rannoch Rd. SR5-2A 98
Ranson Cres. NE34-3E 67
Ranson St. SR4 & SR2
-3F 109
Raphael Av. NE34-4A 68
Rathmore Gdns. NE30-2C 34
Ratho Ct. NE10-4C 80
Ravel Ct. NE32-1A 66
Ravenburn Gdns. NE15-1E 57
Ravenna Rd. SR5-2A 98
Ravensbourne Av. NE36
-2B 86
Ravensburn Wlk. NE15-2E 37
Ravenscar Clo. NE16-5D 75
Ravenscleugh Ct. NE6-3B 62
(off Harbottle St.)
Ravenscourt Pl. NE8-1C 78
(off Airey Ter.)
Ravenscourt Rd. SR5-2A 98
Ravensdale Cres. NE9-4E 79
Ravenshill Rd. NE5-3F 39
Ravenside Rd. NE4-4A 42
Ravenstone. NE37-1A 104
Ravenswood Clo. NE12-2A 30
Ravenswood Gdns. NE9
-2D 91
Ravenswood Rd. NE6-3D 45
Ravenswood Rd. SR5-1A 98
Ravenswood Sq. SR5-1A 98
Ravensworth. SR2-4B 120
Ravensworth Av. DH4-4E 125
Ravensworth Av. NE9-3B 92
Ravensworth Clo. NE28
-2B 48
Ravensworth Ct. NE3-2F 25
Ravensworth Ct. NE11-1F 77
Ravensworth Gdns. DH3
-3A 102
Ravensworth Rd. DH3
-3A 102
Ravensworth Rd. NE11-2E 77
Ravensworth St. NE28-2B 48
Ravensworth St. SR4-1F 109
Ravensworth Ter. DH1
-2D 139
Ravensworth Ter. DH3
-3B 102
Ravensworth Ter. NE4
-2A 60 & 4A 142
Ravensworth Ter. NE11
-2E 77
Ravensworth Ter. NE32
-4A 66
Ravensworth Ter. NE33
-5E 51
Ravensworth Vs. NE9-2B 92
Raven Ter. DH3-3B 102
Ravine Ter. SR6-2D 101
(in two parts)
Rawdon Ct. NE28-4D 47
Rawdon Rd. SR5-2C 98
Rawling Rd. NE8-2C 78
Rawlston Way. NE5-1E 41
Rawmarsh Rd. SR5-2A 98
Raydale Av. NE37-4A 94
Raylees Gdns. NE11-3E 77
Rayleigh Dri. NE13-5A 6
Rayleigh Gro. NE8-2C 78
Raynham Clo. NE23-1E 7
Raynham Ct. NE33-3E 51
Readhead Av. NE33-3F 51
Readhead Dri. NE6-3E 63
Readhead Rd. NE34-4A 52
Reading Rd. NE33-1B 68
Reading Rd. SR5-2B 98
Reading Sq. SR5-2B 98
Reasby Gdns. NE40-2A 54
Reasby Vs. NE40-2A 54
Reay Cres. NE35-2F 85
Reay Gdns. NE5-2C 40
Reay Pl. NE3-4C 26
Reay St. NE10-5F 63
Reay St. NE34-3A 68
Rectory Av. NE3-1F 43
Rectory Bank. NE36-3E 85
Rectory Cotts. NE40-1B 54
Rectory Dri. NE3-1F 43
Rectory Grn. NE36-3E 85
Rectory Gro. NE3-5F 27
Rectory La. NE16-3A 76
Rectory La. NE21-1F 73
Rectory Pl. NE8-1C 78
Rectory Rd. DH5-5F 129
Rectory Rd. NE3-1F 43
Rectory Rd. NE8-1C 78
Rectory Rd. NE10-3B 80
Rectory Rd. E. NE10-3C 80
Rectory Ter. NE3-5F 27
Rectory Ter. NE36-3E 85
Red Admiral Ct. NE11-3A 78
Red Barns. NE1
-2E 61 & 3F 143
Red Briar Wlk. DH1-2A 136
Red Bungalows. NE9-3D 93
Redburn Clo. DH4-5B 126
Redburn Rd. DH4-1A 128
Redburn Rd. NE5-1A 40
Redcar Rd. NE6-3F 45
Redcar Rd. NE28-1C 48
Redcar Rd. SR5-2C 98
Redcar Sq. SR5-2C 98
Redcar Ter. NE36-3E 85
Redcliffe Way. NE5-2D 41
Redcroft Grn. NE5-2D 41
Redditch Sq. SR5-2B 98
Rede Av. NE31-1C 64
Rede Ho. NE1
-2E 61 & 4F 143
Redemarsh. NE10-4D 81
Redesdale Av. NE3-4B 26
Redesdale Av. NE21-2E 73
Redesdale Clo. NE12-2E 29
Redesdale Clo. NE15-5A 40
Redesdale Gdns. NE11-3E 77
Redesdale Gro. NE29-4E 33
Redesdale Rd. DH2-4D 123
Redesdale Rd. NE29-4E 33
Redesdale Rd. SR5-1A 98
Rede St. NE11-5A 78
Rede St. NE32-2F 65
Redewater Gdns. NE16-4F 75
Redewater Rd. NE4-4A 42
Redford Pl. NE23-2E 17
Red Hall Dri. NE7-1E 45
Redheugh Ct. NE8-2A 78
Redheugh Rd. NE25-2C 20
Redhill. SR6-2D 89
Redhill Dri. NE16-5D 75
Redhill Rd. SR5-2B 98
Redhills La. DH1-2A 138
Red Hills Ter. DH1-2B 138
Redhill Vs. DH1-2B 138
Redhill Wlk. NE23-2D 5
Red Ho. Dri. NE25-1E 21
Red Ho. Rd. NE31-2E 65
Redland Av. NE3-4F 25
Redlands. DH4-4F 115
Redland Wlk. NE3-4F 25
Red Lion Building. NE9-4C 92
Red Lion La. NE37-3A 94
Redmayne Ct. NE10-2B 80
Redmond Rd. SR5-2C 98
Redmond Sq. SR5-2C 98
Rednam Pl. NE5-3D 41
Red Rose Ter. DH3-3E 123
Redruth Gdns. NE9-3D 91
Redruth Sq. SR5-2B 98
Red Wlk. NE6-2B 44
Redwell Ct. NE34-5E 53
Redwell La. NE34-1B 70
Redwing Clo. NE38-5E 103
Redwood Clo. DH5-4E 129
Redwood Gdns. NE11-5F 77
Reed Av. NE12-2D 17
Reedham Ct. NE5-5D 25
Reedside. NE40-2C 54
Reed St. NE30-4D 35
Reed St. NE33-4D 51
Reedswood Cres. NE23-4F 5
Reestones Pl. NE3-5E 25
Reeth Rd. SR5-2C 98
Reeth Sq. SR5-2C 98
Reeth Way. NE15-3E 37
Regal Rd. SR4-1E 109
Regency Dri. NE16-4E 75
Regency Dri. SR3-2A 120
Regency Gdns. NE29-3A 34
Regent Av. NE3-4D 27
Regent Cen. NE3-4E 27
Regent Ct. NE8-5D 61
Regent Ct. NE12-5C 16
Regent Ct. NE31-2C 64
Regent Ct. NE33-3D 51
Regent Dri. NE16-5E 75
Regent Farm Rd. NE3-4C 26
Regent Rd. NE3-4E 27
Regent Rd. NE28-2C 46
Regent Rd. NE32-1B 66
Regent Rd. SR2-5F 121
Regent Rd. N. NE3-4D 27
Regents Ct. NE28-1A 46
Regents Dri. NE30-1E 35
Regents Pk. NE28-1A 46
Regent St. DH5-3F 129
Regent St. NE8-5D 61
Regent St. NE33-3D 51
Regent Ter. NE8-5D 61
Regent Ter. NE29-3F 33
Regent Ter. SR2-5D 111
Reginald St. NE10-1A 80
Reginald St. NE35-2E 85
Reginald St. SR4-1E 109
Regina Sq. SR5-1C 98
Reid Av. NE28-1C 46
Reid Pk. Clo. NE2-3A 44
Reid Pk. Ct. NE2-3A 44
Reid Pk. Rd. NE2-3A 44
Reid's La. NE23-3C 8
Reigate Sq. NE23-2D 5
Rekendyke Ind. Est. NE33
-4D 51
Rekendyke La. NE33-3D 51
Relly Path. DH1-3A 138
Relton Av. NE6-3C 62
Relton Clo. DH4-5F 125
Relton Ct. NE25-2A 22
Relton Pl. NE25-2A 22
Relton Ter. DH3-4E 123
Relton Ter. NE25-2A 22
Rembrandt Av. NE34-4B 68
Remus Av. NE15-2A 36
Remus Clo. NE13-2C 14
Rendel St. NE11-1E 77
Rendle Rd. NE6-3F 63
Renforth St. NE11-1E 77
Renfrew Clo. NE29-1E 33
Renfrew Grn. NE5-1D 41
(in two parts)
Renfrew Pl. DH3-1B 112
Renfrew Rd. SR5-2C 98
Rennie Rd. SR5-2A 98
Rennie Sq. SR5-2A 98
Rennington. NE10-4E 81
Rennington Av. NE30-1E 35
Rennington Clo. NE30-5E 23
Rennington Pl. NE5-3E 41
Renny's La. DH1
-4A 140 to 3E 141
Renny St. DH1-2E 139
Renoir Gdns. NE34-5C 68
Renwick Av. NE3-3A 26
Renwick St. NE6-1C 62
Renwick Ter. DH3-5B 124
Renwick Ter. NE8-2B 78
Rescue Station Cotts. DH5
-1D 129
Resida Clo. NE15-4E 39
Retail World. NE11-3B 90
Retford Gdns. NE29-1F 49
Retford Rd. SR5-2B 98
Retford Sq. SR5-2B 98
Retreat, The. NE15-5A 38
Retreat, The. SR2-2A 110
Revell Ter. NE5-3F 41
Revelstoke Rd. SR5-2A 98
Revesby St. NE33-1A 68
Reynolds Av. NE12-5C 16
Reynolds Av. NE34-4B 68
Reynolds Av. NE38-4D 105
Reynolds Clo. DH9-3C 130
Reyrolle Ct. NE31-2C 64
Rheims Ct. SR4-5B 98
Rheydt Av. NE28-2B 46
Rhoda Ter. SR2-2E 121
Rhodesia Rd. SR5-2B 98
Rhodes St. NE6-2F 63
Rhodes Ter. DH1-4A 138
Rhondda Rd. SR5-2A 98
Rhuddlan Ct. NE5-1D 41
Rhyl Pde. NE31-5F 65
Rhyl Sq. SR5-2C 98
Ribbledale Gdns. NE7-1C 44
Ribble Rd. SR5-2A 98
Ribblesdale. DH4-3A 116
Ribblesdale. NE28-1B 46
Ribble Wlk. NE32
-4A 66 & 5A 66
Richard Av. SR4-3F 109
Richard Browell Rd. NE15
-3F 37
Richardson Av. NE34-3E 67
(in two parts)
Richardson Rd. NE2
-5D 43 & 1A 142
Richardson St. NE6-4E 45
Richardson St. NE28-2E 47
Richardson Ter. NE37-4C 94
Richardson Ter. SR2-4E 121
Richard St. DH5-4F 129
Richmond. SR2-3B 120
Richmond Av. NE10-1A 82
Richmond Av. NE16-1F 75
Richmond Av. NE38-1B 104
Richmond Ct. DH1-2D 137
Richmond Ct. NE8-1E 79
Richmond Ct. NE9-5E 79
Richmond Ct. NE32-5C 48
Richmond Gdns. NE28-1A 48
Richmond Gro. NE29-5A 34
Richmond M. NE3-1D 43
Richmond Pk. NE28-1A 46
Richmond Rd. DH1-2D 137
Richmond Rd. NE34-1A 68
Richmond St. SR5-5B 100
Richmond Ter. NE8-1D 79
Richmond Ter. NE10-2C 80
Richmond Ter. NE15-3B 38
Richmond Ter. NE26-5E 13
Richmond Way. NE23-1E 7
Rickaby St. SR1-5D 101
Rickgarth. NE10-5E 81
(in three parts)
Rickleton Av. DH3-5C 112
Rickleton Way. NE38-1D 113
Riddell Av. NE15-2B 58
Riddell Ct. DH2-4E 123
Riddell Ter. NE3-4C 26
Riddings Rd. SR5-1C 98
Riddings Sq. SR5-1C 98
Ridge Ct. NE13-3D 15
Ridge, The. NE40-3B 54
Ridgeway. DH3-2A 102
Ridgeway. NE4-4A 42
Ridgeway. NE10
-4F 81 to 3A 82
Ridgeway. NE25-3D 11
Ridgeway. SR2-4B 120
Ridgeway Cres. SR3-4F 109
Ridge Way, The. NE3-1A 42
Ridgeway, The. NE34-4E 69
Ridgewood Cres. NE3-4A 28
Ridgewood Gdns. NE3-5A 28
Ridgewood Vs. NE3-4A 28
Riding Hill. DH3-5A 124
Riding Lea. NE21-1F 73
Ridings, The. NE25-1D 21
Riding, The. NE3-1A 42
Ridley Av. DH2-3C 122
Ridley Av. NE28-5C 32
Ridley Av. SR2-3D 121
Ridley Clo. NE3-2B 26
Ridley Ct. NE1
-3C 60 & 5C 142
Ridley Gdns. NE16-1F 75
Ridley Gro. NE34-5B 52
Ridley Ho. NE3-4E 27
Ridley Pl. NE1
-1C 60 & 2C 142
Ridley St. DH9-1C 130
Ridley St. NE8-2C 78
Ridley St. NE23-4E 5
Ridley St. SR5-3F 99
Ridley Ter. NE10-2D 81
Ridley Ter. SR2-3D 111
Ridsdale Av. NE5-3F 39
Ridsdale Clo. NE25-1B 10
Ridsdale Clo. NE28-5D 31
Rievaulx. NE38-4B 104
Riga Sq. SR5-2B 98
Riggs, The. DH5-5D 127
Rignall. NE38-3F 105
Riley St. NE32-5B 48
Ringmore Ct. SR2-5A 110
Ringwood Dri. NE23-2D 5
Ringwood Grn. NE12-3D 29
Ringwood Rd. SR5-2B 98
Ringwood Sq. SR5-2B 98
Ripley Av. NE29-5A 34
Ripley Ct. NE9-4F 91
Ripley Dri. NE23-1E 7
Ripley Ter. NE6-1D 63
Ripon Clo. NE23-1E 7
Ripon Gdns. NE2-4C 44
Ripon Gdns. NE28-1A 48
Ripon Rd. DH1-1D 137
Ripon Sq. NE32-1A 84
Ripon St. DH3-4E 123
Ripon St. NE8-1D 79
Ripon St. SR6-3C 100
Rise, The. NE3-1A 42
Rise, The. NE8-1F 79
(off Duncan St.)
Rise, The. NE21-3F 55
Rise, The. NE26-1C 12
Rishton Sq. SR5-1B 98
Rising Sun Cotts. NE28
-5D 31
Rising Sun Vs. NE28-5D 31
Ritson Clo. NE29-3A 34
Ritson St. DH9-3C 130
Ritson St. SR6-1D 101
Riverbank Rd. SR5-3B 98
Riverdale. SR5-4A 98
River Dri. NE33-1D 51
River Garth. SR1-5D 101
(off High St. E.)
River La. NE40-1A 54
Rivermead. NE38-1C 114
Riversdale Ct. NE15-1A 16
Riversdale Rd. NE8-4C 60
Riversdale Ter. SR2-3F 109
Riversdale Way. NE15-1A 56
Riverside Ct. NE11-1F 77
Riverside Ct. NE33-2D 51
Riverside Pk. SR4-5A 98
Riverside Rd. SR5-3C 98
Riverside Studios. NE4-5E 59
Riverside View. NE6-4E 63
River St. NE33-4C 50
River Ter. DH3-2E 123
River View. NE21-5A 56
River View. NE30-3E 35
River View. NE40-2C 54
River View Ter. NE38-2C 114
Roachburn Rd. NE5-2F 39
Roadside Cotts. NE21-2E 55
Robert Owen Gdns. NE10
-3B 80
Robertson Rd. SR5-2A 98
Robertson Sq. SR5-2A 98
Robert Sq. SR7-4F 133
Roberts St. NE15-3E 57
Roberts Ter. NE32-2F 65
Robert St. NE33-3F 51
Robert St. SR3-3F 119
Robert St. SR4-1F 109
Robert St. SR7-4F 133
Robert Ter. DH9-1D 131
Robert Wheatham Ct. SR2
-1D 121
Robin Ct. DH5-4B 128
Robin Gro. SR5-3A 98
Robin La. DH5-5A 128
Robinson Gdns. NE28-1B 48
Robinson Gdns. SR6-1D 89
Robinson Ho. SR8-2E 135
Robinson St. NE6-1A 62
Robinson St. NE33-3E 51
Robinson Ter. NE38-3D 105
Robinson Ter. SR2-3D 111
Robinson Ter. SR3-3A 120
Robsheugh Pl. NE5-5E 41
Robson Av. SR8-2C 134
Robson Pl. SR2-4F 121
Robson's Ter. NE9-3C 92
Robson St. NE6-1F 61
Robson St. NE9-5E 79
Robson Ter. DH1-5F 139
Rochdale Rd. SR5-2B 98
Rochdale St. DH5-5E 129
Rochdale St. NE28-3C 46
Rochdale Way. SR5-2C 98
Roche Ct. NE38-3B 104
(in two parts)
Rochester Est. NE6-3E 63
Rochester Gdns. NE11-2F 77
Rochester Rd. DH1-2D 137
Rochester Sq. NE32-1A 84
Rochester St. NE6-3F 63
Rochester Ter. NE10-2C 80
Rochford Gro. NE23-2E 7
Rochford Rd. SR5-1A 98
Rockcliffe. NE26-2D 23
(off Cheviot View.)
Rockcliffe. NE33-4A 52
Rockcliffe Av. NE26-2D 23
Rockcliffe Gdns. NE15-5B 40
Rockcliffe Gdns. NE26-2E 23
Rockcliffe St. NE26-2D 23
Rockcliffe Way. NE9-3B 92
Rocket Way. NE12-2A 30
Rock Gro. NE9-5E 79
Rockingham Rd. SR5-1B 98
Rockingham Sq. SR5-1B 98
Rock Lodge Gdns. SR6
-1D 101
Rock Lodge Rd. SR6-1D 101
Rockmore Rd. NE21-1B 74
Rock Ter. NE2
-1D 61 & 2E 143
Rock Ter. NE37-5D 95
Rockville. SR6-1C 100
Rock Wlk. DH3-4A 114
Rodham Ter. DH9-1C 130
Rodin Av. NE34-5C 68
Rodney Clo. NE30-3E 35
Rodney Clo. SR2-4B 120
Rodney Ct. NE26-5C 12
(off Woodburn Sq.)
Rodney St. NE6-2A 62
Rodney Way. NE26-5C 12
Rodsley Av. NE8-2D 79
Roeburn Way. NE3-1B 42
Roedean Rd. SR5-1C 98
Roehedge. NE10-3A 82
Rogers Clo. SR8-3F 135
Rogerson Ter. NE5-2A 40
Roger St. NE6-1F 61
Rokeby Av. NE15-1C 56
Rokeby Dri. NE3-1B 42
Rokeby Sq. DH1-5A 138
Rokeby St. NE15-1C 56
Rokeby St. SR4-1F 109
Rokeby Ter. NE6
-3D 45 & 3E 45
Rokeby View. NE9-3F 91
Rokeby Vs. NE15-1C 56
Roker Av. NE25-3A 22
Roker Av. SR6-4C 100
Roker Baths Rd. SR6-3C 100
Rokerby Av. NE16-4A 76
Roker Pk. Rd. SR6-2D 101
Roker Pk. Ter. SR6-2D 101
Roker Ter. SR6-2D 101
Roland Rd. NE28-2A 48
Roland St. NE38-3D 105
Rollesby Ct. NE5-1D 41
Romaldkirk Clo. SR4-2F 107
Roman Av. DH3-3E 123
Roman Av. NE6-1C 62
Roman Rd. NE32-5A 66
Roman Rd. NE33-5E 35
Roman Rd. N. NE33-5E 35
Roman WallWall NE28-4D 47
Roman Way, The. NE5-4F 39
Romford Clo. NE23-1F 7
Romford Pl. NE9-2F 79
Romford St. SR4-1D 109
Romiley Gro. NE10-2C 82
Romilly St. NE33-2E 51
Romley Gro. NE10-2C 82
Romney Av. NE34-4B 68
Romney Av. NE38-4C 104
Romney Av. SR2-5D 111
Romney Dri. DH1-1D 141
Romney Gdns. NE9-3A 80
Romney Vs. NE38-4C 104
Romsey Clo. NE23-2D 5
Romsey Dri. NE35-2C 84
Romsey Gro. NE15-4E 39
Ronald Dri. NE15-1F 57
Ronald Gdns. NE31-3C 64
Ronaldsay Clo. SR2-2C 120
Ronald Sq. SR6-2C 100
Ronsdorf Ct. NE32-1A 66
Rookery La. NE16-5D 75
Rookhope. NE38-2E 113
Rooksleigh. NE21-1A 74
Rookwood Dri. NE13-4B 6
Rookwood Rd. NE5-4B 40
Roosevelt Rd. DH1-1F 139
Ropery La. DH3-3E 123
Ropery La. NE28-2A 48
Ropery Rd. NE8-1A 78
Ropery Rd. SR4-4F 99
Ropery, The. NE6-4C 62
Ropery Wlk. SR7-4F 133
Rosalie Ter. SR2-3D 111
Rosa St. NE38-3F 51
Rose Av. DH4-4E 125
Rose Av. DH9-4A 130
Rose Av. NE16-3A 76
Rose Av. NE23-1A 4
Rosebank Clo. SR2-2C 120
Rosebank Cotts. NE9-3E 93
Rosebank Hall. NE28-2A 48
Roseberry Ct. NE37-4C 94
Roseberry Ter. NE35-1D 85
Rosebery Av. NE8-2E 79
Rosebery Av. NE29-2B 34
Rosebery Av. NE33-3F 51
Rosebery Ct. NE25-2A 22
Rosebery Cres. NE2-4B 44
Rosebery Pl. NE2-4B 44
Rosebery St. SR5-4B 100
Roseby Rd. SR8-3D 135
Rose Ct. NE31-2C 64
Rose Cres. DH4-2C 124
Rose Cres. SR6-5E 71
Rosedale. NE28-5A 30
Rosedale Av. SR6-3D 89
Rosedale Ct. NE5-3F 39
Rosedale Cres. DH4-3A 126
Rosedale Rd. DH1-2D 141
Rosedale St. SR1-1A 110
Rosedale Ter. DH4-2C 126
Rosedale Ter. NE2
-1E 61 & 1F 143
Rosedale Ter. NE30-3D 35
Rosedale Ter. SR6-1C 100
Rosedale Ter. SR8-3E 135
Rosedale Vs. NE23-3E 5
Rosefinch Lodge. NE9-5E 79
Rose Gdns. NE28-5D 31
Rosegill. NE37-1A 104
Rosehill. NE28-2A 48
Rosehill Rd. NE28-2B 48
Rosehill Ter. NE28-2A 48
Rose Hill Way. NE5-3D 41
Roselea. NE32-1B 84
Roselea Av. SR2-3D 121
Rosella Pl. NE29-4B 34
Rosemary Gdns. NE9-3C 92
Rosemary La. NE1
-3C 60 & 5C 142
Rosemary Rd. SR5-2C 98
Rosemount. DH1-1D 137
Rosemount. NE5-2B 40
Rosemount. SR4-2F 107
Rosemount Av. NE10-3A 82
Rosemount Clo. NE37-3A 94
Rosemount Ct. NE36-3F 85
Rosemount Way. NE7-5E 29
Rosemount Way. NE25-2E 21
Rose St. DH4-5C 126
Rose St. NE8-5A 60
Rose St. NE31-2B 64
Rose St. SR4-1A 110
Rose St. E. DH4-2A 116
Rose St. W. DH4-2A 116
Rose Ter. DH2-1A 122
Rose Ter. NE5-3F 41
Rose Ter. NE40-5A 54
Rosetown Av. SR8-3F 135
Rosetree Cres. NE29-1A 50
Rose Villa La. NE16-3A 76
Rose Vs. NE4-2E 59
Roseville St. SR4-2F 109
Rosewell Pl. NE16-5E 75
Rosewood. NE12-4B 18
Rosewood Av. NE3-3F 27

Rosewood Cres. NE6-4B 46
Rosewood Cres. NE26-1C 12
Rosewood Gdns. DH2-1C 122
Rosewood Gdns. NE3-5A 26
Rosewood Gdns. NE9-4F 79
Rosewood Sq. SR4-5F 107
Rosewood Ter. DH3-2A 102
Rosewood Ter. NE28-2B 48
Roseworth Av. NE3-1E 43
Roseworth Clo. NE3-1E 43
Roseworth Cres. NE3-1E 43
Roseworth Ter. NE3-5E 27
Roseworth Ter. NE16-3A 76
Roslin Way. NE23-1E 7
Ross Av. NE11-1E 77
Rosse Clo. NE37-5F 93
Rossendale Pl. NE12-3B 28
Ross Garth. DH5-1D 129
Ross Gro. NE23-2A 4
Ross Lea. DH4-1F 125
Rosslyn Av. NE3-5F 25
Rosslyn Av. NE9-4E 79
Rosslyn Av. SR2-3D 121
Rosslyn M. SR4-2F 109
Rosslyn Pl. DH3-1C 112
Rosslyn St. SR4-1F 109
Rosslyn Ter. SR4-2F 109
Ross St. SR5-3A 100
Ross St. SR7-3E 133
Ross Way. NE3-2B 26
Ross Way. NE26-5D 13
Rosyth Rd. SR5-1C 98
Rosyth Sq. SR5-1D 99
Rotary Way. NE29-2A 50
Rothay Pl. NE5-3D 41
Rothbury. SR2-4B 120
Rothbury Av. NE3-3C 26
Rothbury Av. NE10-1F 81
Rothbury Av. NE32-3E 65
Rothbury Av. SR8-1E 135
Rothbury Clo. DH2-5B 122
Rothbury Clo. NE12-3E 17
Rothbury Gdns. NE11-5F 77
Rothbury Gdns. NE13-1D 15
Rothbury Gdns. NE28-1A 48
Rothbury Rd. DH1-2D 137
Rothbury Rd. SR5-2C 98
Rothbury Ter. NE6-4D 45
Rothbury Ter. NE29-5E 33
Rotherfield Clo. NE23-2D 5
Rotherfield Gdns. NE9-3F 91
Rotherfield Rd. SR5-2A 98
Rotherfield Sq. SR5-2B 98
Rotherham Clo. DH5-1C 128
Rotherham Rd. SR5-2B 98
Rothley. NE38-5D 105
Rothley Av. NE5-5E 41
Rothley Av. SR8-1E 135
Rothley Clo. NE3-4F 27
Rothley Ct. NE12-4E 17
Rothley Gdns. NE30-5C 22
Rothley Gro. NE25-1A 10
Rothley Way. NE26-5D 13
Rothwell Rd. NE3-4E 27
Rothwell Rd. SR5-2A 98
Roundhill. NE32-1B 84
Roundhill Av. NE5-3D 41
Roundway, The. NE12-3D 29
Rowan Av. NE38-1A 114
Rowanberry Rd. NE12-4C 28
Rowan Clo. SR4-2F 107
Rowan Ct. NE12-2B 30
Rowan Dri. DH1-1F 137
Rowan Dri. DH5-4E 129
Rowan Dri. NE3-4A 26
Rowans, The. NE9-3B 92
Rowan Tree Av. DH1-2A 140
Rowantree Rd. NE6-4B 46
Rowanwood Gdns. NE11 -5F 77
Rowedge Wlk. NE5-2B 40
Rowell Clo. SR2-4B 120
Rowell St. NE4-4F 59
Rowes M. NE6-3B 62
Rowhope St. NE31-5F 47
(off Argyle St.)
Rowlands Bldgs. NE23-3E 7
Rowlandson Ter. NE10-2C 80
Rowlandson Ter. SR2-4C 110
Rowsley Rd. NE32-2B 66
Row's Ter. NE3-5A 28
Roxburgh Clo. NE21-2F 73
Roxburgh Pl. NE6-5D 45
Roxburgh St. SR6-2B 100
Roxburgh Ter. NE26-2C 22
Roxby Gdns. NE29-4F 33
Royal Cres. NE4-4F 41
Royal Ind. Est. NE31-5B 48
Royal Ind. Est. NE32-5B 48
Royal Rd. DH9-2C 130
Royalty, The. SR2-2A 110
Roydon Av. SR2-4D 111
Royle St. SR2-5D 111
Royston Ter. NE6-3F 63
Ruabon Clo. NE23-2E 7
Rubens Av. NE34-4B 68
Ruby St. DH4-3B 126
Rudby Clo. NE3-2F 27
Rudchester Pl. NE5-4E 41
Ruddock Sq. NE6-3A 62
Rudyard Av. SR2-5D 111
Rudyerd Ct. NE29-5C 34
Rudyerd St. NE29-4C 34
Rugby Gdns. NE9-1B 92
Rugby Gdns. NE28-1A 48
Ruislip Pl. NE23-1E 7
Ruislip Rd. SR4-2F 107
Runcorn. SR2-3B 120
Runcorn Rd. SR5-2A 98
Runhead Est. NE40-3C 54
Runhead Gdns. NE40-2C 54
Runhead Ter. NE40-2C 54
Runnymede. DH3-4A 124
Runnymede. SR2-3B 120
Runnymede Rd. NE16-4F 75
Runnymede Rd. SR5-2C 98
Runnymede Way. NE3-5F 25
Runnymede Way. SR5-2C 98
Runswick Av. NE12-3B 28
Runswick Clo. SR3-3A 120
Rupert Sq. SR5-1C 98
Rupert St. SR6-1D 89
Rupert Ter. NE15-4A 38
Rushall Pl. NE12-4D 29
Rushbury Ct. NE27-2E 19
Rushford. SR2-4B 120
Rushie Av. NE15-2B 58
Rushley Cres. NE21-4A 56
Rushsyde Clo. NE16-5D 75
Rushton Av. SR2-4D 111
Rushyrig. NE37-2F 103
Ruskin Av. DH2-3A 122
Ruskin Av. NE11-1E 77
Ruskin Av. NE12-1E 29
Ruskin Clo. DH9-2E 131
Ruskin Cres. NE34-4F 67
Ruskin Dri. NE35-2F 85
Ruskin Rd. DH3-3B 102
Ruskin Rd. NE10-3A 80
Ruskin Rd. NE16-2F 75
Russell Av. NE34-2F 69
Russell Sq. NE13-4A 6
Russell St. NE29-4C 34
Russell St. NE32-5E 49
Russell St. NE33-1E 51
Russell St. NE37-5B 94
Russell St. SR1-5C 100
Russell Ter. DH3-1A 102
Russell Ter. NE2 -2E 61 & 3F 143
Russell Way. NE11-5B 58
Ruswarp Dri. SR3-4F 119
Ruth Av. NE21-5B 56
Rutherford Av. SR7-2A 132
Rutherford Rd. NE37-3C 94
Rutherford Rd. SR5-1A 98
Rutherford Sq. SR5-1A 98
Rutherford St. NE1-2B 60
Rutherford St. NE4 -2B 60 & 4B 142
Rutherford St. NE28-2C 48
Rutherglen Rd. SR5-1C 98
Rutherglen Sq. SR5-1C 98
Rutland Av. NE6-5B 46
Rutland Av. SR3-3E 119
Rutland Pl. NE29-4A 34
Rutland Pl. NE37-3C 94
Rutland Rd. NE28-3B 46
Rutland Rd. NE31-4E 65
Rutland Sq. DH3-2A 102
Rutland St. DH5-4E 129
Rutland St. NE34-2A 68
Rutland St. SR4-1E 109
Rutland St. SR7-2C 132
Rutland Wlk. SR8-1B 134
Ryal Clo. NE25-1C 10
Ryall Av. NE13-2B 14
Ryal Ter. NE6-3E 63
Ryal Wlk. NE3-5E 25
Rydal. NE10-2E 81
Rydal Av. DH9-4A 130
Rydal Av. NE30-5B 22
Rydal Clo. NE12-4A 18
Rydal Clo. NE36-2B 86
Rydal Cres. NE21-2A 74
Rydal Cres. SR8-3D 135
Rydal Gdns. NE34-1C 68
Rydal Mt. SR5-5F 97
(Castletown)
Rydal Mt. SR5-1B 100
(Seaburn)
Rydal Rd. DH2-4D 123
Rydal Rd. NE3-4F 27
Rydal Rd. NE15-5E 39
Rydal St. NE8-1C 78
Rydal Ter. NE13-2D 15
Ryde Pl. NE23-2D 5
Ryde Ter. NE11-1E 77
Rye Clo. NE15-3F 37
Ryedale. DH1-3D 141
Ryedale. NE28-5A 30
Ryedale. SR6-3D 89
Ryedale Ct. NE34-3F 67
Rye Hill. DH2-2D 123
Rye Hill. NE4-3A 60 & 5A 142
(in two parts)
Ryelands Way. DH1-1C 136
Ryemount Rd. SR2-3B 120
Rye View. SR2-3D 121
Ryhope Beach Rd. SR2 -4F 121
Ryhope Gdns. NE9-1C 92
Ryhope Grange Ct. SR2 -1E 121
Ryhope Rd. SR2-3C 110
Ryhope St. DH5-5E 127
Ryhope St. SR2-5E 121
Ryhope St. N. SR2-3C 120
Ryhope St. S. SR2-4E 121
Ryknield Way. NE34-3F 67
Ryton Ct. NE33-3E 51
Ryton Crawcrook By-Pass. NE40 & NE21-4A 54
Ryton Cres. DH9-1D 131
Ryton Cres. SR7-3B 132
Ryton Gdns. NE28-1A 48
Ryton Hall Dri. NE40-1A 54
Ryton Ind. Est. NE21-2E 55
Ryton Sq. SR2-4D 111
Ryton Ter. NE6-3E 63
Ryton Ter. NE27-1F 31

Sackville Rd. NE6-3D 45
Sackville Rd. SR3-4C 108
Sacriston Av. SR3-5E 109
Sacriston Gdns. NE9-3A 92
Saddleback. NE37-5A 94
Saddler St. DH1-2D 139
Saffron Pl. NE6-2F 63
Sage Clo. NE15-4E 39
St Aidan's Av. NE12-1D 31
St Aidan's Av. SR2-1E 121
St Aidans Clo. NE29-2E 33
St Aidans Ct. NE30-2E 35
St Aidan's Cres. DH1-2A 138
St Aidan's Rd. NE28-3C 46
St Aidan's Rd. NE33-1E 51
St Aidan's Sq. NE12-1D 31
St Aidans St. NE8-1C 78
St Aidan's Ter. DH4-4C 116
St Aiden's Av. DH1-4B 136
St Albans Clo. DH3-5B 124
St Alban's Clo. NE25-2B 20
St Alban's Cres. NE6-3E 45
St Alban's Cres. NE10-3A 80
St Alban's Pl. NE10-3A 80
St Albans Pl. NE30-3F 35
St Albans St. SR2-4D 111
St Albans Ter. NE8-1D 79
St Albans View. NE27-5A 20
St Aldwyn Rd. SR7-2C 132
St Andrew's. DH4-5A 126
St Andrew's Av. NE37-4F 93
St Andrew's Ct. NE7-5E 29
St Andrew's Dri. NE9-2D 91
St Andrews Rd. DH9-1C 130
St Andrew's St. NE1 -2B 60 & 4B 142
St Andrew's St. NE31-5E 47
St Andrew's Ter. SR6 -3D 101
St Andrew's Ter. SR7-5A 132
St Anne's Clo. NE1 -2E 61 & 3F 143
St Anne's Clo. NE21-1A 74
St Anne's Ct. NE25-4F 21
St Anne's Yd. NE2-2F 61
St Ann's Sq. NE1 -2E 61 & 4F 143
(off Quayside)
St Anselm Cres. NE29-2E 33
St Anselm Rd. NE29-2E 33
St Anthony's Rd. NE6-2D 63
St Anthony's Wlk. NE6-4D 63
St Asaph Clo. NE7-1E 45
St Aubyns Way. DH9-2E 131
St Austell Clo. NE5-5E 25
St Austell Gdns. NE9-2E 91
St Barnabas. DH4-2C 124
St Barnabas Way. SR2 -3D 111
St Bede's. NE36-3C 86
St Bede's Clo. DH1-3A 138
St Bede's Clo. DH5-4F 129
St Bede's Dri. NE8-5E 61
St Bede's Pk. SR2-2C 110
St Bede's Ter. SR2-2C 110
St Benet's Clo. SR6-4C 100
St Brelade's Way. DH9-2F 131
St Buryan Cres. NE5-1E 41
St Catherines Gro. NE2-5B 44
St Chad's Cres. SR3-3A 118
St Chad's Rd. SR3-3A 118
St Chad's Vs. NE36-3C 86
St Christopher's Rd. SR3 -5F 109
St Christopher Way. NE29 -2E 49
St Clement's Ct. NE3-2A 26
St Columbia Ct. SR5-3A 100
Saint Ct. SR3-5F 119
St Cuthbert Av. DH3-3F 123
St Cuthbert's Av. DH1-4A 136
St Cuthberts Av. NE34-5C 52
St Cuthbert's Clo. DH5 -3F 129
St Cuthbert's Ct. NE3-5B 26
St Cuthbert's Ct. NE8-5C 60
St Cuthbert's Dri. NE10-3D 81
(in two parts)
St Cuthbert's Grn. NE5-5D 41
St Cuthbert's Pl. DH1-1B 138
St Cuthbert's Pl. NE8-1C 78
(in two parts)
St Cuthbert's Rd. DH4-2C 126
(Newbottle)
St Cuthbert's Rd. DH4-3E 117
(West Herrington)
St Cuthbert's Rd. NE5-5D 41
(in two parts)
St Cuthbert's Rd. NE8-5C 60
(in two parts)
St Cuthbert's Rd. NE27-1D 31
St Cuthbert's Rd. NE28-1F 47
St Cuthberts Rd. SR8-4C 134
St Cuthbert's Ter. NE8-1C 78
St Cuthbert's Ter. SR4-5F 99
St Cuthbert's Ter. SR7 -5B 132
St Cuthbert's Wlk. DH3 -2E 123
St Cuthbert's Way. NE21 -4C 56
St David's Clo. NE26-4D 13
St David's Ct. NE26-4D 13
St David's Way. NE26-4D 13
St David's Way. NE32-1A 84
St Edmund's Dri. NE10-3D 81
St Edmund's Rd. NE8-1E 79
St Etienne Ct. NE10-1C 80
(off Carlisle St.)
St Gabriel's Av. NE6-4D 45
St Gabriel's Av. SR4-2E 109
St George's Av. NE33 & NE34 -4F 51
St George's Clo. NE2-2A 44
St George's Ct. NE10-3A 82
St George's Cres. NE25-3A 22
St George's Cres. NE29-4A 34
St George's Est. NE38-2A 114
St George's Pl. NE15-2C 56
St George's Rd. NE15-2C 56
St George's Rd. NE30-3D 23
St George's Ter. NE2-3A 44
St George's Ter. NE15-2C 56
St George's Ter. NE36-3C 86
St George's Ter. SR6-2D 101
St George's Way. SR2-2B 110
St Gregorys Ct. NE34-2E 69
St Helen's Cres. NE9-5D 79
St Helen's Ter. NE9-5D 79
St Heliers Way. DH9-1E 131
St Hilda Ind. Est. NE33-2D 51
St Hilda's Av. NE28-1F 47
St Hilda's La. NE33-2D 51
St Hilda St. NE33-2E 51
St Hilds La. DH1-2E 139
St Ignatius Clo. SR2-2D 111
St Ives Way. NE5-1E 41
St James Ct. NE10-1A 80
St James' Cres. NE15-3C 58
St James' Gdns. NE15-3C 58
St James' Mall. NE31-2C 64
St James Rd. NE8-5F 61
St James' Rd. NE15-3C 58
St James Sq. NE8-4F 61
St James St. NE1 -1B 60 & 3B 142
St James St. NE3-5F 27
St James Ter. NE1 -1B 60 & 3B 142
(off St James St.)
St James' Ter. NE29-2F 49
St John's Av. NE31-2C 64
St John's Clo. NE26-4D 13
St John's Ct. NE27-2E 19
St John's Grn. NE29-1F 49
St John's Ho. NE33-2F 51
(off Beach Rd.)
St John's Mall. NE31-2C 64
St John's Pl. DH3-4B 102
(in two parts)
St John's Pl. NE10-2C 80
St John's Pl. NE26-4D 13
St John's Rd. DH1-3A 138
St John's Rd. NE4-3D 59
St John's Sq. SR7-3F 133
St John's Ter. NE29-2F 49
St John's Ter. NE32-1A 66
St John's Ter. NE36-3C 86
St John's Ter. SR7-1A 132
St John St. NE1 -3C 60 & 5C 142
St John St. NE29-1E 49
St John's Wlk. NE4-3D 59
St John's Wlk. NE29-1E 49
St John's Wlk. NE31-2C 64
St Joseph's Clo. DH1-4A 140
St Joseph's Ct. DH3-3B 102
St Joseph's Ct. NE31-4B 64
St Joseph's Way. NE32-1A 84
St Judes Ter. NE33-4D 51
St Julien Gdns. NE7-2E 45
St Julien Gdns. NE28-1C 48
St Just Pl. NE5-1D 41
St Keverne Sq. NE5-1E 41
St Kitts Clo. NE26-4D 13
St Lawrence Ct. NE6-1B 62
St Lawrence Rd. NE6-3A 62
St Lawrence Sq. NE6-2F 61
St Leonards. DH1-1B 138
St Leonards Clo. SR8-4A 134
St Leonard St. SR2-4D 111
St Lucia Clo. NE26-4C 12
St Lucia Clo. SR2-2C 110
St Luke's Rd. NE29-2E 49
St Luke's Rd. SR4 -2A 108 to 1D 109
St Luke's Ter. SR4-1D 109
St Margarets Av. NE12-3E 29
St Margaret's Av. SR5-4F 97
St Margarets Ct. DH1-3B 138
St Margaret's Ct. SR5-4F 97
St Margaret's Rd. NE15-3F 57
St Mark's Clo. NE6-1A 62
St Mark's Ct. NE27-4F 19
St Mark's Ct. NE29-2E 49
St Mark's Cres. SR4-1F 109
St Mark's Rd. SR4-1F 109
St Mark's St. NE6-1B 62
St Mark's St. SR4-1F 109
St Mark's Ter. SR4-1F 109
St Mark's Way. NE33-3E 51
St Martin's Clo. NE26-5C 12
St Martin's Ct. NE26-5C 12
St Martin's Way. NE26-5D 13
St Mary's Av. NE28 -5D 13 & 5E 13
St Mary's Av. NE34-1E 69
St Mary's Clo. DH1-5F 139
St Mary's Clo. DH2-4D 123
St Mary's Ct. NE8-5E 61
St Mary's Pl. NE1 -1C 60 & 2D 143
St Mary's Pl. NE15-3F 37
St Mary's Pl. E. NE1 -1C 60 & 2D 143
St Mary's Rd. DH1-2D 141
St Mary's Ter. NE10-2D 81
St Mary's Ter. NE33-5D 51
(off Dean Rd.)
St Mary's Ter. NE36-3C 86
St Mary's Ter. NE40-2A 54
St Mary's Way. SR1-1B 110
St Matthew's Ter. DH4 -1B 126
St Matthews View. SR3 -3E 119
St Michael's. DH4-5A 126
St Michael's Av. NE33-3F 51
St Michael's Av. N. NE33 -3F 51
St Michael's Mt. NE6-2B 62
St Michael's Rd. NE6-2A 62
St Michael's Way. NE11 -5A 58
St Michaels Way. SR1-2B 110
St Monica Gro. DH1-2A 138
St Nicholas Av. NE3 -5E 27 & 5F 27
St Nicholas Av. SR3-4F 109
St Nicholas' Bldgs. NE1 -3C 60 & 5D 143
St Nicholas Chyd. NE1 -3C 60 & 5D 143
St Nicholas Dri. DH1-5A 136
St Nicholas Precinct. NE1 -2C 60 & 4D 143
St Nicholas Rd. NE36-3E 85
St Nicholas Sq. NE1 -3C 60 & 5D 143
St Nicholas St. NE1 -3C 60 & 5D 143
St Nicholas View. NE36-3E 85
St Nicholas Vs. NE36-3E 85
St Omers Rd. NE11-5D 59
St Oswald Av. NE6-1D 63
St Oswalds Av. NE6-1D 63
St Oswald's Ct. NE10-2B 80
St Oswald's Grn. NE6-5A 46
St Oswald's Heb NE31-5B 48
(in two parts)
St Oswald Sq. DH1-1B 136
St Oswald's Rd. NE28-1F 47
St Oswald's Rd. NE31-5B 48
St Oswald's Ter. DH4-4A 116
St Oswin's Av. NE30-4D 23
St Oswin's Pl. NE30-2F 35
St Oswin's St. NE33-5E 51
St Patrick's Clo. NE10-2C 80
St Patrick's Garth. SR1 -1D 111
St Patrick's Wlk. NE10-2C 80
St Pauls Dri. DH4-2C 114
St Paul's Gdns. NE25-3C 22
St Paul's Pl. NE4-2F 59
St Paul's Rd. NE32-5E 49
St Paul's Ter. SR2-4E 121
St Peter's Av. NE34-1D 69
St Peter's Rd. NE6-3B 62
St Peter's Rd. NE28 -2F 47 to 1F 47
St Peter's Stairs. NE29-5C 34
St Peter's View. SR6-4C 100
St Peter's Way. SR6-5C 100
St Peters Wharfe. NE6-3B 62
St Philips Clo. NE4-2F 59
St Phillip's Wlk. NE4-2F 59
St Rollox St. NE31-2B 64
St Ronan's Rd. NE25-2A 22
St Ronan's View. NE9-3F 91
St Simon St. NE34-3E 67
St Stephens Clo. NE25 -1A 10
St Stephen's Way. NE29 -2E 49
St Stevens Clo. DH4-2D 115
St Thomas Cres. NE1 -1B 60 & 2C 142
St Thomas Sq. NE1 -1B 60 & 2B 142
St Thomas St. NE1 -1B 60 & 2C 142
St Thomas St. NE9-5E 79
St Thomas St. SR1-1C 110
St Thomas' Ter. NE1 -1B 60 & 2B 142
(off Queen Victoria Rd.)
St Vincent Ct. NE8-1F 79
St Vincent's Clo. NE15-5A 40
St Vincent's Pl. NE26-4D 13
St Vincent St. NE33-3F 51
St Vincent St. SR2-2C 110
St Vincent's Way. NE26 -4D 13
Saker Ct. NE28-3C 46
Salcombe Av. NE32-2C 66
Salcombe Clo. SR7-4C 132
Salcombe Gdns. NE9-3D 91
Salem Hill. SR2-3C 110
Salem Rd. SR2-2C 110
Salem St. NE32-5D 49
Salem St. NE33-1D 51
Salem St. SR2-2C 110
Salem St. S. SR2-3C 110
Salem Ter. SR2-2C 110
Salisbury Av. DH3-4E 123
Salisbury Av. NE29-2B 34
Salisbury Clo. DH3-5A 124
Salisbury Clo. NE23-3A 4
Salisbury Gdns. NE2-4C 44
Salisbury Pl. NE33-2F 51
Salisbury Rd. DH1-1E 137
Salisbury St. DH9-4A 130
Salisbury St. NE10-1E 81
Salisbury St. NE33-2F 51
Salisbury St. SR1-2C 110
Salisbury St. SR4-1F 107
Salisbury Way. NE32-1F 83
Salkeld Gdns. NE9-2E 79
Salkeld Rd. NE9-3F 79
Sallyport Cres. NE1 -2D 61 & 4E 143
Salmon St. NE33-1E 51
Saltburn Clo. DH4-4B 126
Saltburn Gdns. NE28-1C 48
Saltburn Rd. SR3-4C 108
Saltburn Sq. SR3-4C 108
Salter Ct. NE3-4A 28
Salterfen La. SR2-2E 121
Salter La. SR3-2A 118
Salters Clo. NE3-4A 28
Salters La. NE3 & NE12 -4A 28
Salters La. Ind. Est. NE12 -1C 28
Salters Rd. NE3-1C 42
Saltford. NE9-3E 91
Saltmeadows Rd. NE8-3F 61
Saltwell Pl. NE8-2C 78
Saltwell Rd. NE8-2C 78
Saltwell Rd. S. NE9-5D 79
Saltwell St. NE8-2C 78
Saltwell View. NE8-2D 79
Sams Ct. NE23-4E 7
Samson Clo. NE12-5D 17
Sancroft Dri. DH5-1C 128
Sandalwood. NE34-4C 68
Sandalwood Sq. SR4-5F 107
Sandalwood Wlk. DH9 -2D 131
Sandbach. DH3-4A 124
Sanderlings, The. NE28 -3D 47
Sanderlings, The. SR2 -4E 121
Sanders Gdns. DH3-2B 102
Sanders' Memorial Homes. DH2-3D 123
Sanderson Rd. NE2-3A 44
Sanderson Rd. NE26-2B 22
Sanderson's Ter. NE23-1B 8
Sanderson St. NE4-4E 59
Sandfield Rd. NE30-4C 22
Sand Flats, The. DH1-1D 139
Sandford M. NE13-2B 14
Sandgate Ho. NE1 -3D 61 & 5F 143
Sandgate Sq. NE1 -2D 61 & 4F 143
(off Quayside)
Sandgrove. SR6-1E 87
Sandhill. NE1 -3D 61 & 5D 143
(off Quayside)
Sandhoe Gdns. NE15-2A 58
Sandhoe Ter. NE6-3B 62
Sandholm Clo. NE28-4B 32
Sandhurst Av. NE30-4D 23
Sandiacres. NE32-1B 84
Sandmere Pl. NE15-2F 57
Sandmere Rd. SR2-1C 120
Sandon Clo. NE27-2E 19
Sandown. NE25-2E 21
Sandown Clo. NE25-2E 21
Sandown Ct. NE28-5B 32
Sandown Gdns. NE8-2B 78
Sandown Gdns. NE28-5B 32
Sandown Gdns. SR3-2D 119
Sandpiper Clo. NE38-5E 103
Sandpiper Ct. NE30-1F 35
Sandpiper Pl. NE12-3C 28
Sandray Clo. DH3-4C 112
Sandrigg Sq. NE34-2C 68
Sandringham Av. NE12 -3E 29
Sandringham Clo. NE25 -3D 21
Sandringham Cres. SR3 -4A 118
Sandringham Dri. NE16 -3E 75
Sandringham Dri. NE25 -3D 21
Sandringham Gdns. NE29 -3B 34
Sandringham M. NE28-5B 32
Sandringham Rd. NE3-5A 28
Sandringham Rd. NE5-4A 40
Sandringham Rd. SR6 -3C 100
Sandringham Ter. NE8-5D 61
Sandringham Ter. SR6 -3C 100
Sandsay Clo. SR2-2C 120
Sands Ind. Est. NE16-1F 75
Sands Rd. NE16-1E 75
Sandstone Clo. NE34-4E 67
Sand St. DH9-2D 131
Sandwell Dri. DH4-2D 115
Sandwich Rd. NE29-1A 34
Sandy Chare. SR6-2D 89
Sandy Cres. NE6-3D 63
Sandyford Ho. NE2 -5A 44 & 1E 143
Sandyford Pk. NE2-5B 44
Sandyford Rd. NE1 & NE2 -1C 60 & 2D 143
Sandy La. NE3 & NE13-2E 15
Sandy La. NE9-4C 92
Sandy La. NE13-1A 14
Sans St. SR1-1C 110
Sans St. S. SR1-1C 110
Sargent Av. NE34-5C 68
Satley Gdns. NE9-3A 92
Satley Gdns. SR3-5A 110
Saturn St. SR7-3B 132
Saunton Ct. DH4-2B 126
Sava Shopping Cen. NE38 -2A 104
Saville Lodge. NE33-2E 51
(off Saville St.)
Saville Pl. NE1 -1C 60 & 3D 143
(off Durant Rd.)
Saville Pl. SR1-1C 110
Saville Row. NE1 -1C 60 & 3D 143
Saville St. NE29 & NE30 -4C 34
Saville St. NE33-2E 51
(in two parts)
Saville St. W. NE29-5C 34
Savory Rd. NE28-1A 48
Saxon Clo. SR6-1D 87
Saxon Cres. SR3-5E 109
Saxondale Rd. NE3-4F 25
Saxon Dri. NE30-1E 35
Saxon Way. NE32-5D 49
Saxton Gro. NE7-1C 44
Sayer Wlk. SR8-4D 135
Scafell. DH3-1C 112
Scafell Clo. SR8-3D 135
Scafell Ct. SR3-4E 119
Scafell Dri. NE5-1F 41
Scafell Gdns. NE11-4F 77
Scalby Clo. NE3-1F 27
Scarborough Ct. NE6-1B 62
Scarborough Ct. NE23-4C 4
Scarborough Pde. NE31 -5F 65
Scarborough Rd. NE6-1B 62
(in two parts)
Scarborough Rd. SR3-2D 119
Scarborough Ter. DH3 -3F 123
Scardale Way. DH1-2E 141
Sceptre Ct. NE4-3F 59
Sceptre Pl. NE4-3E 59
Sceptre St. NE4-2E 59
Schimel St. SR5-3F 99
School App. NE34-1E 69
School Av. NE11-2D 77
School Ct. DH6-4F 141
(off Hallgarth St.)
School La. DH1-4D 139
School La. DH9-4A 130
School La. NE16-3A 76
School Loaning. NE34-2F 67
School Rd. DH5-4B 128
School St. DH3-4B 102
School St. NE8-5C 60
School St. NE16-3F 75
School St. NE31-5A 48
(in two parts)
School St. SR7-5F 133
School Ter. DH4-3D 125
School Ter. DH9-4B 130
Scorer's La. DH3-4B 124
Scorer St. NE29-4A 34
Scotby Gdns. NE9-1F 91
Scotland Ct. NE21-1F 73
Scotland Head. NE21-2F 73
Scotland St. SR2-4F 121
Scotswood Rd. NE15, NE4 & NE1-1C 56 & 5A 142
Scotswood Sta. App. NE15 -3E 57
Scotswood View. NE16-4A 58
Scott Av. NE23-2A 4
Scott Ct. NE34-4F 67
Scott's Bank. SR5-3F 99
Scotts Ct. NE10-4A 82
Scotts Gdns. DH1-2A 138
Scott's Ter. DH5-4F 129
Scott St. DH4-4C 126
Scott St. DH9-2B 130
Scrogg Rd. NE6-5A 46
Scruton Av. SR3-5D 109
Sea Banks. NE30-1F 35
Sea Beach Rd. SR2-5E 111
Seaburn Clo. SR6-5D 89
Seaburn Ct. SR6-1D 101
Seaburn Dri. DH4-5B 126
Seaburn Gdns. NE9-2C 92
Seaburn Gdns. SR6-5D 89
Seaburn Hill. SR6-1D 101
Seaburn Ter. SR6-5D 89
Seacombe Av. NE30-4D 23
Seacrest Av. NE30-4D 23
Seafields. SR6-4C 88
Seafield Ter. NE33-1F 51
Seafield View. NE30-2E 35
Seaforth Rd. SR3-4E 109
Seaham Gdns. NE9-3A 92
Seaham Grange Ind. Est. SR7 -1A 132
Seaham Rd. DH5-5E 127
Seaham Rd. SR2-4F 121
Seaham St. NE4 -2A 60 & 3A 142
Seaham St. SR3-3F 119
Seaham St. SR7-5F 133
Seahouses Wlk. NE8-5C 60
Sea La. SR6-3E 89
Sea Rd. NE33-1A 52
Sea Rd. SR6-1C 100
Seascale Pl. NE9-1A 92
Seaside La. SR6-5D 89
Seatoller Ct. SR3-4E 119
Seaton Av. DH5-5E 127
Seaton Av. NE23-3A 8
Seaton Clo. NE10-4A 82
Seaton Cres. NE25-2E 11
(Holywell)
Seaton Cres. NE25-2A 22
(Monkseaton)
Seaton Cres. SR7-1A 132
Seaton Croft. NE23-2E 9
Seaton Gdns. NE9-2B 92
Seaton La. SR7-1A 132
Seaton Pl. NE6-4D 63
Seaton Pl. NE13-1C 14
Seaton Rd. NE27-3B 20
Seaton Rd. SR3-4C 108
Seatonville Cres. NE25-3F 21
Seatonville Gro. NE25-3F 21
Seatonville Rd. NE25-3F 21
Sea View. SR2-4F 121
(in two parts)
Sea View E. SR2-5E 111
Sea View Gdns. SR6-2C 100
Sea View Ind. Est. SR8 -1F 135
Sea View Pk. NE23-3E 5
Sea View Pk. SR6-2C 88
Sea View Rd. SR2-5C 110
Sea View Rd. W. SR2-5C 110
Sea View St. SR2-1E 121
Seaview Ter. NE33-1F 51
Seaview Ts. NE23-3E 5
Sea Way. NE33-2A 52
Second Av. DH2-3A 112
(Bog La.)
Second Av. DH2-4C 122
(Chester-le-Street)
Second Av. NE6-5D 45
Second Av. NE11-4A 78
Second Av. NE29-5D 33
Second St. NE8-1B 78
Sedbergh Rd. NE30-5C 22
Sedgefield Ct. NE12-4E 17
Sedgeletch Ind. Est. DH4 -3F 125
Sedgeletch Rd. DH4-4F 125
Sedgemoor. NE12-2F 17
Sedgemoor Av. NE15-3F 57
Sedgewick Pl. NE8-1D 79
Sedley Rd. NE28-4C 46
Sedling Rd. NE38-5F 103
Sefton Av. NE6-3D 45
Sefton Sq. SR3-4D 109
Segedunum Way. NE28 -3C 46
Seine Ct. NE32-1A 66
Selborne Av. NE9-1D 91
Selborne Clo. NE23-3A 4
Selborne Gdns. NE2-4B 44
Selborne St. SR6-4C 100
Selbourne St. NE33-2F 51
Selby Clo. NE23-1D 5
Selby Ct. NE6-3D 63
Selby Ct. NE32-5C 48
Selby Gdns. NE6-4B 46
Selby Gdns. NE28-1C 46
Selby Sq. SR3-5D 109
Selkirk Cres. DH3-1B 102
Selkirk Gro. NE23-1D 5
Selkirk Sq. SR3-4C 108
Selkirk St. NE32-4D 67
Selkirk Way. NE29-2E 33
Selsdon Av. SR4-5F 107
Selsey Ct. NE10-4C 80
Selwyn Av. NE25-4F 21
Selwyn Clo. NE5-1F 41
Seton Av. NE34-3E 67
Seton Wlk. NE34-3E 67
Setting Stones. NE38-2F 113
Sevenacres. DH3-5B 124
Sevenoaks Dri. SR4-5E 107
Seventh Av. DH2-2D 123
Seventh Av. NE6-5D 45
Seventh Av. NE11-1C 90
Seventh St. SR8 -2F 135 & 3F 135
Severn Av. NE31-4D 65
Severn Clo. SR8-5A 134
Severn Ct. SR3-4E 119
Severn Cres. DH9-4B 130
Severn Dri. NE32-5B 66
Severn Gdns. NE8-1F 79
Severn Houses. NE37-5F 95
Severus Rd. NE4-1D 59
Seymour Ct. NE11-1F 77
Seymour Sq. SR3-4D 109
Seymour St. NE11-1E 77
Seymour St. NE29-5B 34
Seymour St. SR8-3F 135
Shadfen Pk. Rd. NE30-4C 22
Shadforth Clo. SR8-5A 134
Shadon Way. DH3-4C 102
Shaftesbury Av. NE26-5D 13
Shaftesbury Av. NE32 & NE34 -2C 66
Shaftesbury Av. SR2-3C 120
Shaftesbury Cres. NE30 -4B 22
Shaftesbury Cres. SR3 -5D 109
Shaftesbury Gro. NE6-5D 45
Shaftesbury Wlk. NE8-5B 60
Shaftoe Ct. NE3-3C 26
Shaftoe Ct. NE12-4E 17
Shaftoe Ct. NE15-2A 58
Shaftoe Rd. SR3-5C 108
Shaftoe Sq. SR3-5C 108
Shafto St. NE15-3E 57
Shafto St. NE28-2A 48
Shafto Ter. DH9-1D 131
Shafto Ter. NE37-5C 94
Shakespeare Av. NE31-1D 65
Shakespeare Clo. DH9-2E 131
(in two parts)
Shakespeare St. DH5-1D 129
Shakespeare St. NE1 -2C 60 & 4D 143
Shakespeare St. NE8-5E 61
Shakespeare St. NE28-2A 48

Shakespeare St. NE32-5D 49
Shakespeare St. NE33-3E 51
Shakespeare St. SR5-3F 99
Shakespeare St. SR7-3F 133
Shakespeare Ter. DH2-2A 122
Shakespeare Ter. SR2-2A 110
Shalcombe Clo. SR3-4F 119
Shallcross. SR2-3A 110
Shalstone. NE37-4D 95
Shamrock Clo. NE15-4E 39
Shandon Wlk. NE3-4F 25
Shandon Way. NE3-4F 25
Shanklin Pl. NE23-3A 4
Shannon Clo. SR5-4D 97
Shannon Ct. NE3-3E 25
Shap Clo. NE38-4C 104
Shap Ct. SR3-4E 119
Shap La. NE5-4C 40
Shap Rd. NE30-5C 22
Sharnford Clo. NE27-2E 19
Sharon Clo. NE12-5D 17
Sharp Cres. DH1-3A 140
(in two parts)
Sharpendon St. NE31-5A 48
Sharpley Dri. SR7-2A 132
Shaw Av. NE34-3A 68
Shaw Gdns. NE10-2A 82
Shaw St. SR7-3F 133
Shaw Wood Clo. DH1-1B 138
Shearlegs Rd. NE8-4F 61
Shearwater. SR6-4E 71
Shearwater Av. NE12-3C 28
Shearwater Clo. NE5-5D 25
Sheelin Av. DH2-5D 123
Sheen Ct. NE3-4D 25
Sheepfolds Rd. SR5-5B 100
Sheepfolds S. SR5-5B 100
Sheldon Ct. NE12
-5D 17 & 1D 29
Sheldon Gro. NE3-2B 42
Sheldon Rd. NE34-4B 52
Sheldon St. NE32-5C 48
Shelford Gdns. NE15-5A 40
Shelley Av. NE9-4D 93
Shelley Av. NE34-2F 69
Shelley Av. NE35-2F 85
Shelley Clo. DH9-2E 131
Shelley Ct. DH2-2A 122
Shelley Dri. NE8-5E 61
Shelley Gdns. DH2-2A 122
Shelley Rd. NE15-1E 55
Shelley St. SR7-3F 133
Shellin Av. DH2-5D 123
Shepherd Clo. NE23-1D 17
Shepherd St. SR4-5E 99
Shepherds Way. NE36-3F 85
Shepherd Way. NE38-5D 105
Sheppard Ter. SR5-4A 98
Sheppey Ct. SR3-4E 119
Sheraton. NE10-5F 81
Sheraton St. NE2
-5D 43 & 1A 142
Sherborne. DH3-4B 124
Sherborne Av. NE29-2E 33
Sherburn Grange N. NE32
-2F 65
Sherburn Grange S. NE32
-3F 65
Sherburn Gro. DH4-4B 126
Sherburn Rd. DH1-2F 139
Sherburn Rd. Est. DH1
-5A 140
Sherburn Rd. Flats. DH1
(off Sherburn Rd.) -2F 139
Sherburn Ter. NE9-2B 92
Sherburn Way. NE10-3A 82
Sherfield Dri. NE7-2E 45
Sheridan Grn. NE38-1F 113
Sheridan Rd. NE34-4F 67
Sheridan St. SR4-1D 109
Sheriff Mt. N. NE9-3F 79
Sheriff Mt. S. NE9-3F 79
Sheriff's Highway. NE9-3F 79
Sheringham Av. NE29-2F 33
Sheringham Dri. NE23-3A 4
Sheringham Gdns. NE15
-2D 37
Sherringham Av. NE3-5A 26
Sherwood. NE27-4D 21
Sherwood Clo. NE27-5D 21
Sherwood Clo. NE38-3C 104
Sherwood Ct. SR3-4E 119
Sherwood Pl. NE3-5E 15
Sherwood View. NE28-5B 30
Shetland Ct. SR3-4E 119
Shibdon Bank. NE21-1B 74
Shibdon Cres. NE21-5C 56
Shibdon Pk. View. NE21
-5C 56
Shibdon Rd. NE21-4B 56
Shibdon Way. NE21-5D 57
Shield Av. NE16-1A 76
Shieldclose. NE37-1E 103
Shield Ct. NE2
-1D 61 & 2F 143
Shieldfield Ind. Est. NE2
-2E 61 & 3F 143
Shieldfield La. NE2
-1E 61 & 3F 143
(in two parts)
Shield Gro. NE3-3F 27
Shield Row. DH9-1C 130
Shield Row Gdns. DH9
-1C 130
Shields Pl. DH5-4D 127
Shields Rd. DH3-1F 123
(in two parts)
Shields Rd. NE6
-1A 62 to 3C 46
Shields Rd. NE10
-2D 81 to 5A 64
Shields Rd. NE25-4A 22
Shields Rd. SR6
-4E 69 & 4A 88
Shields Rd. By-Pass. NE6
-1F 61 to 1B 62
Shields Rd. W. NE6-1F 61
Shield St. NE2
-1D 61 & 3F 143
Shiel Gdns. NE23-3A 4
Shillaw Pl. NE23-1D 17
Shillmoor Clo. DH2-5B 122
Shilmore Rd. NE3-5A 26
Shilton Clo. NE34-2F 69
Shincliffe Av. SR5-2B 98
Shincliffe Gdns. NE9-1B 92
Shipby. SR3-4E 119
Shipcote La. NE8-2D 79
Shipcote Ter. NE8-2E 79
Shipley Av. NE4-1D 59
Shipley Av. SR6-5D 89
Shipley Ct. NE8-1D 79
Shipley Pl. NE6-1A 62
Shipley Rise. NE6-1A 62
Shipley Rd. NE30-2E 35
Shipley St. NE15-1B 56
Shipley Wlk. NE6-2A 62
Shipton Clo. NE35-1C 84
Shire Clo. DH1-1D 137
Shirley Gdns. SR3-4F 109
Shirwood Av. NE16-5F 75
Shopping Cen., The. NE5
-2E 39
Shop Row. DH4-5B 116
Shop Spouts. NE21-4B 56
Shoreham Ct. NE3-3D 25
Shoreham Sq. SR3-4C 108
Shorestone Av. NE30-3D 23
Shore St. SR6-4C 100
Shortridge St. NE33-1F 51
Shortridge Ter. NE2-4B 44
Short Row. DH4-1D 125
Shot Factory La. NE4-4B 60
Shotley Av. SR5-2A 100
Shotley Gdns. NE9-3E 79
Shotton Rd. SR8-2D 135
Shrewsbury Clo. NE7-1E 45
Shrewsbury Clo. SR8-4A 134
Shrewsbury Cres. SR3
-5D 109
Shrewsbury Dri. NE27-2E 19
Shrewsbury St. NE11-2E 77
Shrewsbury St. SR7-5E 133
Shrewsbury Ter. NE33-5E 51
Shrigley Gdns. NE3-4B 26
Shropshire Dri. DH1-3C 140
Sibthorpe St. NE29-5C 34
Side. NE1-3C 60 & 5D 143
(in two parts)
Side Cliff Rd. SR6-2C 100
Sidegate. DH1-1C 138
Sidgate. NE1-2C 60
(off Eldon Sq.)
Sidlaw Av. DH2-4C 122
Sidlaw Av. NE29-5A 22
Sidmouth Clo. SR7-4B 132
Sidmouth Rd. NE9-1E 91
Sidmouth Rd. NE29-4E 33
Sidney Clo. DH9-2E 131
Sidney Gro. NE4-1E 59
Sidney Gro. NE8-1B 78
Sidney St. NE29-4C 34
Sidney St. NE35-2E 85
Silkeys La. NE29-4A 34
Silkstun Ct. SR3-3F 119
Silksworth Clo. SR3-2D 119
Silksworth Gdns. NE9-3A 92
Silksworth Hall Dri. SR3
-4D 119
Silksworth La. SR3
-3D 119 to 4F 109
Silksworth Rd. SR3-4A 118
Silksworth Row. SR1-1A 110
Silksworth Ter. SR3-3F 119
Silksworth Way. SR3-4C 118
Silloth Av. NE5-4C 40
Silloth Dri. NE37-2B 94
Silloth Pl. NE30-5D 23
Silloth Rd. SR3-5C 108
Silverdale. SR3-5F 119
Silverdale Av. NE10-2C 82
Silverdale Dri. NE21-1E 73
Silverdale Rd. NE23-1D 5
Silverdale Ter. NE8-2D 79
Silverdale Way. NE16-5E 75
Silverdale Way. NE34-4E 67
Silverhill Dri. NE5-5C 40
Silverlink, The. NE28-3B 32
Silver Lonnen. NE5-5C 40
Silverstone. NE12-4A 18
Silverstone Way. NE37-4D 95
Silver St. DH1-2C 138
Silver St. NE1
-2D 61 & 4E 143
Silver St. NE30-2F 35
Silver St. SR1-5D 101
Silverwood Gdns. NE11-5F 77
Simonburn. NE38-3E 103
Simonburn Av. NE4-4A 42
Simonburn Av. NE29-4E 33
Simon Pl. NE13-2C 14
Simonside. NE26-1C 12
Simonside Av. NE28-1A 48
Simonside E. Ind. Pk. NE34
-2D 67
Simonside Hall. NE34-2D 67
Simonside Ind. Est. NE32
-2C 66
Simonside Pl. NE9-2B 92
Simonside Rd. NE21-1A 74
Simonside Rd. SR3-5B 108
Simonside Ter. NE6-4D 45
Simonside View. NE16-3F 75
Simonside View. NE32-3A 66
Simonside Way. NE12-3B 18
Simon's St. NE33-4C 50
Simpson Clo. NE35-2D 85
(in two parts)
Simpson St. DH9-1C 130
Simpson St. NE29-4A 34
Simpson St. NE30-3E 23
Simpson St. NE40-3D 55
Simpson St. SR4-5F 99
Simpson Ter. NE2
-1D 61 & 3E 143
Simpson Ter. NE15-3D 39
Sinclair Dri. DH3-2B 112
Sinclair Gdns. NE25-1B 10
Sinderby Clo. NE3-2F 27
Sir Godfrey Thomson Ct.
NE10-2B 80
Sitwell Rd. DH9-2E 131
Sixth Av. DH2-2C 122
Sixth Av. NE6-5D 45
Sixth Av. NE11-1B 90
Sixth St. SR8-3F 135
Skaylock Dri. NE38-5F 103
Skegness Pde. NE31-5F 65
Skelder Av. NE12-3D 29
Skelton Ct. NE3-2F 25
Skerne Clo. SR8-5B 134
Skiddaw Clo. SR8-3D 135
Skiddaw Dri. SR6-5A 88
Skiddaw Pl. NE9-1A 92
Skinnerburn Rd. NE4 & NE1
-5A 60
Skipsea View. SR2-3B 120
Skipsey Ct. NE29-2F 49
Skipton Clo. NE23-1D 5
Skipton Grn. NE9-3A 92
Skirlaw Clo. NE38-3B 104
Ski View. SR3-2D 119
Skye Ct. SR3-4E 119
Skye Gro. NE32-5D 67
Slaidburn Rd. DH9-2D 131
Slake Rd. NE32-4F 49
Slake Ter. NE34-1F 67
Slaley. NE38-1D 115
Slaley Clo. NE10-3B 82
Slaley Ct. SR3-4E 119
Slater's Row. DH3-5A 124
(in two parts)
Slatyford La. NE5-5B 40
Sledmere Clo. SR8-2B 134
Slingley Clo. SR7-2A 132
Slingsby Gdns. NE7-2F 45
Sloane Ct. NE2
-5F 43 & 1D 143
Smailes St. DH9-3C 130
Smeaton Ct. NE28-3C 48
Smeaton St. NE28-3C 48
Smillie Clo. SR8-2C 134
Smillie Rd. SR8-1D 135
(in two parts)
Smithburn Rd. NE10-3C 80
Smith Gro. SR2-4C 120
Smith St. SR2-4E 121
Smith St. S. SR2-4E 121
Smith Ter. NE8-1A 78
Smithy La. NE11-4D 91
Smithy Sq. NE23-3C 4
Smithy St. NE33-2E 51
(South Shields)
Smithy St. NE33-4C 50
(Tyne Dock)
Smyrna Pl. SR1-1D 111
Snowdon Gdns. NE11-3F 77
Snowdon Gro. NE36-3F 85
Snowdon Pl. SR8-4A 134
Snowdon Ter. SR2-4E 121
Snowdrop Av. SR8-2E 135
Snowdrop Clo. NE21-5F 55
Soane Gdns. NE34-4C 68
Softley Pl. NE15-5B 40
Solway Av. NE30-5C 22
Solway Rd. NE31-3D 65
Solway Sq. SR3-4D 109
Solway St. NE6-3B 62
Somerford. NE9-3D 93
Somersby Dri. NE3-5A 26
Somerset Cotts. SR3-2E 119
Somerset Gdns. NE28-2C 46
Somerset Gro. NE29-1F 33
Somerset Pl. NE4-3F 59
Somerset Rd. NE31-4E 65
Somerset Rd. SR3-5B 108
Somerset Sq. SR3-4C 108
Somerset St. SR3-2E 119
Somerset Ter. NE36-3B 86
Somerton Ct. NE3-4D 25
Somervyl Ct. NE12-3B 28
Sophia. SR7-3E 133
Sophia St. SR7-3E 133
Sophy St. SR5-3A 100
Sorley St. SR4-1E 109
Sorrel Gdns. NE34-4C 68
Soulby Ct. NE3-2F 25
Sourmilk Hill La. NE9-4F 79
Souter Rd. NE3-5B 26
Souter View. SR6-5D 71
South App. DH2-3D 123
South Av. NE16-5A 76
South Av. NE34-2D 69
South Av. NE37-4A 94
South Av. NE40-2B 54
S. Bailey. DH1-3C 138
S. Bend. NE3-1D 27
S. Bents Av. SR6-4D 89
S. Benwell Rd. NE15-3B 58
Southburn Clo. DH4-5A 126
S. Burns. DH3-2E 123
S. Burns Ter. DH4-4B 116
Southcliff. NE26-3E 23
S. Cliff. SR6-3D 101
South Clo. NE34-2E 69
South Clo. NE40-3A 54
Southcote. NE16-5E 75
South Cres. DH1-1B 138
South Cres. DH4-4D 125
South Cres. NE35-2E 85
South Cres. NE38-2A 114
South Cres. SR7-3F 133
South Cres. SR8-1D 135
South Croft. NE12-2F 29
Southcroft. NE38-1C 114
S. Cross St. NE3-5E 27
Southdowns. DH2-3D 123
South Dri. NE13-1B 24
South Dri. NE31-3B 64
South Dri. SR6-1D 87
S. Durham Ct. SR1-1D 111
S.E. View. SR8-2F 135
S. Eldon St. NE33-5D 51
S. End. SR6-2D 87
Southend Pde. NE31-5F 65
Southend Rd. NE9-1F 91
Southend Rd. SR3-5C 108
Southend Ter. NE9-4A 80
Southen Way. NE40-3B 54
Southern Rd. NE6-3E 63
Southernwood. NE9-3F 91
Southey St. NE33-4E 51
Southfield Gdns. NE16-3B 76
Southfield Grn. NE16-4B 76
Southfield Rd. NE12-4E 29
Southfield Rd. NE16-4B 76
Southfield Rd. NE34-4B 52
Southfields. DH9-4B 130
Southfield Ter. NE6-3E 63
Southfield Ter. NE16-4B 76
Southfield Way. DH1-5A 136
Southfork. NE15-4D 39
S. Frederick St. NE33-5D 51
S. Front. NE2-4F 43
Southgate. NE12-5E 17
Southgate Ct. NE12-3B 28
S. Grange Pk. SR7-1A 132
South Gro. NE40-3C 54
S. Hill Cres. SR2-2A 146
S. Hill Rd. NE8-1B 78
Southill Rd. NE34-1E 69
S. Johnson St. SR1-1A 110
Southlands. NE7-2C 44
Southlands. NE9-3B 92
Southlands. NE30-1C 34
Southlands. NE32-1B 84
South La. NE36-3A 86
South Lea. NE21-1B 74
Southleigh. NE26-2D 23
S. Market St. DH5-4F 129
Southmayne Rd. SR4
-3C 108
Southmead Av. NE5-3D 41
S. Moor Rd. DH9-5B 130
Southmoor Rd. NE6-5A 46
S. Nelson Ind. Est. NE23-1A 4
S. Nelson Rd. NE23-1A 4
South Pde. NE10-5F 63
South Pde. NE26-2C 22
Southport Pde. NE31-4F 65
S. Preston Gro. NE29-4B 34
S. Preston Ter. NE29-4B 34
S. Promenade. NE33-1A 52
S. Railway St. SR7-3E 133
S. Ridge. NE3-1D 27
South Rd. DH1-5C 138
South Row. NE8-3F 61
S. Shore Rd. NE8
-3D 61 & 5F 143
South St. DH1-3C 138
South St. DH2-1D 123
South St. DH4-2C 126
South St. DH5-3B 128
(East Rainton)
South St. DH5-5E 127
(New Town)
South St. NE1
-3C 60 & 5C 142
South St. NE3-4B 26
South St. NE8-1E 79
South St. NE27-3B 20
South St. NE31-5A 48
South St. SR1-1B 110
(in two parts)
Southstreet Banks. DH1
-3C 138
South Ter. DH1-3A 136
South Ter. NE28-3F 47
South Ter. SR5-3F 99
South Ter. SR7-3F 133
South Ter. SR8-2E 135
S. Thorn. DH9-1C 130
S. View. DH1-2F 139
S. View. DH3-3B 102
S. View. DH4-5A 116
S. View. DH9-5E 131
S. View. NE5-4A 40
S. View. NE13-2C 14
S. View. NE23-3A 8
S. View. NE32-1F 65
S. View. NE38-1D 115
S. View. NE40-5A 36
S. View. SR4-3F 107
S. View. SR6-2C 100
(Roker)
S. View. SR6-4D 71
(Whitburn Colliery)
S. View. SR7-5A 132
South View Pl. NE23-3D 5
S. View Rd. SR4-3F 107
S. View Ter. DH4-5A 126
S. View Ter. NE10-2C 80
S. View Ter. NE16-2F 75
(Swalwell)
S. View Ter. NE16-4A 76
(Whickham)
S. View W. NE6-1F 61
Southward Way. NE25-3D 11
Southway. NE9-4F 79
Southway. NE15-1D 57
Southway. SR8-4B 134
Southwick Ind. Est. SR5
-3D 99
Southwick Rd. SR5-3F 99
Southwold Gdns. SR3
-2D 119
Southwold Pl. NE23-3A 4
S. Woodbine St. NE33-2F 51
Southwood Gdns. NE3-5A 26
Sovereign Ct. NE4-3F 59
Sovereign Ho. NE30-3F 35
Sovereign Pl. NE4-3F 59
Spalding Clo. NE7-5E 29
Spanish City Bldgs. NE26
-1C 22
Spartylea. NE38-1D 115
Spa Well Clo. NE21-2A 74
Spa Well Dri. SR5-2A 98
Spa Well Rd. NE21-4B 74
Speculation Pl. NE37-5C 94
Speedwell. NE9-5B 80
Spelter Works Rd. SR2
-5D 111
Spencer Gro. NE16-2F 75
Spencers Bank. NE16-1F 75
Spencer St. NE6-4E 45
Spencer St. NE29-5C 34
Spencer St. NE31-1D 65
Spencer St. NE32-5D 49
Spencer Ter. NE15-3D 39
Spence Ter. NE29-4B 34
Spenfield Rd. NE5-2F 41
Spenser Clo. DH9-2E 131
Spenser Wlk. NE34-4F 67
Spen St. DH9-3B 130
Spicer La. NE1
-3D 61 & 5E 143
Spinneyside Gdns. NE11
-3E 77
Spinney Ter. NE6-1D 63
Spinney, The. NE7-2C 44
Spinney, The. NE12-5A 18
Spinney, The. NE23-4A 8
Spinney, The. NE38-5C 104
Spire Hollin. SR8-3B 134
Spire Rd. NE37-5E 95
Spires La. NE6-1B 62
Spital Ter. NE3-4E 27
Split Crow Rd. NE8 & NE10
-2E 79
Spohr Ter. NE33-3F 51
Spoors Cotts. NE16-4F 75
Spoor St. NE11-1E 77
Spout La. NE38-1C 104
Springbank Rd. NE2-5B 44
Springbank Rd. SR3-5C 108
Springbank Sq. SR3-5C 108
Springfell. DH3-4C 102
Springfield. NE10-5E 81
Springfield. NE29-4B 34
Springfield Av. NE9-3B 92
Springfield Cres. SR7-4D 133
Springfield Gdns. DH3
-1E 123
Springfield Gdns. NE28-1B 46
Springfield Gro. NE25-3A 22
Springfield Pk. DH1-1A 138
Springfield Pl. NE9-4F 79
Springfield Rd. DH4-2C 126
Springfield Rd. NE5-3E 41
(in two parts)
Springfield Rd. NE21-5A 66
Springfield Ter. DH2-1A 122
Springfield Ter. NE9-4E 93
Springfield Ter. NE10-2B 80
Spring Garden La. NE4
-2A 60 & 3A 142
Spring Gdns. NE29-4B 34
Springhill Gdns. NE15-1C 58
Springs, The. DH3-5C 102
Spring St. NE4
-2A 60 & 3A 142
Springsyde Clo. NE16-5D 75
Spring Ter. NE29-4B 34
Springwell Av. DH1-1A 138
Springwell Av. NE6-3D 63
Springwell Av. NE9-2B 92
Springwell Av. NE32-1A 66
Springwell Bldgs. SR8-3F 135
Springwell Clo. NE21-1B 74
Springwell La. NE9-2D 93
Springwell Rd. DH1-1A 138
Springwell Rd. NE9
-3D 93 to 5E 93
(Springwell)
Springwell Rd. NE9-2B 92
(Wrekenton)
Springwell Rd. NE32-2A 66
Springwell Rd. SR4 & SR3
-4C 108
Springwell Ter. DH5-5E 129
Springwell Ter. NE9-2C 92
Springwood. NE31-5E 47
Square Ho. NE10-3A 80
Square, The. NE16-3F 75
Squires Building. NE1-2D 143
Squires Gdns. NE10-3B 80
Stadium Ind. Pk. NE10-4A 62
Stadium Vs. NE28-2D 47
Stafford Gro. SR2-4C 120
Stafford La. SR6-2D 89
Stafford Pl. SR8-2A 134
Staffordshire Dri. DH1
-3D 141
Stafford St. DH5-4E 129
Stafford St. SR1-5D 101
Stafford Vs. NE9-4E 93
Staindrop. NE10-5F 81
Staindrop Rd. DH1-3D 137
Staines Rd. NE6-3C 62
Staines Wlk. NE23-3A 4
Stainmore Dri. DH3-5B 124
Stainton Dri. NE10-2C 80
Stainton Gdns. NE9-3B 92
Stainton Gro. SR6-5A 88
Stainton Way. SR8-3B 134
Staithe Ho. NE38-4F 105
Staithes Av. NE12-4D 29
Staithes Rd. NE11-5F 59
Staithes St. NE6-1F 63
Staith La. NE21-3F 55
Stalks Rd. NE13-1D 15
Stamford. NE12-2F 17
Stamford Av. NE25-2C 10
Stamford Av. SR3-4D 109
Stamfordham Av. NE29-4E 33
Stamfordham Clo. NE28
-2C 46
Stamfordham M. NE5-3E 41
Stamfordham Rd. NE5
-1F 39 to 3F 41
Stampley Clo. NE21-1E 73
Stamps La. SR1-5D 101
Standerton Ter. DH9-5E 131
Standish St. DH9-3E 131
Stanelaw Way. DH9-1C 130
Staneway. NE10-5D 81
Stanfield Gdns. NE10-2B 82
Stanfield Ho. DH9-2C 130
Stang Wlk. NE12-3E 29
Stanhope. NE38-3E 103
Stanhope Chase. SR8-5C 134
Stanhope Clo. DH1-2D 137
Stanhope Clo. DH4-5B 126
Stanhope Pde. NE33-4E 51
Stanhope Rd. NE32-3C 66
Stanhope Rd. NE33
-1A 68 to 4E 51
Stanhope Rd. SR6-1D 101
Stanhope St. NE4
-1F 59 & 3A 142
Stanhope St. NE33-1E 51
Stanhope Way. NE4-1F 59
Stank La. DH1-1A 136
Stanley By-Pass. DH9-3B 130
Stanley Clo. DH6-4F 141
Stanley Ct. DH9-1D 131
Stanley Cres. NE26-3D 23
(off Alma Pl.)
Stanley Gdns. NE9-3A 92
Stanley Gdns. NE23-3D 9
(off The Crescent)
Stanley Gro. NE7-1C 44
Stanley St. DH5-4D 127
Stanley St. NE4-4E 59
Stanley St. NE28-2B 48
Stanley St. NE29-5C 34
Stanley St. NE32-5D 49
Stanley St. NE34-2A 68
Stanley St. SR5-4A 98
Stanley St. SR7-2C 132
Stanley St. W. NE29-5C 34
Stanley Ter. DH3-4E 123
Stanley Ter. DH4-4F 115
Stanmore Rd. NE6-3E 45
Stannerford Rd. NE40-5A 36
Stannington Av. NE6-5D 45
Stannington Gdns. SR2
-5B 110
Stannington Gro. NE6-5D 45
Stannington Gro. SR2-5B 110
Stannington Pl. NE6-5D 45
Stannington Rd. NE29-4E 33
Stansfield St. SR6-3C 100
Stanstead Clo. SR5-4F 97
Stanton Av. NE34-1C 68
Stanton Clo. NE10-3B 82
Stanton Gro. NE30-5B 22
Stanton Rd. NE27-4A 20
Stanton Rd. NE30-5B 22
Stanton St. NE4-2F 59
Stanway Dri. NE7-1C 44
Stanwick St. NE30-2F 35
Stapeley View. NE3-5F 25
Staple Rd. NE32-5D 49
Stapylton Dri. SR2-4F 109
Starbeck Av. NE2
-5B 44 & 1F 143
(in two parts)
Starbeck M. NE2
-5B 44 & 1F 143
Stargate Gdns. NE9-2A 92
Stargate La. NE40 & NE21
-2C 54
Stargate La. Ind. Est. NE40
-4C 54
Starlight Cres. NE25-1B 10
Station App. DH1-2C 138
Station App. NE11-1C 90
Station App. NE12-3F 29
Station App. NE33-1D 51
Station App. NE36-2C 86
Station Av. DH5-5F 129
Station Av. N. DH4-4E 125
Station Av. S. DH4-4E 125
Station Bank. DH1-2C 138
Station Bank. NE40-1B 54
Station Cotts. NE8-2B 78
Station Cotts. NE12-3F 29
Station Cotts. NE13-3B 26
Station Cotts. NE23-3F 9
Station Cotts. NE34-1A 68
Station Cres. SR7-2C 132
Stationfield Rd. DH9-1C 130
Station Houses. DH2-1A 122
Station Ind. Est. NE12-4D 17
Station La. DH1-2E 139
Station La. DH2-1A 122
Station La. DH3-4A 102
Station La. Ind. Est. DH3
-4A 102
Station Rd. DH3-3E 123
Station Rd. DH4-4C 126
Station Rd. DH4-2D 115
(Penshaw, in two parts)
Station Rd. DH5-5F 129
Station Rd. DH9-2C 130
Station Rd. NE3-5A 28
Station Rd. NE6-5F 63
Station Rd. NE9-5D 79
Station Rd. NE10-5F 63
Station Rd. NE12-2D 17
(Camperdown)
Station Rd. NE12-2F 29
(Forest Hall)
Station Rd. NE13-3C 24
Station Rd. NE15-2A 36
(Heddon-on-the-Wall)
Station Rd. NE15-5A 38
(Newburn)
Station Rd. NE16-1F 75
Station Rd. NE23-3B 4
Station Rd. NE23-4E 7
(Dudley)
Station Rd. NE23-3E 9
(Seghill)
Station Rd. NE26-2C 22
Station Rd. NE27-3E 19
Station Rd. NE28-3B 30
(Wallsend)
Station Rd. NE28-3C 48
(Willington Quay)
Station Rd. NE29-1E 49
Station Rd. NE30-4D 23
Station Rd. NE31-1C 64
Station Rd. NE33-2D 51
Station Rd. NE35-5C 66
Station Rd. NE36-3C 86
Station Rd. NE38-3C 104
Station Rd. SR2-4E 121
Station Rd. SR6-1B 100
Station Rd. SR7-2B 132
Station Rd. E. DH4-2D 115
Station Rd. N. NE12-2F 29
Station Sq. NE26-3C 22
Station St. NE32-5C 48
Station St. SR1-1B 110
Station Ter. DH4-4E 125
Station Ter. NE30-2E 35
Station Ter. NE36-3C 86
Station Ter. NE37-5D 95
Station View. DH2-2D 123
Station View. DH5-5F 129
Station Vs. DH9-1D 131
Staveley Rd. SR6-4A 88
Staveley Rd. SR8-3D 135
Stavordale St. SR7-4F 133
(in three parts)
Stavordale St. W. SR7-5E 133
Stavordale Ter. NE9-3F 79
Staward Av. NE25-2C 10
Staward Ter. NE6-3E 63
Staynebrigg. NE10-4E 81
Stead St. NE28-2C 48
Steep Hill. SR3-3A 118
Stella Bank. NE21-2E 55
Stella Gill Ind. Est. DH2
-1A 122
Stella Hall Dri. NE21-3F 55
Stella La. NE21-3E 55
Stella Rd. NE21-2E 55
Stephen Ct. NE32-1B 66
Stephenson Clo. DH5-4F 129
Stephenson Ct. NE30-4D 35
Stephenson Ho. NE12-5E 17
Stephenson Ind. Est. NE12
-5D 17
Stephenson Ind. Est. NE37
-3C 94
Stephenson Rd. NE7-3C 44
Stephenson Rd. NE12-5E 17
Stephenson Rd. NE37-2B 94
Stephenson Rd. SR8-1B 134
Stephenson's La. NE1
-3C 60 & 5C 142
Stephenson St. NE8-2B 78
Stephenson St. NE28-3C 48
Stephenson St. NE30-4C 34
(North Shields)
Stephenson St. NE30-2F 35
(Tynemouth)
Stephenson Ter. NE10-2C 80
Stephenson Ter. NE15-2E 37
(Throckley)
Stephenson Ter. NE15-3D 39
(Walbottle)
Stephenson Trail, The. NE12
-1A 30
Stephenson Way. NE21-2F 73
Stephen St. NE6-1F 61
Stepney Bank. NE1
-2E 61 & 3F 143
Stepney La. NE1
-2D 61 & 4E 143
Stepney Rd. NE1
-1E 61 & 3F 143
Sterling Cotts. NE10-3A 80
Sterling St. SR4-2F 109
Stevenson Rd. DH9-3D 131
Stevenson St. DH4-4C 126
Steward Cres. NE34-1A 70
Steward St. SR3-3E 119
Stewart Av. SR2-4C 120
Stewart Dri. NE36-2F 85
Stewart St. SR4-2F 109
Stewart St. SR7-4F 133
Stewart St. E. SR7-4F 133
Stileford. NE10-3F 81
Stirling Av. NE32-3C 66
Stirling Clo. NE38-4E 105
Stirling Ct. NE11-2D 91
Stirling Dri. NE29-1D 33
Stobart St. SR5-5B 100
Stockbridge. NE1
-2D 61 & 4E 143
Stockdale Gdns. NE6-3F 63
Stockfold. NE38-5C 104
Stockholm Clo. NE29-5D 33
Stockley Av. SR5-2A 98
Stockley Rd. NE38-2E 105
Stocksfield Av. NE5-5E 41
Stocksfield Gdns. NE9-2F 91
Stockton Av. SR8-2E 135
Stockton Rd. DH1-4D 139
Stockton Rd. SR1 & SR2
-2B 110 to 3B 110
Stockton Rd. SR2-5D 121
Stockton Rd. SR7-1A 132
Stockton St. SR7-2C 132
Stockton Ter. SR2-5D 111
Stockwell Grn. NE6-4B 46
Stoddart St. NE2
-1E 61 & 2F 143
Stoddart St. NE34-2A 68
Stoker Av. NE34-3E 67
Stokesley Gro. NE7-1C 44
Stokoe St. SR2-3D 111
Stone Cellar Rd. NE37-3F 93
Stonechat Clo. NE38-4D 103
Stonechat Mt. NE21-3F 55
Stonechat Pl. NE12-3C 28
Stonecrop. NE9-5B 80
Stonefold Clo. NE5-1D 41
Stoneleigh Av. NE12-3B 28
Stoneleigh Clo. DH4-3A 126
Stoneleigh Pl. NE12-3B 28
Stonesdale. DH4-3D 115
Stone St. NE10-4B 80
Stoneycroft E. NE12-4A 18
Stoneycroft W. NE12-4A 18
Stoneygate Gdns. NE10
-1D 81
Stoneygate La. NE10-1C 80
Stoneyhurst Av. NE15-3A 58
Stoneyhurst Rd. NE3-5F 27
Stoneyhurst Rd. W. NE3
-5F 27
Stoney La. NE9-4E 93
Stoney La. SR5-3F 99
Stoneylea Rd. NE5-4B 40
Stonycroft. NE37-1B 104
Store Bldgs. NE15-2D 85
Store St. NE15-1B 56
Store St. NE21-1A 74
Storey La. NE21-3E 55
Storey St. NE23-4E 5
Stormont Grn. NE3-1A 42
Stormont St. NE29-5B 34
Stotfold Clo. SR7-2A 132
Stothard St. NE32-5D 49
Stotts Rd. NE6-4B 46
Stowell Sq. NE1
-2B 60 & 4B 142
Stowell St. NE1
-2B 60 & 4B 142
Stowell Ter. NE10-2D 81
Stow, The. NE12-4C 28
Straker St. NE32-1B 66
Straker Ter. NE34-2A 68
Strand, The. SR3-3C 118
Strangford Av. DH2-4D 123
Strangford Rd. SR7-3D 133
(in two parts)
Strangways St. SR7-4F 133
Stranton Ter. SR6-3C 100
Stratfield St. SR4-5D 99
Stratford Av. SR2-4D 111
Stratford Clo. NE12-3F 17
Stratford Clo. NE23-3A 4
Stratford Gdns. NE9-4E 79
Stratford Gro. NE6-5C 44
Stratford Gro. Ter. NE6-5B 44
Stratford Gro. W. NE6-5B 44
Stratford Rd. NE6-5C 44
Stratford Vs. NE6-5C 44
Strathearn Way. NE3-3A 26
Strathmore. DH3-4A 124
Strathmore Clo. DH9-2F 131
Strathmore Cres. NE4-2C 58
Strathmore Rd. NE3-3E 27
Strathmore Rd. NE9-3A 80
Strathmore Rd. SR3-5C 108
Strathmore Sq. SR3-5C 108
Stratton Clo. SR2-2E 121
Stratus Ct. SR3-4F 119
Strawberry Gdns. NE28
-1B 46
Strawberry La. NE1
-2B 60 & 3B 142
Strawberry Pl. NE1
-2B 60 & 3B 142
Strawberry Ter. NE13-3B 14
Strawberry Ter. NE23-1E 17
St. Benet's Way. SR6-4C 100
Stretford Ct. NE9-3F 91
Stretton Clo. DH4-5F 125
Stretton Way. NE27-2E 19
Stridingedge. NE37-2F 103
Stronsay Clo. SR2-2C 120

Struan Ter. NE36-3C 86
Strudders Farm Ct. NE21 -5E 57
Stuart Ct. NE3-3D 25
Stuart Gdns. NE15-2E 37
Stuart Ter. NE10-1C 80
Stubbs Av. NE16-2F 75
Studdon Wlk. NE3-4F 25
Studland Clo. NE29-1A 34
Studley Gdns. NE9-5D 79
Studley Gdns. NE25-3C 22
Studley Ter. NE4-1E 59
Studley Vs. NE12-2F 29
Sturdee Gdns. NE2-1A 44
Styan Av. NE26-2D 23
Styford Gdns. NE15-5A 40
Success Rd. DH4-1A 126
Sudbury Way. NE23-3A 4
Suddick St. SR5-3F 99
Suez St. NE30-4C 34
Suffolk Gdns. NE28-1F 47
Suffolk Gdns. NE34-5D 53
Suffolk Pl. DH3-1C 112
Suffolk Pl. NE8-3E 61
Suffolk Rd. NE31-4E 65
Suffolk St. DH5-4D 129
Suffolk St. NE32-1F 65
Suffolk St. SR2-2D 111
Suffolk Wlk. SR8-1B 134
Suffolk Way. DH1-1D 137
Sugley Ct. NE15-4A 40
Sugley St. NE15-1B 56
Sugley Vs. NE15-1C 56
Sulgrave Rd. NE37-4D 95
Sullivan Wlk. NE31-2D 65
Summerfield Rd. NE9-3E 79
Summerhill. NE21-4F 55
Summerhill. NE32-1B 84
Summerhill. SR3-3A 118
Summerhill Av. NE3-5F 15
Summerhill Gro. NE4 -3A 60 & 5A 142
Summerhill Rd. NE34-5B 52
Summerhill St. NE4 -3A 60 & 5A 142
Summerhill Ter. NE4 -3A 60 & 5A 142
Summerhouse Farm. DH5 -3B 128
Summerson St. DH5-4F 129
Summer St. NE10-1B 80
Summerville. DH1-3B 138
Sunbury Av. NE2-3A 44
Sunderland Av. SR8-1E 135
Sunderland By-Pass. NE36, SR5 & SR4-4C 84 & 5A 118
Sunderland Enterprise Pk. SR5-4B 98
Sunderland Highway. NE37 & NE38-2A 104 to 1D 107
Sunderland Rd. DH1-2F 139
Sunderland Rd. DH4-2C 126
Sunderland Rd. NE8 & NE10 -5E 61 to 2B 82
Sunderland Rd. NE33 & NE34 -4F 51 to 4E 69
Sunderland Rd. NE36 & SR5 -3C 86
Sunderland Rd. SR5-3F 99
Sunderland Rd. SR6-1F 87
Sunderland Rd. SR8-1E 135
Sunderland Rd. Vs. NE10 -2E 81
Sunderland St. DH4-4C 126
Sunderland St. DH5-4D 127
Sunderland St. NE1 -3B 60 & 5A 142
Sunderland St. SR1-5C 100
Sundew Rd. NE9 & NE10 -5A 80
Sundridge Dri. NE10-3A 82
Sun Hill. DH5-4E 129
Sunholme Dri. NE28-4B 30
Sunlea Av. NE30-4D 23
Sunley Ho. NE3-4E 27
Sunnidale. NE16-5D 75
Sunnilaws. NE34-4E 69
Sunningdale. NE25-2E 21
Sunningdale. NE33-3A 52
Sunningdale Av. NE6-1F 63
Sunningdale Av. NE28-3D 47
Sunningdale Clo. NE10-3C 80
Sunningdale Dri. NE37-3A 94
Sunningdale Rd. SR3-5C 108
Sunnirise. NE34-3F 69
Sunniside. NE29-4F 33
Sunniside. SR4-1E 107
Sunniside Dri. NE34-4E 69
Sunniside Gdns. NE9-2A 92
Sunniside Gdns. NE15-1F 57
Sunniside La. SR6-5F 69
Sunniside Rd. NE16-5A 76
Sunniside Ter. SR6-5F 69
Sunnybank Av. NE15-2B 58
Sunny Blunts. SR8-5B 134
Sunnybrow. SR3-2E 119
Sunnycrest Av. NE6-1D 63
Sunnyside. NE23-3B 4
Sunny Ter. DH9-1C 130
Sunnyway. NE5-2E 41
Sunrise Enterprise Pk. SR5 -5E 97
Sun View Ter. SR6-1D 87
Surrey Av. SR3-4F 119
Surrey Pl. DH4-5B 116
Surrey Pl. NE4-2F 59
Surrey Rd. NE29-3F 33
Surrey Rd. NE31-4E 65
Surrey St. DH4-4B 116
Surrey St. DH5-4D 129
Surrey St. NE32-1F 65
Surrey Ter. DH3-1B 112
Surtees Dri. DH1-2A 138
Surtees Rd. SR8-3C 134
Surtees St. SR2-3E 111
Sussex Ct. SR1-1C 110
Sussex Gdns. NE28-1F 47
Sussex Pl. NE37-3C 94
Sussex St. NE32-1F 65
Sussex St. SR3-2F 119
Sutherland Av. NE4-1D 59
Sutherland Building. NE1 -2D 143
Sutherland Ct. NE34-5B 68
Sutherland Grange. DH4 -4C 116
Sutherland Pl. DH1-5A 140
Sutherland St. NE8-5E 61
Sutherland St. SR6-3B 100
Sutherland St. SR7-2C 132
Sutton Clo. DH4-4F 115
Sutton Ct. NE28-4A 30
Sutton Dwellings. NE4 -1A 60 & 2A 142
Sutton St. DH1-2B 138 (in two parts)
Sutton St. NE6-5A 46
Sutton Way. NE34-2F 69
Swainby Clo. NE3-2F 27
Swale Cres. DH3-5B 124
Swaledale. NE28-4B 30
Swaledale. SR6-3D 89
Swaledale Cres. DH4-3F 115
Swaledale Gdns. NE7-1D 45
Swaledale Gdns. SR4-2D 109
Swallows, The. NE28-2A 32
Swallow St. SR7-2C 132
Swallow Tail Ct. NE34-3A 68
Swalwell Bank. NE16 -1F 75 to 3F 75
Swan Av. NE28-1F 47
Swan Ct. NE8-1F 77
Swan Ind. Est. NE38-4D 105
Swan Rd. NE6-3A 64
Swan Rd. NE38-4E 105
Swan St. NE8-4E 61
Swan St. SR5-3A 100
Swanton Clo. NE5-5D 25
Swanway. NE9-3F 79
Swards Rd. NE10-3D 81
Swarland Av. NE7-5D 29
Swarland Rd. NE25-2C 10
Swinbourne Gdns. NE26 -1A 22
Swinbourne Ter. NE32-4A 66
Swinburne Pl. DH3-5B 102
Swinburne Pl. NE4 -2A 60 & 4A 142
Swinburne Pl. NE8-4D 61
Swinburne St. NE8-4D 61
Swinburne St. NE32-1D 67
Swinburn Rd. NE25-2B 10
Swinburn Ter. NE10-5F 63
Swindon Rd. SR3-4C 108
Swindon Sq. SR3-5C 108
Swindon St. NE31-1C 64
Swindon Ter. NE6-3D 45
Swinhoe Gdns. NE13-5A 6
Swinhope. NE38-2E 113
Swinley Gdns. NE15-1E 57
Swinside Dri. DH1-2C 140
Swirral Edge. NE37-1B 104
Swiss Cotts. NE38-1A 114
Swyntoft. NE10-3A 82
Sycamore. DH2-1C 122
Sycamore Av. NE16-2A 76
Sycamore Av. NE25-3B 22
Sycamore Av. NE34-3E 69
Sycamore Av. NE38-1A 114
Sycamore Clo. NE2-3A 44
Sycamore Dri. SR5-2A 100
Sycamore Gro. NE9-4E 93
Sycamore Gro. NE10-2C 80
Sycamore Rd. NE21-5B 56
Sycamore Rd. SR6-1D 89
Sycamores, The. NE4-4F 59
Sycamores, The. SR2-5D 111
Sycamore St. NE15-2F 37
Sycamore St. NE28-3D 47
Sydenham Ter. NE33-2F 51
Sydenham Ter. SR4-3E 109
Sydney Ct. NE8-4D 61
Sydney Gdns. NE34-4D 67
Sydney Gro. NE28-4C 30
Sydney St. DH4-3D 125
Sydney Ter. DH9-1A 130
Sylverton Gdns. NE33-4A 52
Sylvia Ter. DH9-1C 130
Symington Gdns. SR3 -2D 119
Syon St. NE30-2F 35
Syron. NE16-3E 75
Syston Clo. DH4-5F 125

Taberna Clo. NE15-2A 36
Tadcaster Rd. SR3-1A 118
Tadema Rd. NE33-3A 52
Talbot Clo. NE38-3C 104
Talbot Cotts. DH3-3B 102
Talbot Grn. NE6-4B 40
Talbot Pl. SR7-3E 133
Talbot Rd. NE34-1B 68
Talbot Rd. SR6-2D 101
Talbot Ter. DH3-3B 102
Talgarth. NE38-3F 105
Talisman View. NE9-3F 91
Talley Ct. NE38-2B 104
Tamar Clo. NE29-2E 33
Tamar Clo. SR8-4B 134
Tamar Ct. SR3-4E 119
Tamerton Dri. DH3-5C 102
Tamerton St. SR4-1D 109
Tamworth Rd. NE4-2F 59
Tamworth Sq. SR3-1A 118
Tanfield Gdns. NE34-1F 69
Tanfield Lea S. Ind. Est. DH9 -1C 130
Tanfield Pl. NE9-3B 92
Tanfield Rd. NE9-3B 92
Tanfield Rd. NE15-1F 57
Tanfield Rd. SR3-1B 118
Tanfield St. SR4-1D 109
Tangmere Clo. NE23-3D 5
Tankerville Pl. NE2-4A 44
Tankerville Ter. NE2-4F 43
Tanners Bank. NE30-3E 35
Tanners Ct. NE1 -2B 60 & 4B 142 (off Friar St.)
Tantallon. DH3-5C 102
Tantobie Rd. NE15-1F 57
Tarlton Cres. NE10-2B 80
Tarn Clo. SR8-3D 135
Tarn Dri. SR2-2E 121
Tarragon Way. NE34-4C 68 (in two parts)
Tarrington Clo. NE28-5B 32
Tarset Pl. NE3-3C 26
Tarset Rd. NE25-2C 20
Tarset St. NE1-2E 61
Tasmania Rd. NE34-4D 67
Tasman Rd. SR3-2B 118
Tatham St. SR1-1C 110
Tattershall. SR2-4F 109
Taunton Av. NE29-1E 33
Taunton Av. NE32-2C 66
Taunton Clo. NE28-5B 32
Taunton Pl. NE23-1D 5
Taunton Rd. SR3-1C 118
Taunton Sq. SR3-1B 118
Tavistock Ct. DH4-2B 126
Tavistock Pl. NE32-2C 66
Tavistock Pl. SR1-1C 110
Tavistock Rd. NE2-2A 44
Tavistock Sq. SR3-2F 119
Tavistock Wlk. NE23-1D 5
Taylor Av. NE13-1E 15
Taylor Gdns. NE10-1F 81 (in two parts)
Taylor Gdns. SR2-5D 111
Taylor's Ct. NE1 -2B 60 & 4C 142
Taylor St. NE27-3A 20
Taylor St. NE33-5D 51
Taylor Ter. NE27-1F 31
Taylor Ter. NE34-3E 67
Taynton Gro. NE23-2E 9
Tay Rd. SR4 & SR3-5A 108
Teal Clo. NE7-4D 29
Teal Clo. NE38-5E 103
Team St. NE8-1F 77
Team Valley Shopping Village. NE11-5B 78
Team Valley Trading Est. NE11-4B 78 & 1C 90
Teasdale Ho. NE5-1B 40
Teasdale St. SR2-3D 111
Teasdale Ter. DH1-3B 140
Tebay Dri. NE5-4B 40
Teddington Clo. NE3-3D 25
Teddington Rd. SR3-1B 118
Teddington Sq. SR3-1B 118
Tedham Rd. NE15-5D 39
Tees Clo. SR8-5B 134
Tees Ct. NE34-2A 68
Tees Ct. SR3-4E 119
Tees Cres. DH9-3C 130
Teesdale Av. DH4-2F 115
Teesdale Gdns. NE7-1D 45
Teesdale Gro. NE12-2E 29
Tees Rd. NE31-4D 65
Tees St. SR7-3F 133
Tees St. SR8-2E 135
Tees Ter. NE37-4B 94
Teign Clo. SR8-5B 134
Teindland Clo. NE4-3D 59
Tel-El-Kebir Rd. SR2-4D 111
Telford Clo. NE27-2E 19
Telford Ct. NE28-2E 49
Telford Rd. SR3-1B 118
Telford St. NE8-3C 78
Telford St. NE28-3E 49
Tempest Rd. SR7-3E 133
Tempest St. NE21-3F 55
Tempest St. SR3-3F 119
Temple Grn. NE8-2B 78
Temple Grn. NE34-2C 68
Temple Pk. Rd. NE33 & NE34 -1B 68
Temple St. NE1 -3B 60 & 5B 142
Temple St. NE10-1C 80
Temple St. NE33-5D 51
Temple Town. NE33-4C 50
Tenbury Cres. NE12-2E 29
Tenbury Cres. NE29-1A 34
Tenby Rd. SR3-2A 118
Tenby Sq. NE23-2D 5
Ten Fields. DH5-5E 129
Tennant St. NE31-2B 64
Tennant St. NE34-3E 67
Tennyson Av. NE31-1D 65
Tennyson Av. NE35-2A 86
Tennyson Ct. NE8-5F 61
Tennyson Cres. NE16-2F 75
Tennyson Grn. NE3-1A 42
Tennyson Rd. DH2-2A 122
Tennyson St. NE33-2F 51
Tennyson St. SR5-3E 99
Tennyson Ter. NE29-5C 34
Tenter Garth. NE15-2E 37
Tenter Ter. DH1-2C 138
Tenth Av. DH2-2C 122
Tenth Av. NE6-4D 45
Tenth Av. NE11-2C 90
Tenth Av. W. NE11-2B 90
Tenth St. SR8-3E 135
Terrace Pl. NE1 -1B 60 & 3B 142
Terraces, The. NE38-3D 105
Terrace, The. NE35-1D 85
Terrace, The. NE36-3C 86
Terrace, The. SR4-1E 107
Territorial La. DH1-2D 139
Tesla St. DH4-1B 126
Tetford Pl. NE12-3E 29
Teviot. NE38-1F 113
Teviotdale Gdns. NE7-1D 45
Teviot St. NE8-1F 79
Teviot Way. NE32-2F 65
Tewkesbury. NE12-2E 17
Tewkesbury Rd. NE15-5E 39
Thackeray Rd. SR3-5C 108
Thackeray St. DH4-5C 126
Thames Av. NE32-4B 66
Thames Ct. DH9-4C 130
Thames Cres. DH4-5F 125
Thames Cres. DH9-4C 130
Thames Gdns. NE28-3C 46
Thames Rd. NE31-4D 65
Thames Rd. SR3-2A 118
Thames Rd. SR8-4B 134
Thames St. NE8-2F 79
Thanet Rd. SR3-1C 118
Tharsis Rd. NE31-3B 64
Thatcher Clo. NE16-5F 75
Theatre Pl. NE29-5C 34
Thelma St. SR4-2F 109
Theme Rd. SR3-2A 118
Theresa Russell Ho. NE6 -1A 62
Theresa St. NE21-4B 56 (in two parts)
Theresa St. SR7-5F 133
Thetford. NE38-3B 104
Third Av. DH2-3C 122
Third Av. DH2-3A 112 (North Lodge)
Third Av. NE6-5D 45
Third Av. NE11-4B 78
Third Av. NE29-5D 33
Third St. SR8-2F 135
Thirkeld Pl. DH4-3F 115
Thirlmere. DH3-5C 102
Thirlmere. NE10-2F 81
Thirlmere. SR6-1F 87
Thirlmere Av. DH2-4D 123
Thirlmere Av. NE30-5B 22
Thirlmere Clo. NE12-4A 18
Thirlmere Ct. NE31-3E 65
Thirlmere Cres. DH4-4A 116
Thirlmere Cres. NE21-2F 73
Thirlmere Rd. SR8-3D 135
Thirlmere Way. NE5-4D 41
Thirlmoor. NE37-1F 103
Thirlwell Bank. SR5-4F 99
Thirlwell Rd. SR5-3F 99
Thirsk Rd. SR3-1C 118
Thirston Dri. NE23-3D 5
Thirston Pl. NE29-2E 33
Thirston Way. NE3-5F 25
Thirteenth St. SR8-3E 135
Thirwell Gro. NE32-4F 65
Thirwell Rd. NE8-4E 61
Thistle Ct. NE31-2C 64
Thistledon Av. NE16-4E 75
Thistle Rd. SR3-1B 118
Thistley Clo. NE6-4A 46
Thistley Grn. NE10-1A 82
Thomas Bell Ho. NE34-3F 67
Thomas Horsley Ho. NE15 -2A 58
Thomas Husband St. DH5 -5E 127
Thomas St. DH3-3E 123
Thomas St. DH5-3F 129 (in two parts)
Thomas St. DH9-5F 131
Thomas St. NE5-2A 40
Thomas St. NE9-4C 92
Thomas St. NE16-3F 75
Thomas St. NE33-2E 51
Thomas St. NE37-5D 95
Thomas St. SR2-4E 121
Thomas St. N. SR6-4C 100
Thomas St. S. SR2-4E 121
Thomas St. S. SR5-4E 99
Thomas Taylor Cotts. NE27 -2D 19
Thompson Av. NE12-2D 17
Thompson Cres. SR5-4F 97
Thompson Gdns. NE28-2C 46
Thompson Pl. NE10-2B 80
Thompson Rd. SR5-3F 99
Thompson's Bldgs. DH4 -5B 116
Thompson St. SR8-2F 135
Thompson Ter. SR2-4E 121
Thorburn St. SR6-1C 100
Thornbank Clo. SR3-5E 119
Thornbridge. NE38-3F 105
Thornbury Av. NE23-2E 9
Thornbury Clo. NE3-4D 25
Thornbury Clo. NE35-1C 84
Thornbury Dri. NE25-1E 21
Thornbury St. SR4-1E 109
Thorncliffe Pl. NE29-4A 34
Thorn Clo. NE13-2C 14
Thorndale Rd. DH1-3D 141
Thorndale Rd. NE15-2E 57
Thorndale Rd. SR3-1B 118
Thorne Av. NE10-2A 82
Thornebrake. NE10-3F 81
Thorne Rd. SR3-1A 118
Thornes Clo. SR8-4E 135
Thorne Sq. SR3-1A 118
Thorne Ter. NE6-5A 46
Thorneyburn Av. NE25-2C 20
Thorneyburn Clo. DH4 -3B 126
Thorney Clo. Rd. SR3-1B 118
Thorneyfield Dri. NE12-5C 16
Thorneyholme Ter. DH9 -2C 130
Thorneyholme Ter. NE21 -4B 56
Thornfield Gro. SR2-5C 110
Thornfield Rd. NE3-5D 27
Thorngill. NE37-1A 104
Thornhaugh Av. NE16-4D 75
Thornhill Clo. NE25-3B 10
Thornhill Cres. SR2-2B 110
Thornhill Gdns. SR2-3A 110
Thornhill Pk. SR2-3A 110
Thornhill Rd. NE12-3F 29
Thornhill St. DH4-5C 126
Thornhill Ter. SR2-2A 110
Thornholme Av. NE34-1A 70
Thornholme Rd. SR2-3A 110
Thornhope Clo. NE38-2D 105
Thornlea Gdns. NE9-4E 79
Thornleigh Gdns. SR6-5E 69
Thornleigh Rd. NE2-3A 44
Thornley Av. NE10-4A 82
Thornley Av. NE23-3D 5
Thornley Clo. NE16-5F 75
Thornley La. NE21 & NE39 -3F 73 to 5F 73
Thornley Rd. NE5-4A 40
Thornton Av. NE33-5C 50
Thornton Clo. DH4-3F 115
Thornton Cotts. NE40-1B 54
Thornton Ct. NE38-2B 104
Thornton Cres. NE21-4A 56
Thornton Pl. SR1-1A 110
Thornton St. NE1 -3B 60 & 5B 142 (in two parts)
Thornton Ter. NE12-1B 30
Thorntree Av. NE13-3A 6
Thorntree Clo. NE25-3D 21
Thorntree Cotts. NE13-3A 6
Thorntree Ct. NE12-1B 30
Thorntree Dri. NE15-1F 57
Thorntree Dri. NE25-3D 21
Thorntree Gill. SR8-4F 135
Thorntree Ter. DH9-2E 131
Thorntree Wlk. NE32-5B 66
Thornwood Gdns. NE11 -4F 77
Thornygarth. NE10-3C 80
Thorp Cotts. NE40-3A 54
Thorp Dri. NE40-2C 54
Thorpe Clo. NE4-1F 59
Thorpe Cres. SR8-1D 135
Thorpeness Rd. SR3-1B 118
Thorpe Rd. SR8-1B 134
Thorpe St. NE4-1F 59
Thorpe St. SR8-2F 135
Thread Gdns. NE28-1A 48
Three Mile Ct. NE3-2E 27
Three Rivers Ct. NE36-3F 85
Threlkeld Gro. SR6-5B 88
Thrift St. NE29-5C 34
Thristley Gdns. SR2-5A 110
Throckley Way. NE34-2F 67
Thropton Av. NE7-5D 29
Thropton Clo. DH2-5C 122
Thropton Clo. NE10-3B 82
Thropton Cres. NE3-3C 26
Thropton Pl. NE29-2E 33
Thropton Ter. NE7-2D 45
Thrush Cross Pl. DH1 -3B 140
Thrush Gro. SR5-4A 98
Thurlow Way. DH5-1C 128
Thursby. DH3-1C 112 (in two parts)
Thursby Av. NE30-5D 23
Thursby Gdns. NE9-1F 91
Thurso Clo. SR3-1A 118
Tilbeck Sq. SR3-5F 119
Tilbury Gro. NE30-4B 22
Tilbury Rd. SR3-2A 118
Tilbury Sq. SR3-2A 118
Tileshed La. NE38-1B 86
Till Av. NE21-5A 56
Tilley Rd. NE38-3D 103
Tillmouth Pk. Rd. NE15-3E 37
Till St. NE6-3B 62
Tilmouth Av. NE25-2C 10
Tilmouth Gdns. NE4-1B 58
Tilson Way. NE3-4A 26
Timlin Gdns. NE28-2C 48
Tindal Clo. NE4 -2A 60 & 4A 142
Tindale Av. DH1-3A 136
Tindale Av. NE23-3E 5
Tindale Dri. NE16-3F 75
Tindal St. NE4 -2A 60 & 4A 142
Tinkler's La. DH1-2D 139
Tinkler Ter. DH3-4A 124
Tintagel. DH3-4B 124
Tintagel Clo. NE23-1D 5
Tintagel Clo. SR3-2A 118
Tintagel Dri. SR7-2E 133
Tintern. NE38-4B 104
Tintern Clo. DH4-3B 126
Tintern Cres. NE6-5D 45
Tintern Cres. NE29-1F 33
Tintern St. SR4-1F 109
Tiree Ct. SR3-4E 119
Tirril Pl. NE5-4C 40
Titan Ho. NE6-2E 63
Titan Rd. NE6-1E 63
Titchfield Rd. NE38-3B 104
Titian Av. NE34-5B 68
Titlington Gro. NE31-4B 64
Tiverton Av. NE4-2D 59
Tiverton Av. NE29-1E 33
Tiverton Clo. NE28-4B 32
Tiverton Gdns. NE9-2D 91
Tiverton Pl. NE23-1D 5
Tiverton Sq. SR3-1A 118
Tivoli Bldgs. DH4-5A 116
Toberty Gdns. NE10-2F 81
Todd's Nook. NE4-2A 60
Togstone Pl. NE5-3E 41
Toll Bar Rd. SR2-1C 120
Tollerton Dri. SR5-4E 97
Toll Ho. Rd. DH1-2A 138
Tolls Clo. NE25-1E 21
Toll Sq. NE30-4D 35
Tomlinson Ct. NE25-1E 21
Tonbridge Av. NE29-5A 34
Toner Av. NE31-4C 64
Topaz St. SR7-3B 132
Topcliff. SR6-4D 101
Topcliffe Grn. NE9-3F 91
Toppings St. NE35-1D 85
Torcross Way. NE23-1D 5
Toronto Rd. SR3-5C 108
Toronto Sq. SR3-5C 108
Torquay Gdns. NE9-2E 91
Torquay Pde. NE31-4E 65
Torquay Rd. SR3-1C 118
Torrens Rd. SR3-5B 108
Torver Clo. NE13-2C 14
Torver Clo. SR8-4D 135
Torver Cres. SR6-5B 88
Torver Pl. NE9-1A 92
Torver Way. NE30-5B 22
Tosson Pl. NE29-4F 33
Tosson Ter. NE6-4D 45
Totnes Clo. SR3-1A 118
Totnes Dri. NE23-1D 5
Toward Rd. SR1 & SR2 -1C 110
Toward St. NE6-1F 61
Tower Ct. NE11-1F 77
Tower Gdns. NE40-2B 54
Tower Pl. SR2-3D 111
Tower Rd. NE37-1D 105
Towers Av. NE2-2F 43
Towers Pl. NE34-2D 67
Towers, The. SR4-2A 108
Tower St. NE1 -2D 61 & 4E 143
Tower St. SR2-3D 111
Tower St. W. SR2-3D 111
Tower View. NE15-2A 58
Towne Ga., The. NE15-2A 36
Towneley Ct. DH9-3B 130
Towneley St. DH9-3C 130
Townfield Gdns. NE15-4A 38
Townsend Rd. SR3-2B 118
Townsend Sq. SR3-2B 118
Townsville Av. NE25-4F 21
Towton. NE12-3F 17
Toynbee. NE38-3F 105
Tracey Av. NE36-2F 85
Trafalgar Ho. NE30-3F 35
Trafalgar Rd. NE37-4D 95
Trafalgar Sq. SR1-1D 111
Trafalgar St. NE1 -2D 61 & 4E 143
Trafford. NE9-3E 91
Trafford Rd. SR5-4F 99
Trafford Wlk. NE5-2F 39
Trajan Av. NE33-5E 35
Trajan St. NE33-5E 35
Trajan Wlk. NE15-2A 36
Transbrittania Enterprise Pk. NE21-3D 57
Tranwell Clo. NE3-2B 26
Tranwell Dri. NE25-2C 10
Travers St. DH4-4B 116
Treby St. SR4-5E 99
Trecone Ho. SR3-5F 119
Tredegar Clo. NE5-1D 41
Treecone Clo. SR3-5E 119
Tree Ct. SR3-4E 119
Trefoil Rd. DH9-1A 130
Treherne Rd. NE2-1F 43
Trent Av. NE31-4D 65
Trent Cres. DH3-4B 124
Trent Dri. NE32-5B 66
Trent Gdns. NE8-2A 80
Trentham Av. NE7-5D 29
Trenton Av. NE38-1B 104
Trent Rd. SR3-1B 118
Trevarren Dri. SR2-3E 121
Trevelyan Clo. SR3-1A 118
Trevelyan Ct. NE12-3B 28
Trevelyan Dri. NE5-1B 40
Trevelyan Pl. SR8-5A 134
Trevethick St. NE8-2B 78
Trevone Pl. NE23-2E 9
Trevor Gro. SR6-2E 87
Trevor Ter. NE30-3C 34
Trewhitt Rd. NE6-4D 45
Trewitt Rd. NE26-2C 22
Tribune Pl. NE9-4F 79
Trident Rd. SR3-3F 119
Trimdon Gro. NE9-2C 92
Trimdon St. SR4-5A 100
Trimdon St. W. SR4-5F 99
Trinity Bldgs. NE30-4D 35
Trinity Chare. NE1-3D 61
Trinity Ct. NE8-4E 61
Trinity Ct. NE29-5C 34
Trinity Courtyard. NE6-3B 62
Trinity Gro. NE23-2F 9
Trinity Pl. NE29-5C 34
Trinity Sq. NE8-4D 61 (in two parts)
Trinity St. NE29-5C 34
Trinity St. SR5-3E 99
Trinity Ter. NE29-5C 34
Trinity Wlk. NE33-3D 51
Trojan Av. NE6-5F 45
Tromso Clo. NE29-5D 33
Trool Ct. SR3-5E 119
Troon Clo. NE37-2B 94
Trotter Ter. SR2-4D 121
Troutbeck Av. NE6-2D 63
Troutbeck Gdns. NE9-2F 91
Troutbeck Rd. SR6-5B 88
Troutbeck Way. NE34-4E 67
Troutdale Pl. NE12-3B 28
Troves Clo. NE4-3D 59
Trowbridge Way. NE3-5A 26
Truro Gro. NE29-1F 33
Truro Way. NE32-1A 84
Tuart St. DH3-2E 123
Tudor Av. NE29-3A 34
Tudor Gro. SR3-4E 109
Tudor Rd. DH3-1E 123
Tudor Rd. NE33-3D 51
Tudor Wlk. NE3-4E 25
Tudor Way. NE3-4D 25
Tudor Wynd. NE6-3F 45
Tulip Clo. NE21-5F 55
Tulip Ct. DH4-2A 116
Tulip St. NE10-1A 80
Tummel Ct. SR3-5E 119
Tumulus Av. NE6-4C 46
Tunbridge Rd. SR3-1C 118
Tundry Way. NE21-3E 57
Tunis Rd. SR3-5C 108
Tunstall Av. NE6-1B 62
Tunstall Av. NE34-1A 70
Tunstall Bank. SR3 & SR2 -3B 120
Tunstall Hill Clo. SR2-5B 110
Tunstall Hope Rd. SR3 -1A 120
Tunstall Pk. SR2-4A 110
Tunstall Rd. SR1, SR2 & SR3 -5A 110 to 2B 110
Tunstall Ter. SR2-3C 120 (Ryhope)
Tunstall Ter. SR2-2B 110 (Sunderland)
Tunstall Ter. SR3-3F 119
Tunstall Ter. W. SR2-2A 110
Tunstall Vale. SR3-2B 110
Tunstall View. SR3-2F 119 (off Hawthorn Av.)
Tunstall Village Grn. SR3 -3A 120
Tunstall Village Rd. SR3 -3F 119
Tunstall Vs. SR3-3A 120
Turbinia Gdns. NE7-2E 45
Turfside. NE10-3F 81 (in two parts)
Turfside. NE32-1C 84
Turnberry. NE25-2E 21
Turnberry. NE33-3A 52
Turnberry Clo. NE37-3B 94
Turnberry Ct. NE10-3A 82
Turnberry Way. NE3-4A 28
Turnberry Way. NE23-3E 5
Turnbull Ho. SR5-3A 100
Turnbull St. SR1-5D 101
Turner Av. NE34-4C 68
Turner Clo. NE40-3B 54
Turner Cres. NE3-4C 26
Turner St. NE27-5F 19
Turnham Rd. SR3-2B 118
Turnstone Dri. NE38-4D 103
Turo Rd. SR3-1B 118
Turret Rd. NE15-5B 40
Tuscan Rd. SR3-2A 118
Tuthill Stairs. NE1 -3C 60 & 5D 143
Tweed Clo. SR2-2E 121
Tweed Clo. SR8-4B 134
Tweed Gro. NE15-5D 39
Tweed Ho. NE1 -2E 61 & 5F 143
Tweedmouth Ct. NE3-1F 43
Tweeds St. NE8-1F 79
Tweed St. NE4-2E 59
Tweed St. NE31-1C 64
Tweed St. NE32-3F 65
Tweed St. NE38-3D 105
Tweed Ter. DH9-4C 130
Tweedy's Bldgs. NE40-2A 54
Tweedy Ter. NE6-2E 63
Twelfth Av. DH2-2D 123
Twelfth St. SR8-3E 135
Twickenham Rd. SR3-1B 118
Twizell Av. NE21-5A 56
Two Ball Lonnen. NE4-1B 58
Twyford Clo. NE23-2D 5
Tyldesley Sq. SR3-1A 118
Tyndal Gdns. NE11-1E 77
Tyne Av. NE21-1A 74
Tynebank. NE21-5F 55
Tyne Bri. NE1 & NE8 -3D 61 & 5D 143
Tynedale Av. NE26-1A 22
Tynedale Av. NE28-5D 31
Tynedale Cres. DH4-3A 116
Tynedale Rd. NE34-4A 52
Tynedale Rd. SR3-1B 118
Tynedale Ter. NE12-4F 29
Tyne Gdns. NE37-4B 94
Tyne Gdns. NE40-3C 54
Tyne Ho. NE1-2E 61 & 4F 143
Tyne Ho. SR3-4E 119
Tynell Wlk. NE3-4D 25
Tyne Main Rd. NE10-4A 62
Tynemouth Clo. NE6-1A 62
Tynemouth Ct. NE6-5D 45 (off Elvet Clo.)
Tynemouth Ct. NE29-4B 34
Tynemouth Gro. NE6-1A 62
Tynemouth Pl. NE30-3F 35
Tynemouth Rd. NE6 -1A 62 & 5E 45
Tynemouth Rd. NE28-2B 48
Tynemouth Rd. NE30-3D 35
Tynemouth Rd. NE32-5F 65
Tynemouth Sq. SR3-1B 118
Tynemouth Ter. NE30-3F 35
Tynemouth Way. NE6-5D 45
Tynepoint Ind. Est. NE32 -2C 66
Tyne Rd. DH9-3C 130
Tyne Rd. E. DH9-4C 130
Tyne Rd. E. NE8-5B 60
Tyneside Retail Pk. NE28 -4C 32
Tyneside Rd. NE4-4A 60
Tyne Sq. NE1-2E 61 & 4F 143
Tyne St. NE10-5D 63
Tyne St. NE21-4B 56 (Blaydon)
Tyne St. NE21-1A 74 (Bleach Green)
Tyne St. NE30-4D 35
Tyne St. NE31-1C 64
Tyne St. NE32-4D 49
Tyne St. SR7-3F 133
Tyne Ter. NE34-2A 68
Tyne Tunnel. NE32-4D 49
Tyne Tunnel Trading Est. NE29-5D 33
Tynevale Av. NE21-1A 74
Tynevale Ter. NE8-1B 78
Tynevale Ter. NE15-1B 56
Tyne View. NE15-1B 56
Tyne View. NE40-5A 36
Tyne View Av. NE16-2A 76
Tyne View Gdns. NE10-1E 81
Tyne View Pl. NE8-1A 78
Tyne View Ter. NE28-3D 49
Tyne Wlk. NE15-3F 37
Tyzack Cres. SR6-3C 100

Uldale Ct. NE3-2F 25
Ullardale Clo. DH1-2E 141
Ullswater Av. NE32-4C 66
Ullswater Cres. NE21-2A 74
Ullswater Dri. NE12-4A 18
Ullswater Gdns. NE34-1C 68
Ullswater Gro. SR5-1B 100
Ullswater Rd. DH2-5C 122
Ullswater Way. NE5-4C 40
Ulverstone Ter. NE6-5A 46
Ulverston Gdns. NE9-1F 91
Underhill. NE9-4F 79
Underhill Rd. SR6-2E 87
Underhill Ter. NE9-3E 93
Underwood. NE10-3E 81
Underwood Gro. NE23-1C 4
Unicorn Ho. NE30-4C 34
Union All. NE33-1D 51
Union Ct. DH3-3E 123
Union Hall Rd. NE15-1B 56
Union La. SR1-5D 101
Union Pl. DH1-4D 139 (off Stockton Rd.)
Union Quay. NE30-4D 35
Union Rd. NE6-1B 62
Union Rd. NE30-4E 35
Union St. DH5-4F 129
Union St. NE2 -1E 61 & 3F 143
Union St. NE10-4B 80
Union St. NE28-4D 47
Union St. NE30-5C 34
Union St. NE32-5D 49
Union St. NE33-1A 68
Union St. SR1-1B 110
Union St. SR4-1F 107
Union St. SR7-4E 133
Uplands. NE25-2F 21
Uplands, The. DH3-3C 102
Uplands, The. NE3-1A 42
Uplands Way. NE9-3E 93
Up. Camden St. NE30-4C 34
Up. Chare. SR8-3C 134
Up. Crone St. NE27-3B 20
Up. Elsdon St. NE29-5B 34
Up. Nile St. SR1-1C 110
Up. Norfolk St. NE30-4C 34
Up. Pearson St. NE30-4D 35
Up. Penman St. NE29-5B 34
Up. Queen St. NE30-4D 35
Up. Sans St. SR1-1C 110
Up. Yoden Way. SR8-3C 134
Upton St. NE8-1A 78
Urban Gdns. NE37-5C 94
Urfa Ter. NE33-1E 51
Urpeth Ter. NE6-3B 62 (off St Peter's Rd.)
Urswick Ct. NE3-4D 25
Urwin St. DH5-4F 129
Ushaw Rd. NE31-2E 65
Usher Av. DH6-4F 141
Usher St. SR5-3F 99

sk Av. NE32-4B 66
sworth Rd. NE37-3A 94
sworth Sta. Rd. NE37
-5C 94 & 5D 95
xbridge Ter. NE10-1C 80

alebrooke. SR2-3B 110
alebrooke Av. SR2-3B 110
alebrooke Gdns. SR2
-3B 110
alehead. NE25-2F 21
ale Ho. NE2-4C 44
alentia Av. NE6-5F 45
aleria Clo. NE28-3F 31
alerian Av. NE15-2B 36
aleshead Ho. NE28-3D 47
aleside. DH1-1B 138
aleside. NE15-3D 37
ale St. SR4-2F 109
ale St. E. SR4-2F 109
ale Wlk. NE2-5C 44
alley Ct. SR2-3C 110
alley Dri. NE9-3E 79
alley Dri. NE11-3E 77
alley Dri. NE16-2F 75
alley Forge. NE38-2B 104
alley Gdns. NE9-2E 79
alley Gdns. NE25-2F 21
alley Gdns. NE28-2E 47
alley La. NE34-1A 70
alley Rd. DH2-2A 122
alley Rd. NE25-2E 11
alley View. DH3-1A 102
alley View. DH9-4B 130
alley View. NE2-3B 44
alley View. NE15-5D 39
alley View. NE32-3A 66
alley View. NE38-1C 114
allum Ct. NE4-2F 59
allum Pl. NE9-4A 80
allum Rd. NE6-1D 63
allum Rd. NE15-2F 37
allum Way. NE4-2F 59
anburgh Ct. NE25-2C 10
ance Bus. Pk. NE11-2F 77
ancouver Dri. NE7-2F 45
ane St. SR3-3F 119
ane Ter. SR2-2E 111
ane Ter. SR7-2E 133
ane Vs. DH1-4B 140
anguard Ct. SR3-4E 119
(in two parts)
an Mildert Clo. SR8-5A 134
ardy Ter. DH4-4D 117
auxhall Rd. NE6-4B 46
aux's Cotts. NE36-3B 86
edra St. SR5-3F 99
elville Ct. NE3-4D 25
entnor Av. NE4-2D 59
entnor Cres. NE9-4C 78
entnor Gdns. NE9-4C 78
entnor Gdns. NE26-1B 22
erdun Av. NE31-1C 64
ermont. NE37-5B 94
ermont Ho. NE37-5D 95
erne Rd. NE29-4E 33
ernon Clo. NE33-4D 51
ernon Dri. NE25-3A 22
ernon St. NE37-4C 94
eryan Gdns. SR3-4F 109
espasian Av. NE33-5E 35
espasian St. NE33-1E 51
iador. DH3-1E 123
icarage Av. NE34-1D 69
icarage Clo. SR3-3E 119
icarage Ct. NE10-2E 81
icarage La. SR4-1F 107
icarage Rd. SR3-3E 119
icarage St. NE29-5B 34
icars Holme Clo. SR3
-5D 119
icars La. NE7-4B 28
icars Way. NE12-4B 28
iceroy St. SR7-3F 133
ictor Ct. SR6-4D 101
ictoria Av. NE10-2B 80
ictoria Av. NE12-3E 29
ictoria Av. NE26-2D 23
ictoria Av. NE28-2C 46
ictoria Av. SR2-5D 111
ictoria Av. SR4-1F 107
ictoria Av. W. SR2-5C 110
ictoria Cotts. DH1-3A 136
ictoria Ct. NE30-3E 23
ictoria Ct. NE31-2C 64
ictoria Cres. NE29-5B 34
ictoria Cres. NE30-3E 23
ictoria Ho. NE4-5F 59
ictoria Ho. NE8-1A 78
ictoria Ind. Est. NE31-4B 64
ictoria M. NE2-4B 44
ictoria M. NE26-2C 22
ictoria Parkway. NE7-1F 45
ictoria Pl. NE25-2A 22
ictoria Pl. NE37-5C 94
ictoria Pl. SR1-2C 111
ictoria Pl. SR4-2F 109
ictoria Rd. NE8-1A 78
ictoria Rd. NE33-3E 51
ictoria Rd. NE37-5B 94
ictoria Rd. E. NE31-2C 64
ictoria Rd. W. NE31-5B 64
ictoria Sq. NE2
-5A 44 & 1D 143
ictoria Sq. NE10-2B 80
ictoria St. DH5-4F 129
ictoria St. NE4
-3A 60 & 5A 142
ictoria St. NE11-1E 77
ictoria St. NE29-1C 50
ictoria St. NE31-1B 64
ictoria St. SR7-3E 133
ictoria Ter. DH1-2B 138
ictoria Ter. DH2-1A 122
ictoria Ter. DH4-3A 116
ictoria Ter. NE9-3E 93
(Springwell)
ictoria Ter. NE9-2B 92
(Wrekenton)
ictoria Ter. NE10-2C 80
ictoria Ter. NE15-2F 37
ictoria Ter. NE26-2C 22
ictoria Ter. NE32-1F 65
ictoria Ter. NE36-3A 86
ictoria Ter. S. SR5-4B 100
ictor St. DH3-3E 123
Victor St. SR6-4D 101
Victory Cotts. NE23-3E 7
Victory Ho. NE30-3F 35
Victory St. SR4-5D 99
Victory St. E. DH5-4F 129
Victory St. W. DH5-4F 129
Viewforth Dri. SR5-2A 100
Viewforth Grn. NE5-3D 41
Viewforth Rd. SR2-5E 121
Viewforth Ter. SR5-2A 100
Viewforth Vs. DH1-2A 138
View La. DH9-1C 130
Vigodale. DH3-1C 112
Vigo La. DH3-2B 112
Vigo La. NE38
-2D 113 to 2B 114
Viking Precinct. NE32-5D 49
Villa Clo. SR4-1E 109
Village Ct. NE26-2B 22
Village E. NE40-1B 54
Village La. NE37-1B 104
Village Pl. NE6-2B 62
Village Rd. NE23-3D 5
Village, The. SR2-4E 121
Villa Pl. NE8-1D 79
Villas, The. NE13-2E 15
Villas, The. NE23-4E 7
Villas, The. SR2-5D 121
Villas, The. SR5-3A 98
Villa View. NE9-4F 79
Villers St. S. SR1-1C 110
Villette Brooke St. SR2
-3C 110
Villette Path. SR2-3D 111
Villette Rd. SR2-4C 110
Villettes, The. DH4-2B 126
Villiers Pl. DH3-2E 123
Villiers St. SR1-1C 110
Vimy Av. NE31-1C 64
Vincent St. SR7-4E 133
Vine Clo. NE8-5B 60
Vine La. NE1-1C 60 & 2C 142
Vine La. E. NE1
-1C 60 & 2D 143
Vine Pl. DH4-5C 126
Vine Pl. SR1-1B 110
Vine St. NE28-3D 47
Vine St. NE33-1A 68
Viola St. NE37-4C 94
Viola Ter. NE16-3A 76
Violet Clo. NE4-3C 58
Violet St. DH4-5C 126
Violet St. SR4-1F 107
(South Hylton)
Violet St. SR4-1A 110
(Sunderland)
Violet Ter. DH4-2C 124
Violet Wlk. NE4-4C 58
Viscount Rd. SR3-3F 119
Vivian Cres. DH2-3D 123
Vivian Sq. SR6-2C 100
Voltage Ter. DH4-1B 126
Vulcan Pl. SR6-3C 100
Vulcan Ter. NE12-1F 29

Waddington St. DH1-2B 138
Wadham Clo. SR8-4A 134
Wadham Ter. NE34-2A 68
Wadsley Sq. SR2-5D 111
Wagon Way. NE28-3F 47
Wagonway Ind. Est. NE31
-4A 48
Wagonway Rd. NE31-5F 47
Wakefield Av. NE34-2A 70
Wakenshaw Rd. DH1-1F 139
Walbottle Hall Gdns. NE15
-3C 38
Walbottle Rd. NE15-4B 38
Waldo St. NE29-5C 34
Waldridge Gdns. NE9-1C 92
Waldridge La. DH2
-5A 122 to 4C 122
Waldridge Rd. DH2
-4A 122 to 3E 123
Waldron Sq. SR2-5C 110
Walkerburn. NE23-1A 8
Walkerdene Ho. NE6-4C 46
Walkergate. DH1-2C 138
Walker Ho. NE6-2F 63
Walker Pk. Clo. NE6-3E 63
Walker Pk. Gdns. NE6-3E 63
Walker Pl. NE30-4D 35
Walker Riverside. NE6-4F 63
Walker Rd. NE6-2F 61
Walker Ter. NE8-4D 61
Walker View. NE10-2C 80
Wallace Av. NE16-2A 76
Wallace Gdns. NE9-1D 93
Wallace St. DH4-5C 126
Wallace St. NE2
-5D 43 & 1A 142
Wallace St. NE11-1E 77
Wallace St. SR5-3A 100
Wallace Ter. NE40-2B 54
Wall Clo. NE3-5C 26
Waller Ter. DH5-1D 129
Wallflower Av. SR8-2E 135
Wallinfen. NE10-5D 81
Wallingford Av. SR2-5C 110
Wallington Av. NE13-1C 14
Wallington Av. NE30-1C 34
Wallington Ct. NE3-3F 25
Wallington Ct. NE12-4E 17
Wallington Ct. NE25-1C 10
Wallington Ct. NE30-5C 22
Wallington Dri. NE15-4A 40
Wallington Gro. NE33-2E 51
Wallis St. DH4-3A 116
Wallis St. NE10-2C 80
Wallis St. NE33-2D 51
Wallridge Dri. NE25-3D 11
Wallsend Rd. NE29-1D 49
Wall St. NE3-5C 24
Wall Ter. NE6-5F 45
Walmer Ter. NE9-4C 92
Walnut Gdns. NE8-2B 78
Walnut Pl. NE3-2B 42
Walpole Clo. SR7-4A 132
Walpole Ct. SR4-1E 109
Walpole St. NE6-5A 46
Walsh Av. NE31-5A 48
Walsingham. NE38-4B 104
Walter St. NE13-1B 14
Walter St. NE32-5D 49
Walter Ter. NE4-1F 59
Walter Thomas St. SR5-3E 99
Waltham. NE38-4B 104
Waltham Clo. NE28-1B 46
Waltham Pl. NE5-2D 41
Walton Av. NE29-3B 34
Walton Av. SR7-4A 132
Walton Clo. DH9-3D 131
Walton Garth. SR1-1D 111
Walton La. SR1-5D 101
Walton Pk. NE29-2B 34
Walton Rd. NE5-4B 40
Walton Rd. NE38-2F 105
Walton St. NE8-1B 78
Walwick Av. NE29-3E 33
Walwick Rd. NE25-2D 21
Walworth Av. NE34-1A 70
Walworth Gro. NE32-4F 65
Walworth Way. SR1-1B 110
Wandsworth Rd. NE6-5C 44
Wanlass Ter. DH1-2D 139
Wanlock Clo. NE23-1A 8
Wansbeck. NE38-1F 113
Wansbeck Av. DH9-3C 130
Wansbeck Av. NE30-4D 23
Wansbeck Ct. SR3-4E 119
Wansbeck Ct. SR8-5B 134
Wansbeck Rd. NE3-4C 26
Wansbeck Rd. NE23-4E 7
Wansbeck Rd. NE32-2F 65
Wansbeck Rd. N. NE3-3C 26
Wansbeck Rd. S. NE3-4C 26
Wansbeck Ter. NE23-4E 7
Wansfell Av. NE5-1F 41
Wansford Av. NE5-3C 40
Wansford Way. NE16-5E 75
Wantage Av. NE29-5F 33
Wantage Rd. DH1-1D 141
Wantage St. NE33-5E 51
Wapping St. NE33-5D 35
Warbeck Clo. NE3-4D 25
Warburton Cres. NE9-2F 79
Warcop Ct. NE3-2F 25
Ward Ct. SR2-3D 111
Warden Gro. DH5-1E 129
Wardenlaw. NE10-5D 81
Warden Law La. SR3-4D 119
Wardill Gdns. NE9-3A 80
Wardle Av. NE33-3A 52
Wardle Dri. NE23-4A 8
Wardle Gdns. NE10-3D 81
Wardles Ter. DH1-2C 138
(off Allergate)
Wardle St. DH9-5B 130
Wardley Ct. NE10-2B 82
Wardley Dri. NE10-2B 82
Wardley La. NE10-5B 64
Wardroper Ho. NE6-3F 63
Ward St. SR2-3D 111
Warenford Clo. NE23-1A 8
Warenford Pl. NE5-5D 41
Warenmill Clo. NE15-5D 39
Warennes St. SR4-1D 109
Warenton Pl. NE29-1C 32
Warick Dri. SR3-3A 118
Waring Ter. SR7-4B 132
Wark Av. NE27-3B 20
Wark Av. NE29-4E 33
Wark Ct. NE3-1A 44
Wark Cres. NE32-5F 65
Wark St. DH3-4E 123
Warkworth Av. NE26-2B 22
Warkworth Av. NE28-5D 31
Warkworth Av. NE34-5C 52
Warkworth Av. SR8-1E 135
Warkworth Clo. NE10-2A 80
Warkworth Clo. NE38-3F 103
Warkworth Cres. NE3-4D 27
Warkworth Cres. NE15-5A 38
(off Newburn Rd.)
Warkworth Cres. SR7-3A 132
Warkworth Dri. DH2-4B 122
Warkworth Dri. NE13-5A 6
Warkworth Rd. DH1-2C 136
Warkworth St. NE6-1A 62
Warkworth St. NE15-1B 56
(in two parts)
Warkworth Ter. NE30-1F 35
(in two parts)
Warkworth Ter. NE32-4A 66
Warnham Av. SR2-5C 110
Warpole St. NE33-4D 51
Warren Av. NE6-4B 46
Warrenmor. NE10-3F 81
Warren Sq. SR1-5D 101
Warren Sq. SR8-3E 135
Warren St. SR1-5D 101
Warren St. SR8-3E 135
Warrens Wlk. NE21-1E 73
Warrington Rd. NE3-3A 26
Warrington Rd. NE4-3F 59
Warton Ter. NE6-4D 45
Warwick Av. NE16-5F 75
Warwick Clo. NE16-5F 75
Warwick Clo. NE23-3D 9
Warwick Ct. DH1-5A 138
Warwick Ct. NE3-3F 25
(in two parts)
Warwick Ct. NE8-5D 61
Warwick Dri. DH5-1D 129
Warwick Dri. NE16-5F 75
Warwick Dri. NE37-3B 94
Warwick Hall Wlk. NE7-2F 45
Warwick Pl. SR8-2A 134
Warwick Rd. NE5-4A 40
Warwick Rd. NE28-3C 46
Warwick Rd. NE31-4E 65
Warwick Rd. NE33 & NE34
-5F 51
Warwickshire Dri. DH1
-3D 141
Warwick St. NE2
-1E 61 & 2F 143
Warwick St. NE8-5D 61
Warwick St. SR5-3B 100
Warwick Ter. SR3-2E 119
Warwick Ter. N. SR3-2E 119
(off Warwick Ter.)
Warwick Ter. W. SR3-2E 119
Wasdale Clo. NE23-1A 8
Wasdale Clo. SR8-3D 135
Wasdale Ct. SR6-5A 88
Wasdale Cres. NE21-2A 74
Wasdale Rd. NE5-4C 40
Washington Gdns. NE9-2B 92
Washington Highway. NE37
& DH4-5F 93 to 4F 115
Washington Rd. NE37 &
NE36-5E 95
Washington Rd. SR5-2E 97
Washington St. SR4-1E 109
Washington Ter. NE30-3D 35
Washingwell La. NE16-3B 76
Waskerley Gdns. NE9-1B 92
Waskerley Rd. NE38-2E 105
Waterbeach Pl. NE5-3C 40
Waterbeck Clo. NE23-1A 8
Waterbury Clo. SR5-1E 99
Waterbury Rd. NE3-1D 27
Waterford Clo. DH5-3B 128
Waterford Cres. NE26-3D 23
Watergate. NE1
-3D 61 & 5D 143
Waterloo Ct. NE37-4D 95
Waterloo Pl. NE29-3C 34
Waterloo Pl. SR1-1B 110
Waterloo Rd. NE25-2C 20
Waterloo Rd. NE37
-4D 95 to 2D 95
Waterloo Sq. NE33-2E 51
Waterloo St. NE1
-3B 60 & 5B 142
Waterloo St. NE21-1F 73
Waterloo Wlk. NE37-4D 95
(off Edith Av.)
Waterlow Clo. SR5-1D 99
Watermill. NE40-2B 54
Watermill La. NE10-2C 80
Water Row. NE15-5A 38
Waterside Dri. NE11-5C 58
Water St. NE4-4F 59
Waterville Pl. NE29-5B 34
Waterville Rd. NE29
-1F 49 to 5B 34
Waterville Ter. NE29-5B 34
Waterworks Rd. SR1-1A 110
Waterworks Rd. SR2-5D 121
Watford Clo. SR5-1E 99
Watling Av. SR7-4A 132
Watling Pl. NE9-4A 80
Watling St. NE34-2F 67
Watson Av. NE23-4E 7
Watson Av. NE34-2A 70
Watson Clo. SR7-4B 132
Watson Gdns. NE28-2B 48
Watson Pl. NE34-2A 70
Watson St. DH9-1D 131
Watson St. NE8-1A 78
Watson St. NE32-5E 49
Watson Ter. NE35-3E 85
Watt's Rd. NE26-1C 22
Watt St. NE8-3C 78
Wavendon Cres. SR4-3C 108
Waveney Gdns. DH9-4C 130
Waveney Rd. SR8-5A 134
Waverdale Av. NE6-5C 46
Waverdale Way. NE33-1A 68
Waverley Av. NE25-2B 22
Waverley Clo. NE21-2E 73
Waverley Cres. NE15-5F 39
Waverley Rd. NE4-3A 60
Waverley Rd. NE9-3F 91
Waverley Ter. SR4-5D 99
Waverton Clo. NE23-1A 8
Wawn St. NE33-4F 51
Wayfarer Rd. SR5-4F 99
Wayland Sq. SR2-1D 121
Wayman St. SR5-3B 100
Wayside. NE15-2A 58
Wayside. NE34-1A 70
Wayside. SR2-3A 110
Wealcroft. NE10-5E 81
Wealcroft Ct. NE10-5E 81
Wear Ct. NE34-2A 68
Wear Cres. DH3-5B 124
Weardale Av. NE6-1F 63
Weardale Av. NE12-1E 29
Weardale Av. NE28-5D 31
Weardale Av. NE37-5A 94
Weardale Av. SR6-3C 88
Weardale Cres. DH4-3F 115
Weardale Ho. NE38-3A 104
Weardale Ter. DH3-3E 123
Wear Garth. SR1-5D 101
Wear Ind. Est. NE38-5A 104
Wear Lodge. DH3-4B 112
Wearmouth Av. SR5-3B 100
Wearmouth Bri. SR5 & SR6
-5B 100
Wearmouth Dri. SR5-3B 100
Wearmouth St. SR6-4B 100
Wear Rd. DH9-3C 130
Wear Rd. NE31-4D 65
Wearside Dri. DH1-1D 139
Wear St. DH3-3E 123
Wear St. DH4-5F 125
Wear St. DH5-5F 129
Wear St. NE32-5C 48
Wear St. SR1-1D 111
Wear St. SR4-1F 107
Wear St. SR5-4E 99
Wear St. SR7-3F 133
Wear Ter. NE38-3D 105
Wear View. DH1-2D 139
Wear View. SR4-1F 107
Wear Way. SR1-1D 111
Weathercock La. NE9-5E 79
Weatherside. NE21-1A 74
Webb Av. SR7-3A 132
Webb Gdns. NE10-2F 81
Webb Sq. SR8-1D 135
Wedgewood Cotts. NE15
-2C 56
Wedgewood Rd. SR7-4A 132
Wedmore Rd. NE5-2F 39
Weetman St. NE33-3C 50
Weetslade Cres. NE23-5E 7
Weetslade Rd. NE23-4E 7
Weetslade Ter. NE23-2D 17
Weetwood Rd. NE23-5E 5
Weidner Rd. NE15-2C 58
Weir Pl. SR8-2D 135
Welbeck Grn. NE6-2C 62
Welbeck Rd. NE6-2B 62
Welbury Way. NE23-1F 7
Weldon Av. SR2-5D 111
Weldon Cres. NE7-2C 44
Weldon Pl. NE29-2F 33
Weldon Rd. NE12-3C 28
Weldon Rd. NE23-4F 5
Weldon Ter. DH3-4E 123
Weldon Way. NE3-4C 26
Welfare Rd. DH5-4E 129
Welford Av. NE3-4C 26
Welland Clo. SR8-5A 134
Wellands Clo. SR6-1D 89
Wellands Ct. SR6-1D 89
Wellands Dri. SR6-1D 89
Wellands La. SR6-1D 89
Well Bank Rd. NE37-3A 94
Wellburn Pk. NE2-4B 44
Wellburn Rd. NE37-4A 94
Well Clo. Wlk. NE16-3F 75
Wellesley Ct. NE33-5E 35
Wellesley St. NE32-2F 65
Wellesley Ter. NE4-2E 59
Wellfield Clo. NE15-3E 37
Wellfield La. NE5-2C 40
Wellfield M. SR2-5D 121
Wellfield Rd. NE4-2C 58
Wellfield Ter. NE10-3B 80
Wellfield Ter. SR2-5D 121
Wellgarth Rd. NE37-3A 94
Wellhope. NE38-2E 113
Wellington Av. NE25-2C 20
Wellington Ct. NE10-2B 80
Wellington Ct. NE37-4D 95
Wellington Dri. NE33-1D 51
Wellington La. SR4-5A 100
Wellington Rd. NE11-1C 76
Wellington Row. DH4-5B 116
Wellington St. NE4
-2A 60 & 3A 142
Wellington St. NE8-4D 61
Wellington St. NE10-2B 80
Wellington St. NE15-1C 56
Wellington St. NE31-2C 64
Wellington St. W. NE29
-4C 34
Wellington Wlk. NE37-4D 95
(off Edith Av.)
Well La. NE27-5D 21 & 4D 21
Wellmere Rd. SR2-1D 121
Well Ridge Clo. NE25-1E 21
Well Ridge Pk. NE25-1E 21
Wells Clo. NE7-5E 29
Wells Cres. SR7-3A 132
Wells Gdns. NE9-2E 91
Wells Gro. NE34-5B 52
Wellshede. NE10-3F 81
Wells St. NE35-1D 85
Well St. SR4-1E 109
Wellway. NE32-5A 66
Welwyn Clo. NE28-1A 46
Welwyn Clo. SR5-4E 97
Wembley Av. NE25-3F 21
Wembley Clo. SR5-1E 99
Wembley Rd. SR5-1D 99
Wendover Clo. SR5-1D 99
Wendover Way. SR5-1D 99
Wenham Sq. SR2-4F 109
Wenlock. NE38-3B 104
Wenlock Dri. NE29-1A 34
Wenlock Lodge. NE34-2E 67
Wenlock Pl. NE34-3F 67
Wenlock Rd. NE34-2E 67
Wensley Clo. NE5-5D 25
Wensleydale Av. DH4-3F 115
Wensleydale Av. NE37-5A 94
Wensleydale Dri. NE12-2E 29
Wensleydale Wlk. NE3-4F 25
Wensleydale Wall NE28
-4B 30
Wensley Ho. SR3-5E 119
Wentworth. NE33-3A 52
Wentworth Clo. NE10-3C 80
Wentworth Ct. NE4-3F 59
Wentworth Dri. NE37-2A 94
Wentworth Gdns. NE25
-2D 21
Wentworth Grange. NE3
-1F 43
Wentworth Pl. NE4-3F 59
Wentworth Ter. SR4-1A 110
Werhale Grn. NE10-2C 80
Wescott Ter. DH4-2A 116
(off Penshaw La.)
Wesley Clo. DH9-2E 131
Wesley Ct. NE10-1B 80
Wesley Ct. NE21-1B 74
Wesley Dri. NE12-1D 31
Wesley St. NE9-5E 79
Wesley St. NE33-1E 51
Wesley Ter. DH2-1A 122
Wesley Ter. DH3-3E 123
Wesley Way. NE12-1D 31
Wesley Way. SR7-3A 132
Wessex Clo. SR5-1E 99
Wessington Ter. NE37-5C 94
Wessington Way. SR5-5E 97
Westacre Gdns. NE5-1A 58
W. Acres. NE21-5C 56
W. Acres Av. NE16-5F 75
Westacres Cres. NE15-1A 58
West Av. NE3-5D 27
West Av. NE5-2A 40
West Av. NE12-3F 29
(Benton)
West Av. NE12-1B 30
(Forest Hall)
West Av. NE25-2F 21
West Av. NE29-4F 33
West Av. NE34-1D 69
West Av. NE38-2A 114
West Av. SR6-1C 88
W. Bailey. NE12-3D 17
Westbourne Av. NE3-3E 27
Westbourne Av. NE6-4B 46
Westbourne Av. NE8-2D 79
Westbourne Cotts. DH4
-4F 115
Westbourne Dri. DH4-5F 115
Westbourne Gdns. NE6-1E 63
Westbourne Rd. SR1-1A 110
Westbourne Ter. DH4-4F 115
Westbourne Ter. NE25-1C 10
W. Bridge St. DH4-2C 114
Westburn Gdns. NE28-1B 46
Westburn Ter. SR6-3C 100
Westbury Av. NE6-4B 46
Westbury Rd. NE29-1A 34
Westbury St. SR4-1F 109
W. Chirton Ind. Est. NE29
-5D 33
W. Chirton N. Ind. Est. NE29
-2C 32
Westcliffe Rd. SR6-1D 101
Westcliffe Way. NE34-4E 67
W. Copperas. NE15-5A 40
(in two parts)
Westcott Av. NE33-3A 52
Westcott Dri. DH1-4A 136
Westcott Rd. NE34-2B 68
Westcott Rd. SR8-2C 134
Westcott Ter. DH4-2A 116
West Ct. NE3-5B 26
West Cres. NE10-2B 82
W. Dene Dri. NE30-2C 34
Westcroft Rd. NE12-2F 29
W. Denton Clo. NE15-4F 39
W. Denton Rd. NE15-4E 39
W. Denton Way. NE5-3F 39
West Dri. SR6-1D 87
West End. NE26-1C 12
Wester Ct. SR3-5E 119
Westerdale. DH4-2D 115
Westerdale. NE28-5B 30
Westerdale Pl. NE6-1F 63
Westerham Clo. SR5-1E 99
Westerhope Gdns. NE5-4F 41
Westerhope Rd. NE38
-2D 105
Westerkirk. NE23-1A 8
Western App. NE33
-5D 51 to 3E 51
Western App. Ind. Est. NE33
(off Western App.) -2E 51
Western Av. NE4-2D 59
Western Av. NE5-4F 39
Western Av. NE11-1B 90
Western Av. NE25-1A 10
Western Ct. NE26-4E 13
(off Western Way)
Western Dri. NE4-2D 59
Western Highway. NE38
-1D 113
Western Hill. DH1-1B 138
Western Hill. SR2-2F 109
(Ford Estate)
Western Hill. SR2-3C 120
(Ryhope)
Westernmoor. NE37-1E 103
Western Riverside Route.
NE16-4F 57
Western Rd. NE28-3B 48
Western Rd. NE32-5C 48
Western Ter. DH3-3E 123
Western Ter. NE23-4D 7
Western Ter. NE36-3F 85
Western Ter. NE37-5C 94
Western View. NE9-3A 92
Western Way. NE21-5D 57
Western Way. NE26-4D 13
Western Way. NE40-3A 54
W. Farm Av. NE12
-4A 28 to 4D 29
W. Farm Ct. NE12-4F 17
W. Farm Ct. NE23-3C 4
W. Farm Rd. NE6-5A 46
W. Farm Rd. NE28-1A 48
W. Farm Rd. SR6-2F 87
W. Farm Wynd. NE12-4B 28
Westfield. NE3-2D 43
Westfield. NE10-4C 80
Westfield. NE23-4D 7
Westfield. NE32-1B 84
Westfield Av. NE3-2D 43
Westfield Av. NE13-1C 14
Westfield Av. NE25-3E 21
Westfield Ct. NE28-5C 46
Westfield Ct. SR4-3D 109
Westfield Cres. NE9-4E 93
Westfield Dri. NE3-1D 43
Westfield Gro. NE3-2D 43
Westfield Gro. SR4-3D 109
Westfield La. NE40-1A 54
Westfield Pk. NE3-2D 43
Westfield Rd. NE8-2D 79
Westfield Rd. NE15-2A 58
Westfields. DH9-3B 130
Westfield Ter. NE8-2D 79
Westfield Ter. NE9-3D 93
(off Windsor Rd.)
Westgarth. NE5-5A 24
Westgarth Ter. NE37-5D 95
Westgate. NE1-3D 61
Westgate Av. SR3-2E 119
Westgate Clo. NE25-1D 21
Westgate Gro. SR3-2E 119
Westgate Hill Ter. NE4
-3A 60 & 5A 142
Westgate Rd. NE4 & NE1
-2D 59 & 4A 142
W. George Potts St. NE33
-4E 51
W. Grange. SR5-2A 100
West Gro. SR4-2F 107
West Gro. SR7-3A 132
Westheath Av. SR2-1C 120
(in two parts)
W. Hill. SR4-3D 109
W. Holborn. NE33-3C 50
Westholme Gdns. NE15
-2B 58
Westholme Ter. SR2-5D 111
(off Ryhope Rd.)
Westhope Clo. NE34-5B 52
Westhope Rd. NE34-5B 52
W. Jesmond Av. NE2-3F 43
Westlands. NE5-3E 39
Westlands. NE7-2C 44
Westlands. NE30-1D 35
Westlands. NE32-1B 84
Westlands, The. SR4-3D 109
West La. DH3-3E 123
West La. NE12-5F 17
West La. NE21-2E 73
W. Lawn. SR2-3B 110
W. Lawrence St. SR1-1D 111
West Lea. DH4-4C 116
West Lea. NE21-2B 74
Westlea Rd. DH4-2B 126
Westlea Rd. SR7-3A 132
W. Leigh. DH9-1A 130
Westleigh Ct. SR4-1E 109
Westley Av. NE26-3D 13
Westley Clo. NE26-3D 13
Westline Ind. Est. DH3
-5A 102
Westlings. DH5-4E 129
Westloch Rd. NE23-1A 8
Westmacott St. NE15-4A 38
W. Meadows. NE5-1F 39
W. Meadows Dri. SR6-2F 87
W. Meadows Rd. SR6-2F 87
Westminster Av. NE29-2D 33
Westminster Cres. NE31
-4D 65
Westminster Dri. NE11-4E 77
Westminster St. NE8-2C 78
Westminster St. SR2-5D 111
Westminster Way. NE7-1E 45
W. Moffett St. NE33-3F 51
W. Moor Ct. NE12-5D 17
Westmoor Dri. NE12-5D 17
Westmoor Dri. SR6-3F 87
Westmoor Rd. SR4-1C 108
Westmorland Av. NE28-3C 48
Westmorland Av. NE37-3B 94
Westmorland Ct. NE31-2C 64
Westmorland Gdns. NE9
-5D 79
Westmorland La. NE1
-3B 60 & 5B 142
Westmorland Rise. SR8
-1A 134
Westmorland Rd. NE4 & NE1
-3E 59 & 5A 142
Westmorland Rd. NE29
-3D 33
Westmorland Rd. NE34-5E 53
Westmorland St. NE28-3E 47
Westmorland Wlk. NE4-4E 59
Westmorland Way. NE23
-3B 4
West Mt. NE12-4E 17
West Mt. SR4-3D 109
Westoe Av. NE33-3F 51
Westoe Dri. NE33-4A 52
Westoe Rd. NE33-2E 51
Westoe Village. NE33-4F 51
Weston Av. NE16-5D 75
Weston View. SR8-3B 134
Westover Gdns. NE9-3E 79
West Pde. NE4-3A 60
West Pde. NE31-3C 64
West Pk. NE11-1D 77
(off Meadow La.)
West Pk. SR3-4F 117
W. Park Gdns. NE21-1A 74
W. Park Rd. NE8-3D 79
W. Park Rd. NE33-5D 51
W. Park Rd. SR6-1E 87
W. Pastures NE36-5A 84
W. Percy Rd. NE29-5A 34
W. Percy St. NE29-4B 34
Westport Clo. SR5-1D 99
Westray. DH2-4C 122
Westray Clo. SR2-2C 120
West Rig, The. NE3-1A 42
West Rd. NE5, NE15 & NE4
-5B 40 to 1D 59
West Row. DH3-4D 103
W. Shield Row Vs. DH9
-1B 130
W. Spencer Ter. NE15-3C 38
W. Stainton St. NE33-4E 51
W. Stevenson St. NE33-4E 51
West St. DH3-3A 102
West St. DH9-1A 130
West St. NE8-4D 61
West St. NE16-3F 75
West St. NE27-5F 19
West St. NE28-2B 46
West St. NE31-5A 48
West St. SR1-1B 110
West St. SR3-3E 119
West St. SR7-3F 133
West St. Bungalows. NE28
-2B 46
W. Sunniside. SR1-1C 110
W. Temple St. NE33-5D 51
West Ter. DH1-2B 138
W. Thorn Wlk. NE16-4F 75
W. Thorp. NE5-5B 24
W. Vale. NE15-2D 37
W. Vallum. NE15-5B 40
W. View. DH1-2E 139
W. View. DH3-2E 123
W. View. DH4-2D 125
(Bournmoor)
W. View. DH4-3C 126
(Grasswell)
W. View. DH4-2A 116
(Penshaw)
W. View. DH4-1A 126
(Philadelphia)
W. View. DH9-5B 130
(Stanley)
W. View. DH9-1C 130
(Tanfield Lea, off View La.)
W. View. NE4-3D 59
W. View. NE9-1B 92
W. View. NE12-1F 29
W. View. NE13-5A 6
W. View. NE15-1B 56
W. View. NE21-4B 56
W. View. NE23-4E 7
W. View. NE23-4E 5
(Cramlington)
W. View. NE23-3E 9
(Seghill)
W. View. NE25-2B 20
W. View. NE35-1C 84
W. View. NE37-5C 94
W. View. SR2-4D 121
W. View. SR5-4A 98
W. View. SR6-2C 100
W. View. SR8-2F 135
W. View Bldgs. NE30-3C 22
W. View Gdns. DH9-1C 130
W. View Ter. NE11-5D 59
West Wlk. DH3-5F 113
W. Walpole St. NE33-4D 51
Westward Ct. NE5-1A 40
Westward Grn. NE25-3E 21
Westward Pl. NE38-2A 114
West Way. NE11-2E 77
Westway. NE15-2F 37
Westway. NE21-5A 56
West Way. NE33-5D 51
Westway. SR8-4B 134
Westway Ind. Pk. NE15-1F 37
W. Wear St. SR1-5C 100
Westwell Ct. NE3-5B 28
W. Windsor Ter. NE9-3D 93
Westwood. NE8-5B 60
Westwood Av. NE6-3D 45
Westwood Gdns. NE3-5A 26
Westwood Gdns. NE9-2B 92
Westwood Gdns. NE38
-3C 104
Westwood Rd. NE3-5D 15
Westwood St. SR4-2D 109
Westwood Ter. DH3-4E 123
Westwood View. DH3-4E 123

W. Wynd. NE12-3E 17
Wetheral Gdns. NE9-2F 91
Wetheral Ter. NE6-3E 63
Wetherby Gro. NE8-3B 78
Wetherby Rd. SR2-1E 121
Weybourne Sq. SR2-5D 111
Weyhill Av. NE29-5F 33
Weymouth Dri. SR7-4B 132
Weymouth Gdns. NE9-3E 91
Weymouth Ho. NE4-5F 59
Weymouth Rd. NE49-4D 33
Whaggs La. NE16-4A 76
Whalton Av. NE3-4C 26
Whalton Clo. NE10-3B 82
Whalton Ct. NE3-3C 26
Whalton Ct. NE34-1D 69
Wharfdale Dri. NE33-5D 51
Wharfdale. DH4-3F 115
Wharfedale. NE28-4B 30
Wharfedale Av. NE37-5A 94
Wharfedale Grn. NE15-4B 40
Wharfedale Pl. NE6-1F 63
Wharmlands Gro. NE15
-5B 40
Wharmlands Rd. NE15-5B 40
Wharncliffe St. SR1-1A 110
Wharrier St. NE6-3D 63
Wharton Clo. DH5-3B 128
Wharton St. NE33-3F 51
Wheatall Dri. SR6-5D 71
Wheatall Way. SR6-5E 71
Wheatear Clo. NE38-4E 103
Wheatfield Gro. NE12-3D 29
Wheatfield Rd. NE5-2B 40
Wheatley Gdns. NE36-3F 85
Wheatley Ter. NE23-4E 7
Wheatridge. NE25-1A 10
Wheler St. DH4-4C 126
Whernside Av. SR3-4E 119
Whernside Pl. NE23-1A 8
Whernside Wlk. NE40-3C 54
Whickham Av. NE11-2E 77
Whickham Bank Ind. Est.
NE16-2E 75
Whickham Clo. NE34-5B 126
Whickham Gdns. NE6-2B 62
Whickham Highway. NE16 &
NE13-3C 76
Whickham Lodge. NE16
-3B 76
Whickham Lodge Rise. NE16
-3B 76
Whickham Pk. NE16-3A 76
(in two parts)
Whickham St. NE31-2C 64
Whickham St. E. SR6-4C 100
Whickham St. SR6-4C 100
Whickham View. NE9-5E 79
Whickham View. NE15-1E 57
Whickhope. NE38-1D 115
Whinbrooke. NE10-4F 81
Whinbush Pl. NE15-2F 57
Whinfell. NE37-5A 94
Whinfell Ho. NE23-1A 8
Whinfell Ct. SR3-4E 119
Whinlatter Gdns. NE9-1F 91
Whinlaw. NE9-5B 80
Whinmoor Pl. NE5-3A 42
Whinney Clo. NE21-2F 73
Whinneyfield Rd. NE6-5A 46
Whinney Hill. DH1-4E 139
Whinshaw. NE10-3E 81
Whinship Garden. NE6-1B 62
Whinside. DH9-1B 130
Whinway. NE37-5A 94
Whistler Gdns. NE34-4C 68
Whitbeck Ct. NE5-3C 40
Whitbeck Rd. NE5-4B 40
Whitburn Bents Rd. SR6
-4D 89
Whit Burn Gdns. NE9-2C 92
Whitburn Pl. NE23-1A 8
Whitburn Rd. SR6-2D 87
(East Boldon)
Whitburn Rd. SR6-4D 89
(South Bents)
Whitburn Rd. E. SR6-1F 87
Whitburn St. SR6
-4C 100 & 5C 100
Whitburn Ter. NE36-3B 86
Whitburn Ter. SR6-1C 100
Whitby Av. SR6-4D 89
Whitby Cres. NE12-4D 29
Whitby Dri. NE38-4C 104
Whitby St. NE30-3D 35
Whitchurch Clo. NE35-1C 84
Whitchurch Clo. SR5-1E 99
Whitchurch Rd. SR5-1E 99
Whitebeam Pl. NE4-4F 59
Whitebridge Clo. NE3-2E 27
Whitebridge Ct. NE3-2E 27
Whitebridge Pk. NE3-2F 27
Whitebridge Wlk. NE3-2F 27
Whitcliff Clo. NE29-1A 34
White Cotts. NE32-3E 65
Whitcroft Rd. NE12-5C 16
Whitecross Way. NE1
-2B 60 & 4C 142
Whitefield Cres. DH4-3F 115
Whitefield Gro. NE10-2C 80
Whitefield Ter. NE6-3E 45
White Ford Rd. DH3-2E 9
Whitefriars Pl. NE1-3C 60
(off Hanover St.)
Whitefriars Way. NE12-4C 28

Whitegate Clo. NE11-5E 59
Whitegates Rd. DH6-3F 141
White Hall Cotts. NE7-2F 45
Whitehall Rd. NE8-2C 78
Whitehall Rd. NE15-3B 38
Whitehall St. NE33-1A 68
Whitehall Ter. SR4-2D 109
White Hart Yd. NE1
-2C 60 & 4D 143
Whitehead St. NE33-1A 68
Whitehill. NE10-5E 81
Whitehill Cres. DH2-2A 122
(in two parts)
Whitehill Dri. NE10-4B 80
White Horse View. NE34
-1B 70
Whitehouse Ct. SR8-1A 134
Whitehouse Cres. NE9-5C 80
Whitehouse Enterprise Cen.
NE15-3A 58
Whitehouse La. NE9
-1A 92 & 5B 80
Whitehouse La. NE9
-2E 33 to 2B 34
Whitehouse M. NE28-2D 47
White Ho. Pl. SR2-2D 111
Whitehouse Rd. NE15 & NE4
-2E 59
Whitehouse Rd. NE2
White Ho. Rd. SR2-2D 111
White Ho. Way. NE10-4B 80
White Ladies Clo. NE38
-1C 104
Whitelaw Pl. NE23-5E 5
Whitelea Clo. SR8-4E 135
Whiteleas Way. NE34
-3A 68 & 5B 68
Whiteley Rd. NE21-3C 56
Whitemere Clo. SR2-1D 121
White Mere Gdns. NE10
Whiteoak Av. DH1-3B 140
White Rocks Gro. SR6-4E 71
Whites Gdns. NE31-1B 64
Whitesmocks. DH1-5A 136
Whitesmocks Av. DH1
-1A 138
White St. NE6-2F 63
White Swan Yd. NE1
-2C 60 & 4D 143
Whitethorn Cres. NE5-2F 41
Whitethroat Clo. NE38-4E 103
Whitewell Clo. NE40-2B 54
Whitewell La. NE40-2B 54
Whitewell Rd. NE21-5B 56
Whitewell Ter. NE40-2B 54
Whitfield Dri. NE12-3E 29
Whitfield Rd. NE12-1F 29
Whitfield Rd. NE15-2E 57
Whitfield Rd. NE25-2B 10
Whitfield Vs. NE33-1A 68
Whitgrave Rd. NE5-1F 41
Whitlees Ct. NE3-3A 26
Whitley Cl. NE9-2C 92
Whitley Pl. NE25-2D 11
Whitley Rd. NE12 & NE27
-4F 29 to 5E 19
Whitley Rd. NE25-2C 20
Whitley Rd. NE26-2C 22
Whitley Ter. NE25-2D 11
Whitmore Rd. NE21-5B 56
Whitticks, The. NE36-3A 86
Whittingham Ct. NE30
-5D 23
Whittingham Rd. NE30-5D 23
Whittingham Rd. NE30-5D 23
Whittington Gro. NE5-3C 41
Whittleburn. NE10-5D 81
Whitton Gdns. NE29-2F 33
Whitton Pl. NE7-1C 44
Whitton Pl. NE25-1C 10
Whittonstall. NE38-1D 115
Whitton Way. NE3-4C 26
Whitworth Clo. NE6-2F 63
Whitworth Pl. NE6-2F 63
Whitworth Rd. NE37-1E 103
Whorlton Grange Ct. NE5
-5A 24
Whorlton Rd. NE5-1A 40
Whorlton Ter. NE5-1D 39
Whyndyke. NE10-5D 81
Whytrigg Clo. NE25-1A 10
Widdrington Av. NE34-4C 62
Widdrington Gdns. NE13
-1D 15
Widdrington Rd. NE21-5B 56
Widdrington Ter. NE21-3F 55
Widdrington Ter. NE29-4B 34
Widnes Pl. NE12-3E 29
Wigeon Clo. NE38-5E 103
Wigham's Ter. DH4-3A 116
Wigmore Av. NE6-3D 63
Wilber Ct. SR4-1E 109
Wilberforce St. NE28-4D 47
Wilberforce St. NE32-5E 49
Wilberforce Wlk. NE8-5B 60
Wilber St. SR4-1E 109
Wilbury Pl. NE5-2E 41
(in two parts)
Wilden Ct. SR3-5F 119
Wilden Rd. NE38-4E 105
Wildshaw Clo. NE23-1A 8
Wilfred Dri. DH3-3E 123
Wilfred St. NE6-1F 61
Wilfred St. NE25-2E 85
Wilfred St. SR4-5D 99
Wilfrid St. DH3-5B 102
Wilkes Clo. NE5-2A 40

Wilkinson Av. NE31-4C 64
Wilkinson Ct. NE32-5D 49
Wilkinson St. NE34-2A 68
Wilkinson Ter. SR2-4D 121
Wilkwood Clo. NE23-5D 5
Willan's Bldgs. DH1-2F 139
Willerby Clo. NE9-4F 91
Willerby Dri. SR7-2F 27
William Armstrong Dri. NE4
-4D 59
William Clo. NE12-1B 30
William Pl. DH1-2F 139
William St. DH1-2F 139
Williamson Ter. SR6-4C 100
Williams Ter. SR2-4D 121
William St. DH1-2F 139
William St. DH3-2E 123
William St. DH9-4B 130
William St. NE3-5A 84
William St. NE10-1C 80
William St. NE16-3F 75
William St. NE29-5C 34
William St. NE31-1C 64
William St. NE33-2E 51
William St. SR1-5C 100
William St. SR2-2E 107
William St. W. NE29-5C 34
William St. W. NE31-1B 64
William Ter. DH4-2B 126
William Ter. NE31-1B 64
Willington Ter. NE28-2A 48
Willis St. DH5-3F 129
Willmore St. SR4-1E 109
Willoughby Dri. NE26-5C 12
Willoughby Rd. NE29-3F 33
Willoughby Way. NE26-5C 12
Willow Av. NE4-4F 41
Willow Av. NE11-2E 77
Willowbank Gdns. NE2-1A 44
Willow Bank Rd. SR2-4B 110
Willow Clo. NE40-1C 54
Willowdene. NE12-5F 17
Willowfield Av. NE3-4B 26
Willow Grange. NE32-5C 48
Willow Gro. NE10-2C 80
Willow Gro. NE28-3E 47
Willow Gro. NE29-1A 50
Willow Gro. NE34-2E 69
Willow Rd. NE4-5B 126
Willow Rd. NE21-5B 56
Willows Clo. NE13-2C 14
Willow's Clo. NE38-3D 105
Willows, The. NE4-4F 59
Willows, The. NE15-3F 37
Willows, The. NE31-3D 65
Willows, The. NE32-1B 84
Willowtree Av. DH1-2A 140
(Gilesgate Moor)
Willow Tree Av. DH1-5F 139
(Shincliffe)
Willowvale. DH2-1C 122
Wilmington Clo. NE3-4D 25
Wilson Av. NE3-2B 102
Wilson Cres. DH1-3A 140
Wilson Dri. NE36-2F 85
Wilson Gdns. NE3-2C 42
Wilson Pl. SR8-2C 134
Wilson's Ct. NE1
-2C 60 & 4C 142
Wilson's La. NE6-5F 79
Wilson St. NE11-2E 77
Wilson St. NE28-3D 47
Wilson St. NE29-1C 50
Wilson St. N. SR5-5B 100
Wilson Ter. NE12-1F 29
Wilson Ter. SR3-2F 119
Wilsway. NE15-3E 37
Wilton Av. NE6-3C 62
Wilton Clo. NE23-1A 8
Wilton Clo. NE25-1B 10
Wilton Dri. NE25-1B 10
Wincanton Pl. NE29-1A 50
Winchcombe Pl. NE7-1B 44
Winchester Clo. DH3-5A 124
Winchester Ct. NE32-3A 50
Winchester Ct. SR4-1E 109
Winchester Rd. DH1-2E 137
Winchester St. NE33-2E 51
Winchester Ter. NE4
-2A 60 & 4A 142
Winchester Wlk. NE13-1D 15
Wincomblee. NE6-2E 63
Windburgh Dri. NE23-1F 7
Windermere. DH3-5C 102
Windermere Av. DH2-4D 123
Windermere Av. NE10-1E 81

Windermere Clo. NE23-1F 7
Windermere Cres. DH4
-4A 116
Windermere Cres. NE21
-2A 74
Windermere Cres. NE31
-2E 65
Windermere Cres. NE32
-4C 66
Windermere Cres. NE34
-1C 68
Windermere Gdns. NE16
-3B 76
Windermere Rd. NE5-4C 40
Windermere Rd. SR7-3A 132
Windermere St. NE8-3D 135
Windermere St. NE8-1D 79
Windermere St. SR2-1D 121
Windermere St. W. NE8
-1C 78
Windermere Ter. DH9
-4A 130
Windermere Ter. NE29-3B 34
Windhill Rd. NE6-4E 63
Windlass Ct. NE34-2A 68
Windlass La. NE37-1A 104
Windmill Ct. NE2
-5D 43 & 1A 142
Windmill Hill. DH1-5B 138
Windmill Hill. NE33-3D 50
Windmill Sq. SR5-1B 100
Windsor Av. NE8-2D 79
Windsor Av. NE26-3E 23
Windsor Clo. NE16-5E 75
Windsor Clo. NE28-1B 48
Windsor Ct. NE3-3F 25
Windsor Cres. DH5-5D 127
Windsor Cres. NE5-2C 40
Windsor Cres. NE26-3E 23
Windsor Cres. NE31-1D 65
Windsor Dri. DH5-1C 128
Windsor Dri. NE28-1B 48
Windsor Dri. NE29-3B 34
Windsor Dri. SR3-3E 119
Windsor Dri. SR6-1D 89
Windsor Gdns. NE26-1B 22
Windsor Gdns. NE29-3B 34
Windsor Gdns. NE34-5A 52
Windsor Gdns. W. NE26
-1A 22
Windsor Pk. NE28-1A 46
Windsor Pl. NE2
-5F 43 & 1D 143
Windsor Pl. NE27-5D 19
Windsor Rd. DH3-1A 102
Windsor Rd. NE9-3D 93
Windsor Rd. NE25-2F 21
Windsor Rd. SR7-3A 132
Windsor St. NE6-1F 61
Windsor St. NE28-2C 46
Windsor Ter. DH3-5B 124
Windsor Ter. NE2
-5F 43 & 1D 143
Windsor Ter. NE3-3E 25
Windsor Ter. NE5-5A 24
Windsor Ter. NE9-3D 93
Windsor Ter. NE16-5E 75
Windsor Ter. NE26-3E 23
Windsor Ter. SR2-5D 111
Windsor Ter. SR7-3A 118
Windsor Wlk. NE3
-3E 25 to 2F 25
Windsor Way. NE3-3E 25
Windt St. NE13-2C 14
Windyhill Carr. NE16-5E 75
Windy Nook Rd. NE9 & NE10
-4A 80
Windy Ridge. NE10-3B 80
Windy Ridge Vs. NE10-3B 80
Wingate Clo. DH4-5B 126
Wingate Clo. NE15-1C 56
Wingate Gdns. NE9-1C 92
Wingrove Av. NE4-1E 59
Wingrove Av. SR6-1C 100
Wingrove Gdns. NE4-1D 59
Wingrove Ho. NE33-1A 68
Wingrove Rd. NE4-1D 59
Wingrove Rd. N. NE4
-3A 42 & 4A 42
Wingrove Ter. NE9-3E 93
Wingrove Ter. NE10-1A 82
Winifred Gdns. NE28-4D 47
Winifred Rd. SR1-2C 110
Winifred Ter. SR1-2C 110
Winsford Av. NE29-1A 34
Winshields. NE23-1A 8
Winshields Wlk. NE15-3E 37
Winship Clo. NE34-4B 68
Winship Gdns. NE6-1B 62
(off Grace St.)
Winship Ter. NE6-1B 62
Winskell Rd. NE34-3D 67
Winslade Clo. SR3-2A 120
Winslow Clo. NE6-1F 63
Winslow Clo. NE28-1A 46
Winslow Clo. NE35-5D 67
Winslow Clo. SR5-1D 99
Winslow Cres. SR7-3A 132
Winslow Gdns. NE9-5D 79
Winslow Pl. NE6-1F 63
Winson Grn. DH4-2D 115
Winster. NE38-2E 113
Winster Pl. NE23-1F 7
Winton Clo. SR9-4E 93
Winton Clo. NE23-2E 9
Winton Way. NE5-3B 26
Wirralshir. NE10-4F 81
Wisbech Ct. SR4-1E 109

Wiseton Ct. NE7-5B 28
Wishart Ho. NE4-5E 82
Wishaw Clo. NE23-5E 5
Wishaw Rise. NE15-5F 39
Witham Grn. NE32-5B 66
Witham Rd. NE31-4D 65
Witherington Clo. NE7-1F 45
Withernsea Gro. SR2-3B 120
Witney Clo. SR5-1D 99
Witney Way. NE35-3C 84
Witton Av. NE34-1F 69
Witton Ct. NE3-3F 25
Witton Ct. SR3-5A 110
Witton Gdns. NE9-2B 92
Witton Gdns. NE32-4F 65
Witton Gro. DH1-4A 136
Witton Rd. NE34-5B 126
Witton Rd. NE27-4A 20
Witton Rd. NE31-5A 48
Witty Av. NE31-2C 64
Woburn. NE38-3B 104
Woburn Clo. NE28-1B 46
Woburn Dri. SR3-4F 119
Woburn Way. NE5-2B 40
Wolseley Clo. NE8-1B 78
Wolseley Ter. SR4-2F 109
Wolsey Clo. NE34-2B 68
Wolsey Rd. SR7-4A 132
Wolsingham Dri. DH1
-3D 137
Wolsingham Gdns. NE9
-2C 92
Wolsingham Rd. NE3-5C 26
Wolsingham St. NE4-4C 59
Wolsington St. NE4-1E 59
Wolsington Wlk. NE4-4E 59
Wolveleigh Ter. NE3-4F 27
Wolviston Gdns. NE9-1C 92
Woodbine Av. NE3-5E 27
Woodbine Av. NE28-3D 47
Woodbine Av. SR8-2E 135
Woodbine Clo. NE4-3E 59
Woodbine Cotts. DH2-1B 122
Woodbine Cotts. NE10-2A 80
Woodbine Cotts. NE27-5D 21
Woodbine Pl. NE8-1D 79
Woodbine Rd. DH1-3A 136
Woodbine St. NE8-1C 78
Woodbine St. NE33-1E 51
Woodbine St. SR1-1D 111
Woodbine Ter. DH3-3B 102
Woodbine Ter. NE8-1D 79
Woodbine Ter. NE10-2A 80
(High Felling)
Woodbine Ter. NE10-1F 81
(Pelaw)
Woodbine Ter. SR4-5D 99
Woodbrook Av. NE5-4B 40
Woodburn. NE10-5D 81
Woodburn Av. NE4-4A 42
Woodburn Clo. DH4-3D 125
Woodburn Clo. NE21-2E 73
Woodburn Dri. DH4-4B 126
Woodburn Dri. NE26-5C 12
Woodburn Gdns. NE11-4E 77
Woodburn Sq. NE26-4C 12
Woodburn St. NE15-1B 56
Woodburn Way. NE26-5B 13
Woodchurch Clo. NE7-5F 29
Woodcock Rd. SR3-5E 119
Woodcroft Clo. NE23-3F 7
Woodend Way. NE3-2E 25
Woodfield. NE9-3E 91
Woodford. NE9-3E 91
Woodford Clo. SR5-1D 99
Woodgate Gdns. NE10-1A 82
Woodgate La. NE10-5A 64
Wood Grn. NE10-1A 82
Wood Grn. NE15-1D 57
Woodhall Ct. NE25-1B 10
Woodhead Rd. NE6-5A 46
Woodhill Rd. NE23-5D 5
Woodhorn Gdns. NE13-1D 15
Woodhouse Ct. NE34-5D 53
Woodhouses La. NE16
-4D 75 to 2E 75
Woodhurst Gro. SR4-5E 107
Woodkirk Clo. NE23-5E 5
Woodland Av. SR8-3F 135
Woodland Clo. NE25-2B 20
Woodland Cres. NE23-5A 58
Woodland Dri. SR4-3C 108
Woodland Grange. DH4
-4D 125
Woodland M. NE2-2A 44
Woodland Rise. SR3-4D 119
Woodlands. DH3-1E 123
Woodlands. NE3-2E 43
Woodlands. NE15-3E 37
Woodlands. NE29-3B 34
Woodlands. NE38-3D 113
Woodlands Av. NE3-2E 43
Woodlands Ct. NE15-3E 37
Woodlands Dri. SR6-2F 87
Woodlands Grange. NE12
-1A 30
Woodlands Pk. NE13-2E 15
Woodlands Pk. Dri. NE21
-5C 56
Woodlands Pk. Vs. NE13
-2D 15
Woodlands Rd. NE15-5F 39
Woodlands Rd. SR6-2F 87
Woodlands Ter. NE10-2B 80

Woodlands Ter. NE12-1A 30
Woodlands Ter. NE33-1F 51
Woodlands View. SR5-2E 87
Woodland Ter. DH4-2F 115
Woodland Ter. NE37-5C 94
Woodlea Clo. DH5-4E 129
Woodlea Clo. NE29-1F 49
Woodlea Ct. NE29-1F 49
Woodlea Cres. NE38-5B 104
Woodlea Gdns. NE3-3A 28
Woodlea Sq. NE29-1F 49
Woodleigh Rd. NE25-2F 21
Woodleigh View. NE3-1F 61
Woodman St. NE28-2C 48
Woodmans Way. NE16
-5D 75
Woodpack Av. NE16-4D 75
Woodside. DH9-1C 130
(off Quarry Rd.)
Woodside. SR2-3B 110
Woodside. SR3-4B 118
Woodside Av. NE6-5D 47
Woodside Av. NE15-3A 38
Woodside Av. NE25-2C 10
Woodside Clo. NE40-2A 54
Woodside Ct. NE12-2A 30
Woodside Cres. NE12-2F 29
Woodside Gdns. DH9-5F 131
Woodside Gdns. NE11-3E 77
Woodside Gro. SR3-4B 118
Woodside La. NE40-4A 54
Woodside Rd. NE40-2A 54
Woodside Ter. SR3-4B 118
Woodside Way. NE40-2A 54
Woodstock Rd. NE9-3F 91
Woodstock Rd. SR2-5D 111
(in two parts)
Woodstone Ter. DH4-4C 124
Wood St. NE11-2E 77
Wood St. NE16-2F 29
Wood Ter. NE10-5F 63
Wood Ter. NE32-3F 65
Wood Ter. NE33-4B 118
Wood Ter. NE37-4C 94
Woodthorne Rd. NE2-1F 43
Woodvale Dri. NE31-3B 64
Woodvale Gdns. NE10-4A 80
Woodvale Gdns. NE15-5A 40
Woodvale Rd. NE21-5B 56
Wood View. DH1-5F 139
Woodville Ct. SR4-3D 109
Woodville Cres. SR4-3C 108
Woodville Rd. NE15-4F 39
Woodwynd. NE10-4E 81
Wooler Av. NE29-5F 33
Wooler Cres. NE8-2A 78
Wooler Grn. NE15-5C 38
Wooler Sq. NE13-5A 6
Wooler Sq. SR2-5C 110
Woolerton Dri. NE10-5A 80
Woolerton Dri. NE15-5A 40
Wooler Wlk. NE32-3E 65
Wooley St. NE28-3D 47
Woolmer Gdns. NE11-4E 77
Woolsington By-Pass. NE20,
NE13, NE3 & NE5-1A 24
Woolsington Gdns. NE13
-1A 24
Woolsington Pk. S. NE13
-1B 24
Woolwich Clo. NE29-2D 33
Woolwich Clo. SR5-1D 99
Woolwich Rd. SR5-1D 99
Wooperton Gdns. NE5-5E 41
Worcester Clo. DH3-5A 124
Worcester Grn. NE8-5D 61
Worcester Rd. DH1-2E 137
Worcester St. SR2-2B 110
Worcester Ter. SR2-2B 110
Wordsworth Av. DH2-3A 122
Wordsworth Av. DH5-2D 15
Wordsworth Av. NE28-2A 76
Wordsworth Av. NE31-1D 65
Wordsworth Av. W. DH5
-1D 129
Wordsworth Cres. NE9-4D 93
Wordsworth St. NE8-5E 61
Worley Av. NE9-1E 91
Worley Clo. NE4-2F 59
Worley M. NE9-1E 91
Worley St. NE4-2F 59
Worley Ter. NE9-5E 79
Worm Hill Ter. NE38-1C 114
Worsley Clo. NE28-1B 46
Worswick St. NE1
-2C 60 & 4D 143
Worthing Clo. NE28-1A 46
Worthington Ct. NE2-5B 44
Woulshave Ct. NE33-1F 51
Wouldhave St. NE15-3E 37
Wraith Ter. SR2-4D 121
Wraith Ter. SR8-1E 135
Wraysbury Ct. NE3-5A 100
Wreath Quay Rd. SR5
-4A 100
Wreay Wlk. NE21-3A 8
(in two parts)
Wreigh St. NE31-1C 64
Wrekendon Rd. NE10-2A 82
Wrekenton Row. NE29-2B 92
Wren Clo. NE38-5E 103
Wren Gro. SR5-4A 98

Wretham Pl. NE2
-1D 61 & 2F 143
Wright Clo. NE23-5F 7
Wright Ter. DH4-5F 115
Wroxham Ct. NE5-1D 41
Wroxham St. SR2-5D 111
Wroxton. NE38-5B 104
Wuppertal Ct. NE32-1A 66
Wychcroft Way. NE5-3E 41
Wych Elm Cres. NE7-1E 45
Wycliffe Av. NE3-2A 42
Wycliffe Rd. SR4-3E 109
Wycliffe Rd. SR7-3A 132
Wycombe Way. SR4-1E 109
Wye Av. NE32-4A 66
Wye Rd. NE31-4D 65
Wylam Av. NE25-2D 11
Wylam Clo. NE34-2D 69
Wylam Clo. NE37-3D 95
Wylam Gdns. NE28-1B 48
Wylam Rd. DH9-1D 131
Wylam St. NE32-5D 49
Wylam Ter. DH9-1C 130
Wyncote Ct. NE7-3C 44
Wynde, The. NE34-2B 68
Wyndfall Way. NE3-1B 42
Wyndham Av. NE3-2B 42
Wyndham Way. NE29-2D 33
Wynding, The. NE23-4F 7
Wyndley Clo. NE16-5E 75
Wyndley Pl. NE3-2B 42
Wyndrow Pl. NE3-2B 42
(in two parts)
Wyndsail Pl. NE3-1B 42
Wynd, The. NE13-3B 42
Wynd, The. NE15-3F 37
Wyndtop Pl. NE3-1B 42
Wyndward Pl. NE3-1B 42
Wynn Gdns. NE10-1E 81
Wynyard. DH2-2C 122
Wynyard Gdns. NE9-2B 92
Wynyard Gro. DH1-2F 139
Wynyard Sq. SR2-5C 110
Wynyard St. DH4-5F 125
Wynyard St. NE11-2E 77
Wynyard St. SR3-3E 119
Wynyard St. SR7-5F 133
Wythburn Pl. NE9-5A 80
Wyvern Sq. SR2-5C 110

Yardley Gro. NE23-1B 4
Yarmouth Clo. SR7-4C 132
Yarmouth Dri. NE23-1C 4
Yatesbury Av. NE5-2C 41
Yeadon Ct. NE3-3E 25
Yeavering Clo. NE3-5C 26
Yelverton Ct. NE23-1C 4
Yelverton Cres. NE6-4E 63
Yeoman St. NE29-5C 34
Yeovil Clo. NE23-1B 4
Yetholm Av. DH2-3C 122
Yetholm Pl. NE5-1C 40
Yetholm Rd. NE8-1A 78
Yetlington Dri. NE3-5C 26
Yewbank Av. DH1-3B 140
Yewburn Way. NE12-4D 29
Yewcroft Av. NE15-1E 57
Yewdale Gdns. NE9-1F 91
Yewtree Av. SR5-2D 99
Yewtrees. NE6-4B 46
Yewvale Rd. NE5-3E 41
Yewtrees. NE10-5D 81
Yoden Av. SR8-2E 135
Yoden Cres. SR8-1E 135
Yoden Rd. SR8-2C 134
Yoden Way. SR8
-3C 134 & 4D 135
York Av. NE32-3F 65
York Av. SR8-2E 135
York Clo. NE23-1B 4
York Cres. DH1-1E 137
York Cres. DH5-4E 129
Yorkdale Pl. NE6-1F 63
York Dri. NE28-3C 46
York Rd. DH3-1B 112
(in two parts)
York Rd. NE26-2C 22
York Rd. SR8-1A 134
Yorkshire Dri. DH1-3D 141
York St. NE4-2A 60 & 5A 142
York St. NE10-1E 81
York St. SR1-1B 110
York St. SR3-2F 119
York Ter. DH3-4E 123
(in two parts)
York Ter. NE10-1C 80
York Ter. NE29-4B 34
York Way. NE32-2E 69
Yorkwood. NE8-1E 79
Youll's Pas. SR1-5D 101
Young Rd. NE12-1B 30
Young St. DH1-2F 139

Zetland Clo. NE25-4A 22
Zetland Dri. NE25-4A 22
Zetland Sq. SR6-4C 100
Zetland St. SR6-4C 100
Zion St. SR1-1D 111
Zion Ter. NE21-1A 74
Zion Ter. SR5-2B 100